Glenmore Burgess

www.wadsworth.com

wadsworth.com is the World Wide Web site for Wadsworth and is your direct source to dozens of online resources.

At *wadsworth.com* you can find out about supplements, demonstration software, and student resources. You can also send email to many of our authors and preview new publications and exciting new technologies.

wadsworth.com
Changing the way the world learns®

World Civilizations

VOLUME I: TO 1600

World Civilizations

2nd Edition

VOLUME I: TO 1600

Philip J. Adler

EAST CAROLINA UNIVERSITY

Australia • Canada • Denmark • Japan • Mexico • New Zealand
Philippines • Puerto Rico • Singapore • South Africa
Spain• United Kingdom • United States

History Publisher: Clark Baxter

Senior Developmental Editor: Sharon Adams Poore

Developmental Editor: Anne Reid

Assistant Editor: Cherie Hackelberg

Editorial Assistant: Melissa Gleasor

Marketing Manager: Jay Hu

Print Buyer: Barbara Britton

Managing Permissions Editor: Susan Walters

Production Service: Hal Lockwood/Penmarin Books

Photo Research: Stephen Forsling

Photo Editor: Connie Hathaway

Text and Cover Designer: Diane Beasley

Copy Editor: Laura Larson

Page Layout: Diane Beasley

Maps: MapQuest.com

Cover Image: Pamukkale © SuperStock

Cover Printer: Phoenix Color

Compositor: Carlisle Communications

Printer/Binder: R. R. Donnelley & Sons, Roanoke

For permission to use material from this text, contact us by
Web: www. thomsonrights.com
Fax: 1-800-730-2215
Phone: 1-800-730-2214

**Library of Congress
Cataloging-in-Publication Data**
Adler, Philip J.
    World civilizations / Philip J. Adler. — 2nd ed.
        p.   cm.
    Includes bibliographical references and indexes.
    ISBN 0-534-56908-0
    1. Civilization—History.   I. Title.
    CB69.A35   1999
    909—dc21   99-29867

**Wadsworth/Thomson Learning
10 Davis Drive
Belmont, CA 94002-3098
USA
www.wadsworth.com**

International Headquarters
Thomson Learning
290 Harbor Drive, 2nd Floor
Stamford, CT 06902-7477
USA

Asia
Thomson Learning
60 Albert Street #15-01
Albert Complex
Singapore 189969

UK/Europe/Middle East
Thomson Learning
Berkshire House
168-173 High Holborn
London WC1V7AA
United Kingdom

Canada
Nelson/Thomson Learning
1120 Birchmount Road
Scarborough, Ontario M1K 5G4
Canada

For Ben, with love and hope

Contents in Brief

Part ONE

Ancient Civilizations 3500–500 B.C.E. 1

Part TWO

Classic Mediterranean Civilizations 500 B.C.E.–500 C.E. 77

Equilibrium Among Polycentric Civilizations 100 B.C.E.–1500 C.E. 145

Disequilibrium: The Western Encounter with the Non-Western World 1300–1850 C.E. 301

Contents

Part ONE

Ancient Civilizations 3500–500 B.C.E. 1

Part TWO Classic Mediterranean Civilizations 500 B.C.E.–500 C.E. 77

Part FOUR Disequilibrium: The Western Encounter with the Non-Western World 1300–1850 C.E. 301

Maps

Preface

More than most of us are aware, our lives are intertwined not only with one another but with the past. "We live in a global village" and "Those who do not know their history are condemned to repeat it" are familiar clichés. But clichés become clichés because they possess demonstrable truth. A recognition of our cultural interdependency and of the debts that the present owes the past is one of the requisites of an educated individual. By common consent, the study of history is a chief avenue toward that status. That is why surveys of history, national and international, are among the most common and most popular of the social science requirements in most American colleges.

The history of world civilizations can be neither summed up easily nor exhausted in its detail. *World Civilizations* attempts to walk a middle line; its narrative embraces every major civilized epoch in every part of the globe, but the treatment of topics is selective and follows definite patterns.

This book is a brief survey of the history of civilized life since its inceptions in the Middle East some 5,000 years ago. It is meant to be used in conjunction with a lecture course at the introductory level. A majority of the students in such a course will probably be encountering many of the topics for the first time, and this book reflects that fact. The needs and interests of the freshman and sophomore students in two- and four-year colleges and universities have been kept constantly in mind by the author, whose familiarity with those needs has been sharpened by nearly thirty-five years of classroom experience.

While it deals with the history of civilization throughout the globe, this book does not attempt to be comprehensive in detail or evenly balanced among the multiple fields of history. It deliberately tilts toward social and cultural topics and toward the long-term processes that affect the lives of the millions, rather than the acts of "the captains and the kings." The evolution of law and the formative powers of religion upon early government, as examples, receive considerably more attention than wars and diplomatic arrangements. The rise of an industrial working class in European cities garners more space than the trade policies of the European governments. Such selectivity is forced on any author of any text, but the firm intent to keep this a *concise* survey necessitated a particularly close *review* of the material. That this approach was relatively successful and found favor among many teachers is continued by the appearance of this second edition of *World Civilizations.*

Extensive reviews of the book by classroom users and nonusers brought several changes in chapter content and sequence. The treatment of early Africa has been expanded significantly in Chapter 20. Sections on Southeast Asia have been added in Chapters 19 and 31. The discussion of Christian belief and its adoption in the Roman empire has been consolidated with the earlier medieval age in Europe. In Volume II, more space has been given to non-Western states' affairs, and the chapters dealing with them have been moved forward in sequence so as to allow them to be treated simultaneously with preindustrial and prerevolutionary Europe in Part Four. Part Five is now devoted in its entirety to the West, from the scientific revolution to World War I.

Part Six has been slightly reduced in extent and, as before, is global in its coverage of modern and contemporary affairs.

A particular effort to inspire student reflection is the introduction of chapter inserts that are keyed to seven themes: Law and Lawgivers, Religion and Morality, Commerce and Exchange, Family Relations, Nature and Technology, Tradition and Innovation, and Violence and Coercion. All chapters have one or more of these inserts, some of which are based on biography, others on events.

Throughout, the text has been rewritten for clarity and vigor, and many of the illustrations have been replaced. The bibliography has been updated to include many more 1990s imprints, and the glossary and Test Your Knowledge questions have been revised. While retaining those elements that allowed its successful launching, *World Civilizations* in its second edition should be a substantial improvement on the first.

Organization

❀

The organization of *World Civilizations* is largely dictated by its nature: as a history, the basic order is *chronological.* There are six parts, dealing with six chronological eras from ancient civilizations (3000–500 B.C.E.) to recent times (post-1920 C.E.). The parts have several binding threads of development in common, but the main point of reference is the relative degree of contact with other civilizations. This ranges from near-perfect isolation, as, for example, in ancient China, to close and continual interaction, as in the late twentieth-century world.

The second organizing principle is the *prioritization of certain topics and processes.* Sociocultural and economic affairs are generally emphasized, and the longer term is kept in perspective while some short-term phenomena are deliberately minimized. In terms of the space allotted, the more recent epochs of history are emphasized, in line with the recognition of growing global interdependence and cultural contact.

Although this text was from its inception meant as a world history and contains proportionately more material on non-Western peoples and cultures than any other currently in print, the Western nations also receive considerable attention. (In this respect, *Western* means not only European but also North American since the eighteenth century.) The treatment adopted in this book should allow any student to find an adequate explanation of the rise of the West to temporary dominion in modern times and the reasons for the reestablishment of worldwide cultural equilibrium in the latter half of the twentieth century.

Pedagogy
❈

An important feature of *World Civilizations* is its division into a number of short chapters. Each of the fifty-eight chapters is meant to constitute a unit suitable in scope for a single lecture, short enough to allow easy digestion, and with strong logical coherence. Each chapter offers the following features:

- ❧ a chapter outline
- ❧ a brief chapter chronology
- ❧ a chapter summary
- ❧ a Test Your Knowledge section at the end of the chapter,
- ❧ terms and individuals for identification (in boldface type)
- ❧ color illustrations and abundant maps
- ❧ thematic inserts illustrating changing or contrasting attitudes in each chapter
- ❧ frequent boxed sidebars illustrating contemporary events

Other features include the following:

- ❧ An end-of-book glossary gives explanations of unfamiliar terms.
- ❧ Each of the six parts begins with a short essay that describes the chapter contents and major trends covered in that part.
- ❧ A "Links" feature at the beginning of each part provides a comparative capsule overview of the characteristics and achievements of the epoch as experienced by the different peoples and regions.
- ❧ An extensive bibliography organized by chapter appears at the end of each volume.

Supplements
❈

The following supplements are available for the instructor:

Instructor's Manual and Test Bank
Prepared by Raymond Hylton, Virginia Union University. One volume accompanies all three versions of the text. Includes chapter outlines, lecture topics, definitions of terms to know, chapter summaries, and InfoTrac and Web site links. The test bank includes over 3,000 multiple choice, true/false, long and short essay, matching, and fill-in-the-blank questions.

Thomson World Class Learning Testing Tools, Testbank, for Windows and Macintosh
This fully integrated suite of test creation, delivery, and classroom management tools includes Thomson World Class Test, Test Online, and World Class Management software. Thomson World Class Testing Tools allows professors to deliver tests via print, floppy, hard drive, LAN, or Internet. With these tools, professors can create cross-platform exam files from publisher files or existing WESTest 3.2 test banks, edit questions, create questions, and provide their own feedback to objective test questions, enabling the system to work as a tutorial or an examination. In addition, professors can create tests that include multiple-choice, true/false, or matching questions. Professors can also track the progress of an entire class or an individual student. Testing and tutorial results can be integrated into the class management tool, which offers scoring, gradebook, and reporting capabilities. Call-in testing is also available.

Transparency Acetates
Includes over 100 four-color map images from the text.

Powerpoint for Windows and Macintosh
Includes all images from acetate package.

The Sights and Sounds of History Video
Short, focused video clips, photos, artwork, animations, music, and dramatic readings are used to bring life to historical topics and events that are most difficult for students to appreciate from a textbook alone. For example, students will experience the grandeur of Versailles and the defeat felt by a German soldier at Stalingrad. The video segments (average four minutes long) are available on VHS, which make excellent lecture launchers.

New **History Video Library** available to qualified adoptions.

CNN Video—World History
These compelling videos feature footage from CNN. Twelve two- to five-minute segments are easy to integrate into classroom discussions or as lecture launchers. Topics range from India's caste system to Pearl Harbor.

The following supplements are available for the student:

Study Guide, Volume I: To 1500

Prepared by Raymond Hylton, Virginia Union University. Includes chapter outlines, sample test questions, map exercises, and identification terms.

Study Guide, Volume II: Since 1500

Prepared by Raymond Hylton, Virginia Union University. Includes chapter outlines, sample test questions, map exercises, and identification terms.

Study Tips

Prepared by Raymond Hylton, Virginia Union University. One volume accompanies all three versions of the text.

Primary Source Document Workbook

Prepared by Robert Welborn, Clayton State College. One volume accompanies all versions of the text. A collection of primary source documents (approximately two per chapter) with accompanying exercises. Students learn to think critically and use primary documents when studying history.

Map Workbook

Prepared by Cynthia Kosso, Northern Arizona University. Designed to help students feel comfortable with maps, these workbooks include approximately thirty map exercises in each volume. Students work with different kinds of maps and identify places to improve their geographic understanding of world history.

Journey of Civilization CD-ROM—for Windows

This CD-ROM takes the student on eighteen interactive journeys through history with this exciting Windows CD-ROM. Enhanced with QuickTime movies, animations, sound clips, maps, and more, the journeys allow students to engage in history as active participants rather than as readers of past events.

Internet Guide for History

Prepared by John Soares. The introduction includes descriptions and a glossary of important terms to know regarding the Internet, such as Gopher, bulletin boards, Archie, Usenet, and many more. Internet exercises, tips for searching, and lists of URLs are then organized by topic, so that the student can apply these exercises to any subject of interest.

Hammond Historical Atlas

Available to bundle with text for a nominal price.

For a list of the most popular supplements bundled with the version of *World Civilizations* of your choice or to request a customized bundle, please visit the Wadsworth History Web Page or contact your local sales representative.

InfoTrac® College Edition

Create your own collection of secondary readings from more than 900 popular and scholarly periodicals such as *Smithsonian, Historian,* and *Harper's* magazines for four months. Students can browse, choose, and print any articles they want twenty-four hours a day.

Web page

Historic Times: Wadsworth History Resource Center
http://history.wadsworth.com/
From this full-service site, you can access the *World Civilizations,* second edition, home page, where you will find instructor and student resources, an on-line forum, career center, guidelines for searching the Web, and links to history-related Web sites. Chapter-by-chapter resources are available for the student, including interactive quizzing, hyperlinks, and InfoTrac activities. Instructors can access an on-line instructor's manual and Powerpoint slides.

Acknowledgments

❀

The author is happy to acknowledge the sustained aid given him by many individuals during the long incubation period of this text. Colleagues in the History Department at East Carolina University, at the annual meetings of the test planners and graders of the Advanced Placement in European History, and in several professional organizations, notably the American Association for the Advancement of Slavic Studies, are particularly to be thanked.

In addition, the following reviewers' comments were essential to the gradual transformation of a manuscript into a book; I am indebted to all of them and to the students in HIST 1030-1031 who suffered through the early versions of the work.

William S. Arnett
West Virginia University

Kenneth C. Barnes
University of Central Arkansas

Marsha Beal
Vincennes University

Laura Blunk
Cuyahoga Community College

William Brazill
Wayne State University

Alice Catherine Carls
University of Tennessee–Martin

Orazio A. Ciccarelli
University of Southern Mississippi

Robert Clouse
Indiana State University

Sara Crook
Peru State University

Sonny Davis
Texas A & M University at Kingsville

Joseph Dorinson
Long Island University, Brooklyn Campus

Arthur Durand
Metropolitan Community College

Frank N. Egerton
University of Wisconsin–Parkside

Ken Fenster
DeKalb College

Tom Fiddick
University of Evansville

David Fischer
Midlands Technical College

Jerry Gershenhorn
North Carolina Central University

Erwin Grieshaber
Mankato State University

Eric Haines
Bellevue Community College

Mary Headberg
Saginaw Valley State University

Daniel Heimmermann
University of Northern Arizona

Charles Holt
Morehead State University

Kirk A. Hoppe
University of Illinois–Chicago

Raymond Hylton
Virginia Union University

Fay Jensen
DeKalb College–North Campus

Aman Kabourou
Dutchess Community College

Lois Lucas
West Virginia State College

Ed Massey
Bee County College

Bob McGregor
University of Illinois–Springfield

John Mears
Southern Methodist University

Will Morris
Midland College

Gene Alan Müller
El Paso Community College

David T. Murphy
Anderson University

Tim Myers
Butler County Community College

William Paquette
Tidewater Community College

Nancy Rachels
Hillsborough Community College

Enrique Ramirez
Tyler Junior College

Bolivar Ramos
Mesa Community College

Robin Rudoff
East Texas State University

Anthony R. Santoro
Christopher Newport University

Shapur Shahbazi
Eastern Oregon State University

John Simpson
Pierce College

John S. H. Smith
Northern Nevada Community College

Maureen Sowa
Bristol Community College

Irvin D. Talbott
Glenville State College

Maxine Taylor
Northwestern State University

Eugene T. Thompson
Ricks College

Susan Tindall
Georgia State University

Bill Warren
Valley City State University

Robert Welborn
Clayton State College

David Wilcox
Houston Community College

Steve Wiley
Anoka-Ramsey Community College

John Yarnevich
Truckee Meadows Community College–Old Towne Mall Campus

John M. Yaura
University of Redlands

Many thanks, too, to Lee Congdon, James Madison University; Maia Conrad, Christopher Newport University; Theron E. Corse, Fayetteville State University; Dennis Fiems, Oakland Community College, Highland Lakes; Lauren Heymeher, Texarkana College; Maria Iacullo, CUNY Brooklyn College; Rebecca C. Peterson, Graceland College; Donna Rahel, Peru State College; Thomas J. Roland, University of Wisconsin–Oshkosh; James Stewart, Western

State College of Colorado; and Brian E. Strayer, Andrews University.

I want especially to thank Anne Reid for her labor and good ideas in preparing the second edition.

Note: Throughout the work the pinyin orthography has been adopted for Chinese names. The older Wade-Giles system has been included in parentheses as the first mention and retained in a few cases where common usage demands it (Chiang Kai-shek, for example).

About the Author

Philip J. Adler has taught college courses in world history to undergraduates for almost thirty years prior to his recent retirement. Dr. Adler took his Ph.D. at the University of Vienna following military service overseas in the 1950s. His dissertation was in the activity of the South Slav emigrés during World War I, and his academic specialty was the modern history of eastern Europe and the Austro-Hungarian empire. His research has been supported by Fulbright and National Endowment for the Humanities grants. Adler has published widely in the historical journals of this country and German-speaking Europe. He is currently professor emeritus at East Carolina University, where he spent most of his teaching career.

Introduction to the Student

Why Is History Worth Studying?

A few years ago a book about women in the past appeared with an eye-catching title: *Herstory.* Suddenly, the real meaning of a commonly used word became a lot clearer. History is indeed a *story,* not specifically about women or men, but about all those who have left some imprint on the age in which they lived.

History can be defined most simply as the story of human actions in past times. Those actions tend to fall into broad patterns, regardless of whether they occurred yesterday or five thousand years ago. Physical needs, such as the need for food, water, and breathable air, dictate some actions. Others stem from emotional and intellectual needs, such as religious belief or the search for immortality. Human action also results from desires rather than absolute needs. Some desires are so common that they recur in every generation; some examples might be literary ambition, or scientific curiosity, or the quest for political power over others.

History is the record of how people tried to meet those needs or fulfill those desires, successfully in some cases, unsuccessfully in others. Many generations of our ancestors have found familiarity with that record to be useful in guiding their own actions. The study of past human acts also encourages us to see our own present possibilities, both individual and collective. Perhaps that is history's greatest value and has been the source of its continuous fascination for men and women who have sought the good life.

Many people are naturally attracted toward the study of history, but others find it difficult or (even worse) "irrelevant." Some students—perhaps yourself!—dread history courses, saying that they can see no point in learning about the past. My life, they say, is here and now; leave the past to the past. What can be said in response to justify the study of history?

Insofar as people are ignorant of their past, they are also ignorant of much of their present, for the one grows directly out of the other. If we ignore or forget the experience of those who have lived before us, we are like an amnesia victim, constantly puzzled by what should be familiar, surprised by what should be predictable. Not only do we not know what we should know, but we cannot perceive our true possibilities, because we have nothing to measure them against. The nonhistorical mind does not know what is missing—and contrary to the old saying, that can definitely hurt you!

A word of caution here: this is not a question of "history repeats itself." This often-quoted cliché is clearly nonsense if taken literally. History does *not* repeat itself exactly, and the difference in details is always important. But history does exhibit general patterns, dictated by common human needs and desires. Some knowledge of and respect for those patterns has been a vital part of the mental equipment of all human societies.

But there is another, more personal reason to learn about the past. Adult persons who know none of their history are really in the position of a young child. They are *objects,* not subjects. Like the child, they are acted upon by forces, limited by restrictions, or compelled by a logic that they not only can do little about, but may not even perceive. They are manipulated by others' ideas, wishes, and ambitions. They never attain control of their lives, or, at least, not until the young child grows up. The sad thing is that the unhistorical adult *has* grown up, physically, but less so mentally.

The historically unconscious are confided within a figurative wooden packing crate, into which they were put by the accident of birth into a given society, at a given time, in a given place. The boards forming the box enclose these people, blocking their view in all directions. One board of the box might be the religion—or lack of it—into which they were born; another, the economic position of their family; another, their physical appearance, race, or ethnic group. Other boards could be whether they were born in a city slum or a small village, or whether they had a chance at formal education in school (about three-fourths of the world's children never go beyond the third year of school). These and many other facts are the boards of the boxes into which we are all born.

If we are to fully realize our potential as human beings, some (at least some!) of the boards must be removed so we can see out, gain other vistas and visions, and have a chance to measure and compare our experiences with others outside. Here "outside" refers to the cross section of the collective experience of other human beings, either now in the present, or what is more manageable for study, in the knowable past.

Thus, the real justification for studying history is that it lets us see out, beyond our individual birth-box, into the rich variety of others' lives and thoughts. History is a factual introduction into humans' past achievements; its breadth and complexity vary, depending on the type. But whatever the type of history we study, by letting us see and giving us perspective that enables us to contrast and compare our lives with those of others, history liberates us from the invisible boards that confine us all within our birth-box.

For many people, the study of history has been a form of liberation. Through history, they have become aware of the ways other people have dealt with the same concerns and questions that puzzle them. They have been able to gain a perspective on their own life, both as an individual and as a member of the greater society in which they work and act. Perhaps, they have successfully adapted some of the solutions that history has revealed to them and experienced the pleasure of applying a historical lesson to their own advantage. For all these reasons, the study of the historical past is indeed worth the effort. *Not* to have some familiarity with the past is to abdicate some part of our human potential.

About This Book

Organization

The textbook you are holding is a beginning survey of world history. It is meant to be studied as part of a lecture course at the freshman/sophomore level, a course in which a majority of the students will probably be encountering world history for the first time in any depth.

Some students may at first be confused by dates followed by "B.C.E.," meaning "before the common era," and "C.E." meaning "common era." These terms are used to reflect a global perspective, and they correspond to the Western equivalent B.C. (before Christ) and A.D. (*anno Domini*). Also, a caution about the word *century* is in order: the term "seventeenth century" C.E. refers to the years 1601 to 1699 in the common era. "The 1700s" refers to the years 1700–1799. With a little practice these terms become second nature and will increase your fluency in history.

Although this text includes a large number of topics, it is not meant to be comprehensive. Your instructor's lectures will almost certainly bring up many points that are not discussed in the book; that is proper and should be expected. To do well in your tests, you may pay close attention to the material covered in the lectures, which may not be in this book.

Three principles have guided the organization of this book. First, the basic order is dictated by *chronology,* for that is a history text and history can be defined as action-in-time. After an introductory chapter on prehistory, we look first at Mesopotamia and Egypt, then at India and China. In these four river valley environments, humans were first successful in adapting nature to their needs on a large scale, a process that we call civilization. Between about 2500 B.C.E. and about 1000 C.E., the river valley civilizations matured and developed a "classic" culture in most phases of life: a fashion of thinking and acting that would be a model for emulation so long as that civilization was vital and capable of defending itself.

By 500 B.C.E. the Near Eastern civilizations centered in Egypt and Mesopotamia were in decline and had been replaced by Mediterranean-based ones, which drew on the older civilizations to some extent but also added some novel and distinct features of their own. First the Greeks, then the Romans succeeded in bringing much of the known world under their influence, culminating in the great Roman empire reaching from Spain to the Persians. For the West, the greatest single addition to civilized life in this era was the combination of Jewish theology and Greco-Roman philosophy and science. During the same epoch (500 B.C.E.–500 C.E.), the civilizations of East and South Asia were also experiencing growth and change of huge dimensions. India's Hindu religion and philosophy were being challenged by Buddhism, while China recovered from political dismemberment and became the permanent chief factor in East Asian affairs. Japan emerged slowly from a prehistoric stage under Chinese tutelage, while the southeastern part of the Asian continent attained a high civilization created in part by Indian traders and Buddhist missionaries.

From 500 to about 1500 C.E., the various civilized regions (including sub-Saharan Africa and the Americas) were either still isolated from one another or maintained a power equilibrium. After 500, Mediterranean civilization underwent much more radical changes than occurred elsewhere on the globe, and by about 1000, an amalgam of Greco-Roman, Germanic, and Jewish-Christian beliefs called Europe, or Western Christianity, had emerged. By 1500, this civilization began to rise to a position of worldwide domination, marked by the voyages of discovery and ensuing colonization. In the next three centuries, the Europeans and their colonial outposts slowly wove a web of worldwide commercial and technological interests anchored on military force. Our book's treatment of the entire post-1500 age will give much attention to the West, but also to the impacts of Western culture and ideas upon non-Western peoples. In particular, it will look at the Black African civilization encountered by the early European traders and what became of it and at the Native American civilizations of Latin America and their fate under Spanish conquest and rule.

From 1800 through World War I, Europe led the world in practically every field of material human life, including military affairs, science, commerce, and living standards. This was the golden age of Europe's imperial control of the rest of the world. The Americas, much of Asia, Oceania, and coastal Africa all were the tails of the European dog; all became formal or informal colonies at one time, and some remained under direct European control until the mid-twentieth century.

After World War I, the pendulum of power swung steadily away from Europe and toward what had been the periphery: first, North America; then, Russia, Japan, and the non-Western peoples. As we approach the end of the present century, the world has not only shrunk, but has again been anchored on multiple power bases, both Western and non-Western. A degree of equilibrium is rapidly being restored, this time built on a foundation of western technology that has been adopted throughout the globe.

Our periodization scheme, then, will be a sixfold one:

- Ancient Civilizations, 3500 B.C.E.–500 B.C.E.
- Classical Mediterranean Civilizations, 500 B.C.E.–500 C.E.
- Equilibrium among Polycentric Civilizations, 500–1500 C.E.
- Disequilibrium: The Western Expansion, 1500–1800 C.E.
- Industry and Western Hegemony, 1800–1920.
- Equilibrium Reasserted: The Twentieth-Century World.

Each period will be introduced by a brief summary and by an outline comparing the various contemporary civilizations. These six outlines are termed Links and will afford a nutshell overview of the topics covered in the following part of the book.

Text Emphases and Coverage

As a second principle of organization, this book reflects the author's particular concerns, so the material treated is selective.

There is a definite tilt toward social and economic topics in the broadest sense, although these are usually introduced by a treatment of political events. Wars and military matters are treated only as they seem relevant to other topics. Only the most prominent and most recognizably important governmental, military, or diplomatic facts and figures are mentioned in the text. The author believes that students who are interested in such factual details will hear them in lectures or can easily find them in the library or an encyclopedia. Others, who are less interested in such details, will appreciate the relative focus on broad topics and long-term trends.

The third organizing principle of the book is its approach to Western and non-Western history. A prominent place is given throughout to the history of the Western world. Why this emphasis in a world that has grown much smaller and more intricately connected over the last generation?

At least three reasons come to mind: (1) Western culture and ideas have dominated most of the world for the past 500 years, and much of this text deals with that period; (2) the rest of the planet has been westernized in important ways during the twentieth century, either voluntarily or involuntarily; and most importantly (3) the majority of the people reading this book are themselves members and products of Western civilization. If one agrees with the philosopher Socrates that to "know thyself" is the source of all knowledge, then a beginning has to be made by exploring one's own roots—roots growing from a Western soil.

About one-third of the text chapters deal with the period since the end of the eighteenth century, and about one-fifth with history since World War I. This emphasis on the most recent past fits with the interests of most students; but should you be particularly attracted to any or all of the earlier periods, be assured that an immense amount of interesting writing on almost all of the world's peoples in any epoch is available. The end-of-chapter bibliographies will provide a good starting point for further inquiry.

Many instructors will wish to supplement the text by assigning outside readings and/or by material in their lectures. The bibliographies are helpful sources for much of the information omitted from the text and for much else besides; your college library will have many of the titles listed. They have been chosen because they are up-to-date, readily available, and highly readable.

As a good student, your best resource, always, is your own sense of curiosity. Keep it active as you go through these pages; remember, this and every textbook are the *beginning,* not the ending of your search for useful knowledge. Good luck!

World Civilizations

VOLUME I: TO 1600

Part ONE

Ancient Civilizations

3500–500 B.C.E.

How and when did civilization begin? To answer that question, the first seven chapters of this book examine the growth of civilized life in four quite different areas of the globe before 500 B.C.E. The first chapter deals with the enormous stretch of time between the advent of *Homo sapiens* throughout much of the Earth and about 5000 B.C.E. We look at the general conditions of life and the achievements of human beings before history, or systematic written records of the past. These early "breakthroughs" are truly impressive, and it is a mark of their fundamental importance that we so rarely think about them. We cannot envision an existence in which they were unknown. Metalworking, writing, art, settled habitation, and religious belief are just a few of the triumphs of prehistoric humans' imagination and skill.

Most important of all, the commitment to growing, rather than chasing or gathering, food gradually took root among widely scattered groups in the late Neolithic Age (c. 8000–5000). This Agricultural Revolution is one of the two epoch-making changes in human life to date, the other being the Industrial Revolution commencing in the late eighteenth century. Agriculture generated the material basis of civilization as that word is generally understood. Urban living, statutory law, government by officials, writing beyond mere record keeping, military forces, and socioeconomic classes are all indirect products of the adoption of food growing as the primary source of sustenance for a given people or tribe.

Chapters 2 through 7 examine the establishment and development of urban life in the river valleys of western Asia, northeast Africa, India, and China. First in chronology was probably Mesopotamia, but it was quickly rivaled by the civilization of the Nile valley of Egypt. Both of these began to take definite form about 3500 B.C.E. and reached their apex between about 1500 and 1200. Somewhat later, the plains of the Indus River in India's far west produced a highly organized and urban society that prospered until about the middle of the second millennium B.C.E., when it went into decline and was forgotten for many centuries.

Simultaneous with the decline of the Indus valley civilization, the north-central region of China gave birth to a civilized state ruled by the Shang dynasties. Like the others, this society was founded on a mastery of irrigated farming. Unlike the Mesopotamians and the Indus peoples, both the Egyptians and the Chinese maintained the major elements of their early civilizations down to modern days.

Part One also provides brief accounts of a few of the other major contributors to world civilization before 500 B.C.E. Chapter 4 puts the warlike Assyrians and the first of the several Persian empires into perspective and examines the small but crucially important nation of the Jews and their religious convictions. Finally, Chapter 7 offers a comparative glance at the daily lives and social attitudes of the ancient civilizations, as we can know about them from both archaeology and history. In this chapter, as indeed throughout the book, we devote special attention to the nonelite working people and to the relations between the sexes.

Each chapter in the book (with the exception of Chapter 1) contains one or two theme boxes focusing on a broadly drawn human activity, or theme, that recurs throughout history. Seven such themes reappear throughout the text and are highlighted in boxes: Religion and Morality, Tradition and Innovation, Family Relations, Law and Lawgivers, Nature and Technology, Commerce and Exchange, and Violence and Coercion. The boxes usually deal with themes within the context of a specific historical event or life. Comparisons and contrasts with other ages and other peoples are drawn, sometimes by excerpts from documents and sometimes by narrative or biography. Individual experience thus points up the universal nature of the themes. In each box, a final section entitled "For Reflection" poses several thought-provoking questions.

We conclude Part One and each of the other five parts in this book with a "Link" designed to give a thumbnail comparison of peoples in history. The Link consists of a chart summarizing the characteristics and achievements of the epoch as experienced by the different peoples and regions.

Chapter 1

Prehistory

Civilization is a movement and not a condition, a voyage and not a harbor.

ARNOLD J. TOYNBEE

HISTORY, IN THE STRICT SENSE, means a systematic written record of the human past. But most people don't use history in the strict sense. They define the word *history* as whatever has happened in the past to humans, which, of course, is a much bigger proposition. Humans have inhabited the Earth for a very long time. Present-day human beings evolved over millions of years, and the majority of that period is still a totally closed book to modern science. Indeed, you can think of human evolution as a vast black space penetrated by only an occasional pinpoint of light, representing our current knowledge.

Every few years, new evidence is discovered that extends the age of the genus *Homo* further back in time. A human-like creature, or **hominid,** walked about in East Africa well over three million years ago by latest reckoning. (The old-

✿ **Footprints from 2.5 Million B.C.E.** These fossilized prints were found by the Leakeys in Laetoli, in present-day Tanzania in East Africa. The stride and distribution of weight on the foot indicate that they were walking upright and were thus some of the earliest of the hominids. *(Kenneth Garrett/National Geographic Society)*

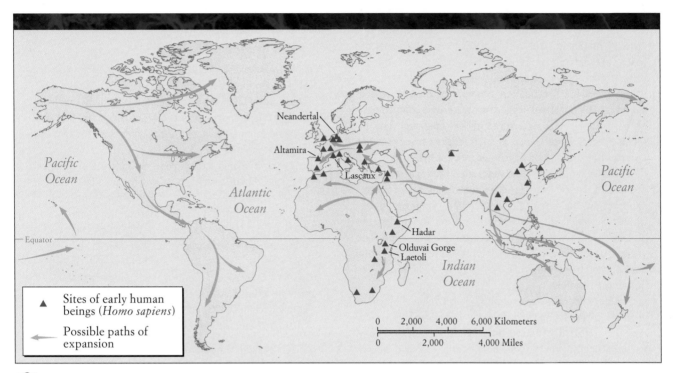

🌼 **MAP 1.1   Spread of *Homo sapiens*.** Anthropologists disagree on the detail but agree that human beings entirely similar to ourselves probably existed in every continent but Antarctica no later than 20,000 B.C.E. Their origin might have been in East Africa.

est hominid generally accepted as such is "Lucy," a female whose fossilized bones were discovered in Ethiopia two decades ago.) *Homo sapiens,* "thinking man," is much younger, however. This modern variety of humans—the originator of all people now living—is apparently no more than about 50,000 years old. Where they first appeared and why they were so successful in extending their habitation over the entire globe in a relatively short time (perhaps 20,000 years) remain mysteries that the anthropologists and their scientific cousins, the archaeologists, would love to solve. Map 1.1 shows the spread of *Homo sapiens* across the continents.

Definition of Terms

❀

Let's start our exploration of the past with some definitions of certain key words and phrases:

- 🕸 **History** is the systematic written record of what people have done in the past. In this context, the past can mean 10,000 years ago or yesterday. History depends on memory; it is remembered activities. What has happened but been forgotten—which is, of course, the vast majority of what has happened—is technically not history.

- 🕸 **Prehistory** is whatever happened to people in the period prior to writing.
- 🕸 **Historiography** is the written-down form of history, as processed through an author's brain and bias working on the raw materials he or she has found.
- 🕸 **Culture** is the human-created part of the environment, the "way of life" of a distinct group of humans interacting with one another. In prehistory, culture is often associated with particular tools.
- 🕸 **Civilization** is a complex, developed culture usually associated with specific achievements such as agriculture, urban life, specialized labor, and a system of writing.
- 🕸 **Archaeology** is the study of prehistoric and/or historical cultures through examination of their artifacts (anything made by humans). The name means "the study of origins," and like almost every other scientific name in the English language, it is derived from Greek.
- 🕸 **Anthropology** refers to the science that studies humans as a species rather than studying a special aspect of their activity. Its name, too, is derived from Greek.

Archaeologists are crucial to the study of prehistoric humans. In that transitional period when writing is just beginning to develop, the **paleontologists** (students of fossils and ancient life forms) and the **paleographers** (students of old writing) are essential to the historian, also.

The Evolving Past

The 1974 discovery of the skeletal remains of a hominid nicknamed "Lucy" by an Anglo-American team of researchers in Ethiopia was a key advance in modern anthropology. Lucy (named whimsically after the Beatles' song) is the first known example of *Australopithecus afarensis*, a bipedal (two-legged) creature who roamed eastern Africa's savannah over three million years ago. The immediate ancestor of *Homo*, as contradistinct from hominid, Lucy and her small-boned fellows were a hybrid between modern man and ape. A few years later, the fossil footprints of similar creatures were found in the volcanic ash of Laetoli, Tanzania, by the British Leakey family of anthropologists. These showed a pair of individuals walking upright for several yards and were dated at about three and a half million years ago. Since then, further discoveries around the globe have pushed the frontier between human and hominid even farther back in time.

Probably no other science, not even nuclear physics or genetic biology, has evolved so swiftly in the past forty or fifty years as archaeology and its associated paleoanthropology. Each season brings its new discoveries about the age, the nature, and the locales of early humans, both before and after the emergence of *Homo sapiens*. In 1998 alone, a random perusal of *Science News* (vol. 154, December 26, 1998) shows the following events recorded:

A million-year-old skull of a hominid found in Africa fills a sizable gap in the fossil record.

Some disputed DNA data point to the possibility that *Homo sapiens* migrated from eastern Africa about 100,000 years ago and founded part of the populations of modern east Asia.

A precursor of *Homo sapiens* reached an island in Indonesia perhaps 800,000 years ago, raising the possibility of much earlier maritime expeditions than was previously thought.

A find in a Brazilian cave may indicate that *Homo sapiens* reached that locale and hence the Americas many tens of thousands of years earlier than had been previously accepted.

An analysis of fossil and modern skulls suggests that speech may have been mastered for sophisticated communication at least 400,000 years ago—again, much earlier than what had been assumed until now.

As the tools and methodology of physical science grow ever more refined, a steady stream of such revisions of "the state of the art" can be expected.

The Paleolithic Age

❖

The very lengthy period extending from about the appearance of the first hominids to about 8000 B.C.E. is known as the Paleolithic Age, or Old Stone Age, so called because tools were made of stone and were still quite crude (*paleo* = old; *lithos* = stone). By the end of the Paleolithic, humans inhabited all the continents except Antarctica. Paleolithic peoples were hunters and foragers, but life was not easy, and famine was always near at hand.

Paleolithic hunting and gathering was done in groups, and success depended more on organization and cooperation than on individual bravery or strength. The family was the basic social unit, but it was normally an extended family that included uncles, aunts, in-laws, and other relatives rather than the nuclear family (mother, father, children) that is common today. A unit larger than the nuclear family was necessary for protection. But the total number able to live and hunt together was probably quite small—no more than forty or so. More than that would have been very difficult to maintain when the hunting was poor or the wild fruits and seeds were not plentiful. Family relations among the Paleolithic hunters were critical to their survival, a fact that we will see reflected in many other groups and locales

in later history. The Family Relations boxes throughout the book will examine this theme.

Although conflicts frequently arose over hunting grounds, water, theft, or other problems, the Paleolithic era probably saw less warfare than any time in later history. So much open space capable of sustaining life was available that the weaker units probably just moved on when they were confronted with force or threats. Violence was a constant factor in determining historical and prehistoric life. The Violence and Coercion boxes throughout the book will help us follow this theme.

Human Development during the Paleolithic

During the Paleolithic, both the physical appearance of humans and their vital capacity to reason and plan changed considerably. Because of the extensive work of anthropologists since World War II, we know that several different hominids evolved during this time. Evidence uncovered in East Africa and Europe indicates that some subspecies came to an evolutionary dead end, however. A good example is the famous **Neanderthal Man** who flourished in western Germany about 30,000 years ago and then disappeared at about the same time that *Homo sapiens* appeared in Europe.

What happened to Neanderthal Man? Climatic changes probably affected and perhaps even caused these evolutionary developments. We know that the end of the last of several Ice Ages coincided with the appearance of *Homo sapiens* throughout the Northern Hemisphere. It is entirely possible that the pre–*Homo sapiens* inhabitants of Europe, such as Neanderthal Man, failed to adapt to the changed climate, in the same way that some zoologists believe that the dinosaurs failed to adapt much earlier.

During the Paleolithic, humans became more upright, and their skull changed shape to encompass a gradually enlarging brain. Their bodies grew less hairy and their arms shorter. Hip structure changed to allow a more erect gait. Eyesight grew sharper and the sense of smell less so. All these changes and many others were adaptations that reflected both humans' changed physical environment and their increasing mastery and manipulation of that environment.

The changed physical environment was reflected in the substitution of semipermanent shelter for the nomadism of an earlier day. By the late Paleolithic, groups were living in caves, lean-tos, and other shelters for long periods of time, perhaps several months. Where earlier a group rarely remained more than a few weeks at a given locale, now they could stay in one place several months to await the ripening of certain fruit or the migration of the animals. Even more important, humans' ability to master their physical environment was constantly increasing as they learned to make clothing for cold seasons, to kindle fire where and when it was needed, and to devise new tools for new tasks. The earliest human artwork came in the late Paleolithic. Certain caves of southern France (Lascaux) and Spain are world famous for their lifelike portraits of deer and other animals.

In such ways, humans began to bend the physical world to their will. As they developed an ability to plan and to remember what had been successful in the past so they could repeat it, humans in the late Paleolithic were making rapid strides toward civilization. They would reach that state in the next age—the Neolithic.

The Neolithic Age: Agriculture

✳

Although the Paleolithic saw notable developments, it was in the Neolithic, or New Stone Age, that humans made the breakthrough to advanced culture and eventually civilization. As we saw, Paleolithic groups were essentially nomadic. They depended on either hunting and gathering or on raising animals for food. Both the hunter-gatherers and the herders had a mobile life. The former moved with the seasons and the migration of the animals they hunted, and the latter had to move with their animals when the grazing was exhausted. Both had no reason to attempt to settle down and every reason not to. In the Neolithic, this situation changed. The gradual adoption of agriculture demanded a *sedentary,* or settled, life.

The beginnings of farming used to be called the "**Agricultural Revolution.**" Now, we know that if this was a revolution, it was a very slow one. Most peoples took about five to ten generations (200–400 years) to complete it. Gradually, hunting-herding as the primary way to gain food

❀ Paleolithic Art. This vivid rendering of a bull was found on the dark walls of a cave in Altamira, Spain, one of hundreds of animal portraits dating from the late Paleolithic Age (c. 15000 B.C.E.) The purpose of these paintings may have been to call forth the spirits of the hunters' quarry. *(AKG London)*

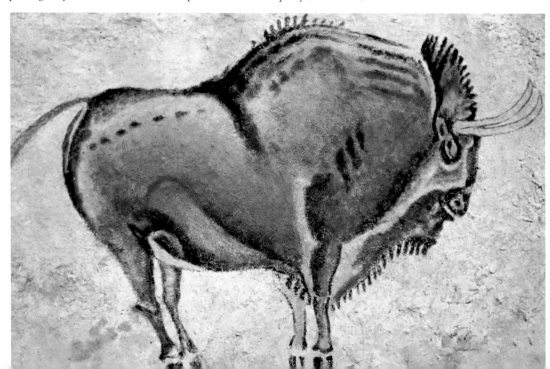

⚘ **Venus of Willemsdorf.** Found near a small Austrian village a hundred years ago, this is one of the better-known "Earth Mothers" found throughout the central and eastern European excavations. Its age is approximately 28,000 years. *(Erich Lessing/Art Resource)*

gave way to sowing and harvesting. Usually, agriculture went hand in hand with hunting for a long, long time. Some members of the group would hunt while others raised some form of grain from wild grasses, the usual form of agriculture. When agriculture became the primary way of getting something to eat, the Agricultural Revolution was complete for that group. Throughout this book, we will be watching traditional beliefs and lifestyles giving way, however grudgingly, to the challenges brought forth by changes in the natural or the manmade environments. The Agricultural Revolution of the Neolithic era was one of the vastest of such changes. The Tradition and Innovation boxes will provide a perspective on others.

With such a slow transition, is *revolution* an appropriate word to describe the adoption of the agricultural lifestyle? In many ways it is, because such adoption did lead to revolutionary changes in the long run. First, it meant that people settled down permanently. To be near the cultivated area, people settled in villages and then in towns, where they lived and worked in many new, specialized occupations that were unknown to preagricultural society. These settlements could not depend on the luck of hunting or fishing or on sporadic harvests of wild seeds and berries to supply their daily needs. Only regularized farming could support the specialists who populated the towns, and only intensive agriculture could produce the dependable surplus of food that was necessary to allow the population to grow. Of course, occasional years of famine still occurred. But the lean years were far less frequent than when people depended on hunting-gathering for sustenance. Thus, one major result of agriculture was a steadily *expanding population* that lived in *permanent settlements.*

Second, agriculture was the force behind creating the concept of "mine versus thine"—that is, *privately owned property* in land. Until farming became common, there was no concept of private property; land, water, game, and fish belonged to all who needed them. But once a group had labored hard to establish a productive farm, they wanted permanent possession. After all, they had to clear the land, supply water at the right time, and organize labor for the harvest. Who would do that if they had no assurance that next year and the next the land would still be theirs?

Third, agriculture necessitated the development of *systematized regulation* to enforce the rights of one party over those of another when disputes arose over property. Codes of law, enforced by organized authority, or government officials, were very important results of agriculture's introduction. Governing relations between individuals and groups so that security is established and the welfare of all promoted is the function of law. Law and the exercise of lawful authority is one of the recurrent themes in this book, and we will look at it in the Law and Lawgivers boxes.

A fourth change was the increasing *specialization of labor.* It made no sense for a Neolithic farmer to try to be a soldier or carpenter as well as a food grower. Efforts were more productive for the entire community if people specialized; the same applied to the carpenter and the soldier, who were not expected to farm.

Agriculture also led to an *enlarged public role for women* in Neolithic society, apparently a direct result of the fact that the very first farmers were probably women. The association of women with fertility, personified in a whole series of Earth Mother goddesses in various cultures, was also important in this development. As the persons who brought forth life, women were seen as the key to assuring that the Earth Mother would respond to the villagers' prayers for food from her womb. In many areas where agriculture became important, *female-centered religious cults* and female priestesses replaced male gods and priests. Changes in reli-

🏵 **Modern Hunter-Gatherers.** The boy is setting a bird trap to supplement his family's diet in Namibia, southern Africa. His Bushmen kin are some of the last of the world's hunting-gathering folk, who range the Kalahari Desert much as their ancient forebears did. *(Peter Johnson/Corbis)*

gious belief and practice carry the widest-ranging consequences for any society, ancient or modern. Often they have been manifested in the concepts of good and bad that dictated public and private behavior patterns, or morality. We will observe many such changes as we progress through this world history, and the Religion and Morality boxes will reinforce the theme.

Alterations in lifestyle came about gradually, of course, as a group learned to depend on crop growing for its main food supply. When that change took place varied sharply from one continent or region to the next. In a few places, it has still not occurred. A few nomadic tribes or hunter-gatherer groups can still be found, although they are fast disappearing under the intrusions of modern communications and technology.

Where were the first agricultural societies? For many years, researchers believed agriculture must have emerged first in the Near or Middle East and spread gradually from there into Asia and Africa. According to this **diffusion theory** of cultural accomplishment, knowledge of new techniques spreads through human contacts, as water might spread on blotting paper. But now it is known that as early as 7000 B.C.E. agriculture had developed in at least four separate areas independent of outside influences: the Near East, Central America, northern China, and West Africa. Slightly later, the first domesticated animals were being raised as a part of village life. The raising of pigs, sheep, cattle, and goats for food and fiber goes back at least as far as 4000 B.C.E. (The horse comes considerably later, as we shall see.) Map 1.2 shows where some common plant and animal species were first cultivated or domesticated.

Irrigation Civilizations

Several of the earliest civilizations developed in the plains bordering on major rivers or in the valleys the rivers created. Not coincidentally, four of the most important civilizations, which we will examine in the next chapters, emerged in this way. The development of high civilization depended on intensive, productive agriculture, and the development of agriculture depended in turn on the excellent

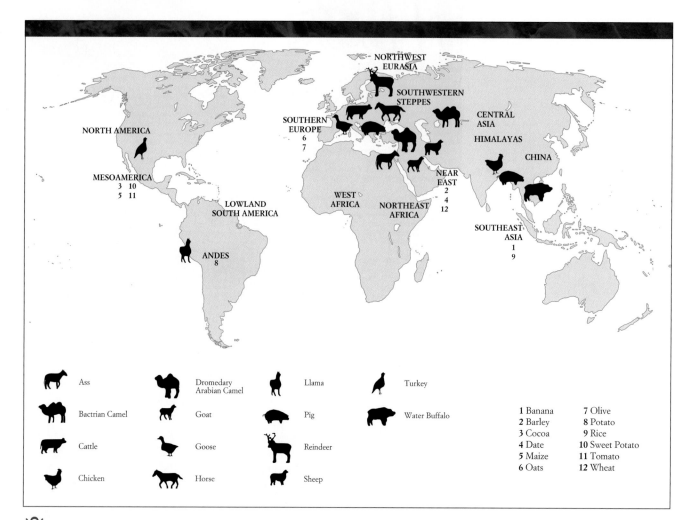

🞧 **MAP 1.2   Origin of Crops and Domestic Animals.** This map shows where particular plant and animal species were first cultivated or domesticated. Did these practices arise independently in different areas, or did they appear by diffusion? In the case of some species (for example, the pig), there seems to have been independent development in different areas. In most cases, however, the contact between neighboring cultures facilitated the rapid rise of plant and animal cultivation around the globe.

soil and regular supply of water provided by the river. In ancient Mesopotamia, the dual drainage of the Tigris and Euphrates Rivers made the first urban civilization possible. In Egypt, the Nile, the world's longest river at more than 4,000 miles, was the life-giving source of everything the people needed and cherished. In India, the beginnings of civilization are traced to the extensive fields on both sides of the Indus River, which flows more than 2,000 miles from the slopes of the Himalayas to the ocean. Finally, in China, the valley of the Yellow River, which is about 2,700 miles long, was the cradle of the oldest continuous civilization in world history. Map 1.3 shows these four early civilizations.

What else did the rivers provide besides good crops and essential water? They also offered a sure and generally easy form of transport and communication, allowing intervillage trade and encouraging central authorities to extend their powers over a much greater area than would have been pos-

sible if they had only overland contacts. The interchange of goods and services between villages or whole regions is a constant in human history, and we will look at this theme in differing contexts in later chapters and in the Commerce and Exchange boxes.

But the rivers had very different natures. The Tigris and the Yellow were as destructive in their unpredictable flooding as the Nile and the Indus were peaceful and friendly. The Yellow River was so ruinous at times that its ancient name was the "sorrow of China." But without its source of water, early farming in northern China would have been impossible.

Climate, too, made a difference among the early civilizations. Egypt and most of the Indus valley have temperate climates that change little over the course of the year and are suitable for crops all year long. It is not at all unusual for an Egyptian family farm to grow three crops annually.

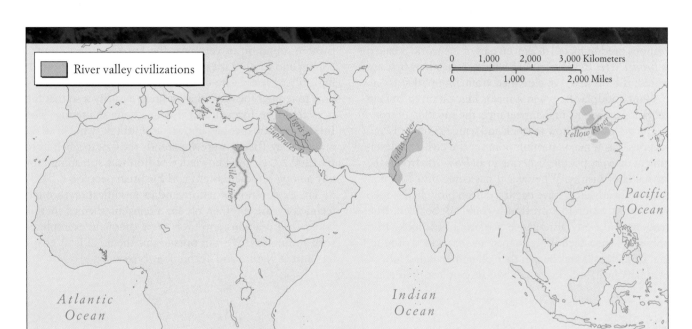

❀ **MAP 1.3 Early Civilizations.** Several of the earliest civilizations were centered around rivers, which provided good soil and water for agriculture. Ancient Mesopotamia grew up around the Tigris and Euphrates Rivers. Egyptian civilization flourished along the Nile. Indian civilization began in fields along the Indus. The Yellow River supported early Chinese civilization.

Northern China and Mesopotamia, on the other hand, experience much more severe changes of weather, not only from season to season but from day to day.

In the Near East, the climate has changed significantly over the past two millennia. What was once a relatively moderate place, with adequate rain for growing grain crops, has gradually become an arid desert, with very intense heat much of the year. Present-day Iraq, which occupies the old Mesopotamia, is a very difficult place to farm even with modern irrigation techniques. This change is a big part of the reason that Mesopotamia, after thousands of years of cultural leadership, sank slowly into stagnation in later days.

Metal and Its Uses

❀

The first metal used by humans seems to have been soft copper. When combined with lead and tin ores, copper becomes the more useful bronze. Bronze has some advantages over copper: it is harder (and therefore more suitable for weaponry) and more resistant to weathering. But it has several disadvantages when compared with other metals: it is relatively difficult to make, its weight is excessive for many uses, and it cannot keep a fine edge for tools and cutting weapons. Above all, bronze was difficult to obtain in the ancient world and very expensive.

❀ **Life in the Iron Age.** The discovery of how to smelt and temper iron tools and weapons changed the life of every people. (© *Superstock*)

The period when bronze art objects and bronze weapons predominated in a given part of the world is called its *Bronze Age.* In western Asia where civilizations first appeared, the Bronze Age extended from about 7000 B.C.E. to about 1500 B.C.E., when a major innovation in human technology made its first appearance: the smelting of iron.

The discovery of how to smelt and temper iron tools and weapons was a major turning point in the civilized development of every people, ushering in an *Iron Age.* Iron is the key metal of history. Wherever it has come into common use, certain advances have occurred. Iron plowshares open areas to cultivation that previously could not be tilled. Iron weapons and body armor give warfare a new look. Iron tools enable new technical progress and expanded production. Iron utensils are cheaper than other metals, last longer, resist fiery heat, and do not easily shatter or lose their edge.

Iron ore is one of the more common metallic ores, and it is often found on or very near the Earth's surface (unlike copper and lead). It is easily segregated from the surrounding soils or rock. The crucial breakthrough was learning how to temper the ore—that is, how to purify it so that the iron could be formed and used without shattering. The Indo-European people known as Hittites, who lived in modern-day Turkey, were apparently the first to smelt iron. By 1200 B.C.E., the knowledge of iron was spreading rapidly among Middle Eastern and Egyptian peoples.

The exploration of nature and its modification through technology are another of our recurrent themes in this book. Iron weapons and tools are a dramatic example of such technology. We will pursue this theme in later chapters and in Nature and Technology boxes.

SUMMARY

The prehistory of the human race is immeasurably longer than the short period (5,000 years or so) of which we have historical knowledge. During the last 50,000 years of the prehistoric period, men and women became physically and mentally indistinguishable from ourselves and spread across the Earth. Developing agriculture to supplement hunting and gathering, humans slowly attained that advanced state we call civilization in the later part of the Neolithic Age, around 3000 B.C.E. Urban life was now possible, a system of government and record keeping evolved, and advanced weapons and tools of metal were invented. In the next chapters of this book, we will examine the four earliest centers of advanced civilization, one by one, and look at the reasons that each of them became such a center. The remarkable similarities and contrasts among these civilizations gave each of them a particular atmosphere that would last for thousands of years and in some cases until the present day.

IDENTIFICATION TERMS

anthropology	culture	history	paleographers
archeology	diffusion theory	hominid	paleontologists
Agricultural Revolution	historiography	Neanderthal Man	prehistory
civilization			

TEST YOUR KNOWLEDGE

1. Which of the following statements most aptly describes Paleolithic society?
   a. The hunt was the only way to obtain food regularly.
   b. There was constant fighting among families and clans.
   c. The individual was more important than the group.
   d. Cooperation was necessary for survival.

2. The Agricultural Revolution occurred first during the
   a. Neolithic.
   b. Bronze Age.
   c. Paleolithic.
   d. Mesozoic.

3. Among the major changes that occur as a result of the adoption of agriculture by any group is
   a. the abandonment of traditional village life.
   b. a decrease in trading.
   c. an increase in population.
   d. a reduction in animal raising.
4. Which of these was of decisive importance to Neolithic agriculture?
   a. The use of beasts of burden for plowing.
   b. The mastery of irrigation techniques.
   c. The development of natural insecticides.
   d. The existence of large cities as marketplaces.
5. The increase in the number of humans during the Neolithic Age was primarily caused by
   a. the disappearance of epidemic disease.
   b. a surplus of food.
   c. decreased intergroup violence.
   d. a greater respect for the aged.
6. The use of bronze as the primary metal for tools and weapons
   a. came after iron.
   b. was dictated by its ease of making.
   c. started about 7000 B.C.E. in western Asia.
   d. came after urban civilizations were established in the Near East.

INFO TRAC COLLEGE EDITION

Enter the search term "antiquities" using the Subject Guide.
Enter the search term "Paleolithic" using Key Words.

Enter the search term "Neolithic" using Key Words.

Chapter 2

Mesopotamia

If a physician performs a major operation . . . and has caused the freeman's death, or he opens the eye-socket and has destroyed the freeman's eye, they shall cut off his hand.

THE CODE OF HAMMURABI

c. 5000 B.C.E.	Sumerians arrive in Mesopotamia
c. 3500 B.C.E.	Cuneiform writing
c. 3000 B.C.E.	Sumerian city-states develop
c. 2300 B.C.E.	Sargon of Akkad
1700s B.C.E.	Hammurabi/oldest surviving law code
c. 1500 B.C.E.	Hittites conquer Mesopotamia
c. 900 B.C.E.	Rise of Assyria
539 B.C.E.	Conquest by Persia

THE LAND THE ANCIENT Greeks called Mesopotamia ("land between the rivers") is now the eastern half of Iraq. The rivers are the Euphrates and the Tigris. They originate in present-day Turkey and parallel one another for about 400 miles before joining together to flow into the head of the Persian Gulf (see Map 2.1).

In the lower courses of the rivers, in the third millennium B.C.E., originated the first extensive urban civilization of the world. This civilization was supported by extensive irrigation farming, pioneered by a people called **Sumerians,** who came into lower Mesopotamia from somewhere to the east about 5000 B.C.E. Gradually, the Sumerians created a series of small competing kingdoms, each of which was centered on a good-sized town. Here they developed a series of ideas and techniques that would provide the foundation of a distinct and highly influential civilization.

Sumerian Civilization

The Sumerians were the first people to do an enormous number of highly significant things. They built the first large cities, as distinct from towns (the largest apparently containing upward of 100,000 people). They developed the first sophisticated system of writing. They built the first monumental buildings, using as the basic principle of support the post-and-lintel system, which is still the normal way of piercing walls for light and air. They probably invented the wheel, and they were the first to design and build a gravity-flow irrigation system. They had the first school system known to history, and they were the first to use sunbaked brick. They were possibly the first to use the plow and among the first to make bronze metal.

What we know of them is extremely impressive. We know a good deal not only because they left extensive records of their own but also because they had enormous influence on their neighbors and their successors in Mesopotamia.

The Sumerians were not the only settlers of the broad plain on either side of the two rivers. In fact, they were not

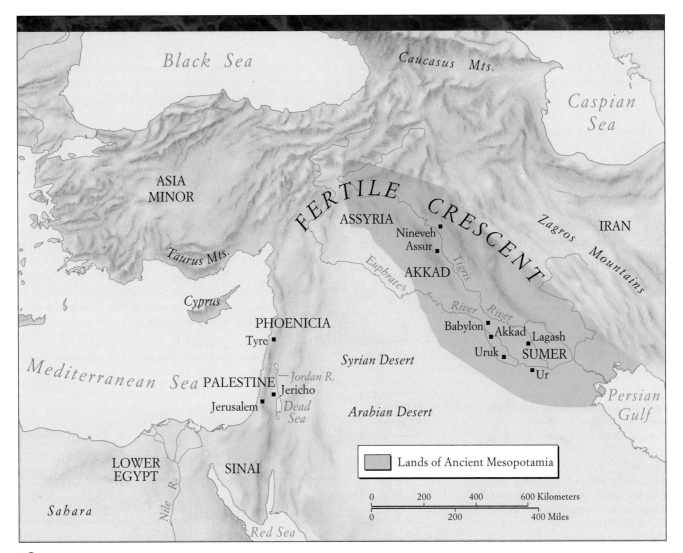

MAP 2.1 The Ancient Near East. The Mesopotamian city-states were concentrated on the rich agricultural plain created by silt from the Tigris and Euphrates Rivers as they flowed toward the head of the Persian Gulf. The wide belt of land reaching from Mesopotamia to Egypt along the Mediterranean coast is known as the Fertile Crescent.

the first people in those regions. Unlike most of their neighboring tribes, the Sumerians were not members of the **Semitic** language family. (Note: A language group or family is related by its grammar and sometimes by its vocabulary and alphabet. The Semitic family is one of the major language families in the world and includes both Hebrew and Arabic as well as many others.)

By somewhere about 3000 B.C.E., the Sumerians had extended their domain upriver into the Semite-inhabited places. Either by coercion or peaceably, they began to civilize these *barbarians* (a Greek word meaning people who speak a different language and are supposedly inferior). Large towns grew up, with neighborhoods of craftspeople, merchants, and laborers. Trade grew rapidly, not only between food-growing villages and the towns but also among the towns scattered for hundreds of miles along the banks of the rivers.

The early history of Mesopotamia under the Sumerians is a tale of great technological and cultural advances, marred by strife, disunion, and unceasing warfare. Trade wars and disputes over water assured that no centralized governing power was possible. Whenever a city managed to seize control of substantial supplies of water and trade, the others upstream or downstream would band together against it, or its subjects would rebel. Conflicts seem to have been the order of the day, with city-state vying against city-state in a constant struggle for mastery over the precious irrigated lands.

Not until about 2300 B.C.E. was the land between the rivers brought under one effective rule, and that was imposed by a Semitic invader known as **Sargon** the Great, who conquered the entire plain. Sargon established his capital in the new town of Akkad, near modern-day Baghdad, capital of Iraq. Although the Akkadian empire lasted less than a century, its influence was great, for it spread Sumerian culture and methods far and wide in the Near and Middle East, through that wide belt of land reaching from Mesopotamia to Egypt that is called the **Fertile Crescent** (see Map 2.1).

Although the Sumerian city-states never united until they were overwhelmed by outsiders, their cultural and religious achievements and beliefs would be picked up by their conquerors and essentially retained by all their successors in Mesopotamia. Perhaps the most important of all the Sumerian accomplishments was the gradual invention of a system of writing.

The Evolution of Writing

Some type of marks on some type of medium (clay, paper, wood, stone) had been in use long, long before 3500 B.C.E.

What did the Sumerians of that epoch do to justify the claim of having invented writing? Significantly, they moved beyond pictorial writing, or symbols derived from pictures, into a further phase of conveying meaning through abstract marks.

All writing derives from a picture originally. This is called *pictography,* and it has been used from one end of the Earth to the other. Pictography had several obvious disadvantages, though. For one thing, it could not convey the meaning of abstractions (things that have no material, tangible existence). Nor could it communicate the tense of a verb, or the degree of an adjective or adverb, or many other things that language has to handle well.

The way that the Sumerians (and later peoples) got around these difficulties was to gradually expand their pictorial writing to a much more sophisticated level, so that it included special signs for abstractions, tenses, and so on—signs that had nothing to do with tangible objects. These are called conventional signs and may be invented for any meaning desired by their users. For example, if both of us agree that the signs "cc~" stand for "the boy in the blue suit," then that is what they mean when we see them on a piece of paper, or a rock surface, or wherever. If we further agree that by adding the vertical stroke "!" we make a verb

✿ **The Development of Cuneiform.**
After earlier experimentation with pictographic writing, the Sumerians devised a script called *cuneiform* (wedge shaped). Because this system of signs transcribed sounds rather than pictures or ideas, it was adaptable to other spoken languages as well. Thus, cuneiform writing was later used by several other peoples.

Original pictograph	Pictograph in position of later cuneiform	Early Babylonian	Assyrian	Original or derived meaning
				Bird
				Fish
				Donkey
				Ox
				Sun Day
				Grain
				Orchard
				To plow To till
				Boomerang To throw To throw down
				To stand To go

into a future tense, then it's future tense so far as we're concerned. Very slowly, the Sumerians expanded their pictographs in this way, while simultaneously simplifying and standardizing their pictures, so that they could be written more rapidly and recognized more easily by strangers.

A big breakthrough came sometime in the third millennium, when a series of clever scribes began to use written signs to indicate the sounds of the spoken language. This was the beginning of the *phonetic written language,* in which the signs had a direct connection with the oral language. Although the Sumerians did not progress as far as an alphabet, they started down the path that would culminate in one about 2,000 years later.

The basic format of the written language after about 3500 B.C.E. was a script written in wedge-shaped characters, the **cuneiform,** on clay tablets about the size of your hand. Tens of thousands of these tablets covered by cuneiform writings have been dug up in modern times. Most of them pertain to contracts between private parties or between a private party and the officials. But other tablets contain prayers of all sorts, proclamations by officials, law codes and judgments, and some letters and poetry. Sumerian cuneiform remained the basic script of most Near and Middle Eastern languages until about 1000 B.C.E., when its use began to fade out.

Mathematics and Chronology

After the invention of writing, perhaps the most dramatic advance made by these early inhabitants of Mesopotamia was in mathematics and chronology. Sumerian math was based on units of sixty, and this, of course, is the reason that we still measure time in intervals of sixty seconds and sixty minutes. Much of our basic geometry and trigonometry also stems from the Sumerians. Their calendar was based on the movement of the moon and was thus a lunar calendar, as were the calendars of most other ancient peoples. The year was based on the passage of seasons and the position of the stars. It was subdivided into lunar months, corresponding to the period between one full moon and the next. In calculating the year's length, the Sumerians arrived at a figure very close to our own, though they were not quite as close as the Egyptians were. All in all, Sumerian math, including its further development by the Babylonians and Persians, has held up very well and has been influential in all later Western theory of science, including that of the Greeks.

✿ **Cuneiform Writing.** This example of cuneiform writing describes an old Babylonian sacred marriage rite. *(Erich Lessing/Art Resource)*

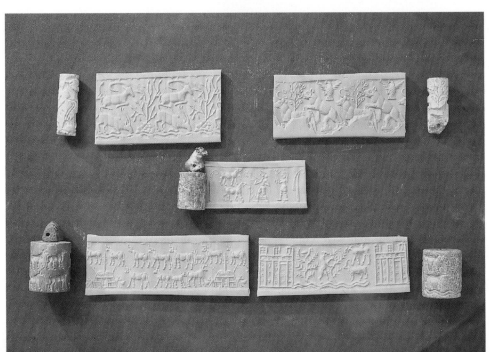

✿ **Sumerian Seals.** These carved cylindrical seals of ivory were equivalent to signatures, identifying the authors of the clay tablet documents they marked. Some have been found as far away as India. *(Scala/Art Resource)*

The *Epic of Gilgamesh*

The collection of stories that are termed the *Epic of Gilgamesh* are one of the earliest approaches to analyzing the relations of gods and humans. It portrays a society in search of a religious basis for human action.

Stories of the Flood occur in many ancient cultural traditions. In each case, the story tells of a disastrous flood that engulfed the entire Earth and nearly annihilated humanity. The most familiar flood story in the Western world is found in the Book of Genesis in the Old Testament.

In the Middle Eastern tradition, the narrative of the Flood is first found in the *Epic of Gilgamesh*. In this version, the main focus of the story is on the inevitability of death and the defeat of the hero as he attempts to achieve immortality. The Mesopotamian counterpart of the biblical Noah is Utnapishtim. Here his description of the flood is contrasted with the version recounted in Genesis:

Gilgamesh

The gods of the abyss rose up; Nergal pulled out the dams of the netherworld, Ninurta the war-lord threw down the dikes . . . a stupor of despair went up to heaven when the god of storms turned daylight into darkness, when he smashed the earth like a teacup. One whole day the tempest raged, gathering fury as it went, and it poured over the people like the tide of battle; a man could not see his brother nor could the people be seen from heaven. Even the gods were terrified at the flood, they fled to the highest heaven . . . they crouched against the walls, cowering . . . the gods of heaven and hell wept . . . for six days and six nights the winds blew, tempest and flood raged together like warring hosts . . . I looked at the face of the earth, and all was silence, all mankind was turned into clay. . . . I bowed low, and I wept. . . .

Genesis

All the fountains of the great deep burst forth and the floodgates of the heavens were opened. And rain fell on the earth for forty days and forty nights. . . . The waters increased and bore up the ark, and it rose above the earth. The waters rose higher and higher, and increased greatly on the earth . . . the waters rose higher and higher, so that all the highest mountains everywhere under the heavens were covered. All flesh that moved on the earth died: birds, cattle, wild animals, all creatures that crawl upon the earth, and all men. Only Noah and those with him in the ark were saved.

Gilgamesh is a grim tale that speaks of death and the afterlife in pessimistic and fearful tones. Indicative is this description by Gilgamesh's companion Enkidu of a vivid dream he had had, foreshadowing his approaching death:

I stood alone before an awful Being; his face was somber like the blackbird of the storm. He fell upon me with the talons of an eagle, and he held me fast, pinioned by his claws until I smothered; then he transformed me so that my arms became wings covered with feathers . . . and he led me away, to the house from which those who enter never return . . . whose people sit in darkness, dust their food and clay their meat. They are clothed like birds with wings for coverings, they see no light, they sit in darkness. . . .

The epic ends with the failure of Gilgamesh's quest for the secret of immortal life. The somber funeral chant seems to underline the poet's sense of resignation and futility:

The king has laid himself down, and will not rise again
The Lord of Kullab [that is, Gilgamesh] will not rise again,
He overcame evil, but he will not rise again,
Though he was strong of arm, he will not rise again,
Possessing wisdom and a comely face, he will not rise again.

For Reflection

Why do you think the ending of the story shows Gilgamesh failing in his search for immortal life? Why do you think the Flood story rather than some other sort of catastrophe was adopted in the Middle East's earliest civilizations?

Religion and the Afterlife

Our knowledge of the Sumerians' religion is sketchy and unsure. Apparently, they believed in a host of gods (**polytheism,** or "many gods") of various ranks. There were many male and female deities, each with specific competencies in human affairs.

The gods were much like superhumans, with all the faults and weaknesses of men and women. Some of them lived forever. Others died just as humans did. Some were immensely powerful, others rather insignificant. Each major city developed its own set of powerful gods and attempted to please its chief gods by building enormous temples, called *ziggurats.* The best-known ziggurat was erected by the powerful city of **Babylon** long after the Sumerian epoch. It was the Tower of Babel of biblical fame.

The gods were frequently cruel toward their human creatures and highly unpredictable. There is no trace of a loving relationship between deity and men. Nor is there any trace of ethics in Mesopotamian religion. The demands of the gods had no intrinsic connection with doing good or avoiding evil on Earth. The gods often punished humans, but not for what we would call sin. When comprehensible at all, the reasons for the punishment were petty and unworthy, but generally, they were simply unknowable. The punishments often took the form of natural catastrophes, such as droughts or floods. To avert punishment, the gods had to be appeased with frequent, costly rituals and ceremonies, which were the responsibility of a hereditary priesthood. The priests used their power as interpreters of the will of the gods to create large and wealthy temple communities, supported by the offerings of the citizens. In some Sumerian cities, the priests seem to have been the true rulers for a time. This practice ended with the conquest by Sargon the Great, who made the royal throne the undisputed center of authority.

The religion was certainly not an optimistic one, and it seems to have had no clear ideas on the nature of the afterlife or who, if anyone, could enjoy immortality. The best approach seemed to be to honor and obey the gods as well as you could, to appease them by making offerings through their very powerful priests, and to hope for the best in the afterlife, if there was one. The concept of a heaven or a hell seems to have been very vague.

Much of what is known about Mesopotamian religious belief derives from their literature, in which several major myths of Western civilization, including the Flood and the Garden of Eden, find their first expressions. Particularly important is the creation myth embraced in the ***Epic of Gilgamesh,*** the first epic poem in world literature. Gilgamesh is a man, a king of one of the city-states, who desires the secret of immortal life, but the gods, jealous of his power, defeat him. The excerpts in the Religion and Morality box show the similarity between the flood stories in *Gilgamesh* and the Book of Genesis of the Judeo-Christian Scripture.

Ishtar Gate. Now in a German museum, this magnificent portal known as the Ishtar Gate was erected in the walls of one of the Mesopotamian cities. It shows the advanced artistic achievement of the age. *(Erich Lessing/Art Resource)*

Law and Government

One of the earliest known complete code of laws originated in post-Sumerian Mesopotamia, in the 1700s B.C.E. during the reign of the emperor **Hammurabi.** He is the first of the historic lawgivers whose work has survived into our times. (His accomplishments are described in the Law and Lawgivers box.) His code certainly had predecessors that have been lost, because its legal concepts and vocabulary are much too sophisticated for it to have been a first effort.

The code is based on two distinctive principles: punishment depended on the social rank of the violator, and offenders were subjected to the same damages or injury that they caused to others. These ideas would be incorporated into many later codes over the next two thousand years. A commoner would get a different, more severe punishment than a noble or official would receive for the same offense. And a slave (of whom there were many) would be treated more harshly still. If in the same social class as the victim,

the offender would have to give "an eye for an eye, a tooth for a tooth." Another basic principle of Mesopotamian law was that the government should act as an impartial referee among its subject citizens, seeing to it that the wronged party got satisfaction from the evildoer. The victim had the right to demand personal compensation from the person who had caused him grief—a legal concept that is gradually being reintroduced into American criminal law.

People were not equal before the law: husbands had a great deal of power over wives, fathers over children, rich over poor, free citizens over slaves. Nevertheless, a definite attempt was made to protect the defenseless and to see that all received justice.

Much of Hammurabi's code dealt with social and family problems, such as the support of widows and orphans, illegitimacy, adultery, and rape. Clearly, the position of women was inferior to men, but they did have certain legal rights and were not just the property of their male relatives. A wife could divorce her husband, and if the husband was found to be at fault, she was entitled to the property she had brought into the marriage. A woman could also enter into contracts and have custody over minor children under certain conditions—two rights that many later civilizations denied them. The "Code of Hammurabi" box gives some examples of Hammurabi's laws.

Government in Mesopotamia can be divided into two types: the **theocracy** (rule by gods or their priests) of the

Hammurabi

The Babylonian emperor Hammurabi, who ruled Mesopotamia from about 1792 to about 1750 B.C.E., is best known for the code of laws that bears his name, one of the earliest law codes yet discovered. Hammurabi's empire stretched from the desolate mountains of Zagros in western Iran, to the edge of the Arabian desert. It was centered on the great city of Babylon in central Mesopotamia. Though nature has not been generous with this region, he was successful in bringing prosperity and peace to the majority of his subjects.

Like all Middle Eastern kingdoms, Hammurabi's empire was originally created by conquest. He formed coalitions with his Semite neighbors and won the loyalty of the smaller Amorite city-states that surrounded his own. Babylon emerged as a center of both manufacturing and trade, and its influence reached from the head of the Persian Gulf to the eastern shore of the Mediterranean.

Hammurabi was a tireless builder, spending much time repairing older temples and constructing new ones dedicated to Babylon's many gods. Among his more important economic undertakings was the construction of several new canals to move the waters of the Tigris farther into the desert and allow new agricultural colonies to flourish. He established a courier service and built roads so the messengers could travel quickly. His government combined a central court with subordinate local lords, a system that would later be used effectively by the Persian Empire.

But the emperor's main concern was to maintain order through good law. To that effect, he gave his subjects a complex law code. Its 282 decrees, collectively termed the Code of Hammurabi, were inscribed on stone stelae or columns and erected in many public places. One was discovered in Persian Susa and is now in the Louvre in Paris.

The code dealt primarily with civil affairs such as marriage and inheritance, family relations, property rights, and business practices. Criminal offenses were punished with varying degrees of severity, depending on the social status of the offender and the victim. Trial by ordeal, retribution by retaliatory action, and capital punishment were common practices. Children were often made to suffer for the sins of their fathers. But judges made a clear distinction between intentional and unintentional injuries, and monetary fines were normally used as punishment where no malicious intent was manifested. The "eye for an eye" morality often associated with Hammurabi's code was relatively restricted in application. The code made theft a serious crime and devoted great attention to crimes against property in general. Marriage and inheritance, business contracts, and commercial transactions of all kinds were strictly regulated and enforced. Workers had to do an adequate job or be punished for negligence. Official fee tables were ordained for medical care, and woe to the doctor who was found guilty of malpractice! Although the code did not concern itself with religious belief or practice, it did accord considerable powers to the administering judges, who were often priests. In general, it established strict standards of justice and public morality.

Hammurabi stands forth after four thousand years as a ruler of exceptional ability. His subjects enjoyed a period of prosperity, in part because of the personal interest he took in all branches of government. In the prologue to the code, he stated, "When Marduk sent me to rule the people . . . I established law and justice in the land, and promoted the welfare of the people." It is a proud boast, and one that apparently has been validated by history. Long after the emperor's death, his law was still the basis of a great civilization.

For Reflection

How does the Hammurabi Code show that property rights were superior to human rights? Is it unusual to show class distinctions in the application of laws?

early city-states of the Sumerians, and the kingdom-empires of their successors, starting with Sargon the Great of Akkad. The cities were ruled by a king, assisted by noble officials and priests. In Sumerian times, the kings were no more than figureheads for the priests, but later they exercised decisive power.

Social Structure

Mesopotamia had three social classes. First was a small group of nobles and priests who were great landlords and had a monopoly on the higher offices of the city. The second group, the freemen, were the most numerous class. They did the bulk of the city's work and trading and owned and worked most of the outlying farmlands. Finally, the slaves, who at times were very numerous, often possessed considerable skills and were given some responsible positions. Freemen had some political rights, but slaves had none.

As we will repeatedly see, slaves were common in most ancient societies, and enslavement was by no means the morally contemptible and personally humiliating condition it would frequently become later. Slavery had nothing much to do with race or ethnicity and everything to do with bad luck, such as being on the losing side of a war or falling

The Code of Hammurabi

Engraved in a stele (a stone pillar) of black basalt, some 282 laws were decreed by King Hammurabi as the basic governance of his wide empire. In the name of the gods, the king demanded that his subjects observe rules of behavior that were strict but nicely calculated to maintain a system of property and social relations already deeply embedded in Mesopotamia. The stele shows the king receiving the laws from the sun god Shamash, and in a long cuneiform text below quotes the laws themselves.

The majority pertain to two categories: (1) property rights and (2) family and interpersonal relations. In the first category there are clear distinctions between the rights of the upper classes and those of the commoners. Money payments are generally allowed as restitution for damage done to the commoners by the nobles. A commoner who causes damage to a noble, however, might have to pay with his head. On the other hand, damage done to the person of a noble by a fellow noble, or to a commoner by another commoner, had to be compensated by a direct equivalent penalty—the famous "eye for an eye" motto.

In the second category, Hammurabi regulated many aspects of interpersonal relations, almost always with a bias toward protection of male and upper-class privileges. For example, a man's wife who has neglected her domestic duties could be drowned by the husband, but a man who went about abusing his (innocent) wife's reputation could only be forced to give back the property she had brought into the marriage (dowry).

Some other examples:

Law 129: If a free man's wife is caught in adultery, both wife and adulterer shall be drowned, unless the husband requests otherwise and allows his wife to return to him.

Law 131: If a free man's wife is accused of adultery but is not caught redhanded and denies the charge as a solemn oath, she shall be allowed to return to her home unpunished.

Law 196: If a free man causes a free woman to have a miscarriage by his action, he shall make restitution for the loss by paying 10 shekels' fine.

 Stele of Hammurabi. (e.t.archive)

into debt. Most slaves in Mesopotamia—and elsewhere—had run up debts that they could not otherwise repay. It was not at all uncommon to become someone's slave for a few years and then resume your freedom when you had paid off what you owed. Hereditary slavery was rare. Many owners routinely freed their slaves in their wills as a mark of piety and benevolence.

Maltreatment of slaves did occur, but mostly to field workers, miners, or criminals who had been enslaved as punishment and had had no personal contacts with their owner. On the other side, in all ancient societies many slaves engaged in business, many had advanced skills in the crafts, and some managed to accumulate enough money working on their own accounts that they could buy their freedom. The conditions of slavery in the ancient world varied so enormously that we cannot generalize about them with any accuracy except to say that slaves were politically and legally inferior to free citizens.

Successors to Sumeria

After the conquest by Sargon of Akkad, Mesopotamia was subjected to a long series of foreign invasions and conquests by nomadic peoples eager to enjoy the fruits of civilized life. These barbaric nomads generally adopted the beliefs and values of those they had conquered. After the Akkadians, the most important of them were as follows, in sequence:

1. The *Amorites,* or *Old Babylonians,* a Semitic people who conquered the plains under their great emperor Hammurabi in the 1700s B.C.E.

Sumerian Art. This golden bull's head adorns a lyre unearthed in the royal tombs of Ur, southern Mesopotamia. It dates from roughly 2500 B.C.E. *(Lynn Abercrombie)*

2. The **Hittites,** an Indo-European group of tribes who came out of southern Russia into modern-day Turkey and constructed an empire there that reached far into the east and south. The first people to smelt iron, the Hittites were a remarkable group who took over the river plain about 1500. They were skilled administrators and established the first example of a multinational state, which worked fairly well.

3. After the Hittites fell to unknown invaders about 1200, the *Assyrians* gradually established themselves, operating from their northern Mesopotamian center at Nineveh. We will deal with the Imperial Assyrian period from about 800 to 600 B.C.E. in Chapter 4.

4. Finally, after a very brief period under the *New Babylonians* (or *Chaldees,* as the Old Testament calls them), the plains fell to the mighty *Persian Empire* in the 500s B.C.E. and stayed under Persian (Iranian) rule for most of the next 1,000 years (see Chapter 4).

The Decline of Mesopotamia in World History

The valley of the Tigris and Euphrates Rivers ceased to be of central importance in the ancient world after the Persian conquest. The Persians did not choose to make their capital there, nor did they adopt the ideas and the cultural models of their new province, as all previous conquerors had. The Persians were already far advanced beyond barbarism when they conquered Mesopotamia and perhaps were not so easily impressed.

Various problems contributed to the decline of Mesopotamia, but it is certain that it proceeded in part from one of the first known examples of long-term environmental degradation. Significantly, the cities' food supply declined as the irrigated farms of the lower plains no longer produced abundant harvests. Thanks to several thousand years of salt deposits from the evaporated waters of the canals and ditches, the fields, unrenewed by fertilizers and exposed to a gradually harshening climate of sandstorms and great heat, were simply not capable of producing as much as the population needed. The once thriving city-states and rich fields were gradually abandoned, and the center of power and culture moved elsewhere.

Mesopotamia slowly receded into the background of civilized activities from the Persian conquest until the ninth century C.E., when for a time it became the political and spiritual center of the far-flung world of Islam. But it was not until the mid-twentieth century, with the rise of Muslim fundamentalism and the coming of the Oil Age, that the area again became a vital world center.

SUMMARY

The Sumerians were the first civilized inhabitants of the dual-river plain and left their several successors-in-power a variety of techniques and attitudes that they adopted and adapted. Of all the Sumerian achievements, none are more important than the invention of writing and the mastery of town building and urban living skills. Their religious beliefs seem harsh and pessimistic now but apparently reflected their perceptions of the world around them.

During the many centuries from 3500 to the Persian conquest, the Mesopotamian valley was the most important single contributor to the spread of civilization in southern Asia and the eastern Mediterranean. Its science and laws, its arts and architecture were strongly reflected in both the classical Greek tradition and the ideas and beliefs of the Hebrews—two very notable ancestors of the Western world.

TEST YOUR KNOWLEDGE

1. The founders of ancient Mesopotamian civilization were the
   a. Sumerians.
   b. Amorites.
   c. Semites.
   d. Babylonians.
2. The Tigris and Euphrates were important to Mesopotamians primarily because
   a. they kept out potential raiders.
   b. they made irrigation possible.
   c. they drained off the water from the frequent storms.
   d. they brought the people together.
3. The Mesopotamian ziggurat was a
   a. military fort.
   b. temple of worship.
   c. household shrine.
   d. royal palace.
4. Pictographs are a form of writing that
   a. uses pictures and words.
   b. uses agreed-on signs to make pictures.
   c. puts abstract ideas into pictorial form.
   d. uses pictures of material objects to form meanings.
5. Mesopotamians considered their gods to be
   a. about equal in power.
   b. the creators of people and the universe.
   c. responsive to human needs and wants.
   d. disembodied spirits.
6. The *Epic of Gilgamesh* deals with the
   a. struggle between good and evil.
   b. details of death and the afterlife.
   c. proof of the existence of gods.
   d. conflict between men and women.
7. The law code of King Hammurabi
   a. ensured equal treatment for all offenders.
   b. was the first law code ever written.
   c. used fines and financial punishments exclusively.
   d. ordered punishments in accord with the social rank of the offender.
8. In Sumerian and later government in Mesopotamia
   a. theocracy succeeded the rule of kings.
   b. a warrior aristocracy was the rule from the beginning.
   c. a monarchy succeeded the rule of priests.
   d. the common people always had the last word.
9. A chief cause for the decline of Mesopotamia in importance after the Persian conquests seems to be
   a. an environmental change.
   b. the unceasing warfare among the Persians.
   c. the conquest of the area by barbarians.
   d. the technological lag from which the area had always suffered.

IDENTIFICATION TERMS

Babylon	*Gilgamesh*	polytheism	**Sumerians**
cuneiform	**Hammurabi**	**Sargon**	**theocracy**
Fertile Crescent	**Hittites**	**Semitic**	

INFOTRAC COLLEGE EDITION

Enter the search term "Mesopotamia" using Key Words.
Enter the search terms "Sumer or Sumerian" using Key Words.

Enter the search term "Babylonian" using Key Words.

Chapter 3

Egypt

To whom can I speak today?/Hearts are rapacious/And everyone takes his neighbor's goods . . ./To whom can I speak today?/Men are contented with evil/And Goodness is neglected everywhere.

FROM A PAPYRUS, "THE MAN WHO WAS TIRED OF LIFE," c. 1800 B.C.E.

IT WOULD BE HARD TO FIND two other ancient civilizations that present as sharp a contrast in some respects as Mesopotamia on one end of the Fertile Crescent and Egypt on the other. Although they were only some 800 miles apart over countryside that is relatively easy to cross and were both based on intensive irrigated farming, the two civilizations evolved very different patterns of beliefs and values. Unlike Mesopotamia, Egypt was an island in time and space that enjoyed a thousand years or more of civilized living with little disturbance from the outside world.

The Natural Environment

Like Mesopotamia, Egypt depended on the waters of a great river system. Egypt is, and has always been, the valley of the Nile—a green strip averaging about thirty miles wide, with fierce desert hills on either side. The 4,000-mile river itself originates far to the south in the lakes of central Africa and flows north until it empties into the Mediterranean Sea at Alexandria.

Unlike the Tigris and Euphrates, the Nile is a benevolent river, and without it life in Egypt would have been unthinkable. In contrast to the frequent destructive flooding of the Tigris, the Nile annually would swell gently until it overflowed its low banks and spread out over the valley floor, carrying with it a load of extremely fertile silt. Two or three weeks later, the flood would subside, and the river would recede, depositing the silt to renew the valley with a fresh layer of good topsoil. The Egyptians trapped receding waters in a series of small reservoirs connected to an intricate system of ditches that would later convey the water into the surrounding fields for irrigation.

Climatic advantages make Egypt an ideal area for intensive agriculture, and it has supported three crops a year for a very long time. The entire year is one long growing season in Egypt. The climate is moderate and constant, with no storms and no frosts ever. The sun shines in modern Egypt an average of 361 days per year, and there is no reason to think that it was any different 4,000 years ago. Rain is almost unknown, and the temperature is in the seventies year-round. In Mesopotamia, by contrast, farmers have always had to cope with excessive heat, drought, sandstorms, occasional floods, and insect invasions.

Egypt's Protective Isolation

But not only in agriculture was Egypt blessed by its environment. Unlike Mesopotamia, which had no real natural boundaries and was repeatedly invaded from all sides, Egypt was secure in its geographic isolation. The country was also protected against invasion by the deserts on the east and west of the valley and by the cataracts (rapids) of the northerly flowing Nile, which prevented easy passage into Egypt from the south, where enemies (Nubians, Ethiopians) dwelled. On the north, the sea gave the Nile delta some protection from unwanted intruders, while still allowing the Egyptians to develop maritime operations. Only on the northeast where the narrow Sinai peninsula links Egypt to Asia (see Map 3.1) was a land-based invasion possible, and most of Egypt's eventual conquerors arrived from this direction.

Egypt's natural walls kept it safe from external danger for a very long time, however. For about 2,500 years, Egyptian civilization developed in almost unbroken safety. But this isolation also had its drawbacks. When serious external challenges finally did come, the Egyptian governing class and general society were not prepared to resist effectively and could not adequately respond to the new situation.

Egypt's Uniqueness

No other ancient civilization was so "different" as Egypt. The country possessed everything needed for a decent life: excellent agriculture, natural barriers against invasion, great natural resources, and a skilled and numerous population. Together, they gave Egypt advantages that could only be envied.

In fact, over time the Egyptian educated class, especially the officials and priests, developed a sort of superiority complex toward foreigners that is rivaled in history only by that of the Chinese. The Egyptians were convinced that the gods smiled on them and their land, that they already possessed the best of all worlds in Egypt, and that they could learn nothing of significant value from others. When the king dealt with foreign traders, he could successfully pretend to his own people that the foreigners had come to "give tribute," while the king showed his own generosity by showering "gifts" in return.

So secure were the Egyptians for so long that their security eventually turned into a weakness. Their conviction of superiority became a kind of mental cage, hemming in their imaginations and preventing the Egyptians from responding to change, even as change became increasingly necessary. In short, they lost their abilities to adapt effectively. But this weakness took a very long time to show itself—about 2,000 years!

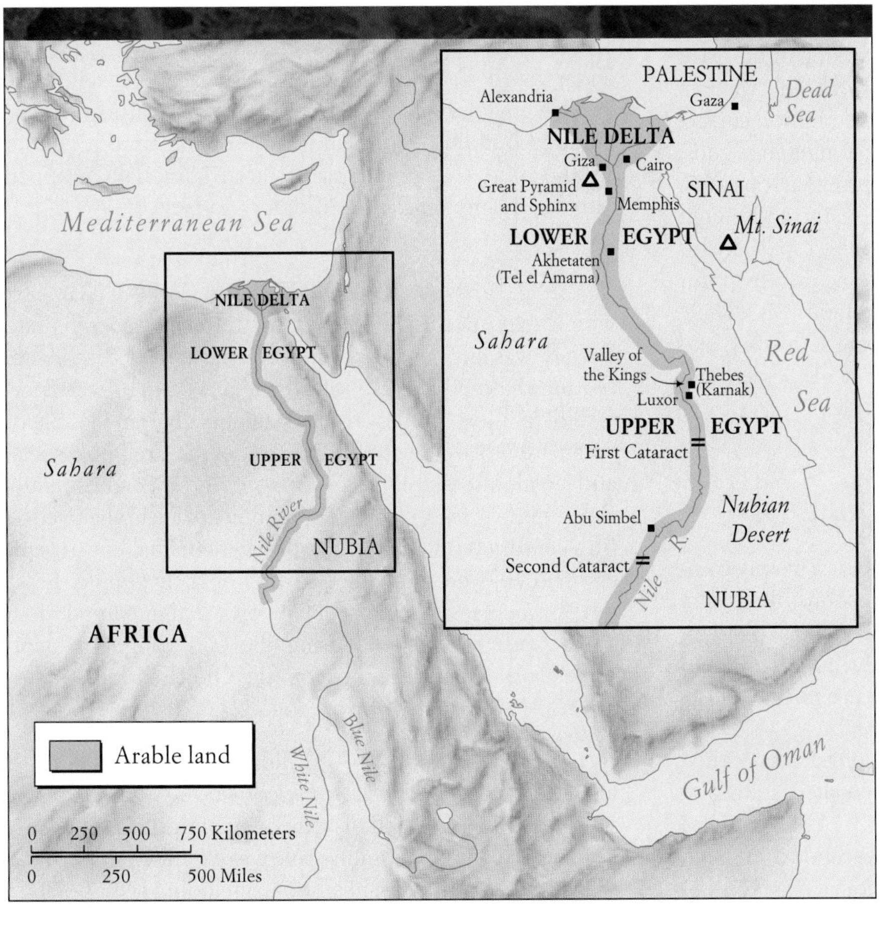

MAP 3.1 **Ancient Egypt and the Nile.** The first tourist to leave an account of Egypt was the Greek Herodotus in the fifth century B.C.E. He called Egypt "the gift of the Nile," a phrase that still describes the relation of the river and the people. The arable portion of the Nile valley extended about 800 miles upriver in ancient times.

The Pharaoh: Egypt's God-King

❉

As is true of almost all early peoples, the Egyptians' religious beliefs reflected their environment to some extent, and the fully developed religion had an enormous impact on the nature of their government.

In contrast to Mesopotamia, Egypt was quickly and easily unified. About 3100 B.C.E. all the middle and lower reaches of the Nile valley came under one ruler. From the Mediterranean Sea southward to the Nubian desert, the country and the numerous already-civilized villagers came under the control of a **pharaoh** (meaning "from the great house"). The first pharaoh was called Menes, but he appears to have been merely a legend—or if he existed in fact, we know nothing of him but his name.

The period from 3100 to about 2500 B.C.E. was Egypt's foundation period and the time of its greatest triumphs and cultural achievements. During these centuries, the land was ruled by an unbroken line of god-kings who apparently faced no serious threats either inside or outside their domain.

It is important to recognize that the pharaoh was not *like* a god. Instead, he *was* a god, a god who chose to live on Earth for a time. From the moment that his days-long coronation ceremony was completed, he was no longer a mortal man. He had become immortal, a reincarnation of the great divinity **Horus.** The pharaoh's will was law, and his wisdom was all-knowing. What he desired was by definition correct and just. What he did was the will of the almighty gods, speaking through him as one of them. His regulations must be carried out without question. Otherwise, the gods might cease to smile on Egypt. His wife and family, especially his son who would succeed him, shared to some degree in this celestial glory, but only the reigning pharaoh was divine. Such powers in the monarch are quite rare in history, and Egypt's god-king was truly extraordinary in his powers and in the prestige he enjoyed among his people.

Government under the Pharaoh

The pharaoh governed through a bureaucracy, mainly composed of noble landowners who were responsible to him but were granted great local powers. When a weak pharaoh came to the throne, the power of the central authority could and occasionally did break down in the provinces, but its memory never disappeared entirely.

There were two intervals in Egypt's long history when the pharaoh's powers were seriously diminished, in the so-called *Intermediate Periods* of 2200–2100 B.C.E. and 1650–1570 B.C.E. The causes of the first breakdown remain unclear, but it was not the result of invasion. The second of these time periods is known to have been triggered by the invasion of the mysterious **Hyksos** people, who crossed the Sinai peninsula and entered the Nile delta. In both cases, a new, native Egyptian dynasty appeared within a century and reestablished strong government. The monarchy's grip on the loyalties of the people was sufficiently strong that it could reform the government in the same style with the same values and officials as before.

What enabled the pharaoh to retain such power over his subjects for so long? For almost 2,000 years, the belief in the divinity of the king (or queen—there were at least three female pharaohs) persisted, as did the conviction that Egypt was specially favored and protected by the gods. This was the result of the happy situation that Egypt enjoyed through climate and geography. Nature provided, as nowhere else, a perpetual abundance, making Egypt the only place in the known world at that time to export grain surpluses. Furthermore, for 3,000 years of civilized life, Egypt was only rarely touched by war and foreign invasion. For a very long time, until the Empire period, no army— that great eater of taxes—was necessary.

The Old Kingdom, Middle Kingdom, and New Kingdom

It has long been customary to divide Egypt's ancient history into *dynasties* (periods of monarchic rule by one family). In all there were thirty-one dynasties, beginning with the legendary Menes and ending with the dynasty that fell to the Persian invaders in 525. The greatest were those of the pyramid-building epoch and those of the Empire, about 1500–1300 B.C.E. The dynasties are traditionally grouped into three kingdoms: Old, Middle, and New.

Old Kingdom　The **Old Kingdom** (3100–2200 B.C.E.), which extended from Menes to the First Intermediate Period, was ancient Egypt's most fertile and successful era. During these 900 years, both form and content were perfected in most of those achievements that made Egypt great: art and architecture, divine monarchy, religion, social and economic stability, and prosperity. (See the Family Relations box for a sample of parental advice in the twenty-fifth century B.C.E.) The pharaohs were unchallenged leaders who enjoyed the willing loyalty of their people. Later developments were almost always only a slight variation on the pattern established during the Old Kingdom or, in some cases, a deterioration from the Old Kingdom model.

Middle Kingdom　The **Middle Kingdom** (2100–1650) followed the *First Intermediate Period* with 500 years of political stability and the continued refinement of the arts and crafts. The country under pharaoh's rule was extended up the Nile to the south. Trade with neighbors, including Mesopotamia

 **The Great Pyramids.** These three massive stone monuments lie just outside the modern city limits of Cairo. The center one is the pyramid of Khufu, or Cheops, the largest masonry construct of all time. Aside from serving as the pharaohs' tombs, the pyramids apparently held great religious significance to the Egyptians, who believed it an honor to contribute their labor and skill to their construction. The pyramids were replaced by underground tombs beginning in the Middle Kingdom, probably because of both the expense and difficulty of keeping them safe from tombrobbers, who were little deterred by religous principles. *(AKG London)*

and Nubia (see Map 3.1), gradually became more extensive. The condition of the laboring poor seems to have gradually worsened. Religion became more democratic in its view of who could enter the afterlife, and a small middle class of officials and merchants began to make itself apparent.

New Kingdom   The **New Kingdom** (1550–700) is also called the *Empire,* although the name really belongs only to its first three centuries (1550–1250). The New Kingdom began after the defeat of the Hyksos invaders in the 1500s (the *Second Intermediate Period*). It lasted through the years of imperial wars against the Hittites and others in Mesopotamia, which ended with Egyptian withdrawal.

Egyptian Hieroglyphics. The *Rosetta Stone* was discovered by French scientists accompanying Napoleon's army during its occupation of Egypt in the 1790s. It contains three versions of the same priestly decree for the second century B.C.E.: hieroglyphic Egyptian, demotic (cursive) Egyptian, and Greek. By comparing the three, the brilliant linguist Jean François Champollion was able in 1822 to finally break the code of hieroglyphic symbols and commence the modern study of the Egyptian language. *(The British Museum/Nawrocki Stock Photo, Inc.)*

The Instruction of the Vizier to His Son

Most of the documents we have from ancient Egypt are prayers and chronologies of the pharaohs. But some more personal writings also survived; they include contracts, wills, some letters, and collections of wise sayings that were thought important to preserve. Among the latter is a collection of parchment scrolls known as the Instruction from the important official Ptah-hotep to his presumably teenaged son. It was composed in the twenty-fifth century B.C.E., but its words could be applied to many a father-son relationship today.

Then he said to his son:

Let not your heart be puffed up because of your knowledge; be not confident because you are a wise man. Take counsel with the ignorant as well as the wise. The full limits of skill cannot be attained and there is no skilled man equipped to his full advantage. Good speech is more hidden than the emerald; but it may be found among maidservants. . . .

Justice is great, and its appropriateness is lasting; it has been shaken since the times of him who made it [that is, since the beginning of the world], but there is punishment for him who passes over its laws. It is the right path. . . . Wrongdoing has never brought its undertaking into port. It may be that fraud gains riches, but the strength of justice is that it lasts. . . .

If you are a man of standing and have founded a household and produce a son who is pleasing to god, if he is correct and inclines toward your ways and listens to your instructions, while his manners in your house are fitting, and if he takes care of your property as it should be, then seek out for him every useful action. He is your son . . . you should not cut your heart off from him. But a man's seed [children] often creates enmity. If he goes astray and transgresses your plans and does not carry out your instruction, so that his manners in your household are wretched, and he rebels against all that you say, while his mouth runs on in the most wretched talk, quite apart from his experience while he possesses nothing [that is, he doesn't know what he is talking about], you should cast him off; he is not your son at all. He was not really born to you. Thus you should enslave him entirely, according to his own speech. He is one whom the gods have condemned in the very womb.

For Reflection

What do you think the vizier meant by "there is no skilled man equipped to his full advantage"? And by his admonition "wrongdoing has never brought its undertaking into port"? Is the vizier too strict by your own standards? Or is he justified?

SOURCE: J. B. Pritchard, ed., Ancient Near Eastern Texts, 3d ed. © Copyright Princeton University Press, 1969. Reprinted by permission.

Then came long centuries of weakness and decline that ended with Egypt's conquest by foreigners.

The Empire was an ambitious experiment in which the Egyptians attempted to convert others to their lifestyle and government. The experiment did not work well, however. Apparently no one else was able to understand the Egyptian view of life or wanted it to be imposed on them. The Empire did not last because of both military reverses starting around the time of Akhnaton (1300s B.C.E.) and internal discontent. By 1100 the pharaoh again ruled only the Nile valley.

During their last 300 years of independent existence, the Egyptians were frequently subjected to foreign invasion, both over the Sinai desert and from the south by way of the great river. Before the Persians arrived in 525, others such as the Kushites (Ethiopians) and the Nubians (Sudanese) had repeatedly invaded—a sure sign that the power of the god-king over his people was weakening (see Chapters 4 and 20). But even after the Persian conquest, which marked the real end of ancient Egypt's existence as an independent state (all the way until the twentieth century!), the life of ordinary people in fields and orchards saw no marked change. Only the person to whom taxes were paid was

different. The lifestyle and beliefs of the inhabitants were by now so deeply rooted that no foreign overlord could alter them.

Cultural Achievements

❧

The wealth of the pharaoh and the willingness and skill of his people allowed the erection of the most stupendous monuments put up by any people or government anywhere: the pyramids and temples of the Old Kingdom. Visitors have marveled at these stone wonders ever since. The Great Pyramid of Khufu (Cheops), located a few miles outside present-day Cairo, is easily the largest and grandest edifice ever built. The pyramids (built between 2600 and 2100 B.C.E.) were designed as tombs for the living pharaoh and were built while he was still alive. They possessed immense religious significance for the Egyptians. Much is still unknown about the pyramids' true purposes, but the perfection of their construction and the art of the burial chambers show Egyptian civilization at its most impressive.

The pyramids were not the only stone monuments erected along the Nile. In the period around 1300, several warrior-pharaohs celebrated the fame of their empire by erecting enormous statues of themselves and their favored gods and even larger temples in which to put them. At the Nile sites of *Karnak* and *Tel el Amarna,* some of these still stand. Most losses of artistic and architectural wonders in Egypt have been caused not by time or erosion but by vandalism and organized tomb and treasure robbers over many centuries. All of the pharaohs' tombs discovered to date, except one, have long since been robbed of the burial treasure interred with the mummy of the dead king-god. The exception is the famous King Tutankhamen—King Tut—whose underground burial chamber was discovered in the early 1920s. (See the Tradition and Innovation box for a discussion of King Tut's significance, then and now.)

Egyptian statuary is distinguished by the peculiar combination of graceful and natural lines in association with great dignity and awesomeness. This awe is reinforced by the art and architecture that surround the great statues, which are designed to impress all onlookers with the permanence and power of the Egyptian monarchy. The Egyptians' mastery of stone is rivaled in Western civilization only by the artistry of the classical Greeks and Romans. And most of this art was apparently created by artists and architects who did not know the principle of the wheel and had only primitive tools and what we would consider very clumsy math and physics!

Other art forms in which Egypt excelled included fresco painting (tinting freshly laid plaster on interior walls), fine ceramics of all sorts and uses, imaginative and finely worked jewelry in both stones and metals, and miniature sculpture. When upper-class Egyptians died, hundreds of small statues would be buried with their mummified remains. The Egyptians believed that what had been precious to a person in earthly life would also be desired in the next (a belief shared by the people of Mesopotamia), so they interred statues representing the person's earthly family and friends. Music and dance were also well developed, as we know from their lively portrayal in thousands of paintings and statuary groups depicting the life of the people of all ranks from the nobles to the poorest peasants. Egypt's artistic heritage is exceeded by few, if any, other peoples of the Western tradition.

Hieroglyphics (sacred carving) were pictographs that could convey either an idea, such as "man," or a phonetic sound, by picturing an object that begins with a strong consonantal sound. The word for *owl,* for example, began with the consonant "m" sound in spoken Egyptian, so a picture of an owl could be used to indicate that sound. This beginning of an alphabet was not fully developed, however. The use of hieroglyphics, which began as far back as 3000 B.C.E., gradually faded out after Egypt lost its independence in the sixth century B.C.E. The complete repertory of 604 hieroglyphic symbols is now deciphered, enabling the reading of many thousands of ancient inscriptions.

Egyptian Female Deity. This figure of Selket, one of the many female deities in the Egyptian pantheon, was probably commissioned by a grateful devotee. Selket was the goddess who healed bites and wounds. (© *Boltin Picture Library*)

Religion and Eternal Life

Egypt's religion was almost infinitely polytheistic. At least 3,000 separate names of gods have been identified in Egyptian writings, many of them the same deities but with different names over the centuries. Chief among them were the gods of the sun, *Amon* and *Ra,* who were originally separate but later combined into one being. Other important deities included **Isis,** goddess of the Nile and of fertility; **Osiris,** god of the afterlife; their son, *Horus,* made visible in the ruling pharaoh; and *Ptah,* the god of all life on Earth.

The Egyptians believed firmly in the afterlife. Originally, it seems to have been viewed as a possibility only for the upper class, but gradually, the afterlife was democratized. By about 1000 B.C.E., most Egyptians believed in a scheme of eternal reward or punishment for their **ka,** which had to submit to Last Judgment by Osiris. "Ka" referred to the life-essence that could return to life, given the correct preparation, even after the death of the physical body.

Mostly, it seems, they expected reward. Egyptians thought of eternity as a sort of endless procession by the *ka* of the deceased through the heavens and the gods' abodes there. In the company of friends and family, watched over by the protective and benevolent gods, the individual would proceed in a stately circle around the sun forever. There was no need to work and no suffering. Such was heaven. The notion of hell as a place for the evil to pay for their sins came along in Egypt only during the New Kingdom, when things had begun to go sour.

The priests played an important role in Egyptian culture, though they were not as prominent as in several other civilizations. At times, they seem to have been the power behind the throne, especially when the king had made himself unpopular.

In the reign of the young and inexperienced **Akhnaton** (1367–1350), the priests opposed a unique experiment: the pharaoh's attempt to change the basic polytheistic nature of Egyptian religion. Why the young Akhnaton (aided by his beautiful wife Nefertiti) chose to attempt to introduce a **monotheist** ("one god") cult of the sun god, newly renamed Aton, we can only guess. The pharaoh announced that Aton was his heavenly father and that Aton alone was to be worshiped as the single and universal god of all creation. The priests naturally opposed this revolutionary change, and as soon as Akhnaton was dead (possibly by poison), they denounced his ideas and went back to the old ways (as described in the Tradition and Innovation box). This attempt at monotheism is a great novelty in ancient civilization, and it was not to be heard of again until the emergence of Judaism five or six centuries later.

Egypt's People and Their Daily Lives

❀

The Egyptian population was composed overwhelmingly of peasants, who lived in the villages that crowded along the Nile. Most were free tenant farmers who worked on the estate of a large landholder or government official, who had been granted the land as payment for services to the crown. Each village followed a similar pattern: the huts were set close together within the village, and the fields lay outside. Several adults lived in each hut. Each day the peasants would go out to work in the fields, care for the irrigation works, or tend the animals.

Besides farmers, many small merchants and craftspeople lived in the villages. But Egypt had no real cities as in Mesopotamia, where neighborhoods were filled with specialized wholesale and retail markets, and dozens of crafts were practiced in hundreds of workshops. Egypt's capital cities, such as Memphis, Tel el Amarna, and Thebes, were really royal palaces and pleasure grounds for the wealthy, not commercial centers. The common people had nothing to do with the capitals except for occasional huge labor projects. Trade and commerce were of relatively minor im-

✿ **Egyptian Fresco.** The Egyptians' love of music and feasting is evident in this fresco from a tomb near Thebes. The emphasis on the eyes of the female figures was one of the many conventions that the anonymous artists were obliged to follow. (© *Werner Forman Archive, British Museum, London/Art Resource*)

King Tutankhamen

The pharaoh **Tutankhamen** (ruled 1347–1339 B.C.E.) died at the age of eighteen without having done anything of consequence during his short reign. The world probably would never have noted him had not the British archaeologist Howard Carter stumbled on his grave 3,000 years later. Tut's real significance lies more in his reign's full restoration of the old polytheism, proving that the priesthood, ignored under Ahknaton, was now back in command. Tradition had prevailed, and it was not going to be challenged again by any pharaoh.

The son-in-law of Queen Nefertiti and King Akhnaton, Tutankhamen came to the throne about 1347 B.C.E. at the age of nine. This was soon after the controversial reign of Akhnaton, the reformer who had attempted to impose a monotheistic religion. Because Akhnaton had no surviving children, Tutankhamen rose to the throne while still very young.

After his accession, the young monarch ruled Egypt through a regency of senior officials. He remained with his court at Tel el Amarna, the city founded by Akhnaton, for only one year. Under the influence of the priests, he moved back to the old capital, Thebes, and changed his name from the original Tutankhaton to Tutankhamen as a token of his attachment to the traditional sun god, Amen (or Amon).

On the priests' advice, he issued a proclamation restoring the ancient cults and ordering his father-in-law's name and deeds to be removed from the monuments. He repaired and reconstructed the old temples, recast the statues of the various gods, and even prohibited the people from speaking the name of Akhnaton. He also reestablished the feast days that had been abolished and eliminated the last vestiges of monotheism. All these actions made him a favorite of the priests, who had been outraged at Akhnaton's actions.

Tutankhamen died suddenly in 1339 B.C.E. from unknown causes. In 1968, British doctors determined that he had died not of tuberculosis as had been previously thought but from a sharp blow to the head, either accidental or murderous. During the next dynasty, his name, along with those of other pharaohs, was also removed from the official list of Egyptian kings.

The young monarch was buried in the Valley of the Kings. There is clear evidence that his tomb, like others in the region, was robbed soon after it was completed. Apparently, the criminals were either caught or frightened off, for the treasure remained almost intact. The tomb was never molested again. Two hundred years later, the architects of the tomb of Ramses VI, excavating just above that of Tutankhamen, ordered the workers to dispose of their waste limestone down the slope, thus completely covering the earlier tomb. The rock chips hid the tomb entry for three millennia, until November 4, 1922, when Carter uncovered the steps leading down to the entrance gallery and the actual burial chamber beyond it.

No other archaeological discovery has received so much publicity. During the following decade, hundreds of articles appeared in the international press. Many of them were written for literary or popular consumption and had little or no scientific value. Many played up the "curse of the pharaohs," pointing out that more than twenty persons connected at some time or other with the unsealing of the tomb had died under somewhat mysterious circumstances in the 1920s and 1930s. The thousands of visitors who flocked to the site constantly interrupted Carter's scientific work. The publicity, however, greatly stimulated interest in Egypt and its ancient history. Many additional archaeological digs were undertaken in the Middle East and Central America, as well as in Egypt, supported by public interest in the new field. All in all, Tutankhamen's relics gave the young king far more fame than anything he did in his lifetime.

The Golden Death Mask of King Tut.
The burial site of young King Tutankhamen became one of the most spectacular archaeological finds of the twentieth century. For eight years, British archaeologist Howard Carter salvaged its magnificent treasure, classifying and restoring more than 5,000 objects, including a beautiful golden death mask, a gilded throne, statues, vases, and hundreds of artifacts made of wood covered in gold leaf and decorated with gems. A magnificent stone sarcophagus held the luxurious coffin, richly wrought in pure gold. The treasure offered scholars and the public a glimpse of the wealth of the ancient Egyptians and their Nile kingdom.
(© Boltin Picture Library)

For Reflection
What significance can the removal of Tut's name from the list of kings possess, in a society as conservative as Egypt's? What does his possible murder say of Egyptian government's nature?

portance in Egyptian history and for a very long period were treated as a monopoly belonging to the government's officials. A small middle class existed by consent of the government officialdom.

As the centuries passed, daily life changed remarkably little. Slavery was originally rare but increased during the Empire when professional soldiers became necessary and prisoners of war became common. As in Mesopotamia, slavery was most often the result of owing debts to a landlord or committing a serious crime. A kind of *serfdom*—lifelong restrictions on one's mobility—also came into existence in later Egypt. Free tenant families were gradually turned into serfs, probably because of debt, and then had to work the land on a system of sharecropping that ensured that they remained in their village.

All in all, however, the common people of Egypt were better off more of the time than the commoners in almost any other ancient society. They were usually free, had enough to eat, lived in one of the world's easiest and most healthful climates, did not have to pay heavy taxes until fairly late in the history of Egypt, and were usually ruled by a relatively just and effective government with honest officials. They even had hopes of pleasing the gods and attaining immortality. Compared with the fate of many others, that was not a bad prospect!

Egypt and Mesopotamia: Contrasts

The two great early centers of civilized life—Egypt and Mesopotamia—were situated fairly close to one another and experienced some cross-cultural stimuli at times. But their differences were notable and permanent. Egypt enjoyed enormous stability. Life was highly predictable: tomorrow was today and yesterday under very slightly changed circumstances. Mesopotamia was frequently subject to violent change. Not only were invasions or war commonplace, but the kings—who were men, not gods—were often challenged by rebels and curtailed in their power by rivals.

Egypt was protected from outsiders for a very long time by natural barriers and could pick and choose among the cultural influences that it wanted to adopt. Mesopotamia was a crossroads between barbarism and civilization, and between barbarian and barbarian. New ideas, new techniques, and new beliefs were introduced by invasion, trade, and simple curiosity.

Egypt had been a unified nation as long as anyone could remember. The Egyptians viewed the world as consisting of the Egyptian people and the rest, whom they regarded as inferiors who had little to teach Egypt. This feeling persisted long after the time when it was clearly no longer true, and it contributed much to the Egyptians' eventual vulnerability to outside forces. As their ability to resist foreign invaders declined, the Egyptian governing class took refuge in a false sense of superiority in culture.

Mesopotamia, on the other hand, was a melting pot. Repeatedly, large groups of outsiders would arrive with sufficient power to force their ideas and beliefs on the conquered people, at least for as long as they needed to strike roots and change some elements of the previous civilization. Stagnation could not occur—challenge was on the daily menu. In Egypt, the sense of superiority seems to have eventually become a sort of "defense mechanism" that prevented the rulers from seeing the truth and choked off badly needed reform. They viewed change as subversive and successfully resisted it for a long time—so long as to make successful adjustment to necessary change almost impossible.

Of these two early civilizations, Mesopotamia proved to be the major cradle of later Western traditions and beliefs. For all its long life and success, Egypt was something of an island in space and time, with relatively little permanent influence on its neighbors or on future generations. In the next chapter, we will look at some of those neighbors in the Near East, including two peoples who eventually conquered Egypt, the Assyrians and the Persians.

SUMMARY

The Nile valley produced a civilized society as early as any in the world, thanks to a unique combination of favorable climate and geography. Long before the emergence of central government under a god-king called pharaoh, the farmers along the river had devised an intricate system of irrigated fields that gave Egypt an enviable surplus of food. The unification of the villages was accomplished about 3100 B.C.E., giving rise to the high civilization of the Old Kingdom and its awesome monuments celebrating the linkage of Egypt and the protective gods. Two thousand years of prosperity and of isolation from contacts with others except on its own terms allowed the pharaohs' government to assume a superiority that, although originally justified, gradually became a clinging to tradition for its own sake. When Egypt faced the challenge of repeated foreign invasions after about 1000 B.C.E., the divine kings lost their stature, and the uniquely static civilization of the Nile fell under the sway of once disdained aliens from the east and south.

TEST YOUR KNOWLEDGE

1. Which of these adjectives would you *not* associate with ancient Egypt?
   a. Stable
   b. Predictable
   c. Poor
   d. Isolated
2. The geographic status of Egypt destined the country to be
   a. vulnerable to repeated invasions.
   b. a crossroads of travelers through the ages.
   c. almost self-contained.
   d. divided into many different natural regions.
3. The key element of Egypt's government was the
   a. pharaoh's efficient police.
   b. code of royal law.
   c. popular respect for the god-king.
   d. powerful military establishment.
4. The Middle Kingdom was ended in Egypt by
   a. the coming of the Hyksos invaders.
   b. the revolt against the pharaoh Ahknaton.
   c. the invasion by the Nubians.
   d. the Persian conquest.
5. The key to understanding the ancient Egyptian hieroglyphics was
   a. the conquest of Egypt by the Persians and their translations.
   b. the discovery of the similarities between them and ancient Sumerian writing.
   c. the translation of the Rosetta Stone.
   d. the ability of modern linguists using computers to compare them with other languages.
6. Slavery in Egypt
   a. became rarer as the New Kingdom expanded Egypt's borders.
   b. was the result mainly of debt and crime.
   c. was quite different from that of Mesopotamia in nature and causes.
   d. was almost unknown.
7. The pharaoh Akhnaton fostered
   a. a belief in a single god.
   b. a return to traditional religious belief.
   c. a major reform in landholding and agriculture.
   d. a major change in government's nature.
8. Which of the following was *least* likely to have occurred in Egypt from 3000 to about 1000 B.C.E.?
   a. A social rebellion against the government
   b. A drastic change in the prestige of various Egyptian deities
   c. An invasion from outside Egypt
   d. An attempt to extend rule over non-Egyptians
9. A chief difference between Egypt and Mesopotamia was their relative degree of
   a. dependence on irrigation farming.
   b. importance of city life and commerce.
   c. degree of democratic government.
   d. artistic creativity.

IDENTIFICATION TERMS

Akhnaton	Isis	monotheism	Osiris
Horus	*ka*	New Kingdom	pharaoh
Hyksos	Middle Kingdom	Old Kingdom	Tutankhamen

INFOTRAC COLLEGE EDITION

Enter the search term "Egypt history" using the Subject Guide.
Enter the search term "pharaoh" using Key Words.

Enter the search term "Tutankhamen" using Key Words.

Chapter 4

Empires and Theology in the Near East: Persians and Jews

The Lord our God made a covenant, not only with our fathers, but with all of us living today. . . . The Lord said, "I am the Lord your God . . . Worship no God but me."

THE BIBLE

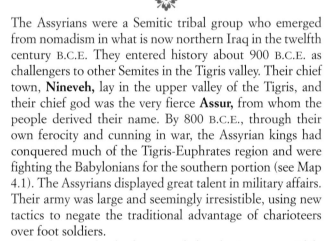

1900s B.C.E.	Hebrews leave Mesopotamia
c. 1250 B.C.E.	Hebrew Exodus from Egypt
c. 1000 B.C.E.	Hebrew kingdom established
	Phoenicians develop alphabet
c. 800 B.C.E.	Assyrian empire founded
	Carthage founded by Phoenicians
722 B.C.E.	Assyrians conquer Samaria
612 B.C.E.	Fall of Nineveh/end of Assyrian empire
500s	Establishment of Persian empire
586–539 B.C.E.	Babylonian Captivity of Jews

THE NEAR EAST BETWEEN the Nile valley and the Sumerians soon became a region of cultural overlap and interchange. First one people and then another would take command of a portion of the region for a century or more, only to fall under the sway of the next onslaught of newcomers. Kingdoms arose whose very names are sometimes forgotten but whose contributions to the ascent of civilization in this region were impressive. In this chapter, we look at three of these—briefly at Assyria and Phoenicia, and in more detail at Persia. Then we review the history of the Hebrews, a small people whose achievement lay in their unusual vision of the relation of God and humans.

The Assyrian Empire

❈

The Assyrians were a Semitic tribal group who emerged from nomadism in what is now northern Iraq in the twelfth century B.C.E. They entered history about 900 B.C.E. as challengers to other Semites in the Tigris valley. Their chief town, **Nineveh,** lay in the upper valley of the Tigris, and their chief god was the very fierce **Assur,** from whom the people derived their name. By 800 B.C.E., through their own ferocity and cunning in war, the Assyrian kings had conquered much of the Tigris-Euphrates region and were fighting the Babylonians for the southern portion (see Map 4.1). The Assyrians displayed great talent in military affairs. Their army was large and seemingly irresistible, using new tactics to negate the traditional advantage of charioteers over foot soldiers.

By this epoch, the horse and the chariot were widely used in warfare. (It is believed that the chariot was introduced to Near Eastern warfare by the Hyksos invaders of Egypt in the 1500s.) For centuries, leather-clad warriors armed with short swords had fought from chariots drawn by two or three horses. The chariots would split the loose ranks of the enemy foot soldiers, and the momentum of the horses combined with the raised platform gave the swordsmen an almost irresistible advantage over opposing infantry.

The early Assyrian kings took away this advantage, however, by fielding tight-knit infantry formations with long

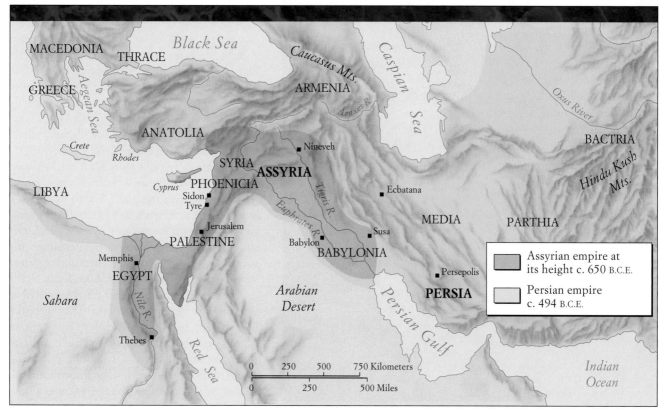

🏵 **MAP 4.1 The Assyrian and Persian Empires.** Although the Assyrians subdued most of the Near East and Egypt for a brief time, the later Persian empire was much more extensive, reaching from Egypt to the borders of the Indus valley. Most of this huge area was held through a network of tributary kingdoms whose rulers regularly acknowledged Persian overlordship.

spears and swords, protected on the flanks by bands of horsemen who engaged the enemy charioteers while they were still far off. The infantry were heavily armored and so disciplined they would stand up to a chariot charge without breaking. The Assyrians were also experts in siege warfare, and no enemy fort could hold for long against their artillery of stone-throwing catapults and rams.

Anyone who resisted the Assyrians and lost suffered a terrible fate: wholesale slavery, execution, pillage, and rape. Once conquered, the enemy was closely supervised, and any effort to spring free of the Assyrian yoke was immediately suppressed. The chronicles left by the Assyrians delight in telling of the huge piles of dead left by the triumphant armies of kings such as Tiglath-Pileser who reigned in the seventh century B.C.E.:

Like the Thunder, I crushed corpses of their warriors in the battle. I made their blood flow over into all the ravines and over the high places. I cut off their heads and piled them at the walls of their cities like heaps of grain. I carried off their booty, their goods, and their property beyond all reckoning. Six thousand, the remainder of their troops who had fled before my weapons and thrown themselves at my feet,

I took away as prisoners and added to the peoples of my country [that is, slaves]. (From J. B. Pritchard, ed., *Ancient Near Eastern Texts,* 3d ed. Princeton, NJ: Princeton University Press, 1969.)

The Assyrians were perhaps the most hated conquerors in ancient history. Only their expertly calculated plans for "divide and conquer" and mass deportations of subject peoples enabled them to remain in power as long as they did. At one point their empire reached from the upper Tigris to central Egypt. It was governed from Nineveh by a network of military commanders who had no mercy for rebels and held large numbers of hostages for the good behavior of the rest of their people.

But less than a century later, Nineveh was in total ruins ("not a stone upon a stone," asserts the Old Testament), and the Assyrians were swept from the pages of history as though they had never existed. Their many enemies and rebellious subjects, led by the Chaldees of New Babylon, finally united against their oppressor and took full revenge for Assyrian atrocities. When they captured Nineveh in 612 B.C.E., the victors even salted the fertile irrigated lands that ringed the city to prevent the site from ever being inhabited

🔸 **Assurbanipal at War.** This Assyrian bas-relief shows King Assurbanipal charging the enemy in his war chariot, accompanied by picked spearmen who thrust away the hostile infantry as the monarch loads his bow. The Assyrian genius for portrayal of violent motion comes through strongly in these reliefs, which date from the 600s B.C.E. (*e.t.archive*)

and Sidon, they became the greatest maritime traders and colonizers of the ancient Near East. Their trade in luxury wares such as copper and dyes took them through the Mediterranean and into the Atlantic as far as the coast of Britain (Cornwall). Here they obtained the precious tin that could be mixed with copper and lead to form bronze, the main metallic resource before 1000 B.C.E. The Phoenicians also apparently spread the art of iron making to the Greeks and westward into Africa. They established a whole series of colonies in the western Mediterranean. Some of these became important in their own right, and one of them, the rich city-state of Carthage, became the great rival to Rome until its final defeat around 200 B.C.E. The Phoenicians themselves were absorbed into the Assyrian and succeeding empires but remained the paramount Mediterranean traders and seafarers until the rise of Greece in the 600s B.C.E.

The Phoenicians' most notable contribution came in the linguistic field. They were the first to use a *phonetic alphabet,* a system of twenty-two written marks ("letters"), each of which corresponded to a specific consonantal sound of the oral language. The Phoenicians' alphabet, which emerged about 1000, was a definite advance in written communication over the cuneiforms of the Sumerians and the hieroglyphs of the Egyptians. The Greeks later improved the Phoenician alphabet, added signs for the vowels, which the Phoenicians did not employ, and thereby created essentially the same alphabet (though in a different letter form) that we use in Western scripts today.

The Persians

❀

Until the twentieth century, present-day **Iran** was called *Persia.* Its ruling group was for a millennium, 500 B.C.E. to 500 C.E., the most powerful of the many peoples in western Asia.

The Persians were an Indo-European-speaking people who had migrated slowly south from the central Asian steppes into Iran. Actually, several related groups, collectively termed Iranians, moved south starting about 1000 B.C.E. At this epoch they were still nomadic and knew nothing of agriculture or other civilized crafts and techniques. They did, however, possess large numbers of horses, and their skill at cavalry tactics enabled them to gradually overcome their rivals and begin a sedentary life. Eventually, through both war and trading contacts with their Mesopotamian neighbors to the west, they learned the basics of agriculture and civilized life.

again. It was indeed forgotten until the middle of the nineteenth century when Nineveh's ruins were unearthed by some of the earliest archaeological expeditions to the Middle East.

With such determined erasure of their history, how can we know anything about the Assyrians' past? Remarkably, they combined their cruelty and delight in slaughter with a sophisticated appreciation for all forms of pictorial and architectural art. Much of our knowledge about the Assyrians comes from this artistic heritage, as well as archaeology.

The Phoenicians

❀

Another small but significant Semitic people were the unwarlike Phoenicians, who originally inhabited a strip along the coast of what is now Lebanon. From their ports of Tyre

🏵 **Lion Attacking a Youth.** This marvelous carved ivory plaque dates from the eighth- or ninth-century B.C.E. Phoenicia. *(Scala/Art Resource)*

Iran is mostly a high, arid plateau, surrounded on the north, west, and east by high mountains and on the south by the Indian Ocean (see Map 4.1). For a long time, the country has been a natural divide for travel from the eastern Mediterranean to China and India, and vice versa. Later, it became the great exchange point between the Arabic-Muslim world and the Indo-Hindu. Thanks to this strategic position, Iran and the Iranians have long been able to play a considerable role in world affairs.

The Persian Empire

In the mid–sixth century B.C.E., the Persians united under a brilliant warrior king, Cyrus the Great, and quickly overcame their Iranian cousins and neighbors, the Medes. In a remarkable series of campaigns between 559 and 530, Cyrus then extended his domains from the borders of India to the Mediterranean coast. By 525 his son and immediate successor, Cambyses, had broadened the empire to include part of Arabia and the Nile valley. The main Persian cities were at Susa, Persepolis, and Ecbatana in Iran, not in Mesopotamia. The gradual decline of Mesopotamia's importance can be dated to this time.

🏵 **Hall of a Hundred Columns.** This is the great assembly and banquet hall erected by Darius I in Persepolis and burned to the ground by the triumphant conqueror Alexander a few years later. Its huge size was symbolic of the great powers exercised by the Persian emperor, the "King of Kings." *(© Giraudon/Art Resource)*

Zarathustra's Vision

We usually think of the connection between religious belief and morality as intrinsic and logical: moral actions are the concrete manifestations of a belief in good and evil, ultimately determined by a supernatural code and/or by conscience. Yet in very ancient times, people did not usually regard the supernatural gods as arbiters of human moral conduct. Rather, gods were seen as personification of natural forces that made men their helpless playthings unless appeased by worship and sacrifice. This attitude was as prevalent among Iranians in the sixth century B.C.E. as any other people. But it would change radically when a prophet arose among them called Zarathustra, or Zoroaster.

About Zarathustra's life we know nothing except that he was a Persian and lived probably in the 500s B.C.E. His teaching, however, was written down long after his death, possibly as late as the third century C.E. This Zoroastrian scripture, known as the *Avesta*, tells in fragmentary fashion the beliefs of a man who founded a new type of religion, a faith that linked the gods and humans in a new fashion.

Zarathustra preached that two principles are in eternal conflict: good and evil, truth and lies. Good is incarnated in the impersonal deity Ahura-mazda, and evil by its twin Ahriman (a close approximation of the Christian Lucifer). The two would struggle for the souls of men, and eventually Ahura-mazda would triumph. Humans, as the possessors of free will, could and indeed must choose between the two gods, serving one and defying the other. In an afterlife, individuals would be made responsible for their choice. They would stand before a divine tribunal and have to answer for their lives on Earth. If the balance was found positive, they would enjoy heaven in eternity; if negative, hell awaited them.

The role of priests was very important, for they interpreted what was right and wrong conduct. The fire worship that had prevailed among Iranians before Zarathustra continued to play a significant role, and a sacred fire was at the heart of the worship of Ahura-mazda. For a time, the teachings of the Zoroastrians became the state cult of imperial Persia, and both Darius I and his son Xerxes were known to be sympathizers.

The similarities between Zarathustra's doctrines and Judaism and Christianity are not coincidental. The Last Judgment that all souls must undergo, the responsibility of the exercise of free will, the eternal bliss of heaven, and the torments of hell entered first Jewish and then Christian belief. Through Zoroastrian preaching and converts in the eastern Mediterranean the image of an all-powerful God who allowed humans the supreme freedom of the choice between good and evil entered the mainsprings of Western religious culture. Zarathustra's teaching that Ahriman was closely bound up with the flesh, while Ahura-mazda was a noncorporeal entity, a spirit, would come to haunt Christianity for ages, and it appeared again and again in various sects. The most famous of these was medieval Manichaeism, which derived its beliefs from the Middle East and spread throughout Mediterranean Europe. It taught that the flesh is essentially evil, the province of the devil. Many people think that the puritanical element in Christianity is largely the product of this belated offshoot of the Zoroastrian creed.

What has become of the religion of Zarathustra? In Persia itself, it gradually declined into superstition and was almost extinguished in the wake of the Muslim conquest of Persia in the 600s C.E. The Parsees of the region around Bombay, India, are the center of the cult in modern times. Their scripture, the *Avesta*, remains one of the very first attempts to unite *religion*, worship of the immortal gods, with *ethics*, a code of proper conduct for mortal men.

For Reflection

Zoroastrianism is called a dualist religion. What is meant by that term? In what ways is the principle of evil as portrayed in Zoroastrian belief similar to the Christian Satan? Why is the concept of free will basic to a belief in good and evil in any religion?

Cyrus had a concept of imperial rule that was quite different from that of the Assyrians. He realized that many of his new subjects were more advanced in many ways than his own Persians and that he could learn from them. Accordingly, his government was a sort of umbrella, sheltering many different peoples and beliefs under the supervision of the "King of Kings" at Persepolis.

The Persian subjects were generally allowed to retain their own customs, laws, and religious beliefs. Their appointed Persian supervisors (*satraps*) only interfered when the central government's policies were threatened or disobeyed. In the provinces **(satrapies)**, the local authorities were kept in power after conquest by Persia, so long as they swore obedience to the monarch, paid their (relatively light) taxes, provided soldiers, and gave aid and comfort to the Persians when called upon. Religion was totally free, and all sorts of beliefs flourished under Persian rule, from the Hebrews to the fire worshipers of the Indian borderlands. Most remarkably, the initial move toward an ethical religion seems to have come with the teaching of **Zarathustra,** as outlined in the Religion and Morality box, "Zarathustra's Vision."

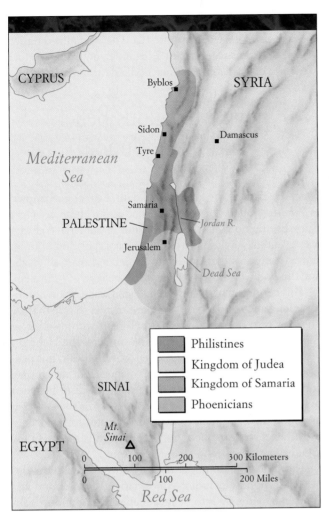

🌸 MAP 4.2   Ancient Palestine and the Jewish Kingdoms. The kingdoms of Judea and Samaria (Judah and Israel) divided the region once occupied by the Philistines and Canaanites prior to the Jews' return to the Promised Land.

Darius I (522–486) was the third great Persian ruler, following Cyrus and Cambyses. During his reign, the empire reached its maximal extent (see Map 4.1). A stable coinage in gold and silver and a calendar that was commonly used throughout the Near East were introduced. Darius's law code was also an advanced and refined distillation of earlier codes from Mesopotamia and Egypt. For the next century the peoples of the empire flourished under enlightened Persian leadership.

The Persian kings eventually made the mistake of biting off more than they could chew. Darius and his successor, Xerxes, invaded the European mainland in an attempt to extend their power and salve their wounded egos. The attempt would cost them dearly, as we will see when we discuss Greek civilization in Chapter 9.

The Hebrews
🌼

What we know of the ancient Twelve Tribes of the Hebrews is derived in large part from the poetic history of the Old Testament. In recent years, the Old Testament's stories have been partially borne out by modern archaeological evidence. It is clear that many events and stories previously regarded as mythological have a strong basis in fact.

The Hebraic tradition of a certain Abraham leading his people out of the wilderness and into the land of Canaan refers to what is generally now accepted as historical fact: nomadic, primitive Semitic tribes departed from someplace in northern Mesopotamia in the twentieth century B.C.E. and wandered for a lengthy time through what is now Saudi Arabia. By the 1500s B.C.E., they were established in Canaan, the southern part of Palestine (see Map 4.2). Here they came under imperial Egyptian rule, and a good portion of the Twelve Tribes went off—perhaps voluntarily, perhaps as coerced slaves—to live in the Nile delta.

We know that in the thirteenth century B.C.E. many semicivilized peoples were moving about the eastern Mediterranean region. The Hebrews' **Exodus** from Egypt under their legendary leader Moses occurred during that century. The exact reasons for the Exodus are not clear, but it is entirely possible that the Old Testament story of brutal treatment by the pharaoh is true. In any case, under Moses, the Hebrews resolved to return to the "land of milk and honey," the Promised Land of Canaan, whose memory had been kept alive by their leaders in Egypt.

Escaping pharaoh's wrathful pursuit (the Old Testament story of the parting of the Red Sea), the Hebrews wandered across the Sinai peninsula until they encountered the Canaanites and the Philistines, who were already settled in coastal Palestine. At first the Philistines were able to hold the newcomers at bay. But by about 1000, the Hebrews had overcome the Canaanites and set up their own small kingdom, with Saul as the first king. Saul carried the war to the Philistines, and his work was carried on by his lieutenant and successor, David. David (the victor over the giant Goliath in the Old Testament) was a great warrior hero, and he was successful in conquering Jerusalem, which then became the Hebrews' capital.

David's son, **Solomon** (ruled 970–935 B.C.E.), was the most renowned king of the Hebrews. During his reign, the Hebrews briefly became a factor in Near Eastern affairs, serving as trading intermediaries between Egypt and the Mesopotamians. The famous Temple of Jerusalem, constructed of stone and cedarwood and decorated inside and out with gold, became a wonder of the ancient world. But many of his subjects hated Solomon because of his heavy taxes and luxurious living, as noted in the Law and Lawgivers box, "King Solomon." When he died, a revolt against his successor split the Hebrew kingdom in two:

 David Beheads Goliath. The poetry of the Old Testament is strikingly exhibited in the story of the battle between the young hero David and the Philistine Goliath. The battle of the two individuals stands for the generations of struggle between the Jews and the Philistines for control of southern Palestine. (© Superstock)

Judea and Samaria, or, as they are sometimes called, Judah and Israel.

Although ethnically very close, the two kingdoms were hostile to one another. As time passed, Samaritans and Judeans (or Jews, as they eventually came to be called) came to look on one another as different peoples. Their differences arose primarily because of differing religious beliefs but also because Judea came under the shadow of a briefly revived Egyptian empire, while Samaria fell to the successive conquerors of Mesopotamia.

The kingdom of Samaria/Israel was ended by a failed rebellion against the Assyrian overlords, resulting in the scattering of the populace far and wide, and the eventual loss of them to Judaic belief (the first **Diaspora,** or scattering). Judea, however, survived under the Assyrians until the defeat of the latter in 612. It then fell under Babylonian overlordship. The ill-fated attempt to throw off this yoke led to the crushing defeat by King Nebuchadnezzar in 586 and the ensuing Babylonian Captivity (586–539 B.C.E.), when thousands of Jews were taken off to Babylon as hostages for the good behavior of the rest. The great temple of Solomon was demolished. Becoming one of the provinces of the Persian empire after 539 B.C.E., the Judeans continued under

Persian rule until Alexander the Great toppled the King of Kings in the 330s (see Chapter 10). They then lived under the Hellenistic successors of Alexander until the gradual extension of Roman power reached Palestine.

Jewish Religious Belief and Its Evolution

From the time of the kingdom of Saul, a great god known as *Yahweh* (Jehovah) was established as the Hebrews' chief deity, but by no means the only one. In Samaria, Yahweh was eventually relegated to an inferior position. But in Judea, Yahweh's cult gradually triumphed over all rivals, and this god became the only deity of the Jews of Jerusalem.

This condition of having a single god was a distinct oddity among ancient peoples. *Monotheism* was so rare that we know of only one pre-Jewish experiment with it—that of Akhnaton in Egypt (see Chapter 3). Some of the Hebrews were living in Egypt during Akhnaton's reign, and it is possible that the pharaoh's doctrines penetrated into Jewish consciousness. Zarathustra's doctrine of dualism between two almost equal deities who wrestled over the souls of men undoubtedly had much to do with the later forms of Hebrew belief, but just how they are related is a subject for argument.

The Judean Jews, under the influence of a whole series of great prophets including Amos, Hosea, Ezekiel, and Isaiah, came by the 600s to believe themselves bound to Yahweh by a sacred contract, the **Covenant,** given to Moses during the Exodus. The contract was understood to mean that if the Jews remained constant in their worship of Yahweh and kept the faith he instilled in them, they would eventually triumph over all their enemies and be a respected and lordly people on Earth. The faith that Yahweh desired was supported by a set of rigid rules given to Moses by Yahweh on Mount Sinai, from which eventually evolved a whole law code that governed every aspect of Hebrew daily life. Coming to be known to later Jews and Christians as the Ten Commandments, these moral regulations (see "The Ten Commandments" box) have been adapted to much different social circumstances.

The Jewish faith was one of the earliest attempts to formalize an ethical system and to link it with the worship of supernatural deities. *Ethics* is the study of good and evil and determining what is right and wrong in human life and conduct. Yahweh's followers gradually came to regard him as an enforcer of correct ethical actions. Those who did evil on Earth would be made to suffer, if not in this world, then in the one to come. In itself, this belief was not unusual, for other religions had made at least some moves toward punishment of evildoers. The laws of Yahweh, however, also assured that the good would be rewarded—again, if not in this life, then in the eternal one to come.

King Solomon

The story of King Solomon is an illuminating example of how historical fact can be adapted to fit the needs of a people. The Old Testament tells us that Solomon ruled the united tribes of the Jews with wisdom and justice and that his people looked up to him as an exemplary ruler. In fact, Solomon's wisdom and justice often seemed conspicuous by their absence, and his kingdom did not long outlast his own life.

The son of King David and his fourth wife Bathsheba, Solomon succeeded his father, despite the existence of an older surviving son. His mother, with the help of the prophet Nathan, persuaded the old king to recognize Solomon as his heir shortly before his death. Several years later, Solomon secured the throne by eliminating his rival on charges of plotting against him.

Under the guidance of counselors, the young king established a form of absolute monarchy. Ignoring Hebrew tradition, he subordinated everything to the splendor of his court, adopting a style of life hitherto unknown to the Hebrew rulers but attractive to many people. The Canaanites, defeated by David but long allowed to go their own way, were now reduced to slaves and forced to work for Solomon's government.

Under Solomon's hand, the city of Jerusalem grew in commercial importance in the Near East. Its residents, formerly impervious to foreign influences, became wealthy and attracted to other lifestyles as a result of expanding contacts with outsiders. Solomon was able to extend his dominions into Mesopotamia and northern Egypt by marrying foreign brides, including the daughter of the pharaoh.

In place of the simple quarters that had sufficed for David, Solomon constructed a large royal home whose size and fittings rivaled those of the Persians. The famous Temple of Jerusalem became a wonder of the ancient world. Visitors from many countries came to marvel and to ask Solomon for solutions to their problems, for the king was reputed to have great wisdom. The little nation of Israelites, so long isolated and ignored, became commercially versatile and sophisticated.

Solomon divided his kingdom into twelve districts and made each responsible for the court's expenses for one month each year. He collected tolls from the expanding overland trade and assessed heavy taxes on his subjects to pay for his projects and his personal luxuries. His extravagances were much resented, and they exacerbated the split that was already developing between Judea and Samaria-Israel.

During Solomon's reign, Judea received commercial advantages and paid few taxes. The northern ten tribes became indignant, threatening to sever their relations with Jerusalem and Judea even before Solomon's death. When the king died in 935, the Hebrew tribes split and formed the two separate, rival kingdoms of Judea and Israel, lessening their ability to rule their satellite peoples and exposing themselves to foreign threats.

The Wailing Wall. In the center of old Jerusalem stands the last remnant of Solomon's temple, where devout Jews such as those shown go to pray to the God of their forebears. (© Comstock)

The vassal kingdoms that David had painfully conquered were lost, and the trading empire that Solomon had labored for forty years to create was destroyed forever. "Vanity of vanities, all is vanity."

For Reflection

Why do you think later Hebrew writers chose to enhance the memory of a king who could not hold the affection of his people or his kingdom's territory? Is Solomon better known as a lawgiver or as a man whose ambitions outgrew his capabilities? What is meant in modern times by "the wisdom of Solomon"?

How did people know whether they were doing good or evil? One way was by following the laws of Yahweh. Increasingly, though, they could also rely on the knowledge of what is right and what is wrong that Yahweh imprinted in every heart: conscience. The Ten Commandments were peculiarly the Jews' property, given them as a mark of favor by their lord and protector Yahweh. But all men and women everywhere were believed to have been given conscience, and insofar as they followed conscience, they were doing the Lord's work and possibly gaining eternal salvation.

Economic Change and Social Customs

❋

Although their religious beliefs would have immense influence on Western civilization, the Jews were at best minor players on the Near Eastern stage in economic affairs and politics. They had never been very numerous, and the split between Israelites and Judeans weakened both. The military victories over the Philistines had allowed the united kingdom to take tribute from the conquered, which eased the Hebrews' own tax burdens. With the rise of Assyria, however, both Israel and Judea had to engage in numerous, expensive wars and suffered economically. Both became relatively insignificant backwaters under the direct or indirect rule of powerful neighbors. Neither Samaria nor Jerusalem ever became an important international trading or commercial center, although Jerusalem was located along the overland travel routes between Egypt and the Middle East.

When the kingdom was founded under Saul, most Hebrews were still rural herders and peasants, living as Abraham had lived. Over the next half millennium, however, many Hebrews made the transition from rural to town life. As many people shifted from subsistence farming to wage earning, social tensions dividing rich and poor began to appear. The strong solidarity that had marked the Hebrews earlier broke down. The prophets of the eighth through fifth centuries remind us that exploitation of widows and orphans and abuse of the weak by the strong were by no means limited to the despised "Gentiles" (all non-Jews).

More than most, the Jews divided all humanity into "we" and "they." This was undoubtedly the result of their religious tradition, whereby they had been selected as the Chosen. Jews looked upon non-Jews as distinctly lesser breeds, whose main function in the divine plan was to act as tempters and obstacles that the pious must overcome. In their preoccupation with the finer points of the Law laid down by Moses and his successors, the Hebrews deliberately segregated themselves from other peoples. Intermarriage with nonbelievers was tantamount to treason and was punished by immediate expulsion from the community. Ancient Judaism was almost never open to converts.

Hebrew society was patriarchal in every respect. The nuclear family (parents and children) was the basic unit of society, with the father enjoying very extensive rights. According to the Old Testament, a husband/father even had life-and-death authority over his wife and children, but this was certainly no longer true by the 500s B.C.E.

Marriage and divorce reflected the patriarchal values of the society. The married state was strongly preferred, and, in fact, bachelors were looked on as failures and shirkers. Young men were to marry by no later than age twenty-four and preferably by twenty. Girls were thought ready for marriage at puberty, roughly about age thirteen. As in every ancient society, marriage was arranged by the parents, usually with a good deal of negotiating about the dowry or bride-price.

A man could have several legal wives and an unlimited number of concubines, but as in other societies, only the wealthy could afford this practice. The wife married into the husband's family and moved into his house. The property she brought into the marriage remained hers, however, and could be removed again should her husband divorce her for any reason but unfaithfulness.

Divorce was easy enough for the husband but very unusual for a wife to initiate. Women caught in adultery could be killed, but typically they were divorced and sent back to their father's home. Infidelity by the husband was a crime only if committed with a married woman.

Children were the whole point of marriage. The continuation of the family was the primary duty of both husband and wife. The oldest male child received the lion's share of the inheritance, but the other boys were not shut out. The girls, on the other hand, received nothing beyond their dowries, because through marriage they would be joined to another family, which would care for them. The education of all children was carried on within the family circle and was religious in nature. Literacy was uncommon among the country folk but not so among the urbanites.

Jewish arts and sciences were relatively undeveloped compared with their more sophisticated and richer neighbors. Excepting the Old Testament's poetry, the Jews produced very little of note in any of the art forms. The representation of living things was thought to be sacrilegious and was banned. There is no record of any important Jewish contributions to the sciences.

A Changing Theology

In the centuries after the fall of the monarchies of Samaria and Judea, the Jews' conception of Yahweh changed in several significant ways, and these changes are linked to their political relations with others. After losing their independence, the Jewish people went through a long spiritual crisis. Their hope for a triumph over their enemies was not realized. Indeed, quite the contrary happened: the *Babylonian Captivity* (586–539 B.C.E.) was a particular low point. Many Jews never returned, having been seduced by the "Great Whore" Babylon into the worship of false gods. Those who returned after release by the Persians under Cyrus were the "tried and true," who had been tested and, strong in their faith, had survived. They rebuilt the Temple and restructured their theology. Aided by new interpretations of the Covenant (the *Talmud*), the Jews reappraised the nature of God and their relation to him.

During this post-Captivity period, the image of Yahweh took on clearer lines. Not only was Yahweh the only god, he was the *universal* god of all. Whether or not the Gentiles worshiped him, he was their judge and would reward or punish them (mostly the latter) as they conformed or not to the demands of conscience.

God was a *just* god, who would reward and punish according to ethical principles, but he was also a *merciful* god who would not turn a deaf ear to the earnest penitent. His ways were mysterious to men such as Job in the Old Testament, but they would someday be seen for what they are: righteous and just.

God was an *omnipotent and omniscient* master (all-powerful and all-knowing), who could do whatever he desired, always and everywhere. There were no other opposing forces (gods) that could frustrate his will, but in his wisdom, Yahweh had granted his creature Man free will

🌣 **The Dead Sea Scrolls.** These historic documents were found by an Arab shepherd boy in 1946. The copper scrolls have been largely deciphered in recent years and have proven a rich source of knowledge of Jewish society and customs around the first century C.E. (© *The Granger Collection*)

and allowed the principle of evil to arise in the form of the fallen angel, Lucifer/Satan. Man could ignore conscience and the Law and choose evil, much as Zarathustra had taught. If he did, he would face a Last Judgment that would condemn him to eternal punishment and deprive him of the fate that Yahweh desired and offered: salvation in blessedness.

Finally, Yahweh gradually came to be a *personal* deity, in a way in which no other ancient god had been. He could be prayed to directly; he was observant of all that affected a man's or a woman's life. His actions were not impulsive or unpredictable. He wanted Man not as a slave but a friend. The relationship between God and Man is meant to be one of mutual love. In a sense, God needed Man to complete the work of creation.

The promise to preserve the Jews as a people that Yahweh had given Moses was what held the Judean Jews together after the Assyrian and Babylonian conquests. But inevitably, some of them, including many of the learned men (*rabbis*), came to think of this promise as one aimed not at simple preservation but at counterconquest by the Jews of their enemies. Instead of being a contemptible minority in the empires of the mighty ones, the Hebrews would be the mighty and make the others bend to *their* will.

In this way grew the hopes for a **messiah,** a redeemer who would take the Jews out of their humiliations and make them a people to be feared and respected. In this manner, the message of the Lord speaking through the great prophets was distorted into a promise of earthly grandeur rather than a promise of an immortal salvation for those who believed. When a man named Jesus appeared claiming to be the messiah and spoke of his kingdom "which was not of this earth," there was disappointment and disbelief among many of his hearers.

By the time of the Roman conquest of the Near East, in the first century before Christ, some of the Jewish leaders had become fanatical, believing in the protection of mighty Yahweh against all odds. These *Zealots* were unwilling to bend before any nonbeliever, however powerful he might be. This was to cause the tension between the Jewish nation and the Roman overlords that eventually resulted in war and the Second Diaspora, the forced emigration of much of this small people from its ancestral home to all corners of the great Roman empire.

Wherever the Jews went, they took their national badge of distinction with them: the unerring belief in their quality as the Chosen and their peculiar vision of the nature of God and his operations in the mind and hearts of humans. This was a vision of the relationship between the deity and his creature man that no other people had: mutually dependent, ethical, just but also merciful on the Lord's side; submissive but not slavish on man's side. It was the relationship between a stern but loving father and an independent, sinful, but dutiful child. The mold for the evolution of Christianity had been formed. All that was needed was the appearance of the long-rumored messiah who would fulfill the promise that the Chosen would enter glory, some day.

SUMMARY

After the decline of Mesopotamia and Egypt in the first millennium B.C.E., several smaller peoples contributed their diverse talents to the spread of civilized life. The Assyrian empire, founded on an efficient army, lasted only a brief time. After it was toppled in the seventh century B.C.E. by a coalition of enemies, most traces of it were wiped away in its Mesopotamian homeland. One of the Assyrians' conquests was Phoenicia, whose people are remembered for their maritime explorations and colonization and for taking the first major steps toward a phonetic alphabet.

For over 200 years after the conquests of Cyrus the Great, the Persian empire brought relative peace and progress to much of the Near East. Learning from their more advanced subjects, the imperial governors allowed substantial freedom of worship, language, and custom, while upholding superior justice and efficient administration. Trade and crafts flourished throughout the immense empire. From the preachings of Zarathustra emerged a new, highly sophisticated ethics that was elevated to a state religion.

The contribution of the Jews to later history was of a different nature. The Twelve Tribes of the Hebrews wandered out of Mesopotamia and entered Palestine sometime in the middle of the second millennium B.C.E. After a long duel with powerful neighbors, the Jews set up a monarchy that broke into two parts in the 900s. The larger segment, Samaria or Israel, gradually fell away from Judaism and was dispersed by Assyrian conquest. The smaller part, Judea with its capital Jerusalem, stayed true to Yahweh and survived as a province of other empires into Roman times.

What distinguished the Jews was their monotheistic religion and their linkage of a universal God with ethical standards in this life and immortal salvation in the next. Their gradually evolving vision of an omnipotent, just, and merciful Lord who would one day send a messiah to lead the Hebrews to glory would be the cement that held this small people together. It was a vision unique to them, and its power carried the Jews through a history of subjugation and torment.

TEST YOUR KNOWLEDGE

1. The key to Assyrian success in empire building was
   a. cultural superiority.
   b. respectful treatment of the conquered peoples.
   c. the bravery of the individual soldier.
   d. effective military organization.
2. The overthrow of the Assyrians was accomplished by
   a. an internal palace plot.
   b. a coalition of their enemies led by the Babylonians.
   c. the Egyptian and Hittite armies.
   d. a general rebellion of the slaves.
3. The outstanding contribution of the Phoenicians to world history was
   a. the marine compass.
   b. the phonetic alphabet.
   c. the invention of coinage.
   d. the gyroscope.
4. The creator of the Persian empire was
   a. Zoroaster.
   b. Xerxes.
   c. Cyrus.
   d. Ahura-mazda.
5. Which of the following is the correct chronological sequence of empires?
   a. Assyrian, Persian, Hittite, Sumerian
   b. Persian, Hittite, Sumerian, Assyrian
   c. Sumerian, Hittite, Assyrian, Persian
   d. Hittite, Assyrian, Sumerian, Persian
6. The Covenant of the Hebrews with their god Yahweh
   a. was given to Moses during the Exodus from Egypt.
   b. had nothing to do with individual conduct, only group survival.
   c. was a contract that was allowed to lapse.
   d. guaranteed each believing Hebrew immortality.
7. The people who conquered Samaria in the eighth century B.C.E. were
   a. Babylonians.
   b. Assyrians
   c. Egyptians.
   d. Hittites.
8. The first king of the Hebrew kingdom founded after the Exodus was
   a. David.
   b. Saul.
   c. Solomon.
   d. Isaiah.
9. Belief in the messiah among Jews of the first century B.C.E. was focused on
   a. hope for a statesman who would lead the Jews to a new homeland.
   b. expectation of a military leader against the Romans.
   c. finding a political leader who would assert Jewish supremacy.
   d. a hermit who rejected society, such as John the Baptist.
10. The critical new factor in the Jews' vision of God by the first century C.E. was
   a. the link between the deity and humans' ethical conduct on Earth.
   b. the belief that God was all-powerful in human affairs.
   c. the belief that God was supreme over all other deities.
   d. the hope for an eternal life given by God to those he favored.

IDENTIFICATION TERMS

Assur	**Exodus**	**Nineveh**	**Solomon**
Covenant	**Iran**	**satrapies**	**Zoroaster/Zarathustra**
Diaspora	**messiah**		

INFOTRAC COLLEGE EDITION

Enter the search terms "Persia or Persian" using Key Words.

Enter the search term "Hebrew" using Key Words.

Chapter 5

India's Beginnings

I renounce all killing of living beings, whether subtle or gross, whether movable or immovable. Nor shall I myself kill living beings, nor cause others to do so, nor consent to it.

MAHAVIRA in *The Book of Righteous Conduct*

∾

∾

HOW OLD ARE THE MOST ancient civilizations? Is it possible that the oldest of all are yet to be discovered? Until fairly recently it was believed that the civilization of India had been founded only some 2,000 years ago, far later than China, Egypt, or Mesopotamia. But in the early twentieth century, archaeologists found that a highly advanced, urbanized civilization had existed since the middle of the third millennium B.C.E. in the valley of the Indus River in what is now Pakistan. The discovery of this chapter in world history is a dramatic story, and much of the detail is still being pieced together. Enough is known, however, to whet our appetite to know much more, especially about the possible contributions of this civilization to one of the world's leading religious beliefs, Hinduism.

Indus Valley Civilization

❀

As in Mesopotamia and Egypt, the earliest Indian civilization was located in the valley of a great stream. The Indus River flows south and west from the foothills of the Himalayan range, the world's loftiest and most forbidding mountains. The Himalayas are the highest of several ranges that separate India and Pakistan from Tajikistan and China (see Map 5.1).

In the 1850s, when India was still under British colonial rule, a railway was extended across the Indus. During the construction, the British engineers noticed that the local workers were bringing in large quantities of hewn stone and brick from somewhere nearby. When the engineers inquired, they learned that the local residents had long been accustomed to go to a certain site, where huge piles of these materials were easily unearthed. The engineers notified the authorities, and the sites were put under archaeological supervision, which has continued ever since.

The major "dig" is at a place in modern Pakistan called **Mohenjo-Daro,** about 300 miles upstream from the mouth of the river. Some years later, another major site was located 400 miles farther up the river at Harappa. In between these large ruins are dozens of smaller sites being slowly uncovered by first British and now Pakistani experts. In terms of area covered, this is by far the largest ancient civilization ever found.

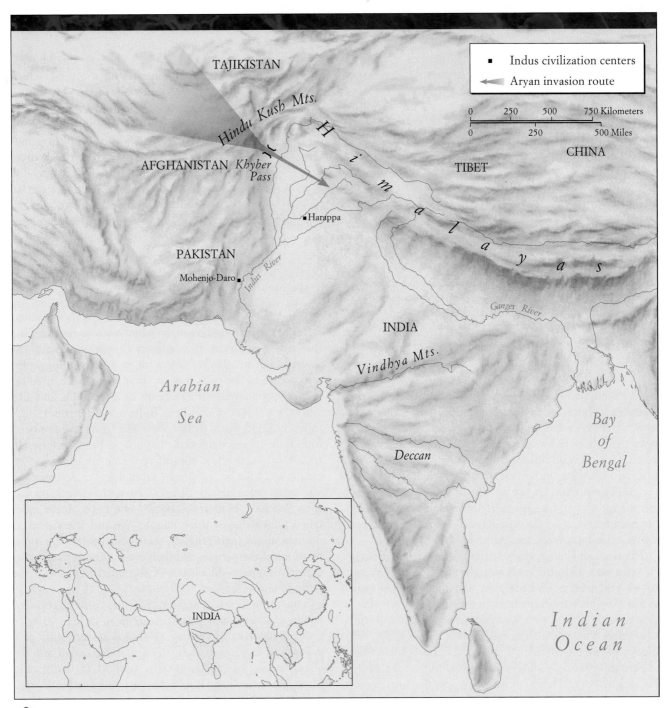

🏵 **MAP 5.1** **The Indian Subcontinent.** India is a very large and diverse geographic entity, ringed by the Himalayas and other high mountains to the north and northeast. The usual routes of contact with other peoples have been from the northwest and by sea from both eastern and western directions. Mohenjo-Daro and Harappa were part of a highly advanced, urbanized ancient civilization that flourished in the valley of the Indus River before the Aryan invasions.

Ruins of Mohenjo-Daro. Systematic excavation commenced in the ruins of Mohenjo-Daro in the late nineteenth century, under the auspices of the British colonial government. It continues today, directed by the Pakistani government. The total extent of the city is an area about three miles in diameter, surrounded by high walls. *(Robert Harding Picture Library)*

Mohenjo-Daro and Harappa

What exactly is being uncovered? At Mohenjo-Daro archaeologists have found the remnants of large, carefully constructed walls and the city they enclosed. The city was more than three miles across and probably housed more than 100,000 people at some time in the distant past. Now, little remains except the brick with which it was built, buried underground by the passage of time, storms, vandalism, and decay. Many smaller towns and villages have also been found under the dust of centuries, scattered along the Indus and its several tributaries in western India.

The cities and villages were built of fired brick and carefully planned. The streets ran at right angles, like William Penn's grid plan of Philadelphia, and they were of two widths. The main thoroughfares were thirty-four feet wide, large enough to allow two large carts to pass safely and still leave room for two or three pedestrians. The smaller avenues were nine feet wide. Many of the buildings had two or even three stories, which was unusual for residences in the ancient world. They were built of bricks that are almost always of two sizes, but only those two. The interior dimensions of the houses were almost identical. A sewage canal ran from each house to a larger canal in the street that carried off household wastes. Small statues of gods and goddesses, almost always of the same size and posture, are frequently found in the house foundations.

All this regularity suggests a government that was very powerful in the eyes of its subjects and probably gained its authority from religious belief. Some experts on Indus civilization believe that it was a *theocracy,* in which the priests ruled as representatives of the gods. In no other way, they

think, could the government's power have been strong enough to command residential uniformity over a period of centuries, as happened in Mohenjo-Daro and Harappa.

Both cities also contain monumental buildings situated on a citadel, which were probably a communal granary and the temples of the local gods. An interesting discovery at Mohenjo-Daro was the "Great Bath," a pool and surrounding cells that clearly existed for ritual bathing. Some have suggested that the emphasis on purification by water in present-day Hinduism may go back to these origins. Harappa differs from Mohenjo-Daro in building style and other details, but the similarities are strong enough that the two cities and the surrounding villages are believed to constitute one civilization.

For their food, the cities depended on the irrigated farms of the surrounding plain, which was very fertile. Like the people of Egypt, the ordinary people apparently enjoyed a high standard of living for many generations. Objects found in the ruins indicate that trade was carried on with Mesopotamia at least as early as 2000 B.C.E. and also with the peoples of southern India and Afghanistan. Although a good many works of art and figurines have been found, the occasional writing has not yet been deciphered. Its 270-odd characters are different from all other known scripts and have no alphabet. Our inability to decipher the writing as well as the long period when this civilization was forgotten have hindered scholars' efforts to obtain a detailed knowledge of these people. We still know next to nothing about their religion, their government, the social divisions of the people, and their scientific and intellectual accomplishments. Much is still shrouded in mystery and perhaps always will be.

One thing now seems clear: the cities and villages were prosperous, expanding settlements from at least 2500 to about 1900 B.C.E. Around 1900, for reasons still only guessed at, they began a long decline, which ended with the abandonment of Mohenjo-Daro about 1200 B.C.E. and Harappa somewhat later. Some evidence indicates that landslides changed the course of the lower Indus and prevented the continuation of the intensive irrigation that had supported the cities. Some people think that the population may have fallen victim to malaria, as the blocked river created mosquito-ridden swamps nearby. Others think that the irrigated land gradually became alkaline and nonproductive, as happened in lower Mesopotamia. Whatever the role of natural disasters, it is certain that the decline of the Indus valley was accelerated by an invasion of nomads called *Aryans,* who descended into the valley from Afghanistan and Iran about 1500 B.C.E.

The Vedic Epoch

The Aryans were one of the earliest horse-breeding people of ancient Asia, and their aggressive ways were the terror of other civilizations besides that of the Indus valley. It is thought that they overwhelmed the civilized Indians in the valley and set themselves up as a sort of master group, using the Indians as labor to do the farming and trading that the Aryan warriors despised as inferior. As we noted, their conquest of the more advanced peoples may have been aided by natural disasters that had weakened the economy severely.

Our knowledge of the Aryans comes largely from their **Vedas,** very ancient oral epics that were written down only long after the Aryan period, so the pictures they present may be deceptive. We know that the Aryans were Indo-European speakers who worshiped gods of the sky and storm and made impressive use of bronze weaponry and horse-drawn chariots in battle. (Apparently, the Indus valley people knew the horse only as a beast of burden and were at a disadvantage against the Aryan chariots.) The **Rigveda,** the oldest and most important Veda, paints a picture of a war-loving, violent folk, led by their *raja,* or chieftain, and their magic-working priests.

In time, the Aryans extended their rule across all of northern India to the Ganges valley. Gradually, they abandoned their nomadic ways and settled down as agriculturists and town dwellers. They never conquered the southern half of India, and the southern culture and religion still differ from those of the north in some respects as a result.

The Beginnings of the Caste System

The Vedas describe the beliefs of a people who saw themselves as the natural masters of the inferior Indians and who underlined their difference by dividing society into four groups or classes. The two highest classes of priests and warriors were reserved for the Aryans and their pure-blooded descendants. The priests were called **brahmins** and originally were superior in status to the warriors, who were called *kshatrija* and evolved over time from warriors to the governing class. The third class, the *vaishya,* was probably the most numerous and included freemen, farmers, and traders. In the fourth and lowest group were the unfree, the serfs or *shudra.*

Over the long course of the Vedic Epoch, these four classes evolved into something more complex by far: multiple social groups defined by birth, or **caste.** A caste is an entity or social unit into which individuals are born and that dictates most aspects of daily life. It confers a status that

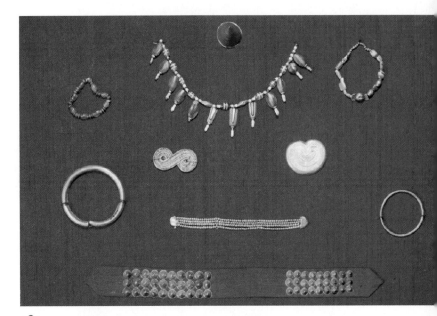

Indus Valley Jewelry. The fine workmanship and imagination exhibited here allow us to draw some conclusions about the state of Indus civilization at this epoch, about 2000 to 1800 B.C.E. Some of the precious stones in this jewelry were brought from as far away as China. (*National Museum of India/The Bridgeman Art Library*)

Shiva in the Dance of Life. One of the great trinity of Hindu deities, Shiva is sometimes portrayed as a male, sometimes as a female. Shiva is the god who presides over becoming and destroying, representing the eternal flux of life. (© *Royal Smeets Offset, Weert*)

Female Dancer, c. 1700 B.C.E. The bronze statuette of a dancer awaiting her turn shows the skill of the Mohenjo-Daro sculptors. It is one of the few surviving examples of their metalwork. *(© Royal Smeets Offset, Weert)*

cannot be changed. Each caste except the very lowest has special duties and privileges, some of which are economic in nature, whereas others are dietary, social, or religious. A high-caste Indian normally has very little contact with lower castes and none at all with the outcastes or *pariahs.* Perhaps a seventh of Indian society still falls into this last category—the untouchables—whose members until recently were treated worse than animals.

The stratification of Indian society begun by the Aryan conquest persists to the present day. The Aryans themselves were gradually absorbed into the Indian peoples through intermarriage with high-status individuals, but the caste system took ever stronger root. By the eighteenth century there were more than 3,000 separate subcastes. Although the number has probably declined since then, the belief that one is born into a group that is fixed by age-old traditions and allows no change is still very strong among rural Indians.

Throughout Indian history, caste has had the effect of inhibiting change, particularly social change. Why? Combined with the beliefs of Hinduism (see the next section), caste made it next to impossible for someone born into a low state to climb the ranks of social prestige and privilege. It also limited political power to the uppermost ranks, in much the same fashion as the exercise of government in medieval Europe was limited to the aristocracy. Caste discouraged or prohibited cultural innovation by those in the lower ranks (the vast majority of Indians). Meanwhile, those on top were very content to have things go on forever as they

were. Under the Aryan-founded caste system, India became a highly stratified and immobile society.

Hinduism

❋

The religion of the overwhelming majority of Indians is Hinduism, the fourth largest in the world with about 700 million adherents. Hinduism is both more and less than a religion as the West understands that term: it is a "way of life," a philosophical system, an inspiration for art, and the basis of all Indian political theory in the past. But it is not a rigid set of theological doctrines that must be believed to find truth or to be saved in eternity. And it possesses almost innumerable localized variations in manner and content.

The Hindu faith is a product of the slow mixing of the Aryan beliefs with those of the native Indians, over a thousand years from 1500 to about 500 B.C.E. Many of Hinduism's basic principles reflect the patriarchal and class-conscious society that the Aryan conquerors founded and that was strengthened in its stratification by the conquerors' beliefs. A revelatory glimpse at early Hinduism is given by the Laws of Manu as excerpted in the Tradition and Innovation box. Family relations are seen to be governed by social class, as is the relation of men to women and husbands to wives.

But Hinduism is quite different from the religions of the West in its insistence on the illusory nature of the tangible world, and the acceptance of the individual's fate in life. Its most basic principles and beliefs are as follows:

1. The nonmaterial, intangible world is the real and permanent one.
2. The soul must pass through a lengthy series of bodily existences, being reincarnated (*samsara*) in accord with its karma.
3. **Karma** is the tally of good and bad committed in a given life. Good karma results in a birth into a higher caste in the next life.
4. One must strive for good karma through following the code of morals prescribed for one's caste, called **dharma,** as closely as one can.

The gods *Brahman* (the impersonal life-force), *Shiva* (the creator and destroyer), and *Vishnu* (the preserver) dominate an almost endless array of supernatural beings. Most Hindus are devotees of either Shiva or Vishnu as the foremost deity, but they worship them in a huge variety of rituals.

When a person has lived a life in perfect accord with his or her dharma, death will lead not to another reincarnation but to final release from the great Wheel of Life. This release is **moksha,** and it is the end for which all good Hindus live. Moksha is sometimes compared with the heaven of the Western world, but it differs in one all-important respect: moksha is the end of individuality, and the individual soul is submerged into the world-soul represented by Brahman.

The Laws of Manu

The Laws of Manu are an ancient compilation of teachings from Hindu India. **Manu** was a being simultaneously human and divine from whom devout Hindus could learn what was needed for perfection and the attainment of *moksha*. Manu's laws were the cornerstone of Hindu traditional opinion on the rights and duties of the sexes and of family members, as well as castes. These opinions and prejudices did not change substantially until very recent times. The attitude of the Laws of Manu toward women and the lower castes are especially revealing. (Note: the *shudra* are the lowest of the original four castes of India established during the Aryan epoch.)

> That place where the shudra are very numerous . . . soon entirely perishes, afflicted by disease and famine.
>
> A Brahmin may confidently take the goods of his shudra, because the slave cannot have any possessions and the master may take his property.
>
> A Brahmin who takes a shudra to wife and to his bed will after death sink into Hell; if he begets a child with her, he will lose the rank of Brahmin. The son whom a Brahmin begets through lust upon a shudra female is, although alive, a corpse and hence called a living corpse. A shudra who has intercourse with a woman of a twice-born caste [that is, a Brahmin] shall be punished so: if she was unguarded he loses the offending part [his genitals] and all his property; if she was guarded, everything including his life.
>
> Women . . . give themselves to the handsome and the ugly. Through their passion for men, through their unstable temper, through their natural heartlessness they become disloyal toward their husbands, however carefully they may be guarded. Knowing their disposition, which the lord of creation laid upon them, to be so, every man should most strenuously exert himself to guard them. When creating them, Manu allotted to women a love of their bed, of their seat and of ornament, impure desire, wrath, dishonesty, malice, and bad conduct. . . .
>
> It is the nature of women to seduce men in this world; for that reason the wise are never unguarded in the company of females. For women are able to lead astray in this world not only the fool, but even a learned man, and make of him a slave of desire and wrath.
>
> But the exhortations of Manu are not completely one-sided:
>
> Reprehensible is the father who gives not his daughter in marriage at the proper time [namely, puberty]; reprehensible is the husband who approaches not his wife in due season, and reprehensible is the son who does not protect his mother after her husband has died.
>
> Drinking spirituous liquors, associating with wicked ones, separation from the husband, rambling abroad, sleeping at unseasonable hours, and dwelling in houses of other men are the six causes of ruin in women.

For Reflection

How do these laws differ, if at all, from the attitudes toward women reflected in the code of Hammurabi? Where did women find better protection and justice, by modern standards?

SOURCE: D. Johnson, ed., Sources of World Civilization, Vol. 1. © 1994, Simon & Schuster.

A good analogy would be a raindrop, which, after many transformations, finds its way back to the ocean that originated it and is dissolved therein.

Vedic Hinduism was highly ritualistic. The priestly caste—brahmins—had power by virtue of their mastery of ceremonies and their semimagical knowledge of the ways of the gods. Gradually, the more educated people became alienated from this ritualism and sought other ways to explain the mystery of human existence. In the fifth century B.C.E., two new modes of thought gradually became established in India: *Jainism* and *Buddhism.*

Jainism is very limited in appeal. It is less a supernatural religion than a philosophy that emphasizes the sacredness of all life (see Chapter 19). In modern India, it has a small number of high-caste adherents representing perhaps 2 percent of the total Indian population.

In contrast, Buddhism is one of the great religions of the world. It has adherents in all south and east Asian nations and includes several sects. Buddhism today has the third largest membership of all faiths.

Buddhism

Buddhism began in India as an intellectual and emotional revolt against the emptiness of Vedic ritualism. Originally an earthly philosophy that rejected the idea of immortal life and the gods, it was turned into a supernatural belief soon after the death of its founder, the Buddha.

Siddartha Gautama (563–483 B.C.E.), an Indian aristocrat, was the Buddha, or "Enlightened One," and his life is fairly well documented (see the Religion and Morality box). As a young man, he wandered for several years through the north of India seeking more satisfying answers to the riddle of life. Only after intensive meditation was he finally able to come to terms with himself and human existence. He then became the teacher of a large and growing band of disciples, who spread his word gradually throughout the subcontinent and then into East Asia. Buddhism eventually came to be much more important in China and Japan than in India, where it was practically extinct by 1000 C.E.

The Buddha

$\mathcal{S}$iddartha Gautama (c. 563–483 B.C.E.) was the pampered son of a princely Indian family in the northern borderlands, near present-day Nepal. A member of the *kshatrija* caste of warrior-governors, the young man had every prospect of a conventionally happy and rewarding life as master of a handful of villages. Married young to a local aristocrat like himself, he dedicated himself to the usual pursuits—hunting, feasting, revelry—of his class and time.

But in his late twenties, a notable change occurred. According to a cherished Buddhist legend, on successive excursions he encountered an aged man, then a sick man, and finally a corpse by the roadside. These reminders of the common fate set the young man thinking about the nature of all human life, in a (for him) novel way. Finally, he abandoned home, wife, and family and set out to find his own answers. In the already traditional Indian fashion, he became a wandering ascetic, begging a handful of rice to stay alive while seeking truth in meditation.

Years went by as Siddartha sought to answer his questions. But for long he found no convincing answers, neither in the extreme self-denial practiced by some nor in the mystical contemplation recommended by others. At last, as he sat under the bodhi tree (the tree of wisdom) through an agonizingly long night of intensive meditation, enlightenment reached him. He arose, confident in his new perceptions, and began to gather around him the beginnings of the community known as Buddhists ("the enlightened ones").

From that point on, the Buddha developed a philosophy that was a revision of the ruling Vedic Hindu faith of India and, in some important ways, a denial of it. By the Buddha's death, the new faith was firmly established, and some version of his teaching would gradually grow to be the majority viewpoint before being extinguished in the land of its birth.

In the original Buddhism, little attention was given to the role of the supernatural powers in human life or to reincarnation. The gods were thought to exist but to have minimal influence on an individual karma, or fate. Gods could not assist a person to find what Hindus call *moksha* and Buddhists *nirvana,* or the state of release from earthly life and its inherent suffering. But in time, this changed among the majority, or Mahayana Buddhists, who came to look on the Buddha himself and other *bodhisattvas* as divine immortals who could be called on for spiritual assistance.

How would this development have been received by the Buddha during his own lifetime? The answer is not hard to guess—his rejection of supernatural deities was well known. But it remains true that the very breadth of Buddhist doctrines and practices, which range from simple repetitive chants to the most refined intellectual exercise, have allowed a sizable proportion of humankind to identify with this creed in one or another of its forms.

For Reflection

Why do you think the nontheological viewpoint on human affairs of Siddartha was soon transformed by his followers? Do you agree that the pursuit of happiness is the root cause of much or all human suffering? Why?

Sri Lankan Buddha. The saffron-robed monk is praying to one of the frequent representations of the Buddha on the island of Sri Lanka, the center of the Theravada school of the religion. *(Hugh Sitton/Tony Stone Images)*

Teachings of the Buddha

What was the essence of the Buddha's teachings? The Buddha taught that everyone, regardless of caste, could attain **nirvana,** which is the Buddhist equivalent of Hindu moksha: release from human life and its woes. Nirvana is attained through the self-taught mastery of oneself: the gods have nothing to do with it, and priests are superfluous. The way to self-mastery lies through the **Four Noble Truths** and the **Eightfold Path,** which the Buddha laid out in his teachings.

Touched by a singular ray of enlightenment as a middle-aged seeker, the Buddha preached that human life can only be understood in the light of the Four Noble Truths he had experienced:

1. All life is permeated by suffering.
2. All suffering is caused by desire.
3. Desire can only be finally overcome by reaching the state of nirvana.
4. The way to nirvana is guided by eight principles.

The Eightfold Path to nirvana demands right (or righteous, we would say) ideas, right thought, right speech, right action, right living, right effort, right consciousness, and right meditation. The person who consistently follows these steps is assured of conquering desire and will therefore be released from suffering, which is the ultimate goal of human life.

The heart of the Buddha's message is that suffering and loss in this life are caused by the desire for an illusory power and happiness. Once the individual understands that power is not desirable and that happiness is self-deception, the temptation to pursue them will gradually disappear. The individual will then find the serenity of soul and the harmony with nature and fellow human beings that constitute true power and happiness.

Buddhism quickly spread among Indians of all backgrounds and regions, carried forth by the Buddha's disciples during his lifetime. What made it so appealing? Much of the popularity of Buddhism stemmed from its *democracy of spirit.* Everyone, male and female, high and low, was able to discover the Four Truths and follow the Eightfold Path. No one was excluded because of caste restrictions or poverty.

Soon after the Buddha's death, his followers made him into a god with eternal life—a thought foreign to his own teaching. His movement also gradually split into two major branches: *Theravada* and *Mahayana* Buddhism.

Theravada (Hinayana) means "the narrower vehicle" and is the stricter version of the faith. It is particularly strong in Sri Lanka and Cambodia. Theravada Buddhism emphasizes the monastic life for both men and women and takes a rather rigorous approach to what a good person who seeks nirvana must believe. It claims to be the pure form of the Buddha's teachings and rejects the idea of the reincarnation of the Master or other enlightened ones (*bodhisattva*) appearing on Earth.

Mahayana Buddhism is much more liberal in its beliefs, viewing the doctrines of the Buddha as a sort of initial step rather than as the ultimate word. The word *Mahayana* means "the larger vehicle," reflecting the belief that there are many ways to salvation. Its faithful believe that there are many buddhas, not just Siddartha Gautama, and that many more will appear. Monastic life is a good thing for those who can assume it, but the vast majority of Mahayana Buddhists will never do so and do not feel themselves disadvantaged thereby. Mahayana adherents far outnumber the others and are found in Vietnam, China, Japan, and Korea. Unlike the history of the Jewish, Christian, and Muslim sects, the two forms of Buddhism take a "live and let live" attitude toward one another, just as the various types of Hinduism do.

The Mauryan Dynasty and Buddhism's Spread

✾

For a century and a half after Buddha's death, the philosophy he founded gained adherents steadily but remained a distinctly minority view in a land of Hindu believers. In the 330s B.C.E., however, the invasion of India by Alexander the Great (see Chapter 10) not only brought the first direct contact with Western ideas and art forms but also introduced a brief period of political unity under the Mauryan dynasty, which moved into the vacuum left by Alexander's retreat. The third and greatest of the Mauryan rulers, Ashoka (ruled 269–232 B.C.E.), is the outstanding native king of premodern times and is beloved by all Indians as the founding spirit of Indian nationhood.

Ashoka's significance stems in large part from his role in spreading the Buddhist faith in India, thereby initiating the tradition of mutual tolerance between religions that is (or used to be) one of the subcontinent's cultural boasts. After a series of successful wars against the Mauryans' neighbors and rivals, Ashoka was shocked by the bloodshed at the battle of Kalinga at the midpoint of his reign. Influenced by Buddhist monks, the king became a devout Buddhist and pacifist. The last twenty years of the reign was marked by unprecedented internal prosperity and external peace. The monarch viewed himself as the responsible father of the people and exerted himself continually for their welfare. In so doing, he set a model of noble authority toward which later Indian rulers aspired but seldom reached. The inscriptions enunciating his decrees were placed on stone pillars scattered far and wide over his realm, and some of them survive today as the first examples of Indian written language. They, and the accounts of a few foreign travellers, are the means by which we know anything of Indian government in this early epoch.

After Ashoka's death, his weak successors soon gave up what he had gained, both in defense against invasion and in internal stability. Wave after wave of barbarian horsemen entered India through the gateway to Central Asia called the Khyber Pass (see Map 5.1). Most of them soon enough became sedentary in habit, adopted Indian civilization, and embraced the Buddhist faith. But the political unity established by the Mauryan rulers disintegrated. Four centuries passed before the Gupta dynasty could reestablish it in the 300s C.E. We will revisit the turbulent course of Indian history in Chapter 19.

India and China

❈

Most of India's land connections with the outer world have been northwestward, across the same routes through the passes of Afghanistan and the Hindu Kush mountains that invaders followed again and again. From the northwest came the Aryans, then the Greco-Macedonians under Alexander, then the Persians in the early C.E. centuries, and eventually the Turks and Afghani Muslims. Most of these intruders, even the savage horsemen from the Asian steppe, soon adopted civilized habits and enriched India's Hindu-Buddhist culture in one way or another. By sea, India's interchange with foreigners reached both the coast of east Africa and into the archipelagos of the Southwest Pacific, as well as the southeast Asian mainland (see Chapter 21).

❀ **The Lions of Sarnath.** The Lions of Sarnath were created by King Ashoka to symbolize the proclamation of Buddhism to the world. Sarnath was the site where Siddhartha Gautama first preached. The lions have been adopted by the modern republic of India as the official symbol of state. *(© Art Resource)*

In contrast, early India had remarkably little cultural interchange with China, its sophisticated and powerful neighbor to the northeast. The main reason for this lack of contact was the extreme difficulty of crossing the Himalaya mountains and the fearsome terrain and sparse population of the Tibetan plateau behind them. The mountains ringing India to the north had no easy routes to the east, nor did the jungles of Burma allow passage in premodern days. There were, however, some exceptions to this mutual lack of contact. By far the most significant one was the export of the Buddhist faith from India to China. Starting in the first century C.E., the new doctrine, in its Mahayana form, penetrated across the mountains and entered deeply into Chinese cultural life. By the fifth or sixth century C.E., much of the Chinese educated class had taken up Buddhism to a greater or lesser degree, blending the new ideas with traditional Confucian practice and ethics.

In fact, the large-scale adoption of Mahayana Buddhism by the Chinese has been called the most far-reaching single cultural event in world history. The Chinese also passed on Buddhism to their satellites Korea and Vietnam, and through Korea, the faith entered Japan. In all these places, Buddhism transformed the previous nature of cultural life. It had enormous impacts on East Asia between roughly 400 and 1000 C.E., by which time Buddhism in one of its variant sects was the primary faith of most of that huge region's populations.

SUMMARY

Civilized life is now known to have emerged in India much earlier than previously believed. By 2500 B.C.E. people of the Indus River valley had developed irrigated fields and good-sized towns that traded widely with both the surrounding villagers and distant neighbors to the west. These towns seem to have been governed by a priesthood, but information on their history is still sparse. The civilization was already in decline, possibly from natural causes, when

it fell to Aryan nomads, who instituted the beginnings of the caste system.

In the 1,000 years after the Aryan conquest (1500–500 B.C.E.), the Hindu religion was gradually constructed from a combination of Aryan belief and the Indus valley faith. When this ritualistic Hinduism was challenged by other, more ethically conscious doctrines such as Buddhism and Jainism, it gave way. Buddhism, in particular, became an international religion and philosophy, as several variants took root throughout East Asia.

Although arts and sciences flourished, the cultural and political unity of India was only sporadically enforced by a strong central government. Many invasions from the north-west kept India in a frequent state of political fragmentation. Religious belief, rather than government, was the cement that held its people together and gave the basis for their consciousness of being a nation.

TEST YOUR KNOWLEDGE

1. The excavation of Mohenjo-Daro indicates that India's earliest civilization
   a. had a strong central government.
   b. was governed by merchants.
   c. had little if any commercial contacts with other civilized lands.
   d. had no dependence on irrigation agriculture.
2. One of the following religions of India emphasizes above all the sacred nature of all life:
   a. Jainism
   b. Buddhism
   c. Hinduism
   d. Mithraism
3. The evolution of Indian castes came about because of
   a. economic necessities.
   b. the application of Vedic beliefs to Indian realities.
   c. the teachings of the Buddhist monks.
   d. climate and geography.
4. In Indian society after the Aryan conquest, the highest social group was that of the
   a. priests.
   b. warriors.
   c. tillers of the soil.
   d. educated.
5. The Laws of Manu show a society in which
   a. there were no essential differences between male and female.
   b. there was a strong sense of social justice.
   c. children were not valued.
   d. women were considered a source of temptation.
6. *Karma* is a Sanskrit word meaning
   a. the soul.
   b. release from earthly life cycles.
   c. the uppermost caste in Hindu society.
   d. the tally of good and bad acts in a previous life.
7. The Buddha taught all but one (identify false answer):
   a. All persons have the prospect of immortal happiness in an afterlife.
   b. Sorrow is generated by desire.
   c. Every individual is capable of attaining nirvana.
   d. Gods are of little or no significance in attaining true happiness.
8. The most significant contribution of India to world history is probably
   a. the model of good government given by Ashoka.
   b. the development of higher mathematics.
   c. the passing of Buddhism to China.
   d. the spiritual precepts of the Vedas.

IDENTIFICATION TERMS

brahmin	Four Noble Truths	Mohenjo-Daro	Siddartha Gautama
caste	*karma*	*moksha*	Theravada
dharma	Mahayana	*nirvana*	Vedas
Eightfold Path	Manu	Rigveda	

INFOTRAC COLLEGE EDITION

Enter the search term "Vedas" using Key Words.
Enter the search term "Hinduism" using the Subject Guide.

Enter the search term "Buddhism" using the Subject Guide.

Chapter 6

Ancient China to 500 B.C.E.

*The people of our race
were created by Heaven
Having from the beginning
distinctions and rules
Our people cling to customs
And what they admire is seemly
behavior.*

THE BOOK OF SONGS

THE MOST STABLE and in many ways the most successful civilization that history has known began in China in the second millennium B.C.E. It continued in its essentials through many changes in political leadership, meanwhile subjecting an enormous area and many different peoples to "the Chinese way." The Chinese educated classes, who considered themselves the hub of the universe, formed the most cohesive ruling group the world has ever seen. They combined scholarship and artistic sensitivity with great administrative abilities. Much of China's permanent culture was already firmly established by about 500 B.C.E., and it would change only very slowly.

Earliest China: The Shang Era

About the time the Aryan invaders arrived in the Indus valley, the Neolithic farming villages along the central course of the **Yellow River** were drawn into an organized state for the first time (see Map 6.1 inset). This state was the product of military conquest by a people closely related to the villagers, the **Shang.** The Shang replaced the villagers' earlier political overseers, but otherwise introduced little if any cultural change. (Note: The Shang dynasty may have been preceded by another, the Hsia, which is mentioned in the ancient histories as the first of the Chinese ruling groups. But unlike the Shang, the Hsia has not been confirmed by archaeological evidence.)

Like other Chinese, the Shang and the people they conquered were members of the Sino-Tibetan language group and the Mongoloid or "yellow-skinned" race. Other members of these groups include the North American Indians and the Turks. The society the Shang took over was already well on the way to civilized life. The villagers were making advanced stone tools and bronze weapons. Farming had long ago replaced hunting and gathering as the mainstay of the economy. The villagers had several types of domesticated animals and were growing wheat on the fertile soil that the north wind blows into the area from Mongolia. In later days, the vast plain on both sides of the river would be China's breadbasket, but life was never easy for the inhabi-

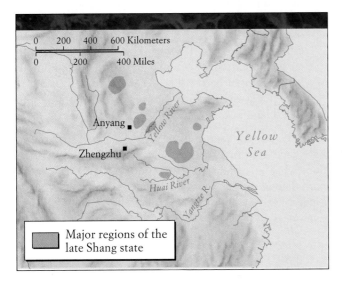

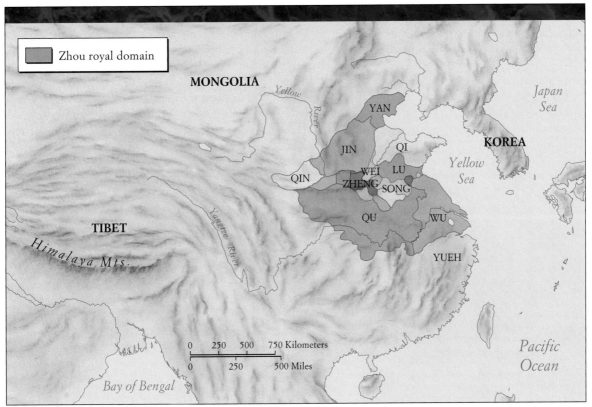

🏵 **MAP 6.1** **Ancient China.** The map at left shows Shang dynasty China, with the chief areas of Shang civilization located in the North China plain on either side of the Yellow River. The larger map shows China in the Era of Warring States. By the 500s B.C.E., the domain of the Zhou dynasts had become only a minor state surrounded by autonomous principalities.

tants of the Yellow River valley. Unlike the floods of the Nile, the floods of the Yellow River were tremendously damaging and had to be controlled by extensive levees.

The central valley of the Yellow River was the cradle of Chinese civilization, but another river would play almost as important a role in China's later history: the **Yangtze.** This great stream is much tamer than the Yellow and runs far to the south through a warmer and wetter landscape. By about the fifth century C.E., it was the center of China's rice culture. Eventually, the rice of the Yangtze became even more

important than the wheat of the Yellow River drainage. The plains along the two rivers and the coastal area between their deltas were the most densely populated and most important regions of ancient China.

Of all the ancient civilizations, China was the most isolated from outside influences, being even more isolated than Egypt. Both agriculture and metalworking apparently originated independently in China. No connections with either Indian or Mesopotamian arts and sciences are known until much later, after the civilization along the Yellow and

Yangtze Rivers had developed its own characteristics and technology.

Most of what we know comes from archaeology rather than history, as Shang writings were not numerous. Several rich grave sites have been excavated starting in the 1920s. Shang society was strictly hierarchical. At the top was a powerful king with his warrior court. War was commonplace, and warriors were favored in every way, much as in feudal Europe. On a level below the warriors were many skilled artisans and a growing class of small traders in the towns. In the countryside lived the great majority, the peasants in their villages. Already by Shang times, the silkworm was being cultivated, and silk was produced for export to India. Scholars are not sure whether the early Chinese had a formal religion in which all participated. Many experts think that the upper class believed in one set of gods, whereas the majority worshiped another.

Several fundamental aspects of Chinese life are already visible in the Shang epoch:

- *The supreme importance of the family.* More than any other culture, the Chinese rely on the family to serve as a model for public life and the source of all private virtue.
- *The reverence shown to ancestors and the aged by the young.* The Chinese believe that experience is far more important than theory and that the young must learn from the aged if harmony is to be preserved and progress achieved.
- *The emphasis on this world.* No other civilization of early times was so *secular* in orientation. China never

had a priestly caste, and the government always subordinated religious affairs to earthly, practical tasks.

- *The importance of education, particularly literacy.* No other culture has made the ability to read and write so critical for success. The ancient Chinese written language was extremely complex (it has since been simplified). Years of hard study were required to master it, but once it was acquired, it opened the doors to both wealth and power.

In the twelfth century B.C.E., the Shang rulers seem to have faced internal conflicts that weakened the dynasty. Somewhat later they fell to the **Zhou** (Chou), a related but barbarian group from farther west. The Zhou would be the longest-lived and most influential of all the Chinese ruling dynasties.

Writing

The written language was critically important in China. How did it differ from other written languages, and how did it develop (apparently without input from non-Chinese sources)? Like most languages, Chinese was originally pictographic, but it soon developed a huge vocabulary of signs that had no picture equivalents. These characters are called **ideographs,** or ideas-in-signs. An ideograph with several parts can take the place of as many as seven or eight words in most languages, conveying whole descriptions or actions in one sign. Some ideographs were derived from certain common roots, but others were not connected in any way, which made learning them difficult. All in all, students had

Oracle Bone. On the flat surface of bones such as this, Shang sages incised the earliest surviving examples of Chinese ideographs. The messages are questions addressed to the gods, and the sages read the answers by examining the patterns of cracks in the bones after hot irons had been pressed against them. (*©Werner Forman Archive, British Library/Art Resource*)

Bronze Elephant. The form of bronze casting known as *cir perdue* (lost wax) was used by the Zhou dynasty artists. It enabled them to achieve a fine detailing of the surface, as seen here. (© *Giraudon/Art Resource*)

to memorize about 5,000 ideographs to be considered literate. Understandably, literacy was rare, and those who knew how to read and write entered a kind of elite club that carried tremendous prestige.

Although writing emerged considerably later in China than in Mesopotamia or Egypt, it developed quickly and had a richer vocabulary and more conceptual refinement than any other written language before the first century C.E. The earliest writing beyond pictography dates to the Shang era around 1500 B.C.E. It is found on **oracle bones,** animal bones and shells that were used to divine the gods' wishes. By the end of the Shang period around 1000 B.C.E., histories and stories were being written, and some have been preserved.

The written language was immensely important in unifying the Chinese. China has dozens of spoken dialects, which are mutually unintelligible, but it has only one way of writing.

Art and Architecture

The greatest artistic achievement of the ancient Chinese was undoubtedly their bronze work. Craftsmen in the late Shang and early Zhou periods turned out drinking cups, vases, wine vessels, brooches, and medallions, whose technical excellence and artistic grace were stunning. Metal technology in general was quite advanced in early China. Besides bronze, cast iron and copper were widely used for both tools and weaponry.

The Shang buildings that have been partially unearthed by modern archaeologists are impressive in both size and design. The upper class built large palaces and strong forts around towns such as Anyang and Zhengzhu (Chengchu)

in the middle reaches of the Yellow River plain. The distinctive style with pagoda-type roof lines and diminishing upper stories was developed at this time, although it was carried out much more elaborately later. Most of the art forms of modern China had their roots in very early times.

The Zhou Dynasty

During the 700 years that they ruled, at least in name, the Zhou greatly extended China's borders. Where the Shang had been content to rule a relatively restricted segment of north-central China on either side of the Yellow River, the Zhou reached out almost to the sea in the east and well into Inner Mongolia in the west. We know much more about the Zhou era than the Shang because an extensive literature survives. Much history was written, and records of all types from tax rolls to lists of imports and exports are found. The dynasty falls into two distinct phases: the unified empire, from about 1100 to about 750, and the Later Zhou, from about 750 to about 400 B.C.E. The earlier period was the more important. The Later Zhou dynasty experienced a series of constant provincial revolts until, finally, the central government broke down altogether (see Map 6.1).

One of the novelties of the Zhou period was the idea of the **mandate of heaven.** To justify their forcible overthrow of the Shang, the first Zhou rulers developed the idea that "heaven"—that is, the supernatural deities who oversaw all life—gave the chosen earthly ruler a mandate, or vote of confidence. So long as he ruled well and justly, he retained the mandate, but it would be taken from him if he betrayed the deities' trust. A ruler who failed to protect his people from invaders or failed to contain internal revolt had betrayed this trust. Thus, if a Chinese ruler fell to superior force or a successful conspiracy, it was a sign that he had "lost the mandate" and should be replaced. This marvelously self-serving theory (it was used to justify innumerable conspiracies and rebellions) was to be highly influential in Chinese history.

The first Zhou kings were powerful rulers, who depended mainly on their swords. The royal court employed hundreds of skilled administrators, and we see the faint beginning of a professional bureaucracy in the Zhou era. China led the world in this development, as in so many others. As the centuries passed, however, power slipped from the monarch's hand and a feudal society developed, as the kings delegated more and more of their military and administrative duties to local aristocrats. These men stood to gain from the acquisition of new territory, and they did so at every chance. As a result, China expanded, but at the same time the control of the royal government weakened. By the 500s, the local aristocrats were in command of much of the empire, and by 400, the central power had broken down completely—one of the few times that has happened in China.

Culture and Daily Life under the Zhou

Although the Zhou rulers eventually failed to keep the nation together, their era saw great advances in every area of arts and crafts. Bronze work, exemplified in all manner of vessels and statues, reached an apex of perfection. Much of it was produced using the lost wax method of casting into molds. This method allowed great delicacy of form and design. Iron came into common use for tools and utensils, as well as weapons.

Wars between the contending aristocrats and against the nomads on China's borders were common also, and the use of the war chariot led to a technical breakthrough of the first rank: a horse harness that allowed the horse to pull with the full strength of its shoulders and body without choking. This type of harness transformed the value of horses, not only in warfare but as beasts of burden. Only much later did other civilizations recognize and copy this fundamental change.

Agriculture was advanced by the invention of the iron-tipped plow, which allowed much more land to be tilled than could be managed with the previous wooden plow. Iron blades of various sorts, sickles, and knives also increased agricultural production and allowed the growth of large cities such as Loyang, the capital of the Later Zhou. The evidence we have suggests that Chinese peasants were moderately prosperous and rarely enslaved at this time. Although their life was undoubtedly hard, it was not miserable. Zhou peasants were in more or less the same economic situation as Egyptian peasants: they were sharecropping tenants with some rights and were protected from grasping landlords by a powerful and respected government.

In the literary arts, most of the classics that have been taught to Chinese children ever since originated in the Zhou era. The earliest surviving books stem from the 800s B.C.E., much earlier than any that survive from other civilized centers. They were written either on strips of specially prepared bamboo, strung together with silken cord, or on silk scrolls. Professional historians, employed by the court, wrote chronicles of the rulers and their achievements. Poetry made its first appearance in Chinese letters during the early Zhou, beginning a tradition of sensitive, perceptive nature poetry that continues to the present day. Calligraphy also began at this time, and officials were expected to master this art form as a qualification for office. Silk was already a major item of luxury trade in the Zhou era. Traces of Chinese silk have been unearthed from as far away as the Greek city-states of the classical age.

Confucius and the Confucian Philosophy

❖

China's greatest single cultural force, the historical figure Kung Fu-tsu (551–479) or **Confucius,** appeared toward the end of the Zhou era. For twenty centuries Confucius was the most respected name in China, the molder of Chinese education and the authority on what a true Chinese should and should not do. (See his biography in the Tradition and Innovation box.)

Confucius's interests were centered on the hierarchy of ethical and political relations between individuals, and especially between the citizenry and the governor. The great model for Confucius's politics was the Chinese family. In his view, the state should be like a harmonious family: the father was the undisputed head, each person had his or her special rights and duties, and the wisdom of the aged guided the young. The oldest male was responsible for protecting and guiding the others, who owed him absolute obedience even when he appeared to be wrong.

Confucius insisted on *gentility*—that is, courtesy, justice, and moderation—as the chief virtue of the public man. He taught that the rich and the strong should feel a sense of obligation toward the poor and the weak. A gentleman was made, not born. An aristocrat might not be a gentleman, whereas a low-born person could learn to be one. The proper calling of a gentleman was government. He should advise the ruler and see to it that government policies were fair and promoted the general welfare. A ruler who followed the advice of his gentlemanly councillors would surely retain the mandate of heaven.

❀ **Bronze Ritual Vase.** This ceremonial vessel was cast between the sixth and fourth century B.C.E. in Zhou dynasty China. The combination of massiveness and adornment has never been excelled by later bronzecasters. (© *Art Resource*)

TRADITION AND INNOVATION

Confucius
(551–479 B.C.E.)

The most revered of all Chinese statesmen and philosophers was Master Kung, or Kung Fu-tzu, who is known as Confucius in the West. As a lasting influence on a nation, he has no match in world history. During his long lifetime, he acquired a devoted group of followers who gave educated Chinese their moral and ethical landmarks for 2,000 years. Confucianism has, of course, evolved considerably over the centuries, and no one now knows precisely what the Master's original thoughts may have been. But by reading what his disciples said about him and about their own understanding of his message, we can appreciate his greatness and his importance in the life of the Chinese people. He established a tradition of cultural values that has changed but in degree of acceptance, not in its essentials.

Confucius was born into an impoverished but aristocratic family in the state of Lu at the time when the Zhou empire was falling apart and the Era of the Warring States was beginning. Given a good education, the young man set out to find a suitable place for himself in the world. His ambition was to acquire a post in the government of his home state, which would allow him to exert a real influence for good and to assist the princely ruler in providing wise and benevolent rule.

Frustrated by the intrigues of his rivals in Lu, where he briefly obtained a post in the ministry of justice, Confucius was forced to seek a position elsewhere. But in the neighboring states, too, he was disappointed in his quest, never securing more than minor and temporary positions before running afoul of backbiting competitors or speaking his mind when that was a dangerous thing to do. He had to return to Lu to earn his living as a teacher, and for the rest of his life, he subsisted modestly on the tuition fees of his wealthier students.

Confucius accepted this fate with difficulty. For many years he continued to hope for appointment as an adviser to the prince and thus to translate his beliefs into government policy. Only gradually did he realize that by his teaching he could have more influence on the fate of his people than he might ever attain as a minister to a trivial and corrupt ruler. By the end of his life, his fame had already reached much of China's small educated class, and his students were going out to found schools of their own, reflecting the principles the Master had taught them.

🔸 **Portrait of Confucius.**
(Field Museum of Natural History, Chicago, Ill.)

Confucius taught that all human affairs, public and private, were structured by the Five Relationships: father and son, husband and wife, elder and younger brother, ruler and official, and friend and friend. The fact that three of these relationships are within the family circle shows the Confucian emphasis on the family. He believed it to be the model and building block of all other social or political arrangements. This emphasis continues in Chinese life to this day.

Confucius was not so much an original thinker as a great summarizer and rephraser of the truths already currently embraced by his people. He did not attempt a complete philosophical system and was not at all interested in theology or what is now called metaphysics. Rather, his focus was always on the relation of human being to human being, and especially on the relation of governor to governed. He was an eminently secular thinker, and this tradition, too, has continued among educated Chinese to the present.

Two of the sayings attributed to him in the *Analects* give the flavor of his teaching:

> Tsi-guang [a disciple] asked about government. Confucius said: "Sufficient food, sufficient armament, and sufficient confidence of the people are the necessities."

> "Forced to give up one, which would you abandon first?"
> "I would abandon armament."
> "Forced to give up one of the remaining two, which would you abandon?"
> "I would abandon food. There has always been death from famine, but no state can exist without the confidence of its people."

The Master always emphasized the necessity of the ruler setting a good example:

> Replying to Chi Gang-tsi who had asked him about the nature of good government, Confucius said, "To govern is to rectify. If you lead the people by virtue of rectifying yourself, who will dare not be rectified by you?"

For Reflection

Do you believe that a governor who "rectifies" himself will always influence his subjects to do the same? What examples in U.S. history of recent date could you give?

Dao de Jing of Lao Zi

Confucian philosophy was by no means universally accepted in ancient China. It had to overcome several rival points of view among the educated class and was only partly successful in doing so. Among the ordinary people, Daoism was always stronger because it lent itself more readily to personal interpretation and to the rampant superstitions of the illiterate. It drew many of its principles from close observation of nature, emphasizing the necessity of bringing one's life into harmony with nature. Rather than the illusions of well-bred Confucians or the brutality of the Legalists, the followers of The Way sought serenity through acceptance of what is.

The *Dao de Jing*, or *Book of Changes*, is a collection of sayings attributed to Lao Zi (Lao-tzu), who supposedly lived in the sixth century B.C.E. Like much Chinese philosophy, the essence of the *Dao de Jing* is the search for balance between opposites, between the *yin* and *yang* principles. Unlike Confucianism, Daoism puts little faith in reason and foresight as the way to happiness. Instead, it urges its followers to accept the mystery of life and stop striving for a false mastery. It delights in putting its truths into paradox.

Chapter II

It is because every one under Heaven recognizes beauty as beauty,
    that the idea of ugliness exists.
And equally, if every one recognized virtue as virtue, this would
    create fresh conceptions of wickedness.
For truly Being and Non-Being grow out of one another;
Difficult and Easy complete one another;
Long and Short test one another;
High and Low determine one another.
The sounds of instruments and voice give harmony to one another.
Front and Back give sequence to one another.
Therefore the Sage relies on actionless activity,
Carries on wordless teaching. . . .

Chapter IV

The Way is like an empty vessel
That yet may be drawn from
Without ever needing to be filled.
It is bottomless; the very progenitor of all things in the world.

In it is all sharpness blunted,
All tangles untied,
All glare tempered,
All dust smoothed.
It is like a deep pool that never dries.
Was it, too, the child of something else? We cannot tell.

Chapter IX

Stretch a bow to the very full
And you will wish you had stopped in time;
Temper a sword edge to its very sharpest,
And you will find that it soon grows dull.
When bronze and jade fill your halls
It can no longer be guarded.
Wealth and position breed insolence
That brings ruin in its train.
When your work is done, then withdraw!
Such is Heaven's Way.

Chapter XI

We put thirty spokes together and call it a wheel;
But it is on the space where there is nothing that the utility of the
    wheel depends.
We turn clay to make a vessel;
But it is on the space where there is nothing that the utility of the
    vessel depends.
We pierce doors and windows to make a house;
But it is on these spaces where there is nothing that the utility of
    the house depends.
Therefore, just as we take advantage of what is, we should
    recognize the utility of what is not.

For Reflection

What application of Daoist thought can you find in your own experiences? Does the paradox of saying that doors and windows can be appreciated only if one keeps in mind the house walls strike you as truthful? As memorable?

SOURCE: The Way and Its Power: A Study of the Dao de Qing, ed. and trans. A. Waley. © 1934.

This philosophy of public service by scholarly, virtuous officials was to have enormous influence on China. Rulers came to be judged according to whether they made use of the Confucian prescriptions for good government. A corps of officials educated on Confucian principles and believing him to be the Great Teacher came into existence. These **mandarins,** as the West later called them, were the actual governing class of China for 2,000 years.

An unfortunate result of this system was the tendency of most rulers to interpret Confucian moderation and distrust of violence as resistance to needed change. The rulers naturally tended to see in Confucius's admonition that the state should resemble a well-run family a condemnation of revolt for any reason. In time many of the Confucian-trained bureaucrats not only agreed but came to believe that the status quo was the only natural and proper way of doing things. The insistence that harmony was the chief goal of politics and social policy sometimes was twisted into an excuse for stagnation. It led to a contempt for the new and a fear of change, however necessary. From time to time in China's long history this resistance to change has led to acute problems.

Rivals to Confucius

❀

In the later Zhou period, two rival philosophies arose to challenge the Confucian view. Neither was as successful in capturing the permanent allegiance of the educated classes, but both were sometimes seized on as an alternative or a necessary addition to the Great Teacher.

Daoism

Daoism (Taoism) is a philosophy centered on nature and following the Way (*Dao*) it shows us. It was supposedly the product of a teacher-sage called **Lao Zi (Lao-tzu),** who purportedly was a near contemporary of Confucius but may be entirely legendary. The book attributed to him, the famous ***Book of Changes (Dao de Jing),*** was probably written by his followers much later.

Unlike Confucius, Daoism sees the best government as the least government, and the people as being inherently unable and unwilling to govern themselves. The responsibility of the ruling class is to give the people the justice and good administration that they are unable to devise for themselves. In so doing, the rulers should follow the Way of Nature, as it is perceived through meditation and observation. The intelligent man seeks a lifestyle that is in tune with the natural world, a harmony of parts into a serene whole.

The excerpt from the *Dao de Jing* in the Nature and Technology box shows this harmony through paradoxical examples drawn from everyday life. All extremes should be avoided, even those meant to be benevolent. The truly good ruler does little except be; excessive action is as bad as no corrective action.

Daoism has taken so many forms through the centuries that it is almost impossible to provide a single description of it. Originally, it was a philosophy of the educated classes, but it eventually degenerated into a superstition of the peasants. Yet for many centuries, it was a serious rival of Confucius's ideas and was often adopted by Chinese seeking harmony with the natural world and escape from earthly conflicts. This dichotomy was summed up in the saying that the educated classes were "Confucian by day, Daoist by night." In their rational, public lives they abided by Confucian principles, but in the quiet of their beds, they sought immersion in mysterious, suprarational nature.

Legalism

Legalism was more a philosophy of government than a philosophy of private life. It was popularized in the **Era of Warring States** (c. 400–c. 225 B.C.E.) between the collapse of central Zhou dynastic authority (around 400 B.C.E.) and the rise of the Qin emperor in the 220s (see Chapter 20). The general breakdown of authority that characterized this period provided the motivation for Legalist ideas.

❀❀ **Warriors.** These clay statuettes of imperial army men date from approximately the third century B.C.E. Their upraised hands once held spears and swords. They were a burial accompaniment for a lord of the Zhou period. (© *Patrick Aventurier/Gamma-Liaison*)

The Legalists were convinced that a government that allowed freedom to its subjects was asking for trouble. Legalism was a rationalized form of governmental manipulation. It was not so much a philosophy as a justification for applying force when persuasion had failed. The basis of Legalism was the conviction that most people are inclined to evil selfishness, and it is the task of government to restrain them and simultaneously to guide them into doing good—that is, what the governors want. This task is to be accomplished by controlling people even before their evil nature has manifested itself in their acts. In other words, the Legalists advocated strict censorship, prescribed education (differing by class), and immediate crushing of any signs of independent thought or action.

In a later chapter, we shall investigate how the Chinese government and state were definitively formed in the second and first centuries B.C.E. But Chinese culture, as distinct from the state, was already shaped by 500 B.C.E. and would not change much until the modern era. The emphasis on the family, the respect due to elders, the subordination of women to men, the focus on this life on Earth rather than on a life to come, and the lofty position of the educated were already deeply rooted in Chinese society long before the Romans had established their empire.

SUMMARY

The civilization of China originated in the Neolithic villages of the northern plains near the Yellow River in the second millennium B.C.E. Under the first historical dynasties of the Shang and the Zhou, this agrarian civilization displayed certain characteristics that were to mark China for many centuries to come: reverence for ancestors, the tremendous importance of the family, and the prestige of the educated. Fine arts and literature were cultivated in forms that persisted: bronzeware, ceramics, silk, historical literature, and nature poetry.

The Shang dynasts were a warrior aristocracy that took over the village folk as their subjects in the eighteenth century B.C.E. What we know of them is almost entirely via archaeology performed in recent times. They were succeeded after several centuries by another warrior group called the Zhou, which established perhaps the most influential of all Chinese dynasties in the realm of culture. The arts flourished and the limits of the state expanded greatly. Gradually, however, power to hold this vast realm together escaped from the ruler's hands and flowed into those of the provincial aristocrats.

The breakdown of central government that ended the long Zhou dynasty and introduced the Era of Warring States demanded further definition of basic values. In response, three great schools of practical philosophy arose between 500 and 250 B.C.E.: Confucianism, Daoism, and Legalism. Of these, the most significant for later Chinese history was the secularist, rationalist thought of Confucius, the Sage of China for the next 2,000 years.

TEST YOUR KNOWLEDGE

1. China's geography
   a. isolated it from other civilizations.
   b. was semitropical.
   c. is much like that of Mesopotamia.
   d. made it a natural marketplace and exchange point.
2. The Shang dynasty was established in northern China at roughly the same time as the
   a. rise of the Assyrians.
   b. Aryan conquest of northern India.
   c. beginnings of Sumerian civilization.
   d. first dynasty in Egypt.
3. Early Chinese religious thought is noteworthy for
   a. its insistence on the existence of only two gods.
   b. its emphasis on devotion to the spirits of the ancestors.
   c. its superstition about heaven and hell.
   d. its clear and detailed theology.
4. A significant long-term advantage of the Chinese style of writing is its
   a. easiness to learn.
   b. independence of regional dialects.
   c. effective use of an alphabet.
   d. small vocabulary.
5. After seizing power from the Shang, the Zhou rulers adopted
   a. a theory of government justifying their action.
   b. a militarized dictatorship.
   c. a theocracy in which the priests had final powers.
   d. a democracy.
6. Which one of the following statements is contrary to Confucian teaching?
   a. The family is the proper model for good government.
   b. The young should be constantly seeking new and more effective modes of action.

c. The gentleman is made and not born.

d. The interactions of social groups should be controlled by formalities and courtesy.

7. In many aspects of philosophy, Chinese thought generally aimed

a. at attaining union with the immortal gods.

b. at inspiring loyalty and fear in the common people.

c. at teaching myths and magical formulas.

d. at attaining harmony and avoiding disorder on earth.

8. Which one of the following products was foreign to ancient China?

a. Iron weaponry

b. Silken cloth

c. Fine bronzeware

d. Porcelain tableware

9. Daoist political views emphasized that

a. people get the government they deserve.

b. people are naturally evil and that government must restrain them.

c. people should be enslaved to ensure peace.

d. people should be left to their own devices as much as possible.

IDENTIFICATION TERMS

Book of Changes (Dao de Jing)

Confucius

Era of the Warring States

ideograph

Lao Zi

Legalism

mandarin

mandate of heaven

oracle bones

Shang dynasty

Yangtze River

Yellow River

Zhou dynasty

INFOTRAC COLLEGE EDITION

Enter the search terms "Confucius or Confucian" using Key Words.

Enter the search term "Taoism" using the Subject Guide.

Chapter 7

Ordinary Lives in the Ancient Past

Fortune, not wisdom, rules the lives of men.

THEOPHRASTUS

WHAT WAS LIFE LIKE for the ordinary people in the distant past? In recent years, many historians of ancient civilizations have shifted their attention from the traditional accounts of the doings of kings and generals to those of average men and women. This history "from the bottom up" is a challenging task. Ancient records and chronicles tell us little about the lives of ordinary people. What is known has had to be reconstructed from the scraps of information available. Much will always remain unknown, of course. Much else can be guessed at but lacks certainty.

In the following pages, we will look at four distinct but related aspects of the four chief centers of early civilization: Mesopotamia, Egypt, India, and China. One aspect will be basic economics: how ordinary persons were employed and how they secured themselves (if indeed they could) against the universal fear of famine and misery. Another will be family relations: parent and child, man and wife, individual and kin. Then we will look at the status of women, both within the home and outside it. Marriage and divorce, differences between free women and slaves, and the clash between patriarchal tradition and the aspirations of talented women will be given special attention. Finally, we will make some observations on the way children were integrated into society. We will draw comparisons and contrasts among the ancient societies wherever enough information is known.

Earning a Living

❀

All early civilizations had an advanced center (town, city) that drew its necessities from a surrounding countryside subject to it. This model seems to have been universal, differing only in the size and complexity of the urban areas.

The largest and most differentiated cities were those of Mesopotamia, some of which may have had populations in excess of 100,000 (about the size of present-day Charleston, South Carolina; Kansas City, Kansas; and Reno, Nevada). The ancient Indus civilization also developed large cities, but Egypt and China were originally much more agrarian in nature. There the normal living environment was the farmers' village rather than the town.

ate poor, or simply a way of getting rid of unwanted females. Certainly, a large number of the prostitutes and tavern girls in the Roman era were picked up as abandoned babies and raised to their later professions by brothel keepers. What seems to us a shocking, heartless crime was, in fact, not considered an offense at all but a matter of private conscience.

Women: Their Status in Society

❀

Recently, there has been much comment on the fact that the history of ancient civilization has been written by and about men. Women play roles within this story only insofar as they are related to or used by the male actors. We know something about queens, royal concubines, and great poetesses, but very little at first hand about ordinary daughters, wives, and mothers. What we do know has been filtered through male consciousness, and we cannot be sure how that has affected the facts we are told. Certainly, there is a difference between the way women themselves see their lives and the way they are seen by the men around them.

In any case, historians generally agree on some categorical statements about the women of ancient Mesopotamia and Egypt:

- In the very earliest stage of civilization, women shared more or less equally with men in social prestige and power.
- This egalitarianism was undermined and overturned by the coming of militarized society (armies), the heavy plow in agriculture, and the establishment of large-scale trade.
- The trend toward patriarchy and male dominance in public affairs of all sorts proceeded at varying speeds in different societies but was impossible to reverse once it started.

Ancient law codes from Mesopotamia show a definite break between about 2000 B.C.E. and 1000 B.C.E., with Hammurabi's code being a transition. In the earliest codes (and to a lesser degree in Hammurabi's), the female enjoys extensive rights; by about 1200, she is an object ruled by men. By the era in which the Old Testament was written (700 B.C.E. on), she scarcely exists as a legal or political entity but has been subordinated to men in every way.

The Judaic Yahweh was very definitely a male lawgiver, speaking to other males in a society where women counted only as the relatives and dependents of men. The nomadic background of the Twelve Tribes of Israel is evident here, for nomads have a universal tendency to subordinate females and to consider them the possessions of their men. In the Old Testament, even when a Jewish woman acts in a self-assertive fashion, the point of her action is to secure some advantage or distinction for her menfolk, and not on her own behalf. Judith slays Holofernes not to avenge herself but to secure the safety of her people. The reward of the heroine is not leadership, to which she never aspires, but an honorable place in the folk memory.

Because of the lack of historical documentation, the general position of women in the earliest Indian civilizations is unclear. Scholars have detected a few signs of equality or even a matriarchal society. With the arrival of the Aryan nomads, female status began a descent that continued in Hindu culture. According to Hindu tradition, Manu, the mythical lawgiver, established the proper relation between the sexes once and for all: the woman was to serve and obey the male (see the Tradition and Innovation box entitled "The Laws of Manu" in Chapter 5). Gradually, the rituals of *sati* (widow's suicide) and *purdah* (isolation from all nonfamily males) became established. The degree of female subordination varied according to caste. In the upper castes, women were subordinate to their men, but not to the extent that was expected in the Jewish or Chinese traditions, for example. The female dharma in all castes, however, was to care for her husband and her sons and honor her parents.

In China the male was always superior to the female in the public arena, and proper observance of religious customs (ancestor "worship") depended on him. It was through his blood that the family was preserved, and he was the equivalent of priest as well as ruler. The good wife was defined as the mother of male children who would keep the family name alive and honor the dead in the proper fashion.

In all four civilizations, most of the routine occupations were open to women as well as to men. Women could engage in business in their own name (but normally under a male relative's supervision). They could be priests, scribes, or tavern keepers, as well as housewives. But their proportional representation in the high-level jobs was much smaller than men's, and in all types of employment, they were normally acting under male supervision or as a man's agent or deputy. Very rarely did a woman operate completely independently. For a woman from an upper-class family, working outside the home was unheard of, unless she became a priestess or took a similar position that brought honor with it.

Female slaves were everywhere, both inside and outside the home. Free women and slaves often worked side by side. Some occupations were dominated by free persons, others by slaves, but most had room for both. Even relatively poor families had a domestic slave or two, who helped with housework and child care and often had a secure place within the household. These slave women had frequently been sold into slavery by destitute parents, who undoubtedly were correct in believing that their daughters would have a longer life expectancy as a slave than as a free person. The painful tradition of selling daughters into slavery persisted in China until well into the twentieth century.

Many house slaves were purchased to serve as a **concubine,** or second wife, to the master of the household. This practice was particularly common in childless marriages, when the husband began to worry about his lack of posterity. The offspring of such arrangements were generally treated as legitimate. The husband in a childless marriage normally was encouraged by his wife to take another woman, because the continuation of the family name was as crucial to her as to him—it had become her name at her marriage. If this second wife did not produce male children, the husband often adopted a son from among his clan relations.

Marriage and Motherhood

Marriage and motherhood were, of course, the chief concerns of females everywhere. Marriage was always arranged by the two families—something so important could never be left to chance attraction. A great many of the clay tablets dug up in the Mesopotamian ruins deal with marital contracts. Some of them were made when the bride and groom were still babies. Such early arrangements were especially common for girls, who normally were considerably younger at marriage than their husbands. The age of menarche (onset of menstruation) seems to have been about fourteen on average in West Asia. Girls were considered capable of bearing children, and therefore marriageable, at age twelve in China and India. One must distinguish, however, between a formal betrothal, or engagement, and the beginning of cohabitation (that is, sharing bed and board), which came later—perhaps years later.

Marriage usually involved the exchange of "bride money" and a dowry. Bride money was a payment by the groom's family to the bride's family as specified in the marital contract. The dowry was also specified in the contract and was paid by the bride's family to the groom when the couple began to cohabit. The dowry remained in the husband's control as long as the marriage lasted. When the wife died, the dowry was distributed among her children, if she had any.

Divorce and lawsuits arising from it were frequent in Mesopotamia, as the tablets attest. Most divorces were initiated by husbands, who were disappointed by childless wives or were sexually attracted to another woman and did not wish to or could not support the first wife as well. The lawsuits resulted when the wife or her father protested the lack of provision made for her support or the husband's attempt to retain her dowry. Then as now, the lawyers must have relied on divorce proceedings for a substantial part of their income.

Of all the ancient civilizations, the Chinese wife's lot was probably the hardest. Wife beating was taken for granted among the ordinary people, as it would be for many generations. Divorce at the wife's request was rare, though it could be granted for abandonment or criminal action. One

Good Husbands, Loving Wives

*I*n the *Instructions of Ani,* an ancient Egyptian scribe recorded his impression of how a husband should behave toward a faithful wife:

> Do not control your wife in her house when you know she is efficient. Do not say to her "Where is it, Get it!" when you know she has put it in its right place. Let your eye observe in silence. Then you recognize her skill, it is joy when your hand is with hers. There are many who do not understand this. If a man desists from strife at home, he will not meet its beginning. Every man who founds a household should hold back the hasty heart.

An inscription has been found in which a fatally ill wife addresses her husband for the last time: "Cease not to drink, to eat, to get drunk, to enjoy making love, to make the day joyful, and to follow your inclination day for day."

SOURCE: *From* Egyptian Life, *a pamphlet from the British Museum, London, 1986.*

of the most admired women in Chinese folklore was a wife who defied her own family's wishes to stay with a husband who was utterly worthless. Virginity before marriage and submissive loyalty afterward were the great virtues for a woman.

In China as in most places, the wife moved in with her husband's family and became a part of it. The mother-in-law was the jealous supervisor of the household, living with the young couple (or couples) who shared the home or the compound of connected houses. China's folk literature is filled with stories about the mean-hearted persecution of young wives by sour mothers-in-law. The older women had the approval of society: they were acting, supposedly, as protectors of their son's honor and property. This is one more instance of the female who can only assert herself as the agent of the male, in this case, her son.

Sexual Life

The sexual nature of the society was more openly discussed in some of the ancient civilizations than others. In China's early literature, sex is treated discreetly, if at all. In contrast, the people of the Near and Middle Eastern centers had little inhibition by modern standards, while the artistic and literary records of ancient India display an absolute joy in the body's sexual powers. Because children and the continuity of the family were the real reasons for marriage, the marital bed was an honorable and even sacred place, and what took place there was in no way shameful. But the male and female had desires that went beyond the creation of children, and these were also nothing to be ashamed of, for these desires were implanted in humans by the all-wise gods. The result was a fundamentally different sexual attitude than we commonly find today. In the Near East, the rites of the "Sacred Marriage" between a god and his high priestess, celebrating the fertility of the earth and of all creatures on it, were central to religious practice. In both the Near East and India, orgies were frequently included in the ceremonies honoring the gods and goddesses.

In India, the female was often seen as being more sexually potent than the male. This conviction, it is now argued, arose from men's fears about the "devouring woman," represented in Hindu art by the ferocious goddess of destruction, Kali. Some equivalent of the devouring woman, who is sexually insatiable and physically overpowering, is found in several ancient religions whose rites were developed by men (as kings and priests). It is notably absent from those that arose during a period of female predominance (matriarchy), or when the sexes were more or less equal in public affairs. The tensions between the sexes are thus reflected in differing views of the sexual instinct and its satisfaction from earliest times.

Every ancient culture insisted that brides should be virgins. This was one of the reasons for the early marriage of women. Although many literary and folk tales describe the horrible fate that awaited a woman who lost her virginity before marriage, it is still quite clear that lovemaking between young unmarried persons was by no means unheard of and did not always result in shame. Loss of virginity was regarded as damage to the family's property rather than a moral offense. As such, it could be made good by the payment of a fine. Punishment for seducing a virgin was less severe than for adultery or rape. Some authorities believe that the early stages of civilization in all areas were more tolerant of nonvirginal marriage for women than were later ones. If premarital relations were followed by marriage, very little fuss was made.

Prostitution was commonplace from very early times in all civilizations and was one of the most profitable employments of female slaves. Married and unmarried males were expected to make use of their services, which were available in every price range. Originating in many places as an element of a religious festival, the so-called temple prostitute soon had counterparts in the taverns found in every town. Women employed in taverns (or "public houses"—pubs—as they are still called in Great Britain) were normally available for commercial sex. Prostitutes were definitely inferior in social standing to other women, free or slave, but they did possess certain legal rights and were protected to

some slight degree from abuse by clients or pimps, as testimony in lawsuits from the Near East as early as 2000 B.C.E. and beyond demonstrates.

Education of Children

❉

How were children raised in ancient times? Our information is limited but sufficient to make some points with certainty. Girls were treated very differently from boys and were given much less opportunity to advance beyond the fundamentals. Only a small proportion of the population, mostly in the urban areas, received any type of formal training.

✿ **Kali.** The Indian goddess of destruction was frequently portrayed in a sexual context, but in this bronze representation (800–1100 C.E.) from south India, she takes a Buddha-like position while extending her four arms with traditional implements of the household. *(Nimatallah/Art Resource)*

Spinning Wool. This recent photo shows how wool thread was spun by a hand spindle for thousands of years, a practice that still goes on in some of the more isolated villages of the Middle East and South Asia. Spinning was perhaps the prime task of women in ancient society, in terms of time consumed. *(Courtesy of Aramco World)*

A male's education depended entirely on his social class. If he was born into an aristocratic or wealthy family, he would usually receive a basic education from a live-in tutor or be sent to school under the aegis of local wise men. If he showed promise, even a boy in a poor family might be sent to such a school by the collective sacrifices of his kinfolk or fellow villagers. A talented young man might undertake higher studies as the protégé of a priest, an official of the king, or a childless man who wished to adopt the pupil (by no means rare). In the Near East and Egypt, this higher study might be focused on mathematics, astrology, or theology. In China and Japan, it would more likely deal with philosophy, music, or etiquette.

Female education usually aimed at preparing the girl to meet the demands of the household. Spinning and weaving were necessary arts in every civilized society, even where slaves did the actual work. Most wives were expected to keep some sort of elementary budget, and a lower-class wife was frequently as involved in the shop or trade as her husband. We have many indications that both in Egypt and in the Mesopotamian cities women were employed as scribes and officials on occasion and that some women rose to high governmental office. (There were at least three female pharaohs, and we know that a queen of the Near Eastern Palmyra rose from slavery.) But these were clear exceptions to the rule and almost always resulted from prior relationships with powerful men.

Girls were invariably instructed in the household arts by their mothers, mothers-in-law, or older sisters before marriage. There were no schools for girls, nor were girls accepted into the male schools so far as is known. For the few girls who were deemed worthy of literacy, tutors were employed.

Summary

The social history of ancient times reveals sharp differences between the classes and between the sexes. Civilized living accentuated the chasm between rich and poor while multiplying the ways in which the two groups could be kept separated in daily life. The great majority worked with their hands, and most of them lived in a rural setting, working on the land in one way or another. Whereas the villages continued to have only one class, the towns were increasingly stratified among the wealthy few, the less wealthy who were slightly more numerous, and working people of various skills who formed the majority.

The condition of women also varied according to class, but the female generally deferred to the male in every sphere of public life. Religion, commerce, government, the arts and sciences, and ownership of property were all dominated by the male in all four civilizations we examined here. Females were cherished largely in relation to their fertility and the assistance they provided to males in the daily labor of life. Although marital affection and romantic passion were by no means excluded, both sexes perceived the common lot of women in terms of willing, permanent subordination to a series of male overseers and protectors.

TEST YOUR KNOWLEDGE

1. Farming or tending animals was the normal way of making a living
   a. for everyone in every ancient society.
   b. for most people in most societies.
   c. for those people who had access to irrigation.
   d. for those who were not someone's slaves.

2. The main cause of misery in society everywhere was probably
   a. warfare.
   b. overpopulation.
   c. religious persecution.
   d. lack of adequate employment.

3. Which of these would most likely be able to read and write?
   a. A Jewish farmer
   b. A Mesopotamian craftsman
   c. An Indian shopkeeper
   d. An Egyptian villager

4. Becoming enslaved in ancient societies was most often the result of one or the other of the following causes:
   a. Commission of crime or personal violence
   b. Prisoner of war or debt
   c. Blasphemy or defiance of the gods
   d. Debt or rebellion

5. Women's participation in ordinary trade and business was normally
   a. possible only in exceptional cases, where no males were available.
   b. a routine affair with full equality with males.
   c. common in the lower-status occupations, usually under some male supervision.
   d. common in the lower-status occupations, usually as independent agents.

6. In most societies that we know much about, the wife
   a. moved in with her husband's family as a junior member of the household.
   b. moved in with her husband but lived apart from the rest of his family.
   c. set up independent housekeeping with her husband apart from both families.
   d. determined where the new couple would live.

7. The most consistently male-oriented society we know of in ancient times was
   a. the Chinese.
   b. the Mesopotamian.
   c. the Persian.
   d. the Indian.

8. The most common example of different standards of punishment for the same offense in ancient society was the handling of
   a. treason against the throne.
   b. adultery in marriage.
   c. theft of others' property.
   d. blasphemy against the gods.

9. As a general rule, the education of the two sexes in ancient times
   a. was similar in the subjects taught and the methods employed.
   b. was sharply divided by gender, with both boys and girls being systematically instructed in schools.
   c. was rarely undertaken except by priests.
   d. was very limited for most girls and was the exception for boys of the lower classes.

10. The usual fashion for educating a female child was
    a. to send her off to a tutor.
    b. to teach her necessary skills at home.
    c. to have her compete with other females for a place in a school.
    d. to charge her older brother with her instruction.

IDENTIFICATION TERMS

concubine	**extended family**	**nuclear family**	**primogeniture**
exposure	**matriarchy**	**patriarchy**	

INFOTRAC COLLEGE EDITION

Enter the search term "antiquities" using the Subject Guide.

Enter the search terms "archaeology research" using the Subject Guide.

	Law and Government	**Economy**
Mesopotamians, Egyptians, Hebrews	*Mesopotamia:* Early law based on different treatment for differing classes. Property better protected than people, but some care for all persons' interests. Government originally theocratic but becomes monarchic after c. 2000 B.C.E. when contesting city-states are conquered by external invader and put under centralized rule. *Egypt:* Law is the divine justice of the pharaoh, administered by his officials. Government displays great stability under god-king until as late as 1000 B.C.E., when foreign invasions multiply after failed attempt at empire. *Israel:* Law is based on Moses' Covenant with Yahweh, which provides a divinely ordained ethical foundation for Hebraic custom. The twelve tribes long for a messiah who will lead them to earthly dominion but are repeatedly disappointed after the collapse of Solomon's kingdom and its division into Israel and Samaria.	Mesopotamia is very active in commerce originating in large towns and cities, which are themselves dependent on intensive irrigation farming. Trade with the Indus valley, the Black Sea region, Egypt, and Persia is attested to by archaeology. Skilled craftsmen as well as priests and governors supply the export trade. Egypt is the most fertile part of the world and can export grain as well as copper to its neighbors, while remaining almost self-sufficient for millennia. Unlike Mesopotamia, no large urban areas and relatively little contact with others through most of this epoch. The Hebrews sporadically play an intermediary role in the trade between the Nile and the eastern Mediterranean civilizations, but their economy is basically agrarian and pastoral throughout this period.
Indians	Government is presumed to be a theocracy in the Indus valley civilization; no evidence as to its nature is available. Law remains customary and unwritten long after the Aryan invasion (c. 1500 B.C.E.). The brahmin priests retain their law-making position as the Aryan-Indian amalgam gradually produces Vedic Hinduism. Important concepts and customs are memorized by succeeding generations, dominated by the self-interest of the uppermost castes. The evolution of Aryan warrior-kings as partners of the brahmins brings a series of petty principalities in northern India and the extension of Aryan colonization from the Indus valley to the Ganges valley. By the end of the period the Aryans have been absorbed into the Indian mass.	Indian and other South Asian cultures are overwhelmingly agrarian into modern times. Large towns exist from earliest times (Harappa, Mohenjo-Daro), but the large majority of people live in villages, with little contact outside their own region. Trade with Mesopotamia and Persia is active from the pre-Aryan period; later, maritime trade with both the eastern and western shores of the Indian Ocean is common and, by the end of the period, with the early Southeast Asian states as well.
Chinese	China develops writing early and keeps extensive records from c. 1000 B.C.E. Chinese law, which is customary in this period, looks to the protection of property and maintenance of the clan/family as determining factors for justice. Government is monarchic and warrior-oriented, with Shang conquerors as models for the succeeding Zhou. Zhou dynasts lose grip on outlying "warlords" by the end of the period, and the Era of Warring States opens.	As in South Asia, most Chinese live in villages, raising grain and engaging in pastoral agriculture. A few large towns exist, but as yet play only a minor role in the economy. Trade with others is negligible in this era. China is still isolated from the rest of the world. Rice culture has not yet begun, as the south remains unconquered. Contact with India, Vietnam, and Japan is not yet undertaken.

Peoples: Mesopotamians, Egyptians, Hebrews, Indians, Chinese

Religion and Philosophy	Arts and Culture	Science and Technology
Religious belief dictates the type of government in the earliest period, but gradually separates the king from the priest. Mesopotamia adopts a pessimistic view of the human-god relationship and the afterlife. Egypt had a uniquely optimistic view of the afterlife and the role of the protecting gods, which lasted more than 2,000 years, until the collapse of its empire and foreign invasions forced a reconsideration. Jews draw on Zoroastrian Persian traditions to pioneer monotheism and to elevate Yahweh into a universal lawgiver to all humanity, with a special relationship with his chosen people, based on love and justice in a life to come.	Mesopotamians produce first monumental architecture, first urban society, first sophisticated writing system, and much else. Arts flourish under priestly and royal patronage, but relatively little has survived time and wars. Egypt's pyramids are the most impressive ancient construction of all; massive sculpture, interior fresco painting, and ceramics are other Egyptian strengths in art. At the end of the period, Hebrews produce the Bible as literature and history of the race.	Mesopotamians play a huge role in early science: chronology, calendar, math, physics, and astronomy are all highly developed by 2500. Technology (mudbrick construction, city sanitation, hydraulics for city and farming, etc.) also has a major place in the daily life of the city-states. Egypt also develops considerable science but is not so consistently innovative. Medicine and pharmacy are strengths, as are skill in construction and stonework. A solar calendar is developed. Jews lag in both science and technology, remaining dependent on others throughout this period.
Religion of India is a mixture of Indus civilization belief and Aryan "sky gods." The Vedas brought by the Aryans become sacred scripture for emerging Vedic Hinduism by 1000. Brahmin priestly castes are corulers with the warriors who conquer North India and impose Aryan rule. South India is not conquered, but is strongly influenced by Vedic beliefs. At the end of the period, Buddhism begins to gain ground rapidly among all Indians and has an enormous impact on philosophy as well as theology.	South Asian art largely reflects the religious mythology, as it does elsewhere until modern times. Much has been lost to the climate. Some sculpture and minor arts survive from ruins of Indus valley towns. Stone temples and carvings survive in limited numbers; the extensive sacred literature is entirely oral into the first centuries C.E., when the Vedas, Upanishads, and other Hindu and Buddhist epics that date in oral form from 1700–500 B.C.E. are first written.	Indians master metalworking (weapons, utensils) early, progressing rapidly through Bronze Age to Iron Age by 1000 B.C.E. Mathematics are especially important, navigation arts are well developed, and engineering skills enable them to erect massive temples and fortresses. Lack of written data hinders detailed knowledge of Indian science in this era.
Chinese religion is conditioned by ancestral continuity; honor of lineage is all-important, with gods playing relatively minor roles. There is no state theology, but the emperor supposedly enjoys the "mandate of heaven" to rule and serves as high priest. At the end of the period, the Confucian ethical and philosophical system, which will be a substitute for supernatural religion for educated classes, is beginning. The peasant majority goes on with superstition-ridden Dao.	Chinese arts in several formats take on lasting features during Zhou dynasty: bronzes, landscape painting, nature poetry, ceramics, silk, and pagoda architecture. Language arts are highly developed, despite difficulties of ideographic language. Reverence for education and for the aged is already apparent. Supreme importance of the family continually emphasized in this patriarchal society.	Metal technology well advanced in China: Bronze Age commences by 3000 B.C.E. and iron introduced, probably from India, by 600s. Shang bronzes finest ever cast, while Zhou dynasty sees major improvements in agricultural productivity and weaponry. Copper coins circulate; lacquer ware and silk processing are major home industries.

Classical Mediterranean Civilizations

500 B.C.E.–500 C.E.

Why do we use the word *classical* to identify the thousand-year epoch from 500 B.C.E. to 500 C.E.? In the eastern Mediterranean and the East and South Asian river valley civilizations, this period saw an impressive cultural expansion and development, especially in philosophy, the arts, and language. The monuments and methodologies created then served as benchmarks for many centuries for the Mediterranean, Indian, and Chinese peoples. Some have even endured to the present day. For example, the use of the architrave and exterior columns to lend both dignity and accessibility to the facade of public buildings (such as the Parthenon shown in Chapter 9) has persisted through 2,500 years in Western architecture.

The two other early centers of civilization—Mesopotamia and the Nile valley—did not undergo similar expansion. In Egypt, the heritage of 2,000 years of cultural and political sovereignty was eroded by invaders from both Asia and Africa. After about 500 B.C.E., Egypt was under foreign masters and became ever more peripheral to the world's affairs. Somewhat similar was the fate of Mesopotamia, where ecological damage intensified the negative effects of the Persians' decision to locate their chief cities elsewhere. The once blooming fields surrounding cities such as Uruk and Lagash have long since been reduced to stark desert. A hallmark of the classical age was the larger territorial size of the civilized societies and their more pronounced cultural attractions for the nomadic barbarians on their fringes. Urban centers were both more numerous and more important. Economic sophistication was evident in the expanded long-distance trade for the more numerous upper classes and in the more refined instruments of payment and credit employed by the merchants. For example, the beginning of the letter of credit was introduced in China to facilitate merchants' exchanges. Social strata were more differentiated and more complex than in the ancient age, and social tensions more evident. Wars were fought on a much larger scale and provided the impetus for much development of government.

Knowledge of the natural world (that is, science) made great strides in certain fields, such as physics, but was paltry in many others, such as geology. Technology, on the other hand, remained primitive in an age of easy access to slave labor. Supernatural and salvationist religions, especially Christianity, came to play an ever-increasing part in daily life after about 300 C.E. in the Mediterranean basin.

In this part of our book, we look at the classical civilization of the Mediterranean and western Europe, established first by the Greeks and then expanded and modified by Romans. (We will turn to the classical age in South and East Asia in Part Three.) Chapters 8, 9, and 10 outline the history of the Greeks. Although we note the Greeks' debts to their Mesopotamian and Egyptian predecessors, our emphasis is on the remarkable two centuries between 500 and 300 B.C.E. Then follows the story of the rise and accomplishments of the Roman empire between about 500 B.C.E. and 200 C.E. in Chapters 11 and 12. We conclude with a comparative look at daily life and work in the Hellenic, Hellenistic, and Roman cultures in Chapter 13.

Chapter 8

The Greek Adventure

The function of the ruler is to use his best endeavors to make his subjects happier.

ISOCRATES

THE SMALL, ROCKY PENINSULA in the eastern Mediterranean Sea now called Greece proved to be the single most important source of later Western civilization. In this unpromising landscape emerged a vigorous, imaginative people who gave the later European and Western world a tradition of thought and values that is still very much alive.

The history of the ancient Greeks can be divided into three epochs: (1) The *Mycenaean* age lasted from about 2000 B.C.E. to the conquest of the Greek peninsula by invaders in the 1100s. (2) The *Hellenic* period extended from the time of Homer to the conquest of the Greek city-states by the Macedonians in the mid-300s. It includes the Classical Age, when Greek philosophical and artistic achievements were most impressive. (3) The *Hellenistic* Age was the final period of Greek predominance, lasting from about 300 B.C.E. to the first century C.E. During this age, Greeks interacted with Eastern peoples to produce a hybrid culture that was extraordinarily influential on the arts and science of both Western and Asian civilizations. In this chapter we will look at the political and social aspects of the Mycenaean and Hellenic periods, and then we will focus on intellectual and artistic developments in Chapter 9. In Chapter 10 we will examine the Hellenistic era.

The Mycenaean Civilization

More than most societies, Greece was shaped by its geography. It is the tip of the European mainland that gradually sank beneath the Mediterranean many tens of thousands of years ago, leaving only the tops of a high mountain range as islands in the Aegean and eastern limits of the Mediterranean. Greece has very little suitable land for large-scale farming, no broad river valleys, and no level plains. No place in modern Greece is located more than eighty miles from the sea. Dozens of protected harbors and bays can be found all along the coast. From a very early time, the Greeks became expert sailors, and ships and shipping have been a major part of their livelihood since ancient days. The mountains of the peninsula make overland travel very diffi-

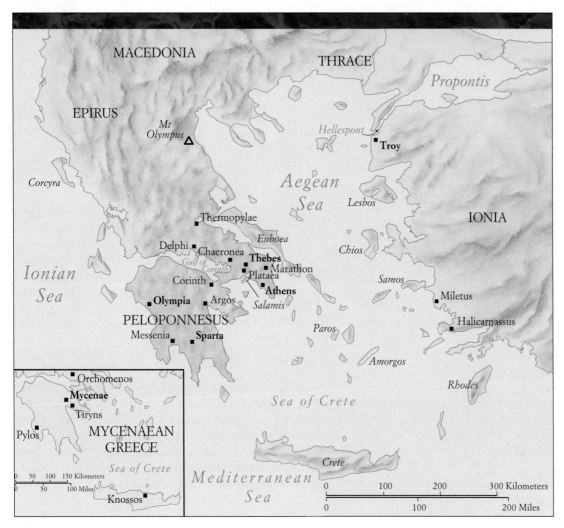

🌸 **MAP 8.1 Early Greece.** At the height of Greek power, there were more than 200 independent *poleis,* many of them on the numerous islands of the Aegean Sea and the Ionian coast. A few were entirely urban, but most combined a town with surrounding rural agricultural areas. The inset shows Mycenaean Greece, the earliest period in the history of the peninsula.

cult, and it has almost always been easier to travel and trade by sea than by land.

Greek geography encouraged political fragmentation. The people in each valley and river basin developed their own sense of patriotism and identity, much as the people of the valleys of our own Appalachians did. Greeks grew up thinking of themselves first as residents of a given place or town and only secondarily as Greeks sharing a common culture and language with the other inhabitants of the peninsula.

The first Greeks to enter the peninsula came about 2000 B.C.E. as wandering nomads from the eastern European plains. By about 1600 they had become semicivilized, and some of them lived in fair-sized towns, notably *Mycenae* on the eastern side of the Peloponnesus (see Map 8.1 inset). The people are known as the **Mycenaeans,** and the first few

hundred years of Greek civilization are called the Mycenaean Age.

Our knowledge of this period comes largely from archaeological excavations and from the **Iliad** and the **Odyssey,** two epics of ancient Greece written by the magnificent poet **Homer** in the eighth century B.C.E. The *Iliad* deals with the Mycenaeans' war against the powerful city-state of Troy, and the *Odyssey* tells of the adventures of the hero Odysseus (Ulysses) after the war (see the Violence and Coercion box). For a long time, historians believed that the Trojan War was simply a fiction created by a great poet about his ancestors. But thanks to archaeology, we know that there actually was a Troy and that it was destroyed about the time that Homer indicates—about 1300 B.C.E. Whether it was destroyed by the Greeks or not, we do not know, but there is no reason not to believe so. Ancient Troy,

🌸 **Ruins of Troy.** This aerial view of the mound where once sat ancient Troy shows the partly reconstituted city walls and the stadium (lower center). Destroyed many times both before and after the Mycenaean Age, the rubble covers the entire hillside, and in places is the hill itself. *(Yann Arthus-Bertrand/Corbis)*

now a great pile of rubble, was situated on a hill commanding the entrance into the straits called the Hellespont. Much evidence indicates that the Greek towns, led by Mycenae, were engaged in commercial rivalry with Troy throughout this period and may well have made war on their nearby enemy.

The Mycenaean civilization was inspired by the model of one of its trading partners and rivals: Crete. This large island supported an urbanized civilization of its own, dating back to at least 1900 B.C.E., when the Greeks on the mainland were still nomads. Historians and archaeologists call the Cretan culture **Minoan** after Minos, the mythical king of Crete. The Minoan towns, led by the town of *Knossos* on the northern coast (see Map 8.1 inset), were evidently masters of a wide-ranging trade empire, including Greece, by about 1600 and had much to do with the civilizing of the Greeks.

The Minoans taught their pupils too well in some ways, however, and about 1400 the warlike Mycenaeans turned on their teachers and destroyed much of the island settlements, aided by either volcanic explosions or earthquakes. By about 1300, the high Minoan civilization was in ashes, and the island of Crete ceased to play an important role in Mediterranean affairs.

The Mycenaeans themselves seem to have engaged in extensive internal warfare among the competing towns. These civil wars weakened them sufficiently that they fell to a new wave of barbarians from the north, the *Dorians*. From about 1100 B.C.E. to about 800, the Greek peninsula declined, so much so that this period is called the *Dark Age.* Not only did arts and crafts decline, but even the ability to

write seems to have been largely lost during these centuries. Were the Dorians to blame, or did the Mycenaeans simply fight one another to mutual exhaustion, as many experts think? The answer is unclear. What is clear is that the achievements of the Mycenaeans were forgotten and the formerly urban civilization reverted to a rural, much less sophisticated one during the Dark Age.

Early Hellenic Civilization

❀

Starting about 800 B.C.E., the Greek mainland slowly recovered the civilization it had created during the Mycenaean age. It then went on to far greater heights during its *Classical Age* (500–325 B.C.E.).

During the Dark Age, the peculiarly Greek institution of the **polis** (plural, *poleis*) gradually developed. In Greek, *polis* means the community of adult free persons who make up a town or any inhabited place. In modern political vocabulary, the word is usually translated as "city-state." A *polis* could be almost any size. Classical Athens, the largest, had almost 300,000 inhabitants at its peak (about the size of our present-day Richmond, Virginia), while the smallest were scarcely more than villages. At one time the Greek mainland and inhabitable islands (all told, about the size of Maryland) were the home to more than 200 *poleis*. Each thought of itself as a political and cultural unit, independent of every other. Yet each *polis* also thought of itself as part of that distinct and superior family of peoples calling themselves "Greek."

Odysseus and the Cyclops

The Homeric hero Odysseus (Ulysses) served as one of the chief role models for the ancient Greeks. He embodied the qualities of craftiness and effective action that the Greeks considered most commendable in a man. The second of the ancient epics, the *Odyssey,* tells how the hero survived a perilous ten-year voyage home after the Trojan War. Living by his wits, he managed to extricate himself from one deadly situation after another until he was finally able to return to his family at Ithaka. In a violent world, Odysseus had to employ violent means when craft failed him.

One of Odysseus's most formidable challenges came when he and his shipboard companions found themselves at the mercy of the dreadful one-eyed giant, the Cyclops. The Cyclops invited the sailors to land on his island and then entertained himself by dismembering and devouring the Greeks two at a time. Then the sly Odysseus devised his counterblow:

I, holding in my hands an ivy bowl full of the dark wine stood close up to the Cyclops and spoke out:

"Here, Cyclops, have a drink of wine, now you have fed on human flesh, and see what kind of drink our ship carried. . . ."

Three times I brought it to him, and gave it him, three times he recklessly drained it, but when the wine had got into the brain of the Cyclops, then I spoke to him, and my words were full of beguilement.

[The Cyclops falls asleep.]

I shoved the sharp pointed beam underneath a bed of cinders, waiting for it to heat. . . . [W]hen the beam of olivewood, green as it was, was nearly at the point of catching fire and glowed, terribly incandescent, then I brought it close up from the fire and my friends about me stood fast. . . .

They seized the beam of olive, sharp at the end, and leaned on it into the eye [of the now sleeping giant], while I from above, leaning my weight on it twirled it . . . and the blood boiled around the hot point, so that the blast and scorch of the burning ball singed all his eyebrows and eyelids, and the fire made the roots of his eye crackle. . . .

He gave a giant, horrid cry and the rocks rattled from the sound. . . .

[The now blinded Cyclops attempts to capture the Greeks by feeling for them, but they escape his wrath by suspending themselves beneath sheep that walk past him to the waiting boat.] When I was as far from the land as a voice shouting carries, I called aloud to the Cyclops, taunting him:

"Cyclops, in the end it was no weak man's companions you were to eat by violence and force in your hollow cave, and your evil deeds were to catch up with you, and be too strong for you, ugly creature, who dared to eat your own guests in your own house, so that Zeus and the rest of the gods have punished you."

For Reflection

How does this story illustrate the qualities most admired by the Greeks in their warriors? Do you think the taunt flung at Cyclops by the escaping Greeks shows reverence for the gods who establish justice or celebrates their own human cleverness?

SOURCE: Excerpts from pages 146, 147, 149, from The Odyssey of Homer by Richard Lattimore. Copyright © 1965, 1967 by Richard Lattimore. Copyright renewed. Reprinted by permission of HarperCollins Publishers, Inc.

The *polis* was much more than a political and governmental unit. It established a frame of reference for the entire public life of its citizens and for private life as well. Yet not everyone who lived in a *polis* was a citizen. There were many resident aliens, who were excluded from citizenship, as were the numerous slaves. Women were also entirely excluded from political life. Basically, only free males of twenty years of age or more possessed full civil rights. That meant that as much as 80 percent of the population might be excluded from political life because of their gender, age, or social status.

Each *polis* had more or less the same economic design: a town of varying size, surrounded by farmland, pasture, and woods that supplied the town with food and other necessities. In the town lived artisans of all kinds, small traders and import-export merchants, intellectuals, philosophers, artists, and all the rest who make up a civilized society. Life was simpler in the countryside. Like all other peoples, the majority of Greeks were peasants, woodcutters, and ditch diggers of whom formal history knows very little except that they existed.

Mycenaean Gold Goblet. This fifteenth-century B.C.E. vessel was used for ritual drinking at the banquets which were an important part of Greek noble society. *(Erich Lessing/Art Resource)*

Athens and Sparta

❀

The two *poleis* that dominated Greek life and politics in the Classical Age were Athens and Sparta. They were poles apart in their conceptions of the "good life" for their citizens. Athens was the center of Greek artistic and scientific activity as well as the birthplace of political democracy. Sparta was a militaristic, authoritarian society that held the arts and intellectual life in contempt. Eventually, the two opposites came into conflict. What was the outcome? Interestingly, the artistic, philosophical, and democratic Athenian *polis* that provoked the war ultimately ruined Athens.

In general, four types of government were known to the Greeks:

1. A **monarchy** is rule by a single person, a king or equivalent (either sex) who has the final word in law by right. Most of the *poleis* were monarchies at one time or another, and many of them apparently began and ended as such.
2. An **aristocracy** is rule by those who are born to the leading families, whether or not they are particularly qualified in other ways. Aristocrats are born to the nobility, but not all nobles are born aristocrats.
3. An **oligarchy** is rule by a few, and almost always the few are the wealthiest members of society. Many *poleis* were ruled by wealthy landlords whose land was worked by tenant farmers.
4. A **democracy** is rule by the people as a whole, almost always by means of majority vote on disputed issues. Voting rights are limited to citizens, and in the Greek *poleis,* this meant freeborn adult males.

Additionally, the Greek word *tyranny* originally meant rule by a dictator who had illegally seized power. That person might be a good or bad ruler, a man or a woman.

Early Athens

Athens went through all these forms of government in the period after 750 B.C.E., when we know something definite about its history. The original monarchy was gradually forced aside by the aristocrats, who ruled the *polis* in the seventh and early sixth centuries. The aristocrats gave way in the 500s to oligarchs, some of whom were nobly born and some of whom were rich commoners. The most important oligarch was **Solon.** When the city faced a social and economic crisis, the other oligarchs gave him supreme power to institute reforms to quell the discontent. Solon responded by establishing a constitution that struck a balance between the desires of the wealthy few and the demands of the impoverished masses. Neither group was satisfied, however, and the contest soon resumed.

Eventually, an aristocratic tyrant named Pisistratus succeeded in making himself the sole ruler and made certain important concessions to the common people to gain their support for his plan to start a new monarchic dynasty with his sons as his successors. But the sons were not nearly as clever as their father and were swept from power by rebellion in 510 B.C.E.

The winner of the ensuing free-for-all was **Cleisthenes,** an aristocrat and the true founder of the Athenian democracy. Cleisthenes believed that the people should have the last word in their own government, both because it was just and because he believed it was the best way to keep civil peace.

Athenian Democracy

Cleisthenes (ruled 508–494 B.C.E.) in effect gave away his tyrannical powers to a series of political bodies that were unprecedentedly democratic in character: the *ekklesia, boule,* and *deme.* The *ekklesia* was the general "town meeting" of all free male Athenians, who had an equal voice in the great decisions of the *polis*. All could speak freely in an attempt to win over the others; all could be elected to any office; all could vote at the meetings of the *ekklesia* in the center plaza of Athens below the Acropolis hill.

The *boule* was a council of 500 citizens who were chosen by lot for one-year terms. It served as a day-to-day legislature and executive, making and implementing policy under the general supervision of the *ekklesia*. The *boule* supervised the civil and military affairs of the *polis* and carried out many of the functions of a modern city council. All male citizens could expect to serve at least one term on it.

The *deme* was the basic political subdivision of the *polis*. It was a territorial unit, something like a modern precinct or ward, but smaller in population. Each *deme* was entitled to select a certain number of *boule* members and was represented more or less equally in the officers of the *polis*.

To enforce the will of the majority, Cleisthenes introduced the idea of *ostracism,* or the "pushing out" of a citizen who would not conform to the will of the majority. An ostracized person lost all rights of citizenship for a certain length of time, normally for ten years. So attached were the Greeks to their *poleis* that many preferred to kill themselves rather than submit to ostracism.

Of all the Athenian political institutions, democracy has attracted the most attention from later history. Americans tend to think of political democracy as a natural and normal way to govern a state, but in actuality, until the twentieth century, democracy was a very abnormal system of government. It was talked about a good deal but was not put into practice outside the West and in only a limited way within it. A great many countries still give only lip service to the idea of democracy, and sometimes not even that. The idea that the ordinary man was capable of governing himself wisely and efficiently was quite daring when it was introduced. After democracy failed in Athens, as it did after about a century, it was so discredited that after the fourth century B.C.E., it was not resurrected until the eighteenth century C.E.

How many other *poleis* became democracies at some time? The answer is not clear, but under the strong pressure of democratic Athens, probably quite a few adopted democratic governments between 500 and 400 B.C.E. But even within Athens (as well as everywhere else), there was strong resistance to the democratic idea that did not cease until democracy had been abandoned and condemned as "the rule of the mob." Ultimately it was the democratic leadership in Athens that created the conditions that allowed the opponents of democracy to win out.

Spartan Militarism

By about 500 B.C.E. Sparta differed from Athens in almost every possible way, although the two were originally similar. The Spartan *polis*, located in the southern Peloponnesus about eighty miles from Athens, was a small city surrounded by pastoral villages. As the population grew in the 700s, the Spartans engaged in a bloody territorial war,

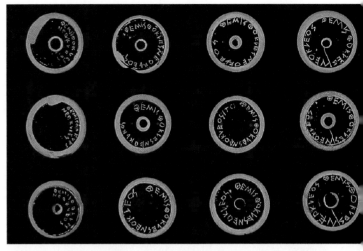

Ostraka Shards. Each year the citizenry of Athens was allowed to vote to ostracize any of their colleagues. The ballot was a ceramic token inscribed in advance with a name (top) or a piece of broken pottery (above). If someone received a predetermined number of votes, he was expelled from the *polis*. (*Courtesy of American School of Athens*)

the **Messenian Wars**, with their nearest Greek neighbor, Messenia, and finally won. The defeated Messenians were reduced to a state of near slavery (*helotry*) to the Spartans, who from this point on became culturally different from most other Greeks. The most striking example of their divergence was their voluntary abdication of individual freedoms. During the 600s, the Messenians rebelled again and again, and as a result the Spartans made themselves into a nation of soldiers and helpers of soldiers so that they could maintain their privileged position. Unlike other Greeks, the Spartans held the arts in contempt and rejected individualism as being unworthy of them. Public life was expressed in total obedience to the state, which was headed by a group of elected officers called *ephors* under the symbolic leadership of a dual monarchy. This strange combination seems to have worked very satisfactorily into the 300s.

Sparta's economic needs were largely met by the captive Messenians. They worked the fields and conducted the necessary crafts and commerce under close supervision. The Spartans themselves devoted their energies to the military arts. Male children entered a barracks at the age of seven and were allowed only sufficient free time thereafter

Plague in Athens

The historian Thucydides has told us of the great plague that struck Athens during the Peloponnesian War in unforgettable fashion. It is now thought to be a variety of bubonic plague, but its cause and nature are still unclear:

For a time, physicians ignorant of the nature of the disease attempted to use remedies. But it was in vain, and they themselves were among the first victims, since they came into contact with it most often. No human art was of any avail. . . . Many persons who seemed to be in perfect health, suddenly and without any apparent reason, were seized with violent pains in the head and with redness and inflammation of the eyes. The throat and tongue were quickly diffused with blood, while the breath became unnatural and foul. Then came sneezing and hoarseness. Soon the disorder, accompanied by a violent cough, reached the chest. Then taking a grip lower down it would move the stomach and cause all the vomits of bile to which physicians have ever given names. It was in truth very distressing. . . . Those affected could not bear to have on them even the finest linen garment. They insisted on being naked, and they longed to throw themselves into cold water. . . .

Appalling was the rapidity with which men caught the infection, dying like sheep if they sought to help others. Indeed, this was the principal cause of mortality. Afraid to visit one another, the sufferers died in solitude. . . .

Apparently, no one was ever attacked a second time, or not without a fatal result. All persons congratulated them, and they themselves, being overcome by joy, innocently believed that they could not die of any other sickness. . . .

The customs which hitherto had been observed at funerals were universally violated. Each buried his dead as best he could. . . . When one man had raised a funeral [cremation] pile, others would come and throw their dead upon it and set it on fire. . . .

The plague brought other and even worse forms of lawlessness to Athens. Men who until this time had concealed their indulgence in pleasure now grew bolder. Observing the sudden changes—how the wealthy died in a moment and those who had nothing immediately inherited their property—they began to reflect that rich and poor alike were transitory creatures. Hence they decided to enjoy themselves as much as they could and think only of pleasure. . . . Such was the grievous calamity that afflicted the Athenians.

SOURCE: Thucydides, The Peloponnesian War, Book II.

---

superior to their own and envied the single-minded purpose displayed by the Spartans in all their public affairs.

Despite its military nature, Sparta was a conservative and nonaggressive state. The Spartan army was so large and so feared that after about 600 Sparta rarely had to use it in war. Sparta actually became a peaceable *polis* and directed all of its attention to keeping the political status quo within its own borders and, so far as possible, outside them.

The Persian Wars

❊

Throughout the early fifth century B.C.E., the foreign policy interests of Athens and Sparta more or less coincided. Both were primarily concerned with maintaining their independence in the face of foreign threats. These threats originated from Persia, which had expanded rapidly in the 500s, as we described in Chapter 4.

The First Persian War ended with an Athenian victory. By 490 B.C.E., the Persian emperor Darius I was faced with spreading rebellion among his subjects, Greeks on the Turkish coast (Ionia). When he attempted to subdue them, Athens went to their aid. Determined to punish the Athenians for their boldness and wishing in any case to expand his domains still further, Darius sent an army across the Aegean Sea to the Greek mainland. Aided by brilliant generalship, the Athenians were waiting and defeated the Persian expedition at the battle of Marathon in 490.

The Second Persian War (480–478 B.C.E.) was fought on both land and sea and resulted in an even more decisive Greek victory. Ten years passed before Darius's successor, Xerxes, could find time to take up the challenge. This time not only Athens but several other Greek *polei* assisted the defensive effort. Spartan troops lived up to their fame at the battle of Thermopylae in 480 and again at the decisive defeat of the Persian force at Platea in 479. The Athenian navy completely routed the larger Persian fleet at Salamis and established Athens as the premier naval force in the eastern Mediterranean.

By the end of these **Persian Wars,** the Greeks had turned back the attempts of the Asian empire to establish a universal monarchy over the entire Mediterranean basin. It was a crucial turning point for Western civilization.

The Peloponnesian War

❊

The Greeks' victory in the Persian Wars did not lead to inter-Greek harmony, however. Athens used its new prestige and growing wealth to form a group of unwilling satellites (the Delian League) among the nearby *poleis*. The democrats, led by the great orator **Pericles,** were now in command and were responsible for bringing Athens into conflict with Corinth, one of Sparta's Peloponnesian

---

to ensure that another generation of Spartan warriors would be born of Spartan mothers.

What did the other Greeks think of Sparta? One might think they would detest such a regime, but on the contrary, most Greeks admired the Spartan way of life, especially its self-discipline, sacrifice, rigid obedience, and physical vigor. Even many Athenians thought the Spartan way was

Pericles

(C. 495–429 B.C.E.)

One of the great figures of democratic politics, the Greek general and statesman Pericles (c. 495–429 B.C.E.) is also a prime example of the dangers of the imperial vision. Desiring to bring his fellow Greeks into a mutually supportive and prosperous defensive alliance against Persia, by the end of his career he was viewed as the chief villain of an imperialist scheme to reduce all Greeks to Athenian subjects. Coercion in this manner always proved difficult to maintain among the poleis, which prided themselves on their traditions of self-government.

Pericles was born into an aristocratic Athenian family and received a traditional education in rhetoric under Anaxagoras, a leading philosopher. Committing himself to the emergent democratic party in the hurly-burly of *polis* politics, he rose quickly to prominence. At the age of thirty-two, he became chief magistrate (the equivalent of mayor). For the next thirty-three years, Pericles was the leading political figure in Athens, a feat that speaks volumes not only about his abilities but also about his sensitivity to popular opinion in a city where every free male saw himself as a comaker of policy.

In power, Pericles showed himself sincerely committed to the extension of democracy, though he was not above using a bit of demagoguery to retain his grip on popular affection. By appealing to the emotions of the populace he reformed the political and judicial systems to allow greater participation by the ordinary citizen. He instituted a system of paying jurors and established new courts to hear criminal cases, thus lessening the powers of the aristocratic judges. He raised the payment citizens received for attending the great debates in the *agora* in the town's center where questions of policy were decided. By paying for jury duty and attendance at the assemblies, Pericles ensured that ordinary men could take time off from work to participate. Pericles himself was a master orator, and his speeches were deemed masterpieces of effective rhetoric. Only one has come down to us: the famous Funeral Oration given near the end of his life to commemorate the Athenians who had fallen in the war. Here is a sample:

Our constitution is called democracy because power is in the hands not of a minority but of the whole people. . . . No one, so long as he has it in him to be of service to the state, is kept in political obscurity because of poverty. . . . [We] do not say that a man who takes no interest in politics is minding his own business; we say that he has no business here at all. . . .

Under Pericles, Athens became the center of the extraordinary intellectual and artistic life that is always associated with the term "Classical Age." But in relations with other Greek city-states, Pericles was not so fortunate. It was he who transformed the Delian League from a defensive alliance against the Persians into an instrument of Athenian empire building. It was he who spent the forced contributions of the other members of the league on the beautification of Athens and the expansion of its navy, which was then used to blackmail the other Greeks into submission to Athens's will. And, finally, it was Pericles who refused to take the warnings of the Spartans seriously when they sought to protect their allies against Athenian aggression.

The Peloponnesian War wrecked all hopes of peaceable unity. It ended in a decisive defeat for Athens and for the Periclean policy of expansion, even though its author had died in the plague that struck Athens many years earlier. The age of Pericles was a time of glorious achievements and stunning defeats. This epoch saw the summit of Greek classical achievement in the arts but also the beginning of the decline of Athens and all Greece into mere provinces of new and alien empires. The Greeks would remain in this condition until modern times.

Pericles. This idealized bust of Pericles—here a Roman copy—was created just after his death.
(© Art Resource)

For Reflection

Pericles tried to warn his fellow Athenians of the dangers of imperial rule, and when he saw that they wouldn't listen, he joined them to maintain his position as leader of the democracy. What does this tell us of popular government's inherent dangers?

 The Phalanx. How did Greek armies fight? This vase painting shows the Greeks' basic military formation, the phalanx. Sixteen columns of heavily armored men marching eight deep attacked the enemy with their spears of graduated length, forming a wall of iron. Having broken the enemy formations, the Greeks dispatched them with their short swords or maces. (© *Scala/Art Resource*)

allies. Corinth asked Sparta for help, and when the Spartans warned the Athenians to back down, Pericles responded with war. Athens was embarked on an imperial adventure, with the goal of extending its authority over not only Greece but the surrounding coasts as well. This coercion of its neighbors was led by a statesman who believed that his polis had earned the right to do so. It turned out to be a fatal error, though Pericles did not live to realize it. (See the Violence and Coercion box.)

With its very strong navy, Athens believed that it could hold off the land-based Spartans indefinitely while building up its alliances. These allied forces would then be able to challenge the Spartan army on Sparta's home territory.

For a long while, the **Peloponnesian War** (431–404 B.C.E.) was an intermittently fought deadlock. Neither side was able to deal the other an effective blow, and long truces allowed the combatants to regain their strength. But after Pericles died in 429, the Athenian democrats argued among themselves while the antidemocratic forces within the *polis* gained strength. An ambitious attempt to weaken Sparta by attacking its allies on Sicily was a disaster for the Athenians. Finally, in 404 the Spartans obtained effective naval aid (from Persia!) and defeated the Athenians at sea. After that, it was a simple matter for their large army to lay siege to Athens and starve it into surrender.

The Peloponnesian War ended with a technical victory for Sparta, but actually this long civil war between the leading Greek cities was a loss for all concerned. Sparta was not inclined or equipped to lead the squabbling Greeks into an effective central government. Defeated Athens was torn between the discredited democrats and the conservatives favored by Sparta.

The Final Act in Classical Greece

After the Peloponnesian War, the Greeks fought intermittently among themselves for supremacy for two generations. Whenever a strong contender emerged, such as the major *polis* of Thebes, the others would band together against it. Once they had succeeded in defeating their rival, they would begin to quarrel among themselves, and the fragile unity would break down once again. The Greek passion for independence and individuality had degenerated into endless quarrels and maneuvering for power with no clear vision of what that power should create.

To the north of Greece were a people—the Macedonians—whom the Greeks regarded as savage and barbarian, although they were ethnically related. Philip of Macedonia, the ruler of this northern kingdom, had transformed it from a primitive society into an effectively governed, aggressive state. One by one he began to absorb the northern Greek *poleis,* until by the 340s he had made himself the master of much of the mainland.

After much delay, the Athenians finally awoke to the danger and convinced Thebes to join with them against the menace from the north. In the battle of Chaeronea in 338 B.C.E., however, Philip's forces defeated the Athenians and Thebans. The former city-states became provinces in a rapidly forming Macedonian empire. Chaeronea was the effective end of the era of Greek independence and of the Classical Age's great triumphs of the spirit and the arts, which we will examine in Chapter 9. From the latter part of the fourth century B.C.E. onward, Greeks were to be almost always under the rule of foreigners.

SUMMARY

The Greeks were an Indo-European nomadic group who entered the Greek peninsula around 2000 B.C.E. and were gradually civilized, in part through the agency of the Minoans on Crete. By 1200 the Greeks had developed to the point that they were able to conquer their former overlords and mount an expedition against Troy. Following the com-

ing of the Dorian invaders, Greece entered a Dark Age of cultural regression. This period ended around 800, and the Greeks began their ascent to high civilization that culminated in the Classical Age from 500 to 325 B.C.E.

Throughout the Classical Age, the democratic *polis* of Athens was the political and cultural leader of the more than 200 city-states, which contended with each other for preeminence. Athens evolved through the various types of Greek government to achieve a limited but real democracy in the early fifth century. Through its commercial and maritime supremacy, it became the richest and most culturally significant of the *poleis.*

Victory over the Persians in the two Persian Wars led democratic and imperialist Athens to attempt dominion over many other city-states. Its main opponent was militaristic and conservative Sparta, and the two came to blows in the lengthy Peloponnesian War, which ended with a Spartan victory in 404. The real winner, however, proved to be the semibarbaric Macedonians, whose king Philip succeeded in imposing his rule over all Greece at the battle of Chaeronea.

TEST YOUR KNOWLEDGE

1. The Mycenaean period of Greek history
   a. preceded the Dark Age.
   b. followed the Dark Age.
   c. was the high point of Greek political culture.
   d. saw the Greeks ruling several other peoples.
2. In Homer's poem, Odysseus (Ulysses) conquered the Cyclops by
   a. killing him in a duel.
   b. blinding him.
   c. tricking him to jump into the sea.
   d. tieing him down while sleeping.
3. The *polis* was a
   a. warrior-king.
   b. community of citizens.
   c. commercial league of merchants.
   d. temple complex.
4. Athenian women were thought to be
   a. suitable only for marriage and then seclusion within the home.
   b. the collective sexual property of all free Greek males.
   c. unsuited for any public political role.
   d. the more talented of the two sexes.
5. Which of the following was *not* a form of classical Greek government?
   a. Monarchy
   b. Hierarchy
   c. Oligarchy
   d. Democracy
6. In early Greece, a tyranny was rule by
   a. the professional military.
   b. a small group.
   c. a person who had illegally seized power.
   d. a person who was evil and vicious.
7. The founder of the Athenian democracy was
   a. Solon.
   b. Cleisthenes.
   c. Pisistratus.
   d. Plato.
8. The critical factor in transforming Sparta from an ordinary *polis* to a special one was
   a. the war against the neighboring Messenians.
   b. the invasions by the Persians.
   c. the war against Athens.
   d. its commercial rivalry with Athens.
9. The Peloponnesian War is best described as
   a. a struggle between Athens and the rest of Greece.
   b. the start of an era of Spartan dictatorship in Greece.
   c. the discrediting of the Athenian democracy as leader of Greece.
   d. the establishment of Persian influence in Greece.

IDENTIFICATION TERMS

aristocracy	*Iliad*	Mycenaeans	Pericles
Cleisthenes	Messenian Wars	*Odyssey*	Persian Wars
democracy	Minoans	oligarchy	*polis*
Homer	monarchy	Peloponnesian War	Solon

INFOTRAC COLLEGE EDITION

Enter the search terms "Greece history" using Key Words.
Enter the search terms "Peloponnesian War" using Key Words.

Enter the search term "Sparta" using Key Words.

Chapter 9

Hellenic Culture

For we are lovers of the beautiful, yet simple in our tastes; we cultivate the mind without loss of manliness.

THE FUNERAL ORATION OF PERICLES

THE GREEK CONTRIBUTION to the creation of Western civilization equals that of the Jews and the Christians. In addition to the concept of democratic government, the Greek achievement was exemplified most strikingly in the fine arts and in the search for wisdom, which the Greeks called philosophy. In both areas, the Greeks developed models and modes of thought that are still valid and inspiring today. The overall achievement of the Greeks during their great age is summed up in the term *Hellenic culture,* and we turn now to look at its specific aspects.

Philosophy: The Love of Wisdom

The Greek word *philosophy* means "love of wisdom." The Greeks used it to mean the examination of the entire spectrum of human knowledge and not just the narrower fields of inquiry, such as the rules of logic, to which it is limited today. The ancient Greeks can legitimately be called the originators of philosophy. Of course, other peoples before them had attempted to work out the nature and meaning of human existence, but none pursued their studies so systematically with as much boldness and imagination as the Greeks starting in the sixth century B.C.E.

Greek philosophy can be divided into two periods: the Pre-Socratic period and the Classical Age. The first period extends from the earliest surviving philosophical writings around 600 B.C.E. to the life of Socrates (470–399 B.C.E.). The second period extends from Socrates through about 300 B.C.E.

Pre-Socratic Philosophy

The Pre-Socratic philosophers devoted themselves mainly to investigating the origin and nature of the physical world. They were less concerned with truth or how to distinguish between good and evil than philosophers would be in the Classical Age and later. The very first philosopher whose writings have survived (in very fragmentary form) is Thales of Miletus, who lived in about 600. During the 500s a group of thinkers attempted to analyze the physical nature of the world and make it intelligible. Some of their ideas have had a lively influence on philosophy ever since, and some of their general concepts, such as Democritus's vision of the atom as the fundamental building block of nature, have been proven correct in modern times.

The greatest contribution of the Pre-Socratics was the concept of law in the universe. Unlike any previous thinkers, these Greeks believed that what happened in the physical cosmos was the result of laws of causation and thus understandable and predictable on a purely natural level. They did not deny the gods or the powers of the gods, but they did not look to the gods as the normal and usual causes of phenomena. Instead, they conceived of what we now call *natural law*—a set of phenomena in nature that, when properly understood, explain why certain things occur.

Two of the greatest of the Pre-Socratics were Anaximander and Hippocrates. Anaximander was the father of the theory of natural evolution of species—long before Darwin ever dreamed of it. He also thought the physical universe had no limits. He conceived of it as boundless and constantly expanding, much as modern astronomers do. Hippocrates is best known as the founder of scientific medicine, but curing people was really only incidental to his intellectual interests. First and foremost, he wished to teach people to observe the life around them. He was the first great **empiricist** in the natural sciences, arriving at his general theories only after careful and prolonged observation of the world that could be weighed and measured.

The Classical Age: Socrates, Plato, and Aristotle

Socrates (470–399 B.C.E.) was the first philosopher to focus on the ethical and epistemological (truth-establishing) questions that have haunted the thoughtful since the dawn of creation. Like most of the Classical Age figures, he concentrated on humans rather than on physical nature. He was more interested in "How do I know?" than in "What is to be known?"

Systematic questioning is the essence of the *Socratic method,* which teachers have used ever since. Socrates believed that intellectual excellence could be acquired. He would systematically question his young Athenian disciples, allowing them to take nothing for granted. He challenged them to fearlessly examine and justify everything before taking it for truth.

Our knowledge of Socrates comes not from him directly but from the numerous works of his pupil and admirer, **Plato** (427–347 B.C.E.), who joined his master in Athens a few years before Socrates' suicide. Socrates, Plato tells us, was accused of poisoning the minds of the youth of Athens by his irreverent questions, which greatly irritated the conservative elders of the *polis.* Brought to trial, he was found guilty and given the choice of exile or suicide. A true Greek, Socrates chose suicide rather than being outcast from his chosen community.

Plato defended his teacher from the unjust accusation, but nevertheless was a very different thinker than his predecessor. Plato tried above all to solve the problem of how the mind can experience and recognize Truth (see the description of his **metaphor of the cave** in the Nature and Technology box). He concluded that it cannot, beyond a certain superficial point. He also ventured into an analysis of politics as it should be (in the *Republic*) and as it existed (in the *Laws*). Plato was an antidemocrat, and his arguments have often been used by conservatives and monarchists ever since. During his lifetime Greece was in constant

Socrates. Plato tells us that his master Socrates was considered extraordinarily ugly, but his mastery of logic and beauty of expression made all those who heard him forget everything else about him. *(© Art Resource)*

Plato's Metaphor of the Cave

The classical Greeks were the ancient West's great pioneers into the question of how the mind works. Seeing Man as a part of the natural world, they wished to know as much as possible about him. Of the great trinity of Greek classical philosophers, Plato distinguished himself by wrestling with the eternal question: how does the human brain penetrate appearances to attain Reality? Our impressions of the outer world originally are entirely dependent on sensory data, what can be touched, or smelled, or seen and heard. How, then, can we formulate ideas that go beyond the specific detail of particular objects that the senses perceive? Or is there any idea, beyond the specific object? Could there be an abstract Idea of, say, a chair? Or only of *this* chair, with rounded legs and a straight back made of walnut wood? Most particularly, are there Ideals of Truth, Beauty, and Goodness that lie behind the weak and unstable versions of those virtues that human experience can conceive of?

Plato thought that such abstractions existed and were far more perfect in their nature than any specific version of them that the senses might perceive. But he also believed that the large majority of people were unable to apprehend such Ideals in anything like their pure forms. Few men and women possessed the mental powers and the desire to allow them to penetrate beyond mere appearances into Truth and Reality.

Seeking to convey his meaning, Plato came to write the Metaphor of the Cave, which has remained one of the best-known philosophical anecdotes in history. Most people, he said, were like prisoners condemned to existence in a dark cave. They peered constantly through the dim light trying to make out what was happening around them:

> Imagine the condition of men living in a cavern underground, with an entrance open to the daylight and a long passage entering the cave. Here they have been since childhood, chained by the leg and by the neck, so that they cannot move and can see only what is directly in front of them. At some higher place in the cave, a fire burns, and between the prisoners and the fire is a track with a parapet built in front of it, like a screen at a puppet show which hides the performers while they show their puppets. . . .
> Now behind this parapet, imagine persons carrying along various artificial objects, including figures of men and of animals in wood or stone or other material which project above the parapet. . . . The

prisoners, then, would recognize as reality nothing but the shadows of those artificial objects.

Our sense impressions, unenlightened by wisdom, deliver us into a prison of ignorance, where men mistake blurred shadows for reality.

Plato further says that if a prisoner were released and forced to go out into the unaccustomed sunlight, he would, of course, be blinded by the light and utterly confused. But this would change as he became accustomed to his new condition; his inability to see this huge new world would gradually cease:

> He would need, then, to grow accustomed before he could see things in the upper world. At first, it would be easiest to make out shadows, and then the images of men and things reflected in water, and later on the things themselves. After that, it would be easier to watch the heavenly bodies and the skies by night, looking at the light of the moon and stars rather than the sun and the light of the sun in daytime . . .

Plato drew his conservative political and social conclusions from these beliefs about the nature of Reality and human ability to perceive it. He thought that relatively few people would ever be released from the cave of ignorance and shadow-play. Those who did attain to the upper world of Truth and slowly and with difficulty worked through the ever-higher, more accurate stages of Reality should be given the leadership positions. They deserved to be leaders not only because they merited power and prestige, but because they—and not the masses who remained in the cave—were able to make proper choices for the welfare of the whole society. Plato, who lived through the Peloponnesian War, remained a convinced antidemocrat all his life.

For Reflection

Does the metaphor employed by Plato explain to you his point about the difference between Reality and appearances? In what way does this story link with Plato's contempt for democratic politics?

SOURCE: F. M. Cornford translation, The Republic of Plato, 1941. By permission of Oxford University Press.

turmoil, which probably influenced his strongly conservative political views.

Aristotle was a pupil of Plato (who founded the first Academy in Athens), but he too was a very different man from his teacher. Aristotle is the nearest equivalent to a universal genius that Greece produced. His interests included practically every field of science yet known, as well as the formal analysis of thought and actions that we know as philosophy in modern times.

Most of what Aristotle wrote has survived and can fill a whole shelf of books. His best-known works are the *Politics, Physics,* and *Metaphysics,* but he was also a first-rate mathematician, an astronomer, the founder of botany, and a student of medicine. So great was his renown in the medieval world that both European Christians and Arab Muslims referred to him simply as the Master. The Christian scholars thought of him as a sort of pagan saint, who lacked only the light of the Revelation as outlined in their scripture. The learned Muslims thought of him as the greatest natural philosopher and man of science the world had yet produced.

Greek philosophy was marked at all times by the strong sense of self-confidence that the philosophers brought to it. The Greeks believed that humans were quite capable of understanding the cosmos and all that lived within it by use of reason and careful observation. In that sense, the Greeks were the world's first real scientists. They were not overawed by the gods but created the gods in their own image and never resorted to supernatural powers to explain what could be explained by law. The wisdom the Greeks sought in their "love of wisdom" was that which was reachable by the unaided human intellect.

Greek Religion

Not all Greeks were able to find the truth they needed in philosophy. Probably, the large majority of people were not exposed to or were quite unable to follow the reasonings of the philosophers. They turned instead to religion. Like most of the other peoples we have discussed, the Greeks were polytheistic. Their gods included Zeus, the father figure; Hera, the wife of Zeus; Poseidon, god of the seas; Athena, goddess of wisdom and also of war; Apollo, god of the sun; and Demeter, goddess of fertility.

Yet Greek religion was rather different from the religions we discussed earlier in at least two ways. First, from early times, the Greek gods were less threatening and less powerful than other peoples' gods. Second, the Greeks never created a priestly class or caste, but used their priests only as informal leaders of loosely organized services. After about 500 B.C.E., the priests and priestesses receded more and more into the background, while many of the gods themselves became mere symbolic figures. Even the great deities whom all Greeks recognized, such as Zeus, were not taken too seriously by the educated. They were certainly not feared in the way that the Sumerians feared their gods or the Jews feared Yahweh. The gods of the classical Greeks were creatures molded in their own image, with the foibles and strengths of men.

How did Greek religion compare with our modern ideas of religion? It differed in many ways. It was not revealed to humans by a supernatural authority. It did not stem from a Holy Book. It made no attempt to impose a system of moral conduct on the faithful. The Greeks never had a centralized ecclesiastical authority or a hierarchy of priests. Greek religion after the fifth century was largely a series of rituals, something like our American celebration of the Fourth of July. Participating in the rituals was an act of *polis* patriotism as much as worship and had little or nothing to do with ethics and morality of private life.

In addition to greater deities whom all Greeks recognized, each *polis* had its own local deities. For example,

Athena was the patron goddess of the city of Athens. The cults of these local gods were forms of civic celebrations in which everyone joined, even those who did not believe in supernatural forces or immortal life. The Greeks did not believe that the gods controlled human destiny in any detailed fashion. Behind and above the gods was an impersonal and unavoidable Fate, which could not be successfully defied by either humans or gods.

The ideal of the **golden mean,** the middle ground between all extremes of thought and action, was a Greek specialty. They distrusted radical measures and tried to find that which embraced the good without claiming to be the best. They believed that the person who claimed to have the perfect solution to a problem was being misled by **hubris,** a false overconfidence. The gods were "setting him up," as we might put it, and disaster was sure to follow. The wise person always kept this in mind and acted accordingly.

The Greeks' adherence to the golden mean should by no means be seen as a sign of humility. The Greeks were not humble by nature but were quite willing to take chances and to stretch their intellectual powers to the utmost. They believed passionately in the human potential. But they did not defy Fate or the gods without expecting to be punished. The great tragedies written by **Sophocles** are perhaps the most dramatically effective expression of this expectation, particularly his trilogy about the doomed **Oedipus Rex** and his vain struggle to avoid the fate that lay in wait for him (see the Religion and Morality box).

As with the Confucians, it was *this world* that engaged the Greeks' attention and provided their frame of reference for good and evil. Normally, the Greeks did not speculate about the afterlife and saw no reason to fear it. By the opening of the Classical Age, most of the educated class apparently no longer believed in immortality, if indeed they ever had. For them at least, philosophy increasingly took the place of religion. The acts of the gods came more and more to be viewed as *myths,* stories that served a useful moral purpose in educating the people to their duties and responsibilities as good citizens of the *polis* and as good Greeks.

The Arts and Literature

The classical Greeks gave at least three major art forms to Western civilization: (1) the drama, a Greek invention that originated in the 600s, presumably in Athens, as a sort of pageant depicting scenes from the myths about the gods; (2) lyric poetry, originating in the pre-Classical era and represented best by the surviving fragments from the work of **Sappho,** a woman who lived on the island of Lesbos in the 600s; and (3) "classical" architecture, most notably the temples scattered about the shores of the Mediterranean by Greek colonists, as well as the Acropolis in Athens. Besides these art forms, which they originated, the Greeks excelled

Oedipus Rex

Greek classical tragedy was built on the conviction that an inexorable Fate had the final word in the life of human beings. Fate might be evaded or even defied for a time, but sooner or later, its commands would be obeyed. In this view (which it seems all educated Greeks held), Man himself assured the punishments and retributions that descended on him by reason of his fatal moral shortcomings. One of the most compelling renditions of this principle is told in the three plays of the fifth century B.C.E. Athenian playwright Sophocles that tell the story of Oedipus, whose *hubris* (false overconfidence) in believing that he could defy the destiny prescribed for him led him into ultimate tragedy. Oedipus's story is a psychologically powerful tale illustrating how the Greeks understood the relation between the gods and man, or between religion and human morals.

Oedipus was the son of King Laius of the city-state of Thebes. Because the oracle of Apollo had prophesied that this boy would one day kill his father and disgrace his mother, King Laius ordered his newborn son to be taken out to a hillside and left to die of exposure. Unknown to the sorrowing parents, a shepherd happened by and rescued the child, taking him to the court of Polybius, the king of neighboring Corinth, who was childless. Brought up as the heir to Corinth's throne, Oedipus was told of the prophecy one day and fled the city, as he loved Polybius and thought him to be his natural father. Wandering through Greece, Oedipus happened to encounter Laius on the road. As a result of a foolish argument over precedence, the hot-tempered Oedipus killed his true father. Some days later, he came to Theban territory and challenged the monster Sphinx who had terrorized the city for many months, devouring anyone who could not solve her riddle: "What goes on four feet in the morning, two at noon, and three in the evening?" Oedipus replied: "Man, in life's three stages."

As a prize for freeing the city, Oedipus was married to the widowed queen Jocasta, his own mother, thus fulfilling the prophecy of years ago. With Jocasta he raised two sons and two daughters before the blind seer Tiresias reluctantly revealed the awful secret. In horror and shame, Jocasta committed suicide. Oedipus in despair blinded himself with the pins of her brooches and was driven from the palace by public outrage to a life of exile. Only his daughter Antigone accompanied him.

The story is told in the play *Oedipus Rex*, which was first produced in Athens about 429 B.C.E. at the height of the Peloponnesian War and the same year as the death of Pericles. The story of the unhappy ex-king is continued in Sophocles' *Oedipus at Colonus*. Colonus is a place near Athens where Antigone helps her father comprehend what has happened and prepare for death. Antigone herself is the protagonist of the final play in the Oedipus cycle, in which the heartbreaking tragedy of a man who thought he might triumph over Fate by his wisdom and willpower is brought to an end. The moral that Sophocles wished to teach is that intelligence and will alone are not sufficient for a good life. Compassion and consideration, qualities that Oedipus lacked until his last days but then learned from his daughter, are more important. Antigone, the faithful daughter who overcomes her revulsion and elects to share her father's misery, is the real hero of the piece.

For Reflection

Does Oedipus's end seem too harsh? Why do you think the Greeks, so much advanced in thought over earlier peoples regarding moral choices, retained their strong condemnation of incest?

---

in epic poetry (the *Iliad* and *Odyssey*); magnificent sculpture of the human form and face at a level of skill not previously approached; dance, which was a particular passion for both men and women; fine ceramic wares of every sort; and painting, mainly on ceramic vessels and plaques.

The particular strengths of Greek pictorial and architectural art were the harmony and symmetry of the parts with the whole; the ability to depict the ideal beauty of the human form, while still maintaining recognizable realism in their portrayals; and the combination of grace and strength balanced in vital tension. The models established during the Classical Age have remained supremely important to artists of the West ever since. Most plastic forms of European art are derived from these models, at least until the twentieth century.

Most Hellenic art was anonymous. The artist worked as a member of the *polis,* contributing what he did best to the benefit of his fellow citizens just as others contributed by paying taxes or working on the roads. We do know that the main Athenian temple, the **Parthenon,** was erected by order of Pericles during the Peloponnesian War as a shrine to Athena, the patron goddess of the city. Within the Parthenon stood an enormous marble statue of Athena by Phidias, the most famous of all the Athenian sculptors.

Greek literature took several distinct forms. Poetry of all types was very highly developed from the time of Homer (eighth century) onward. The outstanding names besides Sappho are Hesiod, Euripides, Aeschylus, Sophocles, Aristophanes, and Pindar. Most of these were dramatists as well as poets. The great trio of Euripides, Aeschylus, and Sophocles created the tragic form, while Aristophanes is the first noted comic playwright.

The drama was one of the Greeks' most popular arts, and the plays that have survived represent possibly a hundredth of what was written in the fifth and fourth centuries. Playwrights and actors were originally amateurs, but soon became professionals. Every citizen was expected to take part occasionally in the dramatic productions, which soon came to be a central element in the numerous civic celebrations that marked the life of the *polis.*

Dance and music were intensely cultivated, both by professionals and amateurs. Greek literature of all types refers abundantly to both, and they are depicted as well as in Greek painting and sculpture. The god Dionysius was particularly connected with orgiastic out-of-doors dancing, accompanied by reed and string instruments, which celebrated the god's triumphant return from the dead. His cult was also instrumental in creating the first drama.

The ancient Greeks prized craftsmanship. They evidently learned much of their skill in ceramics and metalwork from the Egyptians and the Minoans, but they improved on their models. Greek ceramics were in great demand throughout the Mediterranean world, and Greek

ships frequently set sail loaded with wine jugs, olive oil vessels, and other household utensils made from clay, as well as fine work. Much of the Athenian population evidently worked for the export trade, making objects of clay, metal, leather, and wood.

Social Relations in the Classical Age

The average Athenian was a laborer, small artisan, merchant, or slave. The freeman and his family generally lived very simply. He made a modest income working for others or for the *polis* (all *poleis* usually had an ongoing public works program) or as an independent shopkeeper. His wife

🌸 **Discobolus.** This Roman copy of a fifth-century Greek original by the great sculptor Myron is deservedly famous for its combination of manly strength and graceful control. The athlete prepares his body for an extreme effort at tossing the heavy stone disc; this was one of the feats at the Olympic Games. (*Scala/Art Resource, NY*)

🔅 **The Parthenon.** Atop the hill in central Athens called the Acropolis, the Parthenon was designed to be the center of Athenian spiritual life and its most sacred temple. Constructed in the fifth century, the now-empty interior featured a massive statue of the patroness of the city, the goddess of both war and wisdom, Athena. The style of its building has been emulated and imitated throughout the Western world. *(AKG London)*

normally worked inside the home, performing the usual domestic duties. She also generally had considerable control over the children's education.

Ancient Greece was very definitely a male-dominated, even misogynous, society. Outside the home in public life, the women were very much inferior to men, except for the trained and educated entertainer-prostitutes, called ***hetairai,*** who were uniquely respected and allowed to do as they pleased. Few men could afford their services, however, and the usual Greek household seems to have been much like the modern one: husband, wife, and children.

Wives could divorce their husbands and had control over any property they brought into the marriage. (For more information about gender relations and the position of women in ancient Greece, see Chapter 13.)

Homosexuality seems to have been relatively common, at least among the educated, and to have been looked on as a tolerable, though somewhat disreputable, practice. It was viewed as particularly disreputable for the older man, because he was sometimes led to ignore his family responsibilities by a younger lover. From the glancing attention paid to the subject in the surviving literature, it is impossible to know how common such relations were, what the nonhomosexual majority thought of them, or indeed much else regarding the sexual practices of the time (see Chapter 13).

The economic life of the *polis* always centered on freemen. It has frequently been remarked that Athenian democracy was built on and supported by a large population of slaves. This statement is true, but it may not be as damning as it seems at first. Certainly, slaves were numerous (perhaps 30 percent of the total population). Both

Greeks and foreigners could be enslaved, usually as the result of debt. Slaves were normally not abused by their masters, and many slaves were prized workers and craftsmen who worked for pay but were not free to go off at will to other employment. The kind of plantation agriculture that depended on coerced labor was not found in Greece because of the unpromising terrain. The individual slaveholder usually did not own more than one or two men or women and used them more as servants and assistants than as laborers. Slaves did not enjoy civil rights in politics, nor could they serve in the military. Only in the *polis*-owned silver mines near Athens were slaves abused as a matter of course, and these slaves were normally criminals, not debtors.

Most of the Greek population lived in the villages, where the vast majority of people were, of course, simple farmers and herders. In theory, they were free and politically equal to the townsmen. It is difficult to determine how much attention these rural people paid to the public affairs of the town, how often they participated in the *ekklesia* and *boule,* or whether they were elected to public office. Certainly, though, they could not participate to the same extent as the townsmen. Politics was basically an urban pursuit, as it would remain until a century or two ago everywhere.

The general level of education among the urban Greeks of the Classical Age was remarkably high and was not approximated again in the Western world until very much later. Neither the Romans nor the medieval Europeans came close. Yet like politics, education was also basically an urban phenomenon. Most of the country people must have been illiterate.

Sport

❀

The Greeks were the first people to look on the nurture of the physique (the word itself is Greek) as an important part of human life. They admired a healthy body and thought it was a duty to cultivate its possibilities. As part of this effort, they organized the first athletic events open to all male citizens. The most important was the great pan-Hellenic festival known to us as the *Olympic Games.*

According to the records, the Olympics were first held in 776 B.C.E. and then every four years thereafter in the small *polis* of Olympia on the west coast of the Peloponnesian peninsula. The games were originally more a religious festival than a sports event, but soon became both. The best Greek athletes competed for their hometowns in foot races, chariot drives, the discus throw, weightlifting, and several other contests. Prizes were limited to honors and a crown of laurel leaves.

The games lasted for about a week and were immensely popular. They served an important function as a sort of patriotic reunion for people from all over the Greek world. After the Macedonian conquest, the games declined and then ceased for twenty-three centuries until they were revived in the late nineteenth century.

The Greek Legacy

❀

The dimensions and lasting importance of the Greeks' bequest to Western civilization cannot be overemphasized. When the *poleis* fell to the Macedonians, this bequest was retained, though in diluted forms. When the Macedonian world was then itself overtaken by the all-conquering Romans a couple of hundred years later, the new masters adopted much of the Greek heritage with great enthusiasm and made it their own. In this way, the Greek style and the content of their art, philosophy, science, and government gradually infiltrated much of Europe. In the process, though, parts were lost permanently, and much of it was radically altered by other views and conditions of life.

The mixture of Greek with non-Greek produced a peculiar form of civilization that spread through much of the Mediterranean and the Near East after the Macedonian conquest and during the Roman era. We will look at this civilization in the following chapter and see that it was very different from Hellenic civilization in many ways, but it never severed all connections with the original Greek model.

❀ **The Conversation.** This glimpse of ordinary affairs is unusual for Greek art in that it portrays females who have no visible connection to the more often depicted male life. It is a product of the third century B.C.E. (*Courtesy of Trustees of the British Museum*)

✿ **Temple of Poseidon at Paestum.** This temple by the sea in Sicily is the best preserved of all the Greek classical structures outside Greece proper. Its simple and harmonious lines are reminiscent of the Parthenon, which was built slightly earlier. *(Nimatallah/Art Resource)*

SUMMARY

Hellenic culture represents a high point in the history of the Western world. The two centuries embraced by the Classical Age produced a series of remarkable achievements in the fine arts and in the systematic inquiry into humans and nature that we call philosophy. In some of these affairs, the Greeks built on foundations laid by others including the Egyptians and the Phoenicians. In other, such as drama and lyric poetry, they were pioneers. In philosophy, the mighty trio of Socrates, Plato, and Aristotle defined most of the questions that the Western world would ask of the universe ever since. In drama, Aeschylus, Sophocles, and Euripides played the same pathbreaking role. Poets such as Sappho and Pindar, sculptors such as Phidias, and the mostly unknown architects of the Classical Age created monuments that remain models of excellence.

In all of their efforts, the Greeks' intellectual fearlessness and respect for the powers of reason are strikingly apparent. They believed, as they said, that "Man is the measure" and that what could not be analyzed by the educated mind was probably best left alone as being unworthy of their efforts. Their legacies in intellectual and artistic activities rank with those of their predecessors, the Hebrews, in religion and with their successors, the Romans, in government and law.

TEST YOUR KNOWLEDGE

1. The pre-Socratic philosophers sought most of all to explain the
   a. human capacity to reason.
   b. motion of the stars.
   c. composition and laws of the natural world.
   d. reasons for the existence of good and evil.
2. The cave metaphor in Plato's writings refers to
   a. the need of humans to have a place of refuge from their enemies.
   b. the ability of humans to form a community.
   c. the difference between reality and falsely understood images.
   d. the importance of a stable physical environment.
3. Greek religion was
   a. controlled by a powerful priesthood.
   b. the same from one end of the country to the other.
   c. filled with gods created in man's image.
   d. dominated by fear of the afterlife.
4. Hubris meant to the Greeks
   a. an unjustified sense of proud self-confidence.
   b. an excellent command of physical strength.
   c. an apparent mastery of some talent that was deceptive in nature.
   d. an attempt to defy the gods' will.
5. Sophocles and Euripides are two of the greatest Greek
   a. dramatists.
   b. poets.
   c. sculptors.
   d. painters.
6. The Athenian women who enjoyed the most free lifestyles were the
   a. aristocrats.
   b. mothers.
   c. unmarried girls.
   d. entertainer-prostitutes.
7. Slavery in classical Greece was
   a. common and harsh.
   b. nonexistent.
   c. rare.
   d. common and usually mild.
8. The classical Olympics Games shared all but one of these features:
   a. They were open to all male citizens.
   b. They were aimed at establishing a "pecking order" of physical strength.
   c. They were held on a regular schedule.
   d. The visitors were rewarded with honors rather than prizes.
9. Which adjective is *least* appropriate for the classical Greeks?
   a. Intimidated
   b. Rational
   c. Proud
   d. Curious

IDENTIFICATION TERMS

Aristotle	hubris	*Oedipus Rex*	Sappho
empiricist	hetairai	Parthenon	Socrates
golden mean	Metaphor of the Cave	Plato	Sophocles

INFOTRAC COLLEGE EDITION

Enter the search terms "Greek mythology" using the Subject Guide. Enter the search terms "Greece history" using Key Words.

Enter the search terms "Plato or Aristotle or Socrates" using Key Words.

Chapter 10

Hellenistic Civilization

To one who asked him the proper time for taking meals, he said, "If a rich man, when you will; if a poor man, when you can."

DIOGENES THE CYNIC

336–323 B.C.E.   Alexander the Great's campaigns
c. 300–50 B.C.E. Hellenistic Age in eastern Mediterranean

THE NEW STYLE OF CIVILIZED life created by the Greeks of the Classical Age is called *Hellenism.* After the Greeks fell to the Macedonian barbarians in 338 B.C.E., Hellenism in a diluted form was spread into the East and Egypt by the conquerors and their Greek associates. This altered form of Hellenism is known as *Hellenistic* culture or civilization. It retained many of the values and attitudes of the classical Greek *polis,* but it also dropped many in favor of the very different values and attitudes of the Eastern kingdoms and empires.

Alexander and the Creation of a World Empire

After the battle at Chaeronea, which brought him mastery of Greece, King Philip of Macedonia was assassinated and his young son, Alexander, succeeded to the throne. In his thirteen-year reign (336–323 B.C.E.), Alexander conquered most of the world known to the Greeks and proved himself one of the most remarkable individuals in world history. His boldness and vigor became the stuff of legend among the Greeks who fought under him. Both are attested to by the story Plutarch tells in the anecdote in this chapter. Alexander's break with previous military tradition regarding the status of the conqueror is also memorable, as the Tradition and Innovation box describes.

At the time of his death, Philip had been organizing a large combined Macedonian-Greek army with the announced purpose of invading the huge Persian empire. After swiftly putting down a rebellion in Thebes, Alexander continued this plan, and crossed the Dardanelles in 334 with an army of about 55,000 men (very large for the times). In three great battles, the young general brought down the mightiest empire the world had yet seen, the empire of Darius III of Persia, who was slain by his own troops after the third and decisive loss at Gaugamela in present-day Iraq (see Map 10.1).

Conquering an unresisting Egypt, Alexander then invaded the Persian heartland and proceeded eastward into

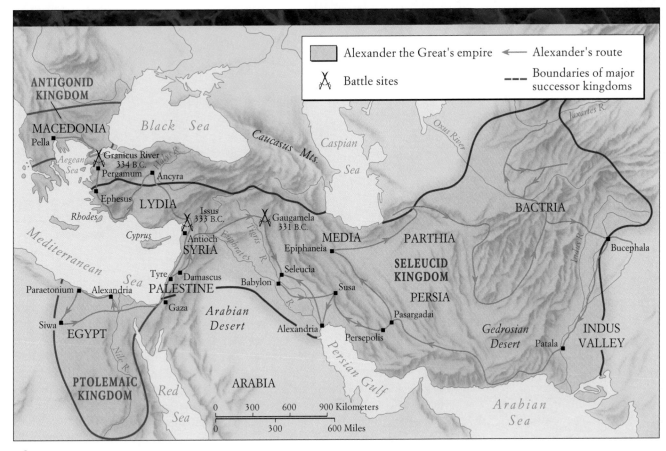

🏵 **MAP 10.1 Alexander's Empire and the Successor Kingdoms.** The huge area conquered by Alexander between 334 and 324 B.C.E. was too large to control from a single center. It quickly broke down after the conqueror's death into regional kingdoms under several of his generals.

the unknown borderlands of India. After spending five years marching up and down the Indus basin and the wild highlands to its north (present-day Pakistan and Afghanistan), his remaining troops finally mutinied and refused to go farther. In 324 Alexander led his exhausted men back to Persia. A year later, he died in Babylon at the age of thirty-three. The few years of his reign would have a lasting effect on much of the world's history.

A Mixed Culture

Alexander the Great (as he was soon called) founded the largest empire yet seen in history, but it began to disintegrate almost on the day of his death. He left an infant son by his last and favorite wife Roxana, but the child became a mere pawn as Alexander's generals struggled to succeed him as sole ruler. (The son was eventually put to death at age sixteen by one of the contestants.) Finally, the exhausted combatants tired of the civil war and split up the vast territories conquered by Alexander into a whole series of kingdoms,

each ruled by one of Alexander's generals. Collectively, these successor states in southwestern Asia and the eastern Mediterranean are called the **Hellenistic kingdoms.**

Everywhere Alexander led his armies, he founded new cities or towns, many of which bore his name. He then recruited Greeks from the homeland to come and establish themselves as a ruling group in the new cities. He encouraged them to follow his own example and intermarry with the locals. Tens of thousands of Greeks took up the invitation, leaving overcrowded, impoverished Greece to make their names and fortunes in the new countries now under Greco-Macedonian control. Inevitably, they brought with them the ways of thought and the values they had cherished in their native land. As the conquerors, the Greeks could and did impose their ideas on the Asiatics and Egyptians with whom they had contact or intermarried.

The result was Hellenistic culture, a mixed culture that blended Greek and Asiatic attitudes. A major example of this is the fate of the Greek civic community. The conquering Greeks first tried to reconstruct the *polis* mode of government and community in their new homes but quickly

Alexander the Great
(356–323 B.C.E.)

In the midst of his fantastic campaign of world conquest, Alexander the Great lost his dearest friend and companion, Hephaestion. The young man had died of a fever, and Alexander was overcome with grief. He cut off all his hair, refused to eat, and executed the physician who had failed to save his friend. Then he sacrificed an entire enemy tribe to honor Hephaestion's memory. In the funeral pyre that consumed the remains of the dead warrior, Alexander also burned many articles of gold and silver, works of art, jewels, fine garments, and oriental spices worth millions. This spectacular display was not a unique occurrence in Alexander's life. Hundreds of similar stories about this extraordinary individual have been told through the centuries.

✿ Alexander. This marble bust of the conqueror was copied from a Greek statue by Eufranor, completed in 338 B.C.E. It emphasizes Alexander's youthful beauty, but may have been close to the reality of his appearance. *(e.t. archive)*

Alexander the Great was perhaps the most renowned of all the world's military heroes. He possessed an active imagination and a lively curiosity, both of which were stimulated by the tutoring of Aristotle himself. The young king possessed a talent for practical matters and a wonderful gift for command. He achieved his most brilliant victories against great odds. But he also committed errors of judgment in his dealings with subordinates. The suspicion of disloyalty was enough to ensure speedy death, and from the accounts of several eyewitnesses, we know that innocent men died because of Alexander's unjustified rages.

During an era when no distinction was drawn between myth and history, he was hailed in his lifetime as a god. People accepted his extraordinary feats as the work of supernatural forces. How else could his achievements be explained?

Alexander the Great's intents and policies have been the subjects of much debate from his own day forward. Some think that he intended to create a world empire in which all peoples would be equal—a sort of world federation. This would have been a stunning break from previous military tradition, in which the conquerors occupy the highest rank for an indefinite period, and the conquered must abase themselves. There is no doubt that his efforts to reconcile Greeks with Asians offended many of his Greek and Macedonian followers. When Alexander himself adopted some Asian customs such as prostration, his men protested so vehemently that the new ceremonies had to be dropped.

They did not appreciate Alexander's vision or his habit of making the local prince and princess practically the equal of the conquering commanders. Alexander himself married several Asian women in an attempt to establish lasting ties. The last was Roxana, who bore him his only son.

Alexander's imprint on history is only partly the result of his military genius. He also spread Hellenic culture to much of the East through his conquering armies. He was the beginner of the Hellenistic civilization, the blend of Greek and Eastern ideas and institutions that dominated western Asia and the Mediterranean for the next several centuries. But his empire fell apart almost immediately, and his attempt to found an Alexandrine dynasty collapsed in intra-Greek wars for dominance. Eventually, the all-conquering Romans took over much of what had once been Alexander's empire in the eastern Mediterranean and Asia. They proudly saw themselves as continuers of the Alexandrine tradition of glorious conquest.

For Reflection

Why might the figure of Alexander have left so deep an impression on the non Greek peoples he briefly ruled? And why would the Greeks themselves be less enthusiastic about his career and his legacies in government?

Plutarch on Alexander: *Parallel Lives*

Alexander of Macedonia is known to us through several eyewitness accounts. The best biography of all, however, was written by a Greek citizen of the Roman empire who lived several hundred years after Alexander. Plutarch wrote his *Parallel Lives* to provide the youth of Rome with examples of both Greek and Roman heroes for them to emulate. It has been a favorite ever since and includes this famous anecdote:

> Philonicus the Thessalian brought the horse Bucephalus to Philip, offering to sell him for thirteen talents of silver; but when they went into the field to try him they found him so very vicious and unmanageable that he reared up when they endeavored to mount him and would not suffer even the voices of Philip's attendants. Upon which, Alexander, who stood nearby, said "What an excellent horse do they lose for want of boldness to manage him! . . . I could manage this horse better than the others do."

Philip, who was a harsh father, challenged his son to prove his boast:

> Alexander immediately ran to the horse and taking hold of his bridle turned him directly toward the sun, having, it seems, observed that he was disturbed by and afraid of the motion of his own shadow. . . . Then, stroking him gently when he found him begin to grow eager and fiery with one nimble step he securely mounted him, and when he was seated by little and little drew in the bridle and curbed him so, without either striking or spurring him. Presently, when he found him free from all rebelliousness and only impatient for the course, he let him go at full speed, inciting him now with a commanding voice and urging him also with his heel. Philip and his friends looked on at first in silence and anxiety, till seeing him turn at the end of the course and come back rejoicing and triumphing for what he had performed, they all burst out into acclamations of applause; and his father, shedding tears of joy, kissed Alexander as he came down from the horse and in his exultation said "O my son, look thee out for a kingdom equal to and worthy of thyself, for Macedonia is too little for thee!"

found that this was impossible. The Easterners had no experience of the *polis* form of government and did not understand it. They had never governed themselves but had always had an all-powerful king who ruled through his officials and generals. Soon the Greeks themselves adopted the monarchical form of government. Thus, instead of the small, tight-knit community of equal citizens that was typical of the *polis* of the Classical Age, a Hellenistic state was typically a large kingdom in which a bureaucracy governed at the king's command. The inhabitants, whether Greek or native, were no longer citizens, but subjects—a very different concept.

Although Alexander never conquered India's heartland, the Greek invasion also had lasting effects on the Indians. It introduced them to the Western world, and from this time onward, there were direct trade contacts between India and the eastern end of the Mediterranean. The invasion also disrupted the existing political balance in northern India and paved the way for the conquering Mauryan dynasty, including the great Ashoka (see Chapter 5). Finally, the Greek models introduced into Indian arts at this time were to have lasting impacts.

Hellenistic Cities

During the Hellenistic Age, a true urban civilization, in which the towns and cities were far more important than the more numerous rural dwellers, came into existence for the first time since the decline of the Mesopotamian cities. Large cities—such as Alexandria in Egypt, Antioch in Syria, and Susa in Persia—dominated the life of the Hellenistic kingdoms. Like modern cities, Hellenistic cities were centers of commerce and learning with great museums, libraries, and amusement halls. A few of them had more than 500,000 inhabitants, drawn from a vast variety of ethnic backgrounds.

What was life in these cities like, and who populated them? Most of the people in these cities were free, but there were also many slaves. Slavery became more common in the Hellenistic era than it had been in the Classical Age—another example of the Eastern tradition dominating the Greek. Even the free majority felt little sense of community, largely because they came from so many different social and ethnic groups. On the contrary, the feeling of alienation, of being apart from others in the psychic sense, was very common. Many city people were peasants who had fled from the civil wars after Alexander's death. Many others were former prisoners of war who had been uprooted from their homes and forced into the cities. They had little in common with their neighbors except that they were all the subjects of the powerful rulers and their bureaucrats.

Originally, the Greeks were the governing class of the cities, but gradually they were absorbed by the larger group that surrounded them. The Greek language remained the tongue of the cultured, but in most other respects, the Eastern way of life and thought won out. In the arts, a hybrid of classical Greek and traditional Eastern forms and content came into existence. Hellenic forms became a thin veneer, covering the underlying Syrian, Egyptian, or Persian traditions. Some of the new forms were truly excellent, but later ages have deemed most of them a deterioration from what the Greeks had achieved during the Hellenic period.

✿ **Temple of Apollo at Didyma.** These massive steps led up to an even more massive hall, dedicated to Apollo by the grateful citizenry of Seleucid Ionia. Begun in the late fourth century B.C.E., the temple was not completed until the early Christian era. Its ruins stand in modern Turkey. *(Erich Lessing/Art Resource)*

Greeks and Easterners in the Hellenistic Kingdoms

✿

The civil wars after Alexander's death resulted in the formation of three major successor kingdoms, each ruled by a former Greek general who had fought his way into that position (see Map 10.1):

1. **The Ptolemaic kingdom of Egypt.** A general named Ptolemy succeeded in capturing Egypt, the richest of all the provinces of Alexander's empire. There he ruled as a divine king, just as the pharaohs once had. By the 100s B.C.E., the many immigrant Greeks and the Egyptian upper class had intermixed sufficiently to make Egypt a hybrid state. Many Greeks adopted the Egyptian way of life, which they found very pleasant. Meanwhile, ordinary Egyptians remained exploited peasants or slaves.

2. **The Seleucid kingdom of Persia.** The Seleucid kingdom, which was the successor to most of the once mighty empire of Darius III, reached from India's borders to the shores of the Mediterranean. It was founded by a former general named Seleucus, and, like Ptolemaic Egypt, it lasted until the Roman assault in the first century B.C.E. Many tens of thousands of Greek immigrants came here as officials, soldiers, or craftsmen, and the contact between the locals and Greeks was very extensive in the western parts of the kingdom, especially Syria and Turkey. The kingdom was too large to govern, however, and began to lose pieces to rebels and petty kings on its borders as early as the 200s. By the time the Ro-

mans were assaulting the western areas, most of the east was already lost.

3. **The Antigonid kingdom.** This kingdom was also founded by a general, who claimed the old Macedonian homeland and ruled part of what had been Greece as well. The rest of Greece was divided among several leagues of city-states, which vied with each other for political and economic supremacy, until both they and the Macedonians fell to the Romans in the middle 100s B.C.E.

Religion

✿

In form and content, the Hellenistic religions that evolved after the conquests of Alexander were different from both the Greek religion of the Classical Age and the earlier religions of China and India. In form, the new religions were frequently modeled on Greek beliefs: worship was often conducted outdoors, and the priests played a relatively minor role and were accorded little prestige. In content, however, Eastern contributions far outweighed those of the Greeks. Despite the prestige of the conquering Greeks, the worship of the traditional Greek gods such as Zeus and Athena soon died out completely in the East.

Why did this happen? Recall that participation in the cults of the traditional Greek gods did not imply a specific belief, or an ethical viewpoint, or even an emotional attachment to the gods. The rites were essentially civic ceremonies rather than a moral guide to living well or a promise of salvation. As such, they held no appeal to non-Greeks, who neither understood the patriotic meaning of the ceremonies nor found any moral or emotional "message."

As time passed, instead of the natives adopting the Greek religion, the Greek immigrants turned more and more to the native religions, which were allowed full freedom under Greek rule. These religions *did* offer some promise of eternal life or earthly prosperity. They provided some concrete emotional support, and they also responded to human longing for security and a guide to right and wrong.

In the second century B.C.E., these Eastern religions became immensely popular among many of the Eastern Greeks, especially the lower classes. Three of the most important were the cults of Isis, goddess of the Nile and renewal; Mithra, god of eternal life; and Serapis, the Egyptian god of the underworld and the judge of souls. All three shared certain characteristics, which allow them to be called **mystery religions.** They demanded faith rather than reason. To believers, who followed the instructions of the priests, they promised eternal life. Life would overcome death, and the afterworld would be an infinitely more pleasant place than this one. These deities were universal gods, who had final jurisdiction over all people everywhere whether they recognized the god or not. The stage was thus being set for the triumph of the greatest of the mystery religions, Christianity.

 The Cult of Isis. One of the most popular mystery religions in the Hellenistic world, the cult of Isis, is shown in this fresco from Herculaneum in Italy. It depicts a religious ceremony in front of the temple of Isis. At the top, a priest holds a golden vessel, while below him another priest leads the worshippers with a staff. A third priest fans the flames at the altar.
(© Gemeinnutzig Stiftung, Leonard von Matt/Photo Researchers)

Philosophy: Three Hellenistic Varieties

The mystery religions were especially appealing to the less educated and the poor. These people were the most likely to suffer the alienation and desperation that were often part of life in the cold, impersonal Hellenistic towns. For them, the promise of a better life in the next world became the true reason for living at all.

The better-educated upper class was more inclined to look askance at such "pie in the sky." They turned, instead, to philosophies that seemed more realistic and did not demand a difficult leap of faith. In addition, they sought a concept of human community that could satisfy them as the *polis* ideal faded.

Three philosophies in particular attracted the Hellenistic Greeks. The first to appear was **Cynicism,** which emerged as an organized school in the middle 300s but became more popular later. Its major figure was the famous **Diogenes,** who reportedly toured the streets of Athens with a lantern in full daylight, searching for an honest man. Cynicism has come to mean something very different from what it signified originally. In his teachings, Diogenes called for a return to absolute simplicity and a rejection of artificial divisions, whether political or economic. Cynicism was the opposite of what is now called *materialism.* Relatively

few people could adapt themselves to the rigid poverty and absence of egotism that the Cynics demanded, but the philosophy nevertheless had a great impact on Hellenistic civilized life, in much the same way that St. Francis would later influence thirteenth-century Christianity.

The second philosophy was **Epicureanism,** named after its founder, **Epicurus,** who taught at his school in Athens during the early third century B.C.E. (After the Macedonian conquest, Athens continued to be the undisputed intellectual center of the Greek world for many years despite its loss of political importance.) Like *cynicism,* the word *epicurean* has undergone a major transformation of meaning. Epicurus taught that the principal good of life was pleasure, which he defined as the avoidance of pain. He was not talking about physical sensation so much as mental or spiritual pleasure and pain. He believed that inner peace was to be obtained only by consciously rejecting the values and prejudices of others and turning inward to discover what is important to you. Epicureanism resembles Buddhism in certain respects, and some feel that this is no coincidence. Epicurus may have had knowledge of the Indian philosophy, which was spreading rapidly in the East during this period. Epicureanism led to political indifference and even withdrawal, as it said that political life led to delusive excitement and false passion: better to ignore the public affairs of the world, and focus on finding your own serenity.

The third philosophy, **Stoicism,** captured the largest following among the Hellenistic population. It was the

Hellenistic Scientists

Egyptian Alexandria under the dynasty of the Ptolemaic kings was the largest city of the Hellenistic world. Founded and named by the world conqueror in the late fourth century B.C.E., it grew steadily, fattened by the increasing trade of the Nile valley with the remainder of the Greco-Roman world. At some point in the third century B.C.E., a museum and library were established there, which quickly became the intellectual and scientific center of the Mediterranean region. A recent British historian of science tells us about the type of research carried on, the nature of the museum, and three of the Hellenistic researchers. Quoting the Roman author Cicero, he says:

"Strato the physicist was of the opinion that all divine power resides in nature, which is a power without shape or capacity to feel, containing within itself all the causes of coming-to-be, of growth, and of decay." Final causes, such as Aristotle posited, are out; nor is there any place in Strato's world for divine providence. Further . . . it seems clear that Strato endeavored to solve his problems by means of experimentation [a much debated question in the history of science].

[T]he second of our Hellenistic scientists, Philo of Byzantium, worked in Alexandria around 200 B.C. Philo's work was concerned with artillery, comprising mechanical arrow-firing catapults and stone-throwing ballistas. . . . The most important fact revealed by recent research is the indication of *repeated experiment* as a means of establishing a method and a formula to be incorporated in the specification for the construction of different types of missile launchers.

While Philo's name is associated with a variety of writings on scientific subjects, that of Ktesibios is linked with an equally wide range of inventions, most of which are based on the application of the principles of hydraulics. . . . His inventions included, in addition to the twin-cylinder water pump, a water-clock, a pipe organ powered by an ingenious combination of water and compressed air, and an improved catapult which operated by bronze springs instead of twisted animal sinews. He is also credited with a considerable number of inventions designed for entertainment, the so-called automata. . . .

It is an easy step from the most famous inventor of his day [that is, Philo] to the Museum with which he was associated. The House of the Muses [the Museum] was evidently a research organization, supported, like the Library, by a royal endowment. Traditional accounts . . . assume that the Library, which rapidly acquired a worldwide reputation was separate from the Museum; but it is more likely that both were parts of what might be called a research institute, which provided facilities for workers in a wide variety of disciplines belonging to what we would now call the humanities and the sciences.

Contrary to the commonly held opinion that under Rome the Museum and the Library suffered a rapid decline into total obscurity, we have evidence that both were still operating many centuries later, even if not as vigorously as in their heyday. . . . Medicine was in the most flourishing condition of all the sciences there, enjoying such a high reputation that the only qualification an intending practitioner needed to produce was a statement that he had received his training at Alexandria. The most important scientific advances seem to have been made in pure mathematics, mechanics, physics, geography, and medicine.

For Reflection

Why do you think it was important whether scientists of this age employed experiments to determine factual knowledge? What might be a modern equivalent to the Alexandria institute?

SOURCE: K. D. White, in Hellenistic History and Culture, ed. P. Green (Berkeley: University of California Press, 1991), p. 216f.

---

product of a freed slave, a Phoenician named **Zeno** who had been brought to Athens around 300 B.C.E. The name *Stoicism* came about because Zeno taught at the *stoa*, a certain open place in the city's center. Zeno emphasized the brotherhood of all men and disdained the social conventions that falsely separated them. He taught that a good man was obliged to participate in public life to help the less fortunate as best he could. Whether he was successful or not was not so important as the fact that he had tried. The Stoics (again, the word has undergone a huge change in meaning from ancient times to the present) thought that it was not whether you won or lost but how you played the game that mattered. Virtue was, and had to be, its own reward.

The Stoics made popular the concept of an overarching natural law that governed all human affairs. One law for all, which was implanted in the brain and heart of all humans by the fact of their humanity, was the Stoics' guiding principle. This concept was to gain a following among the Romans after they came into the Eastern Hellenistic world. Stoicism eventually became the chief philosophy, by far, of the Roman ruling class. It was a philosophy of noble acts, guided by lofty ideals of what a human being could and should be. It strongly emphasized the necessity of service to one's fellows and the recognition that all are essentially equal under the skin.

Science and the Arts

❋

The common belief that Greek science had its heyday during the Classical Age is erroneous. Science did not really come into its own until the Hellenistic period. The most im-

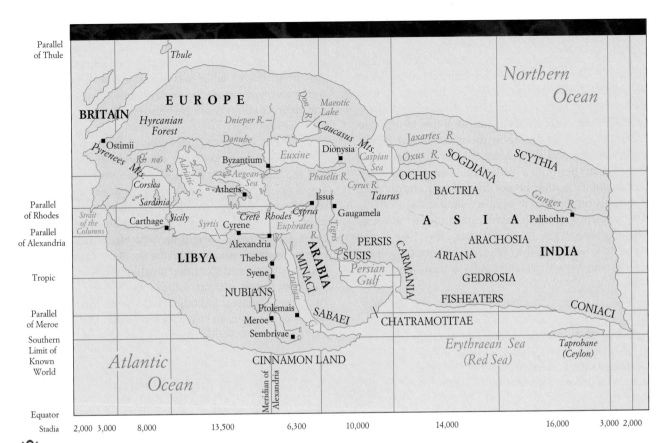

MAP 10.2 **The World According to Eratosthenes.** This is the first world map that bears substantial relation to the globe as modern people know it. It was drawn by the Greek geographer Eratosthenes in the third century B.C.E., relying on reports by mariners and other travelers and on his own observations.

portant areas of inquiry were biology, astronomy, geography, physics, and math. The medical arts were particularly prominent during this period. The third and second centuries B.C.E. produced a number of major contributors to medical knowledge and theory. The biggest single center of science was in the great city of Alexandria, Egypt, where the very rich Ptolemaic kings established and supported many research centers. The contemporary world's largest library and museum there were destroyed much later by fire and earthquake (see the Nature and Technology box).

Why did science flourish in the Hellenistic period? On one hand, the Greek habit of rational and logical thought was especially useful in the sciences. Aristotle, who had tutored young Alexander, insisted on the necessity of careful observation of phenomena before attempting to explain their causes. His successors at the *Lyceum,* the famous school he founded in Athens, proceeded along those lines and obtained worthwhile results in several fields.

On the other hand, one of the chief stimuli to scientific work was the new exposure of the Greeks to the Babylonian mathematicians and astronomers/astrologers, thanks to the conquests of Alexander. Now in the Hellenistic Age, the Greek world was brought into contact with the knowl-

edge of the Middle East. Scientists profited from the work done by Mesopotamian, and especially Babylonian, scholars during the previous three centuries.

The work in astronomy done at this time would stand without serious challenge until the sixteenth century C.E. Among the outstanding astronomers were Aristarchus of Samos (310–230 B.C.E.) and Hipparchus of Nicaea (260–190 B.C.E.). Aristarchus proposed a **heliocentric** model of the universe in which the Earth revolved around the sun. It was attacked by Hipparchus and others, however, and in the second century C.E., a later astronomer named Ptolemy picked up the theory of a **geocentric** universe (that is, centered on the Earth). The geocentric model became the standard wisdom of astronomy for the next 1,500 years, until Copernicus questioned it. The most important figures in geography were the Greek **Eratosthenes** (c. 276–c. 194 B.C.E.) and Strabo (c. 64 B.C.E.–c. 23 C.E.). Eratosthenes calculated the circumference of the Earth very accurately. His data provided the first reliable maps of the globe (see Map 10.2).

In physics, the outstanding researcher was **Archimedes** (c. 287–212 B.C.E.), who was equally important in mathematics. In the third century B.C.E., Euclid, an

Egyptian Greek, produced the most influential math treatise ever written, the *Elements of Geometry.*

The Greeks in general were not interested in the practical aspects of science, which we now call technology. Most of Hellenistic science was not driven by the desire to ease men's burdens or to save labor. Many discoveries and experimental results were allowed to be forgotten because no one saw any need to transform these theoretical breakthroughs into practical applications for daily life. The physical experiments performed by the brilliant Archimedes are a good example: neither he nor his fellow scientists ever tried to apply his findings to ordinary work tasks.

Why were the Greeks so uninterested in practical applications of science? The reasons are not clear. One factor seems to have been that the Greeks' reverence for the intellect was coupled with a contempt for manual labor. They seemed to think that hard labor was fitting only for beasts, not for intelligent human beings. Then, too, labor-saving devices were not much in demand in the Hellenistic period. An abundance of labor was available for all tasks: slaves were much more numerous now than they had been earlier, and their situation could be only marginally affected, if at all, by technology.

By about 200 B.C.E., Hellenistic science had begun a slow decline. Astronomy was being replaced by astrology, and the initial advances in physics and math were not followed up. Only in medicine were some significant advances made, notably by the so-called Empiricists, doctors who were convinced that the answer to the ills of the body was to be found in the careful analysis of diseases and their physical causes. Building on the work of the great Hippocrates, these men identified much of the body's anatomy, including the circulation of the blood and the functions of the nerves, the liver, and other vital organs. Medical knowledge would not reach so high a level again in the West until the end of the Middle Ages.

Art and Literature

The fine arts in the Hellenistic world were generally modeled on the art of the Hellenic Age but tended to be more realistic. They also lacked some of the creative vigor and imagination that had so marked Greek art in the earlier period, and they sometimes tended toward a love of display for its own sake—a sort of boastfulness and pretentiousness. In the Hellenistic Age many individuals became immensely rich through trade or manufacturing, and they wanted to show off their new wealth. The new rich indulged their desires by adorning their homes with works of art or sponsoring a piece of sculpture for the community.

A chief hallmark of Hellenistic art was the new emphasis on the individual artist as creator. In this epoch, for the first time, the name of the artist is almost always found on a work of art. We even hear of architects who took money for their plans, rather than being satisfied by the honor given by his associates or the community. This emphasis on the individual is another aspect of the decreased sense of community and the growing alienation that we noted earlier in this chapter.

Much more literature has survived from the Hellenistic Age than from the Classical Age. Unfortunately, the Hellenistic Age produced many second-rate but few first-rate talents. Both artistic inspiration and execution seem to have declined. There were many imitators, but few original thinkers. The main centers of literature were in Alexandria, Rhodes, Pergamum, and other eastern areas rather than in Athens or Greece itself.

The same was generally true of the plastic arts. Great sculpture and buildings were more likely to be created in the East than in Greece, in large part because the richest cities of the Hellenistic Age were found there, along with

The Old Market Woman. Hellenistic artists were often intent on producing both a realistic portrayal and on demonstrating their technical mastery. Both intentions are fully achieved in this life-sized statue of an old woman. (© *Art Resource*)

the wealthiest inhabitants. In imagination and execution, much Hellenistic sculpture and architecture was very impressive. Indeed, it was much superior to the literary works. The absolute mastery of stone that was already established by the artists of the Classical Age continued and even developed further. Such great works as the *Laocoön, The Dying Gaul,* and *The Old Market Woman* (see the photo) show an ability to "make the stone speak" that has been the envy of other ages. But even in sculpture, there was a great deal of copying of earlier forms and an abundance of second-class work.

The Hellenistic Economy

As we have seen, Hellenistic civilization was much more urban than Greece had been during the Classical Age. The Hellenistic economy was characterized by large-scale, long-distance enterprises. Big cities such as Pergamum, Alexandria, and Antioch required large-scale planning to ensure that they would be supplied with food and consumer necessities of all types. Manufacturing and commerce were common and also were sometimes on an impressively large scale. Trade was carried on in all directions, even with China and Spain. The uppermost classes became very wealthy indeed.

The goods traded included ceramic and metal housewares, olive oil, wine, and, perhaps most commonly, grain. They were carried by land and sea to all corners of the Near and Middle East and most of coastal Europe, as well as to India. A mercantile contract, written in what is now Somalia in Africa, has survived. It was signed by a Greek from Greece, a Carthaginian from North Africa, and a black from the African interior. In this era, the Greeks really came to the fore as tireless and daring mariners of the world's seas.

Outside the cities and towns, the economy depended as ever on farming and related activities such as fruit growing, timber, beekeeping, and fishing. The plantation system of agriculture, based on large gangs of unfree labor, was introduced wherever it could flourish. Consequently, the Hellenistic economy depended more heavily on slavery than had been the case in previous civilizations. For the first time, large groups of people were pulled into lifelong slave status, which was hereditary and passed on to their children. In many places, small farmers were forced into debt, and the family farms that had been typical of earlier Greece, for example, gave way to some form of bondage to a large landlord.

In Ptolemaic Egypt, the old system went on without change: small sharecroppers tilled the land for the great landlords, except now the lords were mostly Greeks, and the exploitation was more severe. Egypt was the wealthiest of all the successor kingdoms, and the Ptolemaic dynasty, which ruled Egypt for three centuries until it fell to the Romans, was the envy of the other Hellenistic kings. Cleopatra, who died in 30 B.C.E., was the last of these Greek-Egyptian monarchs.

In the next two chapters, we will see how the unimportant and provincial city of Rome became the inheritor of the Hellenistic East. We will also look at the way the Romans altered Hellenistic culture until it became a specifically Roman civilization.

Nike, Goddess of Victory. This marvelous statue, now in the Louvre in Paris, portrays Nike, the Hellenistic goddess of victory. One can almost see the wind blowing through the stone folds. Unfortunately, the head was lost in ancient times. *(© Art Resource)*

SUMMARY

The Hellenistic Age is a convenient though deceptively simple label for a widely varying mix of peoples and ideas. For about three centuries, from the death of Alexander to the Romans' coming into the East, the world affected by Greek ideas increased dramatically in physical extent, encompassing Mediterranean and western Asian cultures. This period also saw the first large-scale contacts between the civilization of the Mediterranean basin and those of East Asia, mainly India but also China.

Pagan and Christian Rome was very much a part of the Hellenistic culture, and through it, the civilization of the Mediterranean was passed on to Europe in later years. The philosophies and religious thought of the Hellenistic world eventually became the basic lenses through which the entire European continent (and its North American offspring) would perceive the world of the spirit. Our cultural debts to these Greco-Eastern forebears that include both science and Christianity are beyond easy measure.

TEST YOUR KNOWLEDGE

1. *Hellenistic* refers to a
   a. blend of Greek and eastern ideas and forms.
   b. blend of Greek and Roman ideas and forms.
   c. purely Greek style later transferred to Rome.
   d. mixed style limited in extent to Europe.
2. According to Plutarch, Alexander most impressed his father by
   a. slaying the giant Hercules.
   b. riding a wild horse.
   c. leading the Macedonian army.
   d. constructing a bridge over the Hellespont.
3. The Greek immigrants to Hellenistic Asia were usually
   a. resented and resisted by the local authorities.
   b. given favored official and financial positions.
   c. poverty-stricken workers and craftsmen.
   d. eager to mix with the native populations.
4. In the Hellenistic period, the sociopolitical unit replacing the classical *polis* was the
   a. village.
   b. city.
   c. province.
   d. family.
5. Which of these adjectives is the *least* appropriate description of Hellenistic society and customs discussed in this chapter?
   a. Alienated
   b. Stratified
   c. Urban
   d. Communal

6. In public affairs, the Epicureans insisted
   a. on active participation by their followers.
   b. that all politics and governments were equally corrupt.
   c. that democracy was superior to all other types of government.
   d. on indifference to government.
7. Stoicism believed in
   a. the brotherhood of all men.
   b. the natural superiority of Greeks over all others.
   c. the quest for personal pleasure being the only meaning in life.
   d. the impossibility of finding an honest man or woman.
8. Which of the following does *not* describe the Egypt of the Ptolemies?
   a. A backwater in the sciences
   b. A very wealthy government
   c. One of the most important of the Hellenistic kingdoms
   d. A highly centralized political and economic authority
9. The scientific interests of the Hellenistic period
   a. were limited to math.
   b. led to an industrial revolution.
   c. were limited to agriculture.
   d. had little connection with technology.

IDENTIFICATION TERMS

Alexander the Great

Antigonid kingdom

Archimedes

Cynicism

Diogenes

Epicureanism

Epicurus

Eratosthenes

geocentric

heliocentric

Hellenistic kingdom

mystery religions

Ptolemaic kingdom of Egypt

Seleucid kingdom of Persia

Stoicism

Zeno

INFOTRAC COLLEGE EDITION

Enter the search terms "Greece history" using Key Words.

Enter the search terms "Alexander the Great" using Key Words.

Enter the search term "Archimedes" using Key Words.

Chapter 11

The Roman Republic

*I*t is the nature of a Roman
to do, and to suffer bravely.

LIVY

THE SUCCESSOR TO THE GREEK and Persian civilizations in the Mediterranean basin and the Near East was Rome, the Italian city-state that grew to be the dominant power in the East and West alike. Although Rome is usually called the successor to Hellenistic Greece, they actually overlapped in time. Chronologically, Rome emerged as a community during the same era as Athens and Sparta, but did not become important until much later. In this chapter we will look at the initial stages of Rome's growth, the era of the Roman republic, which lasted until the first century C.E.

Roman Foundations

Rome is situated about halfway down the western coast of the Italian peninsula, where one of the country's very few sizable rivers, the Tiber, flows through a good-sized fertile plain before emptying into the sea (Map 11.1). This river and the plain (*Latium*) were the reason early settlements were located here, and it is only in modern times that their significance to the city's prosperity has faded.

Very early Italy and the Italians are even more a mystery than Greece and the Greeks. We do know that Indo-European peoples settled central and south Italy at least as early as Minoan days (c. 1500 B.C.E.), reaching a high degree of Neolithic culture. They developed farming and villages, but lagged seriously behind the peoples of the eastern Mediterranean and the Near East. Among other things, there is no sign that they had a written language until as late as 700 B.C.E.

About 800 B.C.E., three peoples from the East began to enter Italy first as colonists and then as rulers of various segments of the peninsula: the Etruscans, the Greeks, and the Phoenicians. Each of these civilized groups contributed substantially to Italian development, and the first two had a decisive effect on Roman civilization's early forms.

We know very little about the **Etruscans** except that they came into Italy about 800, probably by following a route along the northern Adriatic Sea, and were already highly civilized at that time. They established a series of small city-states in the northern and central areas of the

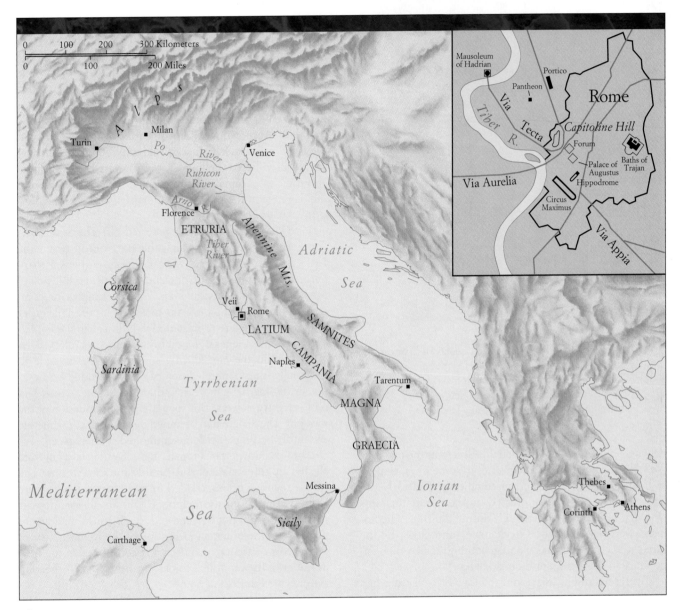

MAP 11.1 Ancient Italy. The Italian peninsula was invaded innumerable times in history. The native Italic peoples of the north and center were taken over by the more civilized Etruscans in the tenth to eighth centuries B.C.E. Rome itself was probably founded by the uniting of several villages under a single government in the eighth century, as Roman legend states.

peninsula, ruling over the native Italians by virtue of their superior weaponry and organization. They left a small amount of writing, but it has never been deciphered, so we have no historical record in the strict sense. We do know that Etruscan kings ruled over early Rome from about 750 to about 500 B.C.E. During that time, they brought civilized life to the Romans. The pictorial record left by the Etruscans, mainly in recently rediscovered underground tombs, makes it clear that the early Romans derived much of their early religious beliefs, art forms, and architecture from the Etruscans.

One thing the Etruscan upper classes prized, but that the Romans held in contempt, was physical comfort. According to Roman sources that may be unreliable, the Romans eventually were able to defeat the Etruscans because they were soft and could not stand up to the rigors of war as long as their rivals. After the Roman victory, the Etruscans gradually fade from history, absorbed by their former subjects and others.

In the long run, the Greeks had even more influence on Roman attitudes and manners than did the Etruscans. Whereas the Romans viewed the Etruscans as rivals and

❀ **Etruscan Winged Horses.** The vivid quality of Etruscan statuary is one of our few sources of knowledge about these people, who were the forerunners of the Romans in central Italy. The superb mastery of anatomy displayed here was to be a particular strength of Roman sculpture at a later date. (© *Scala/Art Resource*)

defeated enemies, they regarded the Greeks as the one people who were superior to themselves in some ways, namely, in culture, imagination, and in commerce. The early Romans were very much impressed by the Greek migrants who had settled in southern Italy during the 700s. The Romans were awed by the Greek towns and cities, by the Greeks' skills in organizing and governing, and by their experience in the great world outside Italy.

Overcrowding at home and the love of adventure had caused these Greek colonists to leave their homes in Corinth, Thebes, and other Greek cities and settle in Italy. They soon transformed southern Italy into a prosperous and commercially advanced civilization but found they had to fight both the Etruscans and the Phoenicians to hold onto it. True to Greek tradition, they made the job much harder by fighting among themselves.

Phoenician influence on Italian events came through **Carthage,** although this great trading city had become independent of its mother country by 700. Before the rise of Rome, Carthage was the most powerful force in the western Mediterranean. It sent ships as far away as Britain and the North Sea, as well as into the Nile, and had founded colonies of its own all over the coasts of Spain and France. The Carthaginians fought the Greek cities of southern Italy and Sicily to a draw until the Romans were able to take advantage of their mutual exhaustion to conquer both of them around 200 B.C.E.

Early Government

According to ancient Roman tradition, Rome was founded by the twin brothers Romulus and Remus, legendary descendants of the survivors who fled burning Troy after the Trojan War. By 753 B.C.E., the population had grown to the point that the settlement could be considered a town. It had walls and its own government. Modern historians agree that the city-state of Rome was founded at approximately that date. According to Roman history written much later, the town was under Etruscan rule until 509 B.C.E. In that year, a bloodless rebellion ousted the last Etruscan king, and the city became a republic ruled by a combination of the Senate and the people—in the original Latin, the *Senatus et populus.*

How did the new republic govern itself? The Senate was composed of the upper class, the **patricians** (from the Latin *patres* or "fathers"), who made up perhaps 5 to 10 percent of the total population and had considerable power even under the Etruscan king. The **plebeians** or commoners (from Latin *plebs,* "the mass") composed the other 90 percent and were represented in political affairs by delegates to the General Assembly whom they elected by wards within the city and by so-called tribes outside it. Originally, the General Assembly was intended to be as powerful—perhaps more so—than the Senate, which had only advisory powers. But soon after the foundation of the republic, the Senate had obtained decisive power while the Assembly became a seldom-summoned rubber stamp.

The executive was a small staff of officials who were elected by the Senate and Assembly for short terms. The chief executive power resided in two **consuls,** who were elected from among the members of the Senate for one-year terms that could not be repeated. Each consul had a veto power over the other, an indication of the Romans' fear of permanent dictatorship. When one consul was in the field as leader of the republic's forces, the other was the head of the civil government at home.

Below the consuls in authority were the **censors,** who were also always drawn from the ranks of the senators. The censors were originally tax assessors, but later they came to have the power to supervise the conduct and morals of their fellow senators. The Roman bureaucracy also included a few other offices, which were dominated by the patricians until a series of plebeian revolts or threats to revolt gradually opened them up to the commoners.

For two centuries, the plebeians struggled to attain equality. Their most important gains were the adoption of the **Law of the Twelve Tables,** the first codified Roman law, in 450 B.C.E.; the expansion of their political influence in 367 after threatening a revolt; and, finally, the enactment of the Hortensian Law (named after the consul of the day) in 287, which expanded the powers of the Assembly, making it supposedly equal to the Senate.

By about 250, the Roman political structure had obtained a nice balance between the aristocrats (patricians) and the common people (plebeians). The chief officers of the plebeians were the **tribunes,** who were representatives of the various tribes. There were about ten tribunes, and they had great power to speak and act in the name of the common Romans. At first, the tribunes were chosen from the common people and were true representatives of them. Later, however, after about 200, the tribunes were offered membership in the Senate, and as they sought to become censors and consuls, they came to identify increasingly with the interests of the patricians and less with those of the plebeians. This development was to be fateful for the republic.

After the passage of the Hortensian Law in 287, plebeians and patricians had equal voting rights and supposedly equal access to office. But in practice, the government was not really democratic. Democracy eventually failed in Rome, just as it had in Athens. When a crisis arose, the Roman republic and democracy died an inglorious death.

Rome's Conquest of Italy

❋

Under this mixed government of aristocrats and commoners, the Roman city-state gradually and painfully became the master of Italy. Down to about 340, the almost constant wars took place in a strip of land along the west coast. The Romans led a federation of tribes living in the plain of Latium, first against the Etruscans and then against other Italians (see Map 11.1).

Although Rome suffered a devastating invasion by Celtic tribes called Gauls in 390, the Romans and their Latin allies ruled most of central Italy by 340 or so. When the Latins attempted to revolt against Roman overlordship, the Romans crushed them. Next they turned their attention to the Samnites, a group of Italic tribes in the south and east of the peninsula. The war against the Samnites was lengthy and very difficult, but it proved significant, for during this conflict the Romans perfected their military organization and created the myth of Roman invincibility.

The surrender of the Samnites in 282 B.C.E. brought the Romans into contact with a new rival: the Greek city-states of southern Italy, who were supported by Pyrrhus, a powerful Greco-Macedonian general. After a couple of costly victories, Pyrrhus was defeated. Rome now inserted itself into the ongoing struggle between the Greeks and the Carthaginians in Sicily. It would be only a matter of time before the two burgeoning powers of the western Mediterranean engaged in a contest for supremacy.

During these almost continuous conflicts, the Romans learned how to assure that yesterday's enemies became today's friends and allies. A pragmatic and flexible people, the Romans very soon realized that their original practice of humiliating and enslaving the conquered was counterproductive. Instead, they began to encourage the subject populations to become integrated with Rome—to become "good Romans" regardless of their ethnic or historical affiliations. The Romans gave partial citizenship rights to the conquered Italians as long as they did not rebel and agreed to supply troops when Rome called. This arrangement was advantageous to the conquered because it eased their tax burden, assured them of Roman assistance against their own enemies, and gave them wide-ranging powers of self-government. Some of the conquered were eventually allowed to become full citizens, which meant they could run for office and vote in Roman elections, serve in the Roman army and bureaucracy, and have protection for property and other legal rights that were not available to noncitizens. The upper classes of the conquered Italians and Greeks were eager to latinize themselves and thus to qualify as full citizens. They achieved this status by intermarrying with Romans, adopting the Latin language, and accepting the basic elements of Roman custom and law.

The Punic Wars

❋

Although the Romans were nearly constantly at war between 500 and 275 B.C.E., these conflicts were generally defensive in nature. Some were responses to the calls of Italian allies for help. In these wars, the Romans were dealing with peoples who were similar to themselves and whose conquered lands were adjacent to Roman possessions.

The two **Punic Wars** against mighty Carthage were decisive in Rome's rise from being a merely Italian power to becoming the center of a great empire. Not until the First Punic War (264–241 B.C.E.) did Rome more or less openly embark on imperial expansion. With that war, Rome became an empire in fact, though it retained the laws and politics of a democratic city-state. This created internal tensions that ultimately could not be resolved. The result was bloody civil strife.

The First Punic War broke out over the question of dominance in Sicily. It lasted for more than twenty years of sporadic combat until both sides were almost exhausted and made a reluctant peace. In this war, Rome for the first time developed a navy, which was necessary to counter the large Carthaginian fleets.

The First Punic War ended with the surrender of Sicily and Sardinia to Rome, but Carthage was far from completely subdued. During the ensuing twenty-year truce, it built up its forces, especially in the large colony of Spain. There, the brilliant general **Hannibal** amassed an army of 50,000 men, which successfully crossed the Alps in midwinter and descended on Italy. The ensuing years were critical to Rome's survival and its eventual imperial glory.

Hannibal won battle after battle against the desperate Romans, but lost the war. Finally, after ravaging Italy for fifteen years in the Second Punic War (218–202), Hannibal was forced to return to Carthage to defend the city against a Roman counterinvasion. (See the Violence and Coercion

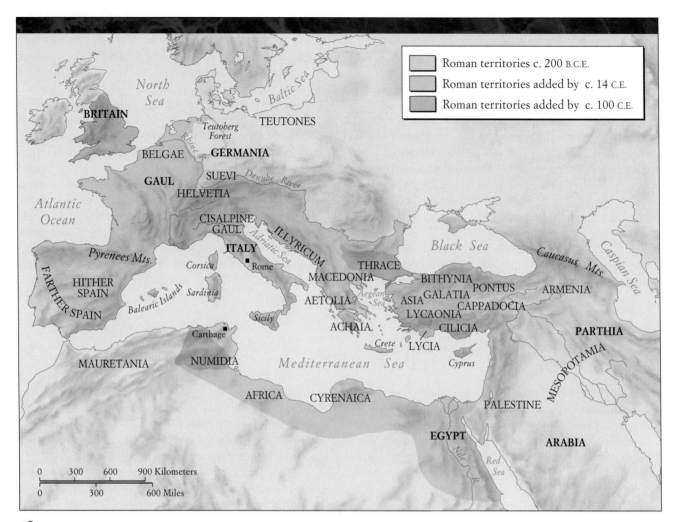

MAP 11.2 Expansion of Roman Territories to 100 C.E. Rome's empire was created not by plan but by a series of wars that had little or no relation to one another. Roman influences were permanently barred from central Europe after the massive defeat in the Teutoburg Forest in 9 C.E. and the establishment of the Rhine and Danube borders thereafter (see Chapter 12). In Asia, the Romans created a series of client kingdoms that relieved them of having to station large numbers of troops there.

box for details about Hannibal's campaign.). The decisive **battle of Zama** in 202 was a clear Roman victory, and Carthage was forced to give up most of its extensive holdings in Africa and Spain. These were made into new provinces of what by now was a rapidly growing empire (see Map 11.2). The Punic Wars determined that Roman, and not Carthaginian, culture and civilization would control the Mediterranean basin for the foreseeable future.

The Conquest of the East

Victorious against Carthage, the Romans at once turned their eyes eastward. Until now they had tried to stay out of the continuous quarreling of the Hellenistic kingdoms. The Roman upper classes were much influenced by Greek cul-

ture and Greek ideas, which they had encountered in conquering the prosperous colonies in southern Italy, but they had shown no interest in actually taking over the Greek homelands.

But in the 190s, immediately after the Punic Wars, ambitious consuls did just that by taking sides in an internal Greek struggle. Within a very short time, the Greco-Macedonian kingdom was under Rome's control.

Roman armies soon defeated the other Hellenistic kingdoms around the eastern edge of the Mediterranean. These kingdoms could have been at once made into Roman provinces. But some senators expressed strong opposition to this, believing that the new, materialistic society being created by military conquests was far from what Roman traditions honored. A seesaw struggle between conservatives, who wished Rome to remain a homogeneous Italian city-state, and imperialists, who wanted expansion (and

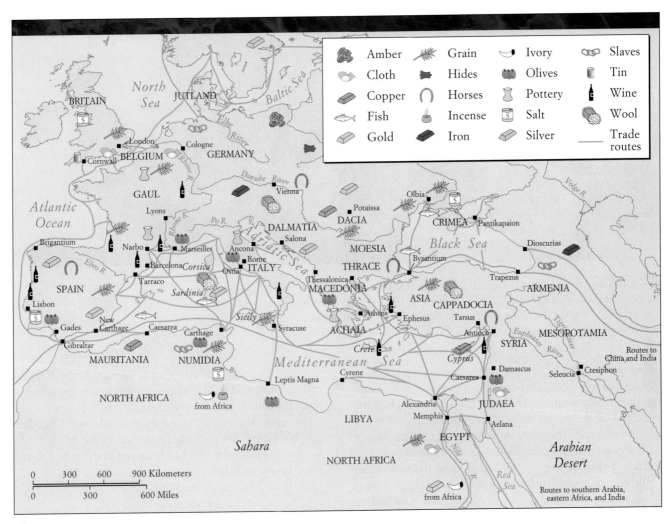

🏵 **MAP 12.1   Products of the Roman Empire c. 200 C.E.** The Romans traded extensively both within and without their borders. Some of the more important items carried are displayed in this map.

behind them. Even though they were effective and wise rulers, they set an ominous precedent that would come back to haunt Rome in the third century.

Unification of the Empire

The successors of Augustus continued his work in bringing together the very diverse peoples over whom they ruled. Gradually, the Latin language became the common denominator of higher culture in the western half of the empire, while Greek continued to serve that function in the East. The imperial government used both languages equally in its dealings with its subjects.

Unification was also assisted by the gradual development of a large bureaucracy for the first time in Roman affairs. This change added greatly to the previously minimal cost of government but also provided many visible ways to reward useful provincials and encourage them to follow a pro-Roman policy. As long as the empire was prosperous, the increased costs of the bureaucracy were bearable.

The imperial government became increasingly centralized. The freedoms of the cities of the ancient East were curtailed by directives and governors sent out from Italy or selected from the romanized locals. In the western half of the empire, the Roman authorities founded many **municipia.** These were towns with their surrounding countryside that formed governmental units similar in size and function to our own counties. The municipal authorities were partly appointed by Rome and partly elected from and by leading local families. The provincial governor (usually an Italian given the job as political patronage) was responsible for their good behavior. He was backed by a garrison commander who had wide-ranging authority in matters both military and civil.

Everywhere, the government became open to non-Italians, as soon as they romanized themselves sufficiently

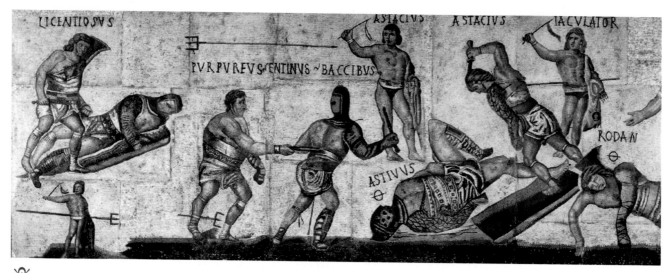

✿ **Gladiators in Combat.** This mosaic from a Roman floor shows the weapons, body armor, and garments of the professional gladiators. Whether they lived or died was of little concern to the Roman crowd, but many of these combatants survived by displaying extraordinary courage in the arena. *(Art Resource)*

to become citizens. (Citizenship was eventually granted to all freemen by a popularity-seeking emperor in 212.) From the time of the emperor Hadrian (the 120s C.E.), half the members of the Senate were of provincial origin. Men of talent could rise swiftly to the highest offices regardless of their ethnic background. Religious differences were ignored, so long as one was willing to make the very undemanding ceremonial tributes to the official Roman gods (Jupiter, Neptune, and the like). Most individuals had no difficulty combining this state cult with the more intimate, traditional religions of their preference.

Roman law made a key contribution to integrating the Roman state and society. Many types of law originally existed within the borders of the empire, but they gradually gave way to the system that the Romans had hammered out by trial and error during the republic and that continued to be developed in the empire. The basic principles of this legal system were (1) the notion of *precedent* as coequal to the letter of the law; (2) the belief that *equity* (fairness) was the goal of all law; and (3) the importance of *interpretation* in applying the law to individual cases.

The Romans had various codes of law. One originally applied only to citizens, and another applied only to aliens and travelers on Roman territory. During the early empire, the law code that governed relations between citizens and non-Romans, known as the **jus gentium** ("law of peoples"), gradually came to be accepted as basic. The rights of citizens and noncitizens, of natives and aliens, came to be seen as worthy of protection by the Roman authorities. These rights were not equal, but they were recognized as existing. This concept paved the way for what we call international law, and it gradually took Roman law far beyond the usual concepts of "us against you" that other peoples employed with foreigners.

Later, in the third and fourth centuries, the Romans evolved *natural law,* the idea that all humans, by virtue of their humanity, possess certain rights and duties that all courts must recognize. As the Romans adopted Christianity, this natural law came to be viewed as the product of a God-ordained order that had been put into the world with the creation of Adam.

Life in the Roman Empire's Heyday

✿

In general, the Romans were very successful in creating a single, unified vision of what life was about—and how it should best be lived—that was accepted from Britain to Egypt and from Spain to Romania. We have a great deal of information about the economic and cultural life of the empire in the first and second centuries C.E. Much of our knowledge has been obtained through archaeology, and every year new digs are started in some part of the former Roman domains.

Trade and manufacturing enjoyed a considerable boom (see Map 12.1). Trade was conducted mainly within the borders of the empire but also extended beyond them to India, Africa, and even China (this was small in volume and was conducted through Asian intermediaries). Increasingly, the balance of trade within the empire shifted to favor the East (meaning from the Adriatic to Mesopotamia and Egypt). Italy itself became more and more dependent on imports from other parts of the empire, mainly from the East where the levels of skills far exceeded those of the West. In the East lived the bulk of the population and the

🏵 **A Roman Apartment House.** This model has been reconstructed from archaeological evidence found at Ostia, Rome's port. The building on the right is the home of a wealthy family, possibly the owners of the multistory tenement to the left. While some tenements were solidly built, many were thrown up to maximize the income for the landlord and allowed to become filthy nests. (© *Scala/Art Resource*)

majority of the urbanites. Here, too, were the sophisticated, civilized traditions of the Hellenistic world. Even the skilled slave labor in Italy came almost exclusively from Eastern sources.

Most Roman subjects, as always, worked the land. But much of this land was now owned either by the imperial government or by wealthy absentee landlords. Small free farmers were a declining species by the second century. They were replaced not so much by slaves as by sharecropper-tenants, who were still free in most of the empire but would not long remain so. Slaves were common in all parts of the empire, but their number stabilized in the first century C.E. The number of slaves stopped increasing because prisoners of war were no longer coming in once the empire ceased expanding and because widespread prosperity meant fewer people were enslaved for debt.

By the 300s, however, in the Italian and western European countryside, the land tenure exemplified by the *villa,* or country estate of the wealthy, was steadily gaining at the expense of the impoverished small farmers. More and more people were tempted or coerced into giving up their independence to obtain regular income and protection against rapacious tax collectors. This trend, too, would be a source of future trouble as the imperial defenses weakened.

Another trend in the early empire was the increasing social stratification, particularly in the towns of Italy. The rich were more numerous and more distinct as a group than ever before, and the poor were both more numerous and more miserable. In the preserved ruins of Pompeii and the

🏵 **Roman Ladies Attended by a Slave.** This first-century C.E. wall painting from the town of Herculaneum displays a group of upper-class matrons who share the hairdressing of a female slave. Romans paid much attention to physical attractiveness in both sexes, and it was not unusual for wealthy females to spend several hours on their daily toilettes. (© *Erich Lessing/Art Resource*)

excavated areas of several other Italian towns, we see many multistory tenements. Here—if they were lucky—lived the unfortunates who did not have steady work or a protector from the propertied class. Wealth seems to have become the main qualification for public office.

Everywhere the early empire saw a major expansion of urban life and its values. The Romans founded numerous towns. Some, like Carthage, were revivals of old towns, but most were quite new. Many of them were the direct descendants of Roman military forts. Perhaps half of the cities of modern Europe west of the Rhine-Danube frontier are originally Roman foundations.

These towns supported a large middle class of merchants, skilled artisans, clerks, and administrators. They were well educated in public and private schools where they studied the disciplines made popular by Hellenistic culture: literature, rhetoric, some math, history, and philosophy of various types. Both Greek and Latin literature flourished in the early empire, although the cultural differences represented by the two languages caused increasing alienation after about 300 C.E.

The Arts and Architecture of the Early Empire

❋

All of the arts flourished under the early emperors, who poured public and private money into celebrations of their military triumphs and what they proudly termed the "Roman mission"—that is, spreading civilization. Some of these monuments were in stone and concrete, such as the triumphal Column of Trajan telling the story of the conquest of Romania. Some were in paint and ceramics, such as the great Golden House of Nero. Others were vast public works such as the Roman Forum and the Coliseum. The Coliseum was built in the first century and is still one of the most impressive arenas of the world.

Rome and several other cities (Antioch, Damascus, Alexandria, Athens, Marseilles, for example) saw a great burst of building, which called for a mastery of masonry and engineering design unapproached even by the Greeks in its imaginative boldness and endurance. In addition to buildings, the Romans constructed roads in all directions, harbors, aqueducts and sewage works, bridges, and fortifications. None exceeded the Romans' abilities to get things done—and done right. A great many of these structures are still in use today 1,700 years later.

Literature

The great age of Roman literature came at the end of the republic and during the first century of the empire. **Virgil** (70–19 B.C.E.) was without doubt the greatest of the Roman

❋ **Roman Ruins in North Africa.** The huge arch and palace was erected by the emperor Trajan in the early second century C.E. to commemorate his victorious reign. The Timgad Arch still stands in Algeria, North Africa. (*Brian Brake/Photo Researchers, Inc*)

poets. His masterwork was the *Aeneid,* the story of Aeneas, a royal refugee from burning Troy. The *Aeneid* follows him through many adventures until he lands in Italy and, by implication, becomes the founding father of Rome. Horace, Ovid, and Catullus were the other leading poets of the Augustan period. Although their work still shows some traces of the Greek models, all four authors developed a style that can accurately be called original. In their hands, the Latin language became an extraordinary instrument, capable of extreme directness and concentration of meaning. Its clarity and accuracy made it into a rival of Greek for both literary and scientific expression.

The historian Tacitus, the satirist Juvenal, and the prose storytellers Pliny the Elder, Petronius, and Suetonius were among the more notable writers in Latin in the first and second centuries. After about the middle of the second century, the quality of Latin literature began to slacken.

Art and Architecture

In the plastic and pictorial arts such as painting, ceramics, mosaics, and sculpture, the Romans were generally content to elaborate, if only slightly, on models drawn from the Hellenistic East. Perhaps the single most impressive triumph of the Romans in this area was the extraordinary portrait sculpture that we mentioned earlier (see Chapter 11). With

🏵 **Roman Aqueduct in Spain.** This modern photo shows the enduring nature of Roman civic architecture all around the Mediterranean basin. This aqueduct might still be employed by the citizens of Segovia, Spain, to bring fresh water to them. Similar structures stand in southern France and in Turkey. Note the Romulus/Remus statue copy in the center. *(Dave G. Houser/Corbis)*

few exceptions, the superb "Greek" statues in the world's museums are Roman copies of originals long since disappeared. In architecture, the Romans' affinity for grand size and their skills in masonry combined to give magnificent expression to public works and buildings. They were the first people to master the large-scale domed roof and the uses of the arch.

Philosophy

"How best to live?" was a question that preoccupied imperial Romans. Perhaps the greatest of all the emperors after Augustus was **Marcus Aurelius** (ruled 161–180 C.E.), the last of the Five Good Emperors who ruled in the second century C.E. He left a small book of aphorisms called *Meditations,* which has been a best-seller ever since (see the Religion and Morality box). Marcus settled on a pessimistic Stoicism as the most fitting cloak for a good man in a bad world, especially a man who had to exercise power. This was a common feeling among upper-class Romans, and it became ever more popular in the third and fourth centuries as civic difficulties multiplied. Like Marcus Aurelius, Roman Stoics often opposed Christianity because they rejected external prescriptions for morality. Instead, they insisted that each person is responsible for searching and

following his own conscience. Seneca, another Stoic and the most persuasive of the Roman moralists, had a somewhat different way of looking at things. He introduced a new note of humane compassion, a belief that all shared in the divine spark and should be valued as fellow creatures.

The Roman character, insofar as one can sum up a heterogenous people's character, leaned toward the pragmatic and the here and now. Romans admired the doer more than the thinker, the soldier more than the philosopher, and the artisan more than the artist. The educated class could and did appreciate "the finer things." They admired and cultivated art in many media and many forms and spent lavishly to obtain it for their own pleasure. But they did not, generally speaking, provide that sort of intense, sustained interest that led to superior aesthetic standards and to the inspiration of superior and original works of art, such as the Greeks possessed in abundance. The early empire's successes in several fields were magnificent and long-lasting, but they were not rooted in an original view of earthly life or a new conception of humans' duties and aspirations.

The really new elements in Roman culture were originated and nurtured not by traditional beliefs and aspirations but by a new sect that was steadily finding more adherents in the empire in the second and third centuries: Christianity. In Chapter 14, we look at what the Christians believed and what they achieved in a faltering imperial society.

The *Meditations* of Marcus Aurelius

Marcus Aurelius (121–180 C.E.) was perhaps the greatest of all the Roman rulers, in the sense of moral grandeur. As the last of the Five Good Emperors who ruled in the second century C.E., he inherited an empire that was still intact and at peace internally. But on its eastern borders, the first of the lethal challenges from the Germanic tribes materialized during his reign (161–180), and he had to spend much of his time organizing and leading the empire's defenses.

Even during his campaigns, his mind was attuned to the Stoic philosophy, which the Roman upper classes had acquired from the Greeks. In his *Meditations* he wrote a personal journal of the adventure of a life consciously lived. His book, which was never meant for publication, has lived on into our day because of its nobility of thought and expression. Some excerpts follow.

Begin each day by reminding yourself: today I shall meet with meddlers, ingrates, insolence, disloyalty, ill-will and selfishness—all of them due to the offenders' ignorance of what is good and what evil. But I have long perceived the nature of good and its nobility, the nature of evil and its meanness, and also the nature of the culprit himself, who is my brother . . . therefore, none of those things can injure me, for no one can implicate me in what is degrading. . . .

Never value the advantages derived from anything involving breach of faith, loss of self-respect, hatred, suspicion, or execration of others, insincerity, or the desire for something which has to be veiled or curtained. One whose chief regard is for his own mind, and for the divinity within him and the service of its goodness, will strike no poses, utter no complaints, and crave neither for solitude nor yet for the crowd. . . .

Hour by hour resolve firmly, like a Roman and a man, to do what comes to hand with correct and natural dignity, and with humanity, independence, and justice. Allow your mind freedom from all other considerations. This you can do if you will approach each action as though it were your last, dismissing the wayward thought, the emotional recoil from the commands of reason, the desire to create an impression, the admiration of self, the discontent with your lot. See how little a man needs to master, for his days to flow on in quietness and piety; he has to observe but these few counsels, and the gods will ask nothing more.

Men seek for seclusion in the wilderness, by the sea, or in the mountains—a dream you may have cherished only too fondly yourself. But such fancies are wholly unworthy for the philosopher, since at any moment you choose you can retire within yourself. Nowhere can man find a quieter or more untroubled retreat than in his own soul; above all, he who possesses resources in himself, which he need only contemplate to secure immediate ease of mind—the ease that is but another word for a well-ordered spirit. Avail yourselves, then, of this retirement, and so continually renew yourself.

SOURCE: Excerpt from Marcus Aurelius Meditations, *trans. Maxwell Staniforth.* © 1964, Penguin Classics. Reprinted by permission of Penguin, Ltd.

SUMMARY

The early Roman empire (27 B.C.E.–180 C.E.) was built on the constitutional and administrative foundations laid down in the reign of the first emperor, Octavian Augustus Caesar. For two centuries, it functioned quite well as a political and economic organism, even though the capital city saw occasional outbursts of civic upheaval or palace coups. Law and order were established securely in an area that reached from Scotland to northern Africa and from Spain to the Iranian borderlands. External raiders were kept at bay without creating an oppressive bureaucracy and expensive armies. Internal malcontents were isolated or put down without much trouble, and the governing system created by Augustus seemed invulnerable.

Though not original contributors in philosophy or the arts, the Romans found their triumphs in the construction of a system of law and government that was flexible enough to serve vastly different subject peoples. Indeed, it served them so well that the statement "I am a Roman" remained a badge of honor and a claim to justice and respect for more than five centuries. Governmental responsibilities were divided between the center and the provinces and municipalities in a way that provided many outlets for talent and inculcated a sense of supraethnic patriotism.

The economy of the empire generally prospered, creating a large middle class of merchants and landowners. But in the cities a growing proletariat underlined the huge differences between poor and rich. The eastern half of the empire was clearly overshadowing the west by the third century. Slavery both urban and rural was common, as was a sharecropping dependency on large landholders in the countryside. Literature and architecture flourished, though both depended for basic forms and inspiration on Greek models and Greek ideas, as was also true of many of the plastic arts.

TEST YOUR KNOWLEDGE

1. In 27 B.C.E. Octavian Caesar began to organize a new government for Rome that was a
   a. republic.
   b. dictatorship.
   c. democracy.
   d. constitutional monarchy.
2. A major problem that confronted Augustus upon taking supreme powers was that the Roman army
   a. had lost its will to fight.
   b. was much too large.
   c. was poorly equipped.
   d. was under the control of Christians.
3. Which of the following modern states was *outside* the Roman empire's borders?
   a. Austria
   b. Greece
   c. Denmark
   d. England
4. Within the Roman sphere, which of the following centuries could most appropriately be described as a period of peace and security?
   a. Sixth century B.C.E.
   b. First century B.C.E.
   c. Second century C.E.
   d. Fourth century C.E.
5. Augustus's most famed successor and Rome's second greatest emperor was
   a. Nero.
   b. Tiberius.
   c. Marcus Aurelius.
   d. Julius Caesar.
6. Roman official cults
   a. insisted on unwavering belief in doctrine.
   b. were religions of ritual without emotional content.
   c. despised the non-Italian subjects of the empire.
   d. sometimes demanded human sacrifices.
7. Virgil's *Aeneid* is a(n)
   a. history of the decline and fall of Greek civilization.
   b. plea for tolerance and justice for the Christians.
   c. argument for pacifism.
   d. explanation of Rome's origin.

IDENTIFICATION TERMS

imperator	**Marcus Aurelius**	**Praetorian Guard**
jus gentium	*municipia*	*princeps*
Livy	*Pax Romana*	Virgil

INFOTRAC COLLEGE EDITION

Enter the search terms "Rome history" using Key Words.
Enter the search terms "Roman empire" using Key Words.

Enter the search terms "Roman law" using the Subject Guide.

Chapter 13

Ordinary Lives in the Classical Age

Censure is blind to the crows, and harasses the doves.

JUVENAL

WHAT WERE THE TYPICAL activities and attitudes of people living in the Greek and Roman civilizations between 500 B.C.E. and 500 C.E.? We return now to the topics of Chapter 7: how people earned a living, women's place in society, what constituted moral and immoral acts, sexual relationships, and how children were treated and educated. Because much more written history survives, we have considerably more choices in trying to reconstruct the daily lives of ordinary Greeks and Romans than was true of the earlier civilizations. Yet what we know is fragmentary at best and is almost always limited to the upper classes. In this epoch, history still refers to the lives and acts of the few.

Earning a Living

A changing social structure resulted from the evolution of the classical economies of the Mediterranean basin. In the 800 years between Greece's high point and the collapse of the western Roman empire, a more urbanized and more stratified society came forth. In this society, slavery and great wealth were the opposing ends of a wide spectrum.

Greece and the Roman Republic

The majority kept body and soul together as always through farming, fishing, and herding. In Greece and Italy, only a small portion of the total area is good farmland. Greece was a country of small farmers, who labored long and hard to make a living from the stony, unrewarding soil. Many pastured a few goats and sheep as well. Both olives and wine grapes supplemented grain farming and inshore fishing.

The Greek *polis* was usually a small place, and its inhabitants were generally racially and culturally homogeneous. The center of the *polis* was a town of moderate size, with a population of 10,000 to 20,000 as a rough average. It supported all of the usual urban trades and crafts. Most adults debated about and participated in civic culture and politics, which were matters of wide concern.

Educated and property-owning Greeks—a minority of the population—thought of manual labor as being beneath the dignity of the free and assigned as much of it as possible to their slaves. But the majority could not afford to keep slaves and had to do the work themselves. Most Greeks active in the labor force were free men and women, working for themselves or for a wage in small-scale enterprises. Athens, the center of the *polis* of Attica, was exceptional in that perhaps as many as half of its total inhabitants were slaves. Many of these men and women were employed directly by the state, and most of the rest were domestic servants of all types, rather than independently productive workers.

Machinery of even primitive design was a rarity. A Greek or Roman woman spent a majority of her waking hours, from childhood to old age, preparing the next day's bread and porridge, carrying water, spinning and weaving cloth, and in general performing the same routine housewifely tasks that occupied her predecessors in the East and in Egypt. In the countryside gender equality was more prevalent, and women did much the same jobs as men, though we know little about the rates of pay or other details.

From the consistent attention given to textile production in classical literature and art, we know that a large part of a woman's life—young or old, married or single (spinsters)—was spent on this task. Among most peoples throughout history, spinning and weaving have been specifically female tasks. No male would be caught doing these jobs, which were identified as "woman's work," just as warfare was "man's work." (The Greek legend of the Amazon female warriors was just that—a legend.)

Probably a higher proportion of people were engaged in commercial business in classical Greece than in any previous civilization, and the proportion grew in the Hellenistic Age. As the Greeks became expert maritime traders, the production of cloth for sale throughout the Mediterranean and Black Sea basins increased dramatically, quite apart from the demand from the domestic markets. The constantly expanding fleets of Athens and other trading towns carried both exports and imports. Leather, ceramics, and metal weaponry were major exports, engaging the efforts of craftsmen in several *poleis.* Imports included much grain, timber, and some luxuries.

The Hellenistic Kingdoms

In the Greek-ruled kingdoms of the East, we have noted that the cities dominated and exploited the countryside. As the *polis* ideal of citizenship grew dim in these multiethnic territories, economic segregation between rich and poor grew more marked. Slaves increased in numbers and in importance to production. Inevitably, they competed for jobs with paid, free laborers. Widespread slavery seriously de-

pressed the income and security of the free, thereby essentially preventing them from exercising their rights of citizenship. The poor are rarely able to afford the luxury of active political participation.

Large enterprises that produced for a wide market became more numerous, indicating the increased economic interdependency of the Mediterranean lands. Some of these enterprises in the Seleucid and Egyptian kingdoms, especially, were manned entirely by slaves, who often were highly skilled. The increased technological capacity and larger markets enabled these large enterprises to supplant the small-scale businesses of the Classical Age Greeks.

The conquests of Alexander paved the way for material wealth unheard of by the classical Greeks. Although the Greek/Macedonian overlords were eventually replaced or absorbed by the Eastern peoples, they retained their business contacts. Silk from the East, for example, now entered the western world as perhaps the most valuable single item of trade. The Chinese monopoly on fine silk production would not be broken until the sixth century C.E., and then only insignificantly. Not until modern times would Euro-

Roman Home with Atrium. The Roman upper and middle classes had a highly developed domestic architecture. All interior space centered on an unroofed opening called the *atrium,* which allowed light and air into the abutting rooms. This style of architecture is still common in countries with a Mediterranean climate. *(©Robert Frerck/Odyssey/Chicago)*

peans understand how to produce silk in quality as fine as the Chinese version.

Trade with the East was conducted both by the traditional overland caravans (see the Silk Road to China on Maps 17.1 and 18.1) and also by new sea routes. The Hellenistic achievements in science had repercussions for navigation and map making, which received considerable attention during the first centuries B.C.E. and C.E. Alexandria in Egypt became a major center of scientific endeavor, much of which was devoted to geography and mapping the heavens.

Agricultural production seems to have risen during the Hellenistic Age. Most of the Mediterranean countries now had agricultural exports, with the major exceptions of Greece and Italy. Thanks to the fertility of the Nile valley, Egypt remained the richest single area in the western world, both under the Ptolemies and later as a province of the Roman empire. Slave labor was widely employed on plantation-like farms, but small subsistence farmers, living in their ancestral villages, were still the norm during Rome's rise to preeminence.

Girl Spinning. This fresco from the first century C.E. shows a young woman at probably the most common household task outside the kitchen: spinning fiber from a hand spindle into thread. (*©Robert Frerck/Odyssey/Chicago*)

The Roman Empire

During the 500 years (100 B.C.E.–400 C.E.) of Rome's empire in Europe, the methods by which the poor made a living changed very little from earlier days. Farming or herding animals remained the paramount occupation in the countryside. At the same time, the urban population grew considerably, especially in the West where the Romans introduced an urban culture for the first time. In the towns, the number of people—both men and women—engaged in skilled or semiskilled labor increased steadily. But the real growth of urban population came from the influx of country people who had lost their land and their livelihood. They came to town hoping for a better life, but many ended up as beggars.

Impoverishment was particularly dramatic in Italy. How did this happen? As we saw in Chapter 11, ongoing wars radically changed the Roman citizen militia of the early republic. Farmer-citizens were away from home for years, fighting one distant enemy or another. Instead of being rewarded, many were taken advantage of by wealthy speculators, who bribed or coerced their way to large-scale estate ownership. The new estates operated a plantation type of agriculture and were staffed by slaves imported from the conquered lands. The increasingly corrupt Senate, itself full of these speculators, made no effort to stop this practice. By the time of the Gracchi (130 B.C.E.), the free peasants who had once formed the backbone of Italian society were a rarity. The "land question" had become Rome's primary social problem—and it was not resolved.

The dispossessed country folk flooded into the towns, above all into Rome, where citizens could sell their votes, if nothing else. Other cities had similar problems, though Rome attracted the bulk of this new proletariat. The formerly honorable relationship of "patron" and "client" now came to mean the dependency of a beggar upon his master and almsgiver. Persons with nothing but the clothes on their back held themselves ready to be of service to some ambitious man: politically, as a voter, and, economically, as casual labor. By the end of the republic, the "Roman mob" was in full flower, living off the handouts of their various patrons, demoralized and in poverty.

To Augustus Caesar's credit, he understood the necessity of linking this unstable mob to the anchor of Roman imperial government. He and his successors did this by the combination of *panem et circenses* ("bread and circuses"). By giving the mob a minimal supply of free food and entertaining it with gladiatorial combats, chariot races, and frequent spectacles, the emperors instilled a commitment to Rome's prosperity and success in much of the lower classes.

But Augustus also transformed the role of the central government, turning it into a massive public works agency, not only in Italy but throughout the far-flung empire. These government measures helped to steady the Roman economy, while the maintenance of peace and order for most of

Gladiators

One unusual way to make a living in classical Rome was to become a gladiator. The first gladiatorial contests seem to have occurred in 264 B.C.E. when three pairs of men fought as part of the funeral celebration of a distinguished senator. Soon, such contests had become a part of the frequent games that marked Roman holidays. Men of rank had private bands of gladiators, whom they maintained and who were ready to engage in any violence on behalf of their master. In the empire, gladiators formed part of the imperial household, paid by the emperor to appear in the games sponsored by the emperor himself. These men were professional athletes, highly paid to engage in highly dangerous work. Many did not survive very long.

The arena contestants were not all professionals, however. Use was also made of criminals condemned to death, who would be put into unequal fights with armed opponents or even wild beasts. Some condemned criminals were offered the chance to become professional gladiators. They thus could escape the death penalty if they could survive for three years in the arena against others like themselves or prisoners of war who were put up as their opponents.

The professional gladiators were trained in special schools under horrific discipline but great solicitude as to their physical condition. Supervised by doctors, their trainers fed the recruits a special diet, massaged them, and regulated every aspect of their lives. On the eve of a fight, the gladiator was entitled to a *libera cena,* a banquet, given in public and attended by spectators who were curious about the men scheduled for combat the next day. For some it would be a final meal. They regarded themselves as soldiers: their task was to kill or to die honorably. In the days of the empire, many gladiators were called to serve in the army; bound by their gladiatorial oath and customs, they proved themselves equal to the best.

---

two centuries encouraged the expansion of private trade and commerce throughout the empire.

Slave and Free The number of slaves climbed sharply in the first century B.C.E.. Roman legions took over one province after another and made off with the human booty. Just as important, the number of debt slaves rose as the Italian countryside came to be dominated by large estates (*villas*).

The slaves brought back as war booty were often more educated and better skilled than the native Italians, and slaves from Greece, in particular, brought high prices in the market. Augustus tried to protect the free citizens by banning the importation of additional slaves into Italy, but his measures were evaded and later revoked. Roman slavery was harsher than had been the case earlier. The large merchant fleet and the navy depended on galley slaves, often criminals, in contrast to Greek practice. The extensive Roman mining industry also depended on slave labor, because this job was so dangerous that few freemen could be lured into it.

Slave families were broken up and sold to the highest bidders. Slaves could own no property of their own, nor could they inherit or bequeath property. The children from a marriage of slaves were automatically the property of the parents' owners. Rape of another's slave was considered a damage to the slave owner, not to the slave, and was paid for accordingly. The rape of a slave by his or her owner was not an offense at all.

Despite such treatment, by the third and fourth centuries C.E. free persons were increasingly selling themselves into voluntary slavery, which promised them a better life than freedom could. Sometimes, too, the self-sale was a dodge to avoid the tax, which a free person had to pay but a slave did not. It is not possible to know which motive predominated.

Gender Relations

The status of the female generally improved from its low point in classical Athens. Women gained some freedoms, but men continued to control public life. Greek prejudices were remedied to some extent by the Romans' sensitivity to the value of the female as property of the male.

Greece in the Classical Age

The degree of freedom accorded women in classical Greek society has been a topic of intense debate in recent years. Perhaps what this really says is that we know much more about the Greeks' preferences and prejudices than we do about any other early society (thanks to the large amount of surviving literature by Greek authors). Historians agree that women were generally excluded from any effective exercise of political and economic powers and that the Greeks were the Western originators of *misogyny,* the distrust and dislike of women by men. The philosopher Thales once said that he was grateful to Fortune for three reasons: that he was born a Greek and not a barbarian, that he was born a man and not an animal, and that he was born a man and not a woman. An authority on Greek women says that they neither had nor sought political power but worked through their husbands or fathers or sons. Any women who took political action did so only under certain closely defined conditions, and unless they did so at least ostensibly on behalf of a male relative, they and those around them came to a bad end. The great tragic heroines such as Electra, Antigone, and Medea and the mythological heroines such as Cassandra and Artemis are examples of women who came "to a bad end."

Greek males' treatment of the other sex exhibits some interesting variations. Another modern scholar notes that the antifemale prejudice exhibited in later Greek literature is not present in the Homeric period. The women of Sparta were quite free and equal with their menfolk. Spartan women allegedly shared the sexual favors of their men, regardless of marriage. The men were so frequently away in the field or in barracks that both they and the government saw this practice as essential to Sparta's survival. Because our knowledge of Sparta comes exclusively from non-Spartan literary sources, it is impossible to know whether this very unusual attitude was actual fact or another example of the antidemocratic Athenian authors' admiration for their powerful neighbor.

In contrast, we have a good deal of definite information about Athens. Respectable Athenian women were limited to the home and could make only rare public excursions under the guardianship of servants and slaves. Their work was closely prescribed for them: management of the household and supervision of children and servants. Within the four walls of the home, one or two rooms were reserved for their use. In multistoried houses, these rooms were normally upstairs, but in any house, they would be in the back away from the street. This segregation was the Greek equivalent of the Muslim *harem* or the Hindu *purdah,* and it fulfilled the same purpose: keeping women, as the valuable possession of men, away from the prying eyes of nonfamily members and all sexual temptations. Poor urban women undoubtedly had more freedom to leave the home and enter the workplace unescorted, as did rural women who had a great many essential tasks to perform daily, some of them outdoors.

Even in the age of democracy (fifth century B.C.E.), Athens was not a happy place for the ambitious woman. Not only was she excluded from politics, but she was also legally and customarily inferior to men in terms of property holding, custody of children, marriage and divorce, and business enterprises. A freeborn, native Athenian woman was recognized as a type of citizen. But her citizenship was limited, and very different from that enjoyed by males. Its main advantage was that Athenian citizenship could be passed on to (male) children through her. Aristotle's attitude was typical. In his *Politics,* he states that the male is by nature superior and the female inferior; the one rules, the other is ruled: "silence is a woman's glory."

Prostitution was common in classical Greece. The upper rank of women who engaged in it were equivalent to the *geisha* of modern Japan. They were the *hetairae*—well-educated, well-paid performers who amused their clients in many nonsexual fashions as well as the essential acts of their trade.

It is thought that male homosexuality or bisexuality was originally a product of Sparta and its militaristic society,

which brought youths together for long periods without women. But this interpretation is open to much question, and certainly, homosexuality existed among the Greeks long before Sparta's transformation. It also existed in other parts of classical Greece—notably, Athens. We know from the writings of several of the philosophers that the Greeks themselves differed sharply about the morality and general advisability of same-sex attraction. Plato has one of his spokesmen (in the *Symposium*) say that in both Athens and Sparta public attitudes on the topic are "complicated."

What happened when wives occasionally found themselves in competition with "boyfriends" for the attention of their husbands? In such situations, they had no more legal grounds to complain than if the man was sleeping with a female slave or a prostitute. Classical society regarded the homosexual relationship between older, experienced males and younger, inexperienced males as potentially the most elevating form of *paideia* (education) possible for the younger person. The fact that it undoubtedly did not always work out that way but sometimes led to the same emotional dead end as a heterosexual romance might was apparently accepted without special comment. Lesbianism was apparently accepted by some Greek males as easily as male homosexuality. But others found it a matter for ridicule and contempt, even when they had no problems with the male variety. We have very little direct evidence on this, as the topic was avoided in the comedies and other dramas, which were otherwise so forceful and direct on human follies.

The Hellenistic Age

Mainly on the basis of literary sources, historians generally agree that women's overall status gradually rose in the Hellenistic and Roman imperial eras. Of course, this statement applies more to the upper classes than to the lower ones. Queens ruled several of the Hellenistic kingdoms, and the incidence of female writers slowly increases from the very low levels of the classical age (the poetess Sappho is one of the very few known before 300 B.C.E.).

In the Hellenistic cities, upper-class women played an active role in business affairs, and the older prohibitions about leaving the family home seem to have faded. By the time of the Roman dominion, women in the East sometimes held positions of importance in politics, such as the queen Cleopatra, the last of the Ptolemies in Egypt. Priestesses such as the female oracles at Delphi were accorded semidivine status by their male adherents and their fellow citizens.

The rights of married women definitely increased. They were no longer regarded as the property of husbands and fathers, but as independent legal personages. In the highly law-conscious Roman society, female status was best revealed by property rights. Dowries were protected from greed and/or stupidity on the husband's side. No "second households" were permitted (though casual affairs with

🌸 **Entertainment at a Banquet.** The Greeks of the classical era were far from prudes, despite their emphasis on a reasonable life. This vase painting shows a scene from a "symposium", or male banquet to which close friends were invited on a rotational schedule to eat, drink, and make merry. Female entertainers were an essential part of the proceedings, often well-paid hetairae.

slaves or prostitutes went on as before). Divorce could be obtained on preordained grounds by either party. When the husband was at fault, he had to return the dowry. But communal property—that is, goods obtained since the start of the marriage—would remain with the husband.

Women also had more opportunities for education in this age. The founder of the Epicurean philosophy, for example, admitted females to his school on the same criteria as males. Even physical exercise, always a justification for segregating males and females in classical Greece, was now opened to some females as well. Illiteracy was the rule for women outside the urban upper classes but was apparently somewhat reduced.

Roman Custom

In Roman times, the earmark of female status was the far-reaching authority of the father over his daughter and, indeed, over all his *familia,* defined as wife, children, grandchildren, and household slaves. This **patria potestas** (literally, the "power of the father") extended even to life and death, though the exercise of the death penalty was very rare. This power originated in the early republic and was reflected in the first Roman code, the Law of the Twelve Tables. It lasted well into the empire, in theory if not in practice.

All Roman law was primarily concerned with the protection of property, and the laws concerning women clearly show that they were considered the property of the male head of the *familia.* It is worth noting that the father's powers exceeded those of the husband. For example, if a wife died without leaving a will, the property she left reverted not to her husband but to her father as head of the *familia* from which she had come.

A woman who passed from her father's control and was not under that of a husband was termed **sui juris** ("of her own law"). This status was quite unusual. Women who were neither married nor possessing *sui juris* had to be under tutelage—that is, a male relative was legally responsible for her.

Roman Marriage and Divorce   Roman girls married young by our standards, and betrothal was often much earlier still. Marriage at age thirteen was not unusual. The girl's consent was not necessary, and the young wife usually (not always) passed under the **manus** ("hand") of her husband. Unlike many other civilizations, the Roman widow was expected to remarry if she could, and she was normally then *sui juris,* legally equal

Male-Female Relations

Among the several acid-tongued commentators on the vices and follies of the imperial Romans, Juvenal stands out. Very few details of the life of this first-century C.E. author's life are known, but his masterly *Satires* have remained a favorite source of information about the daily lives of his Roman contemporaries. Sixteen of these free-verse poems have survived, though he possibly wrote several others. They are filled with allusions to traditional Roman heroes and villains, gods and goddesses, and stories known to all his readers.

In the following selection from the *Sixth Satire*, the poet pretends to be giving advice to an old friend, Postumus, who after many years of carefree bachelorhood is proposing to take a wife for the sake of an easy old age. Juvenal, apparently a Greek-style misogynist about contemporary Roman females, believes he is making a big mistake:

If you don't intend to love the woman who was your betrothed and is now your lawfully wedded wife, why marry at all?

Why waste money on a [wedding] meal? Or hand out pieces of cake to the bloated guests when the company's drifting away? Not to mention the reward for the wedding night. . . .

If your love for your wife is pure and simple, and your heart is devoted to her alone, then bow your head and prepare your neck for the yoke. No woman has any regard for the man who loves her. She may be passionate; still, she loves to fleece and torment him.

And so, the better a husband is, and the more attractive, the smaller the benefit that he receives from having a wife.

You will give no gift without the spouse's permission; no item will be sold when she says no, or bought if she is against it.

She will prescribe your affections. A friend who was known to your door when his beard first grew, now late in life will be turned away.

While pimps and fighters' trainers do what they please when making a will, and while the arena [that is, gladiator-slaves] enjoys a similar right,

She will dictate that some of your rivals figure as your heirs. . . .

The bed which contains a bride is always the scene of strife and mutual bickering. There's precious little sleep to be had there.

She turns on her husband, worse than a tigress robbed of her cubs. She pretends to be injured, covering up her own misdeeds. She rails at his slave boys, or invents a mistress to weep about. Floods of tears are always at hand; they stand at the ready, within the reservoir, waiting to hear the word of command; they flow as she tells them to.

You, poor worm, are delighted, complacently thinking it's love. You set about drying her tears with your lips, little aware of what you'd find in her letters if you ever unlocked the desk of that whore who pretends to be jealous.

SOURCE: Juvenal: The Satires, *trans. Niall Rudd (Oxford: Oxford University Press, 1991).*

to her new husband in terms of control over property. Marriage between close relatives was prohibited as incest. Interestingly, the Egyptian royal habit of marrying one's sister was continued under Roman rule, regardless of this prohibition.

Divorce of wives by husbands was quite common among the upper classes. Augustus, scandalized by the habits of some of his colleagues, decreed that a man catching his wife in adultery must divorce her or be considered her procurer and be punished himself. Divorce was much harder for a woman to obtain, and sexual impotence was one of the few grounds accepted. Because marriage was considered a consensual union rather than a legal obligation of the spouses, the lack of continued consent was itself grounds for its dissolution. This is the source of the modern divorce by "irreconcilable differences."

Abortion was legal until the first century C.E., and when it was declared a crime, it was because the act affected the property of the father of the fetus—a typical Roman viewpoint. Infanticide by exposure also continued, but no one knows how common it may have been or whether it favored the male over the female child, as is frequently assumed. A large proportion of slaves and prostitutes originated as girl babies picked up "from the trash heap," as the Roman saying went.

Law and Morality Like most peoples, Romans attempted to legislate morality. Rape and female adultery were two of the most serious offenses. Both were punishable by death, though actual prosecutions seem to have been few.

The Romans used the legal term **stuprum** to refer to a wide range of crimes and other behavior that was not illegal but considered undesirable. For example, homosexual acts were not illegal, though many considered them immoral and even depraved. Homosexuality does not appear to have been as widespread in Rome as it had been in Greece, although it was certainly not unusual among the upper classes. We have no way of knowing its true frequency or what the population as a whole thought about it.

Prostitution was also not itself illegal, but it carried with it **infamia,** meaning disrepute and shame for the practitioners. Prostitutes were expected to register with the local authorities, and they paid heavy taxes on their earnings. Nevertheless, they were not criminals but were simply engaged in business and were so treated. Brothel keeping in

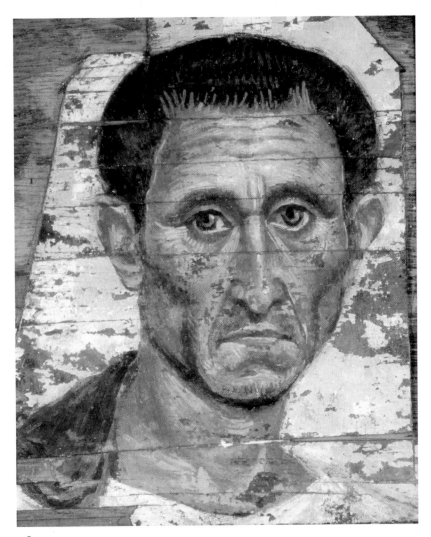

 Roman Portrait. This extraordinary painting was found in Egypt, and probably dates from the early second century C.E. Such lifelike representation was unusual in painting particularly. It was also unusual to paint on wood, as here. *(© The Bridgeman Art Library)*

Roman times, as earlier and later, was one of the more dependable sources of wealth for the (generally female) proprietors. The girls were mostly slave born, but some were free, and some were even married. Dress and hairdos indicated their profession: showy and revealing togas were their trademark. (In Roman times, only men wore the toga in respectable circles; women dressed in a long robe or cloak.)

Female Trades   Women worked in all trades not requiring the heaviest labor. Textile trades were still the most common occupation for women of all classes, slave and free. Midwives, many physicians, scribes, and secretaries were female. Wet nurses were always in heavy demand. Normally, they were country dwellers who cared for the children of urban mothers, either on a live-in basis or by taking the infant to the farm for a year or two. Personal servants, hairdressers, nannies, and masseuses (a Roman passion) were always women.

Entertainers of all sorts—acrobats, clowns, actresses, musicians, dancers—were in high demand. They were often female and frequently combined their stage talents with a bit of prostitution on the side. The tradition that female *artistes* are sexually available continues in Mediterranean folklore to the present day.

Children and Education

We know a bit about Roman attitudes toward young children in the educated class, but not much otherwise. First and foremost, the male child was important as the continuer of the *familia,* and much attention was devoted to his education, sometimes at a school, more often by a live-in tutor. Strict demands for achievement were placed on him oman education aimed at implanting a certain character; its emphasis was on moral rather than intellectual training. Obedience, truthfulness, reverence for the Roman deities, and self-reliance were chief goals; above all, respect for the law and for sacred tradition was emphasized. Much was learned from constant association with parents; children sat with their elders at meals in the family home.

Until about age seven, boys and girls were taught by their mothers in correct language expression and elementary reading and writing. At seven a boy from an educated family went off to a tutor or a school, whereas a girl remained at home. From her female elders she learned to spin, weave, and sew. Reputedly, Augustus Caesar's wife Livia made most of the emperor's clothes herself.

A boy of good family was given a *paedagogus*, a slave, usually Greek, who was given charge of the boy's life as adviser, guardian, and general overseer. Some even had the right to punish their charges. His duties ended only after the boy had put on the toga of an adult male, usually at age fourteen. Many *paedagogi* stayed friends and advisers to their boys until long afterwards, much like an old nanny would. The satirist Martial tells of a *paedogogus* who scolded his former charge after he was a grown man and senator.

✿ **Girl Reading.** This tender rendition of a young girl daydreaming over her studies is marked by a sentiment not often encountered in Roman painting. (© *Werner Forman Archive, Museo Archeologico Nazionale, Naples, Italy/Art Resource*)

from the earliest years. The *patria potestas* was applied here to enforce obedience and learning. External display of affection between adult and child was apparently very rare. In this, the Romans were quite different from the Chinese, say, who were not adverse to a show of sentiment.

As in classical Greece, which served as the model in so many ways, the education of males revolved around future public service. Learning was acquired for a communal purpose: to advance the welfare of the state (in the Roman case) or the *polis* (in Greece). Therefore, the most important subjects to master were law and the principles of government. All men of affairs also needed rhetoric and philosophy. Science and the fine arts were secondary. They were viewed as personal matters, possibly important to the individual but only incidental to the community.

The segregation of the sexes that was so marked in classical Greece was largely overcome in Roman theory and, to some extent, in practice. Roman females continued to be educated along domestic housekeeping lines, but they gradually received increased freedom to enter the "great world" of male concerns. They could do this through advanced studies and larger political responsibilities. Hence, by the second century C.E., it was no longer absurd for a middle-class Roman girl to study mathematics or philosophy or to become an instructor in one of the arts—all careers that had been closed even to upper-class Greek females.

𝒮UMMARY

Between the Classical Age of Greece and the dissolution of the Roman empire 800 years later, a marked evolution of social structure took place. One aspect of this change was the trend toward urban life with its accompanying dislocations and psychic strains on the population at large. Another was the greater prominence of merchants, traders, businessmen, and professionals. Peasants and laborers who still constituted by far the largest segment of the population began to recede into the background. Slaves became more common but were treated considerably worse than earlier. Free individuals were under economic pressures that were hard to resist. By the end of the Roman imperial period in the West, the beginnings of hereditary serfdom were clearly visible.

The status of the female generally improved from its earlier low point in classical Athens. Women gained some freedoms in arranging their own social and economic fates, though men still controlled every important aspect of public life. The male also controlled his female dependents in a legal sense, and this was particularly true of the Roman father. Greek misogyny was remedied to some extent, however, by the Romans' sensitivity to the value of the female as property. Changing sociocultural attitudes in the late empire reflected the changing political and cultural realities of a declining empire.

Test Your Knowledge

1. Educated Greeks generally believed that manual labor
   a. should be engaged in as a healthy remedy for too much thinking.
   b. was fit only for the unfortunate and slaves.
   c. was an absolute necessity for proper living.
   d. was something that only the Spartans could do well.
2. Slavery after about 100 B.C.E. was usually
   a. harsher and more common than had been the case earlier.
   b. a temporary condition that was easily passed through.
   c. a punishment reserved for serious crimes against the state.
   d. reserved for non-Italians.
3. For both Greek and Roman societies, the most dangerous slaves were those made to work
   a. in the plantations.
   b. in the mines.
   c. in metalworking plants.
   d. in the army.
4. The condition of women in classical Greece is best summed up by saying
   a. they had equality with males of the same social status.
   b. they had few rights or duties outside the home.
   c. they often held leading positions in the *polis*.
   d. they were never allowed to leave the house.
5. As a generalization, upper-class women of the Hellenistic Age
   a. were invisible figures in the background of public affairs.
   b. had less prestige than women had enjoyed in Hellenic times in Greece.
   c. were almost all concubines and rarely married.
   d. were able to gain a considerable measure of public prestige.
6. The *patria potestas* of Roman law was
   a. the power to produce legitimate children.
   b. the right to be accepted as a Roman citizen.
   c. the power of a father to do what he chose with his family.
   d. the power of the law to define who was the father of a child.
7. For Roman women, divorce was
   a. as easily obtained as for men.
   b. an absolute impossibility because of *patria potestas*.
   c. granted only for cases of homosexuality in the husband.
   d. difficult but obtainable on a few grounds.
8. Which of these combinations of subjects would be considered most appropriate for educating a Roman boy of good family?
   a. Rhetoric and law
   b. Law and mathematics
   c. Natural science and mathematics
   d. Law and fine arts

Identification Terms

infamia

manus

patria potestas

stuprum

sui juris

InfoTrac College Edition

Enter the search terms "Rome history" using Key Words.
Enter the search terms "Greece history" using Key Words.

Enter the search terms "Roman law" using the Subject Guide.

	Law and Government	**Economy**
Greeks	After the eclipse of the original Greek (Mycenean) civilization and ensuing dark age, the evolution of written law and developed monarchy begins with the reforms of Draco and Solon in the sixth century B.C.E. Although property still outweighs personal rights, there is a noticeable shift towards the latter in lawgiving. Strong differences continue between slave and freemen and between alien and citizen in this wholly patriarchal society. Mass political activity within the framework of the polis is stimulated by the democratic reforms of the fifth century in Athens. Sparta emerges as the opposite pole, and the ensuing Peloponnesian War leads to the "barbarian" Macedonian takeover. The polis ideals gradually die out under alien rule, first under Hellenistic monarchies, then under the conquering Romans.	Small farms, home crafts, and maritime trade were at all times the backbone of the Classical Age economy. The absence of large fertile areas restrict the emergence of plantations and estates. Overpopulation becomes a major problem by the 600s but is solved by large-scale emigration and the establishment of colonies around the Mediterranean. Trade, both maritime and overland, becomes critical to the maintenance of home country prosperity. In the Hellenistic period (after 300 B.C.E.), large numbers of Greeks emigrate to the East as favored citizens. Massive urban development in the Hellenistic monarchies creates a new, socioeconomically stratified society. Slavery becomes commonplace, as does large-scale manufacturing and estate agriculture. Under Roman rule, the Greek homeland diminishes steadily in economic importance and becomes largely impoverished.
Romans	Evolution of Roman law and government forms particularly marked over this millennium. Beginning with usual class-based justice and oral law, Roman republic produces written codes by fifth century B.C.E. and eventual balance of noble-commoner powers. The Punic Wars and resultant imperial outreach corrupt this balance, however, and bring about social problems that cannot be solved peacefully. Augustus's administrative reforms answer most pressing needs for civic peace and stability for next two centuries, while law continues evolution on basis of equity and precedent until final distillation in *Corpus Juris* of Justinian. The central government's authority sharply weakened in West by transfer to Constantinople and then destroyed by successive Germanic invaders after 370s C.E. Eastern provinces remain secure.	Small peasants were the bulk of the original Roman citizenry, but after the Punic Wars are increasingly overshadowed by hordes of slaves and unfree immigrants from Africa and the eastern Mediterranean. Italy becomes dependent on food imports. Plantations and estates replace farms, while the urban proletariat multiplies. After about 200 C.E., the western provinces lose ground to the richer, more populous East, a process hastened by the Germanic invasions. Socioeconomic reforms of Diocletian and Constantine (295–335 C.E.) do not stop declining productivity of western provinces and resultant vulnerability to invaders.

Religion and Philosophy

Greeks of Classical Age are founders of philosophy as a rational exercise. They also explore most of the questions that have occupied Western philosophy in metaphysics, ethics, and epistemology. Religion is conceived of as a civic duty more than as a path to immortality. Lack of fear of the gods and of their priestly agents particularly striking. Gods seen as humans writ large, with faults and virtues of same. Theology and ethics sharply separated; the educated class turns to philosophy as a guide to ethical action. "Man the measure." After c. second century B.C.E., religion-philosophy divergence ever stronger as masses turn to mystery religions from the East.

Romans adopt notions of the supernatural and immortality from the Etruscans and Greeks, modifying them to fit their own civic religion. "In philosophy, the Roman adaptations of Greek Stoicism and Epicureanism become the most common beliefs of the educated classes. No connections between theology and ethics until advent of mystery religions, including Christianity. Christianity is originally adopted by the government of Constantine to sustain faltering imperial rule in the fourth century, and it soon becomes the equal or even senior partner of the civil regime in the West. The Roman papacy assumes governmental powers for Italy when the empire's attempt to recover under Justinian eventually fails.

Arts and Culture

Classical Age brings brilliant flowering of both literary and plastic arts, giving many models for later Western civilization. Particular mastery of sculpture, architecture, poetry of several formats, drama, and history. In Hellenistic period, Roman overlords generally adopt Greek models for their own literature and sculpture, thus spreading them throughout western Europe. Greeks are patriarchal to point of misogyny in their public and private culture. Large cities dominate the culture of the Hellenistic kingdoms and contribute to the continuing differentiation between rich and poor classes.

Art is of high technical quality but lacks creative imagination in contrast to Greeks and Egyptians. Artists generally content to follow models from abroad in both plastic and literary forms. Exceptions: some minor literary genres, mosaic work, and architecture. Public life not so patriarchal as Greece, but more affected by class divisions. Romans give great respect to tradition while demonstrating considerable flexibility in governance and social organization. Urban life is increasingly the dominant matrix of Roman culture as the empire matures, but gives way in the western half as invasions begin.

Science and Technology

In the Classical Age, Greeks profit from their extensive contacts with Mesopotamia and Egypt. Physical science is generally subordinated to philosophy in the broad sense, of which it is considered a branch. In Hellenistic period, physical sciences are selectively advanced, especially mathematics, physics, and medicine. At all times, little or no interest in technology apparent. Scientific knowledge is pursued for its own sake rather than for possible application.

Roman science depends entirely on Hellenistic predecessors, which entered Italy from the East, particularly Egypt. As with the Classical Greeks, abundance of slaves and other cheap labor argues against any search for labor-saving techniques. The only interest shown in technology is in the construction and engineering fields, which are a massively developed specialty in the empire. The novel use of brick and cement, construction of bridges, forts, aqueducts, hydrology systems, road building, and the like are extensive and sophisticated throughout the provinces as well as in Italy.

Part THREE

Equilibrium Among Polycentric Civilizations

100 B.C.E.–1500 C.E.

Prior to about 500 C.E., contacts among the centers of advanced civilized life were limited and tenuous. Usually, they were made through intermediate, less developed societies. Rome, for example, had only the most sparing contacts with China, and they were all indirect. Its contacts with Hindu India were more direct but still very limited. For that matter, India and China had very little contact with one another despite their geographic proximity. Thanks to the mountain walls and the deserts that separated them, few Chinese and still fewer Indians dared that journey.

After 500, however, entirely new centers of civilization emerged, quite detached from the original west Asian and Mediterranean locales. In sub-Saharan Africa, urban life and organized territorial states were emerging by about 800 C.E. Earlier, the Mesoamerican Indians and the Muslims of Asia and northern Africa had achieved a high degree of city-based civilization, the former developing independently of all other models and the latter building on the ancient base in western Asia. As one example of several, commercial relations between Mediterranean Christians and the Hindu/Buddhist regions became closer and more extensive. Both overland and by sea, the Muslims of the eastern fringe of the Mediterranean were the essential mediators between these distant centers and profited from the middleman role.

In the West, the entire thousand-year epoch from 500 to 1500 C.E. carries the title "Middle Age." But this term has no relevance to the rest of the civilized world, of course, and should be avoided when speaking of any culture other than the Christian Europeans. In Europe, the Middle Age began with the gradual collapse of the Roman West under the assaults of the Germanic tribes and ended with the triumph of the new secularism of the Renaissance.

In Asia, this millennium was an era of tremendous vitality and productivity—the South and East Asian Classical Age—which was briefly interrupted by the Mongol conquests of the thirteenth century. But the Mongols were soon assimilated or expelled by their Chinese/Turkic/Persian subjects. At the end of the period in Asia, a reinvigorated Islam extended its conquests in both southern Europe and Africa under the aegis of the Ottoman Turks. In 1500, the Ottoman sultan was in conquered Constantinople, and his armies were menacing the Christian bastion of Vienna. An observer would have been hard put to guess which of the two great contesting religions/polities—Christianity and Islam—would emerge as the determinant of world history in the next century.

In the still isolated America, throughout this period a series of ever more skilled and more populous Indian societies arose in the middle latitudes of the continent and along its western fringe. They were mysteriously (to us) dispersed or overcome by later comers, until the most advanced and skilled of all fell prey to the Spanish conquistadors.

Chapter 14 presents the decline and transformation of Rome and the beginnings of medieval Europe. Chapters 15 and 16 deal with the rise of Islam and its culture. The next several chapters look at the stable and technically advanced South and East Asian societies and the slowly emergent civilizations of the Americas and Africa. The first of this series (Chapter 17) surveys India's flourishing Hindu and Buddhist cultures. The second (Chapter 18) looks at China in the great age of Confucian order and prosperity. Then comes Japan as it evolved from an adjunct of China and Korea into cultural and political sovereignty, along with the early histories of the islands and mainland of southeastern Asia. Sub-Saharan Africa's immense variety is examined in Chapter 20, as parts of the continent emerge into historical light. Chapter 21 surveys the chief actors in the pageant of pre-Columbian America, while Chapter 22 conveys a sense of ordinary lives in the non-Western world. The focus returns to the West in Chapters 23 through 25, as we look at the high medieval age and the decline that followed, through the revival termed the European Renaissance.

Chapter 14

Rome's Transformation and the Beginnings of Europe

They have no fixed abode, no home or law or settled manner of life, but wander.

AMMIANUS MARCELLINUS

c. 6 B.C.E.–29 C.E.	Life of Jesus of Nazareth
284–305 C.E.	Diocletian/Empire divided East and West
313–337 C.E.	Constantine/Christianity tolerated
381 C.E.	Theodosius makes Christianity official religion
late 300s–400s C.E.	Germanic invaders enter western empire
527–565 C.E.	Justinian I/*Corpus juris*
c. 500–800	"Dark Age"/Germanic kingdoms
768–814	Charlemagne/Carolingian renaissance
800s–900s	Rise of feudalism

AFTER MARCUS AURELIUS'S REIGN (ruled 161–180 C.E.), Rome's power and purpose began to decline. Several of the outer provinces were invaded in the mid-200s, and the whole empire was wracked by internal strife that threatened to bring it down entirely. At the beginning of the fourth century came an effort at renewal and realignment based in part on Christianity and absolute monarchy.

Internal Upheavals and Invading Barbarians

After the unfortunate reign (180–193) of the corrupt and incompetent Commodus, son of Marcus Aurelius, the central government fell into the hands of military usurpers for almost a century. Agriculture, which had always provided the livelihood of most Romans, was increasingly dominated by large estates employing unfree labor. Cities declined in size and importance as civil wars among the generals reduced one urban center after another to ashes or strangled its commerce. Some of the provinces were relatively untouched by these conflicts, particularly in the East. This fact reinforced the ever clearer dominance of the eastern half of the empire over the western.

In the half century between 235 and 284, Rome had twenty emperors, eighteen of whom died by violence. This was the Age of the **Barracks Emperors.** An ambitious commander who had the momentary support of a legion or two might attempt to seize power in Rome itself or in one or another of the provinces. Those who had the allegiance of the Italian garrison, the Praetorian Guard, were the most powerful at any given moment, and the guard was easily bought with promises of booty.

Ordinary citizens were not involved in these struggles for raw power, of course, but suffered the effects in many ways. Respect for imperial authority disappeared, the courts of law were overruled by force, and bribery and corruption of officials became commonplace. The long-distance trade that had sustained much of Roman prosperity was badly disrupted.

It was Rome's bad luck that the Barracks Emperors coincided with the first really serious challenges from the barbarian tribes beyond its borders. In the later third century, the great Wandering of the Peoples from Asia and eastern Europe reached the outer provinces from the Low Countries all the way to the Balkans. When these tribal peoples reached the river frontiers (the Rhine and the Danube), they found large gaps in the defenses, caused by the army's dissolution into a series of quasi-private forces. Sometimes peaceably and sometimes by force, the newcomers crossed into the civilized areas in groups both small and large.

Almost miraculously, the last few general-emperors in the 270s were able to beat off the barbarian attacks and manipulate the various tribes and nations into fighting one another more than the Romans. Rome gained breathing space that was utilized by the last of the Barracks Emperors, Diocletian, to reorganize the badly wounded system.

Restructuring of the Empire

Under Diocletian (ruled 284–305), a capable general who had fought his way to supreme power, the fiction created by Augustus Caesar that he was merely first among equals was finally buried. From now on, the emperor was clearly the absolute ruler of a subservient *Senatus et populus.* His bureaucrats were his instrument to effect his will, rather than agents of the Roman people. Diocletian brooked no opposition, not because he was a tyrant, but because he saw that if the empire was to survive, something new must be tried immediately.

To make the huge empire more governable, Diocletian divided it into western and eastern halves and underlined the dominance of the East by taking that half for his personal domain (see Map 14.1). The other he gave to a trusted associate to rule from Rome as his deputy. Each of the two

Trajan's Column. The Roman army was thoroughly trained and equipped in accord with precise regulations issued by the central government. The soldiers' discipline in battle usually won the day against most foes. Here the campaign of the second-century C.E. emperor Trajan that brought Rome the province of Dacia (Romania) is memorialized. (© *Scala/Art Resource*)

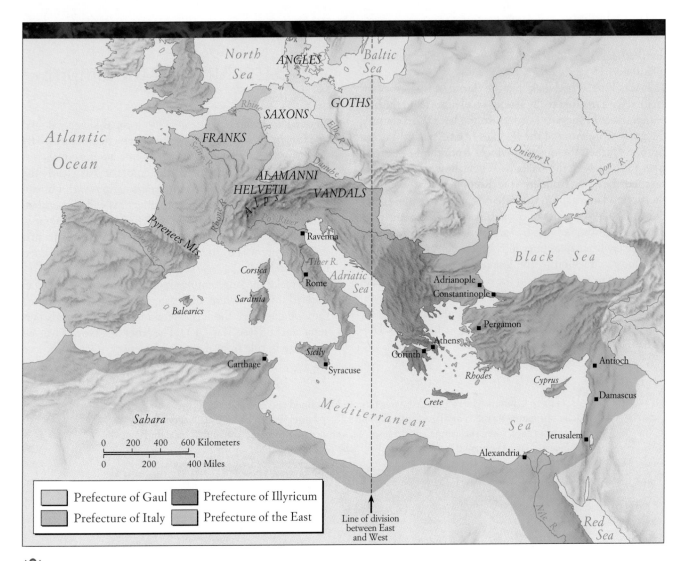

MAP 14.1 The Later Roman Empire. Note the outlines of the four subdivisions of the empire after Diocletian, whose reign ended in 305 C.E. Though the West had more area, the East had much greater population. The total at this era has been estimated at about sixty million, actually a decline from the second century's total of about sixty-five million.

coemperors appointed an assistant, who was to follow him in office. This system, called the **Tetrarchy** (rule of four), was supposed to end the civil wars. It failed as soon as Diocletian retired (305 C.E.), but the political reorganization of the empire into two halves remained.

Diocletian also attempted to revive the economy by lowering inflation, which had been rampant since the early Barracks Emperors. He issued the first governmental "price ceilings" on consumer goods in Western history (which failed, of course). He attempted to restore the badly damaged faith in the value of Roman coinage, whose gold and silver contents had been steadily and surreptitiously reduced. He also increased the tax burden and insisted that the tax collectors were personally responsible for making up any arrearages in their districts. The net result was to make taxes more hated than ever and the tax collectors' posts almost unfillable.

Constantine the Great (ruled 313–337), Diocletian's successor to supreme power after an eight-year civil war, generally continued these policies and increased the restrictions on personal freedoms that the central government was steadily imposing. The measures were aimed especially at the free peasants, who were being forced into debt by big landlords, and often ran away or sold themselves into slavery or were otherwise lost to the tax collector.

In the 330s Constantine took the long expected step of formally transferring the government to the East. Perched on the shore of the strait between Europe and Asia in a highly strategic location, the new capital city of Byzantium was well defensible from both land and sea. In time, the city of Constantine (Constantinople in Greek) became the largest city in the Christian world. Greek was the dominant language in the new capital, and Greeks were the dominant cultural force from the beginning.

What happened to the old Rome in the West? Although the deputy emperor maintained his government there for another century and one half, that city was in steady decline. It was ravaged by two Vandal raids that left parts of it in permanent ruin. Finally, in 476, a German chieftain pushed aside the insignificant deputy of Constantinople and crowned himself, an event conventionally taken as the end of the Roman empire in the West.

Christianity

While the Roman empire weakened and crumbled, a new force—Christianity—developed within it. **Jesus** of Nazareth (c. 6 B.C.E.–29 C.E.), whom about one-third of the world's population assert to be the Son of God and Redeemer of Mankind, was born during the reign of Augustus Caesar, about a generation after Pompey had incorporated Judaea into the growing Roman empire. We summarize his life and influence in the Religion and Morality box.

During the last century B.C.E., the Hellenistic mystery religions (see Chapter 10) had become widely popular. Egyptian, Persian, Greek, and Italian cults promising power and immortality appealed to the lower ranks of a population that was steadily being divided into economic haves and have-nots. The Jews were not immune to this appeal and subdivided into several factions that held different views of the deliverer—the messiah promised to them long ago (see Chapter 4). None of these factions were receptive to the pacifist and provocative message of love and forgiveness that Jesus preached between 26 and 29 C.E. To the Sadducees and Pharisees, Jesus' admonition to stop confusing the letter of the law with its spirit was an attempt to seduce the Jews, who had survived and remained a distinct nation only because of their unbending adherence to their Mosaic laws. Zealots wished to fight the Romans and had no empathy with a prophet who asked them to "render unto Caesar the things that are Caesar's"—that is, to accept the legitimate demands of their Roman overlords.

Meanwhile, the Roman administrators must have regarded Jesus as a special irritant among an already difficult, religiously obsessed people. The Jews' religious doctrines were of no concern to the Romans, but Jesus' challenges to the traditionalist rabbis did create difficulties in governing. In the most literal sense, Jesus was "stirring things up." As a result, when the Jewish leaders demanded that the Roman procurator, Pontius Pilate, allow them to punish this disturber of the peace, he reluctantly agreed, and Jesus was crucified on Golgotha near Jerusalem.

For a couple of decades thereafter, the Christian cult spread slowly in Judaea and was nearly unknown outside it. This situation changed as a result of two developments. First, the educated Jew, Saul of Tarsus (c. 6–67 C.E.), a Roman citizen and sophisticate, was miraculously converted

The Walls of Constantinople. After the move from Rome, the government devoted much money and energy to making the new capital impregnable from both sea and land. On the land side, a series of gigantic walls were erected, which protected Constantinople from all attacks until 1453. *(© Scala/Art Resource)*

to Christianity on the road to Damascus. As the apostle Paul, he insisted on preaching to the Gentiles (non-Jews). Second, the fanatical element among the Jews rebelled against the Roman overlords in the **Jewish War** (67–71 C.E.) After the Romans crushed it, they decided to punish this troublesome people by dispersing them in what came to be known as the **Diaspora** (actually, the second Diaspora: see Chapter 4). One result of this forced eviction from Judaea was the establishment of Jewish exile colonies that became breeding grounds for Christianity throughout the eastern Mediterranean basin and soon in Italy itself. Spurred by the strenuous efforts of the apostle Paul, the Christian doctrine was spreading steadily, if not spectacularly, among both ex-Jews and Gentiles by the end of the first century.

The Appeal of Christianity

What was the appeal of the new religion? First, it distinguished itself from all the other mystery religions by its *universality*. All persons were eligible: men and women, Jew and Gentile, rich and poor, Roman and non-Roman. Second, Christianity offered a message of *hope and optimism* in a Hellenistic cultural world that appeared increasingly grim to the aspirations of ordinary people. Not only were believers promised a blessed life to come, but the prospects for a better life on this earth also appeared to be

Jesus of Nazareth
(C. 6 B.C.E.–C. 29 C.E.)

The life and works of Jesus have affected more people more directly than any other individual in world history. With over two billion formal adherents, Christianity is the world's most widespread faith. As with most other religions, its founder's life is known only in sketchy outline.

In the centuries of Hellenistic civilization, several religions arose in the eastern Mediterranean that shared certain fundamental features. They insisted that there was a better life to come after the earthly existence and that some individuals had the potential to share in that life. They also maintained that it was necessary to follow the teaching of a mythic hero-prophet in order to realize that potential. These were the "mystery" religions, whose appeal depended on an act of faith by the believer, rather than attendance at a priestly ceremony.

Christianity was by far the most important of the mystery religions. Its founder was not a mythic hero such as the Egyptian Osiris or the Greek Cybele, but a real historical person, Jesus of Nazareth, later called by his followers the *Christos*, or Messiah. Jesus was born in the newly romanized province of Judaea, the former Kingdom of Judah and home of the two tribes of Israel that had stayed true to the Mosaic Law.

Of Jesus' early life until he entered on his preaching career about age thirty, we know next to nothing. The Christian disciples who wrote the books of the New Testament did not think it relevant to Jesus' work to tell us of his youth, or the intellectual context in which he grew up.

It is reasonably sure that Jesus was born to a woman and a man—Mary and Joseph—who were quite ordinary, practicing Jews. Their status was undistinguished prior to the miraculous selection of the young virgin Mary as the mother of the Messiah. For many years thereafter, the family (Jesus may have had at least one half-brother, the apostle James) led an obscure life in the region of Galilee, probably in the town of Nazareth.

Around 26 C.E. Jesus was introduced into the teachings of John the Baptist, one of the numerous wandering sages of the day. In that same year, Pontius Pilate was appointed governor of Judaea. He was an average official, mainly concerned with making money out of his position and keeping the subject population sufficiently quiet so as not to create difficulties for his reputation back in Rome.

During the next few years, a group of lower-class Jews attached themselves to Jesus, seeing in him truly the Son of God and the long-awaited Messiah, as he claimed to be. Most of the time, Jesus followed the precepts of Jewish law and tradition quite closely, and he repeatedly said that he did not intend to found a new religion. But his bold insistence on the spirit, rather than the letter of the law, and his flat statement that though he was the Messiah, his kingdom was not of this world, cast him in a dubious light among the rabbis. Before long, his message of faith in God, hope in his mercy, and love of one's fellow man was being seen by the high as potentially revolutionary. They carried their complaints to Pontius Pilate and induced him to let them crucify Christ as an enemy of Roman rule as well as the Mosaic Law.

The Sermon on the Mount gives us the most coherent and concise overview of Jesus' message. It is a message of tolerance, justice, and humility, of turning the other cheek and keeping the peace. Jesus thus differentiated himself and his doctrines from all other mystery religions, in which the prospect of eventually triumphing over enemies and reveling in the "good things" of the world was a major motivation for keeping the faith. Already by the Resurrection three days after his crucifixion, the small cadre of believers in Christ the Messiah felt they were the possessors of a sacred truth. Led by the apostles, they prepared to carry out their heavy responsibility to "make smooth the path of the Lord" on earth.

Christ and the Fishers of Souls. This Ravenna, Italy, mosaic dating from the sixth century shows Christ calling to his disciples Peter and Andrew, and telling them that from henceforth they would be "fishers of souls." Fishing was indeed a common mode of making a living in the Near East, both in fresh and saltwaters. The mosaic was done, like many others, while Ravenna was the capital of the Byzantine government's attempt to regain Italy for the emperor. *(e.t.archive)*

For Reflection

Why do you think the Bible has nothing to say of the early years of Jesus? Is this unusual in the lives of the founders of the various world religions? What is meant by the spirit rather than the letter of the law being the crucial thing? How does the Sermon on the Mount exemplify the spirit of early Christianity?

good. The Second Coming of the Lord and its accompanying Last Judgment, when the just would be rewarded and the evil punished according to their deserts, were thought to be not far off. Third, Christians were far ahead of their rivals in the *spirit of mutuality* that marked the early converts. To be a Christian was to accept an active obligation to assist your fellows in any way you might. It also meant you could count on their help and prayers when needed. Lastly, Christianity featured an *appeal to idealism* that was much more powerful than anything its rivals offered. It emphasized charity and unselfish devotion in a way that had strong appeal to people weary of a world that seemed to be dominated by the drive for wealth and power.

The Gospels ("good news") of the four evangelists Mark, Luke, Matthew, and John were the original doctrinal foundations of the faith. They were written and collected in the late first century C.E., along with the letters of St. Paul to the communities of Christians he had founded in the eastern Mediterranean. By the second century, a written New Testament had appeared that was accepted by all Christians and largely superseded the Old Testament of the Jews in their eyes.

Christianity's Spread and Official Adoption

Slowly, Christian cells sprang up in the major towns all over the Mediterranean basin. The story of Peter the Apostle coming to Rome shortly after the death of Christ may well be factual. Certainly, several disciples, spurred on by Paul, left the strictly Jewish environment in which the religion had begun and "went out into the world" of Roman pagan culture. Paul himself is thought to have died a martyr in Rome under the emperor Nero.

By the early fourth century, it has been estimated that about 10 percent of the population of the East had become Christian and perhaps 5 percent of the West. In this situation, the emperor Constantine (whose mother Helena was a Christian) decided to end the persecution of Christians that had been going on at intervals since Nero's time. In 313 he issued the *Edict of Milan,* which announced the official toleration of Christianity and signaled that the new religion was favored at the imperial court. Constantine himself seemingly became a Christian only on his deathbed in 337, but from this time on, all emperors in East and West, with the exception of Julian (361–363), were Christians. In 381, the emperor Theodosius took the final step of making Christianity the official religion of the empire.

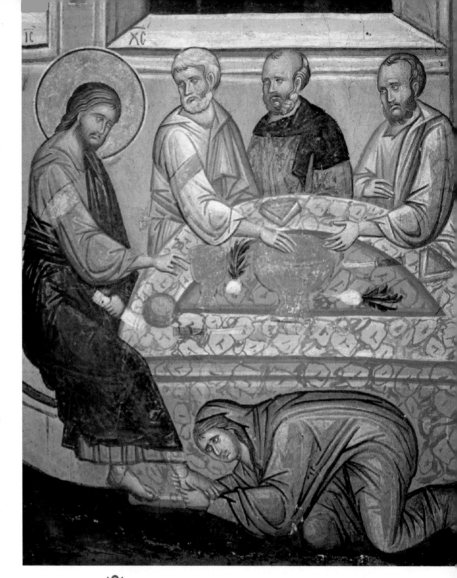

Christ in Bethania. This masterpiece of late Byzantine art shows Christ with his disciples at Bethany. It is a fresco in the Ascension church at Decani, in southern Serbia, painted in the mid-fourteenth century by an anonymous group of Greek and Serbian artists who had been trained in Byzantine technique. Note the use of curvature to focus the viewer's attention on the prostrate figure at the bottom. (*AKG London*)

Constantine's Motives   Why did the suspicious and warlike Constantine decide to stake his own fate, and possibly the fate of the empire, on a new religion that had distinguished itself by its pacifism and its rejection of the traditional Roman state cult? As the story has it, Constantine became convinced that the Christian God had aided him in a crucial battle during the civil war, but historians suspect that something more was behind such a momentous decision. Probably, he expected this move would assist him in shoring up a wounded political system by gradually creating a new unity between governors and governed. Certainly, too, he recognized the growing support that Christianity was attracting among those who counted in Roman society.

Constantine's recognition would both aid and hinder the new religion. Giving Christianity a favored status, and putting the resources of the secular government behind it spurred its growth. Soon Christians were a majority in the cities. (The countryside appears to have been much slower to adopt the new creed.) At the same time, Constantine's decision ensured that the Christian church would be linked with the state and the wishes of the state's governors. Church councils would soon find that civil questions would sometimes override purely religious considerations.

Early Church Organization and Doctrine

Under Constantine, Christians came out into the open and organized their church on Roman civil models. In each community of any size, bishops were elected as heads of a diocese. They in turn appointed priests on the recommendation of the local faithful. The early Christian emperors made the fateful decision to allow the bishops to create their own courts and laws (canon law) for judging the clergy and administering church property—a decision that later led to great friction between revenue seeking kings and wealthy bishops.

Several bishops of important eastern dioceses such as Jerusalem, Antioch, and Alexandria claimed direct office-holding descent from the twelve apostles of Jesus and therefore possessed special prestige and the title of *patriarch.* But the bishop of Rome claimed to be first among equals through the doctrine of *Petrine Succession.* According to this concept, the bishop of Rome was the direct successor of Peter, the first bishop of Rome, whom Christ had pronounced the "rock (*petros*) upon which I build my church." He therefore succeeded Peter as the preeminent leader of the church. This claim was resisted by the patriarchs and other bishops until a pope was able to get it acknowledged by a church council in the sixth century.

The early church experienced many serious disputes in theology, as well. Heated argument about the nature of Christ, the relation between members of the Holy Trinity, the nature of the Holy Spirit, and similar topics broke out repeatedly, especially in the East where the majority of Christians lived. Some segments of Christian believers went their own ways when they could not find majority support. The Copts of Egypt, the Nestorians, and Ethiopian churches are examples. They are not "in communion with Rome" and define their own theology.

The efforts to settle such disputes led to two long-term developments: (1) the council of bishops became the supreme arbiter in matters of faith, and (2) the civil and religious authorities established a close and permanent relationship.

The first council was the **Council of Nicaea,** in Turkey, which was held in 325 during the reign of Constantine. More than 300 bishops attended and defined many impor-

tant questions of theology and church administration. Some of the decisions of the council were implemented by the secular government, thus bringing the second new principle into play. From this time onward, the Roman emperors in East and West saw themselves as possessing executive powers within the Christian community—a development that led to conflict when the emperor and bishops had differing opinions on the civic implications of theological issues.

After the Edict of Milan, many educated Romans still could not bring themselves to adopt the new faith, which they regarded as a mixture of base superstition and a sort of cannibalism (the Eucharist). The challenges that paganism presented to Christianity contributed to the rise of a school of Christian explainers of sacred doctrine, or *apologists,* in the 300s. The most important of these *Fathers of the Church,* as they are called, were **Augustine** and Ambrose, the bishops of Hippo (North Africa) and Milan, respectively. Their writings are the secondary foundation of the Christian faith, as the Gospels are the primary one. St. Augustine has been especially influential in molding belief. His *Confessions* and *The City of God* have been the most important repositories of Christian teaching after the Gospels themselves.

By the early fifth century, the Christian faith was giving the tottering Roman empire a new cast of thought and a system of morality and ethics that challenged the old beliefs in myriad ways. After Theodosius's reign (378–395), the imperial government was a Christian entity, so Christians could actively support it and perhaps even defend it against its external enemies. But if this worldly empire fell, it was no tragedy. It was only the otherworldly kingdom of the Lord that should count in man's eyes. By thus shifting the focus to the next world, Christian doctrine made it easier to accept the sometimes painful ending of the western Roman empire that was occurring at the hands of Germanic warriors.

Only slowly did many Christians acquiesce to the idea of blending Christian and pagan worldviews and realize that there was something to be learned from the Roman secular environment while they awaited the Last Judgment. By the time they had arrived at this realization, however, much of that secular world had already been hammered to pieces.

Germanic Invaders

❁

What we know of the very early Germanic invaders derives entirely from Roman sources, for they left no writings of their own and, in fact, had no written language until they learned Latin from the Romans. They spent much time fighting one another, and the Romans encouraged this to keep the Germans weak. But once they learned to band together, the outer defenses of the Roman empire came under frequent attack from a fierce and determined foe.

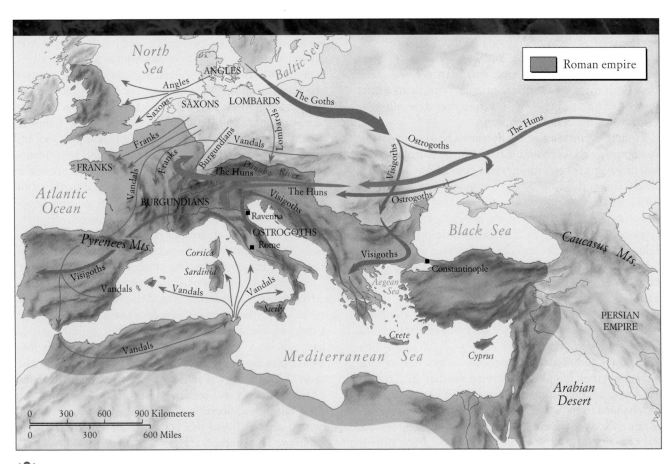

❀ **MAP 14.2   Barbarian Migrations in the Fourth and Fifth Centuries C.E.** This map shows the movements of the major Germanic and Asiatic invaders of Rome's empire.

After the capital was moved to Constantinople, the western provinces were gradually sacrificed to the Germans, who by this time were being pushed from behind by various Asiatic peoples. The invasion of the Huns, an Asiatic nomadic people who suddenly appeared in the 440s and pillaged their way through Italy, confirmed the Romans' decision to more or less abandon the West (see Map 14.2). The Huns dispersed after the death of their warrior leader, Attila, but the vulnerability of the West had been demonstrated, whereas the East was still intact. With the survival of the imperial government at stake, the center of the empire's gravity shifted decisively to the east.

In the fourth and fifth centuries, the Germanic tribes roamed through the western provinces more or less at will (see Map 14.2). Replacing the demoralized Roman officials with their own men, the war chiefs began to create rough-and-ready kingdoms:

1. The *Franks* established the core of the French kingdom in the fifth century.
2. The *Saxons* set up a kingdom in northern Germany from present-day Holland eastward.
3. The *Angles* and *Saxons* invaded and conquered England in the fifth century.

4. The *Vandals* invaded Roman North Africa, established a kingdom there, and from it made the raid on Rome itself (455), which gave their name to history.
5. The *West Goths* (*Visigoths*) took over Spain.
6. The *East Goths* (*Ostrogoths*) took over most of Italy itself.

By the 500s, the western half of the empire was an administrative and sometimes also a physical ruin. Germanic nobles had generally supplanted Italian or romanized officials as the authorities. Small-scale wars, piracy, and general insecurity were the rule. Under such conditions Roman traditions and the Roman lifestyle gradually disappeared except in a handful of cities and larger towns. Even there, trade and manufacturing dwindled, as the population supporting them shrank.

Germanic Customs and Society

❀

It would take centuries for the two cultures—Roman and Germanic—to blend together to form the new culture that we call medieval. The Germans were at first starkly differentiated from their subjects. Most of them wanted to be "Roman," as they understood that term. They certainly did not hate or despise the Roman population or think themselves culturally superior. Intermarriage was practiced from the start. But they brought with them a large number of habits, beliefs, and values that were not at all like those of the conquered.

From the comments of the Romans who observed them, we know that the Germans had a highly personalized concept of government. Authority was exercised by an elected leader. He received the sworn loyalty of his warriors, but the leader's authority only applied in time of war. In peacetime, the Germans remained essentially large families led by the oldest male, each of whom was a little king in his own right. If the war leader was defeated or the warriors were dissatisfied with his leadership, he could be deposed. There was no hierarchy below the chief and apparently no permanent offices of any sort.

Before entering the Roman empire, most of the tribes had led a seminomadic existence, and they at first had little appreciation of town life. For many years, the new Germanic kings had no fixed residences but traveled continuously about their kingdoms "showing the flag" of authority and acting as chief justices to resolve disputes. Gradually, this changed to the extent that the king had a favorite castle or a walled town named for him where he might stay for part of each year.

Very slowly also, the idea made headway that the subject paid tribute and gave loyalty to the *office* of king, rather than to the individual holder of the crown. This last development resulted from Roman influence, and its contribution to peaceable transfer of power and stable government was so clear that all the tribal leaders sooner or later adopted it. The church authorities helped in this by preaching that the crown itself was a sacred object and that its holder was a sacred person, ordained by an all-wise God to exercise civil powers over others.

Conversion to Christianity

The Germans had strong supernatural beliefs when they entered the Roman empire, but we do not know much about their religion because it was rooted out thoroughly in the Christian era. Originally, the Germans were animists, who saw spiritual powers in certain natural objects, such as trees. Their chief gods were sky deities, such as Wotan and Thor, who had no connections with either an afterlife or ethical conduct but served as enforcers of the will of the tribe. The Germans had no priests, no temples, and little, if any, theology.

The various tribes within the old Roman empire converted to Christianity between about 450 and 700. Those beyond the empire's borders converted somewhat later. Last of all were the Scandinavians, some of whom remained pagans as late as 1100.

The method of conversion was similar in all cases. A small group of priests, perhaps headed by a bishop, secured an invitation to go to the king and explain to him the Christian gospel. If they were fortunate (rarely!), conversion of the king, his queen, or important nobles was achieved on the first try. After conversion and baptism (the outward sign of joining the Christian world), the new Christian would exert pressure on family and cronies to join also, and they, in turn, would exhort their vassals and dependents. When much of the upper class was converted at least in name, and some native priests were in place, the tribe or nation was considered Christian, a part of the growing family of ex-pagans who had adopted the new religion.

Why did the Germans accept Christianity? Their reasons were almost always a combination of internal politics, desire for trade, and recognition of the advantages that Christian law could give the ruler in his efforts to create a stable dynasty. It generally took decades for the faith to filter down to the common people, even in a formal sense. Centuries might pass before the villagers could be said to have much knowledge of church doctrine and before they would give up their most cherished pagan customs. Medieval Christianity was in fact a hodgepodge of pagan and Christian images and beliefs. Most priests were satisfied if their faithful achieved a very limited understanding of heaven and hell and the coming Last Judgment. More could not be expected.

Germanic Law

Germanic law was very different from Roman law and much more primitive. It derived from custom, which was unwritten and allowed for no fine points of interpretation. Law was the collective memory of the tribe or clan as to what had been done before in similar circumstances. It did not inquire into motivation but looked simply at the result.

The Germans used trial by fire and by water to determine guilt in criminal cases in which the evidence was not clear-cut. In some capital cases in which the two parties were of equal rank, they sometimes reverted to the extreme measure of trial by combat to get a verdict. As in ancient Mesopotamia, the object of a trial was to ascertain whether damage had been done to an individual and, if so, how much compensation the victim was owed by the perpetrator. As in Hammurabi's Code, the court, which was the general meeting of the elders of the clan or village, acted as a detached referee between the opposing parties.

The ultimate object of Germanic law was preventing or diminishing personal violence, which endangered the whole tribe's welfare. The guilty party, as determined by the assembly, was punished by the imposition of a money fine, or **wergeld,** which was paid to the victim as compensation. In this way, the blood feuds that would have wrecked the tribe's ability to survive were avoided and the honor of the victim maintained.

Female Status

The status of women in pre-Christian Germanic society is a subject of much debate. According to some Roman sources, women who were married had very considerable freedom and rights, more so than Roman matrons did. Although it was a warrior society, an extraordinary amount of attention seems to have been paid to the rights of mothers and wives, in both the legal and the social senses. The legal value (*wergeld*) of women of childbearing age was much higher than that of women who were too young or too old to have children. This reflects the view we have found in other ancient societies that women's chief asset was their ability to perpetuate the male family's name and honor. In some cases, the widows of prominent men succeeded to their husband's position, a phenomenon the Romans found remarkable. After the Germans became Christian, there are many instances of queens and princesses exercising governmental power. The exercise of managerial powers by noble women was routine in their husband's death or absence.

The Romans admired the Germans' sexual morality (though admittedly not to the point of adopting it themselves). Rape was a capital crime when committed against equals, as was adultery by a woman. Both concubinage and prostitution seem to have been unknown.

Beginnings of Feudalism

In the countryside, a process that had begun during the later empire accelerated dramatically. This was the establishment of large estates or **manors,** which were almost entirely self-sufficient and self-governing. The manor normally began as a *villa,* the country hideaway of a wealthy Roman official in quieter days. As order broke down and the province could ignore the central government, some of these officials became the equivalent of Chinese warlords, maintaining private armies to secure the peace in their own localities. Frequently extorting services and free labor from the villagers nearby, they evaded the central government's controls and taxes. These men grew ever more wealthy and powerful and began to acquire the peasants' lands through bribery, intimidation, and in trade for the protection they offered.

When the invasions began, these strongmen simply took over the basic elements of government altogether. In return for physical protection and some assurance of order in their lives, the peasants would often offer part of their land and labor to the "lord" for some period, perhaps life. In this way was born both the later European nobility (or a large part of it) and the feudal system of agricultural estates worked by bound laborers. The serfs of later days were the descendants of these free men and women who were desperately seeking protection in a world of chaos and danger.

As the cities and towns declined, more and more of the population found itself in manorial villages, dependent on

🎗️ **Peasant Labors.** This illustration from the *Tres Riches Heures,* or "Book of Hours," of Jean, Duke of Berry, depicts the month of June. As seen here, men and women worked side by side to reap this duke's hay. (© *The Pierpont Morgan Library/Art Resource*)

and loosely controlled by the Roman or German lord and his small band of armed cronies. Economic life became much simpler, but it was more a daily struggle for survival than a civilized existence. The skills and contacts of Roman days fell into disuse, for there was little demand for them in this rough and sometimes brutal world. Trade in all but the barest necessities over the shortest distances became rare. Neither the roads nor the waters of western Europe were safe from marauders and pirates, and the Roman transport network fell to pieces.

The Dark Age

So backward did much of society become that it was once usual to refer to the centuries between 500 and 800 as the

"Dark Age" in Europe. This name refers as much to the lack of documentation as to the ignorance of people living then. Not only have many documents perished through vandalism and neglect, but relatively few records were kept in the first place. Literacy, that foundation stone of all education, declined sharply. Only the clergy had much need of writing, and many of the priests and monks in the seventh and eighth centuries would do well to read or write more than their names. They were almost always illiterate in the official Latin language of the church and knew their church history and doctrines only by hearsay. Many a bishop could not write his sermon.

The immoral conduct of some clergy gave rise to scandal. Church offices were bought and sold like so many

❀ **Conversion of Clovis.** The Frankish king was reputedly the first monarch among the Germans to accept the papal version of Christianity, thus making him into a revered figure throughout later European history. *(© Giraudon/Art Resource)*

pounds of butter in many places. Rome was far away and could be easily ignored in church affairs, as it was in civil ones. Besides, the pope himself in this era was always a Roman nobleman who rarely gave much attention to things spiritual.

In some countries, notably the German lands east of the Rhine, the bishops were more or less forced by the king to take on secular and even military duties as the king's lieutenant. The churchman was very often the only educated person in the area and the only one who had some concept of administration and record keeping. The combination of civil and religious duties was, however, injurious to the latter. The bishop or abbot (the head of a monastery) often devoted more time and energy to his secular affairs than to his spiritual ones. All too frequently, important clergymen bribed their way into their position with the intention of using it as a means of obtaining wealth and/or influence in political matters. Their ecclesiastical duties played little or no role in these considerations. In the circumstances, it is more remarkable that some clergy *were* good and gentle men who tried to follow the rules than that many were not.

Having said all that, it is still true that the Christian church was the only imperial Roman institution that survived the Germanic onslaught more or less intact. The church was changed, usually for the worse, by German custom and concepts, but it did survive as recognizably the same institution that had won the religious allegiance of most Roman citizens in the fourth century. All the education that was available in early medieval Europe was supplied by the church, which also operated whatever charitable and medical institutions existed. When the higher concepts of Roman law were recovered in Europe, it was the church that adopted them first and spread them to secular life.

The *Age of Faith* had opened, and the church's teachings and preachings about the nature of humans and their relations with God were to have tremendous influence on every facet of human affairs, an influence that did not diminish noticeably for about a thousand years.

Charlemagne and the Holy Roman Empire

❀

The greatest of the Germanic kings by far was **Charlemagne** (Charles the Great), king of the Franks (768–800) and the first **Holy Roman Emperor** (800–814). The kingdom of the Franks had been in a favored position since its founder, Clovis, had been the first important German ruler to accept Roman Christianity, in or about 500. Charlemagne became king through the aggressive action of his father, a

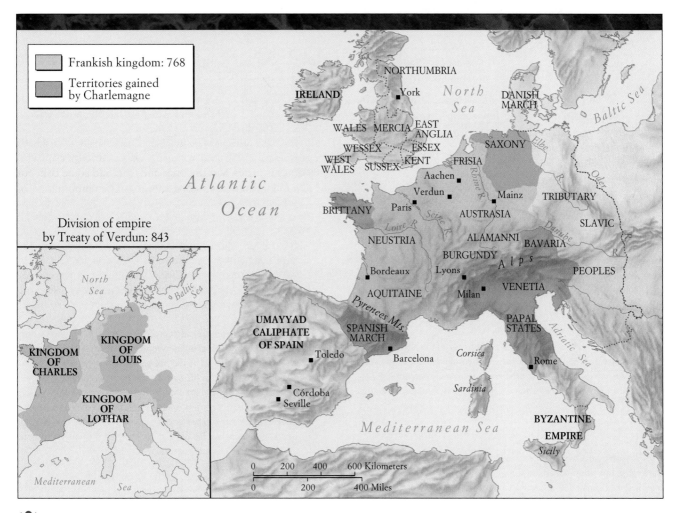

🕸 **MAP 14.3 Charlemagne's Empire.** Charlemagne intended for the territories of the first Holy Roman empire to be divided among his three sons. However, two died before their father, so the entire realm passed to Louis. Louis then repeated his father's plan and divided the empire among three sons: Louis, Lothar, and Charles.

high official who seized royal power. An alliance with the pope in Rome did much to cement the new king's shaky legal position. Charlemagne himself earned the papacy's lasting gratitude by crushing the Lombards, a Germanic people who had settled in northern Italy and were pushing south, threatening Rome.

For thirty years (772–804), Charlemagne was at war with one or another pagan German neighbor. His persistence was rewarded by the establishment of by far the largest territory under one ruler since Roman times and by the granting of the title *emperor* by Pope Leo III. (See Map 14.3.)

Charles's new empire was an attempt to revive the Roman order in Europe, in close cooperation with the Christian church. According to medieval theory, the secular government and the ecclesiastical establishment were two arms of a single body, directed by one head: Christ. Charlemagne's coronation by Leo in the papal city on Christmas Day 800 was looked on as the greatest event since the birth of Christ.

The emperor in Constantinople was not pleased, to put it mildly. But he could do little to hinder or change what was happening in the West. He had his hands quite full with the Muslim attacks at home (see Chapter 15). In fact, it was because of the Byzantine government's inability to defend Rome from the Lombards that the pope had turned to the Franks in the first place.

Carolingian Renaissance

Charlemagne's claims to fame stem more from his brave attempts to restore learning and stable government to Europe than from his position as the first emperor. We know a good deal of his accomplishments as well as his personality from the biography done by Einhard (see the Family Relations box on Charlemagne).

He revived the Roman office of *comes,* or count, as the representative of the king in the provinces. He started the

Charlemagne

The monk Einhard was a German. In the 790s he went to join the school founded by Charlemagne and administered by Alcuin in the Carolingian capital at Aachen. There Einhard came to admire King and Emperor Charles very much and was for many years one of his foremost officials and advisers.

After Charles's death, Einhard found time to write the most famous biography of the Christian Middle Age. He was particularly concerned to give his readers a view of Charles as a human being. The king's strength of character and his love for his children reinforce the image of him as the anointed ruler of his subjects. Very brief and easily read, the *Life of Charlemagne* is our chief source of information about the character of the first Holy Roman emperor.

Chapters 18 and 19: Private Life

At his mother's request he married a daughter of the Lombard king Desiderius but repudiated her for unknown reasons after one year. Then he married Hildegard, who came from a noble Swabian family. With her he had three sons, Charles, Pepin, and Louis, and as many daughters. . . . [H]e had three more daughters with his third wife Fastrada. . . . When Fastrada died he took Liutgard to wife. . . . After her death he had four concubines. . . .

For the education of his children, Charles made the following provisions. . . . [A]s soon as the boys were old enough they had to learn how to ride, hunt, and handle weapons in Frankish style. The girls had to get used to carding wool and to the distaff and spindle. To prevent their getting bored and lazy he gave orders for them to be taught to engage in these and in all other virtuous activities. . . . When his sons and daughter died, Charles reacted to their deaths with much less equanimity than might have been expected of so strongminded a man. Because of his deep devotion to them he broke down in tears. . . . For Charles was by nature a man who had a great gift for friendship, who made friends easily and never wavered in his loyalty to them. Those whom he loved could rely on him absolutely.

He supervised the upbringing of his sons and daughters very carefully. . . . Although the girls were very beautiful and he loved them dearly it is odd that he did not permit any of them to get married, neither to a man of his own nation nor to a foreigner. Rather, he kept all of them with him until his death, saying he could not live without their company. And on account of this, he had to suffer a number of unpleasant experiences, however lucky he was in other respects. But he never let on that he had heard of any suspicions about their chastity or any rumors about them. . . .

Chapter 25: Studies

Charles was a gifted speaker. He spoke fluently and expressed what he had to say with great clarity. Not only was he proficient in his mother tongue (Frankish) but he also took trouble to learn foreign languages. He spoke Latin as well as his own language, but Greek he understood better than he could speak it—He also tried his hand at writing, and to this end kept writing tablets and notebooks under his pillow in bed—But since he had only started late in life, he never became very accomplished in the art.

The Pope Crowns Charlemagne, 800 C.E. Legend states that the pope surprised Charlemagne with the offer of a crown. The Frankish king seems to have been less than impressed with the distinction, as he rarely if ever employed the new title. *(© Giraudon/Art Resource)*

For Reflection

How does Charles's possessiveness toward his daughters make him more believable as a human being? What is the implication of Einhard's statement that Charles "had to suffer a number of unpleasant experiences"?

missi dominici, special officers who checked up on the counts and others and reported directly to the king. Knowing that most people were touched more directly by religion than by government, Charlemagne also concerned himself with the state of the church. Many of his most trusted officials were picked from the clergy, a practice that would lead to problems in later days.

Charles admired learning, although he had little himself (supposedly, he could not sign his name!). From all parts of his domains and from England, he brought men to his court who could teach and train others. Notable among them was **Alcuin,** an Anglo-Saxon monk of great ability, who directed the palace school for clergy and officials set up by the king. For the first time since the 400s, something like higher education was available to a select few. Charlemagne funded the creation of dozens of new monasteries, where many monks devoted much of their time to laboriously copying ancient manuscripts.

A new script was also devised, making the Latin much more readable. Several new editions of the Bible and the works of the church fathers were produced. Not a devout man himself, he still respected and encouraged piety in others. At his orders many new parishes were founded or given large new endowments.

But all Charlemagne's efforts were insufficient to turn the tide of disorder and violence. His "renaissance" was short-lived, and his schools and governmental innovations were soon in ruins. The times were not ripe for them. In the first crises, they collapsed, and the darkness descended again.

Disintegration of the Carolingian Empire
❋

Charlemagne eventually bequeathed his empire to his only surviving son, Louis the Pious, a man who was unfit for the heavy responsibility. By Louis's will, the empire was divided among his three sons: Charles, Lothar, and Louis. Charles received France; Lothar, the midlands between France and Germany reaching down into Italy; and Louis, Germany. Fraternal war for supremacy immediately ensued. The **Treaty of Verdun** in 843, which established the peace, is one of the most important treaties in world history, for the general borders it established still exist today, 1,150 years later (see inset, Map 14.3). When Lothar died a few years later, the midlands were divided between the survivors, Charles and Louis. After a brief period, the title of Holy Roman Emperor was settled on the king of Germany, the successors of Louis, who retained it until the nineteenth century.

❋ **Viking Longboat.** This reproduction shows the type of swift boats used by the Norsemen to ravage the coastal communities and then flee before effective countermeasures could be taken by the victims. (© *Werner Forman Archive/Viking Ship Museum, Bygdoy, Norway/Art Resource*)

❀ **The Farmer's Tasks.** Pastoral life in medieval Europe required the work of men, women, and children. This painting of a farmyard in April is from Da Costa's "Book of Hours."
(© Giraudon/Art Resource)

In the late ninth century, the center and western parts of Europe were attacked from three directions. The Vikings swept down from the north, the Magyars advanced from the east, and the Muslims attacked from the Mediterranean. In the ensuing chaos, all that Charlemagne had been able to do was extinguished, and government reverted back to a primitive military contract between individuals for mutual defense.

The Vikings or Norsemen were the most serious threat and had the most extensive impact. Superbly gifted warriors, these Scandinavians came in swift boats to ravage the coastal communities, then flee before effective countermeasures could be taken. From their headquarters in Denmark and southern Sweden, every year after about 790 they sailed forth and soon discovered that the Franks, Angles, and Saxons were no match. In 834, a large band of Vikings sailed up the Seine and sacked Paris. Seventy years later, they advanced into the Mediterranean and sacked the great city of Seville in the heart of the Spanish caliphate.

By the late 800s, the Vikings were no longer content to raid. They came to conquer. Much of eastern England, Brit-

tany and Normandy, Holland, and Iceland fell to them. In their new lands, they quickly learned to govern by intimidation rather than to plunder and burn, and taxes took the place of armed bands. They learned the advantages of literacy and eventually adopted Christianity in place of their northern gods. By about 1000, the Vikings had footholds ranging from the coast of the North Sea to the eastern Mediterranean. They had become one of the most capable of all the European peoples in government and administration, as well as the military arts.

The Magyars were a different proposition. They were an Asiatic people, who swept into the central European plain from Russia as a horde of horsemen. As such, they were the next to last version of the Asiatic invasions of western Europe, which had begun as far back as the Huns. This resemblance earned their descendants the name *Hungarians* in modern nomenclature. The Magyars arrived in Europe at the end of the ninth century and for fifty years fought the Christianized Germans for mastery. Finally, in a great battle in 955, the Magyars were defeated and retired to the Hungarian plains where they gradually settled down. In the year 1000, their king and patron saint, Stephen, accepted Roman Christianity, and the Magyars joined the family of civilized nations.

The Muslims of the Mediterranean were descendants of North African peoples who had been harassing southern Europe as pirates and raiders ever since the 700s. In the late 800s, they wrested Sicily and part of southern Italy from the Italians and thereby posed a direct threat to Rome. But the Muslims were checked and soon settled down to join the heterogeneous group of immigrants who had been coming to southern Italy for a very long time. The Muslims' highly civilized rule was finally disrupted by the attacks of the newly Christian Vikings, who began battling them for mastery in the eleventh century and eventually reconquered Sicily and the southern tip of the peninsula from them.

Development of Feudalism

The invasions fragmented governmental authority, as the royal courts in France and Germany were unable to defend their territories successfully, particularly against the Viking attacks. It fell to local strongmen to defend their own areas as best they could. Men on horseback had great advantages in battle, and the demand for them rose steadily. Thus, the original **knights** were mercenaries, professional warriors-at-horse who sold their services to the highest bidder. What was bid normally was land and the labor of those who worked it. In this way large tracts passed from the king, technically the owner of all land in his kingdom, to warriors who were the lords and masters of the commoners living on these estates.

The invasions thus greatly stimulated the arrival of the professional army and the feudal military system in north-

Hagia Sophia. Converted into a mosque when the Ottomans finally subdued the Byzantine capital, Hagia Sophia (Holy Wisdom) was the greatest church in Christendom for ten centuries. Its splendid setting near the Bosporus, which separates Europe from Asia, adds to its glory. It is now a museum in present-day Istanbul. *(© Robert Frerck/Tony Stone Images)*

ern Europe, which felt the brunt of the attacks. Any headway Charlemagne had made in restoring the idea of a central authority was soon eradicated. The noble, with control over one or more estates on which manorial agriculture was practiced with serf labor, now became a combined military and civil ruler for a whole locality. The king remained the object of special respect, and the sacred powers of the royal crown were acknowledged by all. But day-to-day administration, military defense, and justice were all carried out by the feudal nobles and their hired men-at-arms.

The Byzantine Empire

❧

The eastern half of the early Christian world is usually known as the **Byzantine empire** (from *Byzantium,* the original name for the town Constantine renamed for himself). It proved to be an extraordinarily resilient competitor among the several rivals for supremacy in the eastern Mediterranean. The Arab Muslims (see Chapter 15) would come to be the most dangerous of these.

In keeping with Eastern traditions, the nature of the imperial throne became even more autocratic than in Rome. The emperor was a semidivine figure, ruling through a large and efficient bureaucracy. Despite occasional religiously inspired revolts (notably the uprising against the imperial decree forbidding worship of images), the government and the population were strongly bonded by Christianity and a belief in the emperor as Christ's deputy on earth. It was, in fact, this spiritual bond that enabled the long life of the empire in the face of many trials, until its ultimate death at the hand of the Ottoman Turks in the fifteenth century.

Unlike the West, the East accepted the emperor as the dominant partner in affairs of church and state. He appointed his patriarchs, and he had the power to remove them. This *caesaro-papism* (the monarch as both head of

state and head of church) was to sharply distinguish the Byzantine from the Latin worlds of faith. The founder of this tradition was the powerful emperor **Justinian,** who also put his stamp on the appearance of the capital by a huge program of public works. The most spectacular was the great central church of Constantinople, the **Hagia Sophia,** or church of Holy Wisdom, which remains today as a magnificent reminder of past glories.

As already noted, after the transfer of imperial government to Constantinople, the western provinces became expendable. In the mid-500s, however, the ambitious Justinian made a concerted effort to recover the West. Justinian's dream of re-creating the empire was ultimately a failure, however. Within just two generations, almost all the reconquered areas had fallen to new invaders. The effort had exhausted the Byzantines and would never be attempted again.

From the early 600s, the Byzantine empire was under more or less constant attack for two centuries. During this period, it lost not only the western reconquests, but also most of its own eastern territories, first to Avars and Persians and then to Arabs and Slavs. The besieging Muslims nearly succeeded in taking Constantinople in 717, when the desperate defenders used "Greek fire," a combustible liquid, to beat them off at sea. While the imperial defenders were occupied, their tributary Slavic subjects in the Balkans (Bulgars, Serbs) established independent states that soon became powerful enough to threaten the Greeks from the north.

In the long term, the most outstanding achievement of the Byzantine rulers was the Christianization of eastern Europe. By the 700s, the missionaries of the western empire, supported by the bishop of Rome, had made many converts among the Germanic tribes and kingdoms. They had not yet ventured into eastern Europe, which had never been under Roman rule. Here, the field was open to the Byzantine missionaries.

The mission to the Slavic peoples of eastern Europe was pursued with energy and devotion. Beginning in the 800s,

Greek monks moved into the nearby Balkans and then to the coast of the Black Sea and into Russia. Their eventual success meant that the present-day states of Russia, Romania, Serbia, Bulgaria, and, of course, Greece itself would look for centuries to Constantinople rather than Rome. Constantinople influenced their religious and cultural values, their laws and their literature, their styles of art and architecture, and, thanks to their ethnically organized churches, their very sense of nationhood.

The conversion of the Slavs to Greek rite Christianity proved to be a crucial and permanent turning point in European history. The split that originated in the rivalry between Rome and Constantinople gradually deepened. It was reflected in the cultural and religious differences between Greek and Latin and between the leaders of the two churches, the Byzantine patriarch and the pope. After many years of alternating friction and patched-up amity, the rift

culminated in the division of Christianity between West and East. In 1054, a headstrong pope encountered a stubborn patriarch who refused to yield to the pope's demands for complete subordination in a matter of doctrine. The two leaders then excommunicated one another in a fit of theological egotism. Despite several efforts—most recently, Pope John Paul's visit to Orthodox Romania—their successors have not been able to overcome their differences to the present day.

One other enormously influential result of Byzantine initiative was the **Corpus Juris.** This sixth-century distillation of Roman law and practice was undertaken at (once again!) the emperor Justinian's command and passed on to posterity. It is the foundation for most Western medieval and early modern law codes, and its basic precepts (see Chapter 12) are operative in many countries of Europe and Latin America to the present day.

ℐummary

The Germanic invasions of the third and fourth centuries found a Roman society that was already sorely tried under the burdens of heavy taxes, declining productivity, and instability at the top. The demoralization was slowed but could not be stopped by the authoritarian reforms of Diocletian and Constantine. In the meantime, the new mystery religion named after Jesus Christ gathered strength within the Roman realm. Christianity spread rapidly after winning the favor of Constantine and his successors, but it could not halt the constellation of forces that were laying waste to the western provinces.

The Germanic tribes took note of Rome's weakness and acted accordingly. A Dark Age of violence and ignorance ensued from which relatively little documentation has survived. In time, the efforts of missionaries from Rome showed results, as the Germanic warriors set up governments of a rough-and-ready sort. By the 700s, these had become stabilized and Christianized, at least in the upper classes.

The most important of the early medieval rulers was Charlemagne, the first Holy Roman Emperor as well as king

of the Franks. His attempts to restore the ancient empire went astray almost as soon as he was dead, and the renaissance that he promoted also proved ephemeral. New invasions by Vikings, Magyars, and Muslims and the chaotic conditions they created in Europe were too much for the personal system of government that Charlemagne had established. It collapsed and was replaced by a highly decentralized administration based on agrarian manors and local military power in the hands of a self-appointed elite, the nobility.

In the eastern half of the old empire, a form of semidivine monarchy possessing great power continued for a thousand years after the collapse in the West. After the failed attempt of Justinian to recover the western provinces, attacks came from all sides. The most persistent and successful attackers were the Arab Muslims, who by the 700s had taken most of the former imperial lands of the eastern Mediterranean. The conversion of the Slavs and some other peoples to Greek rite Christianity was an outstanding achievement, but the split with the Roman church that came in the eleventh century was to be fateful.

ℐest Your Knowledge

1. The reforming emperor who created the Tetrarchy was
   a. Commodus.
   b. Constantine.
   c. Diocletian.
   d. Augustus.

2. Which of the following does *not* help explain the appeal of early Christianity?
   a. Encouragement of military valor
   b. Sense of supernatural mission
   c. Receptivity to all potential converts
   d. Promotion of a sense of community among its adherents

3. Christianity became a universal faith rather than a Jewish sect in large part due to the efforts of
   a. the Roman officials in Judaea.
   b. the apostle Paul.
   c. the apostle Peter.
   d. the Zealots.
4. The emperor Theodosius (378–395 C.E.) is important to Christian history for
   a. his final persecution of Christians.
   b. making Christianity the official religion.
   c. beginning the practice of intervening in internal church affairs.
   d. moving the church headquarters to Constantinople.
5. The bishops of which country were most susceptible to royal pressure to act as the king's officers?
   a. German
   b. France
   c. England
   d. Spain
6. The first Holy Roman Emperor was
   a. Pippin I.
   b. Richard the Lionhearted.
   c. Charlemagne.
   d. Leo III.
7. The biographer of Charlemagne tells us that the king
   a. cared greatly about the manners of his courtiers.
   b. enjoyed the company of his daughters.
   c. despised physical exercise.
   d. read and wrote a great deal.
8. The decisive advantage held by the Vikings in their raids on Europe was
   a. overwhelming numbers.
   b. superior weapons.
   c. great courage.
   d. mastery of naval tactics.
9. The Treaty of Verdun in 843
   a. divided Europe between Muslims and Christians.
   b. created the kingdom of the Franks.
   c. was a compromise between Eastern and Western Christianity.
   d. divided Charlemagne's empire into three states.
10. Which of the following was *not* accomplished by Justinian?
    a. Temporary reconquest of part of the western empire
    b. Construction of Hagia Sophia
    c. Defeat of the Arab invaders
    d. Composition of a new code of law

IDENTIFICATION TERMS

Alcuin	Corpus Juris	Jesus	*missi dominici*
Augustine	Council of Nicaea	Jewish War	Tetrarchy
Barracks Emperors	Diaspora	Justinian	Treaty of Verdun
Byzantine empire	Hagia Sophia	knights	*wergeld*
Charlemagne	Holy Roman Emperor	manor	

INFOTRAC COLLEGE EDITION

Enter the search term "Charlemagne" using Key Words.
Enter the search term "Byzantium" using the Subject Guide.

Enter the search terms "early Christianity" using Key Words.

Chapter 15

Islam

I profess that there is no god save God, and I profess that Muhammad is His Messenger.

MUSLIM PROFESSION OF FAITH

∾

∾

IN THE ARABIAN TOWN OF MECCA, late in the sixth century an individual was born who founded a religion that now embraces about one-fifth of the world's population. **Muhammad** created a faith that spread with incredible speed from his native land throughout the Near and Middle East. Carried on the strong swords of his followers, Islam became a major rival to Christianity in the Mediterranean basin and to Hinduism and Buddhism in East and Southeast Asia. Like these faiths, Islam was far more than a supernatural religion. It also created a culture and a civilization.

The Life of Muhammad the Prophet

The founder of Islam was born into a people about whom little was known until he made them the spiritual and political center of a new civilization. Arabia is a large and sparsely settled peninsula extending from the Fertile Crescent in the north to well down the coast of Africa (see Map 15.1). Mecca, Muhammad's birthplace, was an important interchange where African goods coming across the narrow Red Sea were transferred to caravans for shipment further east. Considerable traffic also moved up and down the Red Sea to the ancient cities of the Near East and the Nile delta. For these reasons, Mecca was a much more cosmopolitan place than one might at first imagine, with Egyptians, Jews, Greeks, and Africans living there, alongside the native Arabs. Long accustomed to trading and living with civilized foreigners, the Arabs in towns were using a written language and had a well-developed system of tribal and municipal government. In such ways, the Arabs of the cities near the coast were far more advanced than the Bedouins (nomads) of the vast desert interior.

Mecca itself was inhabited by several tribes or clans. One of the most important was the Qur'aish, the clan into which Muhammad was born about 570 (see the Religion and Morality box for details of Muhammad's life). The first forty years of his life were uneventful. He married a rich

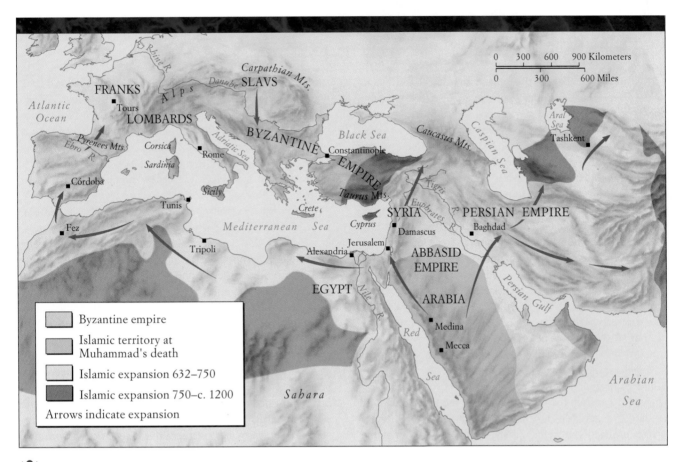

🌸 **MAP 15.1 Spread of Islam.** The lightning-like spread of the new faith throughout a belt on either side of the equator is evident in this map. About one-third of the world's populations known to the Christians converted to Islam in the space of a long lifetime, 630–720 C.E.

widow and set himself up as a caravan trader of moderate means. The marriage produced one daughter, Fatima. Around 610, Muhammad began to talk about his mystical experiences that took the form of visits from a supernatural messenger. For days at a time he withdrew into the nearby desert, where long trances ensued in which he was allowed to speak with the angel Gabriel and others about the nature of life and the true worship of the Almighty. For years he dared speak of these visions only to his immediate kin.

Finally, he began to preach about his visions in the street, but soon ran into condemnation by Meccan authorities, who supported a form of worship centered on the magical qualities of the ***Ka'aba,*** or Black Stone. Muhammad was forced to flee Mecca in 622, which came to be known as the year of the ***Hegira*** ("Flight"). It is the first year of the Muslim calendar.

Muhammad fled to the rival city of Medina, where he found the support he had vainly sought in Mecca. After a few years, he had enough followers to begin a kind of trade

war against the Meccan caravans and to force the city fathers there to negotiate with him on spiritual matters. He also gained support among the Bedouins and by 630 was able to return to Mecca as master. By his death two years later, already a good part of the Arabian peninsula was under Islamic control. A ***jihad,*** a war of holy conquest, was under way.

Islamic Doctrine
❋

What was this message that Muhammad preached that found such ready acceptance? The doctrines of Islam (the word means "submission") are the simplest and most readily understood of any of the world's major religions. They are laid out in written form in the **Qur'an,** the sacred writ of the Muslim world, which was composed a few years after the Prophet's death from the memory of his words. The

Muhammad
(c. 570–632)

The founder of the second largest religion in the world was born into poverty about 570 C.E. in the market town of Mecca, in central Arabia. Of his early life we know next to nothing, as he apparently considered it immaterial, and his early disciples followed his views. Even after he had become a notable person, we have practically no personal information about him, and the sacred book of Islam, the Qur'an, gives us few clues as to the human nature of the Prophet.

Muhammad was orphaned at six and entrusted to his uncle. Sometime about 590 he entered the service of a wealthy widow, Khadija, who had a thriving caravan trade into the interior. Later, he married her and continued the business with such success that he became a respected member of the Meccan community. With Khadija he produced a daughter, Fatima, his only surviving child and the wife of Ali, one of Islam's most notable early warriors.

About 610, at the age of forty, the devout Muhammad began to retire to the surrounding desert for periods of fast and prayer. Here, he had trance-induced visions, in which the angel Gabriel commanded him to heed the divine messages he would be given and preach them to the world as the final Prophet of the Lord. A deeply religious person, Muhammad was frightened at the prospect of this stunning responsibility, and it was not until many other visions had come to him that he began public preaching about 617.

So long as Muhammad was protected by the influential head of his clan, he remained safe from the hostility his preaching aroused in the Meccan establishment. But this changed in 619 when a new clan chief arose, who saw the new doctrine as dangerous to his own social and financial position. Muhammad was forced to flee and take refuge in Medina, Mecca's commercial rival. Muslims see this flight (Hegira) as beginning a new era in human history and use it as the first year of their calendar, conforming to the Christian year 622. In Medina, Muhammad was able to surround himself with a group of dedicated converts; supported for pragmatic commercial reasons by Medina's leaders, he organized and led a small army to attack Mecca. Though repulsed at first, he gradually won over enough Meccans to make the resistance of the rest impossible and entered the city without force of arms in 630. Only two years later, he died, but not before the faith he founded was already sweeping over most of Arabia and preparing to enter the mainstream of Near Eastern and African life.

Muhammad was able to achieve what he did for various reasons. First, he preached a straightforward doctrine of salvation, ensured by a God who never failed and whose will was clearly delineated in comprehensible principles and commands. Second, those who believed and tried to follow Muhammad's words (as gathered a few years after his death in the Qur'an) were assured of reward in the life to come; this included all of those who lost their lives attempting to spread the faith, regardless of their previous conduct.

Lastly, Muhammad's preaching contained large measures of an elevated yet attainable moral and ethical code. It deeply appealed to a population that wanted more than the purely ritualistic animist doctrine could give them but were repelled by the internal conflicts of Christendom or unsympathetic to the complexities of Judaism. His insistence that he was not an innovator, but the completer of the message of the Jewish and Christian prophets and gospel writers was also of great significance in the success of his religion among the Eastern peoples.

For Reflection

Some critics have always attacked Islam as the product of a mere commercial and financial rivalry between aspiring mercantile groups in Mecca and Medina. How would you, as a good Muslim, answer that? Is it unusual for a reformer to insist that he or she was not innovating but returning to the forgotten truths and principles of yesterday? Give some examples from the twentieth century.

---

basic ideas are expressed in the **Five Pillars of Islam** described in the box.

The strict monotheism of Islam was undoubtedly influenced by the Jews and Christians with whom Muhammad had contact in Mecca. Many other aspects of the Muslim faith also derive in some degree from other religions, such as the regulations against pork and against the use of stimulants that alter the God-given nature of man. But the Muslim creed is not just a collection of other, previous beliefs by any means. It includes many elements that reflect the peculiar circumstances of Arabs and Arabia in the seventh century C.E.

Arabia in Muhammad's Day

Much of the interior of the Arabian peninsula was barely inhabited except for scattered oases. The Bedouin tribes that passed from one oasis to the next with their herds were at constant war with one another for water and pasture. The virtues most respected in this primitive society were those of the warrior: bravery, hardiness, loyalty, and honor.

The Arabs' religion prior to Muhammad involved a series of animistic beliefs, such as the important one center-

From the very outset Islam has rested on the Five Pillars taught by Muhammad. In more or less flexible forms, these beliefs are recognized and observed by all good Muslims, wherever and in whatever circumstances they may find themselves.

1. There is one God (whom Muslims call **Allah**), and Muhammad is His prophet. Islam is a thoroughly monotheistic faith.
2. God demands prayer from His faithful five times daily: at daybreak, noon, in the midafternoon, twilight, and before retiring.
3. Fasting and observance of dietary prohibitions are demanded of all who can. The month of Ramadan and some holy days are particularly important in this respect.
4. Almsgiving toward the poor faithful is a command, enforced through the practice of tithing.
5. If possible, every Muslim must make the **hajj** (pilgrimage) to the holy cities of Arabia at least once. In modern days this command has filled Mecca with upward of two million visitors at the height of the holy season.

ing on the Ka'aba stone. *Animism* means a conviction that objects such as rivers, trees, or stones possess spirits and spiritual qualities that have direct and potent impact on human lives. In the coastal towns, these beliefs coexisted side by side with the more developed religions of Judaism, Christianity, and Zoroastrianism.

In towns such as Mecca, commerce had bloomed to such an extent that many Arabs were being corrupted by this newfound wealth, at least in the eyes of others who were perhaps not so fortunate in their affairs. Traditions were being cast aside in favor of materialist values. The cultural gap between town Arab and Bedouin had widened to such an extent that it threatened to become irrevocable. Worship of the *Ka'aba* shrine had degenerated into a business proposition for the merchants of Mecca, who profited greatly from the many thousands of Arabs from the interior who made annual processions there. Superstitions of the most nonsensical sort abounded, making the Arabs contemptible in the view of the foreign traders who dwelled among them.

From this standpoint, Muhammad's religious message was the work of a reformer, a man who perceived many of the problems facing his people and responded to them. The verses of the Qur'an excerpted in the Religion and Morality box contain many references to these problems and propose solutions. For example, the condition of women in pre-Muslim Arabia was apparently very poor. They were practically powerless in legal matters, had no control over their dowries in marriage and could not have custody over minor children after their husband's death, among other things. In his preaching, Muhammad took pains to change this situation and the attitude that lay behind it. In this way he was an innovator, reacting against a tradition that he believed to be ill founded. Though he never said that women were equal to men, he made it clear that women are not mere servants of men; that they do have some inherent rights as persons, wives, and mothers; and that their honor and physical welfare should be protected by the men around them. Indeed, the status of women in early Muslim teaching is relatively elevated. It is actually higher and more firmly recognized than the status accorded women in the contemporary Christian culture of the Latin West or the Greek East.

The Entry into Mecca by the Faithful. In this thirteenth-century miniature from Baghdad the *hajj*, or pilgrimage, is depicted in its glory. Supposedly devoted to pious purposes, the hajj was also an opportunity to display one's wealth. (*Bibliotheque Nationale, Paris*)

provinces put up only halfhearted resistance or none at all, as in Damascus. The religious differences within Christianity had became so acute in these lands that several sects of Christians preferred to surrender to the "pagan" Muslims than continue to live under what they regarded as the wrong-thinking emperor and his bishops. This was true not only in Syrian Damascus but also in several Christian centers in North Africa and Egypt, which were in religious revolt against the church leaders in Constantinople and in Rome.

✾ **The Ka'aba in Mecca.** In this huge mosque courtyard assemble hundreds of thousands of worshipers during the Muslim holy days each year. The Ka'aba is the cubicle of stone in the center. It contains a piece of black meteorite worshiped by the Arabs before their conversion to Islam. It is now a symbol of the ascent of the Arabs from pagan superstitions to Islam's truth. (© *Rulhan Arikan/Photo Researchers*)

The Caliphate
❋

The nature of Muslim leadership changed markedly from epoch to epoch in the 600 years between the founding of Islam in Arabia and 1260 C.E. when it passed from Persian/Arabic to Turco/Mongol hands. Muhammad had been both religious and temporal ruler over his faithful, and he never considered dividing the two powers. He was priest, king, and general, and so also were his immediate successors.

The First Period, 632–661

The first **caliph** (successor to the Prophet) was one of Muhammad's generals, Abu Bakr, who was elected by his colleagues, as were the next three caliphs. Abu Bakr died soon after his election, however, and was succeeded by another general, Omar, who ruled Islam for ten years and was the real founder of the early Muslim empire. His Arab armies pushed deep into North Africa, conquering Egypt by 642. At the same time, he invaded Persia and the Byzantine territory in the eastern Mediterranean. By the time of Omar's death in 643, mounted Arab raiders were penetrating into extreme western India.

This stunningly rapid expansion came to a halt because of a brief civil war for mastery within the Muslim world, which brought Ali, husband of Fatima and the son-in-law of Muhammad, to the fore. Ali was the last "orthodox" caliph for a long time. His assassination by a competitor in 661 marked the end of the first phase of Muslim expansion.

The Ummayad Dynasty, 661–750

The first four caliphs had been elected, but three of the four died by murder. At this point, since the elective system had clearly failed, the system of succession became in fact a dynasty, although the elective outer form was preserved. From 661, two dynasties ruled Islam: the Ummayad to 750, and then the Abbasid from 750 to 1260.

The *Jihad*
✾

One of the unique aspects of Islam is the *jihad,* the war for the establishment of God's law on Earth. Taking part in a *jihad* was the highest honor for a good Muslim. Dying in one assured a direct ticket to heaven.

Aside from the salvation of one's soul, what was the earthly appeal of the *jihad*? It seems to have been based on several aspects of Arabic culture. The desert Bedouins were already a warlike people, accustomed to continual violence in the struggle for pastoral rights. Much evidence also indicates that they faced an economic crisis at the time of Muhammad—namely, a severe overpopulation problem that overwhelmed the available sparse resources. Under such conditions, many were willing to risk their lives for the possibility of a better future. They saw Muhammad as a war leader as much as a religious prophet and flocked to his army from the time he returned to Mecca.

Once the *jihad* was under way, another factor favored its success: exhaustion and division among Islamic opponents. Both of the major opponents, the Byzantine Greeks in Constantinople and the Persians, had been fighting each other fiercely for the previous generation and were mutually exhausted. As a result, by 641, only nine years after the death of the Prophet, all of the huge Persian empire had fallen to Arab armies and much of the Byzantine territory in Asia (present-day Syria, Lebanon, and Turkey) as well (see Map 15.1). In place after place, the defenders of the Byzantine

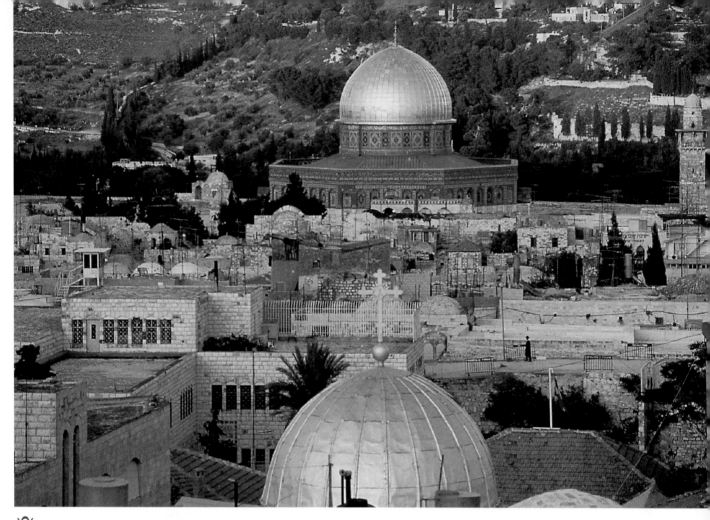

✿ **The Dome of the Rock.** This great edifice, erected by Muslims in Jerusalem in the late seventh century, has been used by three religions as a sacred place of worship. Supposedly Muhammad ascended into heaven from this spot. (*© 1995 Stuart Franklin/Magnum Photos, Inc.*)

The **Ummayad** dynasty was initiated through the murder of Ali by the governor of Syria, Muawiya, and this was to prove fateful. Ali's supporters claimed that because of his family ties with Muhammad and because the Prophet had designated him as a leader, Ali had been the rightful caliph. These supporters of Ali were known as **Shi'ites,** and they formed a significant minority within Islam that continues to the present. They believed that only the blood descendants of the Prophet should become caliph, and they looked on the Ummayad dynasty as murderous impostors.

The supporters of Muawiya and his successors were known as **Sunni,** and they constituted the large majority (currently, about 90 percent) of Muslims at all times. They accepted the principle that the succession should go to the most qualified, regardless of blood connections with the Prophet. They believed that this is what Muhammad desired, and they rejected the claims of the Shi'ites that the family of Muhammad had received some special enlightenment in spiritual matters.

The division of Islam between Shi'ite and Sunni was to have decisive effects on the political unity of the Muslim world. Most members of the Shi'ite minority were concentrated in Persia and the Near East, but they had support in many other areas and were always a counterweight to the policies of the Sunni central government. From their ranks came many of the sects of Islam.

Muawiya proved to be a skillful organizer and statesman. He moved the capital from Medina (where Muhammad had established it) to his native Damascus, where he could be more fully in charge. He made the office of caliph more powerful than it had been before and also laid the foundation for the splendid imperial style that would characterize later caliphs in great contrast to the austerity and simplicity of the first days. Muawiya made clear the dynastic quality of his rule by forcing the reluctant tribal leaders to accept his son as his successor. The caliph under the Ummayads was normally the son or brother of the previous ruler.

The Ummayads continued the advances to east and west, though not quite so brilliantly and rapidly as before. To the east, Arab armies penetrated as far as western China before being checked, and they pushed deep into central Asia (to Tashkent in Uzbekistan). Afghanistan became a Muslim outpost. In the west, the outstanding achievement was the conquest of Christian Spain between 711 and 721. At least part of Spain would remain in Muslim hands until

The Qur'an

The Qur'an is not only the Bible of the Muslims but also an elaborate and poetic code of daily conduct. It is a compilation, like the Christian and Jewish Bibles, formed in the memory of Muhammad's associates of his words and instructions after the Prophet's death. As the literal word of God, the holy book is held by all devout Muslims to be the unfailing source of wisdom, which, if adapted to the changing realities of daily life, can be as usable in the twentieth century as it was in the seventh when it was written. Much of its verses have formed the basis of law in the Muslim countries. Now translated into every major language, the Qur'an was long available only in Arabic, one of the world's most poetic and subtlest languages. This circumstance both helped and hindered the religion's eventual spread. Some excerpts follow:

The Jihad

Fight in the cause of God against those who fight against you, but do not begin hostilities. Surely, God loves not the aggressors. Once they start the fighting, kill them wherever you meet them, and drive them out from where they have driven you out; for aggression is more heinous than killing. But fight them until all aggression ceases and religion is professed for the pleasure of God alone. If they desist, then be mindful that no retaliation is permissible except against the aggressors.

Do not account those who are slain in the cause of God as dead. Indeed, they are living in the presence of their Lord and are provided for. They are jubilant . . . and rejoice for those who have not yet joined them. . . . They rejoice at the favor of God and His bounty, and at the realisation that God suffers not the reward of the faithful to be lost.

Piety and Charity

There is no piety in turning your faces toward the east or the west, but he is pious who believeth in God, and the last day, and the angels, and the scriptures, and the prophets; who for the love of God disburses his wealth to his kindred, and to the orphans, and the needy, and the wayfarer, and those who ask, and for ransoming. . . .

They who expend their wealth for the cause of God, and never follow what they have laid out with reproaches or harm, shall have their reward with the Lord; no fear shall come upon them, neither shall they be put to grief.

A kind speech and forgiveness is better than alms followed by injury. Give to the orphans their property; substitute not worthless things of your own for their valuable ones, and devour not their property after adding it to your own, for this is a great crime.

Women's Place; Marriage

Ye may divorce your wives twice. Keep them honorably, or put them away, with kindness. But it is not allowed you to appropriate to yourselves any of what you have once given them. . . . no blame shall attach to either of you for what the wife shall herself give for her redemption [from the marriage bond].

Men are superior to women on account of the qualities with which God hath gifted the one above the other, and on account of the outlay they make from their substance for them. Virtuous women are obedient, careful, during the husband's absence, because God hath of them been careful. But chide those for whose obstinacy you have cause to dread; remove them into beds apart, and whip them. But if they are obedient to you, then seek not occasion to abuse them.

Christians and Jews

Verily, they who believe and who follow the Jewish religion, and the Christians . . . whoever of these believeth in God and the Last Day, and does that which is right shall have their reward with the Lord. Fear shall not come upon them, neither shall they be grieved.

We believe in God and what has been sent down to us, and what was sent down to Abraham, Ishmael, Isaac, Jacob and their descendants, and what was given Moses, Jesus and the prophets by their Lord. We do not differentiate between them, and are committed to live at peace with Him.

For Reflection

Does some of this excerpt remind you of the Laws of Manu? What similarities are most prominent? Note the fine line walked by the Qur'an between self-defense and aggressive war. What in the background of the Bedouin might have made this close distinction necessary and natural?

SOURCE: From T. B. Irving, trans. The Quran: Selections, 1980.

the time of Christopher Columbus. The Arab horsemen actually penetrated far beyond the Pyrenees, but they were defeated in 733 at Tours in central France by the Frankish leader Charles Martel, in one of the key battles of European history. This expedition proved to be the high-water mark of Arab Muslim penetration into Europe, and soon afterward they retreated behind the Pyrenees to set up a Spanish caliphate.

In the 740s the Ummayad dynasty was overthrown by rebels, and after a brief period of uncertainty, the **Abbasid** clan was able to take over as a new dynasty. One of their first moves was to transfer the capital from unfriendly Damascus to the entirely new town of **Baghdad** in Iraq, which was built for that purpose.

The Abbasid Dynasty, 750–1260

The Abbasid clan claimed descent from Abbas, the uncle of Muhammad, and for that reason were more acceptable to the Shi'ite faction than the Ummayads had been.

The Abbasids also differed from the Ummayads in another important way. Whereas the Ummayads had allowed an Arab elite to monopolize religion and government, the Abbasids opened up the faith to all comers on an essentially equal basis. Arab officials attempted to retain their monopoly on important posts in the central and provincial administration. But gradually, Persians, Greeks, Syrians, Berbers from North Africa and the Sahara, Spanish ex-Christians, and many others found their way into the inner circles of Muslim authority and prestige. In every area, experienced officials from the conquered peoples were retained in office, though supervised by Arabs.

Through these non-Arab officials, the Abbasid administration incorporated several foreign models of government. As time passed, and more natives chose to convert to Islam, the Arab upper class was steadily diluted by other ethnic groups. It was they who made Islam into a highly cosmopolitan, multiethnic religion and civilization. Like the doctrines of Islam, the community of believers was soon marked by its eclecticism and heterogeneity.

Even with the cement of a common faith, the empire was simply too large and its peoples too diverse to hold together politically and administratively. During the Abbasid caliphate, the powers of the central government underwent a gradual but cumulatively severe decline. Many segments of the Islamic world broke away from the political control of Baghdad. Spain became fully independent; Egypt and the eastern regions of Persia almost so.

But the Muslim faith was strong enough to bind this world together, permanently, in a religious and cultural sense. With the sole exception of Spain, where the Muslims were always a minority, those areas captured at one time or another by the Islamic forces after 629 remain majority Muslim today. Those areas reach halfway around the globe, from Morocco to Indonesia.

Conversion to Islam
❊

Contrary to widespread Christian notions, Islam normally did not force conversion. In fact, after the first generation, the Arab leaders came to realize the disadvantages of mass conversion of the conquered and discouraged it. By the time of the Ummayads, conversion was looked on as a special allowance to deserving non-Muslims, especially those who had something to offer the conquerors in the way of talents, wealth, or domestic and international prestige.

No effort was made to convert the peasants or the urban masses. Life in the villages went on as before, with the peasants paying their rents or giving their labor to the new lords just as they had to the old. When and if they converted, it was generally due to specific local circumstances rather than to pressure from above. Centuries passed before the peasants of Persia and Turkey accepted Islam. In Syria and

Lebanon, and Egypt whole villages remained loyal to their Christian beliefs during ten centuries of Muslim rule.

Intermarriage between Muslim and non-Muslim was strictly prohibited. This restriction was supposed to preserve the ruling group indefinitely. In fact, Muslims had very little social contact with non-Muslims, although the two groups did mix together in business transactions, administrative work, and even, at times, intellectual and cultural interchange (especially in Spain).

The Muslims did not view all non-Muslims the same way. Instead, they were categorized according to what the Qur'an and Arab tradition taught about their proximity to spiritual truth. The Jews and the Christians were considered particularly meritorious because both had progressed some way down the Way of Truth and had possessed holy men (such as Jesus of Nazareth) who had tried to lead them onward. The Zoroastrians were viewed in much the same way. All three were classed as ***dhimmis,*** or "Peoples of the Book," and were thought to have risen above what Muslims regarded as the base superstitions of their many other subject peoples.

The *dhimmis* were not taxed as severely as pagans were, and they had legal and business rights denied to others. Restrictions on the *dhimmis* were generally not severe, and in many places there is good evidence that they prospered. They could worship as they pleased and elect their own community leaders. Their position was certainly better in every way than that of either Jews or Muslims under Christian rule.

Everyday Affairs
❊

In the opening centuries of Muslim rule, the Muslims were a minority almost everywhere outside Arabia, so they had to accustom themselves to the habits and manners of their subjects, to some degree. Because the Bedouin pastoralists who formed the backbone of the early Islamic armies had little experience with commerce and finance, they were quite willing to allow their more sophisticated subjects considerable leeway in such matters. Thus, Christian, Jewish, or pagan merchants and artisans were generally able to live and work as they were accustomed to doing without severe disturbance. They managed economic affairs not only for themselves but also for the ruling Arabs. This gradually changed as the Bedouin settled down to civilized urban life, but in the meantime the habit of using the conquered "infidels" to perform many of the ordinary tasks of life had become ingrained.

Somewhat similar patterns could be found in finance and routine administration: the conquered subjects were kept on in the middle and lower levels. Only Muslims could hold important political and military positions, however. The Bedouin maintained an advantage over the neo-Muslim converts as late as the ninth century, but Greek,

The Muezzin. Although the Islamic peoples have no sacred priesthood, men called *muezzin* are appointed to positions of leadership and are responsible for leading the faithful in daily prayer. In former days they called the devout to the mosque five times daily from one of the minarets. Today, tape recordings perform this service. (*Aramco World*)

Syrian, Persian, and other converts to Islam found their way into high posts in the central government in Baghdad under the Abbasids. And in the provinces, it was very common to encounter native converts at the very highest levels. With the native peoples playing such a large role in affairs, it is not surprising that economic and administrative institutions came to be an amalgam of Arab and Greek, Persian, or Spanish customs.

Society in the Muslim world formed a definite social pyramid, with the descendants of the old Bedouin clans on top, followed by converts from other religions. Then came the *dhimmis,* other non-Muslim freemen, while the slaves were at the bottom. All five classes of society had their own rights and duties, and even the slaves had considerable legal protections. Normally, there was little friction between Muslims and non-Muslims, but it was always clear that the non-Muslims were second-class citizens, below every Muslim in dignity. Different courts of law had jurisdiction over legal disputes depending on whether Muslims or non-Muslims were involved. All non-Muslims were taxed heavily, although, as we have seen, the burden on the *dhimmis* was less than on other non-Muslims.

As this suggests, religion was truly the decisive factor in Muslim society. Like Christians and Jews, but even more so, good Muslims believed that a person's most essential characteristic was whether he or she adhered to the true faith—Islam. The fact that all three faiths—Christianity, Judaism, and Islam—believed in essentially the same patriarchal God was not enough to bridge the differences between them. Rather, it seemed to widen them. No one, it seems, hates as well as brothers.

Summary

The surge of Islam from its native Arabia in the seventh century was propelled by the swords of the *jihad* armies. But the attraction of the last of the Western world's major religions rested finally on its openness to all creeds and colors, its ease of understanding, and its assurance of heaven to those who followed its simple doctrines. The Prophet Muhammad saw himself as completing the works of Abraham and Jesus, as the final messenger of the one God. His work was assisted by divisions among the Christians of the Near East, by economic rewards to the Muslim conquerors, and by the momentary exhaustion of both Byzantium and Persia. Already by the middle of the 600s, the new faith had reached Egypt and the borders of Hindustan. By the early 700s, the fall of Spain had given it a foothold in Europe. Not only was this the fastest spread of a creed in world history, but Islam would go on spreading for many years to come.

The political leadership of the faith was held by the caliphs, at first by the Ummayad dynasty at Damascus, then by the Abbasids at their new capital at Baghdad. The unity of Islam was split as early as the first Ummayad caliph by the struggle between the Sunni majority and the Shi'ite minority, the later of which insisted that blood relationship with Muhammad was essential for the caliphate.

The upshot of the Muslim explosion out of Arabia was the creation of a new civilization, which would span a large part of the Afro-Asian world by the twelfth century and be carried into Christian Europe in the fourteenth. In the next chapter, we will look at the cultural aspects of this civilization in some detail.

TEST YOUR KNOWLEDGE

1. Muhammad's religious awakening came
   a. as a result of a childhood experience.
   b. in his middle years, after a vision.
   c. in response to the Christian conquest of Mecca.
   d. after an encounter with a wandering holy man.
2. Muhammad began his mission to reform Arab beliefs
   a. because he was desperate for social prominence.
   b. because he could not tolerate the evil behavior of his associates.
   c. because the angel Gabriel and others told him he was chosen to do so.
   d. because he was inspired by the example of the early Christians.
3. Which of the following is *not* necessary for entry into eternal bliss according to the Qur'an?
   a. Frequent and regular prayer to Allah
   b. Fasting at prescribed times
   c. Passing a Last Judgment
   d. Taking arms against the infidel
4. Which of the following statements about Islamic belief is *false*?
   a. A Last Judgment awaits all.
   b. The faithful will be guided by the Qur'an to salvation.
   c. Mortals must submit to the will of the one all-powerful Lord.
   d. The divinity of Jesus is beyond doubt.
5. The farthest reach of Muslim expansion into Europe was at
   a. Palermo.
   b. Tours.
   c. Córdoba.
   d. Gibraltar.
6. The conflicts between Sunni and Shi'ite Muslims centered on the
   a. divinity of Muhammad.
   b. authenticity of Muhammad's visions.
   c. location of the capital of the Islamic state.
   d. importance of blood kinship to Muhammad in choosing his successor.
7. The basis of all Muslim political theory is
   a. a person's religion.
   b. the wealth possessed by a given group of citizens.
   c. the social standing of an individual.
   d. the historical evolution of a given social group.
8. Which of the following areas had not fallen to Islam by the beginning of the Abbasid dynasty?
   a. Persia
   b. Spain
   c. Iraq
   d. Italy
9. In Islam, the social prestige and position of the Arab Bedouins
   a. varied according to their wealth.
   b. was sometimes below even that of slaves.
   c. was at the top of the pyramid.
   d. was above the *dhimmi* but below that of converts.
10. The *dhimmi* in early Muslim societies were
    a. Christians and Jews who had not converted to Islam.
    b. the merchants.
    c. the original Arabic believers in Islam.
    d. non-Arab converts to Islam.

IDENTIFICATION TERMS

Abbasids	*dhimmis*	*jihad*	Shi'ite
Allah	Five Pillars of Islam	*Ka'aba*	Sunni
Baghdad	hajj	Muhammad	Ummayads
caliph	*Hegira*	Qur'an	

INFOTRAC COLLEGE EDITION

Enter the search term "Islam" using the Subject Guide.

Enter the search terms "caliph or caliphate" using Key Words.

Chapter 16

Mature Islamic Society and Institutions

We believe in God and what has been sent down to us, and was sent down to Abraham, Ishmael, Isaac, Jacob, and their descendants, and what was given Moses, Jesus, and the prophets by their Lord.

THE QUR'AN

750 C.E.	Abbasid caliphate founded in Baghdad
786–809	Harun al-Rashid
1055	Seljuk Turks take power
1096	First Christian Crusade to Holy Land
1258	Mongols plunder Baghdad

THE CONSOLIDATION OF Islamic civilization took place during the period from the founding of the Abbasid dynasty in 750 C.E. through the degeneration of that dynasty in the tenth century. In these 200 years Islam created for its varied adherents a matrix of cultural characteristics that enabled it to survive both political and religious fragmentation, while still expanding eastward into Asia and southward into Africa. In the arts and sciences, the Muslim world now occupied the place once held by the classical Greeks and Romans, whose own accomplishments were largely preserved to a later age through Muslim solicitude.

Challenges to the caliphs' supremacy, not least from the Christian crusades to the Holy Land, checked the faith's expansion after about 900 C.E. A nearly complete breakdown of the Baghdad caliphate ensued in the eleventh and twelfth centuries, before first the all-conquering Mongols from the Central Asian deserts and then the Ottoman Turks took over the leadership of Islam and infused it with new vigor (see Chapter 32).

Even after all semblance of central governance of the vast empire had been destroyed, a clear unity was still visible in Islamic culture and lifestyle, whether in the Middle East, India, or Spain. Conflicts with other civilizations and cultures (African, Chinese, Hindu, Christian) only sharpened the Muslims' sense of what was proper and necessary for a life pleasing to God and rewarding to humans. How well such a sense was converted into actuality varied, of course, from country to country and time to time. But at its height, Islamic civilization was the envy of its Christian neighbor, with achievements in the sciences and arts that could rival even those of the Chinese.

The Caliphate

❀

We have seen how the Abbas clan seized power from the Ummayads and transferred the capital to the new city of Baghdad in the 760s (see Chapter 15). This city quickly became one of the major cultural centers of the entire world, as the Abbasids adorned it with every form of art and en-

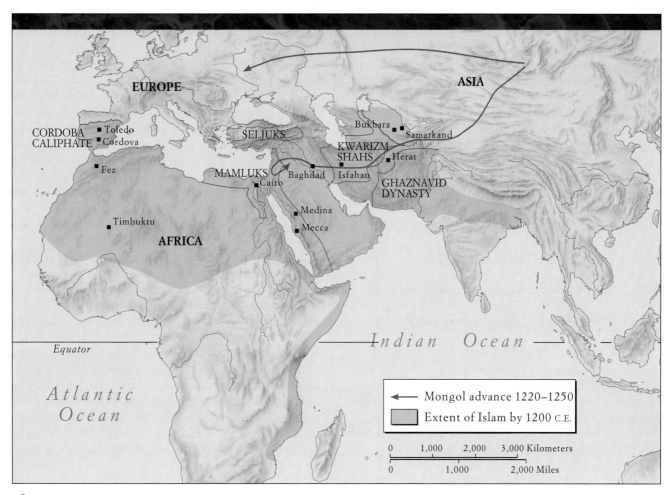

🏵 **MAP 16.1 Islamic Domains, c. 1200 C.E.** At its height, the Muslim world extended from the Atlantic to the Indian Ocean. By about 1200 C.E., the Baghdad caliph's hold on territories beyond Arabia and Iraq was minimal, if it existed at all. Persia and Egypt, as well as Spain and Afghanistan, were autonomous under their own shahs and caliphs. African Muslims had never had direct contact with Baghdad.

couraged its educational establishments with money and personal participation. They also further developed the Ummayad institutions of government.

In Baghdad, governing powers were exercised by an elaborate, mainly Persian bureaucracy. This was headed by a **vizier,** a kind of prime minister for the caliphs who had enormous powers. Many of the other officials were eunuchs, who were thought more likely to be devoted to the government because they could have no family interests of their own. In the provinces, the *emir* or governor was the key man. His tax collecting responsibility was crucial to the well-being of the Baghdad government. Rebellions normally started in the provinces and were led by independent-minded emirs.

The major institutions of the central government were the **ulema,** or high court for religious matters; the *diwan,*

or financial board; and the *kadi,* or local judge who had jurisdiction in all disputes involving a Muslim. The *ulema* operated to gradually bring into existence the **sharia***,* or sacred law, based on the words of the Qur'an. The *sharia* involved far more than religious or doctrinal matters. In the Muslim view, religion entered into many spheres of what we consider civil and private life, so that the decisions of the *ulema* and the applications of the *sharia* affected almost all aspects of public and private affairs.

Unlike the Western world, the Muslims' sacred book remained the basis of all law, and hence of all administration and government, to a very late date. The Qur'an was still the fount of all legal knowledge into modern times, and for some Islamic fundamentalists, it still is (for example, in Iran since the revolution of 1979–1980, Libya, and Saudi Arabia).

The Muslim army in the Abbasid era was very international in composition. Many of the soldiers were slaves, taken from all the conquered peoples but especially from the Africans and Egyptians. They were well trained and equipped, and their commanders came to have increasing political power as the caliph became weaker. Some contemporary estimates of the army's size are incredibly large, running up to hundreds of thousands in the field at one time (which would have been a logistical impossibility for the time). Still, there is little doubt that the Abbasid forces were the most impressive of the era and far overshadowed the Europeans' feudal levies and the Byzantines' professional soldiery. Abbasid raids into Afghanistan and western India established footholds that were gradually expanded by later Muslim forces.

Literature and the Natural Sciences

The Arabic language became an important source of unification in the Muslim world, spreading into its every part. Because the sacred book of the Qur'an could only be written in Arabic, every educated Muslim had to learn this language to some degree. The Arabs also came to possess a cheap and easily made writing medium—paper (picked up from the Chinese, as so much medieval technology would be). A paper factory was operating in Baghdad as early as 793, providing a great stimulus to the making of books and the circulation of ideas.

The university was also a Muslim creation. The world's oldest still functioning higher educational institution is the University in Cairo, founded in the ninth century by Muslim holy men as a place of religious study. Long before the names of Aristotle and Plato were known in the Christian West, the Muslims of the Middle East had recognized the value of classical Greek learning and acted to preserve and expand it. In the academies of Baghdad and other Muslim centers, students of philosophy and the various sciences congregated and debated the writings of the Greek masters. The Muslims especially revered Aristotle, whom they regarded as the greatest teacher of all time. They passed on this esteem for Aristotle to their Christian subjects in Spain, who in turn transmitted it to the rest of Christian Europe in the twelfth and thirteenth centuries.

In the sciences, the Muslim contribution was selective but important. In the medical sciences the four centuries between 800 and 1200 saw the world of Islam considerably ahead of any Western civilization. Pharmacology, physiology, anatomy, and, above all, opthamology and optical science were special strong points. In geography Arabic and Persian writers and travelers were responsible for much new information about the known and the hitherto unknown world. In astronomy and astrology, the Muslims built on and expanded the traditions of careful observation they had inherited in the Near East. In mathematics they developed and rationalized the ancient Hindu system of numbers to make the "Arabic numbers" that are still in uni-

❀ **The University of Cairo.** The University of Cairo is the oldest seat of higher learning in the world still operating in its original site. The modern university has a student body of approximately 50,000, many of whom are adults studying part-time. (© *Nacerdine Zebar/Gamma Liaison*)

The Persian Muslim Avicenna (Ibn Sina in Arabic) was an outstanding example of the Islamic philosophers and men of science who did so much to preserve classical learning in an epoch when the Christian West was unable to appreciate it. His compilation, *The Book of Healing,* is the closest thing to a comprehensive encyclopedia of the medical arts attempted until modern times. And his handbook on clinical practice, *The Canon of Medicine,* is probably the most famous single work on healing ever published.

Avicenna was a child prodigy. At the age of ten, he had already memorized the Qur'an and soon outgrew all his teachers. By the time he was twenty-one, his reputation as a scholar was known throughout Persia. Despite his brilliance, his career was often tempestuous because of the violent changes in dynasties that Persia experienced in the eleventh century. More than once, Avicenna was even imprisoned for a brief period as punishment for having served at the court of the defeated party.

Avicenna was largely responsible for the revived interest in the philosophy of Aristotle that began to percolate into the Christian world (via Spain) in the late eleventh century. Through him the West was able to rediscover the Greek explorations of both the natural and the spiritual worlds and eventually to link them with the teachings of the medieval Christian scholars. His *Book of Healing* was partly translated into Latin in the twelfth century, and the entire *Canon of Medicine* somewhat later. The latter work replaced that of Galen as the standard medical text for several centuries.

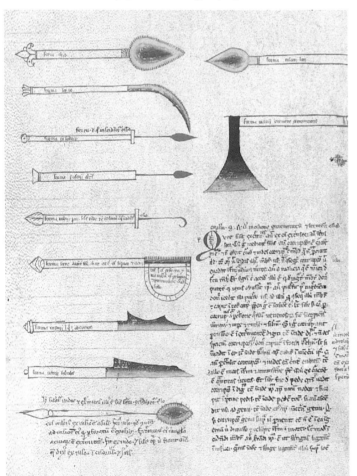

✸ **Surgical Instruments.** Islamic medicine was so far ahead of medieval European practice that, despite the enmity between Christianity and Islam, Arab doctors were frequently invited to spend time teaching in Europe. The Muslim practitioners were particularly adept at eye surgery and amputations. *(Department of Western Manuscripts, Bodleian Library, Oxford)*

versal use. They also introduced the concepts of algebra and the decimal system to the West. One of the most important figures in Muslim science was **Ibn Sina** (**Avicenna**), a physician and scientist of great importance to medieval Europe and author of the famous handbook on clinical practice, *The Canon of Medicine* (see the box). Other important individuals include the philosophers al-Rindi and **Ibn Rushd** (**Averroës**), and al-Zahrawi, a surgeon and medical innovator.

The Arts in the Muslim World

❁

Because the Qur'an prohibited the lifelike representation of the human figure as blasphemous to the creator Allah, the Muslims had to turn to other motifs and developed an intricate geometrically based format for the visual arts. The motifs of their painting, ceramics, mosaics, and inlay work—in all of which the Muslim world excelled—were based on garlands, plants, or geometric figures such as triangles, diamonds, and parallelograms. The Muslims produced no sculpture beyond miniatures and, for a long time, no portrait painting.

In architecture, the Muslims, especially the Persians, developed a great deal of lastingly beautiful forms and executed them with great skill. The "most beautiful building in the world," the Taj Mahal in India, is a thoroughly Muslim creation (see the photo in Chapter 32). The use of reflecting pools and landscapes of great precision and intricate design was common in parks and public buildings. Great wealth and a love of luxury were earmarks of rulers throughout the world of Islam, and it was considered a mark of gentility and good manners for a ruler to spend lavishly on public and private adornments.

Calligraphy was a special strength of the Muslims, whose Arabic script is the product of aesthetic demands as much

🌼 **Decorative Tiles.** The Islamic exhortation that the human figure should be avoided in art, for fear of blaspheming the sole Creator resulted in the adoption of intricate and inventive geometric designs as art's expression. These ceiling tiles in Samarkand, Uzbekistan, date from the days of the Timurid monarchs in late medieval times, and were almost certainly taken from Persian models. *(Geophoto/Art Resource, NY)*

as the desire to communicate. As in ancient China, a beautiful script was considered to be as much a part of good breeding as beautiful clothing. Arabic lettering was incorporated into almost every form of art, generally as quotations from the Qur'an.

Arabs developed storytelling to a high art and are generally credited with the invention of *fiction*—that is, stories told solely to entertain. The most famous book of stories in the history of the world is ***The 1001 Nights*** (also called ***The Arabian Nights***), which was supposedly created by a courtier at the court of **Harun al-Rashid,** one of the greatest of the Baghdad caliphs in the early ninth century. Poetry was also a strongly cultivated and very popular literary art form, especially among the Persian Muslims. The quatrains of Omar Khayyam, a twelfth-century Persian, are famous throughout the world (see the Religion and Morality box in Chapter 32).

Muslim Civilization at Its Apex

🌸

Muslim civilization flourished most brilliantly between about 900 and about 1200. At its height, Islam was the most lavish and innovative civilization of the world, rivaled only by China, with which it had extensive commercial and some intellectual contacts. The Muslim world at this time extended from the Atlantic to the Indian Ocean, and Muslim traders were found on every known continent and sea (see Map 16.1). See the Nature and Technology box for comments on the ways of Christian crusaders by the well-educated Muslim gentleman, Usama ibn Munqidh.

As we will see later in this chapter, the Mongol invasion commencing about 1230 was a huge shock to the Muslims of the Middle East. It is no coincidence that a marked decline in original intellectual work makes itself apparent after this date. Until Mongols and, later, Turks had adopted Islam for themselves and spearheaded two more waves of military expansion in the fourteenth through sixteenth centuries, the Muslim civilization entered a period of retrenchment.

Islam provided a precise place for every person in its social scheme without severely limiting freedom of movement. Believers could move without hindrance all around a huge belt of settlements on either side of the equator, from Spain to the Philippines. Travelers could journey to distant lands, secure in the knowledge that they would be

The *Memoirs* of Usama ibn Munqidh

The Arab Usama ibn Munqidh lived in Christian-ruled Palestine over ninety years. A well educated Muslim gentleman, he had many friends among the Franks (the Muslim term for all Westerners) and made many insightful comments about them in his *Memoirs*. The following excerpts deal with his wonderment at Frankish medical lore and at their incredible absence of jealousy—or gullibility—about their women:

> They brought before me a knight in whose leg an abscess had grown; and a woman afflicted with imbecility. To the knight I applied a small poultice until the abscess opened and became well; and the woman I put on a diet and made her humor wet. Then a Frankish physician came to them, and said, "This man knows nothing about treating them." He then said to the knight, "Which would thou prefer, living with one leg or dying with two?" The latter replied, "Living with one leg." The physician said, "Bring me a strong knight and a sharp ax." A knight came with the ax. And I was standing by. Then the physician laid the leg of the patient on a block of wood and bade the knight strike his leg with the ax and chop it off with one blow. Accordingly he struck it—while I was looking on—one blow, but the leg was not severed. He dealt another blow, upon which the marrow of the leg flowed out and the patient died on the spot.
>
> He then examined the woman and said, "This is a women in whose head there is a devil which has possessed her. Shave off her hair." Accordingly they shaved it off, and the woman began once more to eat the ordinary diet—garlic and mustard. Her imbecility took a turn for the worse. The physician then said, "The devil has penetrated through her head," He therefore took a razor and made a deep cruciform incision on it, peeled off the skin at the middle of the incision until the bone of the skull was exposed, and rubbed it with salt. The woman expired instantly. Thereupon, I inquired whether my services were needed any longer, and when they replied in the negative, I turned home, having learned of their medicine what I knew not before. . . .
>
> One day a Frank went home and found a man with his wife in the same bed. He asked him, "What could have made thee enter into my wife's room?" The man replied, "I was tired, so I went in to rest." "But how," asked he, "didst thou get into my bed?" The other replied, "I found a bed that was spread, so I slept in it." "But," said he, "my wife was sleeping with thee!" The other replied, "Well, the bed is hers. How could I have therefore prevented her from using her own bed?" "By the truth of my religion," said the husband, "if thou shouldst do it again thou and I would have a quarrel."

For Reflection

Does the story of how the Frankish doctor "cured" the madwoman sound plausible? Do you think the Muslim husband really believed the Frank? Or might he have been more concerned about his own reputation?

SOURCE: From "The Memoirs of Usamah," excerpted from The Islamic World edited by McNeill, Waldman, 1973. Reprinted with permission of Oxford University Press.

Arabic Calligraphy. The beauty of written Arabic is rivalled only by the Oriental scripts. Several different styles evolved in different places and times, quite as distinct as the various alphabets of the Western world. Here is an eleventh-century Persian script. *(The Metropolitan Museum of Art, Rogers Fund, 1942)*

Medical Consultation. From a fourteenth-century Arabic manuscript comes this charming miniature showing a pair of doctors consulting about their patient, presumably the woman on the horse. Arab doctors maintained their European reputation as the world's finest well into the later Middle Age. Their instruments and manuals were standard equipment in the West from about the eleventh century onward. *(e.t. archive)*

welcomed by their co-religionists and would find the same laws and prejudices, the same literary language, and the same conceptions of justice and truth that they had known at home. Wherever they were, all Muslims knew they were members of a great community, the Muslim *umma.*

The cities of this world were splendid and varied. Córdoba and Grenada were cities of perhaps a half million people in the tenth century; its ruling class was Muslim, from the North African Berber people, but its inhabitants included many Jews and Christians as well. Anything produced in the East or West could be purchased in the markets of Córdoba. The same was true of Baghdad, which had an even larger population and featured the most lavish imperial court of all under caliph Harun al-Rashid and his ninth-century successors.

Commerce was particularly well developed in the world of Islam, and the exhortation in the Qur'an to "honor the honest merchant" was generally observed. The Muslim faithful saw nothing wrong in getting rich. In contrast to both Christians and Buddhists, they considered a wealthy man to be the recipient of God's blessings for a good life. The rich had an obligation to share their wealth with the poor, however. Most schools, dormitories, hospitals, orphanages, and the like in Muslim areas are to this day the result of private donations and foundations, the ***wakf,*** which are very commonly included in Muslim wills.

Social Customs: Marriage and the Status of Women

How did women fit into the social scheme of the Muslim world? The Qur'an allows but does not encourage a man to marry up to four wives if he can maintain them properly. The marriages may be either serial or simultaneous. There is no limit on the number of concubines he can have. In practice, though, few Muslims had as many as four wives, and fewer still could afford concubines. The children of a concubine, if acknowledged by the father, were provided for in law and custom equally with those of a legal wife.

Many households kept at least one slave (sometimes the concubine). Slavery was very common, but usually not very harsh. Most slaves worked in the household or shop, not in the fields or mines. It was common for slaves to be freed at any time for good behavior or because the owner wished to assure Allah's blessing. Most people fell into slavery for the usual reasons: debts, wars, and bad luck. Muslims were not supposed to enslave other members of the faith; but this seems to have been frequently ignored or rationalized.

The household was ruled absolutely by the man, whose foremost duty toward it and himself was to maintain honor. Muslim society was dominated by honor and shame. Feud-

 Townscape of Grenada. This striking view of one of the strongholds of the Moors (Muslims in Spain, from *moro*, "dark") shows the remnants of the medieval walls and the castle sitting on its hill below the high mountains of southern Spain. (© *Susan McCartney/Photo Researchers, Inc.*)

ing was endemic, and every insult had to be avenged. In the law of the Qur'an, women were granted many rights—far more than in pre-Islamic Arab society—though how many of these were actually put into practice is difficult to know.

One sign of women's inferior social and legal status was the **harem,** the secluded part of every well-to-do Muslim house that was reserved for women and their children. Here they were safe from the insulting eyes of strangers. Shut up in the harem with little to do, the various wives and concubines of a powerful man might occupy their time trying to devise ways to win the favor of the master of the household and advance their own status and that of their children. Sexual jealousy was one of the main hinges around which the society revolved, and the relationship between the sexes was apparently even more one-sided and tension filled than in other civilizations. Some emirs and caliphs spent so much time in the harem that the word came to mean a kind of illicit government by women, who influenced their lords by sexual intrigues. In later Muslim history, the harem system had ruinous effects on the administration and government of the empire. Given the powerlessness of women in these circumstances, it isn't difficult to envision that they pursued distinction and prestige through highly personalized means.

Women were not to be seen or heard outside the house in theory and often in practice as well. This seclusion of women and their total inaccessibility prior to marriage contributed to the relative frequency of male homosexuality in

the Islamic world, where it became even more common than it had been in ancient Greece.

The Decline of the Abbasids and the Coming of the Turks and Mongols

Despite all their efforts, the Abbasids were unable to restore the political unity of the empire they had taken over in 750. Even great caliphs such as Harun al-Rashid, who was well known in the West, could not force the Spaniards and the North African emirates to submit to their rule. Gradually, during the 800s, almost all of the African and Arabian possessions broke away and became independent, leaving the Abbasids in control of only the Middle East. More and more, they came to depend on wild Turkish tribesmen, only some of whom had converted to Islam, for their military power. It was inevitable that the Turks would someday turn on their weak masters and make them into pawns.

In the mid-1000s C.E., a new group of Turks, known as **Seljuks** surged out of Afghanistan into Iran and Iraq. In 1055 they entered Baghdad as victors. Keeping the Abbasid ruler on as a figurehead, the Seljuks took over the government

✿ **The Grand Mosque, Damascus.** Built very early in Muslim history, the Grand Mosque was constructed by the Ummayad dynasty of caliphs. It is considered one of the three most perfect buildings in the Islamic world. (© *Jean-Louis Nou/AKG London*)

for about a century, until they, too, fell prey to internal rivalries. The central government ceased to exist, and the Middle East became a series of large and small Muslim principalities, fighting one another for commercial and territorial advantage.

Into this disintegrated empire exploded a totally new force out of the east: **Chinghis Khan** and the **Mongols.** Chinghis started out as a minor tribal leader of the primitive Mongols, who inhabited the semidesert steppes of northern Central Asia as nomadic pastoralists. In the late twelfth century, he was able to put together a series of victories over his rivals and set himself up as lord of his people. Leading an army of savage horsemen in a great campaign, he managed to conquer most of Central Asia and the Middle East before his death in the early 1200s.

His immediate successor as Great Khan (the title means "lord") was victorious over the Russians and ravaged about half of Europe before retiring in the 1230s. But a few years later, the Mongols felt themselves ready to settle accounts with the Seljuks and other claimants to the Baghdad throne. They took Baghdad in an orgy of slaughter and rape—eyewitnesses claimed that some 800,000 people were killed! In this gory debacle, the Abbasid caliphate finally came to an end in 1258 and was replaced by the Mongol Khanate of Central Asia. This story continues in Chapter 32.

𝒮UMMARY

Muslim civilization was an amalgam of the many civilizations that had preceded it. It was eclectic, taking from any forebear anything that seemed valuable or useful. In the opening centuries, the civilization was dominated by the Arabs who had founded it by military conquest. But it gradually opened up to all who professed the true faith of the Prophet and worshiped the one god, Allah. Much of the territory the Arabs conquered was already highly civilized, with well-developed religions. The Arabs therefore contented themselves with establishing a minority of rulers and traders and intermarrying with the natives as they converted to Islam. Based on the easy-to-understand principles of an all-embracing religious faith, Muslim civilization was a world into which many streams flowed to make up a vast new sea.

Test Your Knowledge

1. Which of the following cities was *not* a center of Muslim culture in this era?
   a. Cairo
   b. Constantinople
   c. Córdoba
   d. Baghdad
2. The impression given by the Arab Usama about Crusader medical knowledge is that
   a. the Muslims had a lot to learn from the West.
   b. the Muslims should send their best students to Europe.
   c. the Franks were delighted to be able to study Muslim technique.
   d. the Franks were too stupid in their practice to learn anything useful from them.
3. The common Muslim attitude toward trade and mercantile activity was
   a. that they were best left to the "infidel."
   b. that nothing was morally or ethically wrong with them.
   c. reluctant acceptance of their necessity.
   d. condemnation as temptations to evildoing.
4. Many Muslim scholars especially revered the work of
   a. Gautama Buddha.
   b. Aristotle.
   c. Confucius.
   d. Socrates.
5. Muslim knowledge significantly influenced the West in all these areas *except*
   a. philosophy.
   b. law.
   c. medicine.
   d. mathematics.
6. The major area from which Muslim culture entered Christian Europe was
   a. Greece.
   b. Spain.
   c. Italy.
   d. Russia.
7. The *Canon of Medicine* was the work of
   a. Aristotle.
   b. Avicenna.
   c. Harun al-Rashid.
   d. Averroës.

Identification Terms

Chinghis Khan

harem

Ibn Rushd (Averroës)

Ibn Sina (Avicenna)

Harun al-Rashid

Mongols

Seljuk Turks

sharia

The 1001 Nights (The Arabian Nights)

ulema

vizier

wakf

InfoTrac College Edition

Enter the search terms "caliph or caliphate" using Key Words.

Enter the search term "Islam" using the Subject Guide.

Chapter 17

Indian Civilization in Its Golden Age

The people are numerous and happy. . . . if they want to go, they go; if they want to stay on, they stay . . . Throughout the whole country the people do not kill any living creature.

FA-HSIEN

The Gupta Dynasty
Economic and Cultural Progress

Political Fragmentation: South and North
South
North

Hindu Doctrines in the Classical Age

Development of the Caste System

Social Customs
Sexuality

India and East Asia

c. 200–500	Ajanta caves constructed and painted
320–480	Gupta dynasty
c. 406	Arrival of Fa-hsien in India
480 onward	India divided between North and South
c. 500–c. 800	Formative period of caste system
711	Arabs invade northwestern India
c. 700–1000:	Hindu revival and decline of Buddhism in India
late 1100s–1400s	Delhi sultanate in North India

UNDER THE GUPTA DYNASTY of kings (320–480 C.E.), India experienced a great flourishing of Hindu culture. At about the time that the Roman empire was weakening, Hindu civilization stabilized. The caste system assured everyone of a definite place in society, and political affairs were in the hands of strong, effective rulers for a century and a half. Vedic Hindu religious belief responded to the challenge of Buddhism and reformed itself so effectively that it began to supplant Buddhism in the country. Indian merchants and emigrants carried Hindu theology and Sanskrit literature to Southeast Asia, where they merged with native religions and cultures. Long after the political unity under the Guptas ended, India continued to produce scientific advances and technological developments that are still not fully recognized in the West. The invasions of Muslim Turks and others from the northwest redivided India into political fragments, but the essential unity of its Hindu civilization carried on.

The Gupta Dynasty

After the fall of the Mauryan dynasty in the 200s B.C.E. (see Chapter 5), India reverted to a group of small principalities fighting one another for mastery. This was the usual political situation in India, where one invader after another succeeded in establishing only partial control, usually in the north, while the rest was controlled by Indian princes.

Not until 320 C.E. was another powerful native dynasty founded—that of the Gupta kings, who ruled from their base in the valley of the Ganges River on the east side of the subcontinent. They overcame their rivals to eventually create an empire over most of India, which lasted until about 500 C.E. when it was destroyed by a combination of internal dissension and external threats. The Gupta dynasty was the last Indian-led unification of the country until the twentieth century. Long after the dynasty had disappeared, memories of its brilliance remained. As time wore on and India remained divided and subject to foreign invaders, the Guptas and their achievements became the standard by which other rulers were measured.

The Gupta period is the first in Indian history for which more or less reliable firsthand accounts have survived. The most interesting is that of the Chinese Buddhist monk *Fa-hsien,* who visited India for a long period around 400 and left a diary of what he saw and did. According to his account, India was a very stable society, well ruled by a king who was universally respected because he brought prosperity and order everywhere. Nevertheless, despite such sources, we know relatively little about Gupta India compared with what we know of other world civilizations of this date. Indians did not begin to keep historical records until very late, so, aside from works such as Fa-hsien's, the main written materials we have are religious poetry and folklore. Even these are quite sparse, for the tradition of both Hinduism and Buddhism was not literary but oral. What was important was memorized, generation after generation, but inevitably with some changes. It was not written down until much later, and then only in a much altered version. For this reason historians have few definite records to work with in India until perhaps as late as 1500 C.E. and must depend heavily on both archaeology and traveler's reports such as Fa-hsien's.

Economic and Cultural Progress

In this classical age, the overwhelming majority of Indians continued to gain their daily sustenance from farming and herding, perhaps even more so than in other parts of the world. The agrarian villages, not the handful of towns and cities were the vital center of Indian life. These villages changed very little in activity or appearance over the centuries. In the Gupta period and for some time thereafter, India was yet free from the problems of insufficient land and overpopulation in its rich river basins. The average villager seems to have been a landowner or tenant who worked a small plot that he had inherited and that he would pass on to an oldest son or sons.

In most of the subcontinent rice was the chief crop, as it had become in most of south Asia. The huge demands this crop imposed on labor determined many aspects of life in the village: the cycle of rice planting and transplanting and harvesting was the fundamental calendar. Water was crucial for rice growing, and control and distribution of water were the source of constant controversy and in some cases even wars between the numerous small principalities. In this respect and in the dependence on intensive, irrigation agriculture, India resembled both Mesopotamia and south China.

The arts flourished during the Gupta period, and several models in architecture and sculpture were developed that remained the standards of beauty for a long time. The greatest of ancient India's playwrights, **Kalidasa,** wrote a series of works that remain popular today. He was a major contributor to the upsurge of Sanskrit literature at this time. Sanskrit, the language of the Aryans, was now formally adopted as a sacred literary script, but literacy remained very exceptional.

The Gupta period also produced notable achievements in the sciences. Mathematicians worked out the concept of zero, which enabled them to handle large numbers much more easily; zero is closely associated with the decimal system, which was probably also an Indian invention. The "Arabic" numbers that are used universally today also originated in Gupta India, so far as historians can determine. Indian astronomers also made several breakthroughs in explaining eclipses of the moon and in calculating geographic distances.

The medical sciences developed significantly during and after the Gupta period. Pharmacy, surgery, and diagnosis of internal ills were Indian specialties, and it was not at all unusual for wealthy Muslims from the west to come to Indian doctors for treatment. In this way began the active interchange between the Muslim and Hindu medical men that so profited the Muslims in the period after 850 C.E. and was eventually passed on to the backward Europeans.

Political Fragmentation: South and North

After the demise of the Gupta dynasty, India divided into political-cultural regions: South and North (see Map 17.1). Each of these further subdivided into several units ruled by hereditary or aristocratic leaders. But each region shared some common features distinguishing each from the other.

South

Below the Deccan plateau, the South was inhabited by dark-skinned peoples whose languages came from the Dravidian and Pali families, quite different from those of the North. The South's political history is almost unknown for several centuries, as it was never brought under direct Gupta rule, and very few written records have survived. The invasions that perennially wracked the North had little effect on the South, whose contacts with foreigners were in the nature of peaceful commerce both east and west over the Indian Ocean.

The culture of the South was strongly influenced by varieties of Hinduism and particularly Buddhism, which differed from those of the North. The Theravada (Hinayana) form of Buddhism became dominant in the South, especially in Sri Lanka. Sri Lankan holy men and monasteries were instrumental in the conversion of much of Southeast

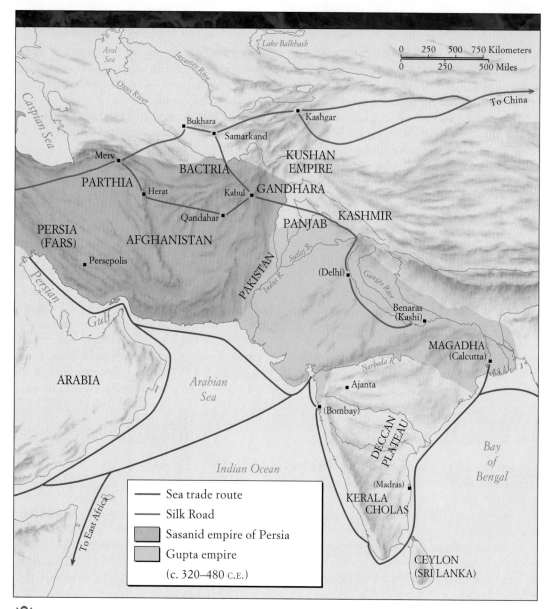

✿ **MAP 17.1   The Gupta Empire and Its Trading Partners.** The Gupta monarchs controlled the northern half of India and made much of the south into their vassals. Their merchants traded with Persia and Africa as well as the Malayan and Indonesian peoples to the east.

Asia. The Theravada devotees tended to look down on the relatively flexible doctrines of the Mahayana adherents and rejected many as unworthy or inauthentic. This attitude contributed to the differentiation of South and North, which was already apparent in linguistic and ethnic spheres. From the Gupta period onward, there was little common political bond between the two regions for many centuries. Only the near extinction of Buddhism and the revival of Hinduism throughout the subcontinent allowed Indians to begin the slow development of a modern, politically expressed sense of nationhood.

The South saw a great flourishing of both Buddhist and Hindu architecture and sculpture between 300 and 700 C.E.

Both religions encouraged the construction of massive stone stupas, rounded temples that stood in the midst of extensive complexes for both worship and living quarters. In the interiors stood statues of the gods and goddesses and all types of holy shrines. Sculpture, mainly in stone but also in bronze, seems to have been the art form of choice among Hindus during most of their history. Some of their life-size and more-than-life-size work has survived to demonstrate the artists' skills. Even more impressive are the many panels and figures that decorate the exteriors of the stupa temples and show us the vigor and life-affirming nature of Hindu art. Much of it was erotic and gave rise to much embarrassment among nineteenth-century British colonial observers. What would have been considered pornographic in a Western context apparently had no such connotations to Indians, either then or now.

Some painting has also survived, most notably in the caves of **Ajanta** in the south. But the climate of tropical India is hard on paint, and little has survived, whether indoors or out. Like most architecture and sculpture of India's Golden Age, all paintings were inspired by religious legends and stories, very much as medieval European artworks were. The paintings portray gods good and bad and all sorts of demons taken from the very rich religious folklore.

North

We have a good deal more political and military data from the North of India during the 700 years between the fall of the Gupta dynasty and the erection of the Muslim sultanate in Delhi. The major question facing all North Indian rulers was how to defend themselves against the repeated and ever fiercer assaults coming from Afghanistan on the northwestern frontier. From the eighth century onward, bands of Muslim raiders and would-be conquerors of the Hindu and Buddhist areas had harassed northwestern India. By the eleventh century, enough of the Turkic tribesmen of central Asia had become Muslims to constitute a fearsome fighting

✿ **Frescos at Ajanta Caves.** The Ajanta cave complex was begun sometime in the second century B.C.E. and completed in 478 C.E. Originally a Hindu project, it became a Buddhist retreat, and the hundreds of frescos and sculptures that grace it are mainly representative of Buddhist belief. The picture shows four seated bodhisattvas behind a row of amorous couples. Such a juxtapositioning of spirit and flesh is not unusual in Indian Buddhist art. *(Vanni/Art Resource)*

✿ **Stupa Reliefs.** The candid emphasis on sexual attributes in Hindu sculpture was considered to be justified recognition of a source of human pleasure. *(© John Elk/Stock Boston)*

The complexities of Hindu religious and philosophical speculations as they developed in the first millennium C.E. are often baffling to the reader. But occasionally help is forthcoming through one or another of the frequent Indian folk sayings that have evolved in the oral tradition:

A learned father wished to instruct his son in the mysteries of the spirit that informs all earthly creatures but can never be apprehended by the senses.

Father: Now you ask for that instruction by which we hear what cannot be heard, by which we perceive what cannot be perceived, by which we know what cannot be known.

Son: What is that instruction, sir?

F: Fetch me a fruit of the Nyagrodha tree.
S: Here is one, sir.
F: Break it.
S: It is broken.
F: What do you see?
S: These seeds, almost infinitesimal.
F: Break one.
S: It is broken.
F: What do you see there?
S: Not anything, sir.
F: My son, that subtle essence which you do not perceive there, of that very essence this great Nyagrodha tree exists.

SOURCE: *Sacred Books of the East, trans. F. Max Mueller, Oxford University Press.*

force under the leadership of Afghani *imams.* Defense against these raiders was haphazard despite the common danger. The princes of North India were as divided among themselves as those in the South, if not more so. As a result, the raiders were successful more often than not and were encouraged to attempt full-scale invasions starting in the late 1000s C.E. and continuing throughout the 1100s over the better part of the North.

In the late twelfth century, at the same time that Chinghis Khan was rising to power far to the north, a force of Turks and Afghans rode down into India from their strongholds in the Afghani hills. This time, they overwhelmed the defenders and came to stay. They created the Delhi Sultanate, based in their newly founded capital city at Delhi. This state continued to govern most of northern India for the next 300 years and ultimately provided the historical foundation for the modern state of Pakistan.

Culturally speaking, the contacts between Islamic and Hindu/Buddhist civilizations were important. Indian visitors to Harun al-Rashid's Baghdad trained Islamic scholars at the request of the caliph himself. When he fell seriously ill, Harun was cured by an Indian physician, who was then rewarded with the post of royal physician. Beginning as early as the 800s, many Arab merchants visited the west coast of India. Some of their travel accounts survive and are important sources of Indian history. So many resident Muslims lived in some of the coastal towns as to justify the building of mosques. In addition to carrying cottons, silks, and fine steel swords from India to the world of Islam, these merchants, traders, and other Muslim visitors took back the Indians' knowledge of algebra and astronomy and other cultural achievements.

Not all the results of the Islamic invasion were positive for India, by any means. Muslim conquest induced the final stage of the long decline of Buddhism in India. Buddhism was a proselytizing religion, like Islam itself, and the two competitors did not get along well. Where the Muslims

were able to ignore or come to terms with Hinduism, they attacked Buddhism and its institutions, especially the numerous monasteries that were the heart of the faith. Already weakened by revitalized Hinduism, the Buddhist faith was now, in the twelfth century, wiped out in the land that had originated it. Its strong roots on the island of Sri Lanka, as well as in China, Korea, Japan, and much of Southeast Asia, guaranteed its continued existence, however.

Hindu Doctrines in the Classical Age

❈

The doctrines of Hinduism stem from a great mass of unwritten tradition but also from three written sources: the **Vedas,** the **Upanishads,** and the *Mahabharata.* The Vedas (see Chapter 5) are four lengthy epic poems that were originally brought to India by the Aryans and were then "nativized" over many centuries. They deal with the relations between the many gods and their human subjects and relate tales of the god-heroes who created the earth and all that lies in it. The most significant is the **Rigveda,** which was written down in relatively modern times; it contains a great deal of information about the Aryan-Indian gods and their relations with humans. The chief deities are Indra and Varuna. Indra, the god of war and revelry, resembles the old Germanic god Thor in several ways. Varuna was the caretaker of proper order in the universe, the first hint of an ethical element in Indian religion. Vedic religion was one of ritual and sacrifice, with priests playing the leading role.

The Upanishads are a series of long and short philosophical speculations, apparently first produced in the eighth century B.C.E.; gradually, they were expanded to number over 100 by a body of poems that deal with the dilemma of being alive on earth as a partial, incomplete be-

An Excerpt from the *Bhagavad-Gita*

Of the myriad Hindu sagas and poems, the *Bhagavad-Gita* is the most popular and the best known among Westerners. It has also been used by Indian holy men and parents to teach lessons of moral behavior to succeeding generations of Hindus. It is a part of the larger poem *Mahabharata*, a tale of the distant and mythical past, when two clans fought for supremacy in India. Just before the decisive struggle, one of the clan leaders, the warrior Arjuna, meditates on the meaning of life. His questions are answered by his charioteer, who is the god Krishna in human disguise. Arjuna regrets having to kill his opponents whom he knows and respects, but Krishna tells him that his sorrow is misplaced because what Arjuna conceives of as the finality of death is not that:

> You grieve for those beyond grief,
> and you speak words of insight;
> but learned men do not grieve
> for the dead or for the living.
> Never have I not existed,
> nor you, nor these kings;
> and never in the future
> shall we cease to exist.
> Just as the embattled self
> enters childhood, youth, and old age,
> so does it enter another body;
> this does not confound a steadfast man . . .
> Our bodies are known to end,
> but the embodied Self is enduring,
> indestructible, and immeasurable;
> therefore, Arjuna, fight the battle!
> He who thinks this Self a killer
> and he who thinks it killed,
> both fail to understand;
> it does not kill, nor is it killed.

> It is not born,
> it does not die;
> having been,
> it will never not be;
> unborn, enduring,
> constant, and primordial,
> it is not killed
> when the body is killed.
> Arjuna, when a man knows the Self
> to be indestructible, enduring, unborn,
> unchanging, how does he kill
> or cause anyone to kill? . . .
> Weapons do not cut it [the Self],
> fire does not burn it,
> waters do not wet it,
> wind does not wither it.
> It cannot be cut or burned;
> it cannot be wet or withered,
> it is enduring, all pervasive,
> fixed, immobile, and timeless. . . .
> The Self embodied in the body
> of every being is indestructible;
> you have no cause to grieve
> for all these creatures, Arjuna!

For Reflection

What does Krishna attempt to show Arjuna about the nature of his duty as a warrior? Is his counsel coldhearted or realistic, in your view? How could devout Hindus take comfort from this poem?

Source: From Bhagavad Gita: Krishna's Counsel in Time of War, *trans.* B. S. Miller, 1986. Bantam Books.

---

ing. The Upanishads are a long step forward from the relatively unsophisticated rituals and anecdotes of the Vedas; with them begins the tradition of very involved speculation that became a characteristic of later Hindu thought.

The *Mahabharata* (*Great Story*) is the world's longest poem. It contains about 200,000 lines, relating the exploits of the gods and some of their favored heroes on earth. The most popular part, known by all Hindus, is the ***Bhagavad-Gita,*** a segment in which the god Krishna instructs a warrior, Arjuna, in what is entailed in being a human being who strives to do good and avoid evil to his fellows (see the Religion and Morality box).

The supreme deities of all Hindus are **Brahman, Vishnu,** and **Shiva.** Though individuals may worship many gods, all Hindus believe in the paramount importance of these

three. In a very general fashion, Hindus are subdivided into the devotees of either Vishnu or Shiva. Brahman is the world-spirit, the source of all life and all objects in the universe. Brahman is roughly equivalent to the Christian God the Father, but entirely impersonal.

Vishnu is the Preserver, a sort of Christ figure without the ethical teachings. He (or sometimes, she; the Hindu deities are often bisexual) has appeared in nine incarnations thus far in world history, and there will be a tenth. The most popular of all Hindu gods, Vishnu is particularly beloved in the form of Krishna, the instructor and protector of all humans.

The last of the Hindu trinity is Shiva, the Destroyer and also Creator. Shiva is best appreciated as the god of becoming, lord of both life and death. At times he or she is

🏵 **Hindu God Vishnu.** *Vishnu Riding the Garuda.* The god of salvation is astride the huge bird-demon as it circles the cosmos in search of prey. (© *Art Resource*)

depicted as a beneficent bringer of joy; at other times he is the ruthless and irresistible destroyer, making way for new life to come.

Some of these beliefs, and particularly the position of the priests who interpreted them—the brahmins—were challenged by the Buddhists and the Jains (see Chapter 6). By the first century C.E., Buddhism and Jainism had attracted the allegiance of a large part of the population (see the second Religion and Morality box). The old Vedic Hinduism proved unable to match the appeal of these religions to persons seeking an ethical and emotionally fulfilling experience.

Just as Buddhism gradually evolved into a ritualistic religion after its founder's death, so did Hinduism respond to the Buddhist challenge by developing a much more formalist and ethical approach to the mysteries of eternal life and the gods who ordained human fate. The Upanishads and the *Mahabharata* are the embodiment of this response, which changed the old Hinduism into something quite different. This new Hinduism was capable of arousing strong adherence among ordinary souls by giving them a meaningful guide to moral and ethical belief. In the first Religion and Morality box, an excerpt from the *Bhagavad-Gita,* one of the best-known sections of the *Mahabharata,* illustrates these teachings.

Both Buddhism and especially Hinduism in time evolved into many subdivisions, or sects, which worshiped somewhat differently and had different gods and prophets. All of these are notable for their tolerance toward others; in contrast with the historical Western religions, they do not assert that there is but one true path to heaven.

🏵 **Borobudur.** Indian influence is strongly visible in the great complex of Borobudur in central Java where Hindu and Buddhist beliefs merged. This eighth-century structure represents in its concentric circles the ascent of the soul to liberation from the great Wheel of Life. (© *Brian Brake/Photo Researchers, Inc.*)

Mahavira Vardhamana

Not all Indians are Hindus; here and there in that vast subcontinent live colonies of other believers, some of whom preceded the sixth-century arrival of the Christians in India by many centuries. Foremost among these are the Jains, who are concentrated in the province of Gujarat, particularly among the members of the mercantile castes. Though not numbering more than a few million, they have exercised an influence on Indian spiritual life that far exceeds their numbers.

The Jain religion owes its origins to the work of a sixth-century B.C.E. sage named Vardhamana, later given the title of *Mahavira,* or Great Hero. He lived from about 540 to 470 and was thus a contemporary of the Buddha, with whom he seems to have had some personal contact. Both men were members of the *kshatriya* caste and, like others of that warrior-governor grouping, resented the exclusive claims of the brahmins to the priestly functions. Animal sacrifice played a major role in the brahmins' Hinduism, and both the Buddha and Mahavira rejected it as inappropriate.

Mahavira later took this rejection to its ultimate form: he and his followers made every possible effort to avoid any form of violence to other creatures, even when that nonviolence represented death or danger to themselves. This doctrine of *ahimsa* was the outstanding characteristic of Jainism in Mahavira's day and remains so to the present.

Mahavira's background strongly resembles that of Siddartha Gautama, the Buddha. He was born into a rich family but began to question the emptiness of his moral life when he was in his twenties. At age thirty, he abandoned his family to become a wandering seeker. Adopting an extreme asceticism (such as the Buddha tried and ultimately rejected), he even dispensed with clothing, preferring to wander naked through the world begging food and sleeping in the open.

After twelve years, he felt he had cleansed himself of worldly ambitions and was qualified to teach others. He preached the Five Great Vows: no killing under any circumstances, no untruth, no greed, total chastity, and no restrictive attachments to any person or object. Certainly, few could maintain these vows fully, but they were meant to be goals that one strived for and did not necessarily attain in one lifetime.

In the present day, Jains often wear gauze masks to avoid inadvertent intake of minute insects and constantly sweep their paths to avoid stepping on some tiny animal or plant. Bathing and moving about in the dark are avoided for the same reason. They set up hostels where they bring sick and aged animals, allowing them to die in peace. And they believe that voluntary starvation is the most admirable death once one has reached a state in which following the Great Vows is no longer possible.

Jainism strongly resembles the other great Eastern faiths in the absence of a Creator God from whom humans receive moral instruction or commands. Like Buddhism, Jainism accepts reincarnation and the concept of *karma,* with the accompanying striving for liberation from an earthly existence, *moksha.* The emphasis on *ahimsa* is its distinguishing mark, and through that pathway the teachings of Mahavira have had an important effect on Hindu and Buddhist belief. Mohandas Gandhi, the father of modern India and the teacher of worldwide nonviolent political action, is the outstanding modern example.

For Reflection

Do you think the Jains' insistence on avoiding violence and coercion is practical in today's world? Could you imagine yourself living as a Jain?

Development of the Caste System

By the end of the Gupta period, the caste system founded by the Aryan conquerors reigned supreme. It had grown ever more refined in its applications and more complex in its structure as time passed. Subcastes had multiplied and were determined by geographic, ethnic, and kinship factors as well as the traditional social and economic categories. Along with the restructured Hindu faith, caste had become one of the two defining factors in the lives of all Indians. At the bottom were the outcastes or untouchables, who were condemned to a marginal existence as beggars, buriers of the dead, and dealers in animal products thought to be polluting. Above them were hundreds of varieties of farmers, craftsmen, and merchants as well as laborers, each of which constituted a more or less closed grouping with its own (unwritten) rules of religious belief and social conduct.

While caste members tended strongly to belong to a distinct occupation, the caste could also be territorial and doctrinal in its nature. For example, members of a caste that specialized in credit and money lending in Calcutta were not members of the caste that dominated the same activity in Bombay or in Delhi, and which could be seen as higher or lower in the intricate gradings of social prestige that caste imposed. Although it was possible to raise one's status by marriage with a higher caste member, it was also possible to

The brief discussion of the concept of karma, so central to Hindu belief, stems from the observations of an outsider, the Muslim Abul Fazl who lived in India during the sixteenth century:

[Karma] is a system of knowledge of an amazing and extraordinary character, in which the learned of Hindustan concur without dissenting opinions. It reveals the particular class of actions performed in a former birth which have occasioned the events that befall men in this present life, and prescribes the special expiation of each sin, one by one. It is of four kinds: The first kind discloses the particular action which has brought a man into existence in one of the five classes into which mankind is divided, and the action which occasions the assumption of a male or female form. . . .

The second kind shows the strange effects of actions on health of body and in the production of manifold diseases.

Madness is the punishment of disobedience to father and mother. . . .

Pain in the eyes arises from having looked upon another's wife. . . .

Dumbness is the consequence of killing a sister. . . .

Colic results from having eaten with an impious person or a liar. . . .

Consumption is the punishment of killing a Brahmin. . . .

The third kind indicates the class of actions which have caused sterility and names suitable remedies. . . .

A woman who does not menstruate [has] in a former existence roughly driven away the children of her neighbors who had come as usual to play at her house. . . .

A woman who gives birth to only daughters is thus punished for having contemptuously regarded her husband, from pride. . . .

A woman who has given birth to a son that dies, and to a daughter that lives has, in her former existence, taken animal life. Some say that she had killed goats. . . .

The fourth kind treats of riches and poverty, and the like. Whosoever distributes alms at auspicious times . . . will become rich and bountiful. . . . Who so at such times visits any place of pilgrimage . . . and there dies, will possess great wealth, but will be avaricious and of surly disposition. Whosoever when hungry and with food before him hears the supplication of a poor man and bestows it all upon him, will be rich and liberal. But whosoever has been deprived of these three opportunities will be empty handed and poor in his present life.

SOURCE: From The Human Record, vol. 2, by A. Andrea and C. Overfield, p. 70.

debase oneself by marriage to a lower one. It seems that the usual rationalizations were attempted by impoverished members of the high-prestige castes who sought material advantage from marriage with a lower, but wealthy, individual. All in all, however, such mixed marriages with their attendant changes of caste were rare in India, and the stratification of society which commenced in Aryan times grew ever stronger.

By about the ninth or tenth century C.E., the system had become so entrenched as to be a fundamental pillar of the revitalized Hindu culture. It was the cement holding the nation together, giving everyone a definite, easily comprehended place in society. Yet at the same time, of course, it created permanent barriers between individuals—separations that persist today. The modern Indian constitution, adopted after independence in 1947 outlaws caste privilege and guarantees all Indians equality before the law. Yet the old categories persist, especially in the villages, where about 75 percent of Indians still live.

Social Customs

❖

How did the Hindu masses organize their day-to-day lives? For Indians as for most early peoples, blood ties were the basis of social life. The extended family was universal: in-laws, cousins, and second and third generations all lived together under the same roof or in the same compound. Authority was always exercised by the oldest competent male.

Polygamy (the practice of having several wives) was common, as was concubinage for those who could not afford another wife. Children, especially the oldest boy, had an honored place and were often pampered.

Females were clearly and unequivocally subservient to the male. Women were expected to be good wives and mothers and to let the husband decide everything that pertained to affairs outside the house. Marriage was arranged very early in life by the parents of the bride and groom. As in most societies, marriage was primarily an economic and social affair, with the feelings of the individuals being distinctly secondary. Ideally, the girl was betrothed (formally engaged) immediately after coming into puberty, at about age thirteen or fourteen, and given into the care of her much older husband soon after. The reality usually differed, however, as many families began to betroth children as young as one to two years of age to assure they would have proper partners, always within the caste. The actual wedding did not take place until both parties were at least at the age of puberty, however. The wife was to be the faithful shadow of her husband and the bearer of children, preferably sons. A barren wife could expect that her husband would take additional wives to assure the continuance of the family name, much as among the Chinese. Divorce was very rare among the upper castes; we know little about the others.

There is considerable evidence that in early times Hindu women, at least in the upper classes, had more freedoms than in other ancient societies. The Rigveda, for example, makes no mention of restricting women from public affairs.

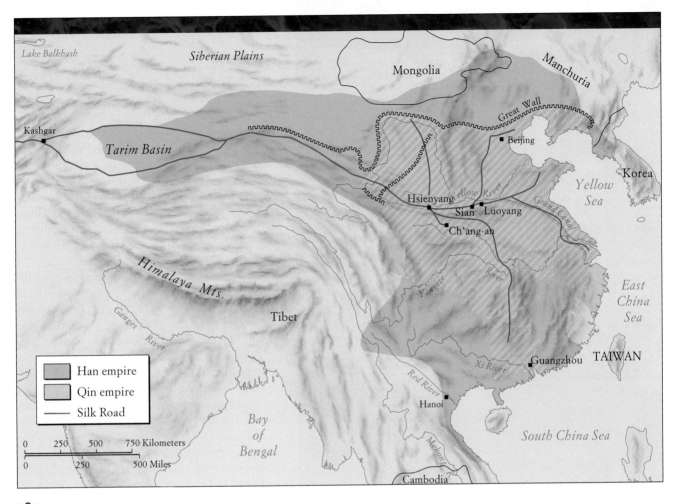

🏵 **MAP 18.1 The Qin and Han Empires.** The Han empire greatly expanded the borders established by the Qin emperor. By the mid-Han period, China's extent westward reached well into central Asia.

Although the king of Qin (246–221 B.C.E.) and later **First Emperor** (221–210 B.C.E.) ruled all China only eleven years, he made an imprint that was to last, as he boasted, "10,000 generations." Shih Huang-di, as he was called, was a man of tremendous administrative gifts and huge personality defects. Both were felt by his subjects. His generalship overwhelmed the rival Chinese states. In only nine years (230–221 B.C.E.), the six largest of them fell to Qin armies or surrendered. At once the process of centralization got under way on ruthless Legalist lines. Guided by the minister Li Si (Li Shu), the emperor set out to make his rule irresistible and eliminate the entrenched feudal aristocracy. The country was divided into administrative units that persisted throughout later history. The emperor fixed weights and measures, made the size of the roads uniform so that all carts would fit the ruts, and introduced the first standard units of money. The system of writing was standardized so effectively that it is almost the same in the twentieth century as it was then.

The disconnected barriers put up by various princes in the north and northwest were unified into the first version of the Great Wall for defense against the constant series of barbarian invaders from Mongolia (see Map 18.1). A whole list of other massive public works were started, including the tremendous imperial palace at Sian and the emperor's tomb in which over 7,000 life-sized clay soldiers were buried with him. (They were recently discovered and dug up.) Under Shih Huang-di China expanded to both north and south. The region around Guangzhou (Canton) was brought under his control; it was to be China's premier port for many centuries to come. First contacts were made with the Vietnamese and with several other civilized and less civilized peoples to the west and south.

The First Emperor's reign also had its negative side. Convinced of the inherent evil of human nature by his Legalist principles, Shih Huang-di apparently became paranoid and engaged in torture and other harsh treatment of his subjects and officials. He especially hated the doctrines

 # The Han Dynasty, 202 B.C.E.–220 C.E.

Han rule occurred almost simultaneously with the Roman heyday, and these two great empires of the East and West had other similarities as well. Both were basically urban in orientation, though the population remained decidedly rural and peasant. Both depended on a nonhereditary officialdom to carry out the distant imperial court's will. Both taxed the peasants heavily, making themselves vulnerable to the loss of loyalty as the central power began to weaken. Both collapsed under the combined impact of invading barbarians and widespread internal revolts.

Why are the Han monarchs considered the shapers of China's national consciousness? Even more than Shih Huang-di, the Han rulers greatly expanded the Chinese frontiers west, north, and south. Under them, China took on the geographic boundaries that it has retained ever since except for the much later conquest of Tibet. These conquests brought the Chinese out of their isolation and into contact with the rest of the world for the first time. In the Han period, the Chinese traded with Indians and even Romans, directly and (mainly) through intermediaries. Chinese commercial contacts soon expanded into massive cultural influence upon the Japanese, Koreans, and Vietnamese. Everywhere on the Asian mainland north of India and east of Cambodia the "men of Han," as the Chinese called themselves, became the controlling factor in military, political, and commercial life.

The Han dynasts were not revolutionaries in any sense. They kept what the Qin had done to assure the state's existence, while relaxing the strictness and brutality that had made the First Emperor hated. The restrictions against Confucianism were thrown out, and the Han rulers in fact adopted Confucius as the quasi-official philosopher of the regime.

This was a changed Confucianism, however, with more emphasis on the obedience owed by the children to the father—that is, by the people to the government. The person of the emperor was given a sacred aura by the renewed emphasis on the "mandate of Heaven," the theory that the gods approved and supported the emperor and all his actions until they showed otherwise. They showed otherwise by allowing the imperial armies to be defeated by the barbarians, by allowing rebels to succeed, or by permitting the provincial administration to break down. In that way, the path was opened to a new dynasty's coming, as the mandate of Heaven was being transferred to

The Great Wall. The golden light of sunset illumines a stretch of "the only earthly object visible from an orbiting space vehicle." The Wall extends more than 1800 miles in the present time, but much of it has been allowed to sink back into the surrounding terrain through lack of upkeep. Started by the First Emperor in the 200s B.C.E., it was last renewed by the early Ching dynasts in the 1600s. (© *Keren Su/Tony Stone Images*)

of Confucius, which he regarded as a menace to his style of autocratic rule, and ordered a **burning of the books** in a vain attempt to eradicate the Confucian philosophy from Chinese consciousness, an episode deeply resented by later generations. Shih Huang-di died of natural causes in 210, but the cruelties and heavy taxation that marked the First Emperor's reign assured that his weaker successor would not last long as ruler. His overthrow in 206 was followed by the establishment of one of the most successful of all the Chinese dynasties, the **Han dynasty,** which lasted until 220 C.E.

The Emperor's Tomb

*I*n the seventh month on *bingyin* the First Emperor passed away at Pingtai. Because the Supreme One had passed away outside the capital, Chief Minister Li Si was afraid that there would be a rebellion among the various princes and also in the empire, and so he kept it a secret, and did not announce the mourning. The coffin was borne in a sleeping carriage, and so the favorite eunuchs attended the carriage, and wherever they came to, food was sent in. Only the son Huhai and Zhao Gao, together with five or six favorite eunuchs knew the Supreme One was dead. Zhao Gao had formerly taught Huhai writing and matters of law, and Huhai privately favored him. Zhao Gao accordingly joined with Prince Huhai and Chief Minister Li Si and secretly plotted to destroy the letter that the First Emperor had sealed for bestowal on Prince Fusu. In its place was fabricated a testamentary edict, which Chief Minister Li Si was supposed to have received from the First Emperor. . . . the letter was rewritten and bestowed on Fusu . . . charging him with crimes and bestowing death on him.

It happened to be hot weather and the Supreme One's sleeping carriage stank, and so there was an imperial mandate to the effect that attendant officials should have carts loaded with a picul of salt fish in order to disguise the smell of it.

Continuing on their journey, they took the direct road back to Xianyang and announced the mourning. Crown Prince Huhai succeeded to the throne and became Second Generation Emperor. In the ninth month, the First Emperor was buried at Mount Li. When the First Emperor had just come to the throne, excavations and building had taken place at Mount Li, but when he unified all under heaven, convicts to the number of more than 700,000 were sent there from all over the empire. They dug through three springs and poured down molten bronze to make the outer coffin, and replicas of palaces, pavilions, all the various court officials and wonderful vessels, and other rare objects were brought up to the tomb, which was then filled with them. Craftsmen were ordered to make crossbows and arrows which would operate automatically, so that anyone who approached was immediately shot. . . .

The emperor's tomb was rediscovered after centuries of searching, in 1974, and it has been almost fully excavated with its rich store of buried treasures.

SOURCE: From Historical Records of Sima Qian, ed. Ray Dawson (New York: Oxford University Press, 1994).

Warriors from the First Emperor's Tomb. The discovery of the tomb of Shih Huang-di, the First Emperor, at Sian in 1974 revealed the terra cotta statues of more than 7,000 warriors buried with him. Armed with spears, swords, and bows, and presumably meant as a bodyguard in the next world, each of the warrior statues has individual features taken from living models. *(© Joe Carini/The Image Works)*

more competent hands. Using this logic, Chinese philosophers and political figures maintained the unbroken legitimacy of government, while recognizing the fairly frequent and violent overturns of individual rulers.

Arts and Sciences

Under the Han rulers, arts and letters experienced a great upsurge in quality and quantity. History came into its own as a peculiarly congenial mode of understanding the world for the Chinese, who are perhaps the globe's most historically conscious people. Records were scrupulously kept, some of which have survived in the scripts of the noted historian Ssu-ma Ch'ien and the Pan family of scholars dating from the first century C.E. As a result, we know far more about ancient China than almost any other part of the civilized world insofar as official acts and personages are concerned. History for the Chinese, of course, was the record of what the uppermost 1 percent did and thought—the peasantry and other ordinary folk were beneath consideration as a historical force. (See the Tradition and Innovation box for anecdotes written by the great classical historian of China, **Ssu-ma Ch'ien.**)

Mathematics, geography, and astronomy were points of strength in Han natural science, all of which led directly to technological innovations extremely useful to Chinese society. Some examples include the sternpost rudder and the magnetic compass, which together transformed the science of navigation. The Han period saw the invention of paper from wood pulp, truly one of the world's major inventions.

The Virtuous Officials

The greatest of the classical historians of China, Ssu-ma Ch'ien (c. 150–90 B.C.E.), wrote during the rule of the ambitious emperor Wu, who had expanded China's borders at the price of imposing a cruel, Legalist-inspired internal regime.

Ssu-ma Ch'ien regretted the emperor's style of governance, but he could not, as court historian, openly oppose it. Instead, he indirectly criticized Wu by writing about the virtue of emperors and officials in the distant past, when Confucian principles guided the government and proper attention was paid to the welfare of the people. These appeals to traditional virtues were well understood by Ssu-ma's audience. Some anecdotes from these histories follow; the first deals with the capable minister Sun Shu-ao, the second with the righteous Kung-i Hsiu, and the third with the relentlessly logical Li Li. All three men served kings of the Zhou dynasty.

The people of Ch'u liked to use very lowslung carriages, but the king did not think that such carriages were good for the horses and wanted to issue an order forcing the people to use higher ones. Sun Shu-ao said, "If orders are issued too frequently to the people they will not know which ones to obey. It will not do to issue an order. If your Majesty wishes the people to use high carriages, then I suggest that I instruct the officials to have the thresholds of the community gates made higher. Anyone who rides in a carriage must be a man of some social status, and a gentleman cannot be getting down from his carriage every time he has to pass through the community gate."

The king gave his approval, and after half a year all the people had of their own accord made their carriages higher so that they could drive over the thresholds without difficulty. In this way, without instructing the people Sun Shu-ao led them to change their ways.

Kung-i Hsiu was an erudite of Lu. Because of his outstanding ability he was made prime minister. . . .

Once one of his retainers sent him a fish, but he refused to accept the gift. "I always heard that you were fond of fish," said another of his retainers. "Now that someone has sent you a fish, why don't you accept it?" "It is precisely because I am so fond of fish that I don't accept it," replied Kung-i Hsiu. "Now that I am minister I can afford to buy all the fish I want. But if I should accept this gift and lose my position as a result, who would ever provide me with a fish again?"

Li Li was director of prisons under Duke Wen. Once, discovering that an innocent man had been executed because of an error in the investigation conducted by his office, he had himself bound and announced that he deserved the death penalty. Duke Wen said to him, "There are high officials and low officials, and there are light punishments and severe ones. Just because one of the petty clerks in your office made a mistake there is no reason why you should take the blame."

But Li Li replied, "I occupy the position of head of this office and I have made no move to hand the post over. . . . I receive a large salary and I have not shared the profits with those under me. Now because of an error in the trial an innocent has been executed. I have never heard of a man in my position trying to shift the responsibility for such a crime to his subordinates!" Thus he declined to accept Duke Wen's suggestion.

"If you insist that as a superior officer you yourself are to blame," said Duke Wen, "then do you mean that I, too, am to blame?" "The director of prisons," said Li Li, "must abide by the laws which govern his post. If he mistakenly condemns a man to punishment, he himself must suffer the punishment; if he mistakenly sentences a man to death, he himself must suffer death. Your Grace appointed me to this post precisely because you believed that I would be able to listen to difficult cases and decide doubtful points of law. But now since I have made a mistake in hearing a case and have executed an innocent, I naturally deserve to die for my offense." So in the end he refused to listen to the duke's arguments, but fell on his sword and died.

For Reflection

How effective do you think Ssu-ma's critiques of his emperor would be, given the Chinese reverence for traditional virtues in their governors? What effect would such an approach have, do you think, in present-day American politics?

SOURCE: Excerpted from Records of the Grand Historian, trans. Burton Watson (New York: Columbia University Press, 1961), vol. 2, pp. 413–418.

By about the fifth century C.E., paper had come into common usage, paving the way for the advent of wood-block printing.

Medicine was a particular interest of the Chinese, and Han doctors developed a pharmacology that was more ambitious than even the later Muslim one. It was also during the Han that acupuncture first entered the historical record. Despite the persistence of superstition and folk medicine, a strong scientific tradition of healing through intensive knowledge of the parts of the body, the functions of internal organs, and the circulation of the blood was established during this period. This tradition has endured and long ago made China one of the permanent centers of the healing arts.

In the fine arts, China continued to produce a variety of metallic and ceramic luxury items, which increasingly found their way into the Near East and even into Rome's eastern provinces. The production of silk was both an economic asset of the first rank and a fine art; for nearly 1,000 years, the Han and their successors in China maintained their monopoly, until the Byzantines were finally able to emulate them. Bronze work, jade figurines, and fine ceramics were partic-

Marco Polo
(1254–1324)

Commerce has often been the driving forces behind the expansion of knowledge. Just as war has often fostered the advances of science, the desire to make a profitable exchange has expanded the boundaries of what has been previously known—or assumed. Few other stories in history illustrate this as well as the history of the life of Marco Polo.

In the thirteenth century, the Italian city-state of Venice was a notable power not only in the Mediterranean but throughout Europe. Based entirely on its merchant navy, the tiny, aristocratically governed republic became rich from its carrying trade with the Byzantine empire and the Muslim lands beyond. Venetian ships carried cargoes of silk, spices, precious stones and woods, ivory, jade, Chinese bronzes, and other luxury items for distribution throughout Europe. Their sailors returned with tales of wealth and wonders that awaited the venturesome in the vast Asian distances.

Among those who listened were Nicolo and Maffeo Polo, members of a merchant family. In 1261 they had journeyed as far as the Black Sea by ship and thence overland along the Silk Road to China. The Italians stayed in the court of the Mongol emperor Kubilai Khan for a few years, then returned to Venice by sea. Several years later, they decided to repeat this strenuous journey, this time taking along Nicolo's seventeen-year-old son, Marco. After a tremendous series of difficulties, they succeeded in reaching Kubilai's capital at Beijing in 1275. Warmly received by the emperor, the Polos settled into a partly commercial, partly official life at the Mongol court.

Marco Polo, who quickly mastered Mongol and at least three other Asian languages, proved a particular asset. Enjoying the emperor's full confidence, he apparently traveled extensively as a government official, not only in China proper but also in other East Asian regions of the immense Mongol empire created by Chingis Khan and his successors. These journeys gave him opportunities to observe the customs, agriculture, commerce, and culture of several parts of Asia. He delighted the Khan with the tales and the information that he brought back from each trip, for he had a curious and informed eye and ear.

For more than fifteen years, the Polos stayed on in Beijing. By this time the older men were anxious to return home, but the emperor was reluctant to part with them. In 1292, however, they persuaded him to allow them to depart as guides for a caravan taking a young Chinese bride to the Persian Shah's court. By the time they reached their destination, many members of the caravan had died or been killed, but the princess and the three Polos had survived. From Persia they were able to return to Venice with relative safety and speed, arriving in their hometown after a twenty-three-year absence in 1295.

Now a famous man, Marco Polo became an admiral in the Venetian navy. During a war with rival Genoa, he was captured and imprisoned briefly. His captors allowed him to pass the time by dictating his memoirs of his years in China, and these were published after Marco's release and return to Venice. The *Description of the World by Marco Polo* soon became a "best-seller" in several languages. It remained the most important source of European knowledge about Asia until the Portuguese explorers reached India in the early sixteenth century. Its detailed observations greatly expanded the very sketchy data brought back by the occasional missionary or merchant who survived the hazards of a central Asian journey. Contemporary readers regarded much of the book, especially the sections on the richness and variety of Chinese urban life, as sheer lies and fantasies and referred to it satirically as "Marco's Millions." He was outraged but could, of course, do nothing. Not until the sixteenth century would his report be validated. A copy of the *Description of the World* accompanied Columbus on his first voyage.

We know almost nothing of Polo's career after his book's appearance. He died in early 1324, leaving a wife and three daughters.

For Reflection

Do you see any equivalent to Marco Polo's voyages and experiences in the contemporary world? Are today's adventures tamer than those of Polo's time, or do you think our sense of wonder has been blunted?

---

ern and western tribes. But in the twelfth century they weakened. Toward the end of the 1100s, they lost any semblance of control over the far west to the Mongols. By the mid-1200s, the Song had been defeated by the descendants of Chinghis Khan and formally gave up the north and center of traditional China to them. The Song were able to hold on for a brief time in the South, but in 1279 there, too, dominion passed into the hands of the Mongols under **Kubilai Khan**—the first and only time China has been conquered in its entirety by outsiders. The Mongol **Yuan dynasty** thus began its century-long reign.

Buddhism and Chinese Culture

The greatest single foreign cultural influence on China during the first millennium C.E.—and possibly ever—was the coming of Buddhism from its Indian birthplace. The Chinese proved very responsive to the new faith, with all social and economic groups finding something in the doctrine that answered their needs. Buddhism believes in the essential equality of all. The enlightenment of the soul, which is the high point of a Buddhist life, is available to all who can find their way to it. Unlike Confucianism and Daoism, which are essentially philosophies of proper thought and conduct in this life and possess only incidental religious ideas, Buddhism, by the time it came to China, was a supernatural religion promising an afterlife of eternal bliss for the righteous. To the ordinary man and woman, this idea had far more appeal than any earthly philosophy. Another aspect of Buddhism's appeal was that the Mahayana version (see Chapter 5) adopted in China was very accommodating to existing beliefs—there was no conflict between traditional ancestor worship and Buddhism in China, for example.

The translation of Sanskrit texts into Chinese stimulated the literary qualities of the language, as the translators had to fashion ways of expressing very difficult and complex ideas. Even more than prose, however, poetry benefited from the new religion and its ideals of serenity, self-mastery, and a peculiarly Chinese addition to classic Indian Buddhism—the appreciation of and joy in nature. Painting, sculpture, and architecture all show Buddhist influences, mostly traceable to India, but some original to China in their conceptions. From about the fourth century onward, China's high-culture arts were strongly molded by Buddhist belief. They not only portrayed themes from the life of the Buddha but also showed in many ways the religion's interpretation of what proper human life should be.

So widespread was Buddhism's appeal that inevitably a reaction set in against it. In part, this reaction was a political phenomenon. In the 800s the Tang dynasty took steps to curb the worrisome powers of the wealthy Buddhist monasteries. Most of their property and prestige was expropriated. But the reaction was also philosophical and intellectual in the form of Neo-Confucianism and a general revival of the Confucian credo.

The Neo-Confucians were philosophers who sought to change the world through emphasis on aspects of the master's thought most fully developed by his later disciple, **Mencius** (370–290 B.C.E.). In Neo-Confucianism, love and the responsibility of all to all were the great virtues. Unlike the Daoists and Buddhists, the Neo-Confucians insisted that all must partake of social life. Withdrawal and prolonged meditation were impermissible. They also thought that formal education in morals and the arts and sciences was an absolute necessity for a decent life—it could not be left to the "enlightenment" of the individual seeker to discover what his fellow's welfare required. The Confucians' efforts to hold their own against their Buddhist competitors were a major reason that the Song period was so fertile in all philosophical and artistic fields.

Tang and Song era formal culture was supremely literary in nature. The accomplished official was also expected to be a good poet, a calligrapher, and a philosopher able to expound his views by quoting the "scriptures" of Confucian and other systems of thought. Skills in painting and music were also considered part of the normal equipment of an educated and powerful man. This was the ideal of the mandarin, the man who held public responsibilities and proved himself worthy of them by virtue of his rich and deep culture. This ideal was often a reality in Tang and later dynastic history.

SUMMARY

The Chinese imperial style was molded once and for all by the ruthless Legalist known as the First Emperor in the third century B.C.E. The Qin dynasty he founded quickly disappeared, but his Han successors built on the foundations he left them to rule a greatly expanded China for four centuries. Softening the brutal Qin policies to an acceptable level, the Han dynasts made Confucianism into a quasi-official philosophy.

After the Han's dissolution and a period of anarchy, the 500 years of the Tang and Song dynasties comprised the Golden Age of Chinese culture. Despite internal dissension at times, the imperial government promulgated and was supported by a vision of proper conduct that was Confucian in essence and very widely subscribed to by the educated classes.

Internally, both the Tang and the Song saw a tremendous development of the economy and its capacity to maintain a rapidly growing and urbanizing population. Thanks in large part to advances in agriculture, few, if any, other civilizations could rival China's ability to supply all classes with the necessities of life. A series of technological inventions had immediate practical applications. It was also a period of extraordinary excellence in the fine arts and literature, which were supported by a large group of refined patrons and consumers in the persons of the landowning gentry and the mandarin officials. Buddhist influences were pervasive in both the popular and gentry cultures, rivaling but not overshadowing traditional Confucian thought.

In foreign affairs, the long seesaw struggle with the northern nomadic barbarians was finally lost when the Mongols of Kubilai Khan defeated the last Song rulers and established the Yuan dynasty. All of China thus fell under alien rule for the first and only time. Also during the Song, China took on more or less its modern territorial outlines, with its withdrawals from Vietnam, Korea, and Mongolia. Cultural and commercial contacts with Japan were expanded, and there was extensive commercial intercourse with the Muslims to the west and the Indians to the south.

TEST YOUR KNOWLEDGE

1. The Qin First Emperor attained power by
   a. a palace coup.
   b. playing on the superstitions of his people.
   c. assassinating the previous emperor.
   d. triumph in battle.
2. Which of the following was *not* a Chinese invention?
   a. The magnetic compass
   b. The waterwheel
   c. Paper from wood
   d. Decimals
3. Which of the following was *not* formally a requirement for joining the Chinese bureaucracy?
   a. Single-minded dedication
   b. Extensive formalized education
   c. Connections with the higher social classes
   d. Passing of written examinations
4. The Tang dynasty was extremely influential in Chinese history as the
   a. developer of the mandarin system of scholar-officials.
   b. creator of the village democracy.
   c. reformer of the military.
   d. originator of the canal system.
5. The Song dynasty was finally overturned by the
   a. Mongol conquerors.
   b. Korean invaders.
   c. Japanese pirates.
   d. Tang dynasty.
6. Marco Polo served as an official in the service of
   a. the Song emperor.
   b. the Mongol emperor.
   c. an Italian embassy to the Chinese government.
   d. Indian visitors to the Chinese court.
7. Chinese Buddhism was different from the original conceptions of Sidhartha Gautama in
   a. the rigidity and uniformity of its doctrine.
   b. its insistence on the lifestyle of a hermit.
   c. its supernatural religious element.
   d. its appeal to only the upper classes.
8. Buddhism found many sympathizers in China because it
   a. offered immortality to all social classes.
   b. was an import from Korea.
   c. came from a civilization that the Chinese regarded as superior to their own.
   d. demanded the rigorous intellectual effort that the Chinese so admired.

IDENTIFICATION TERMS

burning of the books	Hangzhou	Marco Polo	Ssu-ma Ch'ien
Era of the Warring States	Kubilai Khan	Mencius	Tang dynasty
First Emperor	mandarin	Song dynasty	Yuan dynasty
Han dynasty	meritocracy		

INFOTRAC COLLEGE EDITION

Enter the search terms "Han Dynasty or Tang Dynasty or Song Dynasty" using Key Words.

Enter the search terms "China history" using Key Words.

Enter the search terms "China and Buddhism" using Key Words.

Chapter 19

Japan and Southeast Asia

In life there is nothing more than life; in death nothing more than death; we are being born and are dying at every moment.

DOGEN, THIRTEENTH-CENTURY ZEN MASTER

THE ISLAND NATION OF JAPAN emerges from the mists of prehistory in the early centuries C.E., when Chinese travelers begin to report on their adventures there. Geography explains both Japan's receptivity to Chinese influence and its ability to reject that influence when it wished. Japan could adapt foreign ideas and values to its needs without having to suffer military or political domination from abroad. For the first thousand years of recorded Japanese history, until about 1500 C.E., the Japanese state was successful in this adaptation, fitting imported governmental and cultural institutions to existing customs and the requirements of the native society.

Very Early Japan

The Japanese islands (the four main ones are Hokkaido, Honshu, Kyushu, and Shikoku) are situated off the Korean peninsula and Siberia, separated from the mainland by 120 to several hundred miles of open water (see Map 19.1). Together, the islands are about the size of California. Where the original settlers came from is uncertain, but it is clear that the Koreans and Japanese are much closer ethnically than the Chinese and Japanese. The native oral language of Japan is entirely different from Chinese. The written language, which originally borrowed heavily from written Chinese, is still different in many ways.

According to ancient Japanese legends, they are the descendants of the Sun Goddess (Jimmu Tenno), who continues to have a special relationship with the country through the person of the emperor. For many centuries, the Japanese thought of the emperor as divine, a status that was only formally rejected by terms of the Japanese peace treaty after World War II. Archaeological data reveal that as early as the third century C.E., a semicivilized society inhabited the southern island of Kyushu and buried their dead chieftains in elaborate mounds with many pottery figures accompanying them to the next world. The first written records do not appear until the eighth century C.E., how-

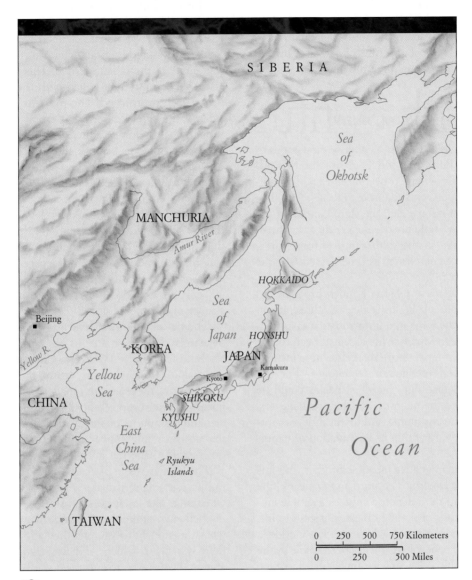

🔆 **MAP 19.1 Japan and Its Neighbors.** The hundred-mile interval between Japan and Korea was not difficult to cross even in ancient times, and Chinese cultural influences came into Japan via Korean intermediaries until direct contacts were established in the seventh century.

ever; prior to that we must rely on the occasional surviving travel reports of Chinese visitors.

For the most part, Japan has a very mountainous and broken terrain, which helps explain why the process of creating a central government with effective controls was so slow and subject to sudden reverses. The leading early political force, the Yamato family, was never able to get real control over the four islands, despite being strong enough to invade southern Korea on several occasions.

During this early period, the relationship between Japan and Korea was important for both. There appear to have been invasions in both directions, and many Koreans lived among the Japanese until well into the first millennium C.E. Commerce between the two countries seems to have been lively. Under Korean influences the Japanese moved gradually northward from the island of Kyushu near Korea to Hokkaido, the most northerly and least developed island. From Korea came several major cultural imports—most important, Buddhism, which arrived in Japan in the sixth century. From Korea also came powerful Chinese influences. During this era, Korea was subjected to a revitalized Chinese imperialism, as the Tang dynasty succeeded in making their northeastern neighbor into a satellite. Korea adopted the Chinese styles of government, law, and writing and passed knowledge of them on to the Japanese.

Buddhism and Shinto

The two major religious beliefs of ancient and modern Japan are the import Buddhism and the native Shinto. Buddhism in Japan, as everywhere, proved itself capable of undergoing many mutations and adapting to local needs. The special Japanese versions are Zen, the Pure Land, and the Nichiren sects, which gradually developed after the introduction of the religion in the sixth century from Korea. Their distinctions became clearer as time passed (see the discussion in Chapter 31).

Buddhism gave Japanese religion a much broader and nobler intellectual content. Its insistence on ethical action and compassion for the weak and unfortunate was as beneficially transforming to Japanese life as it had been earlier in India and China. In Japan more than elsewhere in Asia, Buddhism emphasized meditation techniques. For the more intellectually demanding, Buddhist beliefs could be very complex, but for the majority of Japanese believers, the religion was relatively simple and joyful in its acceptance of things-as-they-are and in its anticipation of happiness in immortality.

The **Shinto** religion is a native Japanese product, but it is fairly close to Chinese Daoism. The word *Shinto* means "the way of the gods," and the religion combines a simple animism, in which all kinds of natural objects possess a spirit, with a worship of great deities, such as the Sun Goddess, who are immortal and benevolent, but not perceivable by the human senses. The Shinto legends with which all Japanese are familiar speak of a time when all things, even stones and trees, could speak and interact with humans. But they were forced into silence later and now must evidence their powers to humans through the *kami* or spirits that inhabit them.

Shinto is a basically optimistic, guilt-free view of the world. It has no theology of the gods or sacred book, no heaven or hell or wrathful Yahweh, and no Fall of Adam. Shinto is supremely adaptable, however, and could serve as a sort of permanent underpinning to whatever more advanced, supernatural religion the individual Japanese might prefer. It persists to this day in that role.

Government and Administration

The beginning of organized government occurred in the Yamato period in the fifth and sixth centuries C.E. At that time Japan was a collection of noble clans, who ruled over the commoners by a combination of military and economic power familiar to students of feudal Europe. The Yamato, the biggest and most potent of these clans, ruled over a good-sized arable area in central Japan near what is now the city of Osaka. The Yamato claimed direct descent from the Sun Goddess and founded what was to become the imperial family of the Japanese state. This family, or more precisely the dynasty that began with the Yamato kings, has never been overturned. The present-day emperor is considered the direct descendant from the earliest Yamato, though he is no longer a divinity.

Buddhism soon became the favored viewpoint of the Yamato state's upper class, and by the beginning of the seventh century, it was used as the vehicle of a general strengthening and clarification of the role of the central government. In 604, **Prince Shotoku,** a devout Buddhist, offered the *Seventeen Point Constitution,* which is the founding document of the Japanese state. It was not really a constitution in the modern sense but a list inspired by Buddhist and Confucian doctrine of what a government and a loyal citizenry *ought* to do. It has had great influence on political science in Japan ever since.

The way of affairs in China was the general model for the Seventeen Points, so to put his constitution into effect, Shotoku sent selected youths to China for a period of study and training under teachers, artists, and officials. In the seventh century, thousands of Japanese were thus prepared for governmental responsibilities and were also trained in the arts and techniques of Tang China. This was one of the earliest and most impressive examples of cultural transfer from one people to another in history.

The Chinese example had a powerful influence in most public and many private spheres, but it was not overwhelming. The Japanese soon showed they were confident of their own abilities to distinguish what was useful and what was not. For example, they adopted the Tang equal field system, in which land was frequently redistributed among the peasants to ensure equity. But the Japanese soon changed this system to allow an individual to have transferable rights to a parcel of productive land no matter who actually tilled it. Another example was the Japanese approach to bureaucracy. Although they admired the Chinese bureaucracy, they did not imitate it. The concept of meritocracy was and remained alien to Japanese thinking. Having competitive exams open to all threatened deep-rooted Japanese social values. Government remained an aristocratic privilege in Japan; the lower classes were not allowed to attain high posts, regardless of their merit.

The Nara and Heian Periods, 710–1185

For seventy years after the death of Prince Shotoku in 622, Japan experienced feudal anarchy. This was followed by a period of reform, during which the first capital, Nara, was established in central Honshu. Buddhism was especially powerful among the Nara clans, and when a Buddhist monk named Dokyo attempted to use his following in the numerous monasteries to usurp political power, there was a strong reaction. Dokyo also used his position as chaplain to the empress to further his political ambitions. When the empress died, he was driven into exile. This experience may explain why in all the remainder of Japanese history there have been only two other female rulers.

The reaction against the Buddhist monks and monasteries did not mean a reaction against the religion itself, which steadily gained new adherents among the educated upper class. In the early ninth century, Japanese visitors to the mainland became acquainted with the Tendai and Shingon sects of Buddhism and took them back to Japan. These sects featured magical elements and promises of salvation to all, which made them highly popular, and they spread quickly. During this period, Buddhism in Japan started a steady transformation from a narrow preoccupation of the court aristocrats to the vehicle of popular devotion it would become.

In 794, owing largely to the bad experience with the Nara monasteries, the imperial court was moved to a new town called Heian (modern **Kyoto**), where it stayed until modern times. At this time, the aristocrats checked further Chinese influence by severing relations with the mainland—one of the several episodes of deliberate seclusion with which Japanese history is studded. For about a century, contacts with China and Korea were strictly limited, while the Japanese aristocracy devoted themselves to organizing the government and creating a cultural/artistic style that was uniquely their own. The process lasted several centuries and was more or less complete by about 1200.

Government during the Heian era quickly became a struggle—almost always concealed—between the Chinese model of an all-powerful emperor ruling through a bureaucracy and the kind of rough-and-ready decentralized feudalism that had marked the Yamato state. The feudal aristocrats soon won out. The emperors were reduced to

The Horyu Temple. The massive wooden stories of the Shinto Horyu temple tower above the park in the ancient Japanese capital city of Nara where it stands. Dating from the seventh century, Horyu is probably the oldest intact wooden building in the world. The pagoda style was borrowed from the Chinese originally, but soon took on a recognizably Japanese format. (© *The Bridgeman Art Library*)

 Samurai Armor. The expenses entailed in outfitting a samurai properly were sometimes borne by the *daimyo,* who was his lord. But the two swords carried by the warrior were always his personal property. By the end of the Kamakura era in the 1300s, the samurai were a separate class in Japanese society, a position retained until the late nineteenth century. (© *Werner Forman/ArtResource*)

ceremonial figures, accorded great respect but essentially without means of imposing their will. A series of provincial noble families—above all, the **Fujiwara clan**—were able to make themselves the real powers. The Fujiwara ruled from behind the throne by arranging marriages between their daughters and the children of the monarchs and then having themselves nominated as regents. They remained content to dominate indirectly and did not try to displace the ruler.

This system of disguised rule by powerful families at court was to become a recurrent part of Japanese life under the name of the **shogunate.** The true head of government was the *shogun,* or commander in chief of the imperial army. The shoguns stayed in the background but decided everything that mattered, while the divine emperors conducted the ceremonies.

After this system had worked fairly well for two centuries, it began to break down as rival clans finally found ways to break the Fujiwara monopoly. In the outlying provinces, and especially in eastern Japan, warriors known as *bushi* were experiencing a rise in power and prestige. The *bushi,* or **samurai,** as they are better known in the West, were the executors of the will of the large landholders and the enforcers of public order in a given locality. In their outlook, means of support, and demanding code of conduct (**bushido**), the *bushi* were very similar to the medieval knights of western Europe. There were, however, some important differences: the samurai's code included no provision for chivalry toward women or for generosity toward a beaten opponent, who expected to die by ritual beheading. This made the samurai a more brutal and menacing figure to the ordinary man and woman.

Using their samurai effectively, the rival clans threw out the Fujiwara regents and then fought one another for supremacy. The house of Minamoto eventually won out and introduced the **Kamakura shogunate.**

The Kamakura Period, 1185–1333

❀

The Kamakura period of Japan's medieval history (it was, in fact, a Japanese version of the European Middle Age) was marked by the complete domination of the country by the samurai and their overlords in the clan aristocracy. The powers of the imperial court in Kyoto declined nearly to the vanishing point. Political leadership at any level depended on two factors: control of adequate numbers of fighting men, and control of adequate **shoen** to support those fighting men.

The *shoen* were parcels of productive land, sometimes including villages. They had originally been created in the early Heian era as support for monasteries or rewards to servants of the emperor for outstanding service. Their critical feature was their exemption from the central government's taxing authority. Whereas most Japanese land was always considered the property of the emperor, lent out to his favored servants, the *shoen* and the rights to their use and income, called **shiki,** were strictly private and remained outside normal laws.

A monastery or official who owned *shoen* would often convey them to a more powerful person, who would allow the original owner to continue as tenant under his protection. Thus, the ownership and use system became ever more complex and eventually resembled the European system of feudal vassalage. It was not unusual for a *shoen* to have three to five "lords" who each had some special rights (*shiki*) to the land and its produce. *Shoen* and *shiki* were thus the currency used by the aristocrats to pay their samurai. In this sense and others we noted earlier, the samurai

The samurai warriors were bound to a strict code of conduct that, among other things, told them that they were expected to die rather than surrender. Because it was commonplace for the victorious commander to order the execution of the captured enemy, they usually had no choice in the matter. An expert in medieval Japanese affairs tells us:

> Those of the defeated who had not been killed in action often had recourse to suicide. We are in possession of many accounts of these suicides, whether the warrior cut open his abdomen with his dagger (*hari-kari* or *seppuku*), or threw himself onto his sword, or preferred to perish in his burning house with his most faithful servants and vassals (*junshi*, or collective suicide). When he was about to be taken prisoner, Yoshitsune "stabbed himself under the left breast, plunging the blade in so deeply it all but came out again in his back; then he made three further incisions, disemboweling himself and wiping the dagger on the sleeve of his robe." Thereupon his wife sought death at the hands of one of their vassals.

Some warriors' suicides were deliberately spectacular for the edification of their descendants:

> Yoshiteru climbed up on the watchtower of the second gate, from where he made sure that the Prince was now far away (for he had taken his place and his clothes in order to deceive the enemy and give his lord time to flee). When the time had come, he cut the handrail of the tower window so that he could be better seen, calling out his lord's name: "I am Son-un, prince of the blood of the first rank, Minister of Military Affairs and second son of Go-Daigo Tenno, ninety-fifth emperor since Jimmu Tenno. . . . Defeated by the rebels, I am taking my own life to avenge my wrongs in the Beyond. Learn from my example how a true warrior dies by his own hand when Fate plays him false!" Stripping off his armor, he threw it to the foot of the tower. Next he took off the jacket of his underdress with its tight fitting sleeves . . . and clad only in his brocaded breeches, he thrust a dagger into his white skin. He cut in a straight line from left to right, cast his entrails onto the handrail, placed the point of the sword in his mouth and flung himself headlong towards the ground.

This kind of death was admired by the samurai and deemed heroic and worthy of praise by generations to come. Many put an end to their life in this way.

For Reflection

How did this suicidal concept of military honor influence the medieval history of Japan? What does the threat of Yoshiteru to "avenge my wrongs in the Beyond" seem to say about the nature of the life to come?

SOURCE: From L. Frederic, *Daily Life in Japan at the Time of the Samurai* (New York: Praeger, 1972), p. 190f.

Burning of the Palace. In this thirteenth-century scroll painting, samurai attack the palace of an enemy by night. The mainly wooden construction of Japanese buildings made fire a constant menace, and besiegers often used flaming arrows in their attacks. *(Fenollosa-Weld Collection)*

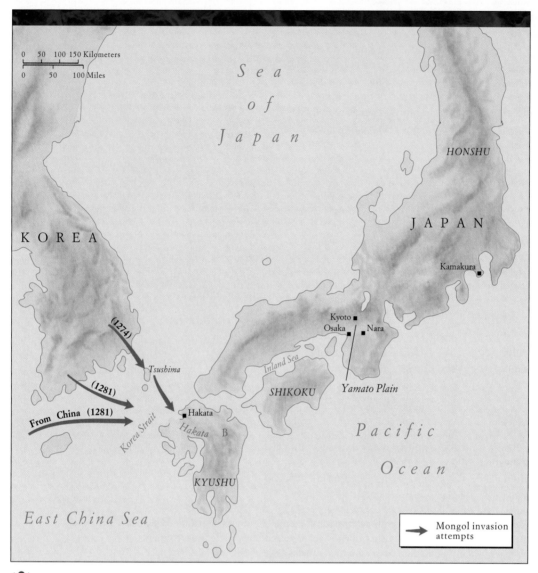

✿ **MAP 19.2 Japan and the Mongol Invasion Routes in the Thirteenth Century.**
From their bases in Korea and northern China, the Mongols mounted two invasion attempts
against Japan within a seven-year period. Both were repulsed by the samurai gathered at the bay
of Hakata, aided by the *kamikaze* wind.

very closely resembled the European knights. But there
were enough differences that some authorities see the
samurai as quite different from the knights and reject the
idea that Japanese society in this era was basically the same
as medieval European.

One of the chief differences between Japanese and medieval European government was the **bakufu,** or military
government under the shogun, which had no European
equivalent. The shogun, always a member of the dominant
clan controlling the emperor, was supposedly the executor
of the emperor's will as generalissimo of the army. In fact,
he was totally independent and the real ruler of Japan. The
Kamakura period derives its name from the small town of
Kamakura where the shogun of the Minamoto clan
resided—quite separate from the imperial court in Kyoto.

Perhaps the most dramatic demonstration of the way the
shogun and his *bakufu* organization could lead the nation
occurred in the late 1200s, when the feared Mongols under
Kubilai Khan prepared to invade the islands (see Map
19.2). Having conquered China in its entirety and all of
eastern Asia to Vietnam, the Mongols sought to do what the
Chinese themselves had never attempted. Twice, the khan
assembled armadas from his bases in Korea and landed on
Kyushu where his forces were met on the beach by the waiting samurai. The effectiveness of the Mongols' most potent
weapon, their cavalry, was sharply limited by the terrain
and by Japanese defenses, including a long wall along the
coast that horses could not surmount. The Mongols called
off the first invasion after fierce resistance led to a stale-
mate. The second attack in 1281 ended in a huge disaster

when a typhoon (the *kamikaze,* or "divine wind") sank most of their ships and the 140,000 men on them. Mongol rule was thus never extended to the Japanese.

The Arts and Culture in Medieval Japan

❀

The partial severance of relations with China following the establishment of the capital in Heian allowed the Japanese full freedom to develop their own culture. Their language and literature shows they were vigorously imaginative. The Japanese and Chinese languages are radically different in both structure and vocabulary; the earliest Japanese writing was a close but necessarily clumsy adaptation of Chinese. This script was used in the eighth-century *Chronicles of Japan* (*Nihongi*) and the *Records of Ancient Matters* (*Kokiki*), the first Japanese books. In the Heian period, it was simplified and brought into closer conformity with oral Japanese. The gradual withdrawal from Chinese vocabulary and modes of expression forced the court authors to invent literary models and expressions of their own. Japanese writers thus evolved two syllabaries, written signs that were based on phonetics, rather than being ideographs or pictographs like Chinese, and could therefore be used to match the syllables of the spoken language—in other words, the beginnings of an alphabet.

The world's first novel, the famous **Tale of Genji** by the court lady Murasaki Shikibu, was written in the early eleventh century and tells us a great deal about the manners and customs of the Japanese aristocracy of the day (see the box on Family Relations for an excerpt from Lady Murasaki in this chapter). It reveals a culture of sensitive, perceptive people, who took intense pleasure in nature and in the company of other refined persons. The impressions left by the *Tale of Genji* are furthered by the other classic court tale of this era, Lady Sei Shonagon's *Pillow Book,* which was a collection of anecdotes and satirical essays centered on the art of love. Neither of these works owes anything to foreign models. The fact that their authors were women gives some indication of the high status of females among the educated class.

Prose was considered the domain of females, but poetry was for everyone—everyone, that is, in the tiny fraction of the population that partook of cultured recreations. In the eighth century a collection of poems entitled *Ten Thousand Leaves* was printed.

Japanese painting in the Heian era exhibited a marvelous sense of design and draftsmanship. Scenes from nature were preferred, but there was also a great deal of lively portraiture, much of it possessing the sense of amusement that marks many of Japan's arts. The well born were expected to be proficient in dance and music, and calligraphy was as revered as it was in China.

❀ **A Japanese Landscape.** Japanese painting strives for a harmonious balance between the works of man and Nature, and this balance is revealed in this sixteenth-century work. Although natural objects are given much space by the artist, the painting's focal point is the house and the human figure within it. (*Chinese and Japanese Special Fund, courtesy of Museum of Fine Arts, Boston*)

Great attention was given to the cultivation of beauty in all its manifestations: literary, visual, plastic, and psychic. Men as well as women were expected to take pains with their appearance; both used cosmetics. (Blackened teeth were the rage among Heian court ladies!) A refined sense of color in dress was mandatory. Both sexes cried freely, and a sensitive sadness was cultivated. The Buddhist insistence on the transitory quality of all good things—the reminder that nothing is permanent—was at the heart of this aristocratic culture. Life was to be enjoyed, not to be worried about or reformed. The wise saw this instinctively and drew the proper conclusions. The Japanese would never have

Lady Murasaki
(C. 976–1026)

In the eleventh century, a Japanese noblewoman, whose very name is uncertain, wrote the world's first work of literature that can be called a novel. The *Tale of Genji*, written between 1015 and 1025, is a long, fascinatingly detailed account of the life of a courtier at the Kyoto imperial palace and his relations with others there.

About the life of the author, we know only some fragments. She was born into an official's family, a member of the large and powerful Fujiwara clan that long occupied a major place in Japanese affairs. Shikibu, as she was named, probably received the minimal education customary for even high-class Japanese women. Presumably, she did not know Chinese, which was the literary language of well-educated males in this epoch. She was married to another official at age twenty, but her husband died soon after, leaving his widow with a young daughter. For some years, Shikibu retired to a chaste widowhood in a provincial town. In 1004, her father received a long-sought appointment as governor of a province and used his influence to have his widowed daughter made lady-in-waiting to the empress Akiko in Kyoto.

From 1008 to 1010, Lady Murasaki (as she was now known at court) kept a diary, which was translated and published not long ago. But her major effort in her years with the empress in the extremely refined Kyoto palace was the *Tale of Genji*. In fifty-four books or chapters, which together are more than twice as long as Tolstoy's *War and Peace*, Lady Murasaki depicts the panorama of Japanese upper-class life in the ceremony-filled, ritualistic court of the emperor and his consort. She thus made a memorable, subtle outline of the traditions that guided the Japanese uppermost class and that would continue to be honored for most of the ensuing millennium.

Prince Genji (Shining One) is a fictional character but presumably was drawn closely on an actual one. Stricken by the death of his mother to whom he was greatly attached, the young man comes to court to forget his sorrow. Popular with both sexes for his gallantry and charm, he engages in a series of love affairs with the court women, in which he displays both his amorous character and his artistic refinement. In a setting where manners are everything, Genji is supreme. But his escapades with the ladies lead to trouble with jealous husbands and suitors, and Genji is banished from the court. He soon obtains forgiveness and returns, only to fall deeply in love with the commoner Murasaki, whom he makes his wife. But she dies young and childless: heartbroken, Genji soon follows her in death.

The action now shifts to Genji's son and grandson by a former marriage. These two are in competition for the same girl, Ukifune, who feels committed to both in different ways. Depressed and ashamed, Ukifune attempts suicide but fails, and she decides to salvage her life by renouncing the world and entering a Buddhist monastery. The competing father and son are both deprived of what they want and are left in bewildered grief at their unconsummated love. The novel ends on a note of deep gloom.

The psychological intricacies of the story have fascinated Japanese readers for 900 years. The novel was first translated into English in the 1930s by Arthur Waley. Of Lady Murasaki's last years, we know nothing.

For Reflection

Why do you think Murasaki chose this anything-but-happy ending to her novel? How much does it relate to what you see as the ordinary lives of Japanese commoners in her day? Would that relationship be of concern to Lady M.?

✿ **Ladies of the Court.** (© *The Granger Collection*)

Malacca on the straits that bear the identical name (see Map 19.3).

Majapahit was the last great Hindu kingdom in southeast Asia, and its demise was caused in large part by the coming of an aggressive Islam, again spearheaded by immigrants from the Indian peninsula. Where Hinayana Buddhism had replaced original Hindu belief in most of the mainland, Islam now replaced it in most of the islands. By the time of the arrival of the Portuguese, who were the earliest Europeans in these latitudes, much of the population of the archipelago had been converted.

Burma and Thailand

After the fall of the Khmers, the mainland was divided gradually among three principal entities. In the far west, the Burmese kingdom centered on the religious shrines at **Pagan** had been founded as far back as the ninth century. It had gradually spread south and east to embrace several minority groups related to the majority Burmans. Originally Hindu thanks to its common borders with India, the governing class adopted Hinayana Buddhism brought to them from the centers of that faith in Sri Lanka during the tenth and eleventh centuries.

In the 1280s the Mongol conquerors of China sent armies to the south that severely ravaged several Southeast Asian states. Chief among these victims were the Burmans, who saw their capital city of Pagan utterly destroyed and their political dominion wrecked as well. Burma disintegrated into several rival principalities for the next three centuries.

To the east of Burma, the Thai people, with their religious and political center at **Ayuthaya,** took advantage of the opportunity afforded by Kampuchea's weakening and the Mongol destruction of the Pagan kingdom. Although the Mongols militarily overwhelmed the Thais in their expeditions of the 1280s, they later favored them as tributaries rather than objects of exploitation. The rise of Thai power was closely linked to this favoritism.

Three great monarchs in the thirteenth, fourteenth, and fifteenth centuries assured the Thai kingdom of central importance in mainland Asia throughout early modern times. Their contributions ranged from adoption of Hinayana Buddhism, to a model land tenure system, an advanced and efficient code of law, and standardization of the language, both written and oral. Collectively, the Thai kings of the Chakri dynasty created the most stable and most administratively advanced state in the area.

Thailand (the name is recent replacement for *Siam*) became the successor-through-conquest of Kampuchea in the fourteenth and early fifteenth centuries. By the fifteenth century, less than a century after its founding, the capital Ayuthaya had a population estimated at 150,000. Its temples and public gardens rivaled those of Anghor in its heyday, and quite overshadowed the now ruined Pagan.

Vietnam

Vietnam is the exception among the states we are now reviewing in its intense, love-hate relationship with China. For a thousand years the Vietnamese were the oft-rebellious subjects of the emperor of the Middle Kingdom. When this "yoke" was finally thrown off in 939 C.E., the educated people had been sinicized (made Chinese) to an extent not otherwise experienced anywhere, even in Korea and Tibet.

Nam viet (land of the Viets) was made into a province of the Chinese empire by a Han ruler in 111 B.C.E. For the next thousand years, it was governed by imperial appointees schooled in Confucian principles and assisted by a cadre of Chinese officials. Mahayana Buddhism was brought to the country by Chinese missionary monks, soon becoming the dominant faith and remaining so when the rest of Southeast Asia had turned to the Hinayana version. The pre–twentieth century Vietnamese script is the only Southeast Asian form of writing based on Chinese ideographs. In many different ways, then, China was the tutelary deity of Viet culture.

Yet this closeness inevitably brought forth a mirror image of rejection and dislike. Heavy-handedness and the serene presumption of superiority that so marked China's upper classes in their contacts with foreigners left their scars on the Vietnamese as deeply as on anyone else. The national heroes are two sisters, Trung Trac and Trung Nhi, who as co-queens led an armed rebellion in 39 C.E. that pushed out the Chinese for two years before being crushed. The sisters committed joint suicide and became the permanent focal point of anti-Chinese patriotism.

After the weakening of the Tang dynasty allowed successful revolt in 939 Vietnam (more precisely *Dai Viet,* the "kingdom of the Viets") remained a sovereign state for another millennium. Its relation with its great neighbor to the north was always delicate, but the adoption of a tributary relationship, with certain advantages to both sides, allowed the Vietnamese effective sovereignty and kept the peace. Even the Mongol conquerors came to accept the right of Dai Viet to exist as an independent entity. Their campaigns aimed at subduing the kingdom in both the 1250s and again in the 1280s were repelled by brilliantly led guerrilla warriors.

In the ensuing centuries the Ly and the Tran dynasties ruling from the city eventually named Hanoi successfully expanded their territories against both the resurgent Champa kingdom to the south, and the Khmers, later the Thais, to the west. In general, these dynasties followed the Chinese administrative style, backed up strongly by the official Confucian culture and the thorough sinicization of the educational system. The Le dynasty was notably successful in organizing resistance against renewed Chinese invasion in the early 1400s, adding another chapter to the Vietnamese saga of rejection of Chinese military pressures while simultaneously pursuing Chinese culture.

SUMMARY

The earliest period of Japan's history is shrouded in mists. The lack of written sources until the eighth century C.E. forces us to rely on archaeology and occasional mentions in Chinese travel accounts. Unlike many other peoples, the Japanese never experienced an alien military conquest that unified them under a strong central government. The imperial court was essentially a symbol of Shinto religious significance and a cultural center rather than a government. Real power was exercised by feudal lords organized loosely in clans who dominated specific localities rather than nationally.

Japan's relations with China and Korea were close through most of its early history but were punctuated with briefer periods of self-willed isolation. In the broadest senses, most of the models of Japanese culture can be traced to Chinese sources. Often these came through Korea. Among Japan's notable borrowings from China were Buddhism, writing, and several art media and forms. But in each instance, the Japanese adapted these imports to create a peculiarly native product. They rejected entirely the Chinese style of imperial government and its accompanying bureaucracy, favoring instead a military feudalism.

The Southeast Asian societies experienced some type of extensive political organization beginning in the early Christian centuries, but very little is known from historical sources until much later. The earliest mainland kingdoms seem to date from the fifth or sixth centuries C.E. and those in the islands a good deal later. The Burman Pagan kingdom was matched by the Khmers of Anghor, and the later Thai kingdom centered on Ayuthaya as major cultural and political factors in the first fourteen hundred years of our era. Originally subscribing to Hindu viewpoints, all these and other mainland countries converted to Hinayana Buddhism. Unlike its neighbors, all of whom were under strong Indian cultural influence, Vietnam emulated Chinese Confucian styles and practice for a lengthy period.

Some of these mainland entities extended their domains into Malaya and the archipelago of Indonesia. But generally speaking, the islands brought forth their own imperial centers that rose and fell depending on control of the lucrative maritime trading routes. At the very end of the period under discussion, a militant Islam was replacing both Hindu and Buddhist religions in most of the islands.

TEST YOUR KNOWLEDGE

1. Very early Japanese history is best summarized as
   a. a complete mystery until the Tang dynasty in China.
   b. unknown except for sporadic Chinese reports.
   c. well documented from native sources.
   d. dependent on the reports of Japan's early invaders.
2. The first Japanese government we know of was organized by the
   a. Yamato clan.
   b. Shinto monasteries.
   c. Buddhist monks.
   d. Heian emperors.
3. Shinto is best defined as
   a. a belief in the infallibility of the emperor.
   b. the original capital city of Japan.
   c. the native religion of the Japanese.
   d. the most important of the Buddhist sects in Japan.
4. The chief original contribution of the Japanese to world literature was the
   a. novel.
   b. epic.
   c. short story.
   d. essay.
5. A shogun was
   a. the high priest of the Shinto temples.
   b. a samurai official.

   c. an illegal usurper of imperial authority.
   d. a general acting as political regent.
6. In the Japanese feudal system, a shoen was
   a. an urban commercial concession.
   b. a property outside imperial taxation and controls.
   c. the preferred weapon of the samurai.
   d. land owned by a free peasant.
7. Which of the following best describes the relationship of China and Japan through 1400 C.E.?
   a. Japan was a willing student of Chinese culture.
   b. Japan selectively adopted Chinese models and ideas.
   c. Japan was forced to adopt Chinese models.
   d. Japan rejected Chinese pressures to conform.
8. In Lady Murasaki's tale, Genji is
   a. a samurai warrior who has no time for love.
   b. a betrayed husband of a court beauty.
   c. a romantic lover of many court ladies.
   d. a wise peasant who avoids courtly snares.
9. Which statement is correct about the early history of Southeast Asia?
   a. The mainland nations normally controlled the islands politically.
   b. The islands clung to their Hindu and animist beliefs throughout this period.

c. The Hinayana Buddhists could not support the idea of divine kingship.

d. The Khmer empire was destroyed by the Chinese.

10. Identify the false pairing of country/nation/empire with a geographic center:

a. Kampuchea—Anghor

b. Dai Viet—Hanoi

c. Burma—Pagan

d. Majapahit—Malacca

IDENTIFICATION TERMS

Ashikaga clan

Ayuthaya

bakufu

bushido

daimyo

Fujiwara clan

Kamakura shogunate

Kampuchea

Khmers

Kyoto

Majapahit

Pagan

Prince Shotoku

samurai

Shinto

shiki

shoen

shogunate

Tale of Genji

INFOTRAC COLLEGE EDITION

Enter the search terms "Asia history" using Key Words.

Enter the search terms "Japan history" using Key Words.

Enter the search term "Shinto" using Key Words.

Chapter 20

Africa from Kush to the Fifteenth Century

Not even God is wise enough.

YORUBA PROVERB

THE HISTORIOGRAPHY OF AFRICANS has made impressive advances in the past fifty years. The greater part of the continent's people had no written language until relatively recent days or employed a language that has not been deciphered. Historiographical research in the usual literary sense was therefore very difficult. But a combination of new methods of obtaining information on the past and new techniques for using that information have changed the situation radically. Now, archaeology, linguistics, art forms, and oral traditions have enabled considerable illumination of Africa's past, and these sources are gradually revealing an extraordinary panorama of peoples and achievements.

Africa is a huge place—the second largest of the world's continents—and the chief characteristic of its history is its variety. Most of its several different climates and topographies have produced civilizations or proto-civilizations. In terms of traditional racial categories, about 70 percent of its present total population is considered Negroid, or black. The remainder is concentrated in the north and northeast and is a mixture of Caucasoid, or white, stocks. More even than elsewhere, Africa has repeatedly demonstrated that traditional racial categories have no relevance for explaining the relative rise or stagnation of peoples in the struggle to achieve a higher civilization. On the contrary, the natural environment and location on trade-and-travel routes have proved the decisive factors.

African Geography and Climates

Before the Europeans arrived during the fifteenth century C.E., Africa was mostly isolated by its geography from other centers of human activity. The great exception was its Mediterranean coast, and the northeastern portion, where both Egypt and the so-called Horn of Africa (present-day Ethiopia and Somalia) were in continuous contact with the Near and Middle Eastern civilizations from at least as early as 2000 B.C.E.

Gold Digging in the Nile Valley

A fourteenth-century geographer, al-`Umari, relates how the medieval black kingdoms of the Sahel found their most vital export northward: gold. In this excerpt, Al-`Umari seems to be saying that gold is a plant, but he means that fine gold dust is found trapped in the roots of plants after being suspended and brought downstream in the Nile flood:

> Gold begins to grow in the month of August . . . when the sun's power is at its peak and the Nile begins to rise to flood level. When the Nile decreases again, prospecting starts where the land has been covered . . . for gold is in the roots of [a certain] plant. Some gravel-like gold is also found.

The mining of surface deposits of fine gold along the upper Nile was a regular source of important income for the black kings, who traded extensively with the Arab and Berber settlements in both the lower Nile and the Maghrib (North Africa) to the west. Another Muslim traveler, al-Idrisi, notes that in the twelfth century, it was already a custom of the Sudan blacks to follow the course of the falling Nile each late summer to obtain the deposited gold-bearing silts.

Source: From Pier Donini, Arab Travellers and Geographers (London: Immel, 1991), p. 57.

quer it, both from the Nile valley and the Red Sea coasts. It also allowed the growth of a unique legend of royal descent, the Solomonic dynasty of Ethiopian Christian kings that commenced in biblical times and lasted until an army rebellion in 1970. According to this history, the royal line was descended from Menelik, son of the Hebrew king Solomon by the queen of Sheba.

Like its predecessor, Axum depended for its prosperity on its function as exchange depot for the Indian Ocean–Red Sea trade, as well as the Nile valley route. The seventh-century Arab conquest of Egypt and south Arabia changed this situation dramatically, and within a century Christian Axum was driven from its Red Sea coast and under siege. Gradually, the city sank into the same forgetfulness that had claimed Kush 500 years before. Its monuments and stelae (columns of stone inscribed with royal laws) fell down and were buried or forgotten by an impoverished remnant.

From the eighth century, the seaborne trade was dominated by Arab Muslims. Axum's place along the Nile was taken by the black Nubians, whose tribally organized society gradually matured into several transitory kingdoms. Little is known about them except for the fact they were converted to Christianity from Egypt in the seventh and eighth centuries and managed to hold out against Muslim pressure until as late as the 1200s in some areas. Throughout this lengthy period from Axum's fall to the coming of Muslim hegemony into the upper Nile, a diminished commercial

❀ **The Ship of the Desert.** The Sahara was never totally impassable, but until the introduction of the camel in the early Christian era, crossing it was very difficult. The camel's superior load-carrying ability and endurance was able to make the north-south crossing a feasible undertaking for large-scale commerce. (© *Raphail Gaillarede/Gamma*)

al-Bakri: Ghana in the Eleventh Century

The Arab and Berber travelers are our chief sources of knowledge about sub-Saharan affairs until as late as the fifteenth century C.E. One of them was al-Bakri, a great Muslim geographer who lived in the eleventh century. Although it is unclear whether he himself ever visited Africa, he was much interested in the continent and wrote extensively about West Africa, where by his day animist and Muslim Africans were living together in many towns. The following excerpt is from al-Bakri's account of the society of Ghana, the name for both the ruler and the location of a kingdom in what is today Mali and Nigeria: Al-Bakri takes particular note of the religious practices of his hosts, wherever he may be. Although eager to show the superiority of Islam over the native practices, he is always the fair-minded observer. Note that the ghana has remained an animist, even while inviting Muslims into his kingdom.

The city of Ghana consists of two towns situated on a plain. One of these towns, which is inhabited by Muslims, is large and possesses twelve mosques, in one of which they assemble for the Friday prayers. There are salaried imams and muezzins, as well as jurists and scholars. . . . The king's town is six miles distant from this one, and bears the name al-Ghaba. Between these two towns there are continuous habitations. The houses of the inhabitants are of stone and acacia wood. The king has a palace and a number of domed dwellings, all enclosed with a city wall. In the king's town and not far from his court of justice is a mosque where the Muslims who arrive at his court pray. Around the king's town are domed buildings and groves and thickets where the sorcerers [shamans] of these people, men in charge of their religious cult, live. In them too are the idols and the tombs of their kings. . . .

All of them shave their beards, and the women shave their heads. The king adorns himself like a woman, with necklaces around his neck and bracelets on his forearms, and he puts on a high cap decorated with gold and wrapped in a turban of fine cotton. He sits in audience or to hear grievances against officials. . . . Behind the king stand ten pages holding shields and swords decorated with gold, and on his right are the sons of the [subordinate] kings of his country, wearing splendid garments and their hair plaited with gold. . . . When the people professing the same religion as the king approach him, they fall on their knees and sprinkle dust on their heads, for this is their way of greeting him. As for Muslims, they greet him only by clapping their hands.

Their religion is paganism and the worship of idols. When their king dies they construct over the place where his tomb will be an enormous dome of wood. Then they bring him on a bed covered with a few carpets and cushions, and place him beside the dome. At his side they place his ornaments, his weapons, and the vessels from which he used to eat and drink, filled with various kinds of food and beverages.

For Reflection

Why didn't the pagan ghana fear that the example ("only by clapping their hands") of the Muslims would spread to his own people? Do you think that Muslims and animist Africans had great difficulties in living and working together? Why or why not?

SOURCE: From N. Levtzion and J. F. P. Hopkins, eds., Corpus of Early Arabic Sources for West African History (Cambridge: Cambridge University Press, 1981), pp. 79–80. Reprinted with permission of Cambridge University Press.

---

traffic along the great river served to bind Egypt with its southern borderlands in Nubia and the Sudan. But the level of civilized sedentary life reached by the Kushite and Axumite kingdoms was not again approached.

The Sudanese Kingdoms

The Sudanese kingdoms were a series of states that were formed starting about 900 C.E. in the bulge of West Africa below the great Sahara Desert. Here, iron tools, good soils, and the transport afforded by the Niger River had enabled agriculture to advance and provide for a rapidly growing population and an active trade northward across the Sahara with the Berbers and Arabs.

Ghana

Ghana, the first of these kingdoms, lasted for about two centuries before it fell apart. It was created by the Soninke people in the tenth century and had extensive dealings with the Muslims to the north. The *ghana* was the title given to the king, a sacred being who ruled through a network of subchieftains in an area that at one point reached the size of Texas. Kumbi, the capital town, was sufficiently impressive that the sophisticated Muslim geographer **al-Bakri** spent some time describing it in a well-known travel and sightseeing guide of the eleventh century. (See a short excerpt of his reaction to this black Muslim stronghold in the Tradition and Innovation box.)

The Muslims, both Arabic and Berber, were very influential in Ghana and, for that matter, in most of the Sudanese West African kingdoms that followed. The peoples of the Sudan were animists, but they had little difficulty converting to the religious doctrines preached by Arab merchants and missionaries. Like the Christians of Rome earlier, the missionaries concentrated their efforts on the upper class, usually in the towns where trade flourished. By adopting the new doctrine, the African merchant partners quickly gained advantages: literacy; access to new commerce and financial connections; treatment as equals by their Arab/Berber colleagues. Soon animist villagers and Muslim urbanites coexisted in these states without apparent friction. The Muslims introduced their concepts of law and administration, as well as religious belief. Kings who chose to remain animist often relied on Muslim advisers for political and administrative advice.

Mali

After Ghana fell to a Berber invasion in the eleventh century, its tribally oriented segments made war on one another until one was powerful enough to intimidate its neighbors into submission. This was the kingdom of **Mali,** which survived from about 1200 to about 1450. Mali was larger and better organized than Ghana, and it too had a sacred king who ruled with the help of his chieftains. The thirteenth-century formal adoption of Islam by the upper class, led by a powerful king, encouraged good relations with the trans-Saharan Berbers, whose trading activities were essential to the prosperity of the kingdom.

Like the earlier Kush and Axum, the Sudanese kingdoms were first and foremost the products of a strategic trading position. In this case, controlling movement along a lengthy stretch of the southern fringe of the Sahara allowed them to monitor the movements of goods from sub-Saharan to North Africa (and on to both Europe and the East). Both Ghana and Mali relied heavily on the taxes imposed on the Saharan traders in three vital commodities: gold, salt, and slaves. Although the king had other means of support for his extensive and expensive court and army, these taxes made the wheels go round, so to speak.

African gold was essential to Roman and medieval European commerce, as well as to the Muslim world. Gold ore was rare in Europe, but it was found in large quantities in parts of sub-Saharan Africa controlled by Mali as well as in some of its African trading partners.

Salt was almost as prized as gold in the ancient world. Though it was a necessity, supplies were limited in most areas except near the sea, and it was difficult to transport without large loss. This made salt highly valuable, and the mines in and on the southern side of the Sahara were a major source.

Slaves were common in the African markets long before the Europeans began the Atlantic slave trade. Neither African nor Muslim culture had any moral scruples about slave trading or possession in this epoch. As in every other part of the ancient world, slavery was an accepted conse-

⚭ **Mosque at Jenne.** This mud brick construction dating from the fourteenth century is located at the ancient caravan town of Jenne, in present-day Mali. It is one of the most striking examples of Muslim penetration into the Sahara. (© *Werner Forman Archives/Art Resource*)

quence of war, debt, and crime. Being captured in raids by hostile neighbors was reason enough for enslavement. Large numbers passed northward through Ghana and Mali, bound for collection points on the Mediterranean coast. From there they were traded all over the known world.

The kingdom of Mali expanded by military conquests in the thirteenth century, until it came to dominate much of West Africa. Early Africa's most noted ruler, the far-traveled **Mansa Musa,** ruled from 1307 to 1332. He extended the kingdom as far north as the Berber towns in Morocco and eastward to include the great mid-Saharan trading post of **Timbuktu.** Perhaps eight million people lived under his rule—at a time when the population of England was about four million.

Mansa Musa

Because of the African tradition of oral literature and history, we have practically no written sources from that continent until the occasional accounts by Muslim traders appear in the twelfth century. One of the first sub-Saharan African rulers known to us in any detail is Mansa Musa (ruled 1307–1332), king of Mali and grandson of the founder of that kingdom, the legendary warrior Sundiata. Both grandfather and grandson were known to their subjects as creative lawgivers, adapting the precepts of Islam to fit their circumstances and their people.

Mansa Musa ruled a kingdom that had been penetrated by Arab trader/missionaries for over fifty years. The ruling group was already converted to Islam. Caravans from North Africa and the upper Nile valley traveled to the major towns of Timbuktu and Walata, where they exchanged their goods for the slaves and gold of Mali.

In 1324, at the height of his powers, Mansa Musa decided to make the *hajj* to Mecca and the holy places of Islam. He did so in a style that endured in the Muslim world's mythology for centuries. According to Egyptian accounts, he arrived in Cairo accompanied by a retinue of soldiers, courtiers, and slaves. One hundred camels carried almost a ton of gold dust in their packs; 500 slaves each carried a staff of gold weighing six pounds!

Staying in Cairo before journeying on to the holy cities across the Red Sea, Mansa Musa spent and gave away so much gold that its price in Egypt declined to a record low and stayed down for a generation! Mali soon became known to the Christian world as well as the Muslim as "the land of gold" and began to appear regularly on the maps of the time with that appellation (see the illustration). The reputation of the country as a source of great wealth was established, and the fame of its king penetrated every mercantile network.

Mansa Musa returned from Mecca with several talented men from the Muslim East, who settled in Mali and contributed to the development of that society. In Timbuktu a Muslim *medresah* (religious school) gradually became a university, similar to the great Muslim center in Cairo. According to a later visitor, Timbuktu had more bookstores than any other type of mercantile establishment and as many scholarly resources as any other city in the Muslim world.

Under Mansa Musa, Mali reached its maximal territorial limits, stretching from the lower Gambia River on the bulge of West Africa well into present-day Nigeria to the south and east. This expansion was accomplished through a standing royal army, which overwhelmed its tribal neighbors. Berber and Arab traders crossing the difficult Saharan trade routes were obliged to seek Mansa Musa's protection. All merchandise sold in his kingdom carried a "sales tax," which went to the royal court. A royal bureaucracy composed of Muslim blacks administered the tax and judicial systems.

Most of the world's supply of gold in the fourteenth century came out of Mali. It supported a notably successful Arab-black mercantile empire that endured for two generations after Mansa Musa's death in 1332.

For Reflection

What advantages did the adoption of Islam possibly hold for the ruling elite in Mali, or any black kingdom of the day? What does the number of bookstores in Timbuktu say about the culture of the urban elite?

This fourteenth-century European map shows Mansa Musa holding a large nugget. (© *The Granger Collection*)

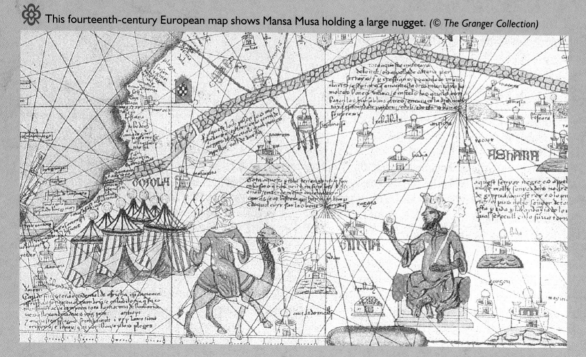

Like his immediate predecessors, Mansa Musa was a Muslim, and in 1324 he made the pilgrimage to the holy places in Arabia. His huge entourage laden with golden staffs and plates entered Cairo like a victory procession and made an impression that became folklore. (For more details about his reign, see the Law and Lawgivers box.)

Thanks to Mansa Musa's enthusiasm and determination, Islam gained much ground in West Africa during his lifetime. Thereafter, the religion gradually passed through the upper classes to the common people. Since then, the Muslim presence in sub-Saharan Africa has been growing slowly for many generations. It has had almost the same impact there as Christianity did in the Germanic kingdoms. Much African law, social organization, literature, and political institutions stem from it.

Songhai

Last of the extensive Sudanese kingdoms was the **Songhai** empire, which arose when Mali collapsed in the wake of civil wars. It dominated the western savanna and the southern edge of the desert for about 200 years. Centered on the bend of the Niger River, Songhai kings ruled almost to the coast and northward to the major trade and administrative center of Timbuktu. On the east, Songhai connected to the Borno kingdom in the Lake Chad area, creating a trade network that allowed caravan-borne commodities to be shipped throughout most of western and much of northern Africa. The empire thus created was defeated by another Moroccan Muslim expeditionary force and broke up into ethnic fragments. This was the situation at the time the first Europeans arrived.

The Swahili City-States
❦

The East African city-states also had a large hand in the gradual commercial development of the continent. Trade between the ports of southeast Africa and India had been carried on since the first centuries C.E., both by Indians and by Roman ships that traveled down the Red Sea to pick up cargoes at ports on the Indian Ocean. But the real entry of these places into history came with the Muslim expansion of the seventh and eighth centuries. Then, a number of Arab traders settled in colonies all up and down the East African coast, where they acted as middlemen between the peoples of the interior and the markets of the north and in South Asia.

Arabs and native Bantu peoples steadily intermarried, and the children of these unions were raised as Muslims, while many native peoples opted to convert to gain credibility as business partners. Persian and even Indonesian Muslims also came to the East African coast, adding to the melting pot of cultures there. Islam served as the one binding thread. By the fourteenth century, a series of small kingdoms or city-states were established. The Bantu controlled some of these sophisticated commercial states, and colonies of Arabs controlled others.

The culture and language of these cities are termed **Swahili,** a Bantu word meaning "mixed." The language is an amalgam of Bantu and Arabic, and it has ever since been a sort of lingua franca, a common ground for communication among all East Africans.

The slave trade was even more extensive in East Africa than in the Sudan. It was highly profitable to send slaves north and east into the Muslim territories where blacks were a novelty that would bring a high price. Although most went to the Red Sea, some were taken as far as Southeast Asia. Ports such as Mombasa, Kilwa, and Mogadishu (in present-day Kenya, Mozambique, and Somalia, respectively) had a rich trade in slaves, gold, ivory, animal skins, amber, and other highly desirable luxuries. When the Portuguese came at the end of the fifteenth century, they were amazed at the wealth and opulent lifestyles in these cities, among the upper class, at least.

Great Zimbabwe
❦

South Africa has a moderate climate and much good agricultural and pastoral soil, which allowed it to shelter the Bantu-speaking migrants who reached it around the 700s C.E. Reports by shipwrecked Portuguese sailors in the early 1500s indicate that Bantu and Bushmen were living either in agricultural villages or in a hunting culture all across the tip of the continent. Archaeology reveals that iron had come into use as early as the fifth century C.E. Nevertheless, development and population growth seem to have been slow. Agriculture did not replace hunting as the normal source of food until around 1500, shortly before the Europeans first appeared.

The chief center of early civilized life in southern Africa was not near the coast, but far inland: **Great Zimbabwe.** Today the ruins of what was once a large capital city and fortress can be seen in the present-day nation of Zimbabwe on the eastern side of the Cape of Good Hope. Great Zimbabwe was not discovered until 1871, and unfortunately, we know nothing of its history from written sources. Nevertheless, its massive walls and towers make it the most impressive monument in Africa south of the pyramids. Apparently, it was built in the tenth and eleventh centuries by kings whose wealth and power rested, once again, on control of rich gold mines. The city flourished as a cultural and trading center until the fifteenth century, when it fell into decline for reasons not known. Perhaps the population exceeded the limits that a backward agriculture could supply, and the city was gradually abandoned. Or perhaps military conquest was threatened or achieved by enemies—we cannot know.

❀ **Great Zimbabwe.** These stone walls are the only remnants of a once-important trade center in the southern African interior. They were discovered only in the late nineteenth century by Europeans. (© *David Reed/Corbis*)

African Arts

❀

In the absence of written languages, art was necessarily visual and plastic, and the sculpture and inlay work of all parts of sub-Saharan Africa have lately aroused much interest and study in the Western world. Perhaps the most famous are the Benin bronzes from the West African kingdom of Benin, one of the successors to Mali. The highly stylized busts and full-length figures in bronze, gold, and combinations of metal and ebony wood are striking in their design and execution. They are obviously the product of a long tradition of excellence. Many of these pieces were vandalized by Benin's enemies during the constant warfare that marred West African history. Many others were carried off as booty by the early Europeans and have since disappeared. Enough remain, however, to give us some appreciation of the skill and imagination of the makers.

The same is true of the wood sculptures of the Kanem and Bornu peoples of central Sudan, who assembled a series of kingdoms in the vicinity of Lake Chad between the twelfth and fifteenth centuries that lasted in one manifestation or another until the eighteenth. The ivory and gold work of the Swahili city-states is also remarkable and much appreciated, especially by Middle Eastern buyers. Some Muslims looked on this infidel artwork depicting human figures as a mockery of Allah and destroyed much of it, ei-

ther in place in Africa or later, in the countries to which it was transported.

The earthenware heads of the Nok people of prehistoric Nigeria, on the other hand, have come to light only in this century. Dating from roughly the first five centuries before the Christian era, these terra cotta portrait heads are the oldest examples yet found of African art. Their probable religious significance is not known.

European Impressions

❀

Unfortunately for the Africans' reputation, the fifteenth-century Europeans arrived on the African coast at about the same time that the most potent and most advanced of the sub-Saharan kingdoms collapsed or were in decline. In the absence of written sources, the causes of decline are not easily identified. They largely seem to have involved a lethal combination of internal quarrels among the nobility who served the king and conquest from outside, generally by other blacks or sometimes by Muslims from Morocco.

As a result, the European explorer-traders perceived the kingdoms as subservient and backward. This impression was reinforced by the Africans' relative lack of knowledge in military matters and later by the readiness of some of the African kings and chieftains to allow the sale of competing

or neighboring people into slavery—a practice that had been commonplace in Europe for a thousand years but that Christian teaching had by that time forbidden.

The Europeans (largely the Portuguese in the first century of contacts) concluded that the Africans were retarded in their sensitivity and degree of civilization and that it would not be wrong to take advantage of them. Africans were perceived as not quite human, so what would have been a despicable sin against God and humanity had it been done back home in Lisbon was quite forgivable—perhaps not worth a second thought—here. This callousness was undoubtedly reinforced by the desperate nature of business enterprise in the first centuries of the colonial era, when it is estimated that those Europeans who went to the African coast had a 25 percent mortality rate *per year*. It was not an

affair that encouraged second thoughts on the morality of what one was doing.

The Portuguese attitude was shared by the other Europeans who came into contact with the Africans, as slavers in West Africa. Early attempts to convert the black Africans to Christianity were quickly subordinated to business interests by the Portuguese and never attempted at all by their English, Dutch, and French successors. The tendency to see Africans as a source of profit rather than as fellow human beings was soon rationalized by everything from biblical quotations to Arab Muslim statements reflecting their own prejudices. The basis of European (and later American) racism directed against the dark skinned is to be found in these earliest contacts and the circumstances in which they were made.

SUMMARY

Africa is a continent of vast disparities in ethnic background, climate, and topography. Much of its interior remained shut off from the rest of the world until a century ago, and little was known of its history either from domestic or foreign sources. Only the Mediterranean coastal region and the Nile valley came to be included in the classical world, while the great Saharan desert long secluded the African heartland from northern penetration. In a prehistoric migration, the Bantu-speaking inhabitants of the western forest regions gradually came to occupy most of the continent in the early Christian era, aided by their mastery of iron and of advanced agriculture.

African state formation proceeded slowly and unevenly. The first were in the northeast, where ancient Egypt was followed by Kush and Axum as masters of the Indian Ocean–Mediterranean trade routes. Their decline followed upon Arab Muslim expansion in the eighth century.

In the tenth and succeeding centuries, several advanced kingdoms arose in the western savanna lands, largely dependent on an active trade in gold and slaves across the desert to the northern Muslim regions. Ghana was the first of these commercially oriented kingdoms, followed by the larger and more permanent Mali and Songhai empires. A black Muslim elite governed in the latter two. In the Swahili city-states along the eastern coast, a mixed Bantu-Arabic group ruled. Indeed, Islam, carried by proselytizing Arab merchants into the interior, was the prime force for political, legal, and administrative organization in much of pre-European Africa.

TEST YOUR KNOWLEDGE

1. The area of Africa in which human habitation was difficult or impossible until very recent times is approximately
   a. 90 percent.
   b. 70 percent.
   c. 50 percent.
   d. 40 percent.
2. An important population movement in Africa around the first century C.E. was the
   a. drift of Bantu speakers from West Africa to the south and east.
   b. movement of the Pygmies from central to northern Africa.
   c. settlement of North Africa by the Tuaregs.
   d. coming of the Portuguese to colonize the coast.
3. The kingdom of Axum
   a. succeeded the kingdom of Kush in northeast Africa.
   b. was crushed by the Egyptians during the New Kingdom of Egypt.
   c. was the original home of the Bantus.
   d. was converted early to Islam.
4. By about the fifth century C.E., the population of the western Sudan had increased dramatically as a result of
   a. immigration from the eastern regions.
   b. changes in climate.
   c. increased food production.
   d. the practice of polygamy.
5. Native African religions were
   a. polymorphic.
   b. animistic.
   c. agnostic.
   d. monotheistic.
6. The outside people having the greatest cultural influence on the kingdom of Ghana were the
   a. European colonists.
   b. Muslim Berbers and Arabs.
   c. Ethiopians.
   d. Egyptian Christians.
7. Trade in slaves in both East and West Africa before the fifteenth century was
   a. commonplace.
   b. limited to extraordinary circumstances.
   c. controlled by the Muslims.
   d. rarely encountered.
8. The Swahili city-states were located
   a. on the northern coast facing the Mediterranean.
   b. on the Cape of Good Hope in the far south.
   c. near the upper Nile.
   d. on the Indian Ocean coast.
9. Mansa Musa was
   a. the outstanding Muslim geographer who described early Africa.
   b. the wealthy African king who journeyed to Arabia on pilgrimage.
   c. the founder of the kingdom of Mali.
   d. the Arab missionary who converted the king of Mali.
10. Identify the art form that was *not* a strength of precolonial Africa:
    a. Silk weaving
    b. Bronze sculpture
    c. Wooden mask making
    d. Ceramic heads

IDENTIFICATION TERMS

al-Bakri	Ghana	Mali	Songhai
Axum	Great Zimbabwe	Mansa Musa	Swahili
Bantu	Kush	matrilineal descent	Timbuktu
Berbers	lineage		

INFOTRAC COLLEGE EDITION

Enter the search term "Bantu" using Key Words.

Enter the search terms "Africa history" using Key Words.

Chapter 21

The Americas Before Columbus

A god, Quetzalcoatl, was expected from the East... Then Hernan Cortes appeared.

VICTOR WOLFGANG VON HAGEN

LIKE AFRICA, THE AMERICAS demonstrate a tremendous range of cultures and physical environments. The first inhabitants came into the Americas much later than humans (*Homo sapiens sapiens*) appeared elsewhere in the world, perhaps as late as 20,000 years ago. They arrived by way of the then-existing land bridge across the northernmost Pacific, now called the Aleutian Islands (see Map 1.1 in Chapter 1). Slowly, they made their way down the Pacific coastal plain through North and Central America into the Andes.

Neolithic America

The Stone Age in the Americas lasted until the coming of the whites. Wooden, bone, and stone tools and weapons supported an impressive array of Neolithic cultures, ranging from the Inuit (Eskimo) of the Arctic to the inhabitants of the Mesoamerican jungle. Hunting and foraging peoples were most common. By about 7000 B.C.E., the western edge of North and South America was supporting populations of Amerindians, who were developing agriculture. Central and South America are the home of many of the world's basic farm crops, such as maize, potatoes, beans, and squashes, all derived from native plants (see Map 1.2 in Chapter 1). The center and eastern parts of North America were penetrated by nomadic hunters considerably later, and eastern South America much later still.

But about 2000 B.C.E. there already existed in what is now the southwestern United States, the central valley of Mexico, and some of the coastal plains of South America the type of intensive agriculture that first supplemented, then supplanted hunting as the major food source.

The arrival of the first Europeans in 1492 found agricultural techniques well advanced in some parts of the Americas, and the crops were sufficient to support a very large population that was organized into states with highly stratified social structures. By the time the Egyptians built the pyramids and the Hebrews were commencing their wanderings in Mesopotamia, Native Americans were living in agrarian villages throughout the western rim of the continent.

First Civilizations

The earliest American civilizations did not locate in river valleys but on the elevated plateaus or the tropic lowlands, inland from the Caribbean Sea.

Olmecs

The earliest civilization we now know about (through archaeology, only) arose in what is now southern Mexico and bears the name **Olmec.** It existed between 1000 B.C.E. and about 300 C.E., when it was overwhelmed by enemies from the north, who then quickly adopted many features of the civilization they had conquered.

The Olmec were the human foundation of all other Amerindian cultures in Central America. Olmec pottery and decorative ceramics have been found throughout Mexico and as far south as Costa Rica. Their main sites thus far discovered, north of Mexico City and near the Caribbean port of Vera Cruz, consist of a central fortified complex of governmental halls and religious shrines. As with all succeeding pre-Columbian civilizations (those before Columbus) a pervasive religious faith centering on worship of gods in feline images, above all the jaguar, was the inspiration for much of the art and architecture.

The Olmecs' skill in stonework is most remarkably expressed by the enormous heads of basalt that they left behind. Standing up to nine feet high and weighing up to twelve tons, these realistically modeled, flat-nosed, thick-lipped heads fulfilled unknown ceremonial functions for the Olmecs. Their Negroid features have given rise to speculation about the possible African origins of the earliest colonists. No evidence of this yet exists.

Olmec masonry skills also enabled them to build ceremonial stone pyramids, one of which reached 110 feet high. This Great Pyramid speaks of a degree of civilized organization and a ready supply of labor, which suggests that the Olmecs' agriculture must have been sufficiently advanced to support a large population. The Olmec had a primitive form of writing and a number system, neither of which is understood, but which enabled them to survey and build a large number of massive edifices. Surviving art (sculpture) indicates that a small elite group centering on the priests of the official religion had great powers, and the ruler was probably a hereditary king/high priest. Unfortunately, more than this is not known.

The Chavin

In South America at the same epoch, the **Chavin** culture centered on the high valleys immediately inland from the Peruvian coast showed a comparable development. Between about 800 and 400 B.C.E., Native American people settled into a Neolithic agrarian lifestyle whose very fragmentary material remnants are best known in the form of the clay and jade sculpture they excelled in. Much goldware has also been found, at sites as high in the forbidding mountains as 11,000 feet. The triumph of the Chavin was above all in the provision of adequate food for a dense population in such topographically difficult areas. This achievement has barely been reproduced aided by the technology of the late twentieth century in modern Peru.

The Maya

Before or around 300 C.E., the Olmec civilization collapsed. Its place as civilized leader in coastal Mexico was taken by the **Maya,** who were the most advanced of all the pre-Columbian Amerindians. Their mysterious demise as an organized state before the arrival of the Spaniards is a continuing problem for archaeologists and historians. The Maya had a written language, a calendar, and an understanding of mathematics that was far more advanced than European mathematics in the twelfth century. The recent decipherment of some of the Mayan written language has enabled scholars to more accurately reconstruct the events

Mayan Palace at Palenque. The Mayan civilization of present-day eastern Mexico was older than the Aztec civilization, but showed many similar characteristics. This seventh-century palace was uncovered from the jungle in the nineteenth century. (© B. Daemmrich/The Image Works)

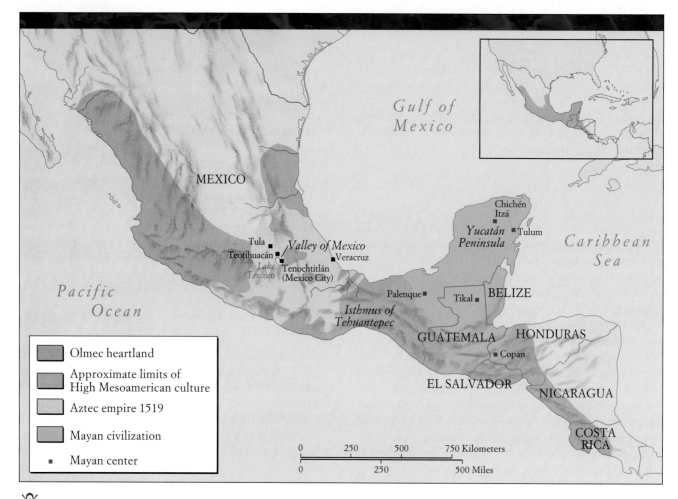

⟨✿⟩ **MAP 21.1 Mesoamerican Civilizations.** The Aztec empire was at its height when the Spanish arrived. The Mayan cities of Palenque and Tikal were abandoned in the tenth century for unknown reasons, possibly failure of the food supply.

portrayed in the rich pictorial images of Mayan stonework, although much remains obscure. All in all, more is known about the life of the Mayan people than any of the other Mesoamericans. They are the model for the classical image of Amerindian civilization.

The historical outline is by now fairly clear. From about 300 C.E., the southern tip of present-day Mexico and Guatemala (the Yucatán) were governed by a hierarchy of Mayan cities ruled by hereditary kings. Some cities contained several tens of thousands of people (see Map 21.1). But the large majority of the population were peasant villagers who lived in satellite settlements on the cities' periphery. The whole population of the Mayan empire or federation may have reached fourteen million—far and away the largest state under one government outside Asia at that time.

Public buildings of truly amazing dimensions were the heart of the cities. Temples, palaces, and ball courts, many of them employing the blunt-tipped pyramid form, are so arranged as to construct a massive arena or assembly ground. To these forums at designated times would stream tens, perhaps hundreds of thousands to experience the

priest-led worship ceremonies, or the installation of a new monarch.

The cities seem to have been more religious/administrative centers than commercial/manufacturing centers. None of them approached the size of the Mesopotamian towns of a much earlier epoch. Trade was a relatively minor part of Mayan life.

The political and social power rested, as with the Olmec, in the hands of a hereditary elite. To judge from their costumes in surviving artwork, they were very wealthy. The common folk seem to have been divided into freemen, serfs, and slaves, as in much of the ancient world.

Religious belief was paramount in ordering the round of daily life. The ruling class included priests, who had magical powers given them by the gods. They also had access to the underworld, which seems to have been as fearsome as that of Mesopotamia. In the Mayan cosmology existed thirteen Heavens and nine Hells. No hint of ethical religion exists, however. The gods, like those of Sumeria, played multiple roles in human affairs, and in their persons they combined beastly and human traits. The jaguar—a species of great cat indigenous to the Americas—was particularly

COMMERCE AND EXCHANGE

Bernal Díaz de Castillo:
The Conquest of New Spain

The long and eventful life of Bernal Díaz de Castillo (?1492–1580) spanned the entire period of the conquest of the Americas. When he was well into his seventies, he set down an eyewitness account of Hernan Cortez's expedition into Mexico (1519–1521); by then he was the last survivor of that expedition. In *The Conquest of New Spain*, Bernal Díaz not only gives us a very exciting account of the entire campaign but also provides a unique description of the advanced civilization of the Aztecs and their capital city, Tenochtitlán (now Mexico City) in the last years of their imperial glory.

Bernal was no particular friend of the Amerindians, but it is plain that he was unexpectedly and deeply impressed by what the "savages" were capable of doing. His account of the marketplace and its lively commerce is particularly breathless, even fifty years after his visit:

On reaching the market place . . . we were astounded at the great number of people and the quantities of merchandise, and at the orderliness and good arrangements that prevailed, for we had never seen such a thing before. . . . Every kind of merchandise was kept separate and had its fixed place marked for it.

Let us begin with the dealers in gold, silver, and precious stones, feathered cloaks and embroidered goods, the male and female slaves who are also sold there. . . . Some are brought there attached to long poles by means of collars around their necks to prevent them from escaping, but others are left loose. Next, there were those who sold coarser cloth and cotton goods and fabrics made of twisted thread, and there were chocolate merchants with their chocolate. . . .

There were those who sold sisal cloth and ropes, and the sandals they wear, which were made of the same plant. All these were kept in one part of the market, in the place assigned them, and in another part were skins of tigers and lions, otters, jackals, and deer, badgers, and other wild animals, some tanned and some not. . . .

There were sellers of beans and sage and other vegetables and herbs in another place, and in yet another they were selling fowls and birds with great dewlaps [that is, turkeys, which the Spaniards had never seen]; also rabbits, hares, deer, young ducks, little dogs, and other creatures. Then there were the fruiterers; and the women who sold cooked food, flour and honey cakes and tripe.

. . . I am forgetting the fisherwomen and the men who sell small cakes made from a sort of weed which they cut out of the great lake, which curdles and forms a kind of bread which tastes rather like cheese. They sell axes, too, made of bronze and copper and tin, and gourds, and brightly painted wooden jars. . . .

Some of our soldiers who had been in many parts of the world . . . said that they had never seen a market so well laid out, so large, so orderly, and so filled with people.

For Reflection

Bernal wrote this account some fifty years later; do you think he had any reason to exaggerate the Amerindians' achievements or to downplay them? Proud of being a warrior even in old age, how would Bernal look on commerce and those who performed it?

SOURCE: Conquest of New Spain, by Bernal Díaz de Castillo, trans. J. Cohen, © Penguin Classics Edition (London: Penguin Ltd., 1991).

To unify their lands, the Inca built great roads running north and south both along the coast and in the mountains. They constructed irrigation systems, dams, and canals and built terraces on the steep hillsides so crops could be planted. The usage of metal was considerably more common in Incan lands than in Mexico. Copper jewelry and bronze tools are found among their grave sites. The llama, a member of the camel family, was used as a beast of burden in the highlands, giving the Inca another advantage over their contemporaries in Mesoamerica. The stone buildings of royal Cuzco are among the finest erected in the Americas, and fine textiles of both cotton and wool were commonplace possessions of the upper class.

One of the most magnificent achievements of Incan rule was **Machu Picchu,** a city in the clouds of the high Andes, whose ruins were discovered only in 1911. The Inca accomplished the awe-inspiring feat of moving thousands of huge stone blocks to build the walls of this fortress-city on a mountaintop, in the absence of almost all technology (probably even without the wheel). No one knows why the city was built or why it was abandoned.

Incan Government and Society

Like most other ancient and premodern societies, Incan society exhibited sharp class divisions. A small elite of nobles were at the top, under their semidivine king, the Inca, from whom all authority issued. A large army maintained obedience. Most rebellions against the Inca were, in fact, fraternal wars in which the rebel leader was a member of the imperial house. The Spaniards under Francisco Pizarro used one of these civil wars to great advantage when they arrived in 1533 to rob the gold of Cuzco.

The basic unit of both society and government was the *ayllu,* or clan. A village would normally possess two to four clans, headed by a male in the prime of life to whom all members of the clan owed absolute loyalty. He handled the

The Americas Before Columbus 245

Moctezuma II
(C. 1466–1519)

The great Moctezuma was about forty years old, of good-height and well proportioned, slender, not very swarthy but of the natural color and shade of an Indian. . . . He was very neat and clean, and bathed once every day, in the afternoon. He had many women as mistresses, and he had two *caciquas* for legitimate wives. The clothes that he wore one day he did not put on again until four days later.

So begins the description of the Aztec emperor in the chronicle of the conquest of Mexico by Bernal Díaz de Castillo, an eyewitness.

We know about Moctezuma II, the last elected ruler of the Aztec empire, mostly through the accounts of his opponents. The early Spanish chroniclers sometimes describe Moctezuma as wise and brave, but most of the time they depict him as the brutal leader of a savage people. Modern historians, on the other hand, picture him either as an insecure individual who was terrified by the supernatural, or as a warrior who overextended himself and proved unable to rise to the demands put on him when the Spanish arrived. He was himself a conqueror of other Amerindians of Mexico, and the violence and coercion he employed against them came back to haunt him.

Born about 1466, Moctezuma was elected to rule by the elders in 1502, when Aztec power was at its zenith. During the seventeen years of his reign, he established a despotic and oppressive government, which governed perhaps as many as fifteen million subjects through force and efficient use of a large army of occupation.

Moctezuma continued the Aztec theocracy, which was organized as a loose confederation of tributary Indian states giving homage to the great city of Tenochtitlán. Fascinated by ceremony, the Aztec rulers separated all citizens and subjects into precise classes. No common folk were allowed to visit the court, and those who wished to see the emperor had to seek permission through an elaborate court bureaucracy. Hundreds of tax collectors, military commanders, accountants, judges, and other officials ran the day-to-day operations of government under the leadership of a supremely important priesthood.

Moctezuma's wars against his rebellious subjects created the conditions that allowed the greatly outnumbered Spanish to gain a foothold in Mexico after they landed at Vera Cruz in 1519. And his own religious heritage led him to a fatal hesitancy in dealing with the strangers who rode enormous "deer" (horses) and fired cannons and muskets at their opponents. Believing for a time that Cortez might indeed be the returning god Quetzalcoatl of Aztec legend, Moctezuma feared to confront him directly and tried instead to win his favor by showing him hospitality. Instead of using his huge advantage in numbers to do battle with the Spaniards, the emperor allowed them to take him hostage for the good behavior of his people.

Moctezuma saw too late that these "gods" were only daring buccaneers, whose sole interest was obtaining mastery over the Aztec lands and treasure. When the showdown finally came between the enraged residents of Tenochtitlán and the Spanish adventurers, Moctezuma's death may well have come at the hands of his own people, as the Spanish chroniclers have said.

For Reflection

Why do you think other Amerindians would join the alien Spanish against one of their own? Why might Moctezuma have hesitated to use the great advantage in numbers that he possessed against Cortez?

---

clan's business dealings with outsiders. After conquering neighboring Indians, the Cuzco emperor broke up the old *ayllus* and replaced them with new ones based on place of residence, rather than common kinship. The head of the new *ayllu* was appointed by the emperor because of good service or demonstrated loyalty. He served the central government in about the same fashion as a feudal baron served the king of France. The ordinary people, organized in these new artificial clans, were his to do with as he liked, so long as they discharged their labor duty and paid any other tax demanded of them by the Inca in Cuzco.

Regimentation was a prominent feature of Incan government, but it also displayed a concern for social welfare that was unusual for early governments. In times of poor harvest, grain was distributed to the people from the government's enforced-collection granaries, as in China. Natural disasters such as flooding mountain rivers were common, and a system of central "relief funds" provided assistance for the areas affected. A sort of old-age pension and provision for the destitute was also in use, enforced by the central authorities. These features of the Incan regime have attracted much attention from modern historians who see in them a tentative approach to the welfare state of the twentieth century.

Fall of the Incan and Aztec Empires

❖

These assistance programs were not enough to win the active loyalty of the Inca's subjects. Just as in Aztec Mexico, the Spaniards found many allies to help them overthrow the

Cuzco government in the 1530s. Also, as in Mexico, the Spanish were immeasurably helped by the coincidence of their arrival with Indian expectations of the return of a white-skinned deity, who had departed in a distant past and, according to legend, would return in triumph. Like Moctezuma, the Inca somewhat naively trusted the newcomers. Pizarro's band, which was even smaller than Cortez's, was able to take the Inca hostage and demolish the regime in a very short time in the Peruvian lowlands and valleys. Some of the imperial family and their officials escaped to the high mountains and attempted to rule from there for another thirty years before being crushed.

The freebooters Cortez and Pizarro were ready to risk everything to win fortune and fame. They used every stratagem and played on every fear among the Indians. Their royal opponents were not used to such dealings and proved unable to counter them effectively. Within two years in both places, the huge wealth and vast territories controlled by the kings fell, like ripe fruit, into the hands of a few hundred bold men. (Chapter 34 outlines the story of how Mexico and Peru became Spanish dominions.)

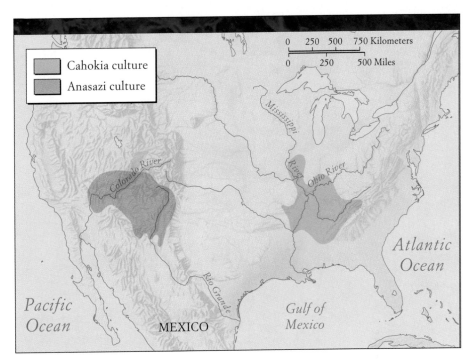

MAP 21.3   Anasazi and Cahokia Cultures of North America. Sometime prior to 500 C.E. the nomads of the southwestern quarter of present-day United States began to farm the riverine wetlands, raising maize, beans, and squashes, which had been developed earlier in Mexico. Their success allowed the maintenance of cliff-side pueblos of more than 200 individuals. Later, the Cahokia Indians of the midwestern Mississippi valley erected large burial mounds near their extensive agricultural villages.

North Americans

While the central American isthmus was seeing the rise of a series of agrarian-based civilizations, the Amerindians of the southwestern and central United States were making a slower and considerably less spectacular ascent from nomadic foraging societies. In what is currently Arizona and New Mexico, the **pueblo culture** of cliff-dwelling farmers took form after about 900 C.E. (see Map 21.3). These **Anasazi,** or "Old Ones," abandoned their hunting habits to begin maize and squash agriculture in the river bottoms below their remarkable "apartment houses" in the recesses of the canyons. By the 1200s, some of these dwelling places contained fifty or more adobe or stone units and sheltered upward of 200 persons.

Sometime after 1300 for reasons not understood, they abandoned most of their settlements and disappeared from view. Thereafter the ruins of their irrigation works and stone dwellings stood empty until they were partly reoccupied by the Native American tribes that came down in the 1700s from the northern Plains. Some basic information about the Anasazi has been worked out from the abundance of cave and rock paintings (pictographs) they left behind them.

In the Mississippi drainage of the American Midwest, another agrarian-based Amerindian culture was shaped in the later part of the first millennium C.E. Called the **Cahokia sites,** it is most easily identified by the great mounds of earth still visible in several river valley locales near St. Louis. The significance of these mounds is not known, but they are thought to have served ceremonial purposes connected with the safe transition of the soul to the next world. The total absence of literary material from the Cahokia culture sites and the scarcity of archaeological artifacts has made it difficult to point out more than the barest outlines. So far as can be known, the sites were abandoned well before the arrival of the Europeans, probably as early as the 1200s.

Neither the Anasazi nor the Cahokia people achieved the urban sophistication of their southern cousins in Central and South America. Lacking beasts of burden and the wheel, their technological progress was limited and tardy. The majority of their Amerindian neighbors remained in a Neolithic hunting-gathering society until the whites' arrival.

✿ **The Mesa Verde Complex.** In these cliff dwellings, the Anasazi lived and tended their extensive gardens below in the creek bottoms. The area is now a national park in Colorado.
(© Henryk T. Kaiser/Envision)

𝒮UMMARY

The achievements of the Amerindian civilizations are imposing in some respects but paltry in others. When compared with the works of the Mesopotamian peoples, the Egyptians, or the Chinese, the relative absence of written documents, and the small number of permanent monuments make it difficult to get a clear and comprehensive view of the Amerindians' abilities. Also, the physical isolation of the American continent from other centers of civilization assured that the Amerindians did not benefit from outside stimuli. What they produced came from their own mental and physical resources, so far as we can now tell. Yet, the physical evidence that survives is certainly impressive. That the Inca could govern a huge empire without benefit of writing or the wheel seems to us almost a miracle. Yet it was done. That the Mayan pyramids in southern Mexico could soar upward of 300 feet without benefit of metal tools or, indeed, any of the technological innovations of the Mesopotamians, Egyptians, and Hindus seems equally incredible. Yet it, too, was done.

The Amerindian civilizations are perhaps the most forceful argument against the diffusion theory of human progress. Most likely, the Amerindians created their own world through their own, unaided, intellectual efforts. What would have been an admirable achievement under any circumstances becomes astounding if the Amerindians did these things alone.

TEST YOUR KNOWLEDGE

1. The most advanced, intellectually speaking, of the Amerindian civilizations, was probably that of the
   a. Maya.
   b. Inca.
   c. Toltecs.
   d. Aztecs.
2. The overridingly important principle of Aztec society and government was
   a. cannibalism.
   b. war and its requirements.
   c. trade and the creation of wealth.
   d. art and excellence in its production.
3. The Aztec society at the time of the Spaniards' arrival
   a. was disorganized, impoverished, and illiterate.
   b. was without social classes.
   c. was tolerant and peaceable.
   d. revolved around the emperor and war.
4. The Aztecs believed that human sacrifices were necessary for the
   a. grain to ripen.
   b. gods to give them victory.
   c. moon to continue its orbit.
   d. rains to fall.
5. Moctezuma II was killed
   a. by the Spanish conquerors as an example to the others.
   b. by being starved to death in Spanish captivity.
   c. by a jaguar.
   d. by unknown hands.
6. South America is the home of which of these Amerindian civilizations?
   a. Aztecs
   b. Inca
   c. Maya
   d. Toltecs
7. The Anasazi were:
   a. rivals to the Incan rulers in Peru.
   b. inhabitants of Mexico City before the Aztecs.
   c. participants in the Pueblo culture in the U.S. Southwest.
   d. part of the Cahokia culture.
8. All the following helped the Inca build and maintain their empire *except*
   a. the Quechua language.
   b. the reformed *ayllu* or clan organization.
   c. their excellent road system.
   d. wheeled transport.
9. All available evidence indicates that the North American Indians
   a. were just as culturally advanced as their Central American contemporaries.
   b. were not entirely dependent on hunting and fishing as their food supply.
   c. remained in an entirely Neolithic culture until the arrival of the Europeans.
   d. were in close contact with the Indians of Mexico and Peru.

IDENTIFICATION TERMS

Anasazi

ayllu

Aztec

Cahokia sites

Chavin

Chichén Itzá

Cuzco

Bernal Díaz de Castillo

Inca

Machu Picchu

Maya

Moctezuma II

Olmec

Pueblo culture

Quechua

Tenochtitlán

Teotihuacán

Toltec

INFOTRAC COLLEGE EDITION

Enter the search terms "Inca or Incan" using Key Words.

Enter the search term "Aztec" using Key Words.

Chapter 22

Ordinary Life Among the Non-Western Peoples

Let a woman modestly yield to others; let her respect others; let her put others first, and herself last.

PAN CHAO in *Lessons for Women*

Keeping Body and Soul Together

Male and Female

Marriage and Divorce

Education and Its Uses

Religious Beliefs

IN THE LAST SEVERAL chapters, we have examined the evolution of the civilizations beyond the boundaries of Europe and the Mediterranean through, roughly, the fifteenth century. By the end of the 1400s, each of these had begun to have contact with the Europeans. What was the impact of these contacts? In the short term, the coming of the European explorers and traders led to only minimal change in the accustomed patterns of living of the masses of ordinary people. Their religions, laws, and customs were untouched or only grudgingly gave way except in parts of the Americas, where the Amerindians were rapidly eliminated or submerged. Even there, however, the ordinary routines of life generally persisted, only under a different master. This chapter will give a brief sketch of how non-Western commoners lived, in the same fashion as Chapters 7 and 13 did for the ancient and Greco-Roman worlds.

Keeping Body and Soul Together

How did the average man or woman outside the Western civilization live? Were there any major differences between West and non-West in this regard? Throughout the world by the end of the first millennium C.E., agriculture had to a large degree supplanted hunting and gathering. The latter mode continued to supply a substantial part of the daily diet only in regions of Africa, which were blessed with more protein-bearing game than any other part of the globe. But even in Africa, in the savanna of the midcontinent where the empires of Ghana and Mali were centered, crops and gardens were at least as important as hunting.

In sub-Saharan Africa clan-demarcated villages depended on both crops and gathering for their food supply. Hunting was a subsidiary resource, especially in the grasslands where big game abounded. Females were by immemorial tradition the main farm labor, tending the gardens and preparing the food. In some regions, such as present-day Kenya and Tanzania, the pastoral lifestyle predominated, and agriculture was very limited. The same was true of the Sahel and the Sahara, where there was too little rainfall for agriculture. But in the more densely settled areas, farming supplied Africans, as all other peoples, with the essentials of life and represented the usual work.

In East and South Asia by the fifteenth century, the growing of basic food grains—notably rice—had been refined by many hundreds or even thousands of years of practice. The Asian village, was a very tightly knit socioeconomic organism, perhaps even more so than most village cultures. Depending on custom, the crops raised, and local ecology, land was variously in the hands of peasants with small holdings, tenant farmers, sharecroppers, or collectives embracing all village families. Large estates worked by gangs of landless peasants were unknown or exceptional. Most people had some direct stake in the cultivation of nearby farmland they considered their own or worked as long-term tenants.

In the Americas the Spaniards discovered a large number of new foods, which they then introduced into the European diet. These included maize (corn), potatoes, manioc, several types of beans, squashes, and sugarcane. All of these had been cultivated by the Amerindians. From the accounts of the conquistadors and the early missionaries, it seems clear that the large majority of the Amerindians engaged in agriculture and that hunting and gathering food was rather exceptional except for specialties such as berries and certain wild fruits. The Spaniards with Cortez were astonished at the variety and abundance of the food grown for the population of Tenochtitlán by the surrounding regions of Mexico (see Chapter 21).

Thus, in the non-Western areas (including the Muslim lands), agriculture in one form or another was by far the most common occupation, just as it was in the West. Climate and terrain were always the controlling factors. In some areas where climate and soil conditions were particularly favorable, such as Vietnam or the Valley of Mexico, tilling the land seems to have been the almost universal occupation. Both sexes engaged in it, with male and female chores clearly delineated. Where agriculture was more difficult or less important, its tasks were assigned to one gender or the other, usually the female.

In the towns—more numerous in Asia and the Americas than in Africa—some better-off people engaged in skilled trades or worked as scribes, artists, or merchants. For most people, of course, unskilled physical labor (porters, cleaners, carters, and the like) was the usual means of staying alive in the towns, just as working with animal and hoe was in the countryside. China was the most

Rice Paddies. This modern photo could have been taken a thousand years ago in any of the South and East Asia lands that depend on rice culture. The terraces are critical for maximal yields and water control. (© B. Daemmrich/The Image Works)

Woman Harvesting Grain. This Bangladeshi woman is cutting the family grain plot with a knife; the process is typical of the huge expenditure of hand labor normally necessary for the most routine tasks in most of the non-Western world.
(© Robert Frerck)

urbanized non-Western society, Africa the least so. The Muslim towns of West Asia and North Africa probably had the highest degree of literacy and thus the most non-agrarian occupations, but, of course, no data on such topics are available until recent times.

Male and Female

It is impossible to generalize accurately about the relative prestige, powers, or social position of males and females, because any rule has too many exceptions. Having said that, we can observe that the female remained nearly always in the male's shadow in public life and could not act publicly except as a reflection of a male's needs or desires. This summary would probably apply most definitely to China and less so to other societies, particularly those of sub-Saharan Africa and Buddhist Asia. As time passed, Muslim Asia became more like China, but this statement must also be qualified. In a stable society that did not face military threats from outside, the role of females, at least those in the upper class, might be enhanced. China is the great exception here. Despite its isolation and military potency, the tradition of female subordination went very deep. It was reinforced by Confucian teachings, but certainly did not originate with them.

In the Americas we have very little information except the sketchy reports of an occasional missionary father or other European observer. Upper-class Aztec women seem to have had some private rights and freedoms that many six-

teenth-century European women might have envied, but the destruction of the Aztec written sources and the absence of others makes it impossible to know for certain. Certainly, the Spanish witnesses in Mexico and Peru give no indication of female governors or high officials, and the major deities that have been identified are male.

In Africa, the female's status varied somewhat between Muslim and non-Muslim areas. As we have seen, Arab travelers remarked on the laxity of black African restrictions on women in public, an indication that females played important roles in social intercourse of all sorts. This continued even after the upper class had accepted Islam. Sub-Saharan African women were never as thoroughly isolated and subordinated as women in the Middle Eastern societies. Among the non-Muslim majority, women presumably held an even more prominent place. Nothing in the animist faith of the majority would exclude females from an honorable or significant place in the clan or family. Formal leadership in the hunting-gathering societies, however, was reserved for the males, as was the norm in all societies where that mode of supply prevailed.

We have noted in earlier chapters the rigid subordination of the female in Confucian China. This inferior condition was ameliorated somewhat by the widespread adoption of Buddhism, especially the Theravada version, a religion that emphasized the basic equality of men and women in cultivation of the Eightfold Path and encouraged the creation of *sangha* (monastic communities) of women as well as men. The Japanese also responded to this impulse after Buddhism was introduced in the sixth century. Upper-class Japanese women were encouraged in unusual freedoms by the refined court culture that Lady Murasaki described in her eleventh-century classic (see Chapter 19). How much of this freedom percolated down to the peasant mass is problematic, however. Certainly, very few of Murasaki's subtleties were experienced or dreamed of in the villages.

Marriage and Divorce

Everywhere, the joining of young persons in marriage was a familial or clan-dictated affair that gave some, but not very much, weight to personal preferences. In Hindu India, the bride and groom often had no direct knowledge of one another prior to the consummation of the marriage, even though they might have been betrothed for years via family

African Marriages

Wilhelm Muller was a perceptive Lutheran pastor who lived for seven years in the later seventeenth century on the coast of what is today Ghana, tending to the presumably minimal religious needs of a tiny flock of German and Danish traders. Among his observations of the local Fetu tribe are these on the nature of their marriage ceremony and the status of various wives:

> As soon as the wedding day arrives, the bride goes out with her playmates to bathe and anoint herself. She adorns herself as splendidly and elegantly as she is able and can afford, with clothes, golden necklaces and bracelets, rings and beads . . . and then goes back and forth in this finery to display herself at public dances. . . .
>
> Toward noon she goes with her companions into the compound in which the bridegroom and the friends he has invited are gathered. Then something to eat is brought, or the bridegroom just treats people to palm wine and perhaps spirits. They enjoy themselves dancing, singing and capering till late at night. When the time for bed arrives, the bride goes with some of her friends into a bedroom in which the wedding bed is prepared, but they bar the bedroom door. A short while after the bridegroom comes and knocks on the barred door; but it is not opened for him unless he has promised to treat people again the following day. Then he is given free entry and all the wedding guests go away. No one remains in the bedroom except the bridegroom and his bride, together with a young girl aged seven or eight, who must sleep in between them and watch that they do not touch each other for seven days. It is hard to believe, however, that this really happens. . . .
>
> The aforementioned wedding festivities are only held when someone marries his first wife, whom he wishes to regard as the principal wife among all the others. If he takes others, the marriage takes place quite quietly, and no special wedding day is celebrated. Here it should be noted that if someone wants to take a wife she must first in the presence of the bridegroom and her friends [take an oath] that she will remain faithful to him and not go near any strange man. If she afterwards does not keep this oath, he has the power to proceed against her according to the law. . . . He divorces her as an ografo [a faithless woman], insulting and mocking her.
>
> The husband, however, is not bound by such an oath. Even if he is unfaithful to his wives, this is not held against him. . . .

SOURCE: As cited in German Sources for West African History, ed. and trans. Adam Jones (Wiesbaden: Steiner, 1983).

contacts and contracts. Everywhere, a bride price or dowry or both had to be carefully calculated and paid. It signified the serious nature of the marital arrangement for the families involved, and it showed the partner (and society at large) that he or she had entered into a respectable relationship of social equals.

Did these careful arrangements mean there were little or no marital friction or divorce? Hardly. Early societies had a substantial amount of the same types of marriage problems that afflict men and women today: jealousy, money, adultery, ill treatment, and so on. Physical abuse of the spouse was tolerated in some societies, but not in others. Wife beating was commonly seen through a caste or class filter: what was allowed to the peasant was condemned in the noble.

As in the West, adultery by the woman was taken very seriously, but for different, nondoctrinal reasons. (There seems to have been little moral outrage about female extramarital escapades except in the Islamic regions.) In Africa and Asia, it was the potential for doubt about the parentage of a child that disturbed people. Because proper honor for the ancestors was of crucial importance in these societies, knowing *who* was a genuine link in the family chain and thus had a claim to receive honor was essential.

Polygamy was the norm among all non-Western societies. Only the Christian West chose to see monogamous marriage as a sacrament that possessed moral value and imposed standards of conduct. Polygamy was usually a function of social and economic standing, rather than the expression of a personal desire (let alone sexual need).

Multiple wives and their children, in other words, were the rewards for a man's high income and status in the community. If additional wives could not be supported properly, they were neither expected nor permitted. This rule was most specific in the Muslim countries, where the Prophet had been quite clear on the obligations of a husband toward his spouse.

In animist Africa, polygamy was the universal rule, regardless of wealth. Taking younger wives as a man matured was considered a natural and desirable way of expanding the clan and its relative importance. The offspring of these unions were considered the responsibility of the females, collectively and without distinction, thus reinforcing the prevalent African custom of seeing the clan or the tribe, rather than the family, as the basic unit of social life.

Divorce was common enough that every society developed some definite rules to regulate it. Grounds varied, but all peoples and religions acknowledged the impossibility of keeping a marriage together when one partner found living with the other intolerable. Like marriage, divorce was viewed not as a question of resolving legal status but rather as a matter of finding a viable compromise between the inclinations of the individual and the demands of the larger community. In some cases, the wife simply abandoned her husband and returned to her parents' home, or the husband commanded his wife to remove herself from his bed and board. More often all the parties involved had to follow specific traditional steps before some authority, such as a council of village elders, would issue directives about the division of property and future obligations.

In some instances, a divorced wife was considered an outcast with no further prospects of marriage, but this seems to have been the exception. More often, if she were still young, a previous marriage had little negative effect on her desirability as a wife and might even enhance it if she had borne healthy children. (See the two boxes on marriage for some contrasting firsthand comments.)

Responsibility for the physical welfare of the minor children (age fifteen and younger) almost always remained with the mother and her female relatives, but parental custody was normally vested in the father as head of the family or keeper of the lineage. In the few matriarchal family systems we know of, responsibility was joined to custody on the mother's side, and the father played a lesser role.

Education and Its Uses

❁

Education was everywhere sharply defined by gender. Boys of the upper classes were given at least a smattering of literacy and rhetorical instruction in the Muslim and East Asian worlds. The more promising students went on to higher institutions such as the great university in Cairo or the medical research academies. In China, both the sons of the gentry and the occasional peasant boy of exceptional promise were tutored in Confucian philosophy and the arts so they could gain access to the mandarin bureaucracy. In both India and Africa, formal schooling outside the home was unknown, and that also appears to have been the case in America. In these societies, young men acquired

Marriage in the Maldives

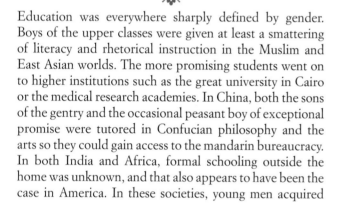

Muhammed ibn Abdallah ibn Batuta was an extraordinary fourteenth-century Muslim traveler. His observant eye registered many of the traditions among fellow worshipers of Allah that sharply differed from his own. In the following excerpt he tells of the Maldive Islands, an outpost in the Indian Ocean where he functioned for a brief time as a *qadi* or judge.

It is easy to get married in these islands on account of the smallness of the dowries and the pleasures of the women's society. When ships arrive, the crew marry wives, and when they are about to sail they divorce them; it is really a sort of temporary marriage. The women never leave the country.

When I was appointed, I strove my utmost to establish the prescriptions of the Sacred Law. There are no lawsuits there like those in our land. The first bad custom I changed was the practice of divorced wives staying in the houses of their former husbands, for they all do so until they marry another husband. I soon put that to rights. About 25 men who had acted thus were brought before me; I had them beaten and paraded in the bazaar, and the women put away from them. Afterward, I gave strict injunctions that the prayers were be observed, and ordered men to go swiftly to the street and bazaar after the Friday services; anyone whom they found not having prayed I had beaten and paraded.

SOURCE: "Travels of Ibn Batuta" excerpted from The Islamic World, *ed. Waldman McNeill, pp. 274–277, 1973. Reprinted with permission of Oxford University Press.*

✿ **Village in the Sudan.** The style of housing as well as construction material varied markedly throughout the habitat of non-Western populations. In this African village, the walls of the huts are of mud and wattle, covered by a sharply angled roof of long grass thatch. The interiors are both well ventilated and cool. *(© Wendy Stone/Odyssey/Chicago)*

the information that was deemed important by emulating the older generation.

For girls everywhere, literacy was not considered important even among the upper class. There were, however, exceptions, such as the Japanese court ladies whom Lady Murasaki so carefully observed. Female education was usually limited to practical instruction in the domestic economy and, among the upper class, to social graces as defined by the male. In Islam, even this aspect was slighted in favor of absolute subordination and passivity.

Outside the Islamic world, the link between education and civil or religious power was most pronounced in China and its Confucian satellites in Korea and Indochina. In Japan, formal education was certainly prized, but was not essential for the exercise of government. Elsewhere, power in sub-Saharan Africa was largely attributable to ancestry and the belief in the sacred nature of the chieftaincy, as created and reinforced by shamans and other quasi-supernatural individuals. The same was true, so far as can be discerned, in the Americas.

For most people, education was associated with attaining or retaining social status—"earning a living," as we would say. It was limited to an apprenticeship in a trade or observing an older model—a father or elder brother for boys, a mother or elder sister for girls. In the more advanced areas such as the Middle East, India, or China, where religion and several millennia of tradition reinforced the high status of the educated minority, occupational mobility was minimal. Only with extraordinary talent or luck could an individual shift from one social stratum to a higher one. In Hindu India, this difficulty was reinforced by caste restrictions, which grew constantly more complex and refined.

All in all, downward mobility was probably more common than upward, as a couple of years of scant crops or floods or any of the myriad potential disasters for a farmer could drive him deeply into debt. But as in the West, the village kinship network and the sense of collectivity cushioned the blow for many. All peasants knew that tomorrow they might themselves need what was needed by a neighbor or kinsman today. They withheld it at their peril.

In much of the non-Western world after about 1000 C.E., the relatively static quality of the village economy and the society it supported contributed to the ignorance of math-based science and technology. These subjects were not considered relevant or useful for the governing classes. Exceptions can, of course, be found from time to time, but on the whole, this attitude was a significant cause of the shift of power from East to West that begins to be visible about 1400. In both East Asia and the Muslim countries, formal education continued to focus on the legal, the literary, and the artistic spheres, whereas in the West these subjects were increasingly rivaled by mathematical and physical science. Nor did any non-Western societies experience a rise in literacy such as that associated with the Protestant sects' insistence on Bible reading after 1500.

Religious Beliefs

✻

Regardless of educational background, the masses of men and women in any civilization are greatly affected by religious belief or the philosophies inspired by religious beliefs. In the non-Western world, such beliefs were as potent as Christianity was in the West. What were some of the

✺ **An Indian Bullock Cart.** In most of rural Asia and Africa, cattle are the usual means of moving heavy items or human beings any distance. Horses are too fragile and too expensive for this type of work, and motorized transport is not available. The construction of this cart has not changed appreciably in 2,000 years. (© *Superstock*)

differences between these non-Western faiths and those of the West?

First, only in the Judeo-Christian West and to a limited degree in the Islamic regions was the link between theology and morality taken for granted. In East Asia, Africa, and the Americas, worship of the gods (often conceived of as ancestors) was only distantly, if at all, related to standards of public conduct or private acts. Even among Muslims, the absence of a priesthood guaranteed the slow and only partial development of a theology that could be translated into a guide to morals.

Second, another distinguishing feature of the Eastern religions when compared with the West or Islam is their universal reluctance to develop a supernatural revelation for the behavior and salvation of the faithful. This was true of the varieties of Buddhism, Hinduism, the animist, ancestor-centered belief of the sub-Saharan Africans, and the Daoist nature worship of China. Confucian China essentially rejected the supernatural as irrelevant to human morality. So far as can be determined now, the religions of the Americas also did not attempt to link the codes of morality they employed with theological speculations or revelation.

What, then, constituted righteousness and acceptable conduct in these societies? Social and economic factors, rather than theology, dictated them. Experience over long periods had shown that a certain mode of action or a certain set of values or convictions contributed to private and public harmony and mutual prosperity. Insofar as possible, the institutions and cultural activity of a given people were then adapted to inculcating and reinforcing these modes of action, beginning with the education of children at their parents' knees. Rarely if ever did a formal education, conducted by a priesthood, constitute the channel for ascertaining right from wrong. This latter approach was a peculiarly Jewish and Christian tradition that was emulated to some extent by orthodox Islam.

Third, the insistence on viewing morals from the standpoint of the community's welfare rather than the attainment of individual salvation is another hallmark of the non-Western religions or philosophies. Although both Jewish and Christian teaching have sometimes emphasized the necessity of finding a balance between individual and social welfare, the Eastern faiths have always refused to permit the individualism that the West has embraced.

Fourth, in the absence of supernatural sources for doctrine, the Eastern faiths have also been less fearful of heresy and more tolerant of doctrinal variation over time and place. This tolerance has led at times to what appears to Western eyes as a chaos of differing, sometimes contradictory beliefs. The non-Western civilizations do not concur in this judgment. They have acknowledged, historically speaking, many paths to Truth, and—with due exceptions—have normally refused to assert a claim on its exclusive possession.

𝒮UMMARY

In the non-Western societies, earning a living usually revolved around agriculture in some form, just as it did in the West. Only here and there in Africa and the steppes of Asia was sufficient game or pasture land available to support a hunting or pastoral lifestyle for large numbers. Before 1500, urbanization was greatest in coastal China and the Muslim societies of West Asia. It was least in sub-Saharan Africa.

Male and female patterns generally followed those already encountered in the West. Females were subordinated in public affairs almost everywhere and in every epoch, although exceptions could be found in non-Muslim Africa and among the highest strata in East Asian societies. The ascendancy of males was normally in direct relationship to the violence and instability of the society, which in turn were often determined by its relative isolation.

Marriage was a matter for the family or clan more than for the individuals involved. Nevertheless, this did not preclude affection and respect between partners. Where these were lacking, divorce followed specified rules just as in the modern West. Children normally were the responsibility of the mother and were sometimes shared with other wives of the same man, as in Africa.

Education was a function of social class or caste. Boys usually received more extensive and formal training than girls. In most societies literacy was rare for either sex. Social mobility was rarely procured by educational achievement except in China.

Religious beliefs in the non-Western world differ in several fundamental ways from the Judeo-Christian traditions and values. In non-Western religions, theology and morality were not closely linked. These religions tended not to develop a supernatural revelation for the behavior and salvation of the faithful. The welfare of the community played a larger role in defining religious belief and morality than it did in the Western tradition. The absence of an official priesthood gave more scope to deviations from the mainstream, and heresies were more likely to find acceptance than to be proscribed.

Test Your Knowledge

1. Both coastal China and western Asia were
   a. strongly subject to Muslim influences.
   b. supported by a pastoral economy.
   c. more urban than most other areas.
   d. very isolated from foreign contacts.
2. From what we know now, it is most accurate to say that the female in the non-Western civilizations
   a. was generally more prominent in public affairs than in the West.
   b. was often in control of public affairs.
   c. was generally treated much worse than in the West in the same epoch.
   d. cannot be generalized about in terms of public prestige or prominence.
3. The most common form of marital relationship in the non-Western world was
   a. polygamy.
   b. monogamy.
   c. polyandry.
   d. informal and unstable.
4. The primary function of marriage in African and East Asian societies was to
   a. enrich the bride's family as recompense for her lost labor.
   b. produce male children to continue the lineage of the husband.
   c. provide an outlet for the sex drive that did not threaten the social order.
   d. assure the happiness of the couple.
5. What is known of non-Western habits of divorce indicates that
   a. the woman was always considered the guilty party and treated accordingly.
   b. the man had to provide for his divorced wife as well as for a second bride.
   c. the children were generally turned over to the husband's family for supervision.
   d. maintenance of children and the divorced wife varied from place to place and case to case.
6. As a general rule, the mobility of labor in non-Western societies was
   a. more often down than up.
   b. frequently set in motion by technical progress.
   c. dependent on the wishes of the lower classes.
   d. probably easier in rural areas than in urban settings.
7. Which of these societies did *not* establish a close link between theology and morality?
   a. Judaism
   b. Christianity
   c. Islam
   d. Buddhism

InfoTrac College Edition

Enter the search terms "animism or animist" using Key Words.

Enter the search terms "agriculture history" using Key Words.

Chapter 23

The High Medieval Age

Consider your origins: You were not born to live like brutes but to follow virtue and knowledge.

DANTE

THE EUROPEAN COMMUNITY that emerged from the trials and troubles of the Dark Age was built on personal status. All people had a place on the social ladder, but their specific rung depended on whether their function was to fight, to pray, or to work. The great majority, of course, fell into the third category. But occasionally they could leave it by entering one of the others. The church was open to entry from below and grew steadily more powerful in both the spiritual and the civil spheres. Its claims in worldly matters brought it into increasing conflict with the kings and emperors, a conflict that hurt both sides. And despite the resistance of both church and nobles, the royal courts gained more and more prestige and power. The High Middle Age (c. 1000–1300 C.E.) saw the faint beginnings of the modern European state and society.

The Workers
❁

The majority of people were peasants who worked on and with the land. Perhaps 90 percent of the population in western Europe, and more in eastern Europe, worked the fields, orchards, and woodlots for a (generally hard) living. Their lives were filled with sweaty labor, but this work was far from continuous. For six months of the year or so in north Europe, they were restricted by climate and habit to their huts and villages. Then they spent a great deal of time on farm and household chores and literally "sitting about." Even during the growing season, from about April to the autumn harvest, many holidays and village festivals interrupted the drudgery.

What the modern world calls labor discipline—that is, the custom of reporting to a given place at a given time daily, prepared to do a given job in a specified manner— was almost unknown. Work was a communal responsibility in large part; people worked with others in a rhythm dictated by the needs of the community and ancient traditions. These traditions left much room for rest and recreation.

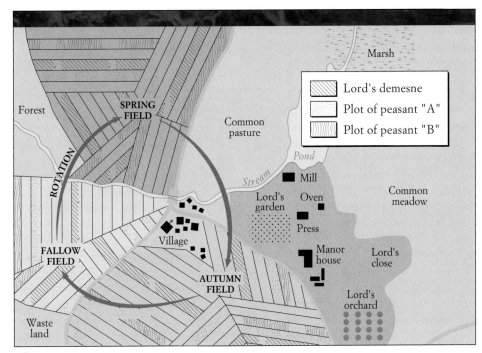

🏵 **MAP 23.1 A Medieval Manor.** The divisions between lord and peasants are shown in this sketch of a typical manor. Note the extent given over to fallow and thus unproductive land; note also the lord's demesne holdings, which had first call on the peasants' labor.

The Feudal Serf

The work on the large manors, which (as we saw in Chapter 14) became dominant in western Europe, was performed by millions of serfs. By the year 1000, serfs had replaced slaves in most places in Europe. Slavery virtually disappeared because the Christian church was opposed to the enslavement of fellow Christians, and gradually this viewpoint prevailed. Because almost the entire continent had been converted to Christianity by 1100, few non-Christians were left who could be enslaved. Asiatics were sometimes encountered, and black slaves from Africa were occasionally purchased from Moorish traders, but they were so expensive that they were viewed as curiosities and kept in noble households rather than used for labor. In some places, particularly east of Germany, serfdom differed little from slavery in practice, and the following remarks apply more to the western region. Legally, however, a serf could not be bought or sold as a slave could, and no one questioned that a serf was a human being with God-given rights and a soul equal in the eyes of Heaven to any other person.

Nevertheless, serfs were in important measure unfree. They were bound by law and tradition to a given place, normally a farm village, and to a given occupation, normally farmwork, under the loose supervision of their lord (*seigneur, Herr, suzerain*). The actual supervision was generally exercised by a steward or some other overseer appointed by the lord. Beyond this general statement, it is difficult to give a specific description of serfdom because conditions varied so much by time and place. Conditions in, say, tenth-century France were not the same as in eleventh-century Spain or England. In general, however, serfs were bound to perform labor services for their lord and to pay certain "dues" and taxes to the lord, which were set by tradition and by sporadic negotiations.

Only rarely were these conditions written. The labor took myriad forms, but usually included work on the **demesne,** the part of the agricultural land of the estate that belonged to the lord directly. The remainder of the estate's cultivable land (most of it, in most cases) was normally given out to the serfs for their own use (see Map 23.1). They did not own it outright, however, but had only a *usufruct* right (that is, a right to use the land, which was still owned by the lord). Serfs who fell into the lord's bad graces could lose their plots.

Serfdom usually became a hereditary condition. People usually had become serfs because they fell into debt or because they offered themselves and their land to a local strongman in exchange for his protection during a period of disorder. In bad times, it was always safer to be the ward of some powerful person than to try to stand alone.

It was not unusual, however, for a serf to gain freedom. The most common way was simply to run away from the lord's manor and start a new life in freedom elsewhere, normally in a town. "Town air makes free" was an axiom of medieval lawyers. In western Europe people who could prove they had resided in a town for a year and a day were considered legally free, whatever their previous condition may have been. Many other serfs gained their freedom with the lord's permission. Some were freed of further obligation by the lord's will; others were rewarded for good services; still others worked their way out of serfdom by paying off their debts. After the eleventh century, freedom could also be won by volunteering to open new lands, particularly in the Low Countries (where dikes were constructed and land was reclaimed from the sea) and in eastern Europe, where much uncultivated land still existed and lords were anxious to gain new labor.

After the tremendous loss of life during the Black Death (see Chapter 24), the serfs who survived were in a strong bargaining position with their masters, and serfdom in western Europe became less onerous. Peasant tenants still had to meet certain feudal dues and minor obligations, but the old hardships and treatment like slaves were over.

Medieval Agriculture

Manorial agriculture made steady, though unspectacular progress during the High Middle Age. Productivity, which was formerly very low (perhaps a 3:1 ratio for return of grain from seed), improved with the invention and introduction of the iron-tipped plow in the twelfth century. Because it could till heavier soils, this implement opened up whole new regions to grain production. The introduction of the horse collar, which was padded to allow the horse to pull a much heavier burden, was another major advance.(It came almost a thousand years after its Chinese invention.) Horses were expensive and difficult to handle and keep fit, but they were so much more flexible and faster than oxen that their widespread use amounted to an agricultural innovation of the first importance—similar in impact to the introduction of tractors. The systematic use of animal manure as fertilizer also improved productivity, although this practice remained the exception.

The productivity of medieval agriculture was above all limited because one-third to one-half of the cultivated land was left **fallow** (unseeded) each year. This practice was necessary because it was the only way the land could recover its nutrients in the absence of fertilizer. Every farmer had a piece or a strip of land in both the cultivated and the fallow segments of the manor, which were rotated from year to year.

Famines were common in years when the harvest was poor; reserves were at best sufficient for one bad harvest, and the miserable state of transportation and roads made it difficult to move foodstuffs. It was not unusual for people to starve in one area, while there was a surplus 100 or 150 miles away.

Urban Workers

The urban workers were not yet numerous and were sharply divided in income and social status. At the top were the craftsmen and shopkeepers. Some of them were highly skilled and enjoyed a solid economic livelihood; they could often afford to educate their children in the hope of advancing them still further. These people benefited from the guild system (see Chapter 24), which restricted competition and assured that their socioeconomic status would be secure.

Below these few fortunates were the semiskilled, unskilled and casual laborers. These men and women worked for others and had few prospects of becoming independent. Many of them lived a hand-to-mouth existence that may have been harder than the lives of the bulk of the manorial peasants. They were often the victims of changed economic conditions (like a new trade route) or local famines. A great many oscillated between seasonal agrarian jobs and town occupations.

Finally, the towns were filled with marginal people who never had steady work. They begged or moved on to more promising places, "living on air" in the meantime. Historians have estimated that as many as one-fourth of the population of seventeenth-century Paris fell into this category. The number in medieval days was smaller, because the towns were still relatively small and residence rights were restricted. But there must have been many then, too.

The Warriors
❁

The European nobility of the Middle Age constituted perhaps 2 to 3 percent of the population on average, though their numbers varied from country to country and region to region. Their rights stemmed generally from **patents of nobility,** royal documents that granted them or their ancestors the status of noble and certain privileges that went with that status.

What type of preferences did they enjoy? The privileges could be almost anything imaginable: economic, political, or social, but above all, they were social. The nobles were thought to be of a different nature than the commoners. They spoke mostly to one another, married other nobles, held exclusive gatherings, and enjoyed an altogether different lifestyle than ordinary people, be they well-off or poor.

Like serfdom, noble status was hereditary, so nobles were generally born noble. Nobility was thus a caste that was more or less closed to outsiders. In medieval times, it was rarely possible to buy one's way into the nobility, although the practice became common later. Women were equally as noble as men, if they were born into the caste. They could not become noble by marriage, however, whereas men occasionally could. In any event, it was very unusual for either male or female nobles to marry beneath their position.

Like serfdom, nobility varied so much that it is impossible to generalize accurately beyond a few facts. Not all nobles were wealthy, though many were. The only type of wealth that was meaningful was land. By the 1300s it was not so unusual to find impoverished nobles who were anxious to have their sons marry rich commoners' daughters. Many once-noble families sank out of sight, pulled down by their ineptitude in business, their mortgages, or their hugely wasteful lifestyle. Their places were taken by newcomers from below, who had obtained a patent for themselves in some way or another (perhaps as a reward for distinguished military service).

Nobles were always free; they could not be bound as an inferior to another. But they were also normally **vassals** of some person of superior rank to whom they owed feudal loyalty and specific duties. In the early Middle Age these duties were military in nature. Later, they often changed into some sort of service. The superior person to whom service was owed was called the vassal's **suzerain.** He (or she) gave something of value to the vassal in return, perhaps political advantage, protection, or administration of justice. The details of a medieval noble's life were dictated by this system of mutual obligations.

Not only were the nobility free, but they were also the sole political factor in medieval life. The king depended on his nobility to run the government and administration. In some countries, churchmen who were not noble by birth also held some offices, but the secular nobles were everywhere the decisive factor in government at all levels from the royal court to the village.

A noble's rank more or less determined his job; there were basically five ranks of nobility, ranging downward from duke to count to marquis to baron to knight. Each country had its variations on this scheme. The knights were seminoble in that their status was solely for their own lifetimes; their sons might be ennobled by the king, but they had no claim to nobility by birth. Knights were by far the most numerous of the nobility and the least prestigious.

The nobles originally claimed their preferred status by virtue of being professional soldiers, policemen, and judges. They supposedly protected the other members of

❀ **Assault at Cherbourg.** In 1450, toward the end of the Hundred Years' War, a French army besieged the British on the Channel coast and forced their surrender. Note the longbows now being employed by both sides, the complete body armor and the armored horses of the officers, the metal helmets and pikes of the infantry, and the howitzers with their stone projectiles. *(e.t.archive)*

society, upheld justice, ensured that the weak were not abused by the strong, and guarded public morals. That, at least, was the nobles' story! In fact, nobles were often noble because they were successful brutes and pirates, who possessed stronger arms than their neighbors and intimidated them into submission. Alternatively, they bought or fought their way into the king's favor or married their way upward.

In any case, the nobles considered themselves as the defenders of society through the command of both God and king and their own sense of honor. Honor was a particularly important aspect of their lives, and every person was supremely conscious of its obligations. Honor meant spending a year's income on the marriage of a daughter or on a proper costume for a court function. Honor meant fighting duels over alleged insults from other nobles and refusing to fight them with commoners. Honor meant living as a nobleman should: as though he had a huge income, while holding money in contempt.

What was life like for women? Female nobles frequently held positions of some power in public life. Queens were generally considered to be a political misfortune, but this did not prevent a few women from attaining that rank. More frequently, widows of royal husbands served as regents, as did **Blanche of Castile** (see the Family Relations box). The widows were usually expected to seek another husband and defer to his advice. Some did, and some did not.

In private life, many noblewomen exerted a strong influence on their husbands or ran the household themselves, as we know from many historical records. They were responsible for the day-to-day management of the estates; when their husband was absent, which was frequent, they moved into his shoes in matters of commerce and even warfare. There are records of duchesses and abbesses who did not hesitate to resort to arms to defend their rights.

But first and foremost, like all medieval women outside the convents, a noblewoman was expected to produce legitimate children to assure the continuity of the (male) family name and wealth. A barren noble wife was in a highly unenviable position; sterility was automatically attributed to the woman, but divorce was next to impossible because of the church's opposition. Hence, sonless fathers sometimes turned to concubines in their search for posterity. A bastard so produced would have only very limited rights, even if he was acknowledged, but for some desperate fathers this was better than nothing. The legal ramifications of bastardy, especially the ability to inherit titles and property, were a preoccupation of medieval lawyers.

The Worshipers

❈

The men and women who worshiped were less numerous than the fighters, but they also filled a social niche that was just as important. In an age of faith, when no one doubted the reality of heaven, hell, or the Last Judgment, those who prayed for others were considered to be absolutely essential. They included both the parish clergy and the regular clergy, or monks, but because the monks were both more numerous and more important than the parish clergy, the following applies particularly to them.

The chief difference between monks and parish priests was that the monks lived somewhat apart from the world in communities called monasteries. The monastery has had a long history in the Christian world. The first ones were founded in the fourth century in Egypt, but the most important monastic institutions were those founded by the Italian St. Benedict in the sixth century. His **Benedictine Rule** for monastic life was the most widely observed, although several others were also in use by the High Middle Age (the Trappist and Cistercian rules, for example).

What was a Benedictine monastery like? The monks believed a mixture of manual and intellectual work was best for a pious and contemplative life. The monks operated extensive farms, which they sometimes leased out to peasants in part. They were also craftsmen, and the abbey house or main center of the monastery was a workshop filled with bustling activity. But the monks never forgot that their intercession with God on behalf of their fellows was at all times the center of their lives. From early morning to night, the Benedictines set aside hours for prayer and contemplation. They also sometimes ran schools for the more talented peasant youth, some of whom were invited to join them in the monastic life.

Monks and nuns (in the convents that were the close equivalent of the monasteries but designed for females) normally came from the aristocracy until the twelfth or thirteenth century, when they became increasingly middle class in origin. They were very often the younger sons or daughters of a noble family, who had little hope of inheriting property sufficient to maintain them in proper style. Their parents therefore put them into a religious institution at the age of twelve or so. Sometimes, the child was miserable in the religious life and left it sooner or later without permission. More often, a compromise was arranged, and the unhappy monk or nun was allowed to leave without the scandal of an open rebellion.

The wealth of the monasteries was considerable. European Christians customarily remembered the church in their wills, if only to assure that masses would be said for their souls in that way station en route to heaven called *purgatory.* Noble sinners often tried to escape their just desserts at the Last Judgement by leaving the local monastery or convent a large bequest on their deathbed. Because most of the charitable institutions of the Middle Age were connected with and run by the clergy, it was natural to leave money or income-producing property to the church. In these ways, the property controlled by the church, and above all by the numerous monasteries, grew to tremendous figures. Historians reckon that, as late as the fifteenth century, the property controlled by the church institutions in western Europe outvalued that controlled by the Crown and nobles together.

This involvement with the business world and large amounts of money often had deleterious effects on the spiritual life of the monks and the nuns. Too often, monastic policy was made by those who oversaw the investments and the rents, rather than the most pious and self-sacrificing individuals. The monasteries repeatedly fell into an atmosphere of corruption, fostered by the indifference of some of their leaders to religious affairs and their close attention to financial ones.

Despite this tendency, the monks and nuns generally did much good work and fulfilled the expectations of the rest of society by their devotions and their actions on behalf of the poor. It should be remembered that medieval government was primitive, and the social welfare services that we expect from government did not exist. Instead, the church institutions—monasteries, convents, cathedrals, and parish

Blanche of Castile
(1187–1252)

*I*n the violent and strongly patriarchal society of the European Middle Age, all women were under some constraints imposed by law and custom. Occasionally, an exception to the rule appeared, a woman who was in every way the equal of her male associates in terms of exercising public power. Blanche of Castile, queen of France, is a good example.

Blanche was a granddaughter of the most famous queen of the entire Middle Age, Eleanor of Aquitaine, and the niece of the unfortunate John of England. Selected by her grandmother as a suitable match, she was married to the heir to the French throne, Louis, at the age of twelve. Her bridegroom was a ripe thirteen! This was not unusual for royal or noble marriages. The legal age of maturity was twelve for females, fourteen for males, conforming to current ideas on mental and moral development. Such a marriage would not be consummated until later, when puberty had been reached at about sixteen for males, fourteen for females.

Blanche gave birth to her first child—of a total of twelve—when she was seventeen. Of the twelve, five lived to adulthood—a relatively high percentage for the time. The oldest surviving boy became King Louis IX, patron saint of the French kingdom. He and his mother remained extraordinarily close throughout their lives.

Blanche had a forceful temperament. At the age of twenty-eight, when her father-in-law, King Philip Augustus, refused to send money to her husband for one of the latter's feudal wars, Blanche swore that she would pawn her two children to get the needed cash. Philip decided to put up some funds after all.

In 1223 Philip died, and Blanche's husband succeeded him as King Louis VIII. Only three years later, he himself died, leaving his queen as the guardian of his twelve-year-old heir, Louis IX.

Blanche thus became not only queen but actual ruler. Although not unheard of in medieval Europe, it was very unusual for a woman to exercise royal powers. Louis apparently knew and appreciated the qualities of his young wife; she did not disappoint his expectations.

Louis IX, a deeply pious person, was content to leave much of the task of governing to his mother even after he had attained his majority. Mother and son had a mutual appreciation that lasted until her death and was undisturbed even by Louis's marriage in 1234. Blanche herself selected Louis's bride, thirteen-year-old Marguerite of Provence, but Joinville, Louis's contemporary biographer, tells us that the mother-in-law was jealous of the young girl and took pains to assert her dominant position: "[Louis] acted on the advice of the good mother at his side, whose counsels he always followed."

Life must have been difficult for young Marguerite, who found that the only way she could be with her husband without his mother was to accompany him on a long-promised crusade against the Muslims in the Holy Land in 1248. During the king's lengthy absence, Blanche again served as regent, and she was the reigning authority in France when she died, at age sixty-five, in 1252. Like her more famous grandmother Eleanor, she was a woman who knew how to handle the levers of power in a masculine age.

For Reflection

Why would it be a severe risk to the kingdom for a female to exercise actual governing duties? What might some of the positive, as well as negative, results be from marriage at the age of thirteen and fourteen into royal powers?

---

churches—supplied the large majority of the "welfare" for the aged, the poor, and the helpless. The clergy founded and managed the hospitals, orphanages, and hospices, using funds contributed by the faithful or generated by the church business and rental income. Then as now, money was used for good ends as well as bad ones.

The New Clerical Orders

In the thirteenth century, **heresies** became much more widespread in the church than ever before. Regular crusades were even mounted against the heretics at times. In southern France, a crusade was mounted against those who insisted that there were two divinities, one who was Good and another who was Evil. This throwback to the age-old Zoroastrian beliefs (see Chapter 4) had come into Christian Europe from the East centuries earlier and had great appeal to those who tended to look upon the flesh as the province of the devil and the spirit as the province of God. These crusades meant to stamp out heresy by killing or suppressing the heretics. Brutal force was their hallmark. To a pair of saintly young priests, this was not the Christian way; they sought a different approach.

St. Francis of Assisi was a young Italian who believed in and practiced a life of total poverty and total service to his fellows (see the Religion and Morality box). St. Dominic, a contemporary of Francis of Assisi, was a young Spaniard who wanted to reform the clergy in a different way. He wanted especially to convert the heretics back to the true

St. Francis of Assisi
(1182–1226)

The man called Francis of Assisi has long been one of the most attractive of the medieval saints to modern eyes. His message was very clear and simple: "Where there is hate, give love; where there is insult and wrongdoing, grant forgiveness and offer hope. Bestow happiness where there is sorrow, and give light where there is darkness." No one lived this high-minded creed better than its originator.

Francesco (Francis) de Bernadone was born the son of a wealthy cloth dealer in the prosperous town of Assisi in northern Italy. Though he apparently had no formal schooling, he was very quick intellectually and early in life was taken into his father's business. He was a member of the "gilded youth" of the town, drinking heavily, getting involved with loose women, and generally enjoying himself as rich, carefree adolescents have always done. His life seems to have been an ongoing party.

But at age twenty he opted to join the local freebooters (*condottieri*) and was taken prisoner during Assisi's squabble with the city-state of Perugia. He spent a year in captivity, a sobering experience. Two years later, ill with fever, he underwent a visionary experience that permanently changed his life. Faced with death, he came to feel that he had been spared for a purpose that he must discover. He renounced his family's wealth and began to dedicate his time to the service of God and the poor.

He visited the lepers and outcasts of the town and practiced a stringently simple life, begging his food. Wherever he was permitted, he preached to anyone who would listen a message of poverty, austerity, and, above all, love for every creature. Braving the inevitable ridicule, he called on his listeners to renounce their fortunes, sell their possessions, and give the proceeds to the poor around them. For his text, Francis took the word of Jesus to his apostles: "Take nothing for the journey, nei-

ther staff nor satchel, neither bread nor money." Trusting fully in the Lord, Francis demanded and practiced absolute poverty.

Some people were touched by the power and sincerity of his preaching and joined him. In a relatively brief time, he had a band of followers, the "Little Brothers of Francis," and came to the attention of Pope Innocent III. Though suspicious at first, Innocent eventually recognized Francis's sincerity and moral stature. His followers, called friars, were allowed to preach where they chose and to solicit the support of good Christians everywhere.

Francis died quite young, but not before he had almost single-handedly made substantial changes for the better in contemporary Christian practice. His example inspired many thousands to reject the materialism that had plagued the thirteenth-century clergy, especially the monastic orders. The Franciscans (who soon had a female auxiliary of nuns) always rejected the idea of the monastery, preferring to live and work among the people as helpmates and fellow sufferers.

Francis of Assisi felt a very strong bond between himself and all other beings. He addressed the birds and the beasts, the sun and the moon and the stars as his brothers and sisters. Once he preached a sermon to the birds, and the legend says that they responded by gathering round him. He did much to instill a love of God's natural world in his followers and should be called one of the Western world's first, and most attractive, ecologists.

For Reflection

What effect on the Franciscan monks' attitude toward people might the founder's insistence that they beg for their food have? Do you know anyone whose lifestyle resembles that of Francis? What do you think of this person?

---

faith by showing them the error of their ways calmly and peaceably. The Dominican Order was therefore an intellectual group, who specialized in lawyerly disputation and preaching. Dominicans were the outstanding professors of law and theology in the early universities of Europe, and they would later take the lead in the Inquisition in Spain against suspected heretics.

In their different ways, both Franciscans and Dominicans attempted to elevate the spiritual life of the clergy and, through them, the people of Europe. They attempted to bring about the reforms of the church that the papal court was ignoring. But their efforts were dulled with the passage of time and checked by a clerical hierarchy that did not want to hear of its failures and corruption or think about how to change.

The Economic Revival

Starting in the eleventh century, the towns of Europe, so long stagnant or semideserted, began a strong revival. Some entirely new cities were founded, including Berlin, Moscow, and Munich. Mostly, however, the eleventh- and twelfth-century revival saw the renaissance of older sites under the influence of (1) increased trade, (2) a more peaceful environment, and (3) a higher degree of skills and entrepreneurial activity.

The basic reason for the resurgence of the towns was the rising volume of trade. After centuries of stagnation, Europe's merchants and moneylenders were again looking for

Liberties of Lorris

In the town charter of the small city of Lorris in northern France is the essence of the "liberties" that the medieval bourgeoisie gradually gained from a reluctant aristocracy, using the king as their protector. The charter of Lorris was granted by King Louis VII in 1155. By this time, the towns had fully recovered from the long centuries of decay and lawlessness after Rome's fall. Most of the rights deal with economic regulations and taxes because the feudal nobility were most likely to apply pressure in these areas. The eighteenth liberty is a good example of the rule that runaways would be free from serf status if they could remain in a town and out of trouble for a year and a day.

The charter of Lorris:

2. Let no inhabitant of the parish of Lorris pay a duty of entry nor any tax for his food, and let him not pay any duty of measurement for the corn [grain] which his labor, or that of his animals may procure him, and let him pay no duty for the wine which he shall get from his vines.

3. Let none of them go on a [military] expedition, on foot or horseback, from which he cannot return home the same day! . . .

15. Let no man of Lorris do forced work for us, unless it be twice a year to take our wine to Orleans, and nowhere else . . .

18. Whoever shall remain a year and a day in the parish of Lorris without any claim having pursued him thither, and without the right [of remaining] having been forbidden him by us or by our provost [equivalent of sheriff], he shall remain there free and tranquil. . .

33. No man of Lorris shall pay any duty because of what he shall buy or sell for his own use on the territory of the parish, nor for what he shall buy on Wednesdays at the town market. . .

Given at Orleans, in the year of our Lord 1155.

SOURCE: As cited in O. Johnson, World Civilization, p. 364.

---

new fields to conquer. The increasing ability of the royal governments to assure a degree of law and order within their kingdoms was a key factor in this increased trade. Others included the steady rise in population, the ability of the townsmen to purchase their liberties from the feudal nobles (see the box "Liberties of Lorris"), and the reappearance of clerical and professional people.

In western Europe, trade approached levels it had last reached in the fourth century. (In this context, "western" means Europe westward from midway across Germany, including Scandinavia and Italy.) Merchants found that a stable coinage and financial techniques such as letters of credit, which they learned from the Muslims, increased their commercial opportunities.

The obvious locations for markets were the strategic, protected places that had been market centers in Roman days. Old municipal centers, such as Cologne, Frankfurt, Innsbruck, Vienna, Lyon, and Paris, which had been almost abandoned in the sixth and seventh centuries, began to come back from the grave. They once again became what they had been under the Romans: commercial and crafts centers with some professionals and administrators, often in the employ of the church. Nevertheless, cities and towns were not yet very large or numerous. By the twelfth century, for example, Cologne's population reached 30,000, which was a large city by medieval standards. The

Medieval Shopping Scene. The bourgeoisie were generally occupied with buying and selling goods. This painting shows the commercial district of a French thirteenth-century town. From left to right, tailors, furriers, a barber, and a grocer are visible at work. Dogs were a constant sight in all medieval towns. *(Biblioteque Nationale, Paris)*

those who destroyed property through war and plunder. The Peace of God and the Truce of God were now enforced across most of the continent. Under the Peace of God, noncombatants, such as women, merchants, peasants, and the clergy, were to be protected from violence. The Truce of God forbade fighting on Sundays and all holy feast days. Violators were subject to spiritual sanctions, including excommunication, and to civil penalties as well in most areas.

The **Crusades** also contributed to peace by giving young nobles an outlet to exercise their warlike impulses in an approved form. Starting with the First Crusade in 1096, tens of thousands of aggressive younger sons of the nobility went off to Palestine or eastern Europe to fight the pagans, seize land and make their fortune (they hoped). Although the first crusade was able to set up a Christian-ruled kingdom in Palestine, these exercises were more often than not destined to end in futility, culminating in the fiasco of the Fourth Crusade (1204). In that, Western knights turned their cupidity on their Greek hosts in Constantinople, rather than on the Muslims in the Holy Land, and after much plundering occupied the city for the next sixty years. So great was the scandal that although there were several more attempts at organizing feudal armies to regain the Holy Land for Christianity, none was successful and most were abortive. By the later 1200s the Near East had reverted to Muslim rule once again.

Finally, the renewed application of Roman law led to the use of legal procedures as a substitute for armed action in disputes. Interest in the *corpus jurisprudentiae* began in the law school founded at Bologna in the eleventh century. Roman law, which had always been retained to some slight degree in the church's administration of its internal matters, was now gradually reintroduced into secular affairs as well. The legal profession was already well developed in the twelfth century.

In part, as a result of the first two factors, people began to develop greater skills and engage in more entrepreneurial activity. As trade and commerce increased and the threat of violence declined, it made sense for people to develop more skillful ways to make goods and provide services. As these skills became apparent to the potential users and buyers, entrepreneurs came into existence to bring the providers of skills and the users together. Along with entrepreneurs came real estate speculators (medieval towns were notoriously short on space), investment bankers (who usually started out as moneylenders), and a host of other commercial and financial occupations that we associate with "doing business." Some of these people succeeded in be-

Moneylending. This manuscript illustration from fourteenth-century Italy shows the moneylender and his clients. Note the monks and other church officials, as well as the women who avail themselves of these forerunners of banks. *(e.t.archive)*

largest cities were Paris, Florence, and Venice, which had populations somewhere well under 100,000 each in the twelfth century.

A number of developments helped create a more peaceful setting for economic activity after the tenth century. One was the increased power of the church to enforce its condemnations of those who fought their fellow Europeans or engaged in random violence. As the church became a major property holder, it began to use its influence against coming quite rich, and they displayed their success in fine townhouses and good living.

Bourgeoisie and Jews

Many people in the towns were what we now call the upper middle class: doctors, lawyers, royal and clerical officeholders, and, first and foremost, merchants. These were the **bourgeoisie,** the educated, status-conscious people who lived within the *bourg* or *burg,* which was a walled settlement meant to protect life and property.

The towns and their inhabitants were by now becoming a major feature of the political and social landscape, particularly in northwestern Europe and northern Italy. In the thirteenth and fourteenth centuries, kings discovered that their surest allies against feudal rebels were the propertied townsmen. The towns were the source of a growing majority of the royal tax revenue, even though they contained only a small fraction (perhaps 10 percent) of the European population. Whereas the villagers' taxes disappeared into the pockets of the nobles and their agents, the towns paid their taxes directly to the royal treasury.

By now, the townsmen were no longer dependents of the local lord; having purchased a charter from the throne, they had the privilege of electing their own government officials and levying taxes for local needs. Their defense costs (town walls were very costly to build and maintain) were borne by the citizenry, not put into the hands of the nobles. The towns often had the privilege of deciding citizens' cases in their own municipal courts; appeal went to the king's officials, not to the local nobleman.

The residents of these reviving towns were not all Christians. A small Jewish population had come to western Europe from the Mediterranean Jewish colonies of the Diaspora. They lived completely segregated from the Christian majority in small urban areas of a block or two called **ghettos.** Initially, Jews provided several of the elementary financial services in medieval cities and in the countryside, too. But by the thirteenth century they were being rivaled by Christians, who no longer paid much attention to the church's official distaste for usury, or the taking of money for the use of money (interest). Most places prohibited Jews from owning land or entering craft guilds so they had little choice but to take up financial and mercantile pursuits.

Until the thirteenth century, attacks on the Jews were relatively rare, but in that century, the kings of both England and France denounced and expelled the Jews on pretexts and seized their property, and the era of sporadic *pogroms,* or anti-Semitic mob actions, began. Fearful for

 Craftsmen and Their Tools. This marvelously detailed miniature painting shows the crafts employed in sixteenth-century construction. Many have not changed significantly since. *(e.t.archive)*

their lives, the Jews began to migrate from western to eastern Europe. The eastern European states such as Poland and Hungary were more hospitable than the West at this juncture. These states badly needed the Jews' experience in trade and finance, which the native Christian populations were almost entirely lacking.

Royal Kingdoms and the Formation of States

❧

The revival of the towns and the growth of urban populations were important factors in the steady strengthening of the royal governments against the nobles' claims for autonomy and feudal fragmentation. The foundations of the modern states of England, France, and Germany can be traced back to the thirteenth and fourteenth centuries.

What is a state? A **state** is a definite territory with generally recognized boundaries and a sovereign government. It recognizes no superior sovereignty within its own borders. It suppresses violence among its subjects in the name of law and defends those subjects from outside oppressors and internal criminals. The state exercises its powers through a group of officials, courts, police forces, and an army.

England and France

England was a pioneer in creating a state. Since the fifth century, when the island was conquered by the barbarian Angles and Saxons, it had been divided among a series of tribal kingdoms that fought one another and the invading Vikings. In the late eleventh century, the recently unified Anglo-Saxon kingdom had been invaded and conquered in 1066 by **William (the Conqueror),** the formidable duke of Normandy, who had a weak claim to the English throne that the English nobility had not recognized. By right of conquest of what he considered a collection of traitors, William proceeded to organize a new type of kingdom, in which the king alone was the source of final authority. Prior to this, the kings of feudal Europe were always being reminded of their dependency on the voluntary collaboration of their nobles in national affairs. Now William could ignore these claims and establish a cadre of noble officials who were all drawn from his supporters. A tangible sign of his power was the incredibly thorough and detailed **Domesday Book** (1086–1087), which was prepared as a royal census for tax purposes. William's successors were not all so clever or determined as he, but by the middle of the twelfth century, the earmarks of a modern state were faintly visible in England. It had, among other things, a loyal corps of royal officials, a system of courts and laws that was more or less uniform from one end of the kingdom to the other, a royal army that looked only to the king, and a single national currency issued by the royal treasury.

France developed a little more slowly. In the early twelfth century, France was still a collection of nearly independent duchies and counties whose feudal lords looked only reluctantly and occasionally to the king in Paris. Some of the French lords, such as the count of Anjou and the duke of Normandy, could figuratively buy and sell the French king; the royal territory around Paris was a fraction of the size of their lands. Furthermore, the king had no royal army worthy of the name.

This situation began to change in the late twelfth century, when the ambitious **Philip II Augustus** (1179–1223) came to the throne and started the process of unifying and strengthening the country. By the end of the thirteenth century, the king had become stronger than any of his nobles and was sufficiently in control of taxation and the military that he could intimidate any of them or even a combination of them. The Crown would experience many ups and downs from this time onward in France, but the outlines of the French state were in place by 1300.

A major difference between the English and French systems of government was that the English Crown relied on unpaid local officials, who were rewarded for their service by social privileges and legislative powers (in the Parliament created in the thirteenth century). The French, on the other hand, created a royal bureaucracy, staffed by highly trained and highly paid officials, who were responsible only to the king and kept clear of local ties. The English system allowed for a maximum of local variations in administration and justice, although the entire kingdom conformed to the common law that the kings had gradually imposed. Each English county, for example, had its own methods of tax assessment, types and rates of taxes, and voting rights, as did the associated kingdoms of Scotland and Wales. The French royal bureaucrats carried out the same duties in the same fashion from one end of France to the other, but they were not able to overcome the large linguistic and customary differences that distinguished Brittany from Normandy or Provence from Anjou. Until the Revolution of 1789, France remained more a series of adjoining semiautonomous countries than a single nation. Thus, England was held together by its national laws and the Parliament that made them, whereas France was unified by the Crown and its loyal hierarchy of officials.

The German Empire

The modern state that we know as Germany was created only in the late nineteenth century. For many hundreds of years before that, its territory was an agglomeration of petty principalities, kingdoms, and free cities. This had not always been the case, however. In the Early Middle Age, Germans had lived under one powerful government headed by an emperor who claimed descent from Charlemagne.

But this state failed and broke up. In the eleventh century, the emperor and the pope in Rome became embroiled in a long, bitter struggle over who should have the right to "invest" bishops in Germany—that is, to select the bishops and install them in office. This **Investiture Controversy** (from about 1075 to 1122) ripped the empire apart, as one noble after another took the opportunity to pull clear of the central government's controls. Another factor weakening the empire was that emperors succeeded to the throne through election. Prospective candidates engaged in all sorts of maneuvering and conspiracy and were even willing to barter away much of their monarchic power to gain votes. Civil wars among the nobility were common at the death of each emperor.

In 1152, the noble electors finally tired of this exhausting sport and agreed on a strong leader in Frederick Barbarossa, who tried his best to reunify the Germans. But his claims to rule in northern Italy—a claim going back to Charlemagne's empire—brought him into conflict with the Italian city-states and the pope in Rome, and he threw away what he had accomplished toward German unity by his costly and vain military expeditions into Italy.

Later, in 1212, his grandson Frederick II became the Holy Roman Emperor of the German Nation (the official title of the German king) and opted to settle in Sicily, which he made into one of the leading states in contemporary Europe. But in the process, he ignored his transalpine possessions, and the Germans looked on him as almost a foreigner rather than their rightful king. By the time he died in 1250, imperial authority in Germany was severely weakened and would not recover. Instead of becoming the dominant state of late medieval Europe as its geographic and demographic destiny seemed to be, the land of the Germans gradually broke up into several dozen competing feudal domains and independent cities. Not until the middle of the nineteenth century did Germany make up the political ground that it had lost in the thirteenth.

Medieval Culture and Arts

❁

What cultural changes accompanied this strengthening of central authority? The appearance of more effective central governments in parts of Europe during the twelfth century went hand in hand with the rising wealth of the urban population. Wealth meant a more lucrative base for taxes levied by the royal Crown and by the church. To manage that wealth properly and to levy and collect the taxes, both institutions needed trained personnel who could plan and oversee the work of others. It is no accident that the first European universities appeared at this time.

The First Universities

The very first were in Italy. In the towns of Bologna and Salerno, specialized academies devoted to law and medicine, respectively, gradually expanded and attracted students from all over Europe. Slightly later, in 1200, the University of Paris was founded by a royal charter; there students studied law, philosophy, and Christian theology.

Much of the university curriculum was devoted to commentaries on the semisacred books of the Greek Classical Age. Pagan authors such as Aristotle had long been forgotten in the Christian West, but they were now being recovered for study through the Muslims, especially in Spain, where the Christian majority had lived for centuries under Muslim rule. Unlike the West, the Muslims were quite aware of the value of the Greco-Roman classics and had preserved and studied them ever since conquering the Greek lands in the East (see Chapter 16).

The greatest Christian teacher of the twelfth and thirteenth centuries was St. Thomas Aquinas. In his *Summa Theologica,* he managed to use the arguments of Aristotle to prove the existence of God. Other great medieval teachers included Albertus Magnus and Peter Abelard, who used reason to teach the truths of faith in an age that was still ruled by universal belief in Christian doctrines.

❁ **A Prospect of Carcassonne.** The best-preserved walled medieval town in France, Carcassonne shows how important protection from enemy armies and marauders was in the Middle Age. Most western European towns once possessed such walls but demolished them later to expand. (© *Wysocki/Explorer/Photo Researchers, Inc.*)

The students at the universities were drawn from all strata of society, but most were apparently from the middle classes or the poor, who sacrificed much to attend their classes. Many lived on the edge of starvation much of the time, but saw a university degree as a passport to a better social position and therefore worth the sacrifice. Many students supplemented their meager funds from home by serving as tutors to the children of the wealthy or as teachers in the "3 R" schools maintained in many towns.

Females were unknown in medieval universities, either as students or teachers. Tension between town and gown was common. Students frequently rioted in protest against the greed of their landlords or the restrictions imposed by town officials. The course of study for a degree in theology (one of the favorites) usually lasted five years, law the same, and medicine somewhat longer. Lectures were the standard approach to teaching, with stiff oral examinations when the student felt ready. (It is remarkable how little the basic methods of university education have changed over 700 years!)

Gothic Architecture

The **Gothic style** of architecture and interior design came to be the norm in Europe during the thirteenth century. The first important example of Gothic architecture was the abbey church of St. Denis, which was built outside Paris in the mid–twelfth century. It was such an artistic success that the style spread rapidly throughout western Europe. The Gothic style's basic elements include a flood of illumination through windows and portals designed to

🏵 **The Gothic Style.** Here the interior of the abbey church of St. Denis is shown in full daylight. This earliest example of the Gothic style was constructed in the mid–twelfth century, a few miles from Paris. Its flooding light and great windows were a revolutionary break from the preceding dark Romanesque buildings. (© *The Bridgeman Art Library*)

throw the sunlight into every corner; an abundance of decoration, inside and out; and the use of arches, buttresses, and complex vaulting to support a sharply vertical, towering architecture.

The great Gothic cathedrals of the thirteenth and fourteenth centuries that were built from Italy north and west to England were expressions not only of building and artistic skills but of the deep faith of those who constructed and used them. The cathedrals were also rich pictorial teaching devices, meant to instruct a still largely illiterate population in the mysteries and lessons of Christianity. Enormously expensive, they were built over generations of time with donations from all classes and the contributed labor of many hundreds of artisans. Each town strove to outdo its neighbors in the splendor of its cathedral. Many of them were destroyed by fire at one time or another and were rebuilt. They could take 50 to 100 years to build or rebuild, and many were not completed until modern times.

Vernacular Literature

Until the end of the thirteenth century, all serious writing between educated persons was normally in Latin, the language of the church everywhere in western Europe and the most highly developed vocabulary and grammar of the day. In the fourteenth century, however, the common people's oral languages (the *vernacular*) began to be used for the first time as vehicles of literature, such as poems, plays, and elementary readers for children. The most important of these early works was Dante Alighieri's *Divine Comedy;* written in Italian, it is one of the great poetic epics of world literature. Somewhat later came the first important work in English: Geoffrey Chaucer's *Canterbury Tales,* which presented a panorama of English society. In the ensuing years, authors writing in the German, French, and Spanish vernaculars also scored artistic breakthroughs in literature. By the end of the fourteenth century, Latin was no longer the automatic choice of the educated for communicating what they held important.

𝒮UMMARY

The High Middle Age was a period of substantial advances for the Europeans, who came back from the long centuries of instability, violence, and ignorance that followed the fall of the western Roman empire. Three segments of society were recognized: the workers, the warriors, and the worshipers. The first were by far the most numerous, but the other two had important roles to fill in government and society. Town life revived after 1000 C.E., especially in the western parts of the continent, where traders, bankers, and artisans of all types began to congregate in the former ghost towns left by the Romans. By the thirteenth century, towns and cities could be found with upward of 80,000 inhabitants. Cities such as Paris, Bologna, and Oxford had universities, and fine goods from the East were familiar, in part through the experiences of the Crusaders.

In the wake of growing population and increasing government stability, traders began to develop long-distance markets in basic goods. Peace was by no means universal, but the invasions had ceased and many of the riotous noblemen were diverted into the Crusades against the heathen in the Near East or in eastern Europe. The professions, particularly law, were also reviving, encouraged by the church and its strong interest in a law-abiding environment. Europe had finally emerged from the shadow of Rome's collapse and was developing a new culture. Noteworthy examples included the magnificent architecture and art of the Gothic style and the literary use of the vernacular languages.

Test Your Knowledge

1. A social group ignored by the original medieval divisions of humanity was the
   a. peasantry.
   b. merchants.
   c. monks.
   d. soldiers.
2. A basic distinction between European slaves and serfs was that slaves
   a. could be sold to another person.
   b. could be severely beaten.
   c. had to work much harder.
   d. could be judged and punished by their master.
3. Which of the following statements about a medieval manor is *false*?
   a. It was normally an economically self-sufficient unit.
   b. It was normally headed by an official of the church or a noble.
   c. It was normally dependent on the labor rendered by unfree peasants.
   d. It was normally a politically independent unit.
4. Members of the medieval nobility
   a. did not have any special legal status.
   b. were uninterested in military affairs.
   c. generally inherited their position.
   d. were limited to males only.
5. The usual path to becoming a monk was to
   a. be handed over by one's parent to a monastery's care.
   b. retire to a monastery in middle age.
   c. enter a monastery after being widowed.
   d. be conscripted into an order from a quota of recruits.
6. Noblewomen in the Middle Age
   a. were strictly confined to domestic duties.
   b. generally married men younger than themselves.
   c. often carried large managerial responsibilities.
   d. played no role in political life.
7. A major difference between England and France was
   a. England's insistence on a strong royal government.
   b. France's royal dependency on officials who volunteered their duties.
   c. France's use of a corps of royally appointed officials in the provinces.
   d. England's attempts to hold the king responsible for the defense of the whole realm.
8. Which of the following was *not* a vital ingredient in the making of medieval European culture?
   a. The Greco-Roman artistic heritage
   b. Roman state paganism
   c. Christian theology
   d. Germanic customs

Identification Terms

Benedictine Rule
Blanche of Castile
bourgeoisie
Crusades
demesne
Domesday Book
fallow land
ghetto
Gothic style
heresies
Investiture Controversy
patent of nobility
Philip II Augustus
St. Francis of Assisi
state
suzerain
vassals
William the Conqueror

InfoTrac College Edition

Enter the search term "feudalism" and also the search term "feudal" using the Subject Guide.
Enter the search terms "Cities and Towns, Medieval" using the Subject Guide.

Enter the search terms "Medieval England" using Key Words.

Late Medieval Troubles

an proposes, and God disposes.

THOMAS A KEMPIS

STARTING ABOUT 1000 C.E., European civilization was revitalized and flourished during several centuries of expansion and consolidation. In the fourteenth century, however, a series of unprecedented disasters sharply reduced the population and caused a decline in the economy that continued for about 150 years. The feudal governing system and the agriculturally based economy reeled under great blows: the Black Death, the Hundred Years' War, and the labor shortage they created.

The leaders of the Christian church became embroiled in one scandalous affair after another: the shameful degradation of the pope in the Babylonian Captivity in France and then the Great Schism. Although the challenge to papal authority embodied in the Conciliar Movement was crushed, the popes never regained their previous moral authority, and the way was prepared for the eventual Protestant revolt against Roman clerical supremacy.

Disasters of the Fourteenth Century

The problems that became manifest in fourteenth-century Europe had their origins in earlier days. By 1300 the population had been steadily growing for two centuries, aided by the new land that had been put into production, several major technical breakthroughs in agriculture, and the unusually benevolent climate, which brought warmer temperatures and appropriate amounts of rain.

These happy circumstances came to an end in the early fourteenth century. Most good land was already being used and the technology to exploit the marginal lands (swamps, marshes, hillsides, and the like) did not exist. The climate reverted to its long-term pattern, and no innovations appeared to improve yields to feed the larger population.

As a result, local famines became commonplace in parts of Europe; those who did not starve were often physically weakened as a consequence of poor nutrition over many years. Europe had too many mouths to feed, and the bal-

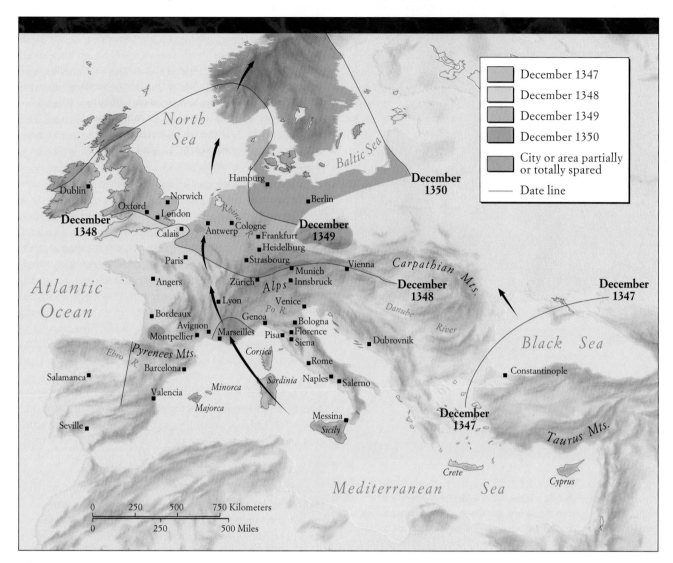

The legend of the map reads:

- December 1347
- December 1348
- December 1349
- December 1350
- City or area partially or totally spared
- Date line

❀ MAP 24.1 Spread of Black Death. The original infections were in Italy and spread rapidly north and west during the years 1346–1350. A pause ensued, but the plague returned on several occasions in parts of Europe until the 1380s.

ance was about to be restored through the natural disasters of famine and disease and the man-made disaster of war.

The Black Death

The **Black Death** of the mid- and late fourteenth century is the most massive epidemic on record and by far the most lethal in European history. What was it, and why did it deal such a blow to Europe? A form of bubonic plague common in the Asian steppes but previously unknown to Europeans was carried to the Mediterranean ports by Italian trading ships in 1346–1347. The plague bacillus was spread by fleas living on rats, and the rats were then (as now) everywhere humans lived. Within two years, this usually fatal disease

had spread all over western Europe and within two more, it had spread from Syria to Sweden and from Russia's western provinces to Spain (see Map 24.1). Hundreds of thousands, perhaps millions of people died in the first years of the plague. To make matters worse, it came back again to some parts of Europe during the 1360s and 1370s, sometimes killing one-third or even one-half of the populations of towns and cities within a few weeks.

No one had any idea of how the disease was spread or what countermeasures should be taken. Fourteenth-century European medicine lagged behind the expertise in several other parts of the world. But even if the Europeans had been on the same level as the Muslims or the Chinese, they would have been unable to halt the spread of the bacilli or prevent flea bites. Because Europeans lacked any immunity to the

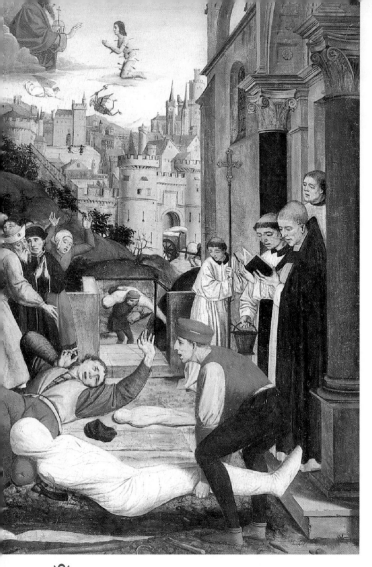

The Black Death. A late medieval painter captures the dismay and despair of the victims of the plague. Note the swelling of the neck of the falling man, one of the most common signs of infection. Above, a devil and an angel battled in the sky, as Saint Sebastian (with the arrow-pierced body) pleads for Christ's mercy on the sufferers. (© *Walters Art Gallery, Baltimore*)

disease, a high death toll was virtually inevitable: death came in about two cases out of three, with the highest mortality being the old and the young. City dwellers died in vast numbers because the crowded conditions aided the spread of the disease. Those who had some place of refuge fled into the countryside, often carrying the disease with them.

Italy, England, and the Low Countries were the most savagely hit, as these were the most urbanized areas. Debate continues on just how many Europeans died from the plague, but historians believe that as many as one-fourth of the English population did, over a period of a few years. Individual cities, such as Venice, Florence, and Antwerp, suffered even more; some cities were practically depopulated for a generation.

The economic consequences of the plague are not easily traced and do not lend themselves to generalizations.

Government revenues were affected: with fewer taxpayers left alive, tax revenues declined sharply; public works such as the cathedrals had to be stopped for a time. Some places experienced a shortage of labor that was not relieved for at least two generations. In the towns, which had been overcrowded, the plague reduced the excess population, and the survivors enjoyed better health and work security. Wages for the surviving craftsmen and common laborers rose sharply despite vain attempts to impose wage and price controls. Merchants and traders found fewer consumers to buy their goods, however, and the volume of trade declined.

Peasants who were still bound in serfdom, those who had to pay high labor rents, and those who were otherwise dissatisfied with their lords took quick advantage of their strong bargaining position—or tried to. France, England, and Germany experienced peasant revolts against their lords. The peasants invariably lost these armed confrontations with the mounted and well-armed nobles, but in the longer run, the settlements made between lords and peasants favored the freedoms of the peasants. Serfdom of the near-slavery sort, which was already weak in western Europe, died as a result of the plague. The mobility of labor increased. Much land that had been previously worked had to be abandoned and reverted to waste.

What were the psychic consequences of the plague? These effects can be detected for the better part of a century after 1347. During the late fourteenth and fifteenth centuries, all types of European Christian art reveal a fascination with death. The figure of the Grim Reaper, the reminder of human mortality and the waiting Last Judgment, became a major motif in pictorial and sculptural art. The Dance of Death, a scene in which skeletons link arms with the living revelers, also appeared frequently. The grave is always present in the background, and morbidity is in the air.

Most Christians believed that a wrathful God had given earthly sinners a horrible warning about what awaited the world if morals and conduct were not improved. Many people joined penitential societies, and some engaged in flagellation (self-whipping). It was at this time that Christianity took on much of the burden of guilt and shame that distinguishes it from other major religions.

The Hundred Years' War: 1337–1453

Even before the outbreak of the Black Death, another European disaster was under way: the Hundred Years' War. This conflict between England and France or, more accurately, between the kings and nobles of England and France, started because of a dynastic quarrel between the English Edward III and his French rival, Philip VI.

Recent interpretations of the causes of the war have stressed economic factors. English prosperity largely depended on the trade with the towns of Flanders across the Channel, where the large majority of woolen cloth was pro-

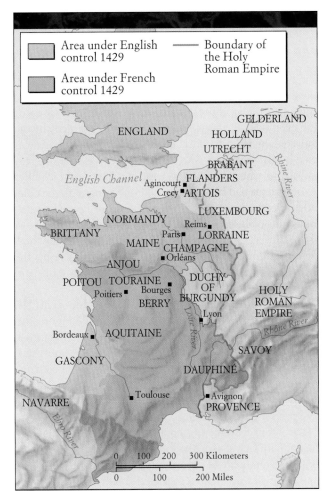

Key:
- Area under English control 1429
- Area under French control 1429
- Boundary of the Holy Roman Empire

GELDERLAND
ENGLAND
HOLLAND
UTRECHT
BRABANT
English Channel
FLANDERS
Agincourt
Crecy
ARTOIS
Rhine River
LUXEMBOURG
NORMANDY
Reims
LORRAINE
BRITTANY
Paris
MAINE
CHAMPAGNE
Orléans
ANJOU
POITOU
TOURAINE
DUCHY OF BURGUNDY
Poitiers
Bourges
BERRY
Lyon
HOLY ROMAN EMPIRE
Loire River
Bordeaux
AQUITAINE
Rhône River
GASCONY
SAVOY
DAUPHINÉ
NAVARRE
Toulouse
Avignon
PROVENCE
Ebro River

0   100   200   300 Kilometers
0   100   200 Miles

✿ **MAP 24.2   The Hundred Years' War.** Much of northern and eastern France, especially the rich duchy of Burgundy, joined with the English invaders in the attempt to escape the reach of the monarchs based in Paris.

✿ **Joan of Arc.** This miniature of the patron saint of France is one of the few contemporary renditions that has survived. A peasant dressed in armor, she was an extraordinary female figure in this age of male warriors drawn from the nobility. *(© Giraudon/Art Resource)*

duced using wool from English sheep. English control of the French duchy of Flanders would assure the continuance of this prosperity and would be popular in both Flanders and England.

Questions of feudal allegiance also contributed to the conflict. The French kings had been trying for generations to increase their powers of taxation at the expense of their feudal vassals in the provinces. Many French nobles saw the English claim as advantageous to themselves, because they thought an English king's control over the French provinces would inevitably be weaker than a French king's. So they fought with the English against their own monarch, saying that the English claim was better grounded in law than Philip's. The war turned out to be as much a civil war as a foreign invasion of France.

The course of the war was very erratic. Several truces were signed, when one or both sides were exhausted. The conflict took place entirely on French soil, mostly in the provinces facing the English Channel or in the region of Paris. The major battles included **Crecy** in 1346, where the English archers used their new longbows effectively against the French (the English may have used a few cannon as well); **Poitiers** in 1356, where the English captured the French king and held him for ransom; and **Agincourt** in 1415, where the English routed the discouraged French a third time.

By the 1420s, the war had long since lost its dynastic element. It had become a matter of national survival to the loyal French nobility, who found themselves being pushed back to the walls of Paris (see Map 24.2). At this juncture appeared the patron saint of France, **Joan of Arc.** This peasant girl who said she had been told by God to offer her services to the embattled (and ungrateful) Charles VII routed the English and their French allies at Orleans in 1429 and changed the trend of the war, which now began to favor the French. In the ensuing twenty years, France recaptured almost all of the lands lost to the English invaders during the previous hundred. In 1453, the costly and sometimes bloody struggle finally ended with the English withdrawal from all of France except the port of Calais on the Channel.

Consequences of the Hundred Years' War

Though originally popular among the English, the war eventually came to be seen as a bottomless pit swallowing up taxes and manpower. The costs of maintaining a large army of mercenaries in France for decades were enormous, and even the rich booty brought home from the captured French towns had not been enough to pay for the war. In addition, the war had disrupted England's commerce with continental markets.

The power and prestige of Parliament had increased, however. Since its origins in the thirteenth century, Parliament had met only sporadically. Now, in thirty-seven of the forty years between the beginning of the war in 1337 and Edward III's death in 1377, Parliament was in session. The king was always looking for money, and Parliament had to be consulted for the necessary new taxes. As a result, by the end of the war, Parliament was a determining voice in matters of taxation and other policy.

France did not experience a similar parliamentary development. The French kings allowed regional assemblies to meet in the major provinces, but they avoided holding a national assembly, which might have attempted to negotiate with the Crown on national issues and policies.

This difference in parliamentary development between the two countries would become more significant as time wore on. France followed the path of most European monarchies in transferring power steadily *to* the royal officials and *away from* the nobles and burgesses of the towns, who would have been representatives to a parliament. England strengthened the powers of its parliament, while checking those of its king.

The Hundred Years' War effectively ended chivalric ideals and conduct in Europe. Warfare changed dramatically during the course of the war. No longer were the heavily armored horsemen the decisive weapon in battle. The infantry, supported by artillery and soon to be armed with muskets, were now what counted. Cavalry would still play an important role in warfare for 400 years, but as an auxiliary force, as it had been for the Romans.

The longbow and cannon at Crecy had initiated a military revolution. With the introduction of gunpowder, war ceased to be a personal combat between equals. Now thanks to the cannon, you could kill your foe from a distance, even before you could see him plainly. The new tactics also proved to be great social levelers. Commoners armed with longbows could bring down mounted and armored knights. The noble horseman, who had been distinguished both physically (by being *above* the infantry) and economically (a horse was expensive to buy and maintain), was now brought down to the level of the infantryman, who could be equipped for a fraction of what it cost to equip a horseman.

Problems in the Church

❦

The fourteenth century was also a disaster for the largest, most omnipresent institution in the Christian world: the Roman Catholic church. Whether a devout Christian or not, everyone's life was touched more or less directly by the church. The church courts determined whether marriages were legal and proper, who was a bastard, whether orphans had rights, whether contracts were legitimate, and whether sexual crimes had been committed. In the church, the chief judge was the pope, and the papal court in Rome handled thousands of cases that were appealed to it each year. Most of the lawyers of Europe from the twelfth through the fourteenth centuries were employed by and trained by the church. As a result, the clergy came to have a more and more legalistic outlook.

Probably the greatest medieval pope, **Innocent III,** reigned from 1198 to 1216. He forced several kings of Europe to bow to his commands, including the unfortunate John of England, Philip II Augustus of France, and Frederick II, the German emperor. But in behaving much like a king with his armies and his threats of war, Innocent had sacrificed much of the moral authority he derived from his position as successor to St. Peter on earth.

Later thirteenth-century popes attempted to emulate Innocent with varying success, but all depended on their legal expertise or threat of armed force (the papal treasury assured the supply of mercenaries). Finally, Pope Boniface VIII overreached badly when he attempted to assert that the clergy were exempt from taxes in both France and England. In the struggle of wills that followed, the kings of both countries were able to make Boniface back down: the clergy paid the royal taxes. It was a severe blow to papal prestige.

A few years later, the French monarch actually arrested the aged Boniface for a few days, dramatically demonstrating who held the whip hand if it should come to a showdown. Boniface died of humiliation, it was said, a few days after his release. His successor was handpicked by Philip, the French king, who controlled the votes of the numerous French bishops.

The Babylonian Captivity

The new pope was a French bishop who took the name Clement V. Rather than residing in Rome, he was induced to stay in the city of **Avignon** in what is now southern France. This was the first time since St. Peter that the head of the church had not resided in the Holy City of Christendom, and to make matters worse, Clement's successors stayed in Avignon as well. The **Babylonian Captivity,** as the popes' stay in Avignon came to be called, created a great scandal. Everyone except the French viewed the popes as

🏵 **The *Jacquerie.*** This brilliant illustration exemplifies the usual end of a peasant rebellion in the fourteenth century; the nobles massacre their challengers and throw them into the river, cheered on by the ladies in the left background. *(Bibliotheque Nationale, Paris)*

captives of the French crown and unworthy to lead the universal church or decide questions of international justice.

In 1377 one of Clement's papal successors finally returned to Rome but died very soon thereafter. In the ensuing election, great pressure was put on the attending bishops to elect an Italian, and one was duly elected, who took the name Urban VI. Urban was a well-intentioned reformer, but he went about his business in such an arrogant fashion that he had alienated all his fellow bishops within weeks after the election. They therefore proceeded to declare his election invalid because of the pressures put on them and elected another Frenchman, who took the name Clement VII. He immediately returned to Avignon and took up residence once more under the benevolent eye of the French king. The bullheaded Urban refused to step down. There were thus two popes and doubt as to which was the legitimate one.

The Great Schism

The final episode in the demeaning decline of papal authority now began. For forty years, Christians were treated to the spectacle of two popes denouncing each other as an impostor and the Anti-Christ. Europeans divided along national lines: the French, Scots, and Iberians supported Clement; the English and Germans preferred Urban (largely because his sentiments were anti-French). Neither side would give an inch, even after the two original contestants had died.

The **Great Schism** hastened the realization of an idea that had long been discussed among pious and concerned people: the calling of a council, a universal conclave of bishops to combat growing problems within the structure and doctrines of the church. The **Conciliar Movement** was a serious challenge to papal authority. Its supporters wished to enact some important reforms and thought that the papal government was far too committed to maintaining the status quo. Its adherents, therefore, argued that the entire church community, not the pope, had supreme powers of doctrinal definition. Such definition would be expressed in the meetings of a council, whose members should include a number of laypersons and not just clerics. These ideas fell on fertile ground and were eventually picked up by other fourteenth-century figures such as the English theologian **John Wyclif.**

Wyclif believed that the clergy had become corrupt and that individual Christians should be able to read and interpret the word of the Lord for themselves. His doctrines were popular with the English poor, and they were emblazoned on the banners of the greatest popular uprising in English history, the revolt of 1381, which very nearly toppled the Crown (see the box later in the chapter). The rebels were called Wyclifites, or **Lollards,** and their ideas about the ability of ordinary people to interpret Scripture for themselves were to be spread to the Continent within a few years.

The scandal of the Schism aroused great resentment among Christians of all nations, and intense pressure was brought to bear on both papal courts to end their quarrel.

Neither would, however, and finally a council was called, at Pisa in Italy in 1409. It declared both popes deposed and elected a new one. But neither of the deposed popes accepted the verdict, and so instead of two there were now three claimants!

A few years later, from 1414 to 1417, a bigger and more representative council met in the German city of Constance. The council had three objectives: to end the Schism and return the papacy to Rome, to condemn the Wyclifite and other heretics, and to reform the church and clergy from top to bottom. The **Council of Constance** was successful in its first goal: a new pope was chosen, and the other three either stepped down voluntarily or were ignored. The council achieved some temporary success with its second goal of eliminating heresy, but the heresies it condemned simply went underground and emerged again a century later. As for the third objective, nothing was done; reforms were discussed, but the entrenched leaders made sure no real action was taken.

Additional councils were held over the next thirty years, but they achieved little or nothing in the vital areas of clerical corruption. The popes who had resisted the whole idea of the council had triumphed, but their victory had come at a very high price. The need for basic reform in the church continued to be ignored until the situation exploded with Martin Luther (see Chapter 27).

 A Medieval Copyist at Work. Thousands of monks labored at the tedious job of copying books for medieval libraries. This example comes from Spain in the thirteenth century. (© *Robert Frerck/Odyssey/Chicago*)

Society and Work in Later Medieval Europe

❖

As we have noted, an upsurge in peasant rebellions followed the Black Death. All of them were crushed. Nevertheless, in the long run, the peasants did succeed in obtaining more freedoms and security.

The *Jacquerie* of 1358 in France shocked the nobility, as the peasants raped and looted, burned castles, and even destroyed chapels. The nobles took a heavy revenge, but the French and Flemish peasants were by no means through. Revolts occurred again and again throughout the 1300s and early 1400s in parts of France.

In England, the Lollard rebellion of 1381 was an equal jolt to the upper classes and the king. One of its leaders was the priest John Ball. His famous couplet would be shouted or mumbled from now on: "When Adam delved and Eva span/Who was then the gentleman?" ("Delved" means plowed, and "span" is old English for spun.)

The causes of the Lollard rebellion were complex and varied from place to place. But almost all England was involved, and in an unusual development, the peasants were joined by a large number of artisans and laborers in the towns. These urban workers had been impoverished by a rigid guild system that prevented newcomers from competing with the established shops and kept pay rates very low for all but the workers at the top.

The **guilds** were medieval urban organizations that controlled what was made, for what price, and by whom. First formed in urban areas in the 1200s, the guilds were very strong by the fourteenth and fifteenth centuries. Their scheme in which a worker advanced from apprentice to journeyman to master as his skills developed was almost universal. Most journeymen never took the final step upward, however, because the guild restricted the number of masters who could practice their trade in a given area.

The guilds aimed at ensuring economic security for their members, not competitive advantage. The members fixed prices and established conditions of labor for employees, length of apprenticeships, pay scales, examinations for proving skills, and many other things. The labor shortages caused by the Black Death actually prolonged and strengthened the monopoly aspects of the guild system. In some European cities, the guilds were the chief determinants of economic activity until the nineteenth century.

Urban areas had been terribly overcrowded, at least until the Black Death.

John Ball's Preaching

*I*n the Lollard rebellion in fourteenth-century England, the peasantry responded violently to the question "When Adam delved and Eva span, who was then the gentleman?" In his *Chronicles*, the medieval author Froissart tells us of what happened:

A crazy priest in the county of Kent, called John Ball, who for his absurd preaching had thrice been confined to prison by the Archbishop of Canterbury, was greatly instrumental in exciting these rebellious ideas. Every Sunday after mass this John Ball was accustomed to assemble a crowd around him in the marketplace and preach to them. On such occasions he would say, "My good friends, matters cannot go on well in England until all things shall be in common; when there shall be neither vassals nor lords; when the lords shall be no more masters than ourselves. How ill they behave to us! For what reason do they thus hold us in bondage? Are we not all descended from the same parents, Adam and Eve? And what can they show, or what reason can they give, why they should be more masters than ourselves? They are clothed in velvet and rich stuffs, while we are forced to wear poor clothing. They have wines, spices, and fine bread, while we have only rye and the refuse of the straw; and when we drink, it must be water. They have handsome seats and manors, while we must brave the wind and rain in our labours in the field, and it is by our labour they have wherewithal to support their pomp. We are called slaves, and if we do not perform our service we are beaten, and we have no sovereign to whom we can complain or who would be willing to hear us. Let us go to the king and remonstrate with him; he is young, and from him we may obtain a favorable answer, and if not we must seek to amend our condition."

Many in the city of London, envious of the rich and noble, having heard of John Ball's preaching, said among themselves that the country was badly governed, and that the nobility had seized upon all the gold and silver. These wicked Londoners began to assemble in parties and show signs of rebellion; they also invited all those who held like opinions in the adjoining counties to come to London: telling them that they would find the town open to them and the commonalty of the same way of thinking as themselves, and that they would so press the king, that there should no longer be a slave in England.

The reduced populations that followed the plague enabled many towns to engage in the first instances of urban planning. Many medieval towns emerged from the crisis with open spaces, parks, and suburbs that made them more attractive. (*Suburb* originally meant a settlement outside the walls of the town.) Again and again, a cramped city found it necessary to tear down the old walls and build new ones further out. This expanding series of defensive earthwork and masonry walls is still quite perceptible in the maps of some modern European cities.

Inside the town walls or just outside, many types of skilled and semiskilled workers plied their trades, generally in home workshops employing one or two workers besides the family members. Factories, or mass employment places of production, were still in the distant future. Machines of any type independent of human or animal energy were unknown. Even water- and wind-powered mechanisms, such as waterwheels and windmills, were relatively rare.

The Role of the Church and Its Clergy

❁

The church was in every way the heart of the community throughout the Middle Age and into modern times. Whether in a village or a great city, the church was much more than a place of worship. Its bells rang out the news and announced emergencies. Popular festivities and the equivalents of town meetings were held there after the Mass. It was also an informal gathering point, a place for business dealings, and a social center. The three great events of ordinary lives were celebrated in the church: birth (baptism), marriage, and death (funeral).

Just as the church was the focal point of everyday life, the parish priest was an important man in the village community. Even if he was ignorant and illiterate, the priest was respected as the representative of an all-powerful, all-seeing lord and final judge. Few, indeed, would attempt to defy or even ignore him in the round of daily life. (For a look at the attractions of the nunnery for young medieval women, see the Family Relations box.)

Late Medieval Art

❁

Gothic cathedrals (see Chapter 23) remain the most impressive example of late medieval art forms. They combined architecture, painting, sculpture, inlay and carving, stained glass, and (in the church services) music and literature. The Gothic churches are some of the supreme examples of the ability to project a vision of life into concrete artistic format.

In the frescoes and alter screens done to decorate the churches' open places, the increasing refinement of European painting is noteworthy, especially from the fourteenth century onward. Experimentation with perspective and more psychological realism in the portrayal of human faces is visible in Italian and Flemish work, particularly. Metalworking still lagged behind the achievements of the Chinese and the Muslims, but the gap was being narrowed and would be overcome by the fifteenth century.

Holy Maidenhood

In the Middle Age literacy was still uncommon among the ordinary folk, so we cannot know very much about their life at first hand. But sometimes a beam of light illuminates it. A good example is *Holy Maidenhood,* by an anonymous author of the thirteenth century. Probably a cleric, he attempts to induce young women to enter the nunnery by arguing against marriage and all its consequences in this unhappy portrait of family relations:

Look around, happy maiden, if the knot of wedlock be once knotted, let the man be idiot or cripple, be he whatever he may be, thou must keep to him. Thou sayest that a wife hath much comfort of her husband, when they are well consorted, and each is well content with the other. Yea; but 'tis rarely seen on earth. . . .

[On childbearing]: Consider what joy ariseth when the offspring in thee quickeneth and groweth. How many miseries immediately wake up therewith, that work thee woe enough, fight against thy own flesh, and with many sorrows make war upon thy own nature. Thy ruddy face shall turn lean and grow green as grass. Thine eyes shall be dusky, and underneath grow pale; and by the giddiness of thy brain thy head shall ache sorely. Within thy belly, the uterus shall swell and strut out like a waterbag; thy bowels shall have pains, and there shall be stitches in thy flank. . . . All thy beauty is overthrown with withering.

After all this, there cometh from the child thus born a crying and a weeping that must about midnight make thee to waken, or her that holds thy place, for whom thou must care [that is, a wet-nurse]. And what of the cradle foulness, and the constant giving of the breast? to swaddle and feed the child at so many unhappy moments. . . . Little knoweth a maiden of all this trouble of wives' woes. . . .

And what if I ask besides . . . how the wife stands that heareth when she comes in her child scream, sees the cat at the meat, and the hound at the hide? Her cake is burning on the stove, and her calf is sucking all the milk up, the pot is running into the fire, and the churl [manservant] is scolding. Though it be a silly tale, it ought, maiden, to deter thee more strongly from marriage, for it seems not silly to her that tries it.

For Reflection

Do you think this warning achieved its purpose? Or is it too one-sided to be effective?

SOURCE: *Cited by Joseph and Frances Gies in* Women in the Middle Ages *(New York: Barnes & Noble, 1980).*

A change in the sponsorship of artwork also gradually came about. The church or individual nobles and kings had directly commissioned most of the artwork of the High Middle Age. The large majority of formal art was done for the church as an institution or for individual clergy who had the wealth and the taste to indulge themselves while allegedly glorifying God.

Toward the end of the medieval period, the members of the commercial class in the towns were at times wealthy enough to begin to play the role that had been monopolized by the nobility and clergy: patrons of the arts. (For a glimpse at the lives of members of the commercial class, see the Commerce and Exchange box.) In the fifteenth century, rich bankers or doctors began to commission portraits, although this was still not a common practice. Most art was still the province of the two privileged classes, the churchmen and the warriors (nobles). Everyone in the medieval town may have contributed to the building of a new church, but the portrait sculpture over the main portal still depicted the bishop, and the front pew was reserved for the local baron.

Medieval Sciences

In later medieval Europe, scientific studies improved somewhat from the very low conditions of theory and practice in the earlier period. The introduction of Arabic numbers made math faster and easier. The Hindu/Arab invention of algebra was becoming known to Europeans. With it, they became much more adept at dealing with unknown quantities. Some faint beginnings of chemistry can be detected. These took the form of alchemy, the search (begun by the Muslims) for the magical substance that would transform base metal into gold and silver.

Geography made considerable progress, borrowing heavily from Muslim cartography and knowledge of the seas. Most educated people already believed the world was a sphere, for instance, before Portuguese voyages proved that it was. But except in anatomy, medicine and surgery made very little headway beyond what the Muslims and Greeks already knew. (See the box for a sample of medieval medicine.) The main European medical center was at Salerno, which depended heavily on teachers from the Muslim countries. Physics and astronomy would only advance after the 1400s. Biological sciences were still in their infancy, the social sciences were not yet heard of, and botany and zoology were basically where the third-century Greeks had left them.

Part of the problem in the lagging development of the sciences was the insistence of the universities now multiplying throughout Europe that scientific knowledge was not as important as the arts and humanities. In places such as Oxford, Paris, Salamanca, and Heidelberg, the majority of the teachers specialized in theology, classical languages,

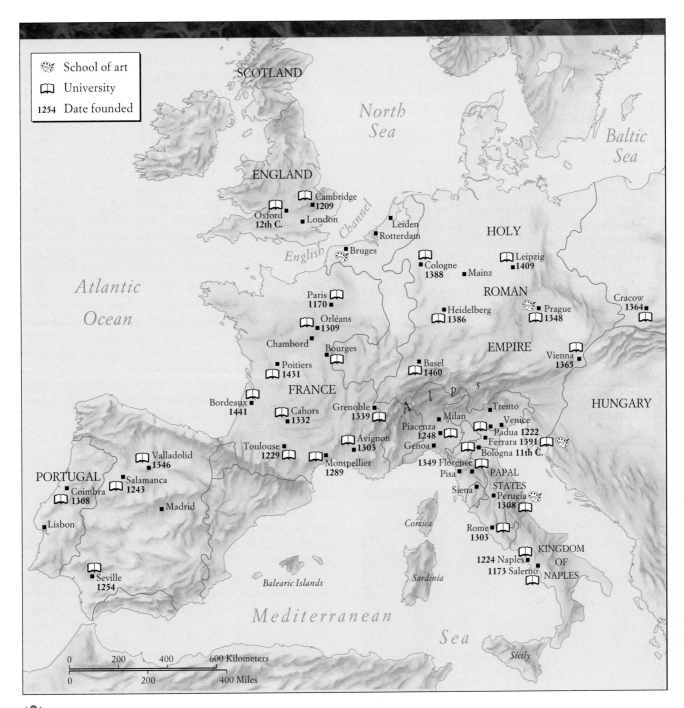

Legend:
- 🎨 School of art
- 📖 University
- 1254 Date founded

SCOTLAND

North Sea

Baltic Sea

ENGLAND

Cambridge 1209
Oxford 12th C.
London

English Channel

Leiden
Rotterdam

HOLY

Bruges
Cologne 1388
Mainz
Leipzig 1409

Atlantic Ocean

Paris 1170
Orléans 1309
Chambord
Bourges
Poitiers 1431

ROMAN

Heidelberg 1386
Prague 1348
Cracow 1364

EMPIRE

Vienna 1365

Bordeaux 1441
FRANCE
Cahors 1332
Grenoble 1339
Basel 1460

Trento
HUNGARY

Valladolid 1346
Toulouse 1229
Avignon 1303
Montpellier 1289

Milan
Piacenza 1248
Venice
Padua 1222
Ferrara 1391
Genoa
Bologna 11th C.

PORTUGAL
Salamanca 1243
Coimbra 1308
Madrid
Lisbon

1349 Florence
Pisa
Siena
PAPAL STATES
Perugia 1308

Corsica

Rome 1303

Seville 1254

Balearic Islands

Sardinia

1224 Naples
1173 Salerno
KINGDOM OF NAPLES

Mediterranean Sea

Sicily

0   200   400   600 Kilometers
0   200   400 Miles

🌸 **MAP 25.1 Renaissance Centers.** The Renaissance was limited to the confines of the old Roman empire and left stronger traces in Italy and northwest Europe than elsewhere. Like most cultural innovations after c. 1200, it was closely tied to the progress and prestige of the urban middle classes. Their absence in eastern Europe and weakness in the Iberian peninsula (Spain and Portugal) meant that the Renaissance was scarcely noticeable there.

The city-states of the fourteenth and fifteenth centuries were princely oligarchies. That is, a small group of wealthy aristocrats, headed by a prince with despotic power, ran the government. No commoners, whether urban workers or peasants outside the city gates, enjoyed even a hint of power. In fact, a huge gap existed between the ruling group of merchants, bankers, and traders and the rest of the population, whom they regarded with a detached contempt. It was possible to rise into the ruling clique, but difficult. The key was money.

The Renaissance Attitude

The wealthy in an Italian city were highly educated and very much aware of and proud of their good taste in the arts. Led by the prince, the members of the oligarchy spared no pains or money to assert their claims to glory and sophistication in the art of living well.

What did "living well" mean to these individuals?

1. *Individualism.* Men and women of the Italian Renaissance believed that the age-old Christian emphasis on submerging one's fate within the general fate of the sons and daughters of Adam was wrong. They wished to set themselves apart from the masses and were supremely confident that they could. They despised Christian humility and encouraged a new pride in human potential. A thirst for fame and a strong desire to put their own imprint on the contemporary world were at the heart of their psychology.

Thomas More. The force of character of Sir Thomas More, English statesman and humanist, comes through strongly in this great portrait by Hans Holbein the Younger. The chain of office worn by More shows that the painting was made between 1529 and 1533, when he was the lord chancellor of King Henry VIII prior to being executed for resisting Henry's divorce and remarriage to Anne Boleyn. *(© Superstock)*

2. *Secularism.* Increasing **secularism** in Italy meant that the focus of the upper classes' attention shifted steadily away from the eternal to worldly affairs. The life to come receded into the background—sometimes, it was pushed off stage entirely. The here-and-now became the critical factor in determining acts and thoughts. The acquisitive instinct was sharpened, and few thought it wrong to pursue riches. Increasingly, people viewed life as an opportunity for glory and pleasure, rather than as a transitory stage on the way to eternal bliss or everlasting damnation. Man was the measure—the hoary Sophist motto—for what life had to offer.

3. *Revival of classical values.* The ancient civilizations of the Greeks and especially the pagan Romans became the focus of artistic and cultural interest. Led by notable scholars such as **Petrarch** and Lorenzo Valla, the thinkers and writers of the fourteenth and fifteenth centuries looked back to pre-Christian Mediterranean culture for their values and standards.

They were not anti-Christian so much as pro-pagan in their admiration for the achievements of Plato, Aristotle, Virgil, Terence, and countless other contributors to the pre-Christian intellectual world. The collection and careful editing of the ancient texts that had somehow survived (many through Muslim caretakers) became an obsession. What the modern world possesses of the Greco-Roman past is very largely the work of the Renaissance.

There were, of course, variations of degree in these attitudes. Even in Italy, there were many sober upholders of the medieval Christian viewpoint, who insisted that humans were made for God and that the new emphasis on pleasure and self-fulfillment could lead only to disaster. Many of the scholars who paged through the Roman manuscripts were devout Christians, looking for holes in the arguments of their secular opponents or for proof of the pagans' search for an all-knowing God.

But, in general, the Italian Renaissance was devoted to the *self*-realization of man as a being whose earthly life was the only sure one he had. It rejected the devotional Middle Age (the term came into first usage at this time) as a dark interlude, which had lasted all too long, between the light of the Classical Age and the rebirth now beginning.

The Northern Renaissance

North of the Alps, the Renaissance was also a powerful force, but with a rather different character than in Italy. Carried to Germany and the Low Countries by students returning from study with the great Italian artists and writers, the new spirit underwent a sort of sea change as it came northward. It became more pietist and less pagan, more reformist, and less self-centered.

The term **humanism** is often applied to the northern Renaissance and its leading figures. The humanists were painfully aware of the corruption of church and society and wished to remedy it by nonrevolutionary means through reforms grounded in ancient Christian teachings. The Renaissance in this context meant a pious attempt to return the church and lay society in general to a purer state; it was an attempt to reawaken a sense of Christians' duties and responsibilities toward themselves and their fellow humans.

In the north as well as in Italy, there was great confidence in the powers of the intellect to find the truth and employ it to bring about necessary reform. The use of reason, rather than dogma, was an important article of faith for humanists everywhere. They believed that if people could be brought to see the good, they would pursue it. The trouble with the world was that the good was everywhere obscured by bad habits, ignorance or malice.

How did the reformers propose to achieve their aims? The English **Thomas More**'s *Utopia* is an excellent example. The book was meant as a satire and a lesson for society. The people of Utopia (Greek for "no place") do not seek wealth because they see no rewards in it. They put their neighbors' welfare ahead of their own. Their education continues throughout their entire lives rather than being limited to a few childhood years. All individuals are absolutely equal in powers and status, and they live by reason rather than passion and ignorance.

It was a radical message: More was saying that a corrupt and ignorant society, not the individual sinner, was responsible for the sorry state of the world. Adam's sin was not enough to explain humans' plight. The very way people lived with one another must be reformed—and by humans themselves.

The best-known and most noble-minded of all the northern humanists was the Dutch Desiderius **Erasmus,** who lived in the late fifteenth and early sixteenth centuries; by his death, his works were being read throughout Europe. His *Praise of Folly* was a scorching indictment of the so-called wisdom of the world and a plea for a return to simple virtues. Even more influential was his new, carefully researched edition of the New Testament, with his commentaries and introduction.

Erasmus's work has two basic themes: the inner nature of Christianity and the importance of education. By the inner nature of Christianity, he meant that the true follower of Christ should emulate Christ's life, not what the theologians have tried to make out of his gospels. Erasmus condemned the empty formalism that was so common in the church of his day. In so doing, he was one of the most important forerunners of the Protestant Reformation, though he absolutely rejected Protestantism for himself and condemned Luther's arrogance (see Chapter 27).

The spirit of north European painting and sculpture also differed from that of the south. Northern art is more overtly religious and avoids the lush sensuousness that marks much Italian art. The outstanding exponents of the northern

Death and the Miser. The Dutchman Hieronymous Bosch was the sixteenth-century master of the grotesque and the damned. Here he shows what happens to the treasure of a miser. As Death comes for him—and the angel implores him to put his faith in the crucified Christ—monsters and thieves make off with his money. (*Samuel H. Kress Collection, © 1995 Board of Trustees National Gallery*)

Renaissance in art were the Flemish portraitists of the fifteenth century such as Van Eyck, Memmling, and Bosch. The Germans of the Rhine valley and Bavaria were also very active in both painting and sculpture. Some of the most accomplished wood carvings of any age were produced in southern Germany and Austria during this era. These, too, display little of the delight in the flesh or the interest in experimentation of the Italians. In general, architecture followed the same pattern. Variations on the Gothic style continued to be the standard in the north, and northern architects made no effort to imitate the revived classicism so popular in Italy.

Family Life and Education of Children

Our knowledge of family life in the Renaissance comes largely from the upper classes, as is usual for premodern history. Men continued to marry quite late, in their thirties and forties, after securing their inheritances. Women were normally much younger at marriage, so there were many middle-aged widows. Marriage to a rich or moderately well-off widow who was still young enough to bear children was perceived as a desirable step for a man. Dowries were expected in every case, even among the poor in the countryside. A girl without a suitable dowry was practically unmarriageable.

Families were often large, especially among the well-to-do. The household might include children from a prior marriage, spinster sisters or elderly widows, servants, and perhaps the husband's illegitimate offspring. We know from surviving records that an Italian merchant's household might easily include as many as twenty persons, including servants. Wealthy households were of a similar size throughout most of the rest of Europe.

The woman of such a house was expected to run this establishment with vigor and economy. If her husband was away (a business trip might last six months or longer), often she was entrusted with full authority. A woman had to be literate to handle these tasks, and all wealthy families had private tutors for their daughters as well as their sons.

In general, however, women did not fare well during the Renaissance as a social group. In fact, the position of upper-class women actually seems to have declined. They no longer enjoyed the liberties afforded upper-class women during the Middle Age. Middle-class women, on the other hand, probably had greater responsibility for the management of household and business affairs and played a role almost equal to that of their husbands. As in the medieval period, the wives of artisans and merchants often were essential partners of the males, whose work could not be performed without them. Of working-class women, we as usual know relatively little, but we can assume that the male-dominated, patriarchal society went on without essential change. A particular crisis was the Europe-wide obsession with witchcraft, which appeared in the sixteenth century and took most of its victims from among the female population (see the Religion and Morality box).

In both town and country, women had to do hard physical work as a matter of course. Spinning and weaving were the particular domain of the female, as well as care of rural livestock. In the towns, records show that women performed just about every task that men did: butchering, baking, metalwork, dyeing cloth, and performing all the handwork trades that they had been doing throughout the medieval period. The separation of work by gender had not yet begun.

Education varied for the sexes, as had long been customary. In the towns, men were educated for an active career in commerce or a craft. Beginning about age seven, they might attend a boarding school for a few years and then were apprenticed to an appropriate firm or craftsman. Literacy was very common by this time among the urban population but still very uncommon in the countryside where most lived. The peasant's son who received any education at all was still the exception, and the peasant woman who could spell out her name was a rare catch.

For girls of the upper and middle classes, education usually meant some study in the home under the supervision of a live-in or outside tutor—usually a seminary student who was trying to keep body and soul together until ordination. Their education focused on literacy in the vernacular with perhaps a bit of Latin, music making, and the domestic arts. Marriage was taken for granted as the fate of most young women. The alternative was a convent, which had little appeal, or spinsterhood, which had less. Intellectual women now had many more opportunities to express themselves in written forms, including history, poetry, religious tracts, and other formats. But their gender was still a severe obstacle to being taken seriously.

How were the earliest years passed? The treatment of young children was slowly changing among the upper classes, but not yet among the lower. Any family that could afford to do so—a minority, certainly—would send a newborn baby to a peasant wet nurse. She would keep the child until it was past the nursing stage—about two years (at times longer, and sometimes without any contacts with the parents!). When the children returned to their parents' house, they were put under the exclusive care of the mother for the next several years. In wealthy homes, the father rarely had much to do with his children until they reached the "age of reason" (age seven), when he would take charge of their education.

The usual attitude among the upper classes was that very young children were of interest to adults only because they represented the continuation of the family line. After reaching age seven or so, they became more worthy of attention not only because they had survived the most dangerous age but also because they were now becoming persons with rec-

Witchcraft

A special example of the relative decline in the social status of females during the Renaissance and early modern eras is the witchcraft mania that raged throughout Europe in the late sixteenth and seventeenth centuries. Although witches could be of either sex, women were by far the more commonly accused of evil deeds. The following are excerpts from seventeenth-century German sources.

> The woman either hates or loves; there is no third way. When she cries, be careful. There's two kinds of feminine tears: one sort for true pain, the other for deceitfulness. . . . There are three other reasons for the fact that more women than men are superstitious: the first is that women are easily swayed, and the Devil seeks them out because he wishes to destroy their faith . . . the second is because Nature has created them from less stable material, and so they are more susceptible to the implantation of evil thoughts and diversions. The third reason is that their tongues are loose, and so when they have learned how to make evil have to share it with others of their own ilk, and attempt to gain revenge by witchcraft, as they don't have the strength of men.
>
> Women's physical weakness was already indicated by her creation from a bent rib [of Adam], thus an imperfect creature from the start.

> It is a fact that woman has only a weaker faith [in God], as the very etymology of her name states: the word *femina* comes from *fe* and *minus* (*fe* = fides, faith, *minus* = less, therefore *femina* = one with less faith). . . . Therefore, the female is evil by Nature, because she is more prone to doubts, and loses her faith more easily, which are the main requisites for witchcraft.

This view of the female nature had bloody consequences: near the German town of Thann, a witch hunt commenced in 1572 that went on at intervals to 1629. In that period 152 witches were put to death, generally by hanging, sometimes by burning. Of that number, only eight were males. Sometimes, five to eight women were put to death at one time. Three hundred six persons, mostly women, were executed as witches in only six years in villages near Trier. In two of the villages, only two women were left alive.

SOURCE: Cited in *Frauen in der Geschichte*, vol. 2, ed. Annette Kuhn and Jorn Rusen (Dusseldorf: Pádigogischer Verlag Schwann, 1982), pp. 114 and 122.

ognizable traits and personalities. By the Renaissance epoch, beating and other severe punishments were applied less often than in earlier centuries but still common enough, as we know from many diaries.

We know less for certain about the lower classes because of the absence of sources. Probably, babies and very young children continued to get little love and cherishing for the sensible reason that the parents could expect that about half of their offspring would die before reaching their seventh year. After that age, they were treated somewhat better, if only because they represented potential labor and "social security" for the aged parent.

The Political Economy of Renaissance Europe

The political theory of the Middle Age was based on a strong monarchy, blessed and seconded by a powerful and respected clergy. The favorite image for government was a man wearing a crown with a cross in his left hand and a sword in his right. But in the Hundred Years' War and other late medieval conflicts, that image suffered serious damage. In country after country, the feudal nobility were able to reassert themselves and again decentralize political power. This decentralization was reversed in the fifteenth and sixteenth centuries. The monarchs, now armed with a new theory of authority, effectively denied the nobles' claims of autonomy and subdued their frequent attempts to rebel. The new basis of royal authority was not church and king in partnership, but the king as executive of the state. What was new here was the idea of the *secular* state.

The Theory of the State

The state in Renaissance thinking was an entity, a political organism that existed independently of the ruler or the subjects. It possessed three essential attributes: legitimacy, sovereignty, and territory.

- *Legitimacy* meant that the state possessed moral authority in the eyes of its subjects. It had a right to exist.
- *Sovereignty* meant that the state had an effective claim to equality with other states and that it acknowledged no higher earthly power over it.
- *Territory* is self-explanatory; the state possessed real estate that could be precisely bounded and contained certain human and material resources.

The royal personage was not the creator or owner, but only the servant, the executive agent and protector of the state. He had every right and duty to use whatever means he deemed fit to assure the state's welfare and expansion. In the fifteenth-century monarch's view, assuring the welfare of the state was about the same as assuring the welfare of the society in general. These so-called "new monarchs" were intent on one great goal: power. To be the proper servants of the state, they felt they must be the masters of all who might threaten it. And that meant being masters of intrigue, deceit, and intimidation. Renaissance politics was a rough game.

All of the Renaissance political theorists spent much time on the relationship between power and ethics, but none had the long-term impact of a young Italian with great ambitions, **Niccolo Machiavelli.** In his extraordinary treatise on politics entitled *The Prince* (1516), Machiavelli described power relations in government as he had experienced them—not as they *should* be, but as they were in *fact.* He thought that human beings are selfish by nature and must be restrained by the prince from doing evil to one another. In so doing, the prince could and should use all means open to him. He must be both the lion and the fox, the one who is feared and the one who is beloved. If it came to a choice between fear and love, the wise prince will choose fear (see the Law and Lawgivers box, which summarizes Machiavelli's position.)

Royal Governments

In the fifteenth century the powers and prestige of various European royal governments increased significantly, especially in France, England, and Russia (see Map 25.2).

France France recovered much more rapidly than might have been expected from the devastation of the Hundred Years' War. The very unpromising monarch who owed his throne to Joan of Arc's help, Charles VII (ruled 1422–1461), turned out to be one of the cleverest and most effective of kings. He created the first truly royal army and used it against those who tried to assert their independence. He also gained much stronger control over the French clergy, particularly the appointment of bishops.

Charles's policies were followed, with even greater cleverness, by his son Louis XI (ruled 1461–1483), the "Spider King," as he was called by his many enemies. Louis was especially effective at gaining middle-class support—and tax money—against the claims of the nobles. He also significantly expanded the size of the royal domain: that part of the country, centered on Paris, under the direct control of the Crown. Louis is credited with laying the foundation for the dimensions the French state attained under the great Bourbon kings of the seventeenth and eighteenth centuries.

England England took more time to establish a centralized monarchy than had France, and never proceeded as far. The strong rule of the early Norman kings ended with weak or unlucky individuals such as John the First

(and Last!). In 1215 John (ruled 1199–1216) had had to accept the *Magna Carta* from his rebellious nobles. Over the centuries, this Great Charter was gradually transformed from a statement of noble privilege against an unloved king to a doctrine that held that the monarch, like all others, was bound to obey the laws.

The Hundred Years' War further weakened the royal powers and strengthened Parliament, as we have noted. By the mid-fifteenth century, Parliament had become the preserve of semi-independent barons and earls, who held the tax purse strings and drove hard bargains with the king in the wake of the lost war. The nobility added to the turbulence by engaging in an obscure struggle over the succession to the throne. Called the **Wars of the Roses,** the conflict lasted fifteen years (1455–1471).

Three late fifteenth-century kings (Edward IV, Richard III, and Henry VII) then gradually threw the balance of power in favor of the Crown. Of these, the most important was Henry VII (ruled 1483–1509), the founder of the Tudor dynasty and a master of intimidation and intrigue. He enlisted the aid of the middle classes and the clergy, both of whom were exasperated by the squabbles of the nobles. Henry not only rebuilt the powers of the royal crown but also avoided foreign wars, which would have meant going back to the noble-dominated Parliament to beg for funds. By the time he died in 1509, the English royal government was in firm control of the state.

The Holy Roman Empire (Germany)

The great exception to the recovery of royal powers in the later fifteenth century was the German kingdom, technically still the Holy Roman Empire of the German Nation. Here there was no central power to recover; it had been utterly destroyed in the medieval struggles between emperor and pope and the struggles between emperor and nobles which then ensued.

Why couldn't the Germans recover from these eleventh- and twelfth-century troubles by the fifteenth? The critical weakness of the monarchy was that the emperor was elected, rather than succeeding by hereditary right. The seven electors, who were all German princes and bishops, could and did negotiate with the various candidates to strike deals aimed at preserving noble autonomy. As a result, Germany had no centralized government in the fifteenth century. The emperor was only the first among equals, and sometimes not even that. He did not have a bureaucracy, a royal army, a national parliament, or the power to tax his subjects. The Holy Roman Empire was really a loose confederation of principalities, dukedoms, and even free cities, some of which were almost always squabbling among themselves. All real power was in the hands of the local aristocrats and the churchmen.

Among the candidates for the throne, the **Habsburgs** had most often been successful. This princely family had its home in Austria. In the late fifteenth and early sixteenth centuries, a series of extraordinary events propelled them

🌸 **MAP 25.2   Europe, the Near East, and North Africa in the Renaissance.** The
political divisions of the Mediterranean basin and Europe in the fifteenth century. Note the division
of the former Abbasid caliphate, centered on Baghdad (not shown), into several independent
sultanates and the Ottoman empire.

into great international prominence for the first time.
Thanks to a series of marriages and the unexpected deaths
of rivals, by 1527 the Habsburg territories had trebled in
Europe and also included the huge overseas empire being
rapidly conquered by Spain, which was now under a Habsburg ruler. It appeared that for the first time since the
twelfth century Barbarossa, the Holy Roman Emperor,
would be able to assert real authority. But the prospects of
establishing royal rule in Germany were not realized: the
burgeoning division between Catholic and Protestant frustrated all efforts to unify the nation until the late nineteenth
century.

Russia   Russia was a brand-new entrant, or rather a
newly rediscovered entrant, on the European scene in the
fifteenth century. The huge expanse of territory east of
Christian Poland and Hungary was practically unknown to

western Europeans after its conquest by the Mongols in the
mid-1200s (see Chapters 15 and 18). Almost all cultural
contacts between Russians and both the Latin and Byzantine Christian worlds had been severed by the primitive
Asiatic tribesmen. The latter's adoption of the Islamic faith
in the fourteenth century deepened the chasm that separated them from their Russian subjects.

The "Mongol Yoke" that lay upon Russia for almost two
and a half centuries (1240–1480) caused a cultural retro-
gression of tremendous import. Prior to its coming, the
Russian **Principality of Kiev** had entertained close relations
with Christian Europe and especially with the Orthodox
Christian empire in Constantinople from which it had received its religion, literature, and law. Situated on the extreme eastern periphery of the Christian world, Russia had
nevertheless felt itself and been considered a full member
of the European family.

Machiavelli, *The Prince*

In the year 1513, the Florentine official and diplomat Niccolo Machiavelli (1469–1527) was arrested for treason and subjected to torture. Although he was soon released, his ambitions for power and wealth lay in ruins. Reluctantly retiring to his country estate, Machiavelli devoted much of his remaining life to writing a series of theoretical works on politics and the eventful history of his native Florence. But he is best remembered for his handbook on the art of governance, *The Prince*, the masterwork of Renaissance political literature. In it he elucidated a coldly realistic view—strongly reminiscent of the Chinese Leyahits—of what law and lawgivers must do to preserve civic harmony.

Machiavelli's denial that common morality should influence a ruler's politics in any way and his insistence that violence and deceit can be justified in the name of good government have earned him a sinister reputation. To the present day, the adjective *Machiavellian* carries a cynical connotation. Yet the author, who had had every chance of observing what he wrote about, was just describing the actual practices of the Italian rulers of his day—and of many wielders of power since then.

> I say that every prince ought to wish to be considered kind rather than cruel. Nevertheless, he must take care to avoid misusing his kindness. Caesar Borgia* was considered cruel, yet his cruelty restored Romagna, uniting it in peace and loyalty. . . . A prince must be indifferent to the charge of cruelty if he is to keep his subjects loyal and united. . . . Disorders harm the entire citizenry, while the executions ordered by a prince harm only a few. Indeed, of all

princes, the newly established one can least of all escape the charge of cruelty, for new states are encumbered with dangers.

> Here a question arises: whether it is better to be loved than feared, or the reverse. The answer is, of course, that it would be best to be both loved and feared. But since the two rarely come together, anyone compelled to choose will find greater security in being feared than in being loved. . . . Men are less concerned about offending someone they have cause to love than someone they have cause to fear. Love endures by a bond which men, being scoundrels, may break whenever it serves their advantage to do so; but fear is supported by the dread of pain, which is always present. . . .

> I conclude that since men will love what they themselves determine, but will fear as their ruler determines, a wise prince must rely upon what he, not others, can control. He need only strive to avoid being hated. Let the prince conquer his state, then, and preserve it; the methods employed will always be judged honorable, and everyone will praise him. For the mob of men is always impressed by appearances, and by results; and the world is composed of the mob. . . .

> How praiseworthy it is, that a prince keeps his word and governs by candor, rather than craft, everyone knows . . . yet, those princes who had little regard for their word, and had the craft to turn men's minds, have accomplished great things, and in the end, they have overcome those who suited their actions to their pledges. . . .

For Reflection

Do you agree that the wise ruler will choose fear over love from his subjects? How do Machiavelli's precepts translate into present-day politics? Can you give some examples from the news this week?

*Caesar Borgia was the illegitimate son of Pope Alexander VI and one of the most ruthless Italian noblemen of the day.

SOURCE: Niccolo Machiavelli, The Prince, trans. Luigi Ricci, as revised by E. A. Vincent (New York: Oxford University Press, 1935). Used by permission.

After the arrival of the Mongols, this situation changed radically. In an effort to escape the ruling group's taxes and cruelties, the clergy and people of Russia sought to isolate themselves and had become vulnerable to all the ills that isolation entails. Ignorance and superstition became rife, even among the diminished number of the formally educated; the levels of technical and theoretical skills declined. Literacy all but disappeared among the laity.

In the absence of a native independent government, the Russian church came to play a particularly vital role in keeping the notion of a national community alive. The church of Rome had been rejected as heretical ever since the split in 1054. After the Turks seized Constantinople in 1453, the belief grew in Moscow that this had been God's punishment for the Greeks' waverings in defense of Orthodoxy. Now, Russia itself was to become the fortress of right belief: the **Third Rome.** As a Russian monk wrote to his ruler in 1511: "Two Romes [that is, the Christian Rome of

the fourth century, and Constantinople] have fallen, but the Third [Moscow] stands and there will be no fourth." Russia's government and church saw themselves as the implements of divine providence that would bring the peoples of Europe back to the true faith and defeat the infidels, wherever they might be.

By the late fifteenth century, the Mongols had been so weakened by internal conflicts that their former partner the prince of Moscow defied them successfully in 1480 and asserted his independence. Already, Moscow had become the most powerful Russian principality by a combination of single-minded ambition and consistent good luck. Soon the prince of Moscow had extended his rule to all parts of the nation and had taken to calling himself *tsar* ("Caesar" in Slavic) of Russia.

A tsar had far more power than any other European ruler of the day. Indeed, a tsar's alleged powers were so impressive as to raise the question whether Russia was still a

European state or whether, under the Mongols, it had become an Asiatic despotism in which the will of the ruler was automatically law of the land. Western European ambassadors and traders sent to Moscow in the sixteenth century felt that they had landed on truly foreign ground. They found themselves in a society that had no middle class and was untouched by the technical and psychological developments of the Renaissance. Its population's superstition and passivity were appalling, and its subservience toward its prince was striking to Western eyes.

🎴 **St. Peter's Cathedral in Rome.** This modern photo also shows the heart of the Vatican City, the papal state and residence by the banks of the Tiber. (*© Robert Frerck/Odyssey/Chicago*)

Art and Its Patrons

🎴

The most visible and historically appreciated form of Renaissance culture is its art, and Italy was the leader in every field. A tremendous creative outburst took place in Florence, Rome, Venice, Milan, and a dozen other city-states during the fifteenth and sixteenth centuries.

The spirit of this art, in whatever form, was quite different from that of medieval art. The latter attempted to portray concretely the collective belief of a community, the Christian community. It subordinated the individual and the particular to the group and the generic. Despite much technical innovation, medieval art was conservative and evolutionary in its spirit.

Renaissance art was intended to show the artist's mastery of technique and his newfound freedoms. It was experimental: new ideas were tried in all directions, and old ideas were put into quite new forms or media. The huge bronze doors of the Florentine cathedral cast by Ghiberti were something quite new: nothing like that had been attempted previously. With their twelve reliefs depicting the life of Christ, the doors were a brilliant success. Similarly, the enormous domes of the Florentine cathedral and St. Peter's were meant as a demonstration of what might be done by the bold human imagination, unfettered from its previous restrictions.

In painting, great talents such as Titian, da Vinci, Michelangelo, Botticelli, and Giotto led the way to an abundance of innovative compositions. All of them opened their studios to teach others, so that a wave of experimentation in the visual art forms swept across Italy and northward into Europe beyond the Alps. One of their great achievements was the mastery of perspective, which was first accomplished by Giotto in the early fourteenth century. He also led the way to a new realism in portraits.

In sculpture, the universal genius of Michelangelo was accompanied by Donatello, Cellini, and Bernini, to mention only some of the better-known names. Both Renaissance sculpture and painting broke sharply from their medieval forerunners. Artists now saw the human figure as a thing of superb animal beauty quite apart from its spiritual considerations or destiny.

Michelangelo was a leader in architecture as well. He designed much of the vast new St. Peter's Cathedral for one of the popes. Other leading architects included Bramante, da Vinci, and Brunelleschi. The basic architectural style of the Renaissance was an adaptation of the classical temple, with its columns, domes, and lofty, symmetrical facades. The Gothic style was now dismissed as primitive and superstition ridden in its striving toward heaven.

The artist's position as a respected member of society was also a Renaissance novelty (one that has generally not been imitated since!). Several of the leading figures of the art world were very well rewarded in money and prestige. They could pick and choose among their patrons and did not hesitate to drive hard bargains for their talents. Leonardo da Vinci was one of the richest men of his time and lived accordingly. So did Michelangelo and Raphael, both of whom enjoyed papal esteem and commissions for the Vatican palaces and libraries.

Art was unashamedly used to display the wealth of the individual or group who had commissioned it, rather than their piety (as in medieval times). Artistic patronage was limited to a smaller group than had been true earlier. The princes and the oligarchies around them were a tiny fraction of Italian society, but they provided most of the artists' commissions. Only rarely would an artist work without a specific commission in the hope of finding a buyer later.

 Equestrian Statue by Donatello. This was the first successful attempt to cast an equestrian statue since Roman days, and it marked a significant breakthrough in artistic achievement for the Renaissance. The statue stands in the main square of Padua. *(© Scala/Art Resource)*

Artists dealt with their patrons as equals. It was not at all unusual for a secure artist to refuse a lucrative commission because of a disagreement. For the most part, the patrons respected talent and allowed the artists to execute their work much as they pleased. The idea of artistic genius came into currency at this time. The artist was thought to possess a "divine spark" or other quality that ordinary souls lacked and therefore should be allowed to develop his talent without too much restriction.

Artists who were not good enough or sufficiently well connected to secure commissions worked for others in their studios as anonymous helpers. Many of the great paintings of the Italian Renaissance were only sketched and outlined by the famous artist: his unknown helpers finished out the brushwork.

The Renaissance Church

Much Renaissance literature satirizes the Christian clergy and focuses attention on the corruption and indifference that had become common in the higher ranks. These attacks are clearly directed at the personnel of the church, not its basic doctrines. At a time when increasing educational opportunity was giving birth to an urban group well read in nonreligious literature, the open immorality of some clergy and the ignorance and selfishness of others gave rise to continual scandal. Many village priests were still illiterate, and many monks had long since forgotten their vows of poverty and chastity. It was not at all unusual for a bishop never to set foot in his diocese because he preferred to live elsewhere. It was equally common for the abbot of a monastery to have produced a couple of illegitimate children with his "housekeeper."

In any Italian town the political and financial interests of the local clergy often nullified their moral leadership. This embittered many of the leading figures of the Italian Renaissance and turned them into raging anticlerics.

The example came from the top. Some of the fifteenth- and sixteenth-century popes were distressingly ignorant of their religious duties and too mindful of their money and privileges. The Italian noble families who controlled the papacy and the papal court were involved in ongoing struggles for political domination of the peninsula and tended to treat the papacy as their hereditary privilege. They regarded the increasing calls for reform as the mumblings of malcontents, which could be safely ignored. Only with the emergence of the Lutheran challenge would they slowly realize their error.

𝒮UMMARY

A rebirth of secular learning derived from classical authors began in fourteenth-century Italy and spread north across the Alps in ensuing years. Between the two areas there were often significant differences in mood and aims. The Renaissance produced the foundations of the modern state. That those foundations were laid along the lines of Machiavelli's *Prince* rather than the lines of the northern Christian humanist tracts would prove fateful.

After the crisis of the Hundred Years' War had been surmounted, the fifteenth century saw a significant rise in monarchic powers and prestige. English and French kings fashioned effective controls over their unruly nobles. The Russian tsar also emerged as a strong ruler, but in Germany and Italy there was no progress in the consolidation of central government.

Individualism and secularism made strong advances among the educated, whereas the moral prestige of the clergy and particularly the Roman papacy continued to sink. The arts flourished under the stimuli of new wealth in the cities and a governing class that placed great store on patronage and fame. Painting and architecture witnessed notable experiments and successful new talents.

TEST YOUR KNOWLEDGE

1. During the fifteenth century, the territory now called Italy was
   a. under the firm control of the Holy Roman Emperor.
   b. broken into several political units centered on cities.
   c. finally brought under the monopolistic control of the papacy.
   d. split in allegiance between Rome and Florence.
2. Which of the following attributes *least* fits the Renaissance world-view?
   a. Ambition
   b. Arrogance
   c. Confidence
   d. Caution
3. Which of the following statements about Renaissance secularism is *false*?
   a. It was vigorously opposed by Roman church leaders.
   b. It was partially a by-product of a changing economy.
   c. Most persons held to the basic tenets of Christian teaching.
   d. It encouraged the acquisition of material things.
4. The Renaissance in northern Europe differed from that of Italy by being
   a. less secular.
   b. more artistic.
   c. less serious.
   d. inferior in quality.
5. The basic message of More's *Utopia* was that
   a. personal wealth is the only sure path to social reforms.
   b. education cannot reduce human sinfulness.
   c. social institutions, not individuals, must be reformed first.
   d. people are inherently evil and cannot really be changed.
6. A new element in Italian city-state politics during the Renaissance was
   a. preferring fear to piety as a basis of government.
   b. a professional army of mercenaries.
   c. an absolute monarchy.
   d. the organization of a taxation agency.
7. One of the peculiar features of Russian Orthodoxy was the belief that
   a. Russians would be the political masters of all Europe.
   b. all Russians would be saved eternally.
   c. Moscow was destined to be the Third Rome.
   d. the state was nonexistent.
8. Titian and Van Eyck were both Renaissance
   a. architects.
   b. painters.
   c. political theorists.
   d. churchmen.

IDENTIFICATION TERMS

Erasmus	Machiavelli, Niccolo	Principality of Kiev	*Utopia*
Habsburg dynasty	More, Thomas	secularism	Wars of the Roses
humanism	Petrarch	Third Rome	

INFOTRAC COLLEGE EDITION

Enter the search term "Renaissance" using the Subject Guide.
Enter the search term "Machiavelli" using Key Words.

Enter the search term "humanism" using the Subject Guide.

	Law and Government	**Economy**
Europeans	Roman institutions are transformed by Germanic admixtures; government evolves slowly from the imperial model through feudal decentralization to the monarchies of the late Medieval Age. A struggle occurs between papacy and monarchs for supremacy within the new kingdoms. Law degenerates badly in the early period, begins comeback on Roman model in high medieval centuries. Faint beginnings of bureaucracy appear at end of period.	Economic activity increasingly mixed between agrarian and nonagrarian fields, but peasant farmers and pastors still make up large majority. By end of this period, the town-dwelling *bourgeoisie* has become significant in western Europe and is challenging the traditional noble-landlord social order. Feudal serfdom in the West diminishes and becomes almost extinct after the Black Death, but is rejuvenated in the eastern countries. Long-distance trade gradually resumes following the establishment of stable monarchic governments in the West. Europeans seek new trade opportunities via ocean routes to the eastern entrepots as the fifteenth century ends. Also, the new economic form called capitalism is promoted by various developments in credit facilities for business and in the new mobility of wealth and wealth-producing production.
East Asians	A thousand-year-long golden age for China, which recovers in late 500s from a second period of disintegration and prospers during the ensuing Tang and Song periods. Mongol conquest in thirteenth century interrupts, but does not severely damage the Chinese "mandate of heaven" monarchy, which resumes under vigorous new Ming dynasty in 1300s. Law and bureaucratic mandarin government operate generally to good effect for peace and stability, particularly in the south where nomads cannot easily reach. Japan selectively emulates Chinese system, but imperial court never exerts control over nation in like fashion to China; feudal nobility resists bureaucratic system, and negates it entirely in later part of this period by erecting the shogunate.	Farming continues in both China and Japan as means of livelihood for huge majority, but in China the cities' growth during the Tang and Song eras is impressive. Towns with populations of more than one million are known. There is very active domestic trade in every type of good, but only limited contacts with Western foreigners until the arrival of seafaring Europeans in the 1500s. Travel and commerce over the Silk Road is stimulated by the Mongol hegemony in the thirteenth and fourteenth centuries, and Chinese–Central Asian contacts multiply. The sudden rise and fall of Chinese maritime expeditions in the fifteenth century demonstrate the powers of the government versus the mercantile class.
Hindus	Written law still exceptional in this oral civilization. Government exercised by tiny minority of high-caste warriors, confirmed by the brahmin priests. Villages govern themselves with little contact with central or regional authorities except taxation. Central government is the exception, due to frequent nomadic invaders from the north.	Village fieldwork is norm throughout Indian history for the majority. Domestic and external trade with Southeast Asia and the Muslims is important in the cities. Colonial outreach to Southeast Asia and Pacific islanders is very strong in south India. Cotton cloth, spices, precious metals exported.

Religion and Philosophy	Arts and Culture	Science and Technology
Roman papal Christianity gradually superimposed upon western and central Europe through missionary activity in 500–800s. Eastern Europe and Russia brought into Byzantine Orthodox orbit in 800–1000s. Politico-religious divisions between East and West reach climax with formal schism between Constantinople and Rome in 1054. Eastern Orthodoxy is closely associated with the state and falls under royal or imperial dominion, especially in Russia. Roman clergy, on the other hand, often in conflict with Western kings after the papal reform in the tenth and eleventh centuries.	Greco-Roman models are lost to northern and central Europe after Roman collapse. After centuries of relative crudity of form, the Gothic architectural style takes root and rapidly spreads in twelfth and thirteenth centuries, giving stimulus to associated plastic arts for church and civic building decor. In the Renaissance, Gothic is supplanted by a neoclassicism based on rediscovered Greek and Roman ideas of beauty. Vernacular literature also comes to replace Latin after 1300s in popular literature. Painting, sculpture, architecture, and metalwork profit from novel techniques and ideas. Secularism and individualism apparent in Renaissance art and civic culture.	Natural sciences stagnate or worse until late medieval period. After universities are founded in 1200s, advances in humanities occur, but little in science. Technology attracts some interest, especially after devastation of Black Death, but few breakthroughs occur except in agriculture, where three-field system, horse collar, use of animal manure, and better plows appear. New energy sources are developed from the introduction of windmills and watermills in northwestern Europe.
In China Buddhism rivals and then blends with Confucian tenets among educated. Peasantry continues ancestor worship and Daoism. In Japan, Buddhism enters from Korea in sixth century, subdivides into several noncompetitive sects, and strongly affects national religion of Shinto. Neither country produces a clergy or much theology; ethics are derived from nonsupernatural sources in both. Warrior creeds become increasingly dominant in feudal Japan. Philosophy is Buddhist-based in both and focuses on questions of daily life rather than abstract ideas. Zen particularly popular in Japan after 1100s.	Landscape painting, porcelain, bronzes, inlay work, silk weaving, and several forms of literature (notably, poetry and the first novels) are highly developed in both nations. Japanese take numerous Chinese forms, alter them to suit Japanese taste. Some art forms, such as Zen gardens and No drama for the Japanese and jade sculpture and porcelain for the Chinese, are peculiar to each nation. Upper-class life allows more freedom to Japanese women than to their counterparts in China.	Both science and technology highly developed in China throughout this period. Many inventions are produced, including gunpowder, printing with movable type, paper made from wood pulp, navigational aids, water pump, and a ship's rudder. Japanese not so active in these areas, depend heavily on Chinese importations but produce exceptional metalwork. Chinese technology leads world throughout this period.
Vedic Hinduism is transformed in response to Buddhist challenge and gradually recaptures almost all of Indians' allegiance while Buddhists disappear. Both religions accept multiple nature of truth, contrasting with both Christians and Muslims. Strong ethical tone, exemplified in the Upanishads in Hinduism, teachings of Mahavira among Jains, and the Eightfold Path of Buddha. Near end of period, Muslim Turks establish their rule in north India and will come to dominate the northern two-thirds of the region via the Delhi sultanate.	Art forms emphasize interweaving of gods and humans and mutual dependency. Much Indian art lost due to climate and repeated invasions. Literature is oral until very late. Buddhist cave shrines and paintings are major repositories of extant art from early part of period. History almost nonexistent in the period. Much sculpture in stone and metal of high quality. Indian artistic influence felt throughout Southeast Asian mainland and Indonesia.	Selective scientific advances. Math is particularly strong (zero concept, decimal system, much algebra). Pharmacy and medicine also well developed. Excellent metalwork. Technology is dormant.

	Law and Government	**Economy**
Muslims	Law is wholly derived from words of the Qur'an as interpreted by *ulema* and the *kadi*. Government is also derived directly from the doctrines of the Prophet. The caliph is head of state and head of religion, as well as commander in chief. No separation of any type between religion and state. Only believers are full citizens; others are excluded from office holding.	A mixed economy, often urban-based. High levels of sophistication in trade and finance. Mercantile activity of all types strongly encouraged, built on previous Eastern civilized life. Wealth open to all, Muslim and infidel. Enormous variations in relative prosperity of Muslim groups, dependent on previous history and regional economy.
Africans	Law is almost always customary until arrival of Muslim traders/conquerors. Government is based on tribal affiliations, ranging from semidivine monarchs with cadres of officials to practically family-level autonomy from all external authority. Large areas never organize formal governments but remain "stateless societies."	Varied lifestyles, dependent on changing climate and terrain. Much nomadism; agriculture important in northern savanna and coastal plains. Long-distance trade from south to north across desert supports large-scale governments beginning in eighth-century Ghana. Gold, slaves, and salt major trade items. Active commerce across Indian Ocean to Arabia and points farther east.
Americans	General absence of writing means reliance on customary law. Government is generally a monarchy of limited powers, with a large group of royal kin sharing in prestige and income from taxes. Priesthood always powerful, sometimes dominant. Conquest of neighbors is usual means of constructing imperial control over large areas. Causes of decline of these governments seldom known or knowable.	Only major ancient civilizations not located in river plain or valley and not dependent on irrigated farms. Both Mexican and Peruvian centers depend on agricultural surplus generated by new crops. Most subjects are farmers, but a few large urban areas (Tenochtitlan, Teotihuacan, Cuzco) appear in time.

Religion and Philosophy	Arts and Culture	Science and Technology
Religious belief is basic organizing principle of public life. No priesthood, but the *ulema* wise men advise caliph and make policy. Strongly exclusivistic, monopolistic in regard to truth. Muslim faith clashes head on with the similar Christianity. Initial pressure to convert soon dropped by the conquering Bedouin. Split between Sunni and Shi'a destroys Islamic unity and adds to political struggles in Middle East.	Art of all types strongly impacted by Qur'anic prohibition of human "counterfeits" of God's work. Architecture, interior decor, landscaping are particular strong points in plastic arts, as are poetry, story telling, and history in literature. Respect for ancient achievements of Greeks in both art and philosophy. Strongly patriarchal society.	Sciences initially and for a long time are fostered by Arab willingness to learn from Greeks and Persians. But by 1300 science is languishing in comparison with West. Technology is selectively introduced, especially in maritime affairs and, for a time, in war. Muslims are frequently first beneficiaries of Hindu and Chinese breakthroughs.
Animism is universal until arrival of Muslims after about 700. Slow conversion of sub-Saharan elite begins then. Christianity isolated in Ethiopia after fourth century. In parts of Africa, distinct two-level religious society forms, with Muslims ruling over the animist majority.	Art is entirely devoted to religion or quasi-religious purposes, few of which are understood today. Fine bronzes and carvings in parts of sub-Saharan west and in southeast. Nok terra-cotta work oldest surviving art (seventh century). The wholly oral culture produced no literature in this era.	Science and technology are stultified in contrast with other parts of globe. Lack of written languages hampers retention and exchange of complex information. Introduction of Arabic in Muslim areas of continent only partially help in alleviating this.
Religious belief usually unknown in detail. The gods are often fearful, demonic rulers of the afterlife. Strongly resembles aspects of Mesopotamia, with human sacrifice on large scale in at least some of the ruling groups (Aztec, Maya). No apparent connections between religion and ethics.	Much pre-Columbian artwork survives. Art serves theology and cosmology. Extraordinary relief sculpture in central America. Architecture (pyramids) highly developed in both Peru and Mexico. Symbolism of much pre-Columbian art unknown to us.	Technology highly developed in certain fashions, notably handling of large stone masses in buildings and fortifications. Mayan mathematics and complex but accurate chronology are other examples. Mastery of hydraulics at Tenochtitlán, Incan road building over very difficult terrain in Andes necessitated basic science knowledge, but no written records exist.

Disequilibrium: The Western Encounter with the Non-Western World

Part FOUR

1500–1850 C.E.

Within fifty years on either side of the year 1500 C.E., a host of events or processes contributed to an atmosphere of rising confidence in the power of European governments and their supportive institutions. In the political and military realm, the Mongol yoke in Russia was lifted; the Turks, victorious at Constantinople, failed in an attempt to seize Vienna and central Europe; the Hundred Years' War had ended and the French recovery commenced. The economy finally recovered from the ravages of the Black Death, and maritime trade had increased significantly, as had the sophistication of commercial and financial instruments. The shameful derogation of the papal dignity brought about by the Babylonian Captivity and the Great Schism had ended. The worst of the peasant *Jaqueries* had been put down, and a peaceable transition from feudal agrarianism seemed possible, at least in the West.

But aside from these general developments, the epoch centered on 1500 is usually heralded as the beginning of the Modern Era because of two specific complexes of events: the questioning of traditional authority manifested in the Protestant Reformation, and the voyages of discovery that revealed the possibilities of the globe to Europeans' imagination—and greed. Both of these complexes contributed, in very different ways, to the expansion of Europe's reach and authority that took place in the next 300 years, until Europeans began to claim a prerogative to decide the fates of others as almost a God-given right. This tendency was particularly striking in the American colonies, where the native Amerindians were either obliterated or virtually enslaved by their overlords. But it was also the case, though in a much more limited way, for eastern and southern Asia, the coast of Africa, and the island or Arctic peripheries of a world that was larger and more varied than anyone had formerly supposed.

The difference between 1500 and 1850 in this regard might well be illustrated by comparing the Aztecs' Tenochtitlán, which amazed the envious Cortez, with the sleepy, dusty villages to which Mexico's Indians were confined later. Similarly, one might compare the army of the Persian Safavid rulers of the early sixteenth century that reduced the mighty Moghuls to supplicants for peace with the raggedy mob that attempted—in vain—to stop a handful of British from installing themselves on the Khyber Pass three centuries later. The West, whether represented by illiterate Spanish freebooters or Oxfordian British bureaucrats, seemed destined to surpass or be invincible against what one unrepentant imperialist called the "lesser breeds."

Part Four examines the massive changes that were slowly evincing themselves during these three centuries of heightening interactions between the West and the rest of the world, interactions that by the end of the period had effected a state of disequilibrium in the oecumene that existed since the early stages of the Common Era.

The voyages of discovery of the fifteenth and sixteenth centuries, the opening of maritime commerce across the Indian and Atlantic Oceans, and the resultant Columbian Exchange and the slave trade are the subject of Chapter 26. In Chapter 27 the successful Lutheran and Calvinist challenges to the papal church and their permanent effects on Western sensibilities are considered in detail. Chapters 28 and 29 examine the absolutist idea, constitutionalism, and their expression in religious warfare and the desire for stability; the evolving differences in the social and economic structures of western and eastern Europe are also considered.

Chapter 30 shifts the focus to East Asia, where China's centuries of glory following the ejection of the Mongols through the early Qing dynasty are analyzed. The history of pre–Meiji Restoration Japan and the colonial epoch in Southeast Asia follow in Chapter 31. In Chapter 32 the rise and fall of the great Muslim empires of central Asia and India are discussed, and this is succeeded by an overview in Chapter 33 of the disparate histories of the regions of precolonial Africa. Finally, the Iberian colonies of America and their struggle for independent existence are outlined in Chapter 34.

Chapter 26

A Larger World Opens

I have come to believe that this is a mighty continent which was hitherto unknown.

CHRISTOPHER COLUMBUS

THE UNPARALLELED OVERSEAS EXPANSION of Europe in the later fifteenth and early sixteenth centuries opened a new era of intercontinental contacts. What were the motives for the rapid series of adventuresome voyages? They ranged from Christian missionary impulses to the common desire to get rich. Backed to varying degrees by their royal governments, Portuguese, Spanish, Dutch, French, and English seafarers opened the world to European commerce, settlement, and eventual dominion. Through the Columbian Exchange initiated in 1492, the New World entered European consciousness and was itself radically and permanently changed by European settlers. In most of the world, however, the presence of a relative handful of foreigners in coastal "factories" or as occasional traders meant little change in traditional activities and attitudes. Not until the later eighteenth century was the European presence a threat to the continuation of accustomed African, Asian, and Polynesian lifestyles.

Maritime Exploration in the 1400s

The Vikings in their graceful longboats had made voyages across the North Atlantic from Scandinavia to Greenland and on to North America as early as 1000 C.E. But the northern voyages were too risky to serve as the channel for European expansion, and Scandinavia's population base was too small. The Vikings' tiny colonies did not last.

Four hundred years later, major advances in technology had transformed maritime commerce. The development of new sail rigging, the magnetic compass, and the astrolabe (an instrument used to determine the altitude of the sun or other celestial bodies); a new hull design; and systematic navigational charts enabled Western seamen, led by the Portuguese, to conquer the stormy Atlantic. Their claims to dominion over their newly discovered territories were backed up by firearms of all sizes. Most of these inventions were originally the products of the Chinese and Muslims. The Europeans had found them in the traditional inter-

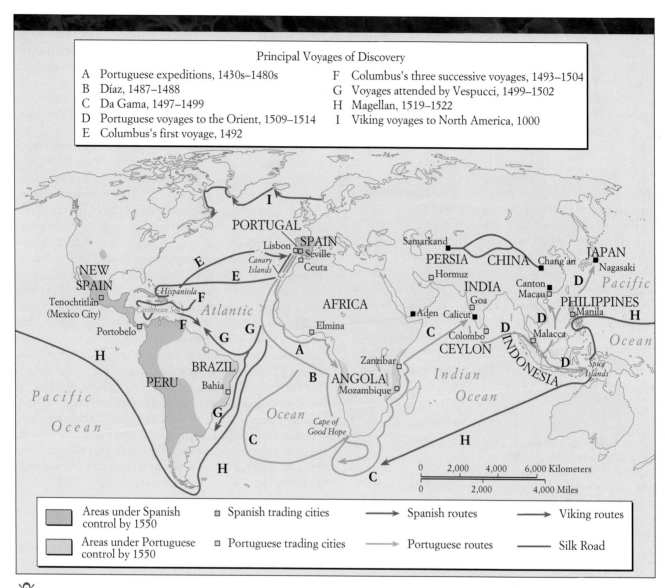

Principal Voyages of Discovery

A   Portuguese expeditions, 1430s–1480s
B   Díaz, 1487–1488
C   Da Gama, 1497–1499
D   Portuguese voyages to the Orient, 1509–1514
E   Columbus's first voyage, 1492

F   Columbus's three successive voyages, 1493–1504
G   Voyages attended by Vespucci, 1499–1502
H   Magellan, 1519–1522
I   Viking voyages to North America, 1000

Areas under Spanish control by 1550   Spanish trading cities   Spanish routes   Viking routes

Areas under Portuguese control by 1550   Portuguese trading cities   Portuguese routes   Silk Road

✿ **MAP 26.1   Spanish and Portuguese Voyages in the Fifteenth and Sixteenth Centuries.**

change ports of the eastern Mediterranean and then improved on them.

By the end of the fifteenth century, the map of the Eastern Hemisphere was gradually becoming familiar to Europeans. Knowledge of the high culture of China was current by the early 1400s. Overland traders, mostly Muslims, had established an active trade with that country via the famous Silk Road through central Asia and served as intermediaries to Europe. Marco Polo's great adventure was well known even earlier, after the appearance of his book about his many years of service to Kubilai Khan (see Chapter 18).

Most of Europe's luxury imports came from China and India, while the Spice Islands (as they were called by Europeans) of Southeast Asia were the source of the most valuable items in international exchange (see Map 26.1). But in the fourteenth century, this trade was disrupted, first by the Ottoman Turkish conquest of the eastern Mediterranean, and then by the breakup of the Mongol empire, which had formed a single unit reaching from China to western Russia. Security of transit across Asia was threatened, as was the Europeans' long-established and profitable interchange of goods with the Arabs and Persians. In 1453 the great depot of eastern wares, Constantinople, fell into the hands of the Turks. Europeans now became much more interested than ever before in finding a direct sea route to the East by circumnavigating Africa. This would allow them to make an "end run" around the hostile Turks and perhaps even cut out the Arab, Persian, and Indian middlemen—a tempting prospect.

Overseas Empires and Their Effects

❀

First the Portuguese and the Spanish and then the Dutch, English, and French created overseas empires that had far-reaching effects both at home and abroad.

Portuguese Pioneers

In the middle of the 1400s, insignificant and impoverished Portugal took advantage of its geographical position to begin the rapid phase of European expansion. Under the guidance of the visionary Prince Henry the Navigator (1394–1460), the Portuguese sponsored a series of exploratory voyages down the west coast of Africa and out into the ocean as far as the Azores (about one-third of the distance to the Caribbean). In 1488 the Portuguese captain **Bartolomeo Diaz** made a crucial advance by successfully rounding the Cape of Good Hope. A few years later, Vasco da Gama sailed across the Indian Ocean to the west coast of India. Trying to go down the west African coast, the cap-

❀ **A Portuguese Galleon.** In what kind of vessel did the early explorers set sail? Ships like these opened the trade routes to the East and to Brazil and the Caribbean for the Lisbon government in the sixteenth and seventeenth centuries. In their later days, two or three rows of cannons gave them heavy firepower as well as cargo space. (*National Maritime Museum Picture Library*)

tain Alvarez Cabral got blown all the way across the Atlantic, making landfall in Brazil, which he promptly claimed for Portugal. By 1510, Portuguese flags were flying over Goa in India and **Macao** on the coast of China (see Map 26.1). In 1511 the extraordinary admiral **Albuquerque** seized the great port-depot of Malacca at the tip of the Malay peninsula. This act established Portugal as the controller of the most profitable sea trade in the world (see Chapter 19). (For a closer look at Albuquerque's exploits, see the Commerce and Exchange box.)

The Portuguese empire was really only a string of fortified stations called "factories," from which the Portuguese brought back shiploads of the much sought-after spices, gold, porcelain, and silk obtained from their trading partners in East Africa and the Southeast Asian mainland and islands. The Portuguese paid for these imports initially with metalwares, cloth, and trinkets and later with firearms and liquor. The Lisbon government was the initiator and main beneficiary of this trade, because Portugal's small upper and middle classes were unable to pay sufficiently to outfit ships for the expeditions.

The era of Portuguese leadership was brief. The country was too poor and its population too small to maintain this fantastic but very thinly spread network. By the late 1500s, the aggressively expanding Dutch merchants had already forced Portugal out of some of its overseas stations. In 1580 previously independent Portugal was incorporated into Catholic Spain, which gave the Dutch and English Protestants an excuse to attack the Portuguese everywhere. Eventually, by the end of the seventeenth century Portugal was left with only Macao, Goa, and a few trading posts scattered along the African and Indian coasts.

How did a relative handful of European intruders establish themselves as regionally dominant authorities in these distant corners of the globe? In the Indian Ocean and Southeast Asia, the patterns established by the Portuguese were followed by all their successors. The European outreach was seaborne, and control of the sea was the crucial element. The militant natives quickly learned that it was not profitable to confront the Europeans by arms, because the Europeans would generally win. Their naval cannon, more advanced methods of rigging, more maneuverable hulls, better battle discipline, and higher levels of training assured them of success in almost all engagements. The intruders avoided land warfare, unless and until mastery of the surrounding seas was assured. In that case, land warfare was rarely necessary.

After an initial display of martial strength, the newcomers were usually content to deal with and through the established native leadership in securing the spices, cotton cloth, silk, and other luxuries that they sought. In the normal course of events, the Europeans made a treaty with the paramount regional ruler that assured them a dominant position in the export market. This meant the elimination of the Muslim or Hindu merchants, who until the sixteenth century controlled the Indian Ocean trade and who were

Alfonso de Albuquerque
(1453–1515)

Tiny Portugal was for a century in the very forefront of European exploration and conquests in the East. The quest for control of the Indian Ocean, for centuries dominated by Muslim traders on both its African and Indian shores, was the driving force. Spices, Chinese porcelain and silk, and Indian cotton goods were the most lucrative commodities in world trade. The profits that might be secured by "cutting out the middlemen" would be enormous for the European importers. But they would have to be conquered. Starting in the epoch of Henry the Navigator, Portuguese guns and daring secured a series of "openings" to the wealth of East Asia. By the 1540s, the flag of the Lisbon court was waving over a chain of ports reaching from Mozambique to the China Sea.

The chief architect of this brief-lived commercial empire was the explorer, administrator, and warrior Alfonso de Albuquerque (1453–1515). An illegitimate relation to the dynasty in Lisbon, he spent his youth at the court of Alfonso V and then served that prince's successor, John II. Albuquerque set out for the first time to the East in 1503 and was rewarded the next year by command of a part of a flotilla that sailed for India in 1506 under the great seaman Tristan da Cunha.

Separating from the main fleet, Albuquerque raided the Arab settlements on the East African coast and then crossed much of the Indian Ocean to the Persian Gulf. Here he temporarily captured the port of Hormuz, halfway up the gulf and one of the most active trade centers in the Muslim world. Proceeding on to India's western coast, he attempted to make good his designation to supersede the previous governor. But this wily opponent threw Albuquerque into jail, and he was only able to regain his freedom after some months.

Albuquerque then undertook a series of maritime raids and conquests that remain among the most remarkable of the Age of Exploration. He secured the important town of Goa on India's western coast, then went on to the Straits of Malacca in Southeast Asia, which controlled all sea traffic from the west to China and the Spice Islands. After a severe struggle against more numerous Muslim fleets, Albuquerque was able to gain control of Malacca for Portugal. On the voyage back to Goa, his ship went down, and the admiral nearly lost his life as well as all the fortune he had captured. In Goa, he established Portuguese rule so solidly that this small colony remained under Lisbon's control until 1960.

An attempt to conquer the gateway to the Red Sea, the port of Aden, in 1513–1514 was foiled by the city's strong defenses, but Albuquerque became the first European to sail into these waters.

In 1515, Albuquerque again sailed up the Persian Gulf and reconquered Hormuz, this time permanently, for Portugal. His reward was bitter: on the homeward voyage to Goa, his ship encountered one newly arrived from Portugal, which carried the new king's command that Albuquerque resign his governorgeneral's post and turn it over to a rival and enemy. Perhaps this humiliation, which was totally undeserved, was the cause of Albuquerque's sudden death at sea. He was buried at Goa, which remained the center of the maritime empire he founded for the next two centuries.

A magnificent seaman, who frequently led his tiny fleets of five or six caravels (small, light sailing ships) against flotillas that outnumbered him by ten to one, Albuquerque was also a skilled and farsighted administrator. His goal was not to crush the natives but to induce them to accept the Portuguese as solicitous overlords and protectors. But the best testimonial to Albuquerque's wisdom and justice is that both Hindus and Muslims used to go to his tomb in Goa as a place of refuge and a gathering point for protests against abusive or unjust Portuguese officials in later days.

For Reflection

How could Albuquerque operate against the numerically superior Muslim fleets so far from his home base in Portugal? What advantages did the Portuguese caravels possess over their enemies at sea?

the instigators of the initial resistance. The local ruler's position was not directly threatened unless he should put up armed resistance—a rare occurrence in view of the Europeans' military superiority.

A kind of partnership thus evolved between the local chieftains and the new arrivals, in which both had sufficient reasons to maintain the status quo against those who might challenge it. The Portuguese frequently made the mistake of alienating the local population by their brutality and their attempts to exclude all competition, but the Dutch and, later, the British were more circumspect. Unlike the Portuguese, they made no attempt until the nineteenth century to bring the Asians into the Christian belief. As a very general rule, after the sixteenth-century Portuguese missionary efforts had subsided, the Europeans interfered little with existing laws, religion, and customs unless they felt compelled to do so to gain their commercial ends. Such interference was rare in both Asia and Africa. There, the European goal was to attain maximal profit from trade, and they avoided anything that threatened to disrupt the smooth execution of that trade. The Spanish and Portuguese empires in the Americas were a different proposition.

The Spanish Empire in the Americas

The newly unified Spanish kingdom was close behind and in some areas simultaneous with Portugal in the race for world empire. A larger domestic resource base and extraordinary finds of precious metals enabled Spain to achieve more permanent success than its neighbor. The Italian visionary Christopher Columbus was able to persuade King Ferdinand and Queen Isabella of his dream of a shortcut to the "Indies" by heading *west* over the Atlantic, which he thought was only a few hundred miles wide. The first of Columbus's Spanish-financed voyages resulted in the discovery of the American continents. He made three more voyages before his death and was still convinced that China lay just over the horizon of the Caribbean Sea.

By then, the Spanish crown had engaged a series of other voyagers, including **Amerigo Vespucci,** who eventually gave his name to the New World that Columbus and others were exploring. In 1519–1521, the redoubtable **Hernan Cortez** conquered the Aztec empire in Mexico. Soon Spanish explorers had penetrated north into what is now California and Arizona. By the 1540s Spain controlled most of northern South America as well as all Central America and the Caribbean islands.

Perhaps the greatest of these ventures was the fantastic voyage of **Ferdinand Magellan.** Starting from Spain in 1519, his ships made the first circumnavigation of the globe. A few survivors (not including the unlucky Magellan) limped back into Sevilla in 1522 and reported that, yes, the world was indeed round. Most educated people already thought so, but Magellan's voyage proved that the Earth had no real ends, and that it was possible to go around the southern tip of the New World into the more or less familiar waters of East Asia.

Like the Portuguese, the Spaniards' motives for exploration were mixed between a desire to convert the heathen to the papal church and thus gain a strong advantage against the burgeoning Protestants (see Chapter 27) and the desire for wealth and esteem. Gold, God, and glory were the motives most frequently in play. It is often difficult to tell which was uppermost. Sometimes, however, as in the cases of Francisco Pizarro in Peru and Cortez in Mexico, it is easier. By whatever motivation, the middle of the 1500s saw the Spanish adventurers creating an empire that reached nearly around the world. In the terms of the royal charters granted to Columbus and his successors, the Spanish Crown claimed the lion's share of special treasures found by the explorers. Indian gold and silver (*bullion*) thus poured into the royal treasury in Madrid. Those metals, in turn, allowed Spain to become the most powerful European state in the sixteenth and seventeenth centuries.

Unlike the Portuguese, the Spanish frequently came to stay at their overseas posts. Whereas the Portuguese were primarily interested in quick profits from the trade in luxury items from the East, the Spanish noble explorers were accompanied by priests, who set up missions among the Indians, and by a number of lowborn men (later women, also), who were prepared to get rich more slowly. They did so by taking land and workers from among the native population.

Finding that the cities of gold and silver, or the *El Dorados,* were mirages, the Spanish immigrants gradually created agricultural colonies in much of Central and South America, using first Amerindian and then black labor. Some of these workers were more or less free to come and go, but an increasing number were slaves, imported from Africa. The Spanish colonies thus saw the growth of a multiracial society—blacks, Indians, and whites—in which the whites held the dominant political and social positions from the outset. The dominance of the whites was to assume increasing importance for the societies and economies of these lands both during their 300 years as colonies and later as independent states.

The African Slave Trade Opens

The African slave trade commenced in the fifteenth century. When the Portuguese ventured down the West African coast, they quickly discovered that selling black houseslaves to the European nobility could be a lucrative business. But the slave trade remained very small scale through the 1490s and only began to grow when slaves started to be shipped across the Atlantic. The first known example occurred in 1502. By the mid-1530s, Portugal had shipped moderate numbers of slaves to the Spanish Caribbean and to its own colony of Brazil, and the transatlantic trade remained almost a Portuguese monopoly until into the next century. At that time, Dutch and then English traders moved into the business and dominated it through its great expansion in the eighteenth century until its gradual abolition.

Few European women traveled to the Americas in the early years of colonization, so the Spaniards often married Amerindian or black women or kept them as concubines. As a result, **mestizos** (the offspring of Amerindians and whites) and **mulattos** (the children of Africans and whites) soon outnumbered Caucasians in many colonies. The same happened in Portuguese Brazil, where over time a huge number of African slaves were imported to till the sugarcane fields that were that colony's chief resource. Here, the populace was commonly the offspring of Portuguese and African, rather than the Spanish-Indian mixture found to the north.

Dutch and English Merchant-Adventurers

Holland   When Portugal's grip on its Indian Ocean trade began to falter, the Dutch Protestant merchants com-

✿ **The Slave Ship.** This engraving shows the usual arrangements for transport of black slaves in the Atlantic trade. The ship was the *Albanez,* with cargo from the Guinea coast and headed for the Caribbean. It was boarded and taken as a prize by HMS *Albatross* in 1840, as part of the British effort to outlaw slave trading. *(e.t.archive)*

bined a fine eye for profit with religious prejudice—the Portuguese were after all minions of the pope and the Spanish king—to fill the vacuum. In the sixteenth century the Netherlands were under Spanish control until the failure of the Spanish *Armada* in 1588 (see Chapter 27). Controlling their own affairs after that, the bourgeois shipowners and merchants of the Dutch and Flemish towns quickly moved into the forefront of the race for trade. By the opening of the seventeenth century, Amsterdam and Antwerp were the major destinations of Far Eastern shippers, and Lisbon had fallen into a secondary position.

Dutch interest in the eastern seas was straightforward and hard-edged. They wanted to accumulate wealth by creating a monopoly of demand, buying shiploads of Southeast Asian luxury goods at low prices and selling the goods at very high prices in Europe. Many of the Asian suppliers were Muslims, and their relationship with the Catholic Portuguese had been strained or hostile. They preferred to deal with the Dutch Protestants, who were simply businessmen with no desire to be missionaries. If the suppliers were for one or another reason reluctant to sell, the Dutch persuaded them by various means, usually involving Dutch superiority in naval gunnery.

The Dutch focused on the East Indies spice and luxury trade, but they also established a settler colony in New Amsterdam across the Atlantic, and several island colonies in the Caribbean. These were less attractive to the Dutch and

eventually surrendered to other powers, such as England. New Amsterdam became New York at the close of the first of two naval wars in the seventeenth century that made England the premier colonial power along the East Coast of the future United States.

How did such a small nation (Holland did not possess more than 2.5 million souls at this juncture) carry out this vast overseas enterprise at the very time it was struggling to free itself from its Spanish overlords? A chief reason for the Dutch success was the East India Company: a private firm chartered by the government in 1602, the company had a monopoly on Dutch trading in the Pacific. The company eventually took over the Portuguese spice and luxury trade from the East and proved an enormous bonanza for its stockholders. The traders were usually temporary partners. A partnership would be set up for one or more voyages with both cost and profits split among the shareholders. The traders hired captains and crews who would be most likely to succeed in filling the ship's hold at minimal cost, whatever the means or consequences. Later in the seventeenth century, the focus of attention shifted from importing spices and luxury goods to the alluring profits to be made in the transatlantic trade in African slaves.

England   The English colonial venture was slow in getting started. When the Portuguese and Spaniards were dividing up the newly discovered continent of America and the Far Eastern trade, England was just emerging from a lengthy struggle for dynastic power called the War of the Roses (see Chapter 25). Starting in the 1530s, the country was then preoccupied for a generation with the split from Rome under Henry VIII and its consequences (see Chapter 27). Then came the disappointing failure of Sir Walter Raleigh's "Lost Colony" on the Carolina coast in the 1580s and a war with Spain.

Only in the early 1600s did the English begin to enter the discovery and colonizing business in any systematic way. Like the Dutch, the English efforts were organized by private parties or groups and were not under the direction of the royal government. The London East India Company founded in 1600 is a good example. Similar to its Dutch counterpart, it was a private enterprise with wide political as well as commercial powers in dealing with foreigners and with its own military resources.

After two victorious wars against the Dutch in the 1650s and 1660s, the English were the world's leading naval power, although the Dutch still maintained their lead in the carrying trade to and from Europe. The East Asian colonial trade was not important to them, however, and they soon gave up their attempts to penetrate the Dutch monopoly on East Indian luxuries, choosing to concentrate on India. (The only important English station in Southeast Asia was the great fortress port of Singapore, which was not acquired until the nineteenth century.)

English colonies in the seventeenth century were concentrated in North America, and an odd mixture they were. The northern colonies were filled with Protestant dissidents who could not abide the Anglican church regime: Puritans, Congregationalists, and Quakers. Maryland was a refuge for persecuted Catholics. Virginia and the Carolinas began as real estate speculations. They were essentially get-rich-quick schemes devised by nobles or wealthy commoners who thought they could sell off their American holdings to individual settlers at a fat profit. Georgia began as a noble experiment by a group of philanthropists who sought to give convicts a second chance.

Elsewhere, the English were less inclined to settle new lands than to make their fortunes pirating Spanish galleons or competing with the Dutch in the slave trade. What the Dutch had stolen from the Portuguese the English stole in part from the Dutch. This was equally true in the New World, where the Dutch challenge to Portuguese and Spanish hegemony in the Caribbean was superseded by the English and French in the eighteenth century.

France The colonial empire of France parallels that of England. Relatively late in entering the race, the French sought overseas possessions and/or trade factories throughout the world to support their prospering domestic economy. From Canada (as early as 1608, one year after Jamestown in Virginia), to the west coast of Africa (as early as 1639) and India (in the early eighteenth century), the servants of the Bourbon kings contested both their Catholic co-religionists (Portugal, Spain) and their Protestant rivals (Holland, Britain) for mercantile advantage and the extension of royal powers. Thus, the French, too, reflected the seventeenth-century trend to allow state policies to be dictated more by secular interests than by religious adherences, a process we will examine in detail in Chapter 28.

Mercantilism

During this epoch, governments attempted to control their economies through a process later termed **mercantilism.** Under mercantilism, the chief goal of economic policy was a favorable balance of trade, with the value of a country's exports exceeding the cost of its imports. To achieve this goal, the royal government intervened in the market constantly and attempted to secure advantage to itself and the population at large by carefully supervising every aspect of commerce and investment. The practice reached its highest development in seventeenth- and eighteenth-century France, but was subscribed to almost everywhere.

As for colonial policy, mercantilism held that only goods and services that originated in the home country could be (legally) exported to the colonies and that the colonies' exports must go to the home country for use there or reexport. Thus, the colonies' most essential functions were to serve as captive markets for home country producers and to provide raw materials at low cost for home country importers. Portugal, Spain, and France practiced this theory of economics rigorously in their colonies, whereas Holland and England took a more relaxed approach in theirs.

The Columbian Exchange

The coming of the Europeans to the New World resulted in very important changes in the resources, habits, and values of both the Amerindians and the whites. Among the well-known introductions by the Europeans to the Western Hemisphere were horses, cattle, sheep, and goats; iron; firearms; sailing ships; and, less tangibly, the entire system of economics we call capitalism.

But the **Columbian Exchange** had another side: a reverse flow of products and influences from the Americas to Europe and through Europe to the other continents. Educated Europeans after about 1520 became aware of how huge and relatively unknown the Earth was and how varied the peoples inhabiting it were. This knowledge came as a surprise to many Europeans, and they were eager to learn more. The literature of discovery and exploration became extraordinarily popular during the sixteenth and seventeenth centuries.

From this literature, Europeans learned, among other things, that the Christian moral code was but one of several;

🌼 **Mining at Cerro Rico.** This contemporary sketch shows the enormous labor involved in getting silver ore out of the Spanish mines in the New World. The Spanish overseer at the base of the ladder supervised perhaps as many as fifty Indian slaves. (© *The Granger Collection*)

that the natural sciences were not of overwhelming interest or importance to most of humanity; that an effective education could take myriad forms and have myriad goals; and that viewpoints formed by tradition and habit are not necessarily correct, useful, or the only conceivable ones. Initially just curious about the Earth's other inhabitants, upper-class Europeans gradually began to develop a certain tolerance for their views and habits. This tolerance slowly deepened in the seventeenth and especially the eighteenth century as Europe emerged from its religious wars. The previously favored view of unknown peoples probably being "anthropophagi" (man-eaters) began giving way to the concept of the "noble savage," whose unspoiled morality might put the sophisticated European to shame.

Contacts with the Americas also led to economic changes in Europe. Some crops such as sugarcane and rice that were already known in Europe but could not be profitably grown there were found to prosper in the New World. Their cultivation formed the basis for the earliest plantations in the Caribbean basin and the introduction of slavery into the New World.

In addition, a series of new crops were introduced to the European Asian and African diet. Tobacco, several varieties of beans and peas, squashes, rice, maize, bananas, manioc, and others stemmed originally from American or Far Eastern lands. First regarded as novelties—much like the occasional Indian or black visitor—they came to be used as food and fodder. The most important was the white or Irish potato, an Andean native, which was initially considered fit only for cattle and pigs but was gradually adopted by northern Europeans in the eighteenth century. By the end of that century, it had become the most important part of the peasants' diet in several countries. The potato was the chief reason European farms were able to feed the spectacular increase in population that started in the later 1700s.

So much additional coinage was put into circulation from the Mexican and Peruvian silver mines that it generated massive inflation. In the seventeenth century, the Spanish court used the silver to pay army suppliers, shipyards, and soldiers, and from their hands, it went on into the general economy. Spain itself suffered most in the long run from the inflation its bullion imports caused. Spanish gold and silver went into the pockets of foreign suppliers, carriers, and artisans rather than into domestic investments or business. This would prove fateful in the next century.

In a period of inflation, when money becomes cheap and goods or services become dear, people who can convert their wealth quickly to goods and services are in an enviable position. Those whose wealth is illiquid and cannot be easily converted are at a disadvantage. As a result, the landholders—many of whom were nobles who thought it beneath them to pay attention to money matters—lost economic strength.

The middle classes, who could sell their services and expertise at rising rates, did well. Best off were the merchants who could buy cheap and hold before selling at higher prices. But even the unskilled or skilled workers in the towns were in a relatively better position than the landlords: wages rose about as fast as prices in this century.

In many feudal remnant areas, where serfs paid token rents in return for small parcels of arable land, the landlord was dealt a heavy blow. Prices rose for everything the noble landlords needed and wanted, while their rents, sanctioned by centuries of custom, remained about the same. Unaware of the reasons for the economic changes and unable to anticipate the results, many landlords faced disaster during the later sixteenth century and could not avoid bankruptcy when their long-established mortgages were called. Many of them had been living beyond their means for generations, borrowing money wherever they could with land as security. Much land changed hands at this time, from impoverished nobles to peasants or to the newly rich from the towns. Serfdom became impractical or unprofitable. Already weakened by long-term changes in European society, it was abolished in most of western Europe.

European Impacts and Vice Versa

How strong was the European impact on the native cultures of the Western Hemisphere and on the peoples of the Far East, sub-Saharan Africa, and the Pacific Rim? Historians agree that it was enormous in some areas, but much less so in others. The Portuguese and others' trading factories on the African and Asian coasts had minimal impacts on the lives of the peoples of the interior. Only in exceptional circumstances was the presence of the Europeans a prominent factor in native consciousness. Even in the areas most directly affected by slaving such as Senegambia and Angola, the consensus of recent scholarly opinion believes that there were few if any massive changes in the course of ordinary affairs, social or economic, brought by slaving alone. Rather, the foreign slavers' interests were filtered through the existing networks of local authority and custom.

Spain's American settler colonies and Brazil were quite different in these respects. Here the intruders quickly and radically terminated existing Amerindian authority structures, replacing them with Spanish/Portuguese models. In the economy, the collectives of the villages with their free laborers were replaced by *encomienda* estates on which first Amerindians and later Africans were forced to reside and labor. Although the *encomiendas* were soon abolished, the exploitation of the helpless by their Spanish and Portuguese overseers continued unabated on the rice and sugar plantations, which replaced gold and silver mines.

As with the exchanges in agricultural products, the stream of external influences was not simply one way, from Europe to the rest of the world. In the Americas there was a noticeable degree of change wrought in the Spanish and Portuguese culture by prolonged exposure to Amerindian habits and attitudes. An example would be the adoption of maize culture by the mestizo Spanish in Mexico. Another would be the incorporation of Amerindian hydraulic farming technique. In another part of the early imperial world created by the voyages of discovery, the architecture of the Dutch colonial town of Batavia (Jakarta), was soon converted from the trim and tight homes and warehouses of blustery Amsterdam to the very different demands of the Javanese climate.

Perhaps it is most accurate to say that in the settler colonies of the Western Hemisphere the local peoples were extensively and sometimes disastrously affected by the arrival of the whites, but in the rest of the world, including sub-Saharan Africa, the Asian mainland, and the South Pacific islands, the Europeans were less disruptive to the existing state of affairs. Sometimes native governments even succeeded in using the Europeans to their own advantage, as in West Africa and Mughal India. This would remain true until the nineteenth century. Promoted by industrialization at that time, the European impacts multiplied, became more profound, and changed in nature so as to subordinate the natives in every sense.

The Fate of the Amerindians

By far the worst human consequences of the European expansion were the tragic fates imposed on the native Amerindians of the Caribbean and Central America in the first century of Spanish conquest (see the report by **Bartolome de Las Casas** in the Violence and Coercion box). Although the Spanish Crown imposed several regulatory measures to protect the Indians after 1540, little could be done to inhibit the spread of epidemic disease (measles and influenza, as well as the major killer, smallpox) in the Amerindian villages. As a general rule, the immune systems of the Amerindians were unable to cope with the diseases brought by the newcomers, whereas the Spaniards were much less affected by the Amerindian maladies. (Which continent is responsible for the appearance of syphilis is much argued.)

Smallpox was a particular curse. The population of Mexico, which was perhaps twenty-five million at the coming of Cortez, was reduced to two million only sixty years later, largely as a result of smallpox epidemics. On the Caribbean islands, no Amerindians remained after a generation of Spanish occupancy. The same story repeated itself in the viceroyalty of Peru, where as many as 80 percent of the native population died in the sixteenth century. Only in modern times have the Amerindians recovered from this unprecedented disaster.

Bartolome de Las Casas's Report on the Indies

Violence toward the conquered is a commonplace in history. But nowhere is this more evident than in the history of the state religions. Propagating Christianity was a useful cover for some of the Spanish conquistadors in their search for gold. They were resisted, however, by one of their own number.

Bartolome de Las Casas (1474–1567), a Dominican priest who had been a conquistador and slaveholder in the Caribbean in his youth, turned his back on his former life and devoted himself to protecting the Amerindians under Spanish rule. In his *Brief Relation of the Destruction of the Indies* (1522), he began an uncompromising campaign to expose the horrendous treatment meted out by his fellow Spanish to the native populations of the New World. So graphic and terrible were his accounts that foreign powers hostile to Spain (notably, England) were able to use them for centuries to perpetuate the so-called Black Legend of the viciousness of Spanish colonialism.

The Conquistadors Arrive. This Aztec painting shows a skirmish between the Spaniards on horse and their Amerindian allies, and Aztec defenders. The Amerindians are armed with obsidian-edge swords capable of cutting off the head of a horse at a single blow. *(© The Granger Collection)*

Of the Island of Hispaniola

The Christians, with their horses and swords and lances, began to slaughter and practice strange cruelties among them. They penetrated into the country and spared neither children nor the aged, nor pregnant women, nor those in childbirth, all of whom they ran through the body and lacerated, as though they were assaulting so many lambs herded into the sheepfold.

They made bets as to who could slit a man in two, or cut off his head at one blow . . . they tore babes from their mothers' breasts by the feet, and dashed their heads against the rocks. Others, they seized by the shoulders and threw into the rivers, laughing and joking, and when they fell into the water they exclaimed, "boil the body of So-and-so! . . ."

They made a gallows just high enough for the feet to nearly touch the ground, and by thirteens, in honour and reverence of our Redeemer and the 12 Apostles, they put wood underneath and, with fire, they burned the Indians alive.

They wrapped the bodies of others entirely in dry straw, binding them in it and setting fire to it; and so they burned them. They cut off the hands of all they wished to take alive, made them carry them pinned on to their bodies, and said "Go and carry these letters," that is, take the news to those who have fled to the mountains. . . .

I once saw that they had four or five of the chief lords [Indians] stretched on a gridiron to burn them, and I think there were also two or three pairs of gridirons, where they were burning others. And because they cried aloud and annoyed the Captain or prevented him from sleeping, he commanded that they should be strangled; the officer who was burning them was worse than a hangman and did not wish to suffocate them, but with his own hands he gagged them, so that they should not make themselves heard, and he stirred up the fire until they roasted slowly, according to his pleasure. I know this man's name, and knew his relations in Sevilla. I saw all the above things and numberless others.

And because all the [Indian] people who could flee, hid among the mountains and climbed the crags to escape from men so deprived of humanity . . . the Spaniards taught and trained the fiercest boarhounds to tear an Indian to pieces as soon as they saw him. . . . And because sometimes, though rarely, the Indians killed a few Christians for just cause, they made a law among themselves that for one Christian whom the Indians might kill, the Christians should kill a hundred Indians. . . .

For Reflection

Beside de las Casas, other Spanish priests attempted protection of the Amerindians against cruelty, but usually in vain. What measures could be undertaken by the clergy to diminish such cruelty? Was it logical to expect the priests or bishops to intervene? What does the colonial record show?

SOURCE: *Bartolome de las Casas*, A Very Brief Account of the Destruction of the Indies, trans. F. A. McNutt (Cleveland: Clark, 1909), pp. 312–319.

Racism's Beginnings

Blacks came into European society for the first time in appreciable numbers during the fifteenth century. At the same time appeared the first faint signs of white racism. The black slaves from Africa, who were brought to Europe through Muslim channels, were mostly regarded as novelties by the rich and were kept as tokens of wealth or artistic taste. Some free blacks lived in Mediterranean Europe where they worked as sailors, musicians, and actors, but they were not numerous enough for the average European to have any firsthand contact.

Many whites thought of blacks in terms dictated either by the Bible or by Muslim prejudices imbibed unconsciously over time. The biblical references were generally negative: black was the color of the sinful, the opposite of light in the world. "Blackhearted," "a black scoundrel," and "black intentions" are a few examples of the mental connection between the color black and the evil and contemptible. The Omani Arab slave traders in East Africa who supplied some of the European as well as the Asiatic markets were another source of prejudice. They were contemptuous of the non-Muslim blacks on the Zanzibar coast whom they ruled and with whom they traded in human flesh. These traders' point of view was easily transferred to their Italian and Portuguese partners.

Summary

The explosive widening of Europe's horizons in the sixteenth century, both in the geographic sense and in the psychological sense, was one side of the Columbian Exchange. A series of colonial empires were created, first by the Portuguese and Spanish and then by the Dutch, English, and French. The original objective of the government-funded explorers was to find new, more secure trade routes to the East, but soon their motives changed to a mixture of enrichment, missionary activity, and prestige: gold, God, and glory.

The import of great quantities of precious metals created severe inflation and promoted the rise of the business/commercial classes. The discovery of customs and values that were quite different from those of Europeans contributed to the beginning of a new attitude of tolerance. The overseas expansion added important new foods to the European diet.

For the non-Western hosts, this colonial and commercial outreach had mainly negative consequences, although circumstances varied from place to place. The most devastating effects were certainly in Spain's American colonies, where the indigenous peoples were almost wiped out by disease and oppression. In West Africa, East Africa, and the Asian mainland, the European trading presence had overall little effect on ordinary life at this time. Racism's beginnings, however, can be traced to its roots in the African slave trade commencing in this era.

Test Your Knowledge

1. The fifteenth- and sixteenth-century voyages of exploration were stimulated mainly by
   a. European curiosity about other peoples.
   b. the determination to obtain more farming land for a growing population.
   c. the individual explorers' hopes of enrichment.
   d. the discovery that the Earth was in fact a sphere without "ends."

2. Which of the following was *not* proved by Magellan's epic voyage?
   a. The globe was more compact than had been believed.
   b. The globe was indeed spherical.
   c. A sea passage existed south of the tip of South America.
   d. The islands called "Spice Lands" could be reached from the East.

3. Which of the following reasons was *least* likely to be the motive for a Dutch captain's voyage of discovery?
   a. A desire to deal the Roman church a blow
   b. A search for personal enrichment
   c. A quest to find another lifestyle for himself in a foreign land
   d. The intention of establishing trade relations with a new partner

4. What is the correct sequence of explorer-traders in the Far East?
   a. Spanish, English, French
   b. Spanish, Portuguese, Dutch
   c. Dutch, English, Spanish
   d. Portuguese, Dutch, English

5. The sixteenth-century inflation affected which group most negatively?
   a. Landholding nobles
   b. Urban merchants
   c. Wage laborers
   d. Skilled white-collar workers
6. Which proved to be the most important of the various new foods introduced into European diets by the voyages of discovery?
   a. Tomatoes
   b. Rice
   c. Potatoes
   d. Coffee
7. Which of the following nations was most persistently committed to converting the natives of the newly discovered regions to Christianity?
   a. Spain
   b. Holland
   c. England
   d. Portugal
8. Albuquerque was instrumental in
   a. bringing the colony of Goa under Portuguese dominion.
   b. bringing the first Christian missionaries to China.
   c. bringing Brazil under the flag of Portugal.
   d. opening the Red Sea passage for Europeans.
9. The most devastating effects on the native population brought about by European discovery was in
   a. India.
   b. Latin America.
   c. West Africa.
   d. Southeast Asia.
10. Mercantilism aimed first of all at
    a. securing financial rewards for the entrepreneurs.
    b. allowing the impoverished a chance at rising in society.
    c. bringing maximal income to the royal throne.
    d. securing favorable balance of foreign trade.

IDENTIFICATION TERMS

Albuquerque, Alfonso de
Columbian Exchange
Cortez, Hernan
de Las Casas, Bartolome
Diaz, Bartolomeo
Macao
Magellan, Ferdinand
mercantilism
mestizo
mulatto
Vespucci, Amerigo

INFOTRAC COLLEGE EDITION

Enter the search terms "Vasco da Gama" using Key Words.
Enter the search terms "Christopher Columbus" using the Subject Guide.

Enter the search term "mercantilism" using the Subject Guide.

Chapter 27

The Protestant Reformation

I have often been resolved to live uprightly, and to lead a true godly life, and to set everything aside that would hinder this, but it was far from being put in execution. I am not able to effect that good which I intend. . . .

MARTIN LUTHER

THE SPLIT IN CHRISTIAN belief that is termed the Protestant Reformation brought enormous consequences in its wake. Its beginning coincided with the high point of the era of discovery by Europeans. Taken together, these events provide the basis for dividing Western civilization's history into the premodern and modern eras around the year 1500. What the opening up of the transatlantic and trans–Indian Ocean worlds did for the consciousness of physical geography in European minds, the Reformation did for the mental geography of all Christians. New continents of belief and identity emerged from the spiritual voyages of the early Protestants. Luther and Calvin worked not only a reformation but also a transformation of the church and its members.

Luther and the German National Church

The upheaval called the Reformation of the early sixteenth century had its roots in political and social developments as much as in religious disputes. The long-standing arguments within the Christian community over various points of doctrine or practices had already led to rebellions against the Rome-led majority on several occasions. In the major affairs in thirteenth-century France, fourteenth-century England, and fifteenth-century Bohemia, religious rebels (the official term is *heretics,* or "wrong thinkers") had battled the papal church. Eventually, all of them had been suppressed or driven underground.

But now, in sixteenth-century Germany, **Martin Luther** (1483–1546) found an enthusiastic reception for his challenges to Rome among the majority of his fellow Germans. Why were they particularly susceptible to the call for reform? The disintegration of the German medieval kingdom had been followed by the birth of dozens of separate, little principalities and city-states, such as Hamburg and Frankfurt, that could not well resist the encroachments of the powerful papacy in their internal affairs. Unlike the nations of centrally governed France, England, and Spain, whose monarchs jealously guarded their sources of revenue, the German populations were systematically milked by Rome and forced to pay taxes and involuntary donations. Many of the German rulers were becoming angry at seeing the tax funds they needed going off to a foreign power and sometimes used for goals they did not support. These rulers were eagerly searching for some excuse to challenge Rome. They found it in the teachings of Luther.

Luther was a monk who had witnessed at first hand the corruption and crass commercialism of the Roman *curia* (court). When he returned to the University of Wittenberg in Saxony, where he had been appointed chaplain, he used his powerful oratory to arouse the community against the abuses he had seen. He especially opposed the church's practice of selling *indulgences*—forgiveness of the spiritual guilt created by sins—rather than insisting that the faithful earn forgiveness by prayer and good works.

In 1517, a major indulgence sales campaign opened in Germany under even more scandalous pretexts than usual. Much of the money raised was destined to be used to pay off a debt incurred by an ambitious noble churchman, rather than for any ecclesiastical purpose. Observing what was happening, the chaplain at Wittenberg decided to take his stand. On October 31, 1517, Luther announced his discontent by posting the famous **Ninety-five Theses** on his church door. In these questions, Luther raised objections not only to many of the papacy's practices such as indulgence campaigns but also to the whole doctrine of papal supremacy. He contended that if the papacy had ever been intended by God to be the moral mentor of the Christian community, it had lost that claim through its present corruption.

Luther's Beliefs

Luther had more profound doubts about the righteousness of the papal church than merely its claims to universal leadership, however. His youth had been a long struggle against the conviction that he was damned to hell. Intensive study of the Bible eventually convinced him that only through the freely given grace of a merciful God might he, or any person, reach salvation.

The Catholic church, on the other hand, taught that men and women must manifest their Christian faith by doing good works and leading good lives. If they did so, they might be considered to have earned a heavenly future. Martin Luther rejected this. He believed that faith alone was the factor through which Christians might reach bliss in the afterlife and that faith was given by God and not in any way earned by naturally sinful man. It is this doctrine of **justification by faith** that most clearly marks off Lutheranism from the papal teachings.

As the meaning of Luther's statements penetrated into the clerical hierarchy, he was implored, then commanded to cease. Instead, his confidence rose, and in a series of brilliantly forceful pamphlets, he explained his views to a rapidly increasing audience of Germans. By 1520 he was becoming a household word among educated people and even among the peasantry. In 1521 he was excommunicated by the pope for refusing to recant, and in the same year, he was declared an outlaw by Emperor Charles V.

The Catholic emperor was an ally of the pope but had his hands full with myriad other problems, notably the Ottoman Turks. Charles had no desire to add an unnecessary civil war to the long list of tasks he faced. He took action against Luther only belatedly and halfheartedly, hoping that in some way an acceptable compromise might be reached.

Threatened by the imperial and papal officials, Luther sought and quickly found the protection of the ruler of Saxony, as well as much of the German princely class. They saw in his moral objections to Rome the excuse they had been seeking for advancing their political aspirations. They encouraged Luther to organize a national church free from papal overlords.

Martin Luther. This contemporary portrait by Lucas V. Cranach is generally considered to be an accurate rendition of the great German church reformer in midlife. Both the strengths and weaknesses of Luther's peasant character are revealed. (© *The Granger Collection*)

With this protection and encouragement, Luther's teachings spread rapidly, aided by the newly invented printing press and by the power and conviction of his sermons and writings, which were in German (rather than the traditional Latin). By the mid-1520s, Lutheran congregations, rejecting the papal authority and condemning Rome as the fount of all evil, had sprung up throughout most of Germany and were appearing in Scandinavia as well. The unity of Western Christianity had been shattered.

Calvin and International Protestantism

❋

It was not Luther, the German peasant's son, but **John Calvin** (1509–1564), the French lawyer, who made the Protestant movement an international theological rebellion against Rome. Luther always saw himself as a specifically German patriot, as well as a pious Christian, and his translations of the Scriptures were written in a powerful idiomatic German. (Luther's role in creating the modern German language is roughly the same as that Shakespeare played in the development of English.) Calvin, on the contrary, detached himself from national feeling and saw himself as the emissary and servant of a God who ruled all nations. Luther wanted the German Christian body to be cleansed of papal corruption; Calvin wanted the entire Christian community to be made over into the image of

❀ **John Calvin.** This Flemish portrait of the "pope of Geneva" in his younger days depicts Calvin in a fur neckpiece. This bit of bourgeois indulgence would not have been worn by an older Calvin. (© *Erich Lessing/Art Resource*)

what he thought God intended. When he was done, a good part of it had been.

Calvin was born into a middle-class family of church officeholders who educated him for a career in the law. When he was twenty-five, he became a Protestant, inspired by some Swiss sympathizers with Luther. For most of the rest of his life, Calvin was "the pope of Geneva," laying down the law to that city's residents and having a major influence on much of the rest of Europe's religious development.

Calvin believed that the papal church was hopelessly distorted. It must be obliterated, and new forms and practices (which were supposedly a return to the practices of early Christianity) must be introduced. In *The Institutes of the Christian Religion* (1536), Calvin set out his beliefs and doctrines with the precision and clarity of a lawyer. From this work came much of the intellectual content of Protestantism for the next 200 years.

Calvin's single most dramatic change from both Rome and Luther was his insistence that God predestined souls. That is, a soul was meant either for heaven or hell for all eternity. But at the same time, the individual retained free will to choose good or evil. The soul destined for hell would inevitably choose evil—but did not have to! It was a harsh theology. Calvin believed that humanity had been eternally stained by Adam's sin and that the majority of souls were destined for hellfire.

Despite its doctrinal fierceness, Calvin's message found a response throughout Europe. By the 1540s, Calvinists were appearing in Germany, the Netherlands, Scotland, England, and France, as well as Switzerland. Geneva had become the Protestant Rome, with Calvin serving as its priestly ruler until his death in 1564.

Calvinism and Lutheranism Compared

What were some of the similarities and differences between the beliefs of Luther and Calvin (who never met and had little affection for one another)? First, Luther believed that faith alone, which could not be earned, was the only prerequisite for salvation. Good works were encouraged, of course, but they had little or no influence on the Last Judgment. Calvin demanded works as well as faith to indicate that a person was attempting to follow God's order on Earth.

Later Calvinists saw their performance of good works as a mark that they were among the Elect, the souls predestined for heaven. The emphasis in some places and times shifted subtly from doing good works as a sign of serving God to believing that God would logically favor the members of the Elect. Therefore, those who were "doing well" in the earthly sense were probably among the Elect. From this, some later students of religion saw Calvinist beliefs as the basis for the triumph of the capitalist spirit in certain parts of Europe. In effect, God could rationally be expected to smile on those who did his bidding in this life as well as the next.

✿ **The Calvinist Church.** This painting is by a Dutch sixteenth-century master, H. Steenwik, who portrays the "purified" interior of the Antwerp cathedral after it was taken over by Calvinists. Contrast this church with the interior of St. Denis presented in Chapter 23. (© *The Bridgeman Art Library*)

Second, Luther saw the clergy as civic as well as spiritual guides for mankind. He believed in a definite hierarchy of authority within the church, and he retained bishops, who maintained their power to appoint priests. In time, the Lutheran pastors and bishops became fully dependent on the state that employed them, rarely defying it on moral grounds. Lutheranism became a state church, not only in Germany but also in Scandinavia where it had become dominant by the mid-1500s. In contrast, Calvin insisted on the moral independence of the church from the state. He maintained that the clergy had a duty to oppose any immoral acts of government, no matter what the cost to themselves. In conflicts between the will of God and the will of kings, the Calvinist must enlist on the side of God.

More than Lutherans, the Calvinists thought of the entire community, lay and clerical alike, as equal members of the church on Earth. Calvinists also insisted on the power of the congregation to select and discharge pastors at will, inspired by God's word. They never established a hierarchy of clerics. There were no Calvinist bishops but only presbyters, or elected elders, who spoke for their fellow parishioners. The government of the church included both clerical and lay leaders. The combination gave its pronouncements great moral force.

By around 1570, Calvin's followers had gained control of the Christian community in several places: the Dutch-speaking Netherlands, Scotland, western France, and parts of northern Germany and Poland. In the rest of France, Austria, Hungary, and England, they were still a minority, but a growing one. Whereas Lutheranism was confined to the German-speaking countries and Scandinavia and did not spread much after 1550 or so, Calvinism was an international faith that appealed to all nations and identified with none. Carried on the ships of the Dutch and English explorers and emigrants of the seventeenth and eighteenth centuries, it continued to spread throughout the modern world.

Other Early Protestant Faiths

✿ *The original name for Baptist is*

The followers of a radical sect called **Anabaptists** (Rebaptizers) were briefly a threat to both Catholics and Lutherans, but they were put down with extreme cruelty by both. The Anabaptists originated in Switzerland and spread rapidly throughout German Europe. They believed in adult baptism, a priesthood of all believers, and—most disturbingly—a primitive communism and sharing of worldly possessions. Both as radicals in religious affairs and as social revolutionaries, the Anabaptists were oppressed by all their neighbors. After their efforts to establish a republic in the Rhineland city of Münster were bloodily suppressed, the Anabaptists were driven underground. They emerged much later in the New World as Mennonites, Amish, and similar groups.

Yet another Protestant creed emerged very early in Switzerland (which was a hotbed of religious protest). Founded by Ulrich Zwingli (1484–1531), it was generally very similar to Lutheran belief, although Zwingli claimed he had arrived at his doctrine independently. The inability of Zwingli's adherents and the Lutherans to cooperate left Zwingli's stronghold in Zurich open to attack by the Catholic Swiss. The Protestants were defeated in the battle, and Zwingli himself was killed. This use of bloody force to settle religious strife was an ominous note. It was to be increasingly common as Protestant beliefs spread and undermined the traditional religious structures.

✤ **A Protestant View of the Pope.** Clothed in hellish splendor and hung about with the horrible symbols of Satan, the Roman pope is revealed for all to see, in this sixteenth-century cartoon. (© *Stock Montage, Inc.*)

The Church of England

As was often the case, England went its own way. The English Reformation differed from the Reformation on the Continent yet followed the general trend of European affairs. The English reformers were originally inspired by Lutheran ideas, but they adopted more Calvinist views as time went on. However, the Church of England, or Anglican Confession, came to be neither Lutheran, nor Calvinist, nor Catholic, but a hybrid of all three.

The reform movement in England had its origins in the widespread popular resentment against Rome and the higher clergy who were viewed as more the tools of the pope than as good English patriots. As we have seen, already in the 1300s a group called the Lollards had rebelled against the clerical claim to sole authority in interpreting the word of God and papal supremacy. The movement had been put down, but its memory persisted in many parts of England.

But it was the peculiar marital problems of King **Henry VIII** (1490–1547) that brought the church in England into conflict with Rome. Henry needed a male successor, but by the late 1520s, his chances of having one with his elderly Spanish wife Catherine were bleak. Therefore, he wanted to have the marriage annulled by the pope (who alone had that power), so that he could marry some young Englishwoman who would presumably be able to produce the desired heir.

After trying to evade the issue for years, the pope refused, for reasons that were partly political and partly moral. Between 1532 and 1534, Henry took the matter into his own hands. Still believing himself to be a good Catholic, he intimidated Parliament into declaring him the "only supreme head of the church in England"—the **Act of Supremacy** of 1534. Now, as head of the church, Henry could dictate to the English bishops. He proceeded to put away his unwanted wife and marry the tragic Anne Boleyn, already pregnant with his child.

Much other legislation followed that asserted that the monarch, and not the Roman pope, was the determiner of what the church could and could not do in England. Those who resisted, such as the king's chancellor Thomas More, paid with their heads or were imprisoned. Henry went on to marry and divorce several more times before his death in 1547, but he did at least secure a son, the future King Edward VI, from one of these unhappy alliances. Two daughters also survived, the half-sisters Mary and Elizabeth.

Henry's Successors Henry's actions changed English religious beliefs very little although the Calvinist reformation was gaining ground in both England and Scotland. But under the sickly boy-king Edward (ruled 1547–1553), Protestant views became dominant among the English governing group, and the Scots were led by the powerful oratory of John Knox into Calvinism (the Presbyterian church). At Edward's death, it seemed almost certain that some form of Protestant worship would become the official church.

But popular support for Mary (ruled 1553–1558), the Catholic daughter of Henry VIII's first wife, was too strong to be overridden by the Protestant party at court. Just as they had feared, Mary proved to be a single-minded adherent of the papal church, and she restored Catholicism to its official status during her brief reign. Protestant conspirators were put to death without hesitation (hence, she is called "Bloody Mary" in English Protestant mythology).

Finally, the confused state of English official religion was gradually cleared by the political skills of Mary's half-sister and successor, **Elizabeth I** (ruled 1558–1603). She ruled for half a century with great success while defying all royal traditions by remaining the Virgin Queen and dying childless (see the Law and Lawgivers box). She was able to arrive at a compromise between the Roman and Protestant doctrines, which was accepted by a steadily increasing majority and came to be termed the Church of England. In most respects, it retained the theology and doctrine of the Roman church, including bishops, rituals, and sacraments. But its head was not the pope but the English monarch, who appointed the bishops and their chief, the archbishop of Canterbury. The strict Calvinists were not happy with this arrangement and wished to "purify" the church by removing all remnants of popery. These **Puritans** presented problems for the English rulers throughout the seventeenth century.

The Counter-Reformation

❊

Belatedly realizing what a momentous challenge was being mounted, the papacy finally came to grips with the problem of Protestantism in a positive fashion during the 1540s. Pope Paul III (served 1534–1549) moved to counter some of the excesses that had given the Roman authorities a bad name and set up a high-level commission to see what might be done to "clean up" the clergy. Eventually, the church decided to pursue two major lines of counterattack against the Protestants: a thorough examination of doctrines and practices, such as had not been attempted for more than 1,000 years, combined with an entirely novel emphasis on instruction of the young and education of all Christians in the precepts of their religion.

The **Council of Trent** (1545–1563) was the first general attempt to examine the church's basic doctrines and goals since the days of the Roman Empire. Meeting for three lengthy sessions divided by years of preparatory work, the bishops and theologians decided that Protestant attacks could best be met by clearly and conclusively defining what Catholics believed. (Protestants were invited to attend, but only as observers; none did.) As a means of strengthening

religious practice, this was a positive move, for the legitimacy of many church doctrines had come increasingly into doubt since the 1300s. But the council's work had an unintended negative effect on the desired reunification of Christianity: the doctrinal lines separating Catholic and Protestant were now firmly drawn, and they could not be ignored or blurred by the many individuals in both camps who had been trying to arrange a compromise. Now one side or the other would have to give in on specific issues, a prospect neither side was prepared for.

The founding of the **Jesuit Order** was the most striking example of the second aspect of the Counter-Reformation. In 1540 Pope Paul III accorded to the Spanish nobleman Ignatius of Loyola the right to organize an entirely new religious group, which he termed the Society of Jesus, or Jesuits. Their mission was to win, or win back, the minds and hearts of humanity for the Catholic church through patient, careful instruction that would bring the word of God and of his deputy on earth, the pope, to everyone. While the Jesuits were working to ensure that all Catholics learned correct doctrine, the *Index* of forbidden books was created and the **Inquisition** revived to ensure that no Catholic deviated from that doctrine. These institutions greatly expanded the church's powers to censor the writings and supervise the beliefs of its adherents. Both became steadily more important in Catholic countries during the next century, as what both sides regarded as a contest between ultimate Truth and abhorrent falsity intensified.

Religious Wars and Their Outcomes to 1600

❊

The Counter-Reformation stiffened the Catholics' will to resist the Lutheran and Calvinist attacks, which had, at first, almost overwhelmed the unprepared and inflexible Roman authorities. By 1555, the **Peace of Augsburg** had concluded a ten-year civil war by dividing Germany into Catholic and Lutheran parcels, but it made no allowances for the growing number of Calvinists or other Protestants.

In the rest of Europe, the picture was mixed by the late 1500s (see Map 27.1). England, as we have just seen, went through several changes of religious leadership, but eventually emerged with a special sort of Protestant belief as its official religion. Scandinavia became Lutheran in its entirety, almost without violence. Austria, Hungary, and Poland remained mostly Catholic, but with large minorities of Calvinists and Lutherans who received a degree of tolerance from the authorities. Spain and Italy had successfully repelled the Protestant challenge, and the counter reform was in full swing. Russia and southeastern Europe were almost unaffected by Protestantism, being either hostile to both varieties of Western Christianity (Russia) or under the

Elizabeth I of England
(1533–1603)

*I*n the late sixteenth century, England became for the first time a power to be reckoned with in world affairs. What had been an island kingdom with little direct influence on any other country except its immediate neighbors across the Channel gradually reached equality with the other major Western military and naval powers: France and Spain. But England's achievement was not just in military affairs. It also experienced a magnificent flowering of the arts and a solid advance in the economy, which finally lifted the nation out of the long depression that had followed the fourteenth-century plague and the long, losing war with France.

The guiding spirit for this comeback was Elizabeth I, queen of England from 1558 until her death in 1603. The daughter of Henry VIII and his second wife, the ill-fated Anne Boleyn, Elizabeth emerged from a heavily shadowed girlhood to become a remarkable queen and one of the most beloved of British lawgivers. Elizabeth was an intelligent, well-educated woman with gifts in several directions. One of her most remarkable achievements was that she managed to retain her powers without a husband, son, or father in the still very male-oriented world in which she moved.

Born in 1533, she was only three years old when her mother was executed. She was declared illegitimate by order of the disappointed Henry, who had wished for a son. But after her father's death, Parliament established her as third in line to the throne, behind her half-brother Edward and her Catholic half-sister Mary. During Mary's reign (1553–1558), Elizabeth was imprisoned for a time, but she was careful to stay clear of the hectic Protestant-Catholic struggles of the day. By so doing, she managed to stay alive until she could become ruler in her own right.

Her rule began amid many internal and external dangers. The Catholic party in England opposed her as a suspected Protestant. The Calvinists opposed her as being too much like her father Henry, who never accepted Protestant theology. The Scots were becoming rabid Calvinists who despised the English halfway measures in religious affairs. On top of this, the government was deeply in debt.

Contrary to all predictions, Elizabeth showed great insight in selecting her officials and maintained good relations with Parliament. She conducted diplomatic affairs with a caution and farsightedness that England had not seen for many years and found she could use her status as an unmarried queen to definite advantage. Philip of Spain, widower of her half-sister Mary, made several proposals of marriage and political unity that Elizabeth cleverly held off without ever quite saying no. She kept England out of the religious wars raging in various parts of Europe for most of her reign. But it was in one of these wars, against her ex-suitor Philip, that the Virgin Queen led her people most memorably.

In 1588, after long negotiations failed, Philip sent the Spanish Armada to punish England for aiding the Dutch Calvinists across the Channel (the Netherlands at that time were a Spanish possession). The queen rallied her own sailors in a stirring visit before the battle. The resulting defeat of the Armada not only signaled England's rise to naval equality with Spain but also made Elizabeth the most popular monarch England had ever seen.

A golden age of English literature coincided with Elizabeth's rule, thanks in some part to her active support of all the arts. Her well-known vanity induced her to spend large sums to ensure the splendor of her court despite her equally well-known miserliness. The Elizabethan Age produced Shakespeare, Marlowe, Spenser, and Bacon. By the end of the sixteenth century, English literature for the first time could hold a place of honor in any assembly of national arts.

Elizabeth's version of Protestant belief—the Church of England—was acceptable to the large majority of her subjects and finally settled the very stormy waves of English church affairs. Although she may not have been beloved by all at the end of her long reign, still "Good Queen Bess" had become a stock phrase that most people believed, from barons to peasants.

Elizabeth I of England. The Armada Portrait, perhaps the most famous, was painted by an anonymous artist in the late sixteenth century. (© Bridgeman/Art Resource)

For Reflection

Given that an unmarried queen was considered a political risk, what reasons of state could have impelled Elizabeth to remain "the Virgin Queen"? What political capital did she make out of creating the hybrid Church of England that otherwise would have been denied her?

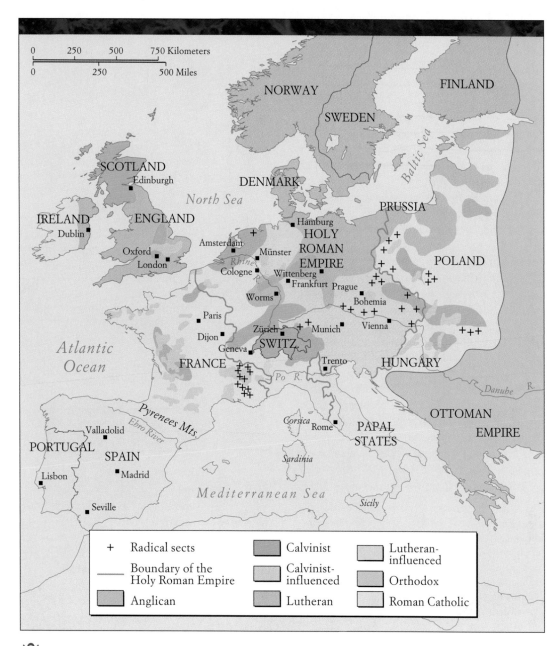

🏵 **MAP 27.1   Catholics, Protestants, and Orthodox Christians in Europe by 1550.** The radical sects included Unitarians in eastern Europe, Anabaptists in Bohemia and Germany, and Waldensians in France. All of these rejected the idea of a privileged clergy and a priestly hierarchy.

political control of Muslims. In two countries, however, the issue of religious affiliation was in hot dispute and caused much bloodshed in the later 1500s.

France

France remained Catholic at the level of the throne, but developed a large, important Calvinist minority, especially among the nobility and the urbanites. For a brief time the Catholic monarchs and the Calvinists attempted to live with one another, but in the 1570s religious wars began that

threatened to wreck the country. The Violence and Coercion box on the St. Bartholomew's Day Massacre gives an eyewitness view of the violence.

After some years, the Calvinists found a politician of genius, Henry of Navarre, who profited from the assassination of his Catholic rival to become King Henry IV of France. In 1593 he agreed to accept Catholicism to win the support of most French ("Paris is worth a mass," he is reported to have said). He became the most popular king in French history. His Protestant upbringing inspired the Calvinist minority to trust him, and he did not disappoint them.

The St. Bartholomew's Day Massacre

During the sixteenth-century religious wars in Europe, no battlefield was contested more ferociously by both sides than France. Not only did France contain Europe's largest population, but it lay between the Protestant North and the Catholic South. Though the bulk of the peasantry and the royal family remained Catholic, an influential and determined minority of nobles and bourgeoisie became Calvinists, or "Huguenots."

By 1572, because of the political astuteness of their leader Gaspard de Coligny, the Huguenots were close to a takeover of the French government. However, the queen mother, Catherine de Medici, and the Catholic warlord Henry, duke de Guise, turned the weak-minded King Charles IX against Coligny. The result was a conspiracy that began with Coligny's assassination on August 24, 1572 (St. Bartholomew's Day) and quickly degenerated into a wholesale massacre of the entire Protestant population of Paris: men, women, and children. The death toll is estimated to have approached 10,000, and the streets and alleys reeked of the stench of decaying corpses for weeks afterward.

According to an anonymous Protestant who was among the fortunate few to escape the carnage, vicious cruelties were committed without number, setting the scene for what would become twenty years of intermittent civil war in France:

> In an instant, the whole city was filled with dead bodies of every sex and age, and indeed amid such confusion and disorder that everyone was allowed to kill whoever he pleased, whether or not that person belonged to the [Protestant] religion, provided that he had something to be taken, or was an enemy. So it came about that many Papists themselves were slain, even several priests. . . . Nevertheless, the main fury fell on our people; and to provide better quarry for the murderers, they were permitted to loot and plunder houses, so that by the same means thieves, pickpockets, and other robbers and loafers, always numerous, moved all the more actively against us in the hope of booty. . . .
>
> No one can count the many cruelties that accompanied these murders. . . . Most of them were run through with daggers or poniards; their bodies were stabbed, their members mutilated, they were mocked and insulted with gibes sharper than pointed swords . . . they knocked several old people senseless, banging their heads against the stones of the quay and then throwing them half dead into the water [the Seine River]. A little child in swaddling clothes was dragged through the streets with a belt round his neck by boys nine or ten years old. Another small child, carried by one of the butchers, played with the man's beard and smiled up at him, but instead of being moved to compassion, the barbarous fiend ran him through with his dagger, then threw him into the water so red with blood that it did not return to its original color for a long time. . . .
>
> [T]he continuous shooting of arquebusses and pistols, the lamentable and frightful cries of those they slaughtered, the yells of the murderers, the bodies thrown from windows . . . can only bring before the eyes of the reader an unforgettable picture of the calamity appalling in every way.

For Reflection

What recent world event or events does this picture of religious hate bring to mind from history of the last several years? Do you think that sixteenth-century Frenchmen were any different in their cruelty and their willingness to assault persons of their own faith from modern religious fanatics?

SOURCE: Excerpted from Julian Coudy, *The Huguenot Wars*, trans. Julie Kernon (Radnor, PA: Chilton, 1969).

In 1598 Henry made the first significant attempt at religious toleration as state policy by issuing the **Edict of Nantes.** It gave the million or so French Calvinists—the Huguenots—freedom to worship without harassment in certain areas, to hold office, and to fortify their towns. This last provision demonstrates that the edict was more in the nature of a truce than a peace. It held, however, for the better part of a century. During that time, France rose to become the premier power in Europe.

The Spanish Netherlands

The Spanish Netherlands (modern Holland and Belgium) were ruled from Madrid by King Philip II, the most potent monarch of the second half of the sixteenth century. He had inherited an empire that included Spain, much of Italy, and the Low Countries in Europe plus the enormous Spanish overseas empire begun by the voyages of Columbus.

But Philip was a man with a mission, or rather two missions: the reestablishment of Catholicism among the Protestant "heretics" and the defeat of the Muslim Turks in the Mediterranean and the Near East. These missions imposed heavy demands on Spanish resources, which even the flow of gold and silver out of the American colonies could not fully cover. Generally successful in his wars against the Turks, Philip could not handle a combined political-religious revolt against Spain's recently acquired province of the Netherlands that broke out in the 1560s. The Netherlands were a hotbed of both Lutheran and

Calvinist doctrines, and the self-confident members of the large middle class were much disturbed at the Spanish aliens' attempt to enforce on them the Counter-Reformation and papal supremacy.

Thanks to Spanish overextension, the revolt of the Netherlanders succeeded in holding Philip's feared professional army at bay. The wars were fought with ferocity on both sides. While Philip saw himself as the agent of legitimacy and the Counter-Reformation, the Dutch rebels were aided militarily and financially by the English Protestants across the Channel. The English support was due in part to religious affinity, but even more to the traditional English dislike of a great power's control of England's closest trading partners.

In the mid-1580s, the friction came to a head. Philip (who had earlier tried to convince Elizabeth I to become his wife) became incensed at the execution of the Catholic queen of Scots by order of Elizabeth, who had imprisoned this possible competitor for England's throne. With the reluctant support of the pope, Philip prepared the vast Armada of 1588 to invade England and reconquer that country for the "True Church."

The devastating defeat of the Armada—as much by a storm as by English ships—gave a great boost to the Protestant cause everywhere. It relieved the pressure on the Huguenots to accept Catholic overlordship in France. It saved the Dutch Calvinists until they could gain full independence some decades later. And the defeat of the Armada marks the emergence of England as a major power, both in Europe and overseas.

Spain remained the premier military power long after the Armada disaster, but the country in a sense never recovered from this event. Other fleets were built, bullion from Mexican and Peruvian mines continued to pour into Madrid's treasury, and the Spanish infantry were still the best trained and equipped of all the European armies, but the other powers were able to keep Spain in check from now on, until its inherent economic weaknesses reduced it to a second-line nation in the seventeenth century.

The Legacy of the Reformation

The Protestant movement made a very deep impression on the general course of history in Europe for centuries. It is one of the reasons European history is conventionally divided into "modern" versus "medieval" around the year 1500. The religious unity of all western Europe was irrevocably shattered, and with the end of such unity inevitably came political and cultural conflicts. For a century and a half after Luther's defiance of the papal command to be

silent, much of Europe was engaged in internal acrimony that wracked the continent from the Netherlands to Hungary. In some countries such as Italy, Spain, and Sweden, one or the other faith was dominant and proceeded to harass and exile those who thought differently. Separation of church and state was not even dreamed of, nor was freedom of conscience. These are strictly modern ideas and were not seriously taken up by educated persons until the eighteenth century.

In the Protestant societies, the abolition of the monasteries and convents and the emphasis on vernacular preaching helped integrate the clergy and the laity and thus blurred one of the chief class divisions that had been accepted in Europe since the opening of the Middle Age. Combined with the important roles of the middle-class Protestants in spreading and securing reform, this development provided new opportunities for the ambitious and hardworking to rise up the social ladder.

Some of the other long-term cultural changes that resulted from the Reformation included the following:

1. *Higher literacy and start of mass education.* In much of Protestant Europe in particular, the exhortation to learn and obey Scripture provided an incentive to read that the common folk had never had before. The rapid spread of printing after 1520 was largely due to Protestant tracts and the impact they were seen to have on their large audiences.
2. *Emphasis on individual moral responsibility.* Rejecting the Catholic assurance that the clergy knew best what was necessary and proper in the conduct of life, the Protestants underlined the responsibility of individual believers to determine through divine guidance and reading Scripture what they must do to attain salvation.
3. *Closer identification of the clergy with the people they served.* Both the Catholic and Protestant churches came to recognize that the church existed as much for the masses of faithful as it did for the clergy—a realization that was often absent previously—and that the belief of the faithful was the essence of the church on Earth.
4. *Increase in conflicts and intolerance.* Much of Europe fell into civil wars that were initially set off by religious disputes. These wars were often bloody and produced much needless destruction by both sides in the name of theological truth. Religious affiliation greatly exacerbated dynastic and the emergent national conflicts.

The Catholic-Protestant clashes led to intellectual arrogance and self-righteousness not only in religion but in general among those who wielded power. Open debate and discussion of contested matters became almost impossible between the two parts of Western Christianity for a century or more.

SUMMARY

As much as the discovery of the New World, the Protestant movement gave birth to the modern era in the West. The protests of Luther, Calvin, and many others against what they saw as the unrighteous and distorted teachings of the Roman papacy had immense long-term reverberations in Western culture. The reformers combined a new emphasis on individual morality with assertions of the ability and duty of Christians to read the Gospels and take into their own hands the search for salvation.

Among Calvinists, the material welfare of the Elect on Earth was linked to their quality of being saved, a link that would gradually produce what later generations called the

"Protestant ethic." The Catholic response was the Counter-Reformation, which, spearheaded by the Jesuits, eventually reclaimed much of the Protestant territories for the Roman church at the cost of an alarming rise in religiously inspired conflict. Warfare of an unprecedentedly bloody nature broke out in the Netherlands and in France and Germany between groups asserting their possession of the only correct theology. Europe entered the Modern Age in a flurry of fierce antagonisms among Christians, some of which were to continue for generations and permanently split apart previous communities.

TEST YOUR KNOWLEDGE

1. The posting of the *Ninety-five Theses* was immediately caused by
   a. Luther's outrage over the ignorance of the clergy.
   b. Luther's conviction that he must challenge papal domination.
   c. Luther's anger over the sale of indulgences.
   d. the tyranny of the local Roman Catholic bishop.
2. Which of the following practices/beliefs is associated with Calvinism?
   a. The basic goodness of humans
   b. Predestination of souls
   c. Religious freedom for all
   d. Indulgences
3. Henry VIII's reform of English religious organization occurred
   a. after study in the Holy Land.
   b. for primarily religious-doctrinal reasons.
   c. for primarily political-dynastic reasons.
   d. at the urging of the pope.
4. The Jesuit Order was founded specifically
   a. to train Catholic soldiers for battle.
   b. to recover through education fallen-away Catholics.
   c. to act as the pope's first-line troop in religious wars.
   d. to open a new type of monastery.
5. Which of the following countries remained most strongly attached to Rome in the wake of the Reformation?
   a. Scotland
   b. France
   c. The Netherlands
   d. Spain

6. The term *Counter-Reformation* applies to
   a. a movement in Germany aimed at extinguishing the Lutherans.
   b. the strong resistance of the Roman clergy to real reforms.
   c. a Europe-wide campaign to win back the Protestants to Rome.
   d. the political and military efforts of the German emperor to crush the Protestants.
7. The St. Bartholomew's Day bloodshed was
   a. the result of the Catholic fanatics' hatred of Protestants in France.
   b. the revenge of the English Calvinists on the English Catholics.
   c. the upshot of a failed attempt to overturn the Catholic dynasty in Spain.
   d. the slaughter of rebel peasantry in Flanders.
8. The *Edict of Nantes*
   a. expelled all Protestants from Catholic France.
   b. gave Protestants in France a degree of official toleration.
   c. brought civic and legal equality to Protestants in France.
   d. ended the war between Catholic France and Protestant England.
9. One of the chief negative effects of the Reformation on Europe was
   a. the lessening of educational opportunity.
   b. the loss of national identities.
   c. the diminished tolerance for variations from official doctrine.
   d. the decreased opportunities for social climbing.

Bibliography

PART ONE

Chapter 1

Cole, S. *The Neolithic Revolution,* 1970. Covers the Near East and parts of Europe.

Hallo, W., and W. K. Simpson. *The Ancient Near East,* 1971. A readable survey that examines both Mesopotamia and Egypt. Discusses mainly political affairs.

Jones, W. D. *Venus and Sothis: How the Ancient Near East Was Rediscovered,* 1982. Very interesting account of early archaeology.

Leakey, R. E., and R. Lewin. *Origins: What New Discoveries Reveal,* 1977. Well illustrated and controversial.

———. *The Making of Mankind,* 1981. Perhaps the best account of early hominids, heavily illustrated and clearly written. The author takes sharp issue with the conclusions of his father Louis Leakey on this topic.

Quennell, M. C., and H. B. Quennell. *Everyday Life in the New Stone, Bronze, and Early Iron Ages,* 1955. One of the very best of the *Everyday Life* series.

Starr, C. G. *Early Man,* 1968. A brief, well-illustrated survey that discusses early Near Eastern civilizations as well as prehistory.

Chapter 2

Crawford, H. *Sumer and the Sumerians,* 1991. More recent than Kramer, but not as witty.

Frankfort, H., et al. *Before Philosophy: The Intellectual Adventure of Ancient Man,* 1946.

Kramer, S. *History Begins at Sumer,* 1981. A classic rendition of why the Sumerians are important.

Mallowan, M. E. *Early Mesopotamia and Iran,* 1966. Strong on the technical achievements.

Saggs, H. F. *Civilization before Greece and Rome,* 1989. Very usable for the findings of the late twentieth century.

Chapter 3

Edwards, I. E. S. *The Pyramids of Egypt,* 1976. Covers the whole topic of pyramid building.

Frankfort, H. *Ancient Egyptian Religion,* 1948. By the grand master of Egyptology in this century.

Gardner, A. *Egypt of the Pharaohs,* 1966. Very readable; covers primarily the political and military events.

Hawkes, J. *King of the Two Lands,* 1966. A historical novel of Egypt by a distinguished archaeologist.

———. *Life in Mesopotamia, the Indus Valley, and Egypt,* 1973. The work of a much admired writer. Good on comparisons among the three places and their societies.

James, T. G. H. *Pharaoh's People: Scenes from Life in Imperial Egypt,* 1984. Interesting and worthwhile.

Michalowski, K. *Art of Ancient Egypt,* 1969.

Montet, P. *Everyday Life in Egypt in the Days of Ramses II,* 1958. An interesting contrast to the James book that looks at the same epoch.

Redford, D. *Akhnaten, the Heretic King,* 1984.

Chapter 4

Assyrians

Countenau, G. *Everyday Life in Assyria and Babylon,* 1954. An identical title was issued by H. W. F. Saggs in a revised edition in 1987.

Saggs, H. W. *The Babylonians,* 1995. Reflects the latest archaeological findings.

———. *The Might That Was Assyria,* 1984. Probably the best single work in English on this topic; perhaps more detail than students may wish.

Phoenicians

Harden, D. B. *The Phoenicians,* 1962. This text deals with the interrelations between Jews and their northern neighbors.

Moscati, S. *The Phoenicians,* 1971. A standard older work.

Sandars, N. *The Sea Peoples,* 1978. A standard work on the Phoenicians.

Persians

Boyce, M. *Zoroastrians: Their Religious Belief and Practices,* 1979.

Cook, J. M. *The Persian Empire,* 1983.

Frye, G. *The Heritage of Persia,* 1963. More concise and easier to read than Olmstead's large work, as is the next entry.

Ghirshman, R. *Persia: From the Origins to Alexander the Great,* 1964.

Olmstead, A. T. *History of the Persian Empire,* 1948. The place to find all the answers, including those to questions you never thought to ask.

Jews

Bright, J. *A History of Israel,* 1981. As near as one can come to a standard American treatment.

Davies, W. D., and L. Finkelstine, eds. *The Cambridge History of Judaism,* 1984–1987. The first volumes to appear of what will be a standard history.

Hopfe, L. M. *Religions of the World,* 1991. Good introduction to Judaism.

Kaufman, Y. *The Religion of Israel,* 1960.

Maly, E. H. *The World of David and Solomon,* 1966. A popularized account of the Jews' daily life.

Schwartz, L. W., ed. *Great Ages and Ideas of the Jewish People,* 1956. A good introduction to the biblical Jews.

Shanks, H. *Ancient Israel: A Short History from Abraham to the Destruction of the Temple,* 1988.

Wurmbrand, M., et al. *The Jewish People: 4000 Years of Survival,* 1967. Less detailed than *The Cambridge History* but brilliantly illustrated.

Chapter 5

Basham, A. L. *The Wonder That Was India,* 1959. With its many photos and maps, possibly the best introduction to the Indus valley civilization. More up-to-date but not as readable as D. P. Agrawal, *The Archaeology of India,* 1982, and S. F. Mahmud, *A Concise History of Indo-Pakistan,* 1988.

Burtt, E. A. *The Teachings of the Compassionate Buddha,* 1955. Recommended for those interested in what this religion has to say to modern men and women.

Chandhuri, N. C. *Hinduism: A Religion to Live By,* 1979.

Humphreys, C. *Buddhism,* 1962, and *The Wisdom of Buddhism,* 1979. Two studies by a leading Western interpreter of Buddhism. Both are meant for beginners.

Radhakrishnan, S. *The Hindu View of Life,* 1926; many reprints. Focuses on Hindu religion and philosophy.

Thapar, R. *History of India,* 1966. A fine work by one of the best Indian historians. There is a good chapter on the Aryan society at the time of the conquest/penetration.

Wheeler, R. E. *Civilization of the Indus Valley and Beyond,* 1966. Looks at the excavations of Harappa in the twentieth century.

Chapter 6

Creel, H. G. *The Birth of China,* 1967. A good introduction to Chinese history.

———. *What Is Taoism?* 1959, and *Confucius and the Chinese Way,* 1960. Outstanding explanations of these religions/philosophies by one of the best interpreters of early China to English speakers.

Fairbank, J. K., et al. *East Asia: Tradition and Transformation,* 1973. Deals with both Japan and China.

Goldschmidt, D. L., and J. C. Moreau-Gobard. *Chinese Art,* 1962. Includes many first-rate photos of early Chinese paintings and bronzework.

Karlgren, B. *The Chinese Language,* 1949. Makes this obscure topic come alive and demonstrates how important a single written language was for Chinese history.

Liu, Z. *Ancient India and Ancient China,* 1988. Sheds light on both nations in early times.

Loewe, M. *Imperial China,* 1965. Its early sections are a good place to begin with Chinese history.

Schirokauer, C. *A Brief History of the Chinese and Japanese Civilizations,* 1989. Shorter than Fairbank et al., *East Asia,* but not better.

Smith, B. *China: A History of Art,* n.d. Many photos of early Chinese paintings and bronzework.

Sullivan, M. *The Arts of China,* 1984. Has good illustrations and a wide range.

Waley, A., trans. *Analects,* 1938. A very readable translation of the Confucian *Analects* and an introduction to Confucius's thought.

———. *Three Ways of Thought in Ancient China,* 1956. An easy introduction to the differences among Confucianism, Daoism, and Legalism.

Chapter 7

Beyond the items listed for Chapters 2 through 7 for specific civilizations, the *Everyday Life* series is a superior source of information on how people ate, worked, dressed, and so on in a given epoch or locale. Some are much more easily digested than others: browse through them to discover what is useful.

Loewe, M. *Everyday Life in Early Imperial China,* 1968.

Potter, K. H. *Guide to Indian Philosophy,* 1988. Casts light on many other topics besides formal philosophy.

Romer, J. *Ancient Lives: Daily Life in the Egypt of the Pharaohs,* 1984. A fine account of village life.

Saggs, H. W. F. *The Greatness That Was Babylon,* 1962, and *Everyday Life in Babylonia and Assyria,* 1987. Both look at society and its structures in the ancient Near East down to about the first century C.E.

Zhongshu, W. *Han Civilization,* 1982. Adds some detail on agriculture and architecture to Loewe's picture of early China.

PART TWO

Chapter 8

Bury, J. B., and R. Meiggs. *A History of Greece to the Death of Alexander,* 1975. One of the best general works on Greek history.

Cartledge, P. *Sparta and Lakonia,* 1979. An introduction to Spartan politics and government.

Fine, J. *The Ancient Greeks,* 1984. Another good general history.

Hornblower, S. *The Greek World 479–323 B.C.,* 1983. A good introduction to politics and government.

Iliad and *Odyssey.* Both are available in several readable translations, notably those in the Penguin Book edition.

Jones, A. H. *Athenian Democracy,* 1957. Deals with classical politics and government. An expert's book for students.

Just, R. *Women in Athenian Law and Life,* 1988. One of many recent books on the Greek female and family relations.

Lazenby, J. F. *The Spartan Army,* 1985. Looks at the institution that was so admired by the Greeks.

Meiggs, R. *The Athenian Empire,* 1972. A modern look at the Peloponnesian War.

Mueller, M. *The Iliad,* 1984. Good background on the Trojan War.

Pomeroy, S. B. *Goddesses, Whores, Wives and Slaves,* 1975. Another well-known book on Greek women and family relations.

Thucydides, *History of the Peloponnesian War.* A major work of ancient history that has come down to us intact. Written by a participant in the war.

Chapter 9

Bulfinch, T. *Mythology.* A classic work that tells the stories of mythology in a most entertaining way.

Burkert, W. *Greek Religion,* 1987. Deals with Classical Age religion and philosophy.

Dodds, E. R. *The Greeks and the Irrational,* 1951. A controversial study that sees the Greeks as a supremely passionate people.

Finley, M. I., ed. *Slavery in Classical Antiquity,* 1960. A good source for Greek slavery.

Kitto, H. D. F. *The Greeks,* many editions. A brief study that is very lucid and easily digested.

Lawrence, A. W. *Greek Architecture,* 1983. A standard treatment of the subject with many illustrations.

Osborne, R. *Demos,* 1985. See for slavery and Athenian society in general.

Pinsent, J. *Greek Mythology,* 1969. A clear overview of the Greeks' beliefs about the gods and the way different classes of society perceived them.

Richter, G. M. *Sculpture and Sculptors of the Greeks,* 1971. A richly illustrated treatment of painting and sculpture.

Sansone, D. *Greek Sport,* 1988. An illustrated work dealing with sport and its place in Greek life.

Chapter 10

Bowman, A. K. *Egypt after the Pharaohs,* 1986. Deals with the mixing of Greek and eastern cultures in Egypt.

Green, P. *Alexander of Macedon,* 1970. One of many biographies of Alexander. Well illustrated and readable.

Hamilton, J. R. *Alexander the Great,* 1973. Another readable and well-illustrated biography.

Lloyd, G. E. *Greek Science after Aristotle,* 1973. Deals with the development of the natural sciences in the Hellenistic Age.

Long, A. *Hellenistic Philosophy,* 1986. Examines the three major philosophies in detail.

Pollitt, J. *Art in the Hellenistic Age,* 1986. Shows how art forms reflect the mixing of Greek and Eastern traditions.

Rose, H. J. *Religion in Greece and Rome,* 1959. An examination of Hellenistic religions.

Tarn, W. W., and G. T. Griffith. *Hellenistic Civilization,* 1966. A good introduction.

Walbank, F. W. *The Hellenistic World,* 1981. Perhaps the best general history for students.

Chapter 11

Adcock, F. E. *Roman Political Ideas and Practice,* 1959. Clear and always to the point.

Gelzer, M. *Caesar, Politician and Statesman,* 1968. An informative biography.

Harris, W. V. *War and Imperialism in Republican Rome,* 1979. A broad treatment of Rome's expansion.

Heurgon, J. *The Rise of Rome to 264 B.C.,* 1973. Examines the Roman military establishment in clear detail.

Huzar, E. G. *Marc Antony,* 1987. A biography of an important late republican figure.

Lazenby, J. F. *Hannibal's War,* 1978. See for Hannibal and the Punic Wars.

Ogilvie, R. M. *The Romans and Their Gods,* 1970. An introduction to Roman religion.

Richardson, E. *The Etruscans: Their Art and Civilization,* 1964. An illustrated handbook to the influences of this rather mysterious people on early Rome.

Scullard, H. H. *Festivals and Ceremonies of the Roman Republic,* 1981. Explains how the Romans viewed their supernatural overseers and assistants.

Sherwin-White, A. N. *The Roman Citizenship,* 1973. A standard study of politics in the late republic.

Syme, R. *The Roman Revolution,* 1984. Another major study of late republican politics.

Note: Social and economic affairs are covered in the bibliography for Chapter 13.

Chapter 12

Benko, S. *Pagan Rome and Early Christianity,* 1985. A comprehensive study of Roman philosophy and pagan religion.

Campbell, J. *The Emperor and the Roman Army, 31 B.C. to A.D. 235,* 1984. Useful study of the military.

Duff, J. W. *Literary History of Rome from the Origins to the Close of the Golden Age,* 1953. A survey of Roman literature.

Gernsey, P., and R. Saller. *The Roman Empire,* 1987. A good general account of politics and administration.

Grant, M. *The Army of the Caesars,* 1974. This and Watson below are the most accessible studies for students interested in the imperial army, its personnel, weaponry, and organization.

Liebeschutz, J. *Continuity and Change in Roman Religion,* 1979.

Rostovtzeff, N. *The Economic and Social History of the Roman Empire,* 1957. The standard treatment of Roman economic and commercial life. A great book on a huge topic.

Schulz, F. *Classical Roman Law,* 1951. A good introduction to the principles guiding the Roman jurists.

Toynbee, J. M. *Art of the Romans,* 1965. A short study of how Roman art strove to fulfill certain civic ideals.

Watson, G. R. *The Roman Soldier,* 1969.

Wells, G. *The Roman Empire,* 1984. A good general study of politics and administration.

Chapter 13

Balsdon, J. P. V. *Roman Women,* 1975. See also his book in the Chapter 14 section.

Bradley, K. R. *Slaves and Masters in the Roman Empire,* 1988. A good overview of this topic.

Carcopino, J. *Daily Life in Ancient Rome,* 1956. A deservedly famous classic, written for students at the undergraduate level.

Dover, K. *Greek Homosexuality,* 1978. A standard work.

Garlan, Y. *Slavery in Ancient Greece,* 1988.

Golden, M. *Children and Childhood in Classical Greece,* 1990. The latest work on this subject.

Humphrey, J. *Roman Circuses and Chariot Racing,* 1985. Will give the student some understanding of how important these mass entertainments were to the Roman way of life.

Keuls, E. *The Reign of the Phallus,* 1987. An interesting, if much-attacked, work on the politics of sexuality in Greece.

Lacey, W. K. *The Family in Classical Greece,* 1984.

MacMullen, R. *Roman Social Relations A.D. 50 to A.D. 284,* 1981. More detailed and broader than Bradley's work cited earlier.

Pomeroy, S. *Women in Hellenistic Egypt,* 1984. Discusses the lives of women from all social classes.

Sherwin-White, A. *Racial Prejudice in Imperial Rome,* 1967. Covers a special topic.

PART THREE

Chapter 14

Balsdon, J. P. V. *Life and Leisure in Ancient Rome,* 1969. An enlightening book on ordinary affairs in Rome.

Barraclough, G. *The Crucible of Europe: The Ninth and Tenth Centuries in European History,* 1976. Discusses the invasions of the ninth century.

Benko, S. *Pagan Rome and Early Christianity,* 1985.

Bridge, A. *Theodora: A Portrait in a Byzantine Landscape,* 1984. A highly entertaining look at a controversial figure.

Bronsted, J. *The Vikings,* 1970. See for the Vikings' role in the invasions of the ninth century.

Bullough, D. *The Age of Charlemagne,* 1965. See for Charlemagne and his empire.

Duby, G. *The Early Growth of the European Economy,* 1974. Covers economic and commercial topics.

Einhard. *Life of Charlemagne,* many editions. A classic thumbnail sketch.

Fichtenau, H. *The Carolingian Empire,* 1972. Takes a critical view of the emperor and his ambitions.

Frend, W. H. *The Rise of Christianity,* 1984. A good study of Christianity's spread within the empire.

Grant, M. *The Fall of the Roman Empire: A Reappraisal,* 1976. See this and the next entry by Jones for different explanations for the collapse of the Roman empire.

Jones, A. M. *The Decline of the Ancient World,* 1966.

MacMullen, R. *Constantine,* 1988.

Mango, C. *Byzantium: The Empire of New Rome,* 1980. A good survey of Byzantine affairs. See also Runciman's work.

Musset, L. *The Germanic Invasions: The Making of Europe A.D. 400–600,* 1975. Looks at the barbarian invaders in some detail, as does Wallace-Hadrill.

Painter, S. *The Rise of the Feudal Monarchies,* 1957. Looks at the period after 1000 C.E.

Richards, P. *Daily Life in the World of Charlemagne,* 1978. A lively survey of the life of the people in the earlier Middle Ages.

Runciman, S. *Byzantine Civilization,* 1956. A standard work, clear and lively.

Stenton, F. *Anglo-Saxon England,* 1971. Deals with the Germanic invaders in a particular country.

Strayer, J. *Western Europe in the Middle Ages,* 1982. A fine survey of the whole period, with a very good bibliography.

Wallace-Hadrill, J. M. *The Barbarian West,* 1967.

Wilken, R. L. *Christians as Romans Saw Them,* 1984. An interesting variation on the theme of the persecutions.

Chapter 15

Andrae, T. *Mohammad: The Man and His Faith,* 1970. A reliable biography. See also Rodinson's work.

Denny F. *An Introduction to Islam,* 1985. Fulfills what the title promises.

Donner, F. M. *The Early Islamic Conquests,* 1986. Looks at the reasons for the rapid expansion of the religion and the concept of the *jihad,* so often misunderstood in the West.

Kennedy, H. *The Prophet and the Age of the Caliphates,* 1986. A good survey of the spread of Islam to the Seljuk era.

Lewis, B., ed. *Islam and the Arab World,* 1976. As good an introduction to the topics covered in this chapter as exists. Excellent illustrations. The same author's *The Arabs in History,* 1961, is focused more sharply on the Arabian peninsula.

Nutting, A. *The Arabs: A Narrative History from Mohammad to the Present,* 1964. Written especially for beginners.

Qur'an. Many translations are available. Perhaps the best for students is that of N. J. Dawood, 1990.

Rodinson, N. *Mohammad,* 1971.

Chapter 16

The Cambridge History of Islam, vols. 1 and 2, 1970. Perhaps the handiest collection of work on every aspect of Islamic culture, but sometimes too specialized for student use.

Dunlop, D. M. *Arab Civilization to A.D. 1500,* 1971. An excellent collection dealing with many facets of this world, including the achievements of women.

Haddawy, H., trans. *Arabian Nights,* 1990. A recent translation that stands out.

Lapidus, I. *Muslim Cities in the Later Middle Ages,* 1967. A standard introduction to the wealth and variety of those urban societies. See also the same author's *A History of Islamic Societies,* 1988.

Lewis, B. *The Arabs in History,* 1968.

Morgan, D. *The Mongols,* 1986. An interesting presentation of Mongol history.

Musallam, B. F. *Sex and Society in Islam,* 1983. Discusses women in Islamic society.

Nasr, S. H. *Science and Civilization in Islam,* 1968.

Rice, D. T. *Islamic Art,* 1975. See for explanations of how the Islamic peoples adapted art to their supernatural ends and pioneered new forms and methods to do so.

Watt, W. *History of Islamic Spain,* 1965.

Yarshater, E. *Persian Literature,* 1988. An illuminating discussion.

Chapter 17

Akira H. *A History of Indian Buddhism from Sakyayuni to Early Mahayana,* 1990. A survey of the fortunes of the religion in its first millennium.

Auboyer, J. *Daily Life in Ancient India,* 1965. Covers ordinary life. See also some chapters in Basham's work.

Basham, A. L. *The Wonder That Was India,* 1954. Remains very informative for this period, as well as earlier.

Bussagli, M. *5000 Years of the Art of India,* n.d. Perhaps the best illustrated of the histories of Indian art.

The Oxford History of India, 4th ed., 1981. A source of general information on India's long history.

Rowland, B. *The Art and Architecture of India: Buddhist/Hindu/Jain,* 1970. The massive impact of Buddhism on Indian art and culture is outlined in Chapters 6 to 8.

Wales, H. G. *The Making of Greater India,* 1974. Goes into the colonizing and cultural diffusion activities of Indians in Southeast and East Asia.

Chapter 18

The general histories cited in the bibliography for Chapter 6 are still useful in this period: the works by C. Schirokauer and J. Fairbank can be recommended. See also the multivolume Oxford and Cambridge histories of the Chinese state.

Cahill, J. *Chinese Painting,* 1960. A good survey.

Ch'en, K. *Buddhism in China,* 1964.

Fitzgerald, C. P. *Son of Heaven: A Biography of Li Shih-min, Founder of the T'ang Dynasty,* 1933. A fine biography. See also his biography of one of the very few Chinese empresses, *The Empress Wu,* 1968.

Gernet, J. *Daily Life in China on the Eve of the Mongol Invasion,* 1948. A look at an unchanging society in the thirteenth century from a worm's eye view.

Grousset, R. *In the Footsteps of the Buddha,* 1931. A modern version of the journal of a Chinese Buddhist pilgrim visiting India.

Waley, A., trans. Several volumes of poetry translated from the original.

Wright, A. F. *Buddhism in Chinese History,* 1959. A straightforward explanation.

Wu-chi, L. *An Introduction to Chinese Literature,* 1966. A readable introduction to Chinese classical literature with a good bibliography.

Chapter 19

Bowring, R., trans. *Tale of Genji,* 1988. A good recent translation.

Coulborn, R., ed. *Feudalism in History,* 1956. See E. O. Reischauer's chapter on Japan.

Craig, A., and E. O. Reischauer. *Japan: Tradition and Transformation,* 1989. A widely used textbook covering the entire sweep of Japan's history.

Duus, P. *Feudalism in Japan,* 1976. Examines decentralized politics in its Japanese variant.

Kidder, J. E. *Japan before Buddhism,* 1959, and *Early Buddhist Japan,* 1972. Two good introductions for the student.

Kitagawa, J. M. *Religion in Japanese History,* 1966. Deals with the differences between Shinto and Buddhism and how they have been accommodated.

Morris, I. *The World of the Shining Prince: Court Life in Ancient Japan,* 1964. Deals with Genji and his environment by examining artistic life at Kyoto.

Reischauer, E. O., and J. Fairbank. *East Asia: The Great Tradition,* 1960. A detailed survey.

Schirokauer, C. *A Brief History of Chinese and Japanese Civilizations,* 2d ed., 1989. A good introduction.

Suzuki, D. T. *Zen and Japanese Culture,* 1959. A standard treatment.

Chapter 20

Ade Ajaji, J. F., and I. Espie, eds. *A Thousand Years of West African History,* 1972. A good summary.

Bohannon, P., and P. Curtin. *Africa and Africans,* 1971. A very useful review of social institutions in precolonial days.

Burstein, S. ed. *Ancient African Civilizations: Kush and Axum,* 1998. Very brief overview.

Curtin, P., et al. *African History,* 1998. Will probably be the definitive treatment at the student level for many years.

Davenport, T. R. H. *South Africa: A Modern History,* 3d ed., 1987. A well-recommended treatment of South Africa.

Fage, J. F. *A History of Africa,* 1978. Considered by many the best textbook treatment of the continent in its entirety.

Hiskett, M. *The Development of Islam in West Africa,* 1984. Deals with Islam in the western and Saharan regions.

The Horizon History of Africa, 1971. Treats individual segments of the continent.

July, R. W. *Precolonial Africa: An Economic and Social History,* 1975. A very straightforward, readable account. Somewhat broader is the same author's *A History of the African People,* 3d ed., 1980.

Manning, P. *Slavery and African Life,* 1988. Very detailed but provides a complete picture as it is now perceived.

Oliver, R., and G. Mathew, eds. *History of East Africa,* 1963. A well-recommended treatment.

Trimingham, J. *Islam in East Africa,* 1974.

Chapter 21

Katz, F. *The Ancient American Civilizations,* 1972. Smoothly written, this is an excellent introduction to a world that seems very far from our own. Deals with all the major civilizations in the Americas prior to the Europeans.

Von Hagen, C. W. *Realm of the Inca,* 1961, and *The Aztec: Man and Tribe,* 1961. Two of the most readable popular accounts.

Aztecs

Davies, N. *The Aztecs,* 1973.

Leon-Portilla, M., ed. *The Broken Spears: The Aztec Account of the Conquest of Mexico,* 1961. A special look at the Aztecs.

Weaver, M. P. *The Aztecs, Mayas, and Their Predecessors: Archaeology of Mesoamerica,* 1981. A very good study.

The Inca in Peru

Baudin, L. *A Socialist Empire: The Incas of Peru,* 1961. Another excellent scholarly survey.

Cobo, B. *History of the Inca Empire,* 1979.

Lanning, C. *Peru before Pizarro,* 1967.

Maya Civilization

Coe, M. D. *The Maya,* 1986.

Sabloff, J. *The New Archaeology and the Ancient Maya,* 1990.

Schele, L., and D. Freidel. *A Forest of Kings: The Untold Story of the Ancient Maya,* 1990.

Stuart, G. E., and G. F. Stuart. *The Mysterious Maya,* 1977. Well-illustrated, popular account.

Chapter 22

Many of the works cited in previous bibliographies dealing with the non-Western peoples will be useful here. Authors of works that are particularly relevant include R. Thapar and A. L. Basham for India; J. Gernet and J. K. Fairbank for China; E. O. Reischauer for Japan; J. Fage, and R. Oliver, and P. Bohannon for Africa; and H. W. Von Hagen for the Americas.

The *Everyday Life* series, most translated from the original French, are often very informative, though the quality and coverage are uneven.

Chang, K. C. *Food in Chinese Culture,* 1977, is an entertaining look at eating habits among people with the widest culinary experience in the world.

Dunn, C. J. *Everyday Life in Traditional Japan,* 1969, is a good example of the series.

Shinnie, M. *Ancient African Kingdoms,* 1966, gives some of the flavor of daily affairs.

Smith, H. *The World's Religions,* 1991, is an excellent introduction to all of the major religions of East and West in their conceptual essences.

Soustelle, J. *Daily Life of the Aztecs on the Eve of the Spanish Conquest,* 1961. Probably the best single book on the topic. He has also written on the Olmec.

Spence, J. *The Death of a Woman Wang,* 1986, gives a unique account of the daily affairs of an ordinary woman of seventeenth-century China.

Waley, A., has brought a most extraordinary man to life in his *The Poetry and Career of Li-po*, 1958, a biography of one of the greatest and most quoted of Chinese poets.

Chapter 23

Barraclough, G. *The Origins of Modern Germany*, 1963. A good survey.

Duby, G. *Rural Economy and Country Life in the Medieval West*, 1968, and *The Chivalrous Society*, 1977. See the former for the manor and peasant life and the latter for essays on aristocratic life.

Dunbabin, J. *France in the Making, 843–1100*, 1957. An introduction to early French history.

Ennen, E. *The Medieval Town*, 1979. One of the best summaries of medieval town life. Discusses who lived in the towns and how they lived between 1000 and 1300.

Ferruolo, S. C. *The Origins of the University*, 1985. Deals with an important part of medieval culture.

Ganshof, F. *Feudalism*, 1961. The standard explanation of European feudalism.

Gimpel, J. *The Cathedral Builders*, 1961. See for Gothic art and cathedrals.

Gold, P. S. *The Lady and the Virgin*, 1985. Deals with images and reality of upper-class women in twelfth-century France.

Haskins, C. *The Renaissance of the Twelfth Century*, 1927. A fine study that has not lost its value.

Landes, D. *Revolution in Time: Clocks and the Making of the Modern World*, 1985. Examines the concept of time and how it was spread through a largely illiterate population.

Macaulay, D. *Cathedral: The Story of Its Construction*, 1973. Fascinatingly written.

McNeill, W. H. *Plagues and People*, 1976. Discusses how disease affected medieval society.

Stuard, S., ed. *Women in Medieval Society*, 1976. A collection of essays on women from different backgrounds.

Chapter 24

Aston, M. *The Fifteenth Century: The Prospect of Europe*, 1968. Reviews the social consequences of the plague in lively style; illustrated.

Cipolla, C. *Before the Industrial Revolution: European Society and Economy, 1000–1700*, 1976. An outstanding survey that discusses, among other topics, the difficulties of producing sufficient food.

Ferguson, W. K. *Europe in Transition, 1300–1520*, 1968. Focuses on the interrelations between the plague and the new spirit of the Renaissance.

Mollat, M., and P. Wolff. *The Popular Revolutions of the Late Middle Age*, 1973. Deals with peasant revolts and their suppression.

Oakley, F. P. *The Western Church in the Late Middle Ages*, 1980. Surveys the problems of the church.

Perroy, E. *The Hundred Years' War*, 1965. A comprehensive survey.

Renovard, Y. *The Avignon Papacy, 1305–1403*, 1970. Looks at the Babylonian Captivity.

Runciman, S. *The Fall of Constantinople, 1453*, 1965. A marvelous account of the Ottomans' long-sought victory over their Christian opponents.

Tuchman, B. *A Distant Mirror*, 1982. A vivid, exciting story of the calamities besetting Western Europe in the fourteenth century; uses an actual French nobleman as the protagonist.

Ziegler, P. *The Black Death*, 1969. A very readable account of the plague.

Chapter 25

Benesch, O. *The Art of the Renaissance in Northern Europe*, 1965. A well-illustrated introduction.

Ferguson, W. K. *The Renaissance*, 1940. A brief, lively account of what the term *Renaissance* meant.

Hay, D. *The Italian Renaissance*, 1977. A gem for students' use; concise and very readable.

Herlihy, D. *The Family in Renaissance Italy*, 1974. A good introduction to the social domain.

Huizinga, J. *Erasmus of Rotterdam*, 1952. The standard biography.

King, M. L. *Women of the Renaissance*, 1991. An introduction to women in the Renaissance.

Marius, R. *Thomas More*, 1984.

Martindale, A. *The Rise of the Artist in the Middle Ages and the Early Renaissance*, 1972. Well illustrated with an extensive bibliography.

Phillips, M. M. *Erasmus and the Northern Renaissance*, 1956. The leading figure of the northern Renaissance.

Woelfflin, H. *Classic Art: An Introduction to the Italian Renaissance*, 1968.

PART FOUR
Chapter 26

Boxer, C. R. *The Portuguese Seaborne Empire, 1415–1825*, 1969. The best account of the achievement of tiny Portugal.

Cipolla, C. M. *Guns, Sails, and Empires*, 1965. A fascinating account of technical progress and its effects on human relationships in an age of exploration.

Crosby, A. W. *The Columbian Exchange: Biological and Cultural Consequences of 1492*, 1972. The most important book on this subject in the last generation.

Curtin, P. *The African Slave Trade*, 1969, and J. L. Watson, ed., *Asian and African Systems of Slavery*, 1980, are among the most interesting and authoritative treatments.

Díaz de Castillo, B. *The Conquest of New Spain*, trans. and ed. J. Cohen, 1988. The best of the conquistador accounts.

Elliot, J. H. *The Old World and the New*, 1970, considers the mutual impacts of the discoveries.

Fernandez-Armesto, F. *Columbus*, 1991. The most recent biography, reflecting new information.

Innes, Hammond. *The Conquistadors*, 1969. A lively illustrated rendition that is also sympathetic.

Kirkpatrick, F. *The Spanish Conquistadores*, 1968, is a standard work on the opening of the Caribbean and Central America.

McNeill, W. *The Pursuit of Power: Technology, Armed Force and Society since 1000 A.D.*, 1992.

Parry, J. H. *The Age of Reconnaissance*, 1981. The classic account of the early voyages. Wonderfully clear prose.

——. *The Spanish Seaborne Empire*, 1966. The standard account of Spain's push into the Americas.

———. *The Discovery of South America,* 1979. Tells how new discoveries affected the Europeans. Excellent illustrations.

———. *The Establishment of European Hegemony 1415–1715,* 1961 is a short treatment.

Sale, K. *Conquest of Paradise,* 1990. Highly critical of the Spanish policies.

Tracy, J. D. *The Rise of Merchant Empires; Long Distance Trade in the Early Modern World 1350–1750,* 1990. An anthology treating various empires and locales.

Wolf, E. *Europe and the People without History,* 1982. Critical of the Westerners' arrogance in dealing with others.

Wright, S. *Stolen Continents,* 1995. The discovery of America, from the points of view of the Aztecs, Inca, and North American Indians.

Chapter 27

Bainton, R. *Here I Stand,* 1950. Remains perhaps the best biography of Martin Luther.

Bouwsma, W. *John Calvin,* 1988. A good recent biography of the most influential of the Protestant leaders.

Jensen, D. L. *Reformation Europe,* 1990. An excellent survey of the Reformation period.

Kelly, H. A. *The Matrimonial Trials of Henry VIII,* 1975. Another good work on English affairs of state and religion.

McNeill, J. *The History and Character of Calvinism,* 1954. The best survey of what Calvinism meant theologically and as a way of living.

Neale, J. *Queen Elizabeth I,* 1934. Still the best biography of this significant ruler. See also J. Ridley, *Elizabeth I,* 1988.

O'Connell, M. *The Counter-Reformation, 1559–1610,* 1974. A fair-minded balancing of Protestant and Catholic claims as well as a history of the Catholic responses.

Ozment, S. *Protestants: The Birth of a Revolution,* 1992. Also useful for students.

Youings, J. *Sixteenth Century England,* 1984. Places the English Reformation in the context of English society and culture.

Answers to Test Your Knowledge

CHAPTER 1
1. d, 2. a, 3. c, 4. b, 5. b, 6. c

CHAPTER 2
1. a, 2. b, 3. b, 4. d, 5. b, 6. b, 7. d, 8. c, 9. a

CHAPTER 3
1. c, 2. c, 3. c, 4. a, 5. c, 6. b, 7. a, 8. a, 9. b

CHAPTER 4
1. d, 2. b, 3. b, 4. c, 5. c, 6. a, 7. b, 8. b, 9. c, 10. a

CHAPTER 5
1. a, 2. a, 3. b, 4. a, 5. d, 6. d, 7. a, 8. c

CHAPTER 6
1. a, 2. b, 3. b, 4. b, 5. a, 6. b, 7. d, 8. d, 9. d

CHAPTER 7
1. b, 2. a, 3. b, 4. b, 5. c, 6. a, 7. a, 8. b, 9. d, 10. b

CHAPTER 8
1. a, 2. b, 3. b, 4. c, 5. b, 6. c, 7. b, 8. a, 9. c

CHAPTER 9
1. c, 2. c, 3. c, 4. a, 5. a, 6. d, 7. d, 8. b, 9. a

CHAPTER 10
1. a, 2. b, 3. b, 4. b, 5. d, 6. d, 7. a, 8. a, 9. d

CHAPTER 11
1. c, 2. b, 3. d, 4. d, 5. c, 6. d, 7. a, 8. c, 9. a, 10. d

CHAPTER 12
1. d, 2. b, 3. c, 4. c, 5. c, 6. b, 7. d

CHAPTER 13
1. b, 2. a, 3. b, 4. b, 5. d, 6. c, 7. d, 8. a

CHAPTER 14
1. c, 2. a, 3. b, 4. b, 5. a, 6. c, 7. b, 8. d, 9. d, 10. b

CHAPTER 15
1. b, 2. c, 3. d, 4. d, 5. b, 6. d, 7. a, 8. d, 9. c, 10. a

CHAPTER 16
1. b, 2. d, 3. b, 4. b, 5. b, 6. b, 7. b

CHAPTER 17
1. a, 2. c, 3. c, 4. d, 5. b, 6. c, 7. a, 8. d

CHAPTER 18
1. d, 2. d, 3. c, 4. a, 5. a, 6. b, 7. c, 8. a

CHAPTER 19
1. b, 2. a, 3. c, 4. a, 5. d, 6. b, 7. b, 8. c, 9. c, 10. d

CHAPTER 20
1. b, 2. a, 3. a, 4. c, 5. b, 6. b, 7. a, 8. d, 9. b, 10. a

CHAPTER 21
1. a, 2. b, 3. d, 4. a, 5. d, 6. b, 7. c, 8. d, 9. c

CHAPTER 22
1. c, 2. d, 3. a, 4. b, 5. d, 6. a, 7. d

CHAPTER 23
1. b, 2. a, 3. d, 4. c, 5. a, 6. c, 7. c, 8. b

CHAPTER 24
1. c, 2. b, 3. b, 4. c, 5. a, 6. a, 7. a, 8. d, 9. a

CHAPTER 25
1. b, 2. d, 3. a, 4. a, 5. c, 6. a, 7. c, 8. b

CHAPTER 26
1. c, 2. a, 3. c, 4. d, 5. a, 6. c, 7. a, 8. d, 9. b, 10. d

CHAPTER 27
1. c, 2. b, 3. c, 4. d, 5. b, 6. c, 7. a, 8. b, 9. c

Glossary

A

Abbasid dynasty The caliphs resident in Baghdad from the 700s until 1252 C.E.

Abbot/abbess The male/female head of a monastery/nunnery.

Abstractionism A twentieth-century school of painting that rejects traditional representation of external nature and objects.

Actium, Battle of The decisive 31 B.C.E. battle in the struggle between Octavian Caesar and Mark Anthony, in which Octavian's victory paved the way for the Principate.

Act of Supremacy of 1534 A law enacted by the English Parliament making the monarch the head of the Church of England.

Age of the Barracks Emperors The period of the Roman empire in the third century C.E. when the throne was repeatedly usurped by military men.

Agincourt The great victory of the English over the French in 1415, during the Hundred Years' War.

Agricultural revolution The substitution of farming for hunting-gathering as the primary source of food by a given people.

Ain Jalut A decisive thirteenth-century battle in which the Egyptians turned back the Mongols and prevented them from invading North Africa.

Ajanta Caves Caves in central India that are the site of marvelous early frescoes inspired by Buddhism.

Allah Arabic title of the one God.

Alliance for Progress The proposal by U.S. president John F. Kennedy in 1961 for large-scale economic assistance to Latin America.

Alliance of 1778 A diplomatic treaty under which France aided the American revolutionaries in their war against Britain.

Anabaptists Radical Protestant reformers who were condemned by both Lutherans and Catholics.

Anarchism A political theory that sees all large-scale government as inherently evil and embraces small self-governing communities.

Anasazi Pre-Columbian inhabitants of the southwestern United States and creators of pueblo cliff dwellings.

Ancien régime "The old government"; the pre-Revolutionary style of government and society in eighteenth-century France.

Anghor Wat A great Buddhist temple in central Cambodia, dating to the twelfth-century C.E. Khmer empire.

Anglo-French entente The diplomatic agreement of 1904 that ended British-French enmity and was meant as a warning to Germany.

Anglo-Russian agreement The equivalent to the Anglo-French entente between Britain and Russia; signed in 1907.

Angola-to-Brazil trade A major portion of the trans-Atlantic slave trade.

Animism A religious belief imputing spirits to natural forces and objects.

Anschluss The German term for the 1938 takeover of Austria by Nazi Germany.

Anthropology The study of humankind as a particular species.

Antigonid kingdom One of the Hellenistic successor kingdoms to Alexander the Great's empire.

Apartheid The Afrikaans term for segregation of the races in South Africa.

Appeasement The policy of trying to avoid war by giving Hitler what he demanded in the 1930s; supported by many in France and Britain.

Archaeology The study of cultures through the examination of artifacts.

Aristocracy A social governing class based on preeminence of birth.

Ark of the Covenant The wooden container of the two tablets given to Moses by Yahweh on Mount Sinai (the Ten Commandments); the Jews' most sacred shrine, signifying the contract between God and the Chosen.

Aryans A nomadic pastoral people from central Asia who invaded the Indus valley in c. 1500 B.C.E.

Ashikaga clan A noble Japanese family that controlled political power as shoguns from the 1330s to the late 1500s.

Assur The chief god of the Assyrian people.

Ataturk, Mustafa Kemal The "father of the Turks"; a World War I officer who led Turkey into the modern age and replaced the sultanate in the 1920s.

Audiencia The colonial council that supervised military and civil government in Latin America.

August 1991 coup The attempt by hard-line communists to oust Gorbachev and reinstate the Communist Party's monopoly on power in the Soviet Union.

Ausgleich of 1867 The compromise between the Austro-Germans and Magyars that created the "Dual Monarchy" of Austria-Hungary.

Austro-Prussian War The conflict for mastery of the German national drive for political unification, won by the Bismarck-led Prussian kingdom in 1866.

Avesta The holy book of the Zoroastrian religion.

Axis pact The treaty establishing a military alliance between the governments of Hitler and Mussolini; signed in 1936.

Axum The center of the ancient Ethiopian kingdom.

Ayllu Quechua name for the clan organization of the Peruvian Indians.

Aztec Latest of a series of Indian masters of central Mexico prior to the arrival of the Spanish; developers of the great city of Tenochtitlán (Mexico City).

B

Babylon Most important of the later Mesopotamian urban centers.

Babylonian Captivity The transportation of many Jews to exile in Babylon as hostages for the good behavior of the remainder; occurred in the sixth century B.C.E.

Babylonian Captivity of the papacy See **Great Schism.**

Bakufu The military-style government of the Japanese shogun.

Balfour Declaration The 1917 public statement that Britain was committed to the formation of a "Jewish homeland" in Palestine after World War I.

Banana republics A dismissive term referring to small Latin American states.

Bantu A language spoken by many peoples of central and eastern Africa; by extension, the name of the speakers.

Barbarian Greek for "noncomprehensible speaker"; uncivilized.

Battle of the Nations October 1813, at Leipzig in eastern Germany. Decisive defeat of the army of Napoleon by combined forces of Prussia, Austria, and Russia.

Bedouin The nomadic inhabitants of interior Arabia and original converts to Islam.

Benedictine Rule The rules of conduct given to his monastic followers by the sixth-century Christian saint Benedict.

Berbers Pre-Arab settlers of northern Africa and the Sahara.

Berlin blockade The 1948–1949 attempt to squeeze the Western allies out of occupied Berlin by the USSR; it failed because of the successful Berlin Airlift of food and supplies.

Berlin Wall The ten-foot-high concrete wall and "death zone" erected by the communist East Germans in 1961 to prevent further illegal emigration to the West.

Bhagavad-gita The best-known part of the *Mahabharata,* detailing the proper relations between the castes and the triumph of the spirit over material creation.

Big bang theory The theory that the cosmos was created by an enormous explosion of gases billions of years ago.

Bill of Rights of 1689 A law enacted by Parliament that established certain limits of royal powers and the specific rights of English citizens.

Black Death An epidemic of bubonic plague that ravaged most of Europe in the mid–fourteenth century.

Boer War/Boers The armed conflict 1899–1902 between the Boers (the Dutch colonists who had been the initial European settlers of South Africa) and their British overlords; won by the British after a hard fight.

Bohemia Traditional name of the Czech Republic, dating from the tenth century C.E.

Bolsheviks The minority of Russian Marxists led by Lenin who seized dictatorial power in the October revolution of 1917.

Boule The 500-member council that served as a legislature in ancient Athens.

Bourgeoisie The urban upper middle class; usually commercial or professional.

Boxer Rebellion A desperate revolt by superstitious peasants against the European "foreign devils" who were carving up China in the new imperialism of the 1890s; quickly suppressed.

Brahman The title of the impersonal spirit responsible for all creation in Hindu theology.

Brahmin The caste of priests, originally found among the Aryans and later spread to the Indians generally.

Bread and circuses The social policy initiated by Augustus Caesar aimed at gaining the support of the Roman proletariat by supplying them with essential food and entertainments.

Brest-Litovsk Treaty of 1918 The separate peace between the Central Powers and Lenin's government in Russia.

Bronze Age The period when bronze tools and weapons replaced stone among a given people; generally about 3000–1000 B.C.E.

Burning of the books China's Legalist first emperor attempted to eliminate Confucian ethic by destroying the Confucian writings and prohibiting its teaching.

Bushido The code of honor among the samurai.

Byzantine empire The continuation of the Roman imperium in its eastern provinces until its fall to the Muslim Turks in 1453.

C

Cahokia sites The locales of North American Indian ceremonial sites in the valley of the Mississippi, established sometime prior to the fifteenth century.

Caliph Arabic for "successor" (to Muhammad); leader of Islam.

Carthage Rival in the Mediterranean basin to Rome in the last centuries B.C.E. before ultimate defeat.

Caste A socioeconomic group that is entered by birth and rarely exitable.

Caudillo A chieftain (that is, a local or regional strongman) in Latin America.

Censors Officials with great powers of surveillance during the Roman republic.

Chaeronea The battle in 338 B.C.E. when Philip of Macedon decisively defeated the Greeks and brought them under Macedonian rule.

Chartists A British working-class movement of the 1840s that attempted to obtain labor and political reform.

Chavin Early Peruvian Indian culture.

Cheka An abbreviation for the first Soviet secret police.

Chichén Itzá Site in the Yucatán of Mayan urban development in the tenth to thirteenth centuries.

Civil Code of 1804 Napoleonic law code reforming and centralizing French legal theory and procedures.

Civil constitution of the clergy 1791 law in revolutionary France attempting to force French Catholics to support the new government and bring clergy into conformity with it.

Civilization A complex, developed culture.

Command economy The name given to communist economic planning in the Soviet version after 1929.

Committee of Public Safety The executive body during the Reign of Terror during the French Revolution.

Commonwealth of Independent States (CIS) The loose confederation of eleven of the fifteen former Soviet republics that was formed after the breakup of the Soviet Union in 1991.

Conciliar movement The attempt to substitute councils of church leaders for papal authority in late medieval Christianity.

Conquistadores Title given to sixteenth-century Spanish American explorers/colonizers.

Consuls Chief executives of the Roman republic; chosen annually.

Coral Sea, Battle of the Naval engagement in the southwest Pacific during World War II resulting in the removal of a Japanese invasion threat to Australia.

Corpus Juris "Body of the law"; the final Roman law code, produced under the emperor Justinian in the mid-500s C.E.

Creationism A cosmology based on Christian tradition that holds that the universe was created by an intelligent Supreme Being.

Crecy Battle in the Hundred Years' War won by the English in 1346.

Crimean War Conflict fought in the Crimea between Russia and Britain, France, and Turkey from 1853 to 1856; ended by the Peace of Paris with a severe loss in Russian prestige.

Criollo Creole; term used to refer to whites born in Latin America.

Cultural relativism A belief common in the late twentieth-century West that there are no absolute values to measure contrasting cultures.

Culture The human-created environment of a group.

Cuneiform Mesopotamian wedge-shaped writing begun by the Sumerians.

Cynicism A Hellenistic philosophy stressing poverty and simplicity.

Dada A brief art movement in the early twentieth century that repudiated all obligations to communicate intelligibly to the public.

Daimyo Japanese nobles who controlled feudal domains under the shogun.

Dao de Jing (Book of Changes) Daoism's major scripture; attributed to Lao Zi.

Daoism (Taoism) A nature-oriented philosophy/religion.

Dawes Plan A plan for a dollar loan and refinancing of post World War I reparation payments that enabled recovery of the German economy.

D day June 6, 1944; the invasion of France from the English side of the English Channel by combined British and American forces.

Declaration of the Rights of Man and Citizen The epoch-making manifesto issued by the French Third Estate delegates at Versailles in 1789.

Deductive reasoning Arriving at truth by applying a general law or proposition to a specific case.

Delian League An empire of satellite *polei* under Athens in the fifth century B.C.E.

Deme The basic political subdivision of the Athenian *polis.*

Demesne The arable land on a manor that belonged directly to the lord.

Democracy A system of government in which the majority of voters decide issues and policy.

Demographic transition The passage of a large group of people from traditional high birthrates to lower ones, induced by better survival chances of the children.

Dependency In the context of national development, the necessity to reckon with other states' powers and pressures in the domestic economy and foreign trade.

Descamisados "Shirtless ones"; the poor working classes in Argentina.

Descent of Man The 1871 publication by Charles Darwin that applied selective evolution theory to mankind.

Détente Relaxation; the term used for the toning down of diplomatic tensions between nations, specifically, the cold war between the United States and the Soviet Union.

Dharma A code of morals prescribed for one's caste in Hinduism.

Dhimmis "People of the Book": Christians, Jews, and Zoroastrians living under Muslim rule and receiving privileged treatment over other non-Muslims.

Diaspora The scattering of the Jews from ancient Palestine.

Diffusion theory The spread of technology through human contacts.

Directory The five-member executive organ that governed France from 1795 to 1799 after the overthrow of the Jacobins.

Divine right theory The idea that the legitimate holder of the Crown was designated by divine will to govern; personified by King Louis XIV of France in the seventeenth century.

Diwan A council of Islamic government ministers in Istanbul during the Ottoman empire.

Domesday Book A complete census of landholdings in England ordained by William the Conqueror.

Dorians Legendary barbaric invaders of Mycenaean Greece in c. 1200 B.C.E.

Dream of the Red Chamber The best known of the eighteenth-century Chinese novels.

Duce, il "The Leader"; title of Mussolini, the Italian dictator.

East India Company A commercial company founded with government backing to trade with the East and Southeast Asians. The Dutch, English, and French governments sponsored such companies starting in the early seventeenth century.

Economic nationalism A movement to assert national sovereignty in economic affairs, particularly by establishing freedom from the importation of foreign goods and technology on unfavorable terms.

Edo Name of Tokyo prior to the eighteenth century.

Eightfold Path The Buddha's teachings on attaining perfection.

Ekklesia The general assembly of citizens in ancient Athens.

Emir A provincial official with military duties in Muslim government.

Empirical data Facts derived from observation of the external world.

Empirical method Using empirical data to establish scientific truth.

Empiricist A school of Hellenistic Greek medical researchers.

Enclosure movement An eighteenth-century innovation in British agriculture by which formerly communal lands were enclosed by private landlords.

Encomienda The right to organize unpaid native labor by the earliest Spanish colonists in Latin America; revoked in 1565.

Encyclopedie, The The first encyclopedia; produced in mid-eighteenth-century France by the philosophe Diderot.

Enlightenment The intellectual reform movement in eighteenth century Europe that challenged traditional ideas and policies in many areas of theory and practice.

Epicureanism A Hellenistic philosophy advocating the pursuit of pleasure (mental) and avoidance of pain as the supreme good.

Equal field system Agricultural reform favoring the peasants under the Tang dynasty in China.

Equity Fairness to contending parties.

Era of Stagnation The era of Brezhnev's government in the Soviet Union (1964–1982), when the Soviet society and economy faced increasing troubles.

Era of Warring States The period of Chinese history between c. 500 and 220 B.C.E.; characterized by the breakdown of the central government and feudal war.

Essay Concerning Human Understanding An important philosophical essay by John Locke that underpinned Enlightenment optimism.

Estates General The parliament of France; composed of delegates from three social orders: clergy, nobility, and commoners.

Ethnic, Ethnicity The racial, cultural, or linguistic affiliation of an individual or group of human beings.

Etruscans The pre-Roman rulers of most of northern and central Italy and cultural models for early Roman civilization.

European Economic Community An association of western European nations founded in 1957; now called the European Union, it embraces fifteen countries with several more in candidate status.

Excommunication The act of being barred from the Roman Catholic community by decree of a bishop or the pope.

Existentialism Twentieth-century philosophy that was popular after World War II in Europe; insists on the necessity to inject life with meaning.

Exodus The Hebrews' flight from the wrath of the Egyptian pharaoh in c. 1250 B.C.E.

Extended family Parents and children plus several other kin group members.

Factory Acts Laws passed by Parliament in 1819 and 1833 that began the regulation of hours and working conditions in Britain.

Factory system Massing of labor and material under one roof with a single proprietorship and management of production.

Fallow Land left uncultivated for a period to recover fertility.

Fascism A political movement in the twentieth century that embraced totalitarian government policies to achieve a unity of people and leader; first experienced in Mussolini's Italy.

Fathers of the Church Leading theologians and explainers of Christian doctrine in the fourth and early fifth centuries.

Fertile Crescent A belt of civilized settlements reaching from lower Mesopotamia across Syria, Lebanon, and Israel and into Egypt.

Feudal system A mode of government based originally on mutual military obligations between lord and vassal; later often extended to civil affairs of all types; generally supported by landowning privileges.

Final Solution Name given by the Nazis to the wartime massacres of European Jews.

First consul Title adopted by Napoleon after his coup d'état in 1799.

First Emperor (Shi Huangdi) The founder of the short-lived Qin dynasty (221–205 B.C.E.) and creator of China as an imperial state.

First Five-Year Plan Introduced in 1929 at Stalin's command to collectivize agriculture and industrialize the economy of the Soviet Union.

First Industrial Revolution The initial introduction of machine-powered production; began in late eighteenth-century Britain.

First International Title of original association of socialists, in 1860s Europe.

Five Pillars of Islam Popular term for the basic tenets of Muslim faith.

Floating world A term for ordinary human affairs popularized by the novels and stories of eighteenth-century Japan.

Forbidden City The center of Ming and Qing government in Beijing; entry was forbidden to ordinary citizens.

Four Little Tigers Singapore, Taiwan, South Korea, and Hong Kong in the 1960s–1980s economic upsurge.

Four Noble Truths The Buddha's doctrine on human fate.

Fourteen Points The outline for a just peace proposed by Woodrow Wilson in 1918.

Franco-Prussian War The 1870–1871 conflict between these two powers resulting in German unification.

Frankfurt Assembly A German parliament held in 1848 that was unsuccessful in working out a liberal constitution for a united German state.

Führer, der "The Leader" in Nazi Germany—specifically, Hitler.

Fujiwara clan Daimyo noble clan controlling the shogunate in ninth- to twelfth-century Japan.

Gendarme of Europe Name given to the Russian imperial government under Czar Nicholas I (1825–1855).

General theory of relativity Einstein's theory that introduced the modern era of physics in 1916.

Gentiles All non-Jews.

Geocentric "Earth centered"; theory of the cosmos that erroneously held the Earth to be its center.

Ghana The earliest of the extensive empires in the western Sudan; also a modern African state.

Ghetto Italian name for the quarter restricted to Jews.

Gilgamesh One of the earliest epics in world literature, originating in prehistoric Mesopotamia.

Glasnost The Russian term for "openness"; along with *perestroika,* employed to describe the reforms instituted by Gorbachev in the late 1980s.

Glorious Revolution of 1688 The English revolt against the unpopular Catholic king James II and the subsequent introduction of certain civil rights restricting monarchic powers.

Golden Horde The Russia-based segment of the Mongol world empire.

Golden mean Greek concept of avoiding the extremes; "truth lies in the middle."

Good Neighbor Policy President Franklin D. Roosevelt's attempt to reform previous U.S. policy and honor Latin American sovereignty.

Gothic style An artistic style, found mainly in architecture, that came into general European usage during the thirteenth century.

Gracchi brothers Roman noble brothers who unsuccessfully attempted reform as consuls in the late republican era.

Grand vizier Title of the Turkish prime minister during the Ottoman era.

Great Elector Frederick William of Prussia (1640–1688); one of the princes who elected the Holy Roman Emperor.

Great Leap Forward Mao Tse-tung's misguided attempt in 1958–1960 to provide China with an instantaneous industrial base rivaling that of more advanced nations.

Great Proletarian Cultural Revolution The period from 1966 to 1976 when Mao inspired Chinese youth to rebel against all authority except his own; caused great damage to the Chinese economy and culture.

Great Purge The arrest and banishment of millions of Soviet Communist Party members and ordinary citizens at Stalin's orders in the mid-1930s for fictitious "crimes against the State and Party."

Great Reforms (Russia) Decrees affecting several areas of life issued by Czar Alexander II between 1859 and 1874.

Great Schism A division in the Roman Catholic Church between 1378 and 1417 when two (and for a brief period, three) popes competed for the allegiance of European Christians; a consequence of the Babylonian Captivity of the papacy in Avignon, southern France.

Great Trek The march of the Boers into the interior of South Africa where they founded the Orange Free State in 1836.

Great Zimbabwe The leading civilization of early southern Africa.

Grossdeutsch* versus *Kleindeutsch The controversy over the scope and type of the unified German state in the nineteenth century; *Kleindeutsch* would exclude multinational Austria, and *Grossdeutsch* would include it.

Guild A medieval urban organization that controlled the production and sale prices of many goods and services.

Gupta dynasty The rulers of most of India in the 300–400s C.E.; the last native dynasty to unify the country.

Habsburg dynasty The family that controlled the Holy Roman Empire after the thirteenth century; based in Vienna, they ruled Austria until 1918.

Hacienda A Spanish-owned plantation in Latin America that used native or slave labor to produce export crops.

Hagia Sophia Greek name ("Holy Wisdom") of the cathedral in Constantinople, later made into mosque by Ottoman Turkish conquerors.

Haiku A type of Japanese poetry always three lines in length. The lines always have five, seven, and five syllables.

Hajj The pilgrimage to the sacred places of Islam.

Han dynasty The dynasty that ruled China from c. 200 B.C.E. to 221 C.E.

Hangzhou Capital city of the Song dynasty China and probably the largest town in the contemporary world.

Hanoverians The dynasty of British monarchs after 1714; from the German duchy of Hanover.

Harem Turkish name for the part of a dwelling reserved for women.

Hegira "Flight"; Muhammed's forced flight from Mecca in 622 C.E.; marks the first year of the Muslim calendar.

Heliocentrism Opposite of geocentrism; recognizes sun as center of solar system.

Hellenistic A blend of Greek and Asiatic cultures; extant in the Mediterranean basin and Middle East between 300 B.C.E. and c. 200 C.E.

Helots Messenian semislaves of Spartan overlords.

Heresies Wrong belief in religious doctrines.

Hetairai High-class female entertainer-prostitutes in ancient Greece.

Hinayana Buddhism A stricter monastic form of Buddhism, claiming closer link with the Buddha's teaching; often called Theravada. Headquartered in Sri Lanka and strong in Southeast Asia.

Historiography The writing of history so as to interpret it.

History Human actions in past time, as recorded and remembered.

Hittites An Indo-European people who were prominent in the Near East around 1200 B.C.E.

Hohenzollerns The dynasty that ruled Prussia-Germany until 1918.

Hominid A humanlike creature.

Homo sapiens "Thinking man"; modern human beings.

Horus The falcon-headed god whose earthly, visible form was the reigning pharaoh in ancient Egypt.

Hubris An unjustified confidence in one's abilities or powers leading to a tragic end.

Huguenots French-speaking Calvinists, many of whom were forced to emigrate in the seventeenth century.

Humanism The intellectual movement that sees humans as the arbiter of their values and purpose.

Hungarian Revolution The Hungarians' attempt to free themselves from Soviet control in October 1956; crushed by the Soviets.

Hyksos A people who invaded the Nile delta in Egypt and ruled it during the Second Intermediate Period (c. 1650–1570 B.C.E.).

Ideographs Written signs conveying entire ideas and not related to the spoken language; used by the Chinese from earliest times.

Iliad The first of the two epics supposedly written by Homer in eighth-century Greece.

Imperator Roman title of a temporary dictator given powers by the Senate; later, emperor.

Impressionists Members of a Paris-centered school of nineteenth-century painting focusing on light and color.

Inca Title of the emperor of the Quechuan peoples of Peru prior to arrival of the Spanish.

Indochina, Union of Official term for the French colonies in Indochina until their dissolution in the 1950s.

Inductive reasoning Arriving at truth by reasoning from specific cases to a general law or proposition.

Infamia Roman term for immoral but not illegal acts.

Inquisition Roman Catholic agency that was responsible for censorship of doctrines and books; mainly active in Iberian lands in the fifteenth through seventeenth centuries.

Institutes of the Christian Religion John Calvin's major work that established the theology and doctrine of the Calvinist churches; first published in 1536.

Intelligentsia Russian term for a social group that actively influences the beliefs and actions of others, seeking reforms; generally connected with the professions and media.

Investiture Controversy A dispute between the Holy Roman Emperor and the pope in the eleventh and early twelfth centuries about which authority should appoint German bishops.

Iranian Revolution The fundamentalist and anti-Western movement led by the Ayatollah Khomeini that seized power from the shah of Iran through massive demonstrations in 1979.

Irredentism The attempt by members of a nation living outside the national state to link themselves to it politically and/or territorially.

Isis A chief Egyptian goddess, represented by the Nile River.

Jacobins Radical revolutionaries during the French Revolution; organized in clubs headquartered in Paris.

Jacquerie A French peasant rebellion against noble landlords during the fourteenth century.

Janissaries From Turkish *yeni cheri,* meaning "new troops"; an elite troop in the Ottoman army; created originally from Christian boys from the Balkans.

Jesuits Members of the Society of Jesus, a Catholic religious order founded in 1547 to combat Protestantism.

Jewish War A rebellion of Jewish Zealots against Rome in 66–70 C.E.

Jihad Holy war on behalf of the Muslim faith.

Judea One of the two Jewish kingdoms emerging after the death of Solomon when his kingdom was split in two; the other kingdom was Samaria.

July Monarchy The reign of King Louis Philippe in France (1830–1848); so called because he came to power through a brief revolution in July 1830.

Junkers The landowning nobility of Prussia.

Jus gentium "Law of peoples"; Roman law governing relations between Romans and others.

Justification by faith Doctrine held by Martin Luther whereby Christian faith alone was the path to heavenly bliss.

Ka The immortal soul in the religion of ancient Egypt.

Ka'aba The original shrine of pagan Arabic religion in Mecca containing the Black Stone; now one of the holiest places of Islam.

Kabuki A type of popular Japanese drama depicting heroic and romantic themes and stories.

Kadi An Islamic judge.

Kamakura shogunate The rule by members of a noble Japanese family from the late twelfth to the mid–fourteenth century in the name of the emperor, who was their puppet.

Kami Shinto spirits in nature.

Kampuchea Native name of Cambodia, a state of Southeast Asia bordered by Thailand and Vietnam.

Karma The balance of good and evil done in a given incarnation in Hindu belief.

Karnak The site of a great temple complex along the Nile River in Egypt.

Kashmir A province in northwestern India that Pakistan also claims.

Kellogg-Briand Pact A formal disavowal of war by sixty nations in 1928.

KGB An abbreviation for the Soviet secret police; used after *Cheka* and *NKVD* had been discarded.

Khmers The inhabitants of Cambodia; founders of a large empire in ancient Southeast Asia.

Kiev, Principality of The first Russian state; flourished from c. 800 to 1240 when it fell to Mongols.

King of Kings The title of the Persian emperor.

Kleindeutsch "Small German"; adjective describing a form of German unification that excluded the multinational Austria; opposite of *Grossdeutsch.*

Knights Type of feudal noble who held title and landed domain only for his lifetime; generally based originally on military service to his overlord.

Korean War 1950–1953 war between United Nations, led by the United States, and North Korea; precipitated by the invasion of South Korea.

Kuomintang (KMT) The political movement headed by Chiang Kai-shek during the 1930s and 1940s in China.

Kush Kingdom in northeast Africa that had close relations with Egypt for several centuries in the pre-Christian epoch.

Kyoto Ancient capital of the Japanese empire and seat of the emperor.

Labour Party Political party founded in 1906 by British labor unions and others for representation of the working classes.

Late Manzhou Restoration An attempt by Chinese reformers in the 1870s to restore the power of the central government after the suppression of the Taiping rebellion.

League of Nations An international organization founded after World War I to maintain peace and promote amity among nations; the United States did not join.

Left The reforming or revolutionary wing of the political spectrum; associated originally with the ideals of the radical French Revolution.

Legalism A Chinese philosophy of government emphasizing strong authority.

Legislative Assembly The second law-making body created during the French Revolution; dominated by the Jacobins and giving way to the radical Convention.

Legitimacy A term adopted by the victors at the Congress of Vienna in 1815 to explain the reimposition of former monarchs and regimes after the Napoleonic wars.

Levée en masse General conscription for the army; first occurred in 1793 during the French Revolution.

Leviathan A book by Thomas Hobbes that supported the necessity of the state and, by inference, royal absolutism.

Liberum veto Latin for "free veto"; used by Polish nobles to nullify majority will in the Polish parliaments of the eighteenth century.

Lineage A technical term for family or clan association.

"Little red book" Contained the thoughts of Chairman Mao Tse-tung on various topics; used as a talisman during the Cultural Revolution by young Chinese.

Locarno Pact An agreement between France and Germany in 1925.

Lollards Name of unknown origin given to the English religious rebels of the 1380s and later who protested against the privileges of the clergy and were vigorously persecuted.

Long March The 6,000-mile fighting retreat of the Chinese communists under Mao Tse-tung to Shensi province in 1934–1935.

Lyric poetry Poetry that celebrates the poet's emotions.

Maastricht Treaty Signed in 1991 by members of the European Community; committed them to closer political-economic ties.

Macao Portuguese colony-island just off China's coast; founded in 1513.

Machtergreifung "Seizure of power"; Nazi term for Hitler's rise to dictatorial powers in Germany.

Maghrib or **Maghreb** Muslim northwest Africa.

Mahabharata A Hindu epic poem; a favorite in India.

Mahayana Buddhism A more liberal, looser form of Buddhism; originating soon after the Buddha's death, it deemphasized the monastic life and abstruse philosophy in favor of prayer to the Buddha and the bodhisattvas who succeeded him.

Mahdi Rebellion A serious rebellion against European rule in the Sudan in the 1890s, led by a charismatic holy man ("mahdi") whose death and British attack ended it.

Majapahit The main town of a maritime empire in fourteenth-century Indonesia.

Mali The African Sudanese empire that was the successor to Ghana in the 1300s and 1400s.

Manchester liberalism The economic practice of exploiting the laboring poor in the name of the free market.

Manchuria Large province of northeastern China, seized in the nineteenth century by Russia and Japan before being retaken by the Maoist government.

Mandarins Chinese scholar-officials who had been trained in Confucian principles and possessed great class solidarity.

Mandate Britain and France governed several Asian and African peoples after World War I, supposedly as agents of the League of Nations.

Mandate of heaven A theory of rule originated by the Zhou dynasty in China, emphasizing the connection between imperial government's rectitude and its right to govern.

Manor An agricultural estate of varying size normally owned by a noble or the clergy and worked by free and unfree peasants/serfs.

Manu Legendary lawgiver in India.

Manus "Hand"; Latin term for the legal power of a person over another.

Manzhou Originally nomadic tribes living in Manchuria who eventually overcame Ming resistance and established the Qing dynasty in seventeenth-century China.

Marathon The battle in 490 B.C.E. in which the Greeks defeated the Persians, ending the first Persian War.

March on Rome A fascist demonstration in 1922 orchestrated by Mussolini as a preliminary step to dictatorship in Italy.

March Revolution of 1917 The abdication of Czar Nicholas II and the establishment of the Provisional Government in Russia.

Maritime Expeditions (China's) Early fifteenth-century explorations of the Indian and South Pacific Oceans ordered by the Chinese emperor.

Marshall Plan A program proposed by the U.S. secretary of state George Marshall and implemented from 1947 to 1951 to aid western Europe's recovery from World War II.

Masscult The banal culture that some think replaced the traditional elite culture in the twentieth-century West.

Matriarchy A society in which females are dominant socially and politically.

Matrilineal descent Attribution of name and inheritance to children via the maternal line.

May Fourth Movement A reform movement of young Chinese students and intellectuals in the post–World War I era; Mao Tse-tung was a member prior to his conversion to Marxism.

Maya The most advanced of the Amerindian peoples who lived in southern Mexico and Guatemala and created a high urban civilization in the pre-Columbian era.

Medes An early Indo-European people who, with the Persians, settled in Iran.

Meiji Restoration The overthrow of the Tokugawa shogunate and restoration of the emperor to nominal power in Japan in 1867.

Mein Kampf *My Struggle;* Hitler's credo, written while serving a prison term in 1924.

Mercantilism A theory of national economics popular in the seventeenth and eighteenth centuries; aimed at establishing a favorable trade balance through government control of exports and imports as well as domestic industry.

Meritocracy The rule of the meritorious (usually determined by examinations).

Messenian Wars Conflicts between the neighbors Sparta and Messenia that resulted in Messenia's conquest by Sparta in about 600 B.C.E.

Messiah A savior-king who would someday lead the Jews to glory.

Mestizo A person of mixed Amerindian and European blood.

Metaphor of the Cave Plato's explanation of the difficulties encountered by those who seek philosophical truth and the necessity of a hierarchy of leadership.

Mexican Revolution The armed struggle that occurred in Mexico between 1910 and 1920 to install a more socially progressive and populist government.

Middle Kingdom The period in Egyptian history from 2100 to 1600 B.C.E.; followed the First Intermediate Period.

Milan, Edict of A decree issued by the emperor Constantine in 313 C.E. that legalized Christianity and made it the favored religion in the Roman empire.

Minoan An ancient civilization that was centered on Crete between c. 2000 and c. 1400 B.C.E.

Missi dominici Agents of Charlemagne in the provinces of his empire.

Modernism A philosophy of art of the late nineteenth and early twentieth centuries that rejected classical models and values and sought new expressions and aesthetics.

Mohenjo-Daro Site of one of the two chief towns of the ancient Indus valley civilization.

Moksha The final liberation from bodily existence and reincarnation in Hinduism.

Monarchy Rule by a single individual, who often claims divine inspiration and protection.

Mongols Name for collection of nomadic, savage warriors of Central Asia who conquered most of Eurasia in the thirteenth century.

Mongol yoke A Russian term for the Mongol occupation of Russia, 1240–1480.

Monotheism A religion having only one god.

Monroe Doctrine The announcement in 1823 by U.S. president James Monroe that no European interference in Latin America would be tolerated.

Mughal A corruption of "Mongol"; refers to the period of Muslim rule in India.

Mulatto A person of mixed African and European blood.

Munich Agreement The 1938 meetings between Hitler and the British and French prime ministers that allowed Germany to take much of Czechoslovakia; the agreement confirmed Hitler's belief that the democratic governments would not fight German aggression.

Munich putsch The failed attempt by Hitler to seize power by armed force in 1923.

Municipia The basic unit of Roman local government; similar to a present municipality.

Muslim Brotherhoods Associations of Islamic groups that have strong fundamentalist leanings and practice mutual aid among members.

Mystery religion One of various Hellenistic cults promising immortal salvation of the individual.

Nantes, Edict of A law granting toleration to French Calvinists that was issued in 1598 by King Henry IV to end the religious civil war.

Napoleonic settlement A collective name for the decrees and actions by Napoleon between 1800 and 1808 that legalized and systematized many elements of the French Revolution.

National Assembly The first law-making body during the French Revolution; created a moderate constitutional monarchy.

Natural selection The Darwinian doctrine in biology that change in species derives from mechanistic changes induced by the environment.

Navigation Acts Laws regulating commerce with the British colonies in North America in favor of Britain.

Nazism The German variant of fascism created by Hitler.

Neanderthal man A species of *Homo sapiens* flourishing between 100,000 and 30,000 years ago and that mysteriously died out; the name comes from the German valley where the first remains were found.

Negritude A literary term referring to the self-conscious awareness of African cultural values; popular in areas of Africa formerly under French control.

Neo-Confucianism An eleventh- and twelfth-century C.E. revival of Confucian thought with special emphasis on love and responsibility toward others.

Neolithic Age The period from c. 7000 B.C.E. to the development of metals by a given people.

New China movement An intellectual reform movement in the 1890s that attempted to change and modernize China by modernizing the government.

New Economic Policy (NEP) A policy introduced at the conclusion of the civil war that allowed for partial capitalism and private enterprise in the Soviet Union.

New imperialism The late nineteenth-century worldwide colonialism of European powers interested in strategic and market advantage.

New Kingdom or **New Empire** The period from c. 1550 to 700 B.C.E. in Egyptian history; followed the Second Intermediate Period. The period from 1550 to c. 1200 B.C.E. was the Empire.

Nicaea, Council of A fourth-century conclave that defined essential doctrines of Christianity under the supervision of the emperor Constantine.

Niger River The great river draining most of the African bulge.

Ninety-five Theses The challenge to church authority publicized by Martin Luther, October 31, 1517.

Nineveh The main city and later capital of the Assyrian empire.

Nirvana The Buddhist equivalent of the Hindu *moksha;* the final liberation from suffering and reincarnation.

NKVD An abbreviation for the Soviet secret police; used after *Cheka* but before *KGB.*

Non-aggression Pact of 1939 The treaty between Hitler and Stalin in which each agreed to maintain neutrality in any forthcoming war involving the other party.

North American Free Trade Agreement (NAFTA) An agreement signed by the United States, Canada, and Mexico in 1993 that provides for much liberalized trade among these nations.

North Atlantic Treaty Organization (NATO) An organization founded in 1949 under U.S. aegis as a defense against threatened communist aggression in Europe.

Nuclear family Composed of parents and children only.

Nuclear test ban The voluntary cessation of aboveground testing of nuclear weapons by the United States and the Soviet Union; in existence from 1963 to the present.

Nuremberg Laws Laws defining racial identity that were aimed against Jews; adopted in 1935 by the German government.

O

October Revolution of 1917 The Bolshevik coup d'état in St. Petersburg that ousted the Provisional Government and established a communist state in Russia.

Odyssey Second of the two Homeric epic poems, detailing the adventures of the homeward-bound Ulysses coming from the siege of Troy; see also *Iliad.*

Oedipus Rex Part of a triad of tragedies written by the classical Greek playwright Sophocles concerning the life and death of Oedipus and his daughter, Antigone.

Oil boycott of 1973 The temporary withholding of oil exports by OPEC members to Western governments friendly to Israel; led to a massive rise in the price of oil and economic dislocation in many countries.

Old Kingdom The period of Egyptian history from 3100 to 2200 B.C.E.

Old Testament The first portion of the Judeo-Christian Bible; the holy books of the Jews.

Oligarchy Rule by a few.

Olmec The earliest Amerindian civilization in Mexico.

Operation Barbarossa Code name for German invasion of the Soviet Union in 1941.

Opium Wars Conflicts that occurred in 1840–1842 on the Chinese coast between the British and the Chinese over the importation of opium into China. The Chinese defeat began eighty years of subordination to foreigners.

Oracle bones Animal bones used as a primitive writing medium by early Chinese.

Orange Free State One of the two political organisms founded after the Boer Great Trek in southern Africa.

Organization for Pan African Unity (OAU) The present name of the association of sub-Saharan African nations founded in 1963 for mutual aid.

Organization of American States (OAS) An organization founded in 1948 under U.S. auspices to provide mutual defense and aid; now embraces all countries on the American continents except Cuba.

Organization of Petroleum Exporting Countries (OPEC) Founded in the 1960s by Arab governments and later expanded to include several Latin American and African members.

Origin of Species, On the Charles Darwin's book that first enunciated the evolutionary theory in biology; published in 1859.

Osiris A chief Egyptian god, ruler of the underworld.

Ostpolitik German term for Chancellor Brandt's 1960s policy of pursuing normalized relations with West Germany's neighbors to the east.

Ostracism In ancient Greece, the expulsion of a citizen from a *polis* for a given period.

P

Paleolithic Age The period from the earliest appearance of *Homo sapiens* to c. 7000 B.C.E., though exact dates vary by area; the Old Stone Age.

Paleontology The study of prehistoric things.

Palestine Liberation Organization (PLO) An organization founded in the 1960s by Palestinians expelled from Israel; until 1994 aimed at destruction of the state of Israel by any means. Superseded by the autonomous Palestinian Authority created in 1997.

Pan-Arabism A movement after World War I to assert supranational Arab unity, aimed eventually at securing a unified Arab state.

Pantheism A belief that God exists in all things, living and inanimate.

Paragraph 231 of the Versailles Treaty The "war guilt" paragraph, imputing responsibility for reparation of all damages to Germany.

Pariah An outcaste; a person having no acknowledged status.

Paris Commune A leftist revolt against the national government after France was defeated by Prussia in 1871; crushed by the conservatives with much bloodshed.

Parthenon The classic Greek temple to Athena on the Acropolis in Athens center.

Patents Royal documents conferring nobility.

Patria potestas The power of the father over his family in ancient Rome.

Patriarchy A society in which males have social and political dominance.

Patricians (*patres*) The upper class in ancient Rome.

Pax Mongolica The Mongol peace; between c. 1250 and c. 1350 in most of Eurasia.

Pax Romana The "Roman peace"; the era of Roman control over the Mediterranean basin and much of Europe between c. 31 B.C.E. and 180 C.E. or later.

Peace of Augsburg Pact ending the German religious wars in 1555, dividing the country between Lutheran and Catholic hegemony.

Peaceful coexistence The declared policy of Soviet leader Khrushchev in dealing with the capitalist West after 1956.

Peloponnesian War The great civil war between Athens and Sparta and their respective allies in ancient Greece; fought between 429 and 404 B.C.E. and eventually won by Sparta.

Peon A peasant in semislave status on a hacienda.

Perestroika The Russian term for "restructuring," which, with *glasnost,* was used to describe the reforms instituted by Gorbachev in the late 1980s.

Persepolis With Ecbatana, one of the twin capitals of the Persian empire in the 500s B.C.E.

Persians An early Indo-European tribe that, along with the Medes, settled in Iran.

Persian Wars The conflict between the Greeks and the Persian empire in the fifth century B.C.E., fought in two installments and ending with Greek victory.

Petrine succession The doctrine of the Roman Catholic church by which the pope, the bishop of Rome, is the direct successor of St. Peter.

Pharoah The title of the god-king of ancient Egypt.

Philosophes A French term used to refer to the writers and activist intellectuals during the Enlightenment.

Phonetic alphabet A system of writing that matches signs with the sounds of the oral language.

Piedmont "Foot of the mountains"; the Italian kingdom that led to the unification of Italy in the mid–nineteenth century.

Plastic arts Those that have three dimensions.

Platea The land battle that, along with the naval battle of Salamis, ended the second Persian War with a Greek victory over the Persians.

Plebeians (*plebs*) The common people of ancient Rome.

Pogrom Mob violence against local Jews.

Polis The political and social community of citizens in ancient Greece.

Polytheism A religion having many gods.

Popular Front The coordinated policy of all antifascist parties; inspired by the Soviets in the mid-1930s as a policy against Hitler.

Porte, The A name for the seat of Ottoman government in Istanbul.

Post-Impressionist A term for late nineteenth-century painting that emphasized color and line in revolutionary fashion.

Praetorian Guard The imperial bodyguard in the Roman empire and the only armed force in Italy.

Precedent What has previously been accepted in the application of law.

Prehistory The long period of human activity prior to the writing of history.

Pre-Socratics Greek philosophers prior to Socrates who focused on the nature of the material world.

Primogeniture A system of inheritance in which the estate passes to the eldest legitimate son.

Princeps "The First" or "the Leader" in Latin; title taken by Augustus Caesar.

Principate The reign of Augustus Caesar from 27 B.C.E. to 14 C.E.

Proconsuls Provincial governors and military commanders in ancient Rome.

Proletariat Poverty-stricken people without skills; also, a Marxist term for the propertyless working classes.

Provisional Government A self-appointed parliamentary group exercising power in republican Russia from March to October 1917.

Psychoanalysis A psychological technique that employs free associations in the attempt to determine the cause of mental illness.

Ptolemaic Kingdom of Egypt The state created by Ptolemy, one of Alexander the Great's generals, in the Hellenistic era.

Pueblo culture Name given to the southwest U.S. Indian culture beginning c. 1000 B.C.E.

Punic Wars The three conflicts between Rome and Carthage that ended with the complete destruction of the Carthaginian empire and the extension of Roman control throughout the western Mediterranean.

Purdah The segregation of females in Hindu society.

Purgatory In Catholic belief, the place where the soul is purged after death for past sins and thus becomes fit for Heaven.

Puritans The English Calvinists who were dissatisfied by the theology of the Church of England and wished to "purify" it.

Pyramid of Khufu (Cheops) The largest pyramid; stands outside Cairo.

Qing dynasty The last Chinese dynasty, which ruled from 1644 until 1911; established by Manzhou invaders after they defeated the Ming rulers.

Quadruple Alliance The diplomatic pact to maintain the peace established by the Big Four victors of the Napoleonic wars (Austria, Britain, Prussia, and Russia); lasted for a decade.

Quanta A concept in physics indicating the expenditure of energy.

Quechua The spoken language of the Incas of Peru.

Qur´an The holy scripture of Islam.

Raison d'état The idea that the welfare of the state should be supreme in government policy.

Raja Turkish for "cattle"; used to refer to non-Muslims.

Red Guard The youthful militants who carried out the Cultural Revolution in China during the 1960s.

Red International See **Third International.**

Reform Bill of 1832 Brought about a reform of British parliamentary voting and representation that strengthened the middle class and the urbanites.

Reign of Terror The period (1793–1794) of extreme Jacobin radicalism during the French Revolution.

Reparations Money and goods that Germany was to pay to the victorious Allies after World War I under the Versailles Treaty.

Republican government A form of governing that imitates the Roman *res publica* in its rejection of monarchy.

Rerum novarum An encyclical issued by Pope Leo XIII in 1890 that committed the Roman Catholic church to attempting to achieve social justice for the poor.

Restoration (English) The period of the 1660s–1680s when Charles II was called by Parliament to take his throne and was thus restored to power.

Revisionism The adaptation of Marxist socialism that aimed to introduce basic reform through parliamentary acts rather than through revolution.

Revolution of 1989 The throwing out of the communist governments in eastern Europe by popular demand and/or armed uprising.

Rigveda The oldest of the four Vedas, or epics, brought into India by the Aryans.

Romanov dynasty Ruled Russia from 1613 until 1917.

Rome, Treaty of The pact signed by six western European nations in 1957 that is the founding document of the European Union.

Rubaiyat The verses attributed to the twelfth-century Persian poet Omar Khayyam.

Safavid The dynasty of Shiite Muslims that ruled Persia from the 1500s to the 1700s.

Sahel The arid belt extending across Africa south of the Sahara; also called the Sudan.

Sakoku Japan's self-imposed isolation from the outer world that lasted until 1854.

Salamis The naval battle that, with the battle of Platea, ended the second Persian War with a Greek victory.

Samaria One of the two kingdoms into which the Hebrew kingdom was split after Solomon's death; the other was Judea.

Samsara The reincarnation of the soul; a concept shared by Hinduism and Buddhism.

Samurai Japanese warrior-aristocrats of medieval and early modern times.

Sanhedrin The Jewish governing council under the overlordship of Rome.

Sanskrit The sacred language of India; came originally from the Aryans.

Sardinia-Piedmont. See **Piedmont.**

Sati The practice in which a widow committed suicide at the death of her husband in ancient India.

Satrapy A province under a governor or *satrap* in the ancient Persian empire.

Savanna The semiarid grasslands where most African civilizations developed.

Schutzstaffel (SS) Hitler's bodyguard; later enlarged to be a subsidiary army and to provide the concentration camp guards.

Scientific method The method of observation and experiment by which the physical sciences proceed.

Second Front The reopening of a war front in the west against the Axis powers in World War II; eventually accomplished by the invasion of Normandy in June 1944.

Second Industrial Revolution The second phase of industrialization that occurred in the late 1800s after the introduction of electricity and the internal combustion engine.

Second International Association of socialist parties founded in 1889; after the Russian Revolution in 1917, the Second International split into democratic and communist segments.

Secret speech Premier Nikita Khrushchev of the USSR gave an account in February 1956 of the crimes of Josef Stalin against his own people that was supposed to remain secret but was soon known internationally.

Secularism The rejection of supernatural religion as the arbiter of earthly action; emphasis on worldly affairs.

Seleucid kingdom of Persia The successor state to the empire of Alexander the Great in most of the Middle East.

Self-strengthening The late nineteenth-century attempt by Chinese officials to bring China into the modern world by instituting reforms; failed to achieve its goal.

Seljuks Turkish converts to Islam who seized the Baghdad government from the Abbasids in the eleventh century.

Semitic Adjective describing a person or language belonging to one of the most widespread of the western Asian groups; among many others, it embraces Hebrew and Arab.

Serfdom Restriction of personal and economic freedoms associated with medieval European agricultural society.

Seven Years' War Fought between France and England, with their allies, around the world, 1756–1763; won by England, with major accessions of territory to the British empire.

Shang dynasty The first historical rulers of China; ruled from c. 1500 to c. 1100 B.C.E.

Sharija The sacred law of Islam; based on the Qur'an.

Shiite A minority sect of Islam; adherents believe that kinship with Muhammad is necessary to qualify for the caliphate.

Shiki Rights attached to parcels of land (*shoen*) in Japan.

Shinto Native Japanese animism.

Shiva A member of the high trinity of Hindu gods; lord of destruction but also of procreation; often pictured dancing.

Shoen Parcels of land in Japan with *shiki* (rights) attached to them; could take many forms and have various possessors.

Shogunate The government of medieval Japan in which the shogun, a military and civil regent, served as the actual leader while the emperor was the symbolic head of the state and religion.

Show trials First used for the staged trials of alleged traitors to the Soviet system in 1936–1937; generically, a political trial in which the conviction of the accused is a foregone conclusion.

Sikhs Members of a cult founded in the sixteenth century C.E. by a holy man who sought a middle way between Islam and Hindu belief; centered on the Punjab region in northern India.

Sino-Soviet conflict Differences in the nature of socialism were accentuated by conflict over proper policy vis-á-vis the United States in the 1950s and 1960s in the twin capitals of Marxist socialism, Moscow and Beijing.

Sino-Tibetan languages The family of languages spoken by the Chinese and Tibetan peoples.

Social Darwinism The adaptation of Darwinian biology to apply to human society in simplistic terms.

Social Democrats Noncommunist socialists who refused to join the Third International and founded independent parties.

Solidarity The umbrella organization founded by Lech Walesa and other anticommunist Poles in 1981 to recover Polish freedom; banned for eight years, but continued underground until it was acknowledged as the government in 1989.

Song dynasty The dynasty that ruled China from c. 1127 until 1279 when the last ruler was overthrown by the Mongol invaders.

Songhai A West African state, centered on the bend of the Niger River, that reached its fullest extent in the sixteenth century before collapsing.

Spinning jenny A fundamental improvement over hand-spinning of cotton thread, developed by an English engineer in the 1780s.

Spirit of the Laws One of the basic tracts of the eighteenth-century Enlightenment, written by Baron Montesquieu and adopted by many reformers of government throughout Europe.

Springtime of the Peoples The spring and summer of 1848 when popular revolutions in Europe seemed to succeed.

Stalingrad The battle in 1942 that marked the turning point of World War II in Europe.

Stalinist economy Involved the transformation of a retarded agrarian economy to an industrialized one through massive reallocation of human and material resources directed by a central plan; imposed on the Soviet Union and then, in the first years after World War II, on eastern Europe.

Stamp Act A law enacted by the British Parliament in 1765 that imposed a fee on legal documents of all types and on all books and newspapers sold in the American colonies.

State The term for a territorial, sovereign entity of government.

Stoicism A Hellenistic philosophy that emphasized human brotherhood and natural law as guiding principles.

Structural Adjustment Programs (SAPs) Programs designed by the World Bank to achieve economic improvement on a national scale in developing countries.

Stuprum A Roman legal term denoting acts that were both immoral and illegal; contrast with *infamia,* which was an immoral but not illegal action.

Sturmabteilung **(SA)** The street-fighting "bully boys" of the Nazi Party; suppressed after 1934 by Hitler's orders.

Successor states Usual term for the several eastern European states that emerged from the Paris treaties of 1919 as successors to the Russian, German, and Austro-Hungarian empires.

Sudan The arid belt extending across Africa south of the Sahara; also called the Sahel.

Sufi Arabic name for a branch of Islamic worship that emphasizes emotional union with God and mystical powers.

Sui dynasty Ruled China from c. 580 to c. 620 C.E.; ended the disintegration of central government that had existed for the previous 130 years.

Sui juris "Of his own law"; Roman term for an individual, especially a female, who was not restricted by the usual laws or customs.

Sultanate of Delhi The government and state erected by the conquering Afghani Muslims after 1500 in north India; immediate predecessor to the Mughal empire.

Sumerians The creators of Mesopotamian urban civilization.

Sunni The majority group in Islam; adherents believe that the caliphate should go to the most qualified individual and should not necessarily pass to the kin of Muhammad.

Supremacy, Act of A law enacted in 1534 by the English Parliament that made the monarch the head of the Church of England.

Suzerain The superior of a vassal to whom the vassal owed feudal duties.

Swahili A hybrid language based on Bantu and Arabic; used extensively in East Africa.

Syndicalism A doctrine of government that advocates a society organized on the basis of syndicates or unions.

Taipings The followers of anti-Manzhou rebels in China in the 1860s.

Taj Mahal The beautiful tomb built by the seventeenth-century Mughal emperor Jahan for his wife.

Tale of Genji First known novel in Asian, if not world, history; authored by a female courtier about life in the Japanese medieval court.

Tang dynasty Ruled China from c. 620 to c. 900 C.E. and began the great age of Chinese artistic and technical advances.

Tel el Amarna The site of great temple complexes along the Nile River in Egypt.

Test Act Seventeenth-century English law barring non-Anglican Church members from government and university positions.

Tetrarchy "Rule of four"; a system of government established by Diocletian at the end of the third century C.E. in an attempt to make the Roman empire more governable; failed to achieve its goals and was not continued by Diocletian's successors.

Theocracy The rule of gods or their priests.

Theravada Buddhism A stricter, monastic form of Buddhism entrenched in Southeast Asia; same as Hinayana Buddhism.

Thermidorean reaction The conservative reaction to the Reign of Terror during the French Revolution.

Third Estate The great majority of Frenchmen: those neither clerical nor noble.

Third International An association of Marxist parties in many nations; inspired by Russian communists and headquartered in Moscow until its dissolution in 1943.

Third Republic of France The government of France after the exile of Emperor Napoleon III; lasted from 1871 until 1940.

Third Rome theory A Russian myth that Moscow was ordained to succeed Rome and Constantinople as the center of true Christianity.

Third World A term in use after World War II to denote countries and peoples in underdeveloped, formerly colonial areas of Asia, Africa, and Latin America; the First World was the West under U.S. leadership, and the Second World was the communist states under Soviet leadership.

Tiananmen Square, massacre on The shooting down of thousands of Chinese who were peacefully demonstrating for relaxation of political censorship by the communist leaders; occurred in 1989 in Beijing.

Tilsit, Treaty of A treaty concluded in 1807 after the French had defeated the Russians; divided Europe/Asia into French and Russian spheres.

Time of Troubles A fifteen-year period at the beginning of the seventeenth century in Russia when the state was nearly destroyed by revolts and wars.

Titoism The policy of neutrality in foreign policy combined with continued dedication to socialism in domestic policy that was followed by the Yugoslav Marxist leader Tito after his expulsion from the Soviet camp in 1948.

Toltec An Amerindian civilization centered in the Valley of Mexico; succeeded by the Aztecs.

Torah The first five books of the Old Testament; the Jews' fundamental law code.

Tories A nickname for British nineteenth-century conservatives; opposite of Whigs.

Totalitarianism The attempt by a dictatorial government to achieve total control over a society's life and ideas.

Transvaal Second of the two independent states set up by the Boer Great Trek in the early nineteenth-century in South Africa.

Trent, Council of The council of Catholic clergy that directed the Counter-Reformation against Protestantism; met from 1545 until 1563.

Tribunes The chief officers and representatives of the plebeians during the Roman republic.

Triple Alliance A pact concluded in 1882 that united Germany, Austria-Hungary, and Italy against possible attackers; the members were called the Central Powers.

Triumvirate "Three-man rule"; the First Triumvirate was during the 50s B.C.E. and the Second in the 30s B.C.E. during the last decades of the Roman republic.

Truman Doctrine The commitment of the U.S. government in 1947 to defend any noncommunist state against attempted communist takeover; proposed by President Harry Truman.

Twelve Tables The first written Roman law code; established c. 450 B.C.E.

Ulema A council of learned men who applied the *sharija* in Islam; also, a council of religious advisers to the caliph or sultan.

Ummayad dynasty The caliphs resident in Damascus from 661 to 750 C.E.

Uncertainty principle The theory in physics that denies absolute causal relationships of matter and, hence, predictability.

Unequal treaties Chinese name for the diplomatic and territorial arrangements foisted on the weak Qin dynasty by European powers in the nineteenth century; also, the commercial treaties forced on just-opened Japan by the same powers and the United States.

Upanishads The Hindu holy epics dealing with morals and philosophy.

Utopia "Nowhere"; Greek term used to denote an ideal place or society.

Utopian socialism The dismissive label given by Marx to previous theories that aimed at establishing a more just and benevolent society.

V

Vakf An Islamic philanthropic foundation established by the devout.

Vassal In medieval Europe, a person, usually a noble, who owed feudal duties to a superior, called a *suzerain*.

Vedas The four oral epics of the Aryans.

Verdun, Treaty of A treaty concluded in 843 that divided Charlemagne's empire among his three grandsons; established what became the permanent dividing lines between the French and Germans.

Vernacular The native oral language of a given people.

Villa The country estate of a Roman patrician or other wealthy Roman.

Vizier An official of Muslim government, especially a high Turkish official equivalent to prime minister.

W

Wandering of Peoples A term referring to the migrations of various Germanic and Asiatic tribes in the third and fourth centuries C.E. that brought them into conflict with Rome.

Wannsee Conference The 1942 meeting of Nazi leaders that determined the "final solution" for the Jews.

Wars of the Austrian Succession Two 1740s wars between Prussia and Austria that gave important advantages to Prussia and its king Frederick the Great.

War of the Roses An English civil war between noble factions over the succession to the throne in the fifteenth century.

Warsaw Pact An organization of the Soviet satellite states in Europe; founded under Russian aegis in 1954 to serve as a counterweight to NATO.

Waterloo The final defeat of Napoleon in 1815 after his return from Elban exile.

Wealth of Nations, The The short title of the pathbreaking work on national economy by Adam Smith; published in 1776.

Wehrgeld Under early Germanic law, a fine paid to an injured party or his or her family or lord that was equivalent to the value of the injured individual.

Weimar Republic The popular name for Germany's democratic government between 1919 and 1933.

Westphalia, Treaty of The treaty that ended the Thirty Years' War in 1648; the first modern peace treaty in that it established strategic and territorial gains as more important than religious or dynastic ones.

Whigs A nickname for British nineteenth-century liberals; opposite of Tories.

"White man's burden" A phrase coined by Rudyard Kipling to refer to what he considered the necessity of bringing European civilization to non-Europeans.

World Bank A monetary institution founded after World War II by Western nations to assist in the recovery effort and to aid the Third World's economic development.

Yalta Conference Conference in 1945 where Franklin D. Roosevelt, Josef Stalin, and Winston Churchill (the "Big Three") met to attempt to settle postwar questions, particularly those affecting the future of Europe.

Yamato state The earliest known government of Japan; divided into feudal subdivisions ruled by clans and headed by the Yamato family.

Yin/yang East Asian distinction between the male and female characters in terms of active versus passive, warm versus cold, and the like.

Yom Kippur War A name for the 1973 conflict between Israel and its Arab neighbors.

Yuan dynasty Official term for the Mongol rule in China, 1279–1368.

Zama, Battle of Decisive battle of the Second Punic War; Roman victory in 202 was followed by absorption of most of the Carthaginian empire in the Mediterranean.

Zambo Term for mulattos in Brazil.

Zhou dynasty The second historical Chinese dynasty; ruled from c. 1100 to c. 400 B.C.E.

Zionism A movement founded by Theodor Herzl in 1896 to establish a Jewish national homeland in Palestine.

Zulu wars A series of conflicts between the British and the native Africans in South Africa in the late nineteenth century.

Index